Student's Encyclopedia
of American Literary Characters

⌗

VOLUME I

A – F

ASSIGNING EDITORS

John Unrue, University of Nevada-Las Vegas
Darlene Unrue, University of Nevada-Las Vegas
Park Bucker, University of South Carolina-Sumter

Student's Encyclopedia
of American Literary Characters

✳

VOLUME I

A – F

edited by

Matthew J. Bruccoli
Judith S. Baughman

☑️Facts On File
An imprint of Infobase Publishing

Student's Encyclopedia of American Literary Characters

Copyright © 2008 by Manly, Inc.

Facts On File, Inc.
An imprint of Infobase Publishing
132 West 31st Street
New York NY 10001

Library of Congress Cataloging-in-Publication Data

Student's encyclopedia of American literary characters //edited by Matthew J. Bruccoli,
Judith S. Baughman.
   p. cm.
  Includes bibliographical references and index.
  ISBN 978-0-8160-6498-4 (acid-free paper)
  1. American literature—Encyclopedias. 2. Characters and characteristics in literature—Encyclopedias.
  I. Bruccoli, Matthew Joseph, 1931- II. Baughman, Judith.
  PS21.S77 2008
  810.9'2703—dc22

                        2008001704

Text design by Erika K. Arroyo

Printed in the United States of America

VB Manly 10 9 8 7 6 5 4 3 2 1

This book is printed on acid-free paper and contains 30 percent postconsumer recycled content

CONTENTS

✳

ALL VOLUMES

Indexes of characters and of literary works included in the set are at the back of volume IV.

Introduction

Action is character.

—*F. Scott Fitzgerald*

Fitzgerald knew what he was talking about. See the Jay Gatsby and Dick Diver entries in this volume. Certain characters become—not types or stereotypes—but one-off figures who represent a response to life. Their names are recognizable and meaningful: thus Yossarian, Ántonia Shimerda, Philip Marlowe, Flem Snopes, Nick Adams, Hester Prynne, Holden Caulfield, Natty Bumppo....

Great fiction is remembered for great characters, who are believable or convincing or recognizable. They endure in the reader's mind long after the details of plot or story have been forgotten. Great characters outlast their books.

These four volumes perforce provide a selection of characters to serve students. Another thousand characters could be usefully included—and may well be in supplementary volumes. The principles of selection are based on the reputations of the character and the work: characters students have heard about—or should have heard about—and need to know more about. They mainly include characters in classic American works of fiction, which are or should be classroom staples, as well as characters in influential current writing. The editors have endeavored to include the most widely recognizable characters across three centuries of American literature. There are missing persons because choices had to be made. This condition is inevitable and even desirable, for one function of a literary reference book is to provide a testing place for its users—a facility for them to determine what they know, what they don't know, and what

they want to know. Good reference works involve their parishioners.

Student's Encyclopedia of American Literary Characters is not another dictionary providing brief indentifications of literary characters. The entries on characters in this set are substantial and analytical in nature, designed to help students think more deeply about the subject. The questions appended to the character entries provide ideas for classroom discussion and topics for student papers. Many of the questions refer to other characters, authors, and books, in order to encourage students to make connections between works of literature.

The inconsistencies in style and focus among these entries are unavoidable as well as functional. Each is intended to reveal the nature of the character as determined by the work. Accordingly, uniformity of the entries is impossible and unnecessary. The entries were not produced by an assembly line: some 300 contributors were involved. Nonetheless, each entry conforms to the same format and employs an accessible prose style, eschewing literary-critical jargon.

Entries are organized by author, then by work, then by character. The expanded table of contents lists all authors, works and characters included. The two indexes in the last volume list the literary works covered and the characters in alphabetical order.

By approaching fiction through its characters—the best of whom live apart from their books—SEALC provides students and serious extra-curricular readers with handles for understanding them and their worlds. Some reference sets for students merely provide plot summaries that mention characters in passing. Such volumes are intended to save students the trouble of reading the works. SEALC is not intended as an instead-of convenience: it is an aid for meaningful, rewarding, and enjoyable reading. Nothing can replace the real thing in fiction. Nothing can be more important than a work of literature.

These entries eschew the criticism of criticism. There is probably something wrong with works of fiction that require a great deal of interpretation. A book belongs to its readers—not to the people who make a living by analyzing it.

—M. J. B.

A

Conrad Aiken

(August 5, 1889 – August 17, 1973)

"SILENT SNOW, SECRET SNOW"

Collected in *Among the Lost People* (New York: Scribners, 1934).

PAUL HASLEMAN

Paul Hasleman, the twelve-year-old protagonist of Conrad Aiken's short story "Silent Snow, Secret Snow," is typical of Aiken's protagonists. His physical appearance and history are withheld; he is progressively obsessed with the struggle to assert his interior reality over the facts of his daily life, and he draws the reader into his (possibly delusional) reality with no promise of resolution. The wonder and ambiguity of the story makes it alluring, and Aiken's protagonist captivates with the beauty and mystery of his secret: "Just why it should have happened, or why it should have happened just when it did, he could not, of course, possibly have said. . . . The thing was above all a secret, . . . and to that very fact it owed an enormous part of its deliciousness." Like his literary ancestor Edgar Allan Poe, Aiken withholds expository information from the reader to create a sense of uncertainty that simulates the protagonist's unbalanced state of mind. Something secret and mysterious has begun happening in the protagonist's life, and he knows that it must be kept secret or it may lose its deliciousness.

The story takes place in one day, but in typical Aiken fashion, the events of more than a week are related via Paul's daydreams and reflections. He sits in Miss Buell's geography class in school, only half paying attention, allowing himself to be distracted by the sweet memory of his first experience of the secret. The experience unfolds over seven mornings, which Paul loves to recall in detail. Each morning, a secret snowfall results in the sound of the postman's footsteps as he delivers mail on Paul's street becoming more muffled, and each day it takes longer to hear the footsteps at all. It is as if snow were falling more and more until, at last, he does not hear the postman's approach at all. Paul succumbs to the hypnotic quality of the snow, noticing its effects on everything: "the same slightly abstracted quality, as if removed by one degree from actuality—as if everything in the world had been insulated by snow."

When Paul looks out of his bedroom window, however, the sun is shining on clean, dry streets. As he realizes there is no snow outside, he becomes inexplicably sad. The snow had brought him a sense of things absent in his daily life: "peace, remoteness, cold, sleep." If there were no snow, he would have to go downstairs to his usual routine as if everything were fine. But now he knows something better, and his ordinary experience will never be acceptable again. He comes to understand that he can bring on the secret snow any time with just a thought: "All the following morning he had kept with him a sense as of snow falling about him, a secret screen of new snow between himself and the world." As the days pass, his control over the snow diminishes as the snow increases.

While Paul becomes more entranced by the delicious progression of the snow, he is also consumed with a problem: what to tell his mother and father. His life becomes a balancing act between his inner world and the outside world of home and school. Mother and Father finally call a doctor to examine

Paul. When the doctor begins to ask probing questions ("Is there anything that worries you?"), Paul's parents close in on him, and the tension increases. For Paul, the sound and sight of the snow also increase, promising to save him. Finally, he escapes to his room, the snow egging him on with promises of "the last, the most beautiful and secret story." As Paul willingly succumbs to that deep, white, cold snow, his mother reaches his bedside. Feeling anger and loathing at her interference, he shouts, "Mother! Mother! Go away! I hate you!" At that moment, "everything was solved. The whole world was a vast, moving screen of snow—but even now it said peace, it said remoteness, it said cold, it said sleep."

Paul is a physically nondescript character involved in a convincingly detailed psychological struggle: how to accept the unacceptable. He has been described as an everyman involved in an archetypal human struggle, the origins of which are worthy of speculation but do not determine its significance. His shift from one world to the next is chilling to observe and experience vicariously. The power of Aiken's fiction is in his expert use of the implements of daily life as portals into the mystery beyond (immanent transcendence as in the American Transcendentalist tradition). The problem of free will, a favorite theme of American fiction, is displayed in the character of Paul. Does he choose the snow or does the snow choose him? The question of knowledge (experience vs. innocence) also comes into play via Paul. As his fascination with the snow develops, he begins to ignore the adults in his life, finally despising them. Is he choosing his truth over an alleged one being forced on him? Or is he being driven into a cold corner by trying to live a lie perpetrated by the adult world? These questions ultimately go unanswered. The focus of the story is on Paul's perception of his interior experience.

Discussion Questions

1. Symbolism is central to any work by Aiken. In "Silent Snow, Secret Snow," Paul, his mother, and his father are all characterized by their shoes, and the secret itself is brought to Paul through the footsteps of the postman. What is the significance of shoes and footsteps in the story?

2. Critic Jay Martin, in *Conrad Aiken: A Life of His Art*, has said that Aiken's finest moments in fiction are when he makes the reader believe that the illusion being created has a "deeper reality," even when we cannot define the deeper reality. What are some of the techniques Aiken uses in "Silent Snow, Secret Snow" to create this sense that the illusion has deep meaning even if we do not understand it?

3. Catharine F. Seigel, in her essay "Conrad Aiken, His Hour Come 'Round at Last" (*Southern Quarterly*, Fall 1982), finds the key to Aiken's short fiction in its "illumination of the amorphous inner world of consciousness." Compare and contrast the inner worlds of the young protagonists of "Silent Snow, Secret Snow" and "Strange Moonlight" as examples of Aiken's focus on the inner world of consciousness.

—*Nancy Story*

REFERENCES

F. W. Bonnell and F. C. Bonnell, comps., *Conrad Aiken, A Bibliography* (San Marino, Calif.: Huntington Library, 1982);

Frederick John Hoffman, *Conrad Aiken* (New York: Twayne, 1962);

Jay Martin, *Conrad Aiken: A Life of His Art* (Princeton: Princeton University Press, 1962);

Catharine F. Seigel, *The Fictive World of Conrad Aiken: A Celebration of Consciousness* (De Kalb: Northern Illinois University Press, 1993);

Southern Quarterly, "Conrad Aiken's Prose," special issue, 21 (Fall 1982);

Ted Spivey and Arthur Waterman, *Conrad Aiken: Priest of Consciousness* (New York: AMS Press, 1990).

Edward Albee
(March 12, 1928 –   )

❦

A DELICATE BALANCE
New York, Martin Beck Theatre, April 22, 1966; (New York: Atheneum, 1966)

AGNES
Agnes is a woman who attempts to maintain equilibrium in her home despite the intrusions of various family and friends in Edward Albee's *A Delicate Bal-*

ance. Because her husband, Tobias, has shirked the role of head of household since the death of their son, Teddy, Agnes has assumed a more commanding, and masculine, role in the family. Additionally, she acts as a guard against the "plague"—which she believes her friends Harry and Edna have brought with them when they came to Agnes and Tobias's while fleeing an unnameable dread—a sickness that threatens the balance and harmony of the traditional nuclear family. At one point in the play Agnes comments, "I do wish sometimes that I had been born a man." According to her, women lead more complicated lives than men, who merely have to worry about "making ends meet until they meet the end."

Albee used as a model for Agnes his own mother, Frankie, who ran their household and, like Agnes, maintained an inflexible definition of what was appropriate and inappropriate. Agnes deals with confrontations and problems by attempting to exile anything that appears foreign or aberrant. She considers herself a defender against outer forces that threaten her household, though Albee undermines her throughout the play. The family already does not conform to many of the conventional notions of American life in the 1950s and 1960s. Harry and Edna's request to stay with them becomes but one of several unorthodox occurrences that night. Agnes is already boarding another outsider, her sister Claire, whose story about angering a salesclerk by asking for a topless bathing suit reveals that her values clash starkly with those Agnes wishes to maintain. After the death of their son, Teddy, her marriage to Tobias has become a charade, with husband and wife sleeping in different bedrooms and refraining from all sexual activity. Especially in light of their daughter Julia's return home after another failed marriage, Agnes's mission to protect her family from the "plague" seems to ignore the fact that the family already suffers from many problems.

Her sister represents everything that Agnes finds threatening to society. As a sort of court jester who plays the accordion, yodels, and tells dirty jokes, Claire provides an ironic, self-aware commentary on the manifold problems in the family. Claire's past love affair with Tobias helps to reveal significant elements of Agnes's character, making her seem less like a faithful wife and more like a servant or obstacle to Tobias's happiness. Tobias, in ceasing all manner of sexual relations with his wife, has left her desire to bear another son unfulfilled, so that she has become, in effect, sterile. Thus, Agnes clings to the illusion of herself as a wife, just as she tries to defend a balance or harmony that has not existed since the death of Teddy.

While she proclaims herself to be the "fulcrum" on which the family depends for its survival, Agnes does inevitably come to express a sense of loss, confusion, and disorientation without Teddy. She relegates herself to domestic tasks in order to hide from the more difficult decisions and issues that afflict the family. In her opinion a wife merely performs household duties and "prepares for the children to become adult strangers." She likens a typical household to "a team of twenty horses, and we sit there, and we watch the road and check the leather . . . if our . . . man is so disposed." She holds that while women are essential to the maintenance of a balanced family unit, the women of the house "don't decide the route." Agnes thus commits the same fault of which she accuses Tobias—shirking responsibility—and she places all the blame for everyone's stagnation on her husband's shoulders. While she criticizes Tobias for his reluctance to make decisions, she exempts herself from the role of decision maker. She lacks even the resolve of Julia, who has at least left her husbands rather than remaining to perpetuate her misery.

When Harry and Edna seek refuge, Agnes's desire to keep them out becomes a defining part of her character. As Albee puts it, she must "figure out whether or not they are strong enough anymore to do what should normally be done: the Christian way, to take you in. . . . Agnes asks which values are more important," the contest being between altruism and self-interest. Ultimately, Agnes believes that she acts out of the best interest of her family, deciding that, in Albee's words, "the people have got to leave. Because the family can't survive." She does not, however, accept the responsibility of asking them to leave. While she aspires to lead the family on this issue, she only reaffirms her role as wife and says, "ultimately I will do whatever you want." Agnes, like the rest of her family, chooses passivity. For her, the family's stability depends on a delicate balance of guardedness and delusion.

Discussion Questions

1. Focusing on his representation of mother figures, what similarities and differences does one find in *A Delicate Balance* and one of Albee's other plays, such as *The American Dream* or *Three Tall Women?*

2. Albee based Agnes's sister, Claire, largely on his mother's sister, Jane. What social values come under revaluation in the play, and how does Claire refute or threaten much of the order Agnes tries to foster?

3. Consider Agnes's comments regarding the absence of a strong patriarchal role in the family, as well as her own buried emotions regarding the loss of Teddy, who is hardly mentioned anywhere throughout the play. In view of these carefully constructed absences, could one say Albee's characterization of void and negation in Agnes's life is a consciously instilled theme rather than a weakness?

—*Brian Ray*

TOBIAS

Tobias is a man who, in deciding whether or not to take in his friends Harry and Edna, runs into conflict with his wife, Agnes, in Edward Albee's *A Delicate Balance*. While the play revolves around this central conflict, Tobias also faces deeper problems, such as his diminishing role in his own family, his reluctance to make decisions, and the general hostility between himself and Agnes, who sees Harry and Edna as a threat to what remains of their family's integrity.

In notes he wrote during the first production of the play, Albee avoids chastising Tobias for his indifferent attitude: "The tragedy of Tobias is that Time has happened to him." Unable to recover from the past death of his son, Teddy, he has chosen to distance himself from Agnes and his daughter, Julia. His sister-in-law and one-time lover, Claire, makes fun of his passivity, calling him "stolid Tobias," someone who will never "proceed by reflex." According to Mel Gussow's biography, *Edward Albee: A Singular Journey*, Albee remembers his own adoptive father as "uncommunicative and disengaged," a man who "hardly ever spoke" to his son.

While Agnes once expressed the desire for another son, Tobias refused and initiated the habit of coitus interruptus to prevent any possible pregnancy.

Eventually, he quit all manner of conjugal affection and then moved into a separate bedroom. While passive, Tobias is also capable of intentional insensitivity. He only complains when daughter Julia comes home after leaving her fourth husband, dragging her "marriage" with her "like some Raggedy Anne doll," to "fill this house" with her "whining." Evidence of his cruelty lies in the story he tells Claire about how he put the family cat to sleep when it began to avoid him. Albee wrote this particular speech "rather quickly," he says, and "after I had written it I became aware that it was a sort of metaphor for the whole play."

Tobias's offer to let Harry and Edna live with them signals a desire to transcend his own passivity. The rest of the family, however, expresses discontent at the idea on the grounds that it will violate the family's integrity. For Agnes and the rest, a household should only consist of kin, and in their view Harry and Edna have brought with them a "plague" that threatens their stability. Julia expresses the belief that Harry and Edna are not Tobias's friends but instead are intruders. Claire as well asks Tobias repeatedly about Harry, "What do you have in common with him?" This particular question reflects the entire family's fear of the unorthodox.

The only moment in the play in which Tobias seems to express genuine emotion occurs in the final act, when Harry says he will not return Tobias's hospitality. Tobias sheds a tear as he watches his friends leave. "You've put forty years into it," he says, begging them to "bring your terror . . . and you live with us. . . . I don't want you here! I don't love you! But by God . . . you stay!" Their departure from the house signals a final defeat for Tobias. According to Albee, "When he says, please stay, he's not begging people to stay so that he can be nice to them, he's saying 'you've taken away my last opportunity to do something worthwhile in my life.' That's really what the play is about."

Tobias sinks into depression because he seems lost and unable to recapture a sense of home and, with it, a sense of belonging. To him and Agnes they do not live at home but instead in "the dark sadness." Neither Agnes nor Tobias seems to realize that, as Albee puts it, "your home is in your head" and that Tobias's dark sadness is the result of a self-awareness he is unable to deny. The family's descent also stems from their refusal to accept social change, evident in the hostility they display toward Harry and Edna, whose relationship to Agnes and Tobias is akin to "looking into a mirror." By exiling them, then, Agnes and Tobias also exile themselves. Their reluctance to accept the couple accompanies a deeper misunderstanding or denial of the self.

Discussion Questions

1. Does the offer Tobias makes to Harry and Edna stem from an actual care for their well-being or, rather, from a need to prove himself capable of compassion? Consider that Tobias does not make the offer until everyone has basically decided to let Harry and Edna leave of their own will.

2. Many of Albee's plays deal with themes of loneliness or existential despair. Consider such plays as *The Zoo Story* and *The American Dream*. What parallels do you find between Tobias's cat story and the dog story Jerry relates in *The Zoo Story?*

—*Brian Ray*

‿❦

THREE TALL WOMEN

Vienna, English Theatre, June 14, 1991; (New York: Dutton, 1995)

A, B, AND C

In Edward Albee's play *Three Tall Women*, A, B, and C represent a multifaceted portrait of a single tall woman who traded her beauty and freedom for a marriage of wealth and stature. The play focuses on her compromises as she consistently chooses the artificial and the comfortable over the real from the time she is twenty-six years old until she is ninety-two.

Albee acknowledges in the introduction to the published play that this character-in-three-parts is directly based on his adoptive mother, from whom he was estranged for decades before reconnecting on a limited basis toward the end of her life: "We had managed to make each other very unhappy over the

years, but I was past all that, though I think she was not. I harbor no ill will toward her; it is true I did not like her much, could not abide her prejudices, her loathing, her paranoias, but I did admire her pride, her sense of self. As she moved toward ninety, began rapidly failing both physically and mentally, I was touched by the survivor, the figure clinging to the wreckage only partly of her making, refusing to go under."

Act 1 focuses on the woman "clinging to the wreckage": character A is ninety-one or possibly ninety-two, with a shattered arm that refuses to heal, a failing mind, and an insistent bladder. She struggles to retain her dignity and control over B, her middle-aged caretaker, and C, the young representative from her attorney. During this act, A moves between being child-like and imperious, from being dependent on B and C to reminding them of their dependence on her. She relates details from her life, similarly bouncing back and forth between recounting the wild days when she and her sister partied and trawled for eligible men, the highs and lows from her married life, and her present struggles with her finances and failing health. Despite her bitterness over the more tawdry experiences of her life, she is proud of her survival and disdainful of her weaker family members: "If I don't have my eye out, who will? I've always had to be on my toes, them sneaking around, conniving. . . . If I didn't have my eye out, we wouldn't have had *any*thing." Her sister, her mother, her husband, and her son may have despised her, but they ultimately depended on her having her "eye out."

B and C function largely as a chorus in act 1; their characters are undeveloped, presented as middle-class women with no personal details beside their professions and age. They alternately ask A probing questions and offer comments as she relates the twists and turns of her life. C is disdainful of A's hypocrisy and physical decline, while B, closer to her in age, is more sympathetic. B has experienced enough in life that she can share part of A's journey and anticipate the rest; C believes that she can avoid the accommodations and indignities of A's life.

While act 1 is a realistic play, act 2 moves into a more imaginative realm, with the three characters representing different aspects of the woman who now lies in a coma, represented on stage by a life mask of A in an upstage bed, obscured by medical equipment. At the start of the act, A, B, and C enter elegantly dressed as the Tall Woman at ages ninety-one or so, fifty-two, and twenty-six respectively. While retaining the full experience of her life, A is no longer hampered by the mental and physical handicaps of act 1, as she delicately shares her memories with her younger personas, B and C.

C resents A and B; she refuses to believe that she will become them, preferring to hope for a good life rather than to hear the unpleasant truths of her future: "I imagine I'll marry and I imagine I'll be happy." C cannot imagine that she would marry an unattractive man that she did not love—who would merely make her laugh and belong to a rich family. However her priorities change after her father dies. B and A can accept their compromises and the ways that compromises have changed them.

While C struggles against her future, B is still struggling with her past: she is still bitter over her husband's constant and tawdry infidelities and over her son's inadequacies. Though A has weathered more than B—including her mother's bitter decline, her husband's lingering death, and her son's resentful return—A has moved past B's bitterness. Though A may not have forgiven her alcoholic sister, her mother, her husband, or her son, she has managed to accept them and the fact that she is stronger than all of them. Overall, the older selves appreciate being able to share their remembered experiences with someone who has their strength and spirit. Despite the disappointments and trade-offs of their life, A, B, or C never indulge in self-pity, all claiming that they are experiencing the happiest age. The Tall Woman has always been a survivor, appreciating each moment while awaiting each new challenge.

Discussion Questions

1. Albee commented that his friends who met his adoptive mother could not "abide her," but those who have seen the play find her "fascinating." Can you find support for both of these reactions in the play?

2. Why is it valuable in act 1 to see A interact with other characters? Is it more or less effective that they are employees rather than family members?

3. How does the realistic portrayal of the woman (as A) in act 1 work with or against her imaginative portrayal (as A, B, and C) in act 2?

4. Which aspect of the Tall Woman (A, B, or C) do you admire the most? Which aspect do you pity the most?

—*Elizabeth Abele*

WHO'S AFRAID OF VIRGINIA WOOLF?

New York, Billy Rose Theatre, October 13, 1962; (New York: Atheneum, 1962)

GEORGE

George, the male lead in Edward Albee's play *Who's Afraid of Virginia Woolf?* characterizes himself as "numb." He feels completely untouched by events or people. Once a promising young academic with considerable career prospects, George is now in midlife stuck with no real prospect of either advancing or getting out of the mire in which he finds himself. He married the boss's daughter, but he failed to replace the boss. He is not—as Martha repeats incessantly—the head of the history department but only a lowly professor. Much of the rest of George's biography is, however, somewhat murky, since it remains unclear whether the novel he wrote is an actual novel or his own autobiography. At various times he claims it as "real" and at others he insists it is fiction. Martha similarly treats it as both. Whatever the truth, audiences quickly become aware that, for whatever reasons, as the world measures people, George is a failure.

During the play, George attempts to overcome his numbness and get his emotional blood circulating once more through a battle of wits with Martha; setting up and taunting his young rival, Nick; exposing the shaky grounds for Nick's marriage to Honey; and finally through destroying the illusion he and Martha have created together to fill the void at the center of their lives. As portrayed by Arthur Hill, who created the part and who won a Tony Award and a Drama Critics Award as best actor of the 1962–1963 season for his performance, George lives by and for his wits. A master of language with a repertoire of appropriate quips, stinging digs, not-quite-insults, and instant replies, he lies in wait for a worthy opponent. Nick quickly gives up attempting to parry his wit. Of all his possible opponents, only Martha appears capable of rising to his level of repartee. Clearly, she admires George as the only man who has ever been able to play the games as fast as she is able to change or invent them.

The play itself depicts a classic battle of the sexes, such as August Strindberg memorably dramatized in *Fadren* (The Father, 1912) and *Dödsdansen* (The Dance of Death, 1905). But in *Who's Afraid of Virginia Woolf?* Albee goes beyond a simple confrontation of the sexes to examine what happens when adults substitute fantasy for reality. Like the Boy and Girl in his later play, *The Play about the Baby* (1998), George and Martha are childless and, also similar to that other couple, they appear to have needed to invent a fictitious baby that binds them together and through the years has acquired a life of his own.

This fictitious child motivates the dramatic crisis of *Who's Afraid of Virginia Woolf?*—a crisis that may or may not change George and Martha's relationship. The evidence that it does or does not force a change may lie in how an audience reacts to George's conducting the service of exorcism held to drive out the evil spirit haunting their home. Audiences generally are divided in how seriously they take his action. (Albee's working title for the play was "The Exorcism.") If George is merely role-playing and not serious, then his action may be seen as just one more in the long series of games that fill the small hours of this night. But if his actions are taken seriously rather than ironically, then George is attempting to exorcize a demon that has warped his relationship with Martha for years. The earlier games then appear to be part of a progressive stripping away of illusion as George attempts to limit self-dramatization. He does not, for instance, make a scene when Nick goes upstairs with Martha but instead quietly reads a book, which infuriates his wife far more than his outright objections might.

George exactly fits the psychological profile of men in a midlife crisis: they question all that they have done or not done, examine exactly where they are and what prospects they may have, and determine whether they will continue on the way they have gone in the past or attempt to alter their future direction. Martha in her early fifties faces a similar crisis. So both together are, in Martha's memorable phrase, "walking what's left of our wits" in an effort to postpone or ignore the crisis. When Martha violates her agreement with George never to speak about their son before others, she precipitates the crisis the fantasy son was invented to overcome, causing George to conduct his service of exorcism. When Nick asks, "You couldn't have . . . any?" both George and Martha reply separately: "We couldn't." Alone with one another, George affirms that it was time to destroy illusions as together they face a new day and the rest of their lives.

Discussion Questions

1. *Who's Afraid of Virginia Woolf?* is verbally one of the wittiest plays in the American repertoire. Discuss the sources and variety of George's wit.

2. Nick sees himself as the future and George as a has-been. Discuss what, if any, advantages George has over Nick.

3. One disgruntled critic commented after seeing the play that "nothing happened because nothing has changed." Argue for or against this proposition, giving evidence for your position drawn from the play.

4. Albee has always insisted on the political and historical dimensions of *Who's Afraid of Virginia Woolf?* beginning with the names of George and Martha that echo those of George and Martha Washington and continuing with the illusion of the child. Discuss George's role in the political and historical dimensions of the play.

—*Donald E. Morse*

MARTHA

Larger than life, witty, sensual yet vulnerable, Martha in Edward Albee's play *Who's Afraid of Virginia Woolf?* commands such a wide range of emotion and action that hers is one of the great roles for actresses in the contemporary theater. Uta Hagen, who originated the role, won both a Tony and a Drama Critics Award as Best Actress for the 1962–1963 theater season. Hagen's performance emphasized

Martha's ability to match wits with her husband, George. Rarely does she come off second-best in these duels.

The daughter of the president of a small New England college, Martha married George in the expectation that he would one day succeed her father, but George's talent and interests lay elsewhere. She never tires of reminding him that he has not and will not become president nor will he even become head of the history department where he teaches. But if George's career is in her eyes a failure, her own cannot be much more than that since she appears to have no roles but those of daughter of the college president and/or professor's wife. She has no job and she has no children, so—perhaps in desperation—she invents a child in order to create a meaningful role for herself, that of mother to her son.

Time magazine, reviewing the original Broadway production, found the play repetitious and too long. (Their reviewer also thought the fantasy son unbelievable.) Yet, an argument could be made that the length and repetition is necessary to establish Martha's character well enough to account both for the fantasy son and the violation of her pact with George not to mention him to outsiders. The boasting of the absent son to Honey precipitates the dramatic crisis in the play as Martha oversteps the boundary she previously agreed to with George.

During the first two acts of the play Martha appears to motivate almost all the action. She invites Nick and Honey over for a nightcap after a welcome party given by her father for new faculty. Then the games begin. Like Eugene O'Neill's characters, Albee's confront one another and, eventually, themselves during a long night of drinking, but along the way no holds are barred. The first game, "Humiliate the Host," appears merely witty and entertaining, but the game-playing becomes serious with "Hump the Hostess" and then hurtful with "Get the Guests" as the characters verbally slug it out with each other. Although Nick boasts that he can play in Martha and George's league, clearly he cannot. Only George is a match for Martha.

Moreover, what begins as a battle of the sexes turns into an existential probing for meaning. Some critics find that "beneath the struggle there is nothing at the core but loneliness," but this assessment may be too superficial. George and Martha, at middle age, childless, restless and dissatisfied with their lives, must affirm some positive values, find meaningful work, become part of a community, or discover some avenue or venture that would make life worthwhile. What they do not need is more self-dramatization, such as Martha proclaiming, "I am the Earth Mother." Nor do they need more skating on the surface of life or toying with easy victims, such as Martha's dwelling on the "crummy, totally pointless infidelities . . . *would*-be infidelities" that come with the Earth Mother role, including that night's nonperformance by Nick. Martha deliberately humiliates Nick by reflecting back on his inability and taunting him—calling him a "houseboy." At the same time, she confesses that there has only been "one man in my life who has ever made me happy," and that is George. To Nick's astonished objection that George is a "has-been" who has been broken by life, Martha acidly asks, "You always deal in appearances?"

On the night on which the play is set, Martha and George go far beneath appearances to confront the pain—what Albee has called "the awful loss and lack" at the center of their relationship. During the play, only liquor appears to numb this pain until the end. The son that had filled the couple's empty life and substituted for shallow relationships becomes exposed as a fantasy in the last game, "Bringing Up Baby." While Martha may object: "You didn't have to let him die, George," the opposite is true: the fantasy child had to die, if the "parents," especially Martha, are to become truly adults facing their own mortality and what is left of their lives. At this point, after all the games and subterfuge, after all the booze and avoidance, Martha appears to connect with George, and as they make contact with one another, they also appear to acknowledge external reality. Revealing this truth before Nick and Honey, that is, before witnesses, ends the fantasy for Martha once and for all. The ending of the play suggests that there may be some basis, however small, for her own maturation and for a renewal of her relationship with George.

Discussion Questions

1. Discuss Martha's role in relation to the title of each act of *Who's Afraid of Virginia Woolf?*

2. Comment on Martha's relationship to Nick. How successful is she as a sexual temptress?

3. Why does Martha admire George?

4. Do you see Martha moving closer to George throughout the play until, as one critic suggests, they "become united?" If so, why? If not, why not?

—*Donald E. Morse*

꩜

THE ZOO STORY

Berlin, Schiller Theater, September 28, 1959; in *The Zoo Story, The Death of Bessie Smith, The Sandbox* (New York: Coward-McCann, 1960)

JERRY

Jerry, one of only two characters in Edward Albee's play *The Zoo Story*, appears at the beginning of the play to be in need of company; he tries to engage Peter in conversation, but when Peter ignores him, Jerry immediately becomes assertive, raising his voice until Peter is forced to listen and unable to stop Jerry's final act.

From the beginning Jerry is judgmental; he tells Peter that because he smokes a pipe that he'll get "cancer of the mouth." Then Jerry criticizes Peter in small ways and chatters until finally Peter is forced to respond. Only then does Jerry ask Peter, "Do you mind if we talk?" Jerry continues to make assertions about Peter, forcing Peter to defend himself. Skillfully, Jerry manipulates the conversation so that he can tell Peter about himself, revealing that he has no one to keep him company. He is alone and considers Peter his only friend. Peter now becomes concerned, not realizing that he is being manipulated and will ultimately be used.

Jerry makes the audience, along with Peter, uncomfortable. Like the world and generation that Albee grew up in, which was a world that lived with fear of another world war, the invention of the atom bomb, and an uneasy ambivalence between two superpowers, the United States and Russia, Jerry, too,

is uneasy and anxious; yet, he also creates his own discord. Pushing Peter too far, Jerry appears to be contrite and apologetic. "I'm sorry. All right? You're not angry?" Yet, Jerry begins to tell a story that Peter reacts to violently. Jerry pushes and pulls Peter to the brink of exasperation, to sympathy, back to being infuriated; still, Peter forgives Jerry, not wanting to anger him. Jerry lives alone on "the edge of society" and does not accept the societal apathy shown to him. In his attempt to live on the edge alone no longer, Jerry has decided to put a placid, perfectly sane individual on the edge of society in his place.

While the discomfort that Jerry creates is at first societal, it becomes psychological and then finally physical as Jerry invades Peter's space. He makes Peter an unwilling accomplice to his suicide, impaling himself on a knife he has given Peter to hold. The impossible position in which Peter is placed is an example of what makes *The Zoo Story* an absurd display. No one will believe Peter when he tells how Jerry died.

Discussion Questions

1. Compare Albee's *The Zoo Story* to Samuel Beckett's *Krapp's Last Tape*, with which *The Zoo Story* was once performed on a double bill. How is loss a factor for both of the main characters? Does loneliness factor into that loss at all?

2. If absurdity is based on a world that has no meaning and communication that becomes babble, pinpoint those areas in *The Zoo Story* where Jerry creates babble. By the time the play ends, is there any meaning in Peter's world?

3. What are the consequences of Jerry's final act for Peter personally, professionally? How does Jerry's suicide ultimately affect how Peter views himself?

4. Is Albee's intent to purposely seduce the reader into thinking Jerry is a sympathetic character because of his delusions of loneliness? How does this sympathy work to create terror by the end of the play?

—*Diana Fox*

REFERENCES

Edward Albee, *Stretching My Mind* (New York: Avalon, 2005);

Richard E. Amacher, *Edward Albee,* revised edition (New York: Twayne, 1982);

Stephen Bottoms, *Albee: Who's Afraid of Virginia Woolf?* (Cambridge: Cambridge University Press, 2000);

Bottoms, ed., *The Cambridge Companion to Edward Albee* (Cambridge: Cambridge University Press, 2005);

Jackson Bryer, *The Playwright's Art: Conversations with Contemporary American Dramatists* (New Brunswick, N.J.: Rutgers University Press, 1995);

Mel Gussow, *Edward Albee: A Singular Journey* (New York: Applause, 2000);

Philip C. Kolin, ed., *Conversations with Edward Albee* (Jackson: University Press of Mississippi, 1988);

Bruce J. Mann, ed., *Edward Albee: A Casebook* (New York: Routledge, 2003).

Louisa May Alcott

(November 29, 1832 – March 6, 1888)

◖◗

LITTLE WOMEN

(Boston: Roberts, 1868, 1869); *Little Men* (London: Sampson Low, Son & Marston, 1871; Boston: Roberts, 1871); *Jo's Boys, and How They Turned Out* (Boston: Roberts, 1886)

MARCH FAMILY

The March family are the main characters of Louisa May Alcott's novel *Little Women* and are also featured prominently in Alcott's *Little Men* and *Jo's Boys, and How They Turned Out*. Although based on the personalities and exploits of Alcott's own family, the Marches and their experiences are shaped by the author so as to explore themes that were important not only in her own life but also in the society around her. One problem that surfaces early in *Little Women* and continues throughout the March trilogy is the struggle between the individual and the community. Like many of her Concord neighbors, including Ralph Waldo Emerson and Henry David Thoreau, Alcott believed in the need for each individual to find herself and follow a distinctive path without regard to arbitrary societal pressures. Yet, in writing about the March family, Alcott overtly acknowledges the conflict between the needs of the individual members for independence and the needs of the family to remain intact. Unlike many heroes and heroines of nineteenth-century American literature, the young March women must balance their aspirations with their duties to one another. While this duty at times forces them to set aside their own ambitions, Alcott demonstrates "that there is something sweeter" than liberty, and the only self worth having, ultimately, is a self intimately connected to others.

The March family consists of Mr. March, Mrs. March ("Marmee"), and four daughters, Meg, Jo, Beth, and Amy. Mr. March is away serving as a chaplain for Union soldiers during the Civil War throughout most of the first half of *Little Women*, and even after his return he remains a somewhat shadowy presence in the novel. Although Alcott insists that he "was still the head of the family" and serves as the "household conscience" and "anchor," Marmee actually runs the household and governs the family members in all of their practical, day-to-day affairs. She guides the March sisters in their search for their vocations, and through her Alcott insists upon the benefits of work for women—whether housework, work done to help support the family, or the work of a true calling. As Marmee counsels, "Work is wholesome, and there is plenty for everyone; it keeps us from ennui and mischief, is good for health and spirits, and gives us a sense of power and independence better than money or fashion." The four sisters and their choices of careers are representative of four different possible paths for women.

Meg, the oldest, follows the most traditional path. Devoted to her husband and children, she is content, at the end of *Little Women*, to be "on the shelf," free "from the restless fret and fever of the world." Yet, even within this traditional frame, Alcott shows the need for balance. Meg's marriage is threatened by her obsession with her children. With Marmee's advice, Meg allows her husband a greater share in the child care, freeing her to take more of an interest in events outside the nursery. Although her husband's death in *Little Men* compels her to become somewhat more engaged with the world, she does so by being a "motherly friend" to the girls at Jo's school. In suggesting, in *Jo's Boys*, that the sisters enlarge their sewing circle to include the female students, Meg hopes to remedy the lack of practical education she believes needs to accompany the study of Latin, Greek, and mathematics; but the circle provides the opportunity for important discussions on education, politics, and careers for women, showing the value of community and the individual growth that springs from it.

Jo, who rebels against the constraints imposed upon young women, also marries and has children by the end of the March family trilogy. Unlike Meg, however, Jo partners with her husband, Friedrich Bhaer, in a joint business venture: the school at Plumfield. Indeed, it is Jo's idea to open the school, having inherited the estate from Aunt March. Thus, Jo is able literally to combine marriage and career. Of the four sisters, she struggles the hardest with trying to balance her need for independence with the needs of the family. As Alcott makes clear, however, she is committed to both: she longs to break out and "do something splendid," but to keep the family intact she also wants to prevent Meg's marrying and Beth's dying. While trying to assume Beth's role after her death, however, Jo quickly becomes desperate at the thought of "spending all her life in that quiet house, devoted to humdrum cares." In opening the school and employing her husband and eventually involving the entire family in the project, Jo arrives at an acceptable compromise—though she remains hopeful that she will still be able to write a good book someday. Her wish is not granted until the end of the trilogy, but she ultimately finds success in her true calling. Her personal, independent success is not sacrificed to the needs of the community, only delayed.

Amy, the youngest of the sisters, like Jo, does not view marriage and child rearing as her only sources of fulfillment. Though she does not become the great artist she had once hoped to be (having learned that "talent isn't genius"), as the wealthy Mrs. Lawrence, she is able to become a "Lady Bountiful," providing exposure to art and culture for Jo's young students, as well as being a patron of the arts. As she tells Laurie soon after their marriage, she is particularly interested in helping "ambitious girls," and Jo's co-educational institution provides her with the opportunity to pursue her own calling.

Beth's death at the cusp of adulthood relieves her from having to choose a path. While Alcott certainly presents her death as one of the saddest moments in March family history, Beth's lack of independence can also be seen as unfitting her for the world. When an eighteen-year-old Beth appears troubled, Jo surmises that growing up causes her to "have hopes and fears and fidgets, without knowing why or being able to explain them." Beth later confides to Jo that she has never thought about what she might do when grown and never imagined herself married. While part of her sadness comes from her inability to participate in the happy plan-making of the others, she also confesses that she never could imagine herself being of any use outside the March family home. Through her short life, however, she is able to teach Jo the values of patience, self-sacrifice, and duty better than "the wisest sermons," and lives on through Jo's newfound appreciation for the "genuine virtues," which temper and ennoble her ambitions.

Discussion Questions

1. In a journal entry written after the first half of *Little Women* was published, Alcott conveys her annoyance at the girls who write to her only to find out whom the March sisters marry, and states definitively: "I *won't* marry Jo to Laurie to please any one." Why? How would the characters and/or the plot be marred by such a match? What does Alcott accomplish by marrying Jo and Professor Bhaer?

2. In the first chapter of *Little Women,* Jo states, "I'm the man of the family now Papa is away, and *I* shall provide the slippers, for he told me to take special care of Mother while he was gone." Later, she resists crying in front of her mother after Amy burns her manuscript because "tears were an unmanly weakness." And in "Tender Troubles," Jo assures Marmee that "if anything is amiss at home, I'm your man." Why does she describe herself in masculine terms? What does she mean by them? Does she really want to be a man, or in adopting these terms is she simply resisting traditional definitions of what it means to be a woman?

3. *Transcendental Wild Oats* is Alcott's satire of her family's experience at her father's utopian community, Fruitlands. Compare and contrast the portraits of Mr. and Mrs. Lamb with Mr. and Mrs. March. What important similarities and/or differences do you notice? Since the March family trilogy

and the novella are supposed to be based, to some extent, on Alcott's own family, how do you account for any of the differences you see?

4. In the chapter "Calls," in *Little Women,* an exasperated Amy tells Jo that if only she would be pleasant to others she would be the better liked of the two, "because there is more of you." What does she mean by this? Is she right about Jo? What does this statement reveal about Amy?

—*Carolyn R. Maibor*

REFERENCES

Sarah Elbert, *A Hunger for Home: Louisa May Alcott's Place in American Culture* (New Brunswick, N.J.: Rutgers University Press, 1987);

Lucile Gulliver, *Louisa May Alcott: A Bibliography* (New York: Burt Franklin, 1973);

Elizabeth Langland, "Female Stories of Experience: Alcott's *Little Women* in Light of *Work,* " in *The Voyage In: Fictions of Female Development,* edited by Elizabeth Abel, Marianne Hirsch, and Elizabeth Langland (Hanover, N.H.: University Press of New England, 1983), pp. 112–127;

Ruth K. MacDonald, *Louisa May Alcott* (New York: Twayne, 1983);

Carolyn R. Maibor, *Labor Pains: Emerson, Hawthorne, and Alcott on Work and the Woman Question* (New York: Routledge, 2004);

Daniel Shealy, ed., *Alcott in Her Own Time* (Iowa City: University of Iowa Press, 2005).

Thomas Bailey Aldrich
(November 11, 1836 – March 19, 1907)

൰

THE STORY OF A BAD BOY
(Boston: Ticknor & Fields, 1869)

TOM BAILEY

Tom Bailey is the central character in Thomas Bailey Aldrich's only novel for children, *The Story of a Bad Boy.* This autobiographical novel is based largely on Aldrich's childhood experiences between 1849 and 1852, a period in Aldrich's life when he lived with his grandfather in Portsmouth, New Hampshire, and attended a well-respected school for boys. Because Aldrich drew so heavily on his own childhood, this character strikes the reader as a real boy, making Tom Bailey one of the first realistically drawn boy characters in American children's literature.

In the beginning of *The Story of a Bad Boy,* Aldrich made a point of distinguishing the character of Tom Bailey from the idealized characters in other books for children: "I call my story the story of a bad boy, partly to distinguish myself from those faultless young men who generally figure in narrative of this kind, and partly because I really was *not* a cherub. . . . I was a real human boy such as you may meet anywhere in New England, and no more like the impossible boy in a story-book than a sound orange is like one that has been sucked dry." Tom often sneaks out of his grandfather's house and meets up with several of the other boys in the town. Together they engage mischievous adventures, and their various escapades are the foci of most of the chapters. These chapters are often humorous. In one, for example, the boys take possession of an abandoned mail coach and set it ablaze as part of their Fourth of July bonfire. In another chapter, the boys fire a battery of abandoned cannons during the middle of the night, resulting in comedic chaos. Other chapters are filled with tension and conflict, such as the one in which the boys from rival sides of the town engage in an escalating war fought first with snowballs and then with dangerous projectiles of ice embedded with bird shot or marbles. Tom willingly participates in these adventures, and he sometimes plays the role of instigator.

Another way in which Tom differs from earlier child characters from American children's literature is in his relationships with adults. There are three adult characters with whom Tom interacts on a daily basis. The most important adult in Tom's life is his grandfather, Captain Nutter. At first glance, this character seems to be a stern authority figure, but as the story progresses it becomes clear that the captain has a playful side as well. Tom also lives with his Aunt Abigail and an Irish housekeeper named Kitty Collins. These two women are often in conflict, but they both love Tom and try their best to keep him out of trouble. Tom clearly has much affection for these adults; he occasionally disobeys them, however, and in a few cases he outwits them. In his interactions with these adult characters, Tom exhibits an independent streak.

The Story of a Bad Boy does not have much of a central plot. Each chapter reads as a short story with its own subplot. Despite the episodic nature of the book, Tom gradually matures over the course of narrative. At the beginning of the book, Tom is an impulsive, generally cheerful twelve-year-old boy who seldom thinks about the future. As the story progresses, he becomes a bit more serious, develops an interest in girls, and even experiences a bout of adolescent angst during which he sets out to "become a blighted being." By the end of the book, he leaves school and prepares to go to work for his uncle in New York.

The Story of a Bad Boy achieved immense popularity. Nearly fifty editions came out during the nineteenth century, and the book continued to sell well into the early decades of the twentieth century. The success of the book encouraged other authors to write realistic boys' books in which the boy characters have exciting adventures. The most notable example is Mark Twain's *The Adventures of Tom Sawyer,* which came out seven years after the publication of Aldrich's novel. Another example is Booth Tarkington's *Penrod* (1914). Although *The Story of a Bad Boy* is not widely read today, it is still considered a classic children's novel because it played such a pivotal role in the rise of realistic characters in the pages of children's literature.

Discussion Questions

1. By titling his novel *The Story of a Bad Boy,* Aldrich emphasizes his character's "badness." In what ways is Tom Bailey bad? Does his "badness" detract from his appeal or add to it?

2. In *The Story of a Bad Boy,* Tom Bailey is described as "a boy of a naturally vivacious disposition" who "liked society." How does this personality trait figure in his interactions with the other boys in the town?

3. *The Story of a Bad Boy* is often described as a boys' book. Is Tom Bailey a character that only boy readers would find appealing? Why or why not?

4. The success of Aldrich's *The Story of a Bad Boy* led to the publication of other realistic adventure stories for boys, such as Mark Twain's *The Adventures of Tom Sawyer.* In what ways is Tom Sawyer similar to Tom Bailey?

—*Mark I. West*

REFERENCES

Lilian Aldrich, *Crowding Memories* (Boston: Houghton Mifflin, 1920);

Thomas Bailey Aldrich, *The Story of a Bad Boy,* introduction by David Watters (Hanover, N.H.: University Press of New England, 1990);

Ferris Greenslet, *The Life of Thomas Bailey Aldrich* (Boston: Houghton Mifflin, 1908);

Alice M. Jordan, *From Rollo to Tom Sawyer and Other Papers* (Boston: Horn Book, 1948);

Charles E. Samuels, *Thomas Bailey Aldrich* (New York: Twayne, 1966);

Frederic Fairchild Sherman, *A Checklist of First Editions of Thomas Bailey Aldrich* (New York: Privately printed, 1921).

Sherman Alexie
(October 7, 1966 –   )

ﶮ

THE LONE RANGER AND TONTO FISTFIGHT IN HEAVEN
(New York: Atlantic Monthly, 1993)

VICTOR

Victor is a young Native American who comes to terms with his heritage and adult responsibilities in Sherman Alexie's *The Lone Ranger and Tonto Fistfight in Heaven,* a collection of twenty-two interconnected short stories. Although many characters move in and out of focus in the stories, Victor is the character around whom a large part of the action flows. In "Every Little Hurricane" he is introduced as a nine-year-old who tries to sleep through his parents' New Year's Eve party. The young Victor is portrayed consistently as an observer, keenly aware of the events around him, yet unable or unwilling to participate in them. He watches what happens in his house, in his town, as if it were on television. His youth is spent dreaming of the past and of alternatives to his present life. Later, in "Somebody Kept Saying Powwow," a story in which Victor makes only a brief appearance, another character asserts the significance of observation for Native Americans: "Didn't you know that Indians are born with two antennas that rise up and field emotional signals? Norma always said that Indians are the most sensitive people on the planet. For that matter, Indians are more sensitive than animals, too. We don't just watch things happen. Watching automatically makes the watcher a part of the happening." In this context, Victor might not be as passive as he first appears.

Victor's parents are the two most important people in his life. In "Every Little Hurricane" he sleeps between his drunk, passed-out parents, trying to absorb some peace from them. In fact, Victor casts his origin as an act fueled by alcohol: "I was conceived during one of those drunken nights, half of me formed by my father's whiskey sperm, the other half formed by my mother's vodka egg. I was born a goofy reservation mixed drink, and my father needed me just as much as he needed every other kind of drink." Victor's father leaves the family in the story "Because My Father Always Said He Was the Only Indian Who Saw Jimi Hendrix Play 'The Star-Spangled Banner' at Woodstock." His father leaves out of a kind of unspoken dissatisfaction with the way his life had been going. He looked back on the days of his youth with intense nostalgia and could not square his life on the reservation with what he thought it could and should be. Victor's response to his father's desertion is anger and sadness, which has a large bearing on how he raises his own adopted son, James, in the story "Jesus Christ's Half Brother Is Alive and Well on the Spokane Indian Reservation." When Victor neglects to bring James home from a party, he is arrested for abandonment: "The tribal police drag me into the cell for abandonment and I'm asking them who they're going to arrest for abandoning me."

"A Drug Called Tradition" introduces an important character in Victor's life, the storyteller and mystic Thomas Builds-the-Fire. Victor and his friends experiment with hallucinogenic drugs in this story, and they have visions of themselves as great cowboys, musicians, and Indian heroes. Victor returns to sobriety with new insight into the power of the past and future to influence the present, especially for one unaware of the "skeletons" walking both in front of him and behind him. His dissatisfaction with the reality he sees around him, and his inability to see a realistic alternative, is a theme that runs through the entire collection. In the story "This Is What it Means to Say Phoenix, Arizona," Victor's father dies suddenly and far away. Victor, with the help of Thomas Builds-the-Fire, flies to Phoenix to claim his father's cremated remains. On the journey, Victor learns to value Thomas's ability as a storyteller, the central figure in Indian culture and the repository of all history.

With his father gone, Victor needs to find his own way to grow up. In the story "The Only Traffic Signal on the Reservation Doesn't Flash Red Anymore," he and his friend Adrian reminisce about their own too-brief basketball careers as they watch the next young hotshot, a kid named Julius Windmaker, about whom Victor says: "he had that gift, that grace, those fingers like a goddamn medicine man." While Adrian never had a basketball career to speak of, Victor nursed dreams of basketball glory throughout his youth, until a realization of his own fragility slowed him forever. Again, from the perspective of an observer, a nonparticipant, Victor is left to imagine a different reality, one that more closely conforms to his dreams for a better life. He takes no satisfaction in watching Windmaker succumb to alcohol and waste his basketball talent. He hopes that the next young reservation star will make it all the way, although he expresses that hope wistfully, uncertain if what he wishes for actually is possible at all.

A turning point for Victor comes when he becomes the guardian of a baby, James, whose parents died in a fire. James was injured in a fall during the fire and develops slowly. Victor tries to take good care of him and matures in the process. For the first time, the circumstances of his life demand he take an active role in someone else's life. He stumbles; alcohol comes close to undoing him, but he tries repeatedly to overcome his dependency. Finally, after seven years without speaking, James begins to say all kinds of wonderful things. Victor finally has a family he can imagine living with all of his life. He sees James taking care of him in his old age. Victor fades out of the mainstream of the stories after this point. Although he stumbles often, he seems to have found a place for himself, a way into a decent future.

Discussion Questions

1. Victor and Thomas Builds-the-Fire come to a new understanding of each other in the story "This Is What It Means to Say Phoenix, Arizona." How does their relationship develop through the course of this story? What does Victor learn about himself and other people as a result of this experience?

2. Victor's parents are important people in his life. Yet, their irresponsibility causes him sadness and anger. How exactly does Victor come to terms with his parents' legacy? Is he completely bitter, or does he find some measure of forgiveness for his imperfect parents?

3. James, the boy Victor adopts, is a curious character who spends most of his early life passively observing the world around him. How does James change Victor? What influence does Victor have on James?

4. Basketball is an ever-present force in reservation life. What role does the sport play in Victor's life? How does the fate of Julius Windmaker in the story "The Only Traffic Signal on the Reservation Doesn't Flash Red Anymore" affect Victor? How does Victor's knee injury affect him?

—*Bill Gillard*

RESERVATION BLUES
(New York: Atlantic Monthly, 1995)

THOMAS BUILDS-THE-FIRE

Sherman Alexie, a Native American storyteller, places Thomas Builds-The-Fire, another Native American storyteller, at the center of his novel *Reservation Blues*. As the lead singer of the blues band Coyote Springs, Thomas, a member of the Spokane tribe of the Northwestern United States, demonstrates many of Alexie's ideas about Indian identity, reservation existence, and freedom of expression. Audiences, white and Native American alike, turn against Coyote Springs for making music they do not think is "Indian" enough. Thomas becomes the main source of humor in the novel, often at Native Americans' expense, but he also addresses the plight of Indian existence with a deeply serious compassion. His music in turn combines indigenous Indian spirit and soulful blues rhythms, as if Thomas tries to sing of ancient Indian heartache and to make it accord with a modern musical style. Through Thomas, Alexie treats the band members' alcoholic excesses comically, portraying their suffering and alcoholism from their point of view: as providing inspiration for their music.

Thomas's frequent jokes do not inspire laughter, in fact, so much as empathetic understanding. His ancestors roamed the plains as fearless braves and unconquerable warriors; but his own generation only has bureaucracy and boredom to look forward to, overseen by the U.S. government's Bureau of Indian Affairs. Indians once told their own legends and passed their own religions on to successive generations; but Thomas's peers only have U.S. government lies to recount and spend more time consuming alcohol than preserving stories of Indian valor. Indian chants once called forth native spirits and evoked animals as the tribe's kindred, totem figures, as braves danced through fireside rituals; but Coyote Springs's music finds its inspiration with African American blues musician Robert Johnson's battered guitar, with the lessons of a spiritual healer named Big Mom, and with the vocal harmonizing of Betty and Veronica, two Caucasian backup singers. Thomas, Victor, and Junior, the original founders of the band, cannot seem to perform well without Johnson's guitar, which has miraculously made its way onto their reservation, and without the white women singing along. They honestly sing of their own stories, then, but do not have what others call a "purely" Indian band. Rather, theirs is an eclectic musical style, harmonizing with their racially mixed composition. Perhaps they are too mixed, in fact, for Coyote Springs never sound or look as their listeners wish. The Spokane tribe cannot accept Coyote Springs because Indians of a different tribe—Chess and Checkers Warm Water, Flatheads from Arlene, Montana—keep them from being an all-Spokane band. The alcohol Victor and Junior consume keeps them from performing their music at the best of their abilities. The reservation, where many Indians barely survive on the checks the government issues on the first of each month, cannot give the band the fan base or the funds it needs. The subject about which they sing, the blues spirit inherent in reservation life, tends also to inhibit the production of their music.

In his characterization of Thomas, Alexie also depicts the career of an artist who claims special license to speak for his tribe as a whole. The fact that Coyote Springs leaves the reservation, headed for a Seattle concert venue or a New York recording studio, might disqualify them from playing "reservation blues." One might not be able to make music about the lonesomeness of reservations, the poverty of Native American life, if one has left the reservation for the city, and if one's music has made one rich. Alexie balances a Native American spokesperson's quest to find a popular musician's stardom with his need to preserve a lonesome, starving Indian's authenticity.

Questions of success and authenticity assume more-serious dimensions when the band plays in New York, and when an all-white company named Calvary Records decides that the braves in the band do not look or sound enough like Indians to sell records—but that two non-Indian vocalists, Betty and Veronica, do. It seems likely that Indian blues cannot survive unless white, mainstream record executives shape how Indian music should sound and even choose singers based on their ideas of how Indians should look. Like James Weldon Johnson or James Baldwin, who connected blues music to complicated lives in impoverished African American ghettos, Alexie lets Coyote Springs's successes and failures as a blues band speak for a minority's experience. Minority blues bands sing songs about their own existence, and yet need to appeal as well to white listeners outside the reservation or ghetto to have commercial success as a band.

Thomas's musical career is ultimately both comic and tragic. Comically, he demonstrates that alcoholism and loneliness, usually seen as disadvantages of Indians' existence, can lead to their musical success. But he also shows that demanding a reservation sound from an Indian band leads to Indians remaining stuck on the reservation. When Thomas's fellow band members devote more time to the bottle than the band, and when the record industry ruins Coyote Springs's authenticity as an Indian blues band, Thomas returns to the reservation in defeat. He has nothing left from Coyote Springs's concert tour, other than the sad stories he can tell others. Indian blues, much like Native American literature, he discovers, needs to find an audience beyond the reservation, but once it leaves the reservation and reaches white listeners, it risks becoming something other than pure reservation blues.

Discussion Questions

1. Alexie could have consistently told the story from Thomas's point of view and in chronological order, but instead, he jumps around chronologically to describe a dream or distant memory and at times writes in surreal and mysterious, rather than realistic, ways. What effects does Alexie achieve by jumping around so much and mingling dreams with reality?

2. In what ways do Alexie, as a Native American novelist, and Thomas, as a Native American lead singer, face similar problems in their writing and singing careers? Consider, for example, their approaches to finding an audience, their ways of deciding what they should write or sing, and their ways of making stories or songs out of familiar subject matter.

3. African American writers from James Weldon Johnson (in *The Autobiography of an Ex-Colored Man*), to Langston Hughes (in *Montage of a Dream Deferred*), to James Baldwin (in "Sonny's Blues"), have drawn connections between literature and blues rhythms. What seems the same about African American blues, as the heroes of these works experience them and sing about them, and Indian blues, as Thomas experiences them? What seems different?

—Adam Sonstegard

REFERENCES

Joseph L. Coulombe, "The Approximate Size of His Favorite Humor," *American Indian Quarterly*, 26, no. 1 (2002): 94–115;

Jerome DeNuccio, "Slow Dancing with Skeletons: Sherman Alexie's *The Lone Ranger and Tonto*

Fistfight in Heaven," *Critique,* 44, no. 1 (2002): 86–96;

Daniel Grassian, *Understanding Sherman Alexie* (Columbia: University of South Carolina Press, 2005);

Paul Paquaretta, "African-Native American Subjectivity and the Blues Voice in the Writings of Toni Morrison and Sherman Alexie," in *When Brer Rabbit Meets Coyote: African-Native American Literature,* edited by Jonathan Brennan (Urbana: University of Illinois Press, 2003), pp. 278–291;

Gordon E. Slethaug, "Hurricanes and Fires: Chaotics in Sherman Alexie's *Smoke Signals* and *The Lone Ranger and Tonto Fistfight in Heaven,*" *Literature Film Quarterly,* 31, no. 2 (2003): 130–141;

Blythe Tellefson, "America Is a Diet Pepsi: Sherman Alexie's *Reservation Blues,*" *Western American Literature,* 40 (Summer 2005): 125–147.

Nelson Algren

(March 28, 1909 – May 9, 1981)

✺

THE MAN WITH
THE GOLDEN ARM

(Garden City, N.Y.: Doubleday, 1949)

FRANKIE MACHINE

Frankie Machine is the drug-addicted protagonist of Nelson Algren's third novel, *The Man with the Golden Arm.* As the novel opens, Frankie and his best friend, Solly "Sparrow" Saltskin (a shoplifter and seller of stolen dogs), are being released after a night in jail. Incarceration, however, is to be expected in Frankie's world; as Sparrow puts it, "everybody got to get arrested now 'n then," or, as police captain "Record Head" Bednar explains, the two are "a couple loose bums livin' off the weaker bums. . . ." However, what Algren explores are the reasons why Frankie is himself one of the weaker bums of society. ("The Weaker Sheep" was among Algren's working titles for the novel.) Indeed, as Algren later remarked, the point (as with most of his fiction) was to elicit in the reader compassion

for Frankie as a man who "had no alternatives: that was the very reason I wrote about him. His frame of reference was the street he worked on, the army he served in and the needle he died by."

Set primarily in the inner-city neighborhood surrounding Chicago's Division Street between autumn 1946 and spring of 1948, *The Man with the Golden Arm* follows Frankie through his days, interrupting his story to detail in often-comic prose the lives of other Division Street denizens. Having become addicted to morphine while recovering from a shrapnel wound received in the war, Frankie has returned to his hopeless dreams (he wants to be a professional jazz drummer) and to a wife, Sophie, whom he married only because he thought she was pregnant and with whom he stays because he was drunk at the wheel when a car crash put Sophie in a wheelchair with injuries more psychological than physical. To ease his guilt, Frankie turns to drugs, to pranks and petty larceny, to hours drinking in the Tug and Maul bar, and to an affair with Molly Novotny, the "girl with the heart-shaped face and the wonder gone out of her eyes."

The wonder has left most of the eyes on Division Street: as the novel progresses and Sophie slips deeper into the gloom of her lonely brooding, Frankie drinks and dreams, deals cards and sticks a hypodermic needle into his arm until a quarrel with his drug dealer, Nifty Louie Fomorowsky, leaves Louie dead. Before suspicion falls on Frankie, he is arrested for shoplifting and sent to prison. The novel offers a detailed account of life behind bars and of the pain of kicking a drug habit. Back on the street, he is soon back on drugs despite Molly's efforts to help him get clean because, as he explains, "nobody can stand gettin' that sick 'n live," that "there ain't no 'will power' to it like squares like to say."

Eventually, the identity of Louie's killer becomes an open secret on Division Street, and the police pursue Frankie until, in pain from a gunshot wound and in need of a fix, the emptiness of his future overwhelms him, and he hangs himself in the flophouse where he has been hiding. Frankie dies as he has lived: a broken machine, a man who never knew who he was: "You know who I am? You know who you are?" he challenges Sparrow. "You know who *anybody* is any more?" He is a poor man with few skills and little education who identifies with a roach drowning in a jail-cell water bucket, a victim whose bad breaks are to a significant degree (like his initial addiction to morphine) the result of forces and circumstances over which he has little control. The only explanation he can offer for the choices he has made is a dismissive "some cats just swing like that, Molly-O."

"Machine" is a nickname acquired by Frankie Majcinek because of his machine-like skill as a professional card dealer for poker games. "It's all in the wrist 'n I got the touch," Frankie is fond of saying, bragging that he "drives like he deals, deals like he lives 'n he lives all the time." If an ability to shuffle and deal seems a small thing, it suggests how narrow Frankie's world is and how little he has of which to be proud. Early in the novel, Sophie laments that "God has forgotten us all." It could be argued that Algren, who believed that "literature is made upon any occasion that a challenge is put to the legal apparatus by conscience in touch with humanity," wrote *The Man with the Golden Arm* so that people like Frankie and Sophie would not be forgotten, and so that readers might recognize that, as one arrested character puts it, "we are all members of one another."

Discussion Questions

1. Nelson Algren is sometimes described as a literary naturalist, which means in part that he sees people as products of heredity, environment, and chance more than of free will and deliberate choice. Is Frankie to blame for what happens to him, or is he a victim of things beyond his control?

2. What purpose is served by interrupting Frankie's story with material about other characters: the "Great Sandwich Battle" between Vi and Stash, for instance, or the scene in which Record Head Bednar interrogates the petty criminals rounded up by the police?

3. *The Man with the Golden Arm* is often very funny. What is the function of the humor in Algren's development of Frankie?

4. Algren's epigraph, taken from the Russian novelist Aleksandr Kuprin, reads, "Do you under-stand, gentlemen, that all the horror is in just this—that there is no horror!" In what ways does this idea provide a means of understanding how Algren wants his readers to respond to Frankie's story?

5. The critic Chester Eisinger once complained that Algren's books were "not very different" from one another. In what ways is the characterization of Frankie psychologically and/or stylistically different from the characterization of Bruno Bicek in *Never Come Morning* or Dove Linkhorn in *A Walk on the Wild Side?*

—*Brooke Horvath*

ᗜ

NEVER COME MORNING
(New York & London: Harper, 1942)

BRUNO "LEFTY" BICEK

Bruno "Lefty" Bicek first appeared in the 1941 short story "Biceps," which was later collected as "A Bottle of Milk for Mother" in Nelson Algren's first story collection, *The Neon Wilderness* (1947). In 1942 Bruno returned as the protagonist of Algren's second novel, *Never Come Morning*, which also incorporated the plot of "Biceps" as part of its larger story. The novel was, Algren later explained, "a thinly fictionalized report on a neighborhood" and on "the lives of half a dozen men with whom the writer had grown up, as well as upon newspaper reports of the trial of Bernard 'Knifey' Sawicki," a nineteen-year-old who went on a killing spree in the summer of 1941.

Set in the west-side Polish neighborhood of Chicago known as the Triangle during the late 1930s and early 1940s, *Never Come Morning* focuses on Bruno and his girlfriend, Steffi Rostenkowski, both fatherless seventeen-year-olds when the novel opens. Their story is as simple as it is heartbreaking: Steffi, betrayed by Bruno's cowardice, is raped by members of Bruno's street gang before Bruno lashes out in his shame, killing a stranger waiting in the rape line. Steffi is forced into a life of prostitution, while Bruno, taking the rap for a mugging he and two friends attempted, is incarcerated for six months. Upon his release, he becomes a pimp and bouncer at the brothel where Steffi works, attempts to set things right with Steffi, and eventually manages to realize a lifelong dream by getting himself a professional boxing match. Doing so, however, means crossing Bonifacy "the Barber" Konstantine, a procurer, fence, fight promoter, and organizer of local teenagers into criminal gangs. Bonifacy, seeking revenge for Bruno's betrayal, gives the police all they need to arrest Bruno for the rape-line murder. The novel ends immediately after Bruno has won his first professional bout with the police arriving and Bruno protesting that he "knew [he'd] never get t' be twenty-one anyhow."

Explaining that his assault upon an old man was just his way of "break'n the old monotony," Bruno hopes to be exculpated by reminding the police that "I'm a neighborhood kid is all." The first eighty pages of the novel offer a detailed picture of what life in that neighborhood is like. It is a life of economic, intellectual, and emotional poverty, enlivened by baseball, petty larceny, and efforts to meet girls who might let one seduce them and thereby prove one's manhood. Honest work is scarce and scorned, and peer pressure is the principal force shaping the lives of Bruno and his friends. Bruno, who protests that he has "been hungry all [his] life, all the time," lives in a world in which the main thing is "to take care of number one." Steffi, following a booze-toting Bruno to the shed where she will soon be raped repeatedly, can only think, "I got nothin', so I got nothin' to lose"—in which respect she is no different from Bruno. The Triangle is a place where, Bruno explains, "ever'thin's crooked"; life is "a ceaseless series of lusts"; survival depends upon brutal cunning and physical strength; and "personal triumphs in public places" (winning a fight or a craps game, committing a successful crime, seducing a girl) are the best life can offer. The world of the Triangle is, Steffi thinks one lonely night, "a curtained brothel," the city "a madhouse" in which a boy like Bruno "wished only to be a man" but carried a burden of guilt, shame, and depravity that grew heavier by the day.

According to a preface for *Never Come Morning* written by Algren in 1963, "the novel attempted to say, about the American outcast, what James Baldwin has observed more recently of the American Negro: if you don't know my name you don't know your own. I felt that if we did not understand what was happening to men and women who shared all the horrors but none of the privileges of our civilization, then we did not know what was happening to ourselves." An example of literary naturalism that combines poetic prose with internal monologues, surreal dreams, expressionistic description, and the replication of the argot and speech rhythms of the street, *Never Come Morning* documents the effects of environment upon those trapped in the sort of world that is the Triangle. The result, according to novelist James T. Farrell, was a "telling social indictment," a novel Ernest Hemingway believed to be "about the best book to come out of Chicago."

Discussion Questions

1. What does Algren mean when he writes that *Never Come Morning* attempted to say about social outcasts such as Bruno "what James Baldwin has observed more recently of the American Negro: if you don't know my name you don't know your own"?

2. *Never Come Morning* was attacked for its unflattering portrait of Polish Americans. Is the book singling out Bruno's ethnicity for condemnation?

3. Does Bruno ever genuinely care for Steffi, or is she simply the focus of his needs and desires and, later, of his guilt and shame?

4. Research the story of real-life criminal Bernard "Knifey" Sawicki (you might begin with Bettina Drew's biography, *Nelson Algren: A Life on the Wild Side*). How did Algren use Sawicki in his creation of Bruno?

5. The writer John Clellon Holmes believed that Algren preferred America's outcasts to its respectable citizens because they were "more honest." In what ways are the protagonists of Algren's novels—Bruno of *Never Come Morning,* Dove Linkhorn of *A Walk on the Wild Side,* and Frankie Machine of *The Man with the Golden Arm*—more honest than the members of the middle class that appear in these same novels?

—Brooke Horvath

ᘝ⚬

A WALK ON THE WILD SIDE
(New York: Farrar, Straus & Cudahy, 1956)

DOVE LINKHORN

Dove Linkhorn is the protagonist of Nelson Algren's fourth novel, *A Walk on the Wild Side*. The novel began as a revision of Algren's first novel, *Somebody in Boots* (1935), but the changes grew so numerous and wide-ranging that the result was an entirely new book. Whereas protagonist Cass McKay of *Somebody in Boots* was intended as a representative of the lumpenproletariat in a novel that preaches Marxist revolution at the same time that it questions the likelihood of such an event occurring in America, Dove is the picaresque, tragicomic hero of a story that indirectly lampoons the American Dream and notions of the self-made man by refusing to take either seriously. If the comic absurdity of the novel seems to mock Algren's earlier earnestness, his complex interweaving of emotions and his affectionate portraits of what he terms "lonesome monsters" yield fiction as comically serious as anything Algren ever wrote. Like another character in the novel, Hallie Breedlove, *A Walk on the Wild Side* smiles precisely because it is so sad.

Set in the early years of the Depression (the spring of 1930 through the spring of 1932), the novel takes Dove from his hardscrabble life in Arroyo, Texas, through a brief series of adventures on the road (where he meets the memorable Kitty Twist) to New Orleans, where he finds work as a shady door-to-door salesman, a manufacturer of O-Daddy condoms, and an actor in a sex show. This last career move leads to an affair with the prostitute Hallie and a vicious beating at the hands of Hallie's legless lover—a beating that leaves Dove blinded and heading for home as the novel closes.

Algren described *A Walk on the Wild Side* as a "reader's book" in which the writer had to think first about amusement. Thus, Dove is cast as an innocent abroad (in the manner of Mark Twain's Huck Finn or Voltaire's Candide): a comic figure of irrepressible optimism and good-natured gullibility trapped in an often horrific world in which no one is to be trusted and along any street of which "the wildest beast of

all roamed free." Dove enters this world convinced of his invulnerability and golden promise: "I don't know what kind of great I'm bound to be," Dove declares early in his story; "all I know for certain is I'm a born world shaker." By the end of the novel, however, Dove feels differently about his lot: "'I feel like I been everywhere God got land,' Dove thought, 'yet all I found was people with hard ways to go. All I found was troubles 'n degradation. . . . All I found was two kinds of people. Them that would rather live on the loser's side of the street with the other losers than win off by themselves; and them who want to be one of the winners even though the only way left for them to win was over them who have already been whipped." Thinking of himself as much as of the "poor bummies [and] poor tarts" he has known, Dove adds, "you could always treat one too good, it was said, but you never could treat one too bad." In short, Dove's story demonstrates the truth of Algren's observation that there is always "room for one more at the bottom."

A Walk on the Wild Side is a book that reveals the results of poverty and stupidity, violence and depravity. As one of Dove's jail mates contends, whether in or out of jail, everyone is "innocent of nothin'! Guilty of everythin'!" It is a world in which the successful are mocked as more corrupt and immoral than any prostitute or con man. As Algren explained on the dust jacket of the first edition, "this is a story that tries to tell something about the natural toughness of women and men. . . . The book asks why lost people sometimes develop into greater human beings than those who have never been lost in their whole lives. Why men who have suffered most at the hands of men are the natural believers in humanity. . . ." However flawed Dove may be, however flawed the world in which he finds himself, he—like the rest of the men and women populating the novel—is capable of acting honorably and selflessly, driven by pride and the desire for dignity, the need for love and redemption. Although reviewers in the mid 1950s faulted Algren for sentimentally valorizing the bottom dogs of society in the outmoded manner of Depression-era literary naturalism, Algren thought *A Walk on the Wide Side* "by sixteen furlongs and eleven lengths" a better book than his award-winning *The Man with the Golden Arm.* "It is," Algren wrote, "a kind of novel that, so far as I know, has never been written before. It is an American fantasy, a poem written to an American beat as true as *Huckleberry Finn.*"

Discussion Questions

1. Dove is in many ways foolish, boorish, reprehensible. How does Algren manage to engage our sympathies for such a character? Is Algren's portrait of Dove sentimental?

2. The novel blames "the city fathers" and other representatives of polite, middle-class society for the vice and immorality that fill its pages. To what extent is Dove a victim of society? To what extent is he a victimizer who deserves to be blamed for what he does?

3. Algren said that *A Walk on the Wild Side* asks "why lost people sometimes develop into greater human beings than those who have never been lost." How does the novel answer this question? How would you?

4. Algren believed that *A Walk on the Wild Side* was "a kind of novel that . . . has never been written before," but he also compared it to Mark Twain's *Huckleberry Finn.* To what novel would you compare *A Walk on the Wild Side?* Why? What other character in American literature most reminds you of Dove?

5. Compare Dove and Cass McKay of *Somebody in Boots:* in what ways are they the same character? In what ways are they radically unlike each other?

—*Brooke Horvath*

REFERENCES

Nelson Algren, *The Man with the Golden Arm,* Fiftieth Anniversary Critical Edition, edited by William J. Savage Jr. and Daniel Simon (New York: Seven Stories Press, 1999);

Matthew J. Bruccoli with the assistance of Judith Baughman, *Nelson Algren: A Descriptive Bibliography* (Pittsburgh: University of Pittsburgh Press, 1985);

Martha Heasley Cox and Wayne Chatterton, *Nelson Algren* (Boston: Twayne, 1975);

James R. Giles, *Confronting the Horror: The Novels of Nelson Algren* (Kent, Ohio: Kent State University Press, 1989);

Brooke Horvath, *Understanding Nelson Algren* (Columbia: University of South Carolina Press, 2005);

Robert Ward, ed., *Nelson Algren: A Collection of Critical Essays* (Madison, Wis.: Fairleigh Dickenson University Press, 2007).

Dorothy Allison
(April 11, 1949 –   )

BASTARD OUT OF CAROLINA
(New York: Plume, 1992)

RUTH ANNE "BONE" BOATWRIGHT

Ruth Anne "Bone" Boatwright is the observant child-narrator of Dorothy Allison's first novel, *Bastard out of Carolina,* published in 1992. A National Book Award nominee, the novel tells Bone's story from her own perspective, and the result is a merciless but relatively nonjudgmental view of lower-class life in post–World War II Greenville, South Carolina. Bone's life also becomes a testimony of abuse and the manner in which one survives it. By the end of the novel, Bone learns how identifying and acknowledging one's personal demons becomes a way of moving beyond them.

What marks Bone's life from the beginning of as well as throughout the novel is, much like the poverty in which she lives, something she has no control over: her illegitimacy. Bone's certification as illegitimate by the State of South Carolina occurs when her grandmother becomes confused while trying to hide Bone's illegitimacy from hospital officials when filling out her birth certificate. Bone's nickname results from her uncle's saying she is "no bigger than a knucklebone." Bone's mother, Anney, tries over the course of the next few years to have the birth certificate corrected, but every time she gets a new copy of the birth certificate it still has the word "Illegitimate" written across the bottom. Bone's illegitimacy becomes even more obvious when her mother marries Lyle, a sweet, gentle man who is estranged from his prosperous family. Anney soon gives birth to Reese, and after Lyle dies in a car accident, Bone is forced to spend time with Reese's rich grandparents, who emphasize her lower-class origins and illegitimacy. Although other children taunt her, Bone's status as a bastard is almost never something that people point out to her explicitly; like her poverty, it becomes a silent burden that sets her apart from her peers, and even her family, throughout the novel. Bone realizes this separation when she reads *Gone with the Wind* and recognizes her mother not as Scarlett O'Hara but as the poor white Emma Slattery: "That's who I'd be, that's who we were. Not Scarlett with her baking-powder cheeks. I was part of the trash down in the mud-stained cabins, fighting with the darkies and stealing ungratefully from our betters, stupid, coarse, born to shame and death."

Bone's acknowledgment of her role as an outsider in society and her family becomes even more apparent when her mother marries Glen Waddell—Daddy Glen to Bone. Bone becomes a victim of both sexual and physical abuse at the hands of her stepfather. Glen's love for Anney is almost psychotic in nature and causes him to be jealous of her love for her children, Bone in particular. The resulting abuse causes Anney to leave Glen for a period and culminates when Glen brutally rapes Bone. Again, the focus is on Bone's illegitimacy when Glen tells her: "You goddamn little bastard. . . . If it hadn't been for you, I'd have been all right. Everything would have been all right." During this scene, and others like it in the novel, Bone learns a hard lesson about the nature of love as her mother flees with Glen after the rape and leaves Bone to live with her aunt. Bone goes from hating her mother to pitying her, just as she both pities and hates other children who make fun of her for being a bastard. As Carolyn E. Megan notes, "In *Bastard out of Carolina*, Allison treads the fragile ground between judgment and understanding, violence and redemption. In the end, Allison suggests, people will suffer the ramifications of their choices by the very lives they lead."

When the novel ends, it is clear that Anney is going to suffer tremendously for the choice she has made, but it becomes apparent that she truly wanted the best for Bone when, before leaving with Glen, she gives her a birth certificate that no longer bears the stamp of illegitimacy. Bone realizes, at age twelve, that she does not understand anything, least of all her mother. Through her main character, Allison presents a realistic vision of emotional trauma as well as the response to it. For Bone, the dramatic stories she invents as well as the gospel revivals she attends become a way of seeking identity and coping with abuse. For example, after Glen breaks her clavicle, Bone imagines a detailed scene in which she forgives him and then dies. Allison has discussed the manner in which Bone's storytelling is a method of survival: "It becomes a technique whereby she retains a sense of power in a situation where she has none. And comfort, just sheer physical comfort or retelling herself the story in which she is not a victim." Admitting a strongly autobiographical element to the novel, Allison has also acknowledged how writing and storytelling have helped her survive her own experiences of sexual and physical abuse.

Discussion Questions

1. There is much discussion on what it means to be a "Boatwright woman" in the novel. Anney supposedly gets the look of one after Lyle dies, and at the end of the novel Bone says she will become one. What does this status mean for these women, Bone in particular? Does it have a social, economic, or personal meaning?

2. Why does Bone become friends with Shannon Pearl and attend church revival meetings? What is her attraction to people like the Pearl family and these religious events? How does it help her cope in the novel?

3. There is great emphasis placed on Bone's reading and storytelling in the novel. What kinds of books does she read, and what do they reveal about her personality and way of coping with the abuse? What kinds of stories does she invent? Does her reading link her with other characters in the novel or only further alienate her?

4. Why does Anney leave with Glen at the end of the novel? Furthermore, why does she give Bone the birth certificate? How does Bone react, and what do these events say about the larger themes of the novel?

—*Brittany R. Powell*

REFERENCES

Leigh Gilmore, *The Limits of Autobiography: Trauma and Testimony* (Ithaca, N.Y.: Cornell University Press, 2001);

Carolyn E. Megan, "Dorothy Allison," in *The History of Southern Women's Literature,* edited by Carolyn Perry and Mary Louise Weaks (Baton Rouge: Louisiana State University Press, 2002), pp. 584–587;

Megan, "Moving toward Truth: An Interview with Dorothy Allison," *Kenyon Review,* 16 (Fall 1994): 71–83.

Julia Alvarez
(March 27, 1950 –   )

‿❧

HOW THE GARCÍA GIRLS LOST THEIR ACCENTS
(Chapel Hill, N.C.: Algonquin, 1991)

THE GARCÍA FAMILY

Julia Alvarez's *How the García Girls Lost Their Accents* is what the author calls a "loosely autobiographical" novel, telling the story of the Garcías, a Dominican family that struggles to find a place in American society. The family consists of four sisters, Carla, Sandi, Yolanda, and Sofia, and their parents, Carlos and Laura. Like Alvarez's own family, the Garcías immigrated to the United States from the Dominican Republic following the father's involvement in a failed rebellion against the dictator Rafael Trujillo. Trujillo's reign lasted for three decades, during which time the Dominican Republic was plagued by violence and corruption. Those who challenged the supreme authority of the dictator frequently "disappeared" and were never heard from again. Part of a wealthy and respected Dominican family, the Garcías are able to escape to the safety of the United States, where their lives are no longer in danger but their cultural identities are.

While all of the chapters are narrated through a mix of third-person narration, each chapter focuses on one or more specific family members, whose perspectives and experiences dominate temporarily. The novel thus offers many intersecting stories about different characters' personal negotiations with American society. The stories of the sisters are particularly important, as each has been marked by Dominican culture in different ways and each encounters her own America despite their shared home life. However, all of the sisters find it difficult to make sense of the Latin American Catholic worldview once it is transplanted to 1960s American soil. As Yolanda's lover complains, sometimes "he felt caught between the women's libber and the Catholic senorita." What makes for a "good daughter" by Papi's standards is often in conflict with what makes for an independent young woman.

Carlos García, Papi, is the character most resistant to the Americanization of his family. A doctor in the Dominican Republic, in the United States he is forced to live on a small fellowship and do unspecified work at a hospital while he earns a license to practice in his new country. Papi retains not only his strong Dominican accent, but his allegiance to Dominican ideas about gender and parenting as well. These ideas regularly lead him into conflict with his children, whose educational and social experiences often make them feel more American than Dominican.

Laura García de la Torres, Mami, is the matriarch of the García family. Having been partially educated in the United States, she has always chosen to raise her children according to a mix of American and Dominican ideas about parenting. Her embrace of American ideas about freedom and women's potential frequently balances out her husband's Old World attitudes. Mami has a revolutionary fantasy of herself as an inventor, an atypical dream for a woman of her class and culture. Nevertheless, in the minds of her daughters, she is "a good enough Mami, fussing and scolding and giving advice, but a terrible girlfriend parent, a real failure of a Mom." Mami, struggling to raise four girls on a tight budget and without the help of the servants and extended family she is used to, tends toward a regimented style of homemaking. For instance, when the girls were young, she "dressed them all alike in diminishing-sized, different color versions of what she wore," feeling that she lacked the time and energy to indulge in individual tastes and preferences.

Mami's color coding is something that upsets Carla, the eldest of the García daughters. Carla is a child psychologist who frequently annoys her siblings and parents with unwanted psychoanalytic commentary and advice. Most memorably, she writes an essay, "I Was There Too," that offends Mami, claiming that her dressing her daughters by a color system "had weakened the four girls' identity differentiation abilities and made them forever unclear about personality boundaries." Carla's childhood experience of America is marked by an encounter with a flasher shortly after her arrival, the first of many confusing encounters with sexuality that the girls experience. As the oldest sister and the most experienced, she is often the one to clear the way for the other girls in their efforts to embrace American culture.

Sandi, the second oldest, is known in her family as the beautiful sister. As Mami explains, "Sandi got the fine looks, blue eyes, peaches and ice cream skin. . . . But imagine, spirit of contradiction, she wanted to be darker complected like her sisters." Mami makes this comment to Dr. Tandlemann, a psychiatrist who is trying to explain to the García parents why Sandi, their beautiful daughter, has been institutionalized and believes that she is rapidly devolving into a monkey. Through Sandi, Alvarez examines the struggles with white standards of beauty that each of the girls must deal with in turn.

Yolanda, or Yo, the third daughter, is the character most like the author. Yo is a poet whose identity struggles center on language and the loss of her mother tongue in her new country. She is also the central character of Alvarez's third novel, *Yo!* (1997). As Alvarez explains in an interview, "She is sort of the centering point of view in *How the García Girls Lost Their Accents* and she plays the role of the storyteller. It seemed appropriate, then, to turn the table on her and see what stories others tell about her." *Yo!* takes as its premise that Yolanda has written a book about her family (presumably *How the García Girls Lost Their Accents*) that has hurt and angered them; it is narrated by each of the other members of the García family in turn. *Yo!* deals with many of the issues of responsibility and ethics that Alvarez herself faces when writing about her experiences with her Dominican family and culture.

Sofia, Fifi, is the baby of the García family. Having grown up in the United States since she was a small child, she is the most Americanized of the girls, and the most rebellious. As a young woman, she is sent to live in the Dominican Republic after taking responsibility for a bag of marijuana that the sisters have been caught with. Later, she runs away from home to marry Otto, a man she meets in Colombia, and with whom she has "gone behind the palms," as her father puts it. Engaging in premarital sex is something Papi threatens never to forgive, though Fifi's marriage to Otto and the birth of their son helps to heal the rift. Fifi's sisters have similar struggles with Papi's Catholic morality and traditional Dominican ideas about women, but Fifi's acts of defiance most clearly demonstrate the difference between American and Dominican attitudes toward women's sexuality.

Alvarez's García family is certainly the best-known Dominican American family in U.S. Latino literature. The sisters' struggles with the intricacies of Latin American and United States sexual mores and gender norms are echoed in a broad range of literature by Latina writers including Esmerelda Santiago's *Almost a Woman* (1998), Ana Castillo's *The Mixquiahuala Letters* (1986), and Sandra Cisneros's *House on Mango Street* (1991).

Discussion Questions

1. Alvarez begins the novel in the present and works backward in time. How does this affect the reader's experience of the characters? How does the movement back to the Dominican Republic relate to this?

2. In *Yo!* Yolanda's family is angry about the ways that she depicts their lives in her novel. They quarrel with her interpretation of events. How is this theme, that events are subject to interpretation, treated in *How the García Girls Lost Their Accents?*

3. At one point Yo objects to the shortening of her name, and her sister explains that "She wants to be called Yolanda now." Why is naming important to Yolanda?

4. As an adult, Carla claims that she felt her individual identity was lost in Mami's tendency to treat

the girls as a unit. Many readers find themselves confusing the sisters. Why do you think this happens? In what ways does Alvarez try to distinguish the girls?

—*Shealeen Meaney*

REFERENCES

Julia Alvarez, "A Note on the Loosely Autobiographical," *New England Review: Middlebury Series*, 21 (Fall 2000): 165–166;

William Luis, "A Search for Identity in Julia Alvarez's *How the García Girls Lost Their Accents*," *Callaloo*, 23 (Summer 2000): 839–849;

Silvio Sirias, *Julia Alvarez: A Critical Companion* (Westport, Conn.: Greenwood Press, 2001).

Laurie Halse Anderson

(October 23, 1961 –   )

❧

SPEAK

(New York: Farrar Straus & Giroux, 1999)

MELINDA SORDINO

Melinda Sordino, the teenage narrator of Laurie Halse Anderson's young-adult novel *Speak,* is a confused victim of sexual abuse. Over the course of a high-school academic year, she describes her surroundings and her situation, demonstrating a witty and bright understanding of certain aspects of her world. The voice employed is believable for a freshman girl, including as it does an ironic sense of humor that undoubtedly serves as a manner of defense against the feelings of alienation, depression, shame, loss, and victimhood Melinda faces after her attack and her status as an outcast from her school's social ranks as a result of her consequential action.

As the novel begins, the reader is unaware of the sexual abuse Melinda has endured and the exact nature of her transgressions against her social peers. She describes her first high-school assembly as a "National Geographic special," where the teachers are predators and young, lost girls such as herself are "wounded zebras." Other situations at the high school are related in a similarly humorous, tongue-in-cheek manner. Revealing a sensitivity to the stark reality she faces, Melinda uses humor to undercut the hypocrisy and insensitivity she observes around her. After an art teacher's speech denouncing the importance of words, for example, she observes, "For someone who questions the value of words, he sure uses a lot of them." Describing her former best friend's habit of "smoking" candy cigarettes, Melinda emphasizes the immaturity of this attempt at appearing mature: "Next thing you know, she'll be drinking black coffee and reading books without pictures." Further, in the midst of the mascot search, Melinda suggests "Overbearing Eurocentric Patriarchs," ironically emphasizing the impossibility of choosing a name that is completely politically correct. When meeting in the counselor's office with her parents and the principal, after a rude outburst by her parents, Melinda describes their apologies as a "show tune" complete with silly rhymes, drawing attention to the lack of true meaning and performative nature of the apologies. Finally, she sums up the misery she experiences after being dumped by her only friend by imagining a mock announcer bursting onto the scene and stating, "Another alternate-reality moment brought to you by Adolescence!"

Melinda's ironic sense of humor is one of the means by which she reshapes her world through words. She habitually gives teachers and others nicknames based on physical characteristics: she calls an overmuscled varsity coach "Mr. Neck," for example, and the frazzled English teacher with "uncombed stringy hair" is "Hairwoman." Hairwoman does not involve the class in discussions or even look directly at them, leading Melinda to conclude that she "has no face." She assigns nicknames to students as well, including "Basketball Pole" for one of the jocks she encounters in the lunchroom and "Donner" and "Blitzen" for two interchangeable members of the cheerleading squad.

Melinda's stereotyping other characters through the nicknames is her way of exerting power over them. She strips them of their personalities, their wills, and their ability to hurt her. Having reduced them to a type, she sees no reason to communicate with them, and thus she feels insulated from the pain she has suffered. Her habit of assigning nicknames seems mostly comic early in the novel but becomes more serious when she begins to refer to

"IT," as she calls her rapist. Melinda cannot say her attacker's name even to herself because doing so would encourage a personal connection and recognize that he is capable of holding power over her.

Discussion Questions

1. Laurie Halse Anderson employs various symbolic motifs in *Speak,* most notably plants, seeds, and trees, to underscore Melinda's emotional state. What is the significance of plants for Melinda?

2. The organization of *Speak* corresponds with Melinda's evolution as a character, in that information is revealed to the reader as Melinda recognizes and accepts her circumstances and reveals facts to herself and those around her. How does this eventual revelation of information affect the reader's experience of the novel?

3. How reliable is Melinda as a narrator? How would the novel change if narrated by one of the other characters (Heather, Rachel, or Mr. Neck, for example)? How would it change if written from an omniscient point of view?

—*Sarah L. Moore*

REFERENCE

Laurie Halse Anderson, "Speaking Out," *ALAN Review,* 27, no. 3 (2000): 25–26.

Maxwell Anderson
(December 15, 1888 – February 28, 1959)

~~~

THE BAD SEED
New York, Forty-sixth Street Theatre, December 8, 1954 (New York: Dodd, Mead, 1955)

RHODA PENMARK

Rhoda Penmark is the titular character of Maxwell Anderson's 1954 play *The Bad Seed* based on a novel by William March. Anderson's stage directions describe her as a "neat, quaint and pretty little girl of eight." Most adults dote on Rhoda; her father, army colonel Kenneth Penmark, says that she is "just too good to be true." While he means the remark as a sincere compliment, over the course of the play Anderson

reveals that it is literally true as well. Beneath her superficial perfection Rhoda is an evil child, perhaps a psychopath, who is capable of remorseless killing. The main action of *The Bad Seed* involves the revelation of Rhoda's true character and the varying capacities of the adults around her to see her as she really is.

In the first scenes, Rhoda appears to be an entirely charming child, adored by her parents and neighbors. Early in the first act, Penmark asks Rhoda, "What will you give me if I give you a basket of kisses?" She replies, "I'll give you a basket of hugs." Variations on this exchange occur at key points throughout the play, including the final words of the last scene. Anderson provides some early clues, however, that Rhoda's apparent perfection masks a darker reality and that most of the adults around her are blinded by her superficial charm. When she greedily responds to the gift of a locket by asking for two gemstones instead of one, her landlady praises her: "How wonderful to meet such a natural little girl! She knows what she wants and asks for it—not like those over-civilized little pets that have to go through analysis before they can choose an ice cream soda!" Rhoda later displays an alarming burst of temper because one of her classmates wins the medal for best penmanship, and Miss Fern, the head of Rhoda's school, tells Christine, Rhoda's mother, that Rhoda has a "disturbing" quality and is not popular with the other children.

Rhoda's psychopathic qualities are revealed in her nonreaction to the loss of her classmate Claude Daigle, whose death she caused by pushing him off a pier and then stamping on his hands when he tried to climb out of the water. Christine tries to comfort her with the words "Darling, you're controlling yourself very well, but just the same it was an unfortunate thing to see and remember. I understand how you feel, my darling," but Rhoda replies, "I don't know what you're talking about. I don't feel any way at all." Leroy, a handyman employed by the Penmarks' landlady, confronts her about her lack of empathy: "Ask me and I'll say you don't even feel sorry for what happened to that little boy." Rhoda says, "Why should I feel sorry? It was Claude Daigle got drowned, not me."

The Bad Seed is in part a "problem play," which deals with a matter of societal concern, in this case whether some people are born evil or if their behavior is a product of their environment. Reginald Tasker, a houseguest and noted crime writer, endorses the first position, telling Christine that some children are "bad seeds—just plain bad from the beginning, and nothing can change them." As evidence mounts against Rhoda, Christine begins to suspect that she is just such a "bad seed," having inherited evil from her grandmother, a murderer. Christine attempts to destroy this inheritance by killing both herself and Rhoda, but she fails. The play ends with a chilling echo of its opening, as Rhoda comes onstage and exclaims: "I love you, daddy! What will you give me for a basket of kisses?" Her father replies: "Oh, my darling—I'll give you a basket of hugs!"

Anderson adapted *The Bad Seed* from the 1954 novel by William March; he kept the main characters and basic plot, while simplifying the story and omitting some minor characters. He wrote *The Bad Seed* quickly, producing a first draft in two months and a completed version in five months, and did not consider it one of his better works; in fact, he referred to it as a "potboiler." Audiences nevertheless found it an effective and well-constructed play, and it ran for 334 performances in New York in 1954–1955 and remains in the active repertoire. It is unique in Anderson's oeuvre, which consists primarily of serious literary works such as *Both Your Houses* (winner of the Pulitzer Prize in 1933) and *Winterset* (winner of the New York Drama Critics Circle Award in 1935). Psychopathically evil child characters are rare in American theater: the clearest precedent to Rhoda may be Mary Tilford in Lillian Hellman's *The Children's Hour* (1934).

Discussion Questions

1. *The Bad Seed* takes place entirely in the Penmark family's apartment. How is the drama of the play intensified by Anderson's restricting the action to this space?

2. Critics have remarked on Maxwell Anderson's effective use of sound in *The Bad Seed*. Describe how Anderson uses music in this play, in particular the piece *Claire de Lune*.

3. Leroy is the first character to see Rhoda for what she really is. Why do you think Anderson included this character, and why did he make him an outsider to the social world of the other characters?

4. Mary Tilford in Lillian Hellman's *The Children's Hour* may be a spiritual predecessor to Rhoda. How are they similar, and how are they different? To what extent to you think these differences were due to differences in popular beliefs about psychology and sociology at the time each play was written?

—*Sarah Boslaugh*

WHAT PRICE GLORY

by Anderson and Laurence Stallings, New York, Plymouth Theatre, September 5, 1924; *Three American Plays* (New York: Harcourt, Brace, 1926).

CAPTAIN FLAGG

Captain Flagg is the rowdy company commander in *What Price Glory*, a three-act play by Maxwell Anderson and Laurence Stallings. Described as "a fine, magnificently endowed man," Flagg is a hard-working, hard-drinking, tough-talking military veteran, having served in both China and Cuba. Though he rules his men with an iron hand, Flagg also has a sensitive side, which is particularly evident at the end of act 2, as he tenderly comforts a dying young soldier.

What Price Glory is set in 1918 on a battlefront in France during World War I. Flagg has fallen in love with Charmaine, the seductive daughter of Cognac Pete, a local tavern owner, who freely shifts her sentiments from one well-dressed officer to another. When Flagg is preparing to head for Paris on leave, he refuses to take her along but asks that she wait for his return. He calls for a replacement to run the platoon while he is gone and, to his surprise, is sent First Sergeant Quirt, who had served as Flagg's superior officer in China and who is a brutal, brash, and battle-hungry womanizer. Flagg and Quirt are lifelong rivals who always fight and insult each other, yet also have a mutual respect. In fact, much of the play centers around this antagonistic relationship, which is by turns comic and threatening. Flagg's introduction of Quirt to his officers reflects this dichotomy. After praising Quirt's abilities, Flagg goes on to say, "As long as he's sober, he'll run this outfit—whether I'm here or absent; but Quirt loves the bottle; and when he's drunk he's the lousiest, filthiest bum that ever wore a uniform. . . . If he tanks up I'll break him."

In Flagg's absence, Quirt engages the affections of Charmaine—not the first time he has stolen a woman from Flagg. Upon returning from his leave—most of which he spent in a military prison after a drunken brawl—Flagg learns that Charmaine's father is distraught that his daughter has been dishonored. He is demanding her marriage to the offending soldier, as well as a large sum of money. Quirt thinks Flagg will take the fall, but Flagg turns the tables on him. Citing Quirt as the scoundrel who ruined her, Flagg tells him, "I'm going to marry you to Charmaine and let you make an honest woman out of her!" and docks an allotment of his pay. Fortunately for Quirt, the unit is suddenly ordered into battle, allowing him to escape the marital and financial traps.

The second act, set in a wine cellar at the war front, exposes the horrors of war as well as Flagg's own sentiments as he tends to several soldiers. Lieutenant Moore, upon seeing a wounded comrade brought in by Flagg, breaks down. "God DAMN them for keeping us up in this hellish town," he cries. "And since six o'clock there's been a wounded sniper in the tree by that orchard angel crying '*Kamerad! Kamerad!*' just like a big crippled whippoorwill. What price glory now? Why in God's name can't we all go home?" Flagg, seeming to attack Moore for his softness, abruptly puts his arm around him and "speaks in a quiet, chastening tone, with a gentility never before revealed." He says, "You are all tuckered out with your side of the line. Don't worry about your platoon. We'll get them out." Even the contention between Flagg and Quirt abates for a while. But when a corporal brings in a couple of new unseasoned lieutenants disguised as officers, Flagg vents his anger. "My name is Flagg, gentlemen, and I'm the sinkhole and cesspool of this regiment. . . . I am a lousy, good-for-nothing company commander. I corrupt youth and lead little boys astray into the black shadows between the lines of hell." The act ends as bombs explode in the bunker, fatally wounding the naive young soldier Lewisohn, who begs Flagg to "stop the blood," but Flagg can only hold his head and reassure him that "You'll be alright, boy. You'll be alright."

Back at Cognac Pete's tavern in act 3, Flagg resumes his clashes with Quirt, culminating in a face-off over Charmaine in a game of blackjack. "The man that wins gets a gun, and the man that loses gets a head start," Flagg dictates. Quirt loses but is out the door before Flagg can even grab the gun. Suddenly, a runner brings news that the outfit has been called back to the front. Weary and angry, Flagg at first refuses to go but ultimately relents. "There's something rotten about this profession of arms, some kind of damned religion connected with it that you can't shake," he laments. "When they tell you to die, you have to do it, even if you're a better man than they are." After he leaves, Quirt returns, and adhering to the same sense of military honor, he leaves, shouting, "Hey, Flagg, wait for baby!"

Discussion Questions

1. Compare the characteristics of Flagg with those of Quirt. How would you evaluate their similarities and their differences?

2. Flagg is not really motivated by patriotic ideals, one aspect of the play that caused outrage when it first opened. What, then, does drive Flagg? Where in the play can you find instances of what compels him?

3. Flagg is a toughened career veteran. What impact do you think that a lifelong confrontation with war has had on Flagg? Does he ever show regrets about this dedication?

4. What comic aspects can you find in the vitriolic relationship between Flagg and Quirt?

—*Karen C. Blansfield*

REFERENCES

Laurence G. Avery, *Dramatist in America: Letters of Maxwell Anderson, 1912–1958* (Chapel Hill: University of North Carolina Press, 1977);

Barrett Harper Clark, *Maxwell Anderson: The Man and His Plays* (New York: S. French, 1933);

Martha Cox, *Maxwell Anderson Bibliography* (Charlottesville: University of Virginia Press, 1974);

Nancy J. Doran Hazelton and Kenneth Krauss, eds., *Maxwell Anderson and the New York Stage* (Monroe, N.Y.: Library Research Associates, 1991);

Barbara Lee Horn, *Maxwell Anderson: A Research and Production Sourcebook* (Westport, Conn.: Greenwood Press, 1996);

Alfred S. Shivers, *The Life of Maxwell Anderson* (New York: Stein & Day, 1983);

Shivers, *Maxwell Anderson* (Boston: Twayne, 1976).

Sherwood Anderson
(September 13, 1876 – March 8, 1941)

"I'M A FOOL"
Collected in *Horses and Men* (New York: Huebsch, 1921).

WALTER MATHERS

Walter Mathers is the name the central character and nineteen-year-old narrator falsely gives himself in Sherwood Anderson's short story "I'm a Fool." Socially insecure, Walter works as a "swipe," rubbing down horses, tending to their minor injuries, and traveling with them to trotting races. Although he promises his mother, who finds his job a disgrace to his family, to "quit the race horses," he takes a swipe job in Sandusky, Ohio, where, on his day off, he mixes with "the dudes" downtown and spends his pay ostentatiously because he likes "to put up a good front." At the races he buys the best grandstand seat possible, from which he "looks down" on other swipes. There Walter begins a conversation with Wilbur Wessen, his sister, Lucy, and Wilbur's "best girl," Elinor Woodbury, young people who invite Walter to sit with them. He is impressed by his new acquaintances, and he seeks to impress them, in particular Lucy, "a peach" with whom he senses a mutual attraction. Observing that a horse he knows, owned by a Mr. Mathers and raced secretly by a man for whom he had groomed, will likely win one of the dishonest races, Walter advises Wilbur to bet on it, and the horse wins. He then begins a foolish lie, telling his new friends that he is Walter Mathers from Marietta, Ohio, the son of the owner of the winning horse, and that his father owns a "grand" house and large stables. His family, he says, is too proud to race horses, and he is at the track to check the honesty of the man racing the horse for his father. After the races, Walter and his friends spend their winnings on supper and champagne and then go to a park with dance halls and beaches. Left alone with Lucy, Walter believes he has found the girl he would like to marry and laments the evening's end. Suddenly, he is intensely aware that he has destroyed all possibilities for any future with Lucy by his lies. When she attempts to write him in Marietta, her letters will be returned, he concludes, stamped with the words "'there ain't any such guy,' or something like that," and he feels a "hard jolt" signaling that he has been a fool.

Anderson acknowledged his debt to Mark Twain when he wrote "I'm a Fool." Several critics have regarded the story as Anderson's attempt to turn a dramatic monologue, a narrative form in which a speaker reveals more about herself or himself than intended, into a story, and Anderson's narrator bares his feelings despite his attempts "to put up a good front" in unconvincing displays of confidence, disparagement of education, and exaggerated assertions of contentment. Thus, as with other Anderson stories, the plot of "I'm a Fool" is unimportant; rather what the character thinks and feels is at the heart of the story. As critic Malcolm Cowley has observed, Anderson preferred "emotional rather than factual truth." Contrary to what the narrator says, he does not leave home because younger boys take jobs away from him or because he is too old to remain there, factual as these statements might be. He leaves to escape frustration and anxiety caused by his mother's and his sister's driving him toward a kind of social respectability he is not prepared to embrace, made detestable for him by his sister's determination to become a teacher and by a neighborhood boy doing menial jobs "to work his way through college." Nevertheless, his refuge as a swipe ultimately proves insufficient because he needs broader human contact, acceptance, and love, underscoring major themes in the story: alienation and initiation. The images of "the dirty horsey pants" worn by the swipes and "the dressed-up people" in the grandstand objectify the conflict the narrator faces. That he takes another identity, albeit to blend with the grandstand crowd and to impress Lucy, and admits one can be educated and be free from pretensions suggests that he is ready to leave the world of horses behind. Furthermore, his "looking down on the swipes" from the grandstand indicates detachment, if not separation, from the job he "had been doing all the year before." A letter Anderson wrote to Alfred Stieglitz, a friend and distinguished photographer and editor, illuminates Walter's character and his emotions. "In my boyhood," he recalled, "I . . . was groom to running and trotting horses . . . because they were the most beautiful things about me. But it did not suffice. Will not suffice. The horse is the horse, and we are men." The consequences of the narrator's lie to Lucy come in the flash of one of Anderson's "moments," or epiphanies, but those consequences remain "after all this time," alive in his inescapable recollection of a specific time and place: "at three o'clock one October afternoon . . . in the grandstand at the fall trotting and pacing meet at Sandusky, Ohio." Critic Danforth Ross sees the narrator displaying "longing for life as it might be" and the necessity of "acceptance of life as it is."

Discussion Questions

1. The narrator of "I'm a Fool" is frequently compared to Mark Twain's Huckleberry Finn. Like Huck, Walter also rejects the values of his home environment. What do you believe is driving Walter upon his quest, and what do you think he hopes to find?

2. Several of Anderson's stories concerning adolescents and the horse-track culture focus upon themes of initiation. Would you agree that Walter Mathers is being initiated? What do his experiences teach him? Can you cite evidence to suggest that Walter has changed, or do you believe that much further progress awaits him?

3. One critic has observed that Walter is "exposed to the unpleasant realities of life" but that "he fails to achieve a mature understanding of them." Do you agree with this observation? What are the "unpleasant realities" that Walter encounters? Discuss what you believe to be Walter's dilemma in the story.

4. The narrator of "I'm a Fool" says that he likes "to put up a good front." Could it be argued that most of the narrator's comments are "a good front"? How do you interpret his comment to the reader, "I'm only telling you to get everything straight"?

—*John C. Unrue*

WINESBURG, OHIO
(New York: Huebsch, 1919)

WING BIDDLEBAUM

Wing Biddlebaum is the main character of "Hands," the second story in Sherwood Anderson's collection of linked stories, *Winesburg, Ohio*. The stories are connected by the presence of George Willard, a young man who listens as the lonely, alienated people of Winesburg—the "grotesques," to use Anderson's phrase—tell him of their emotionally frustrated lives. As the title of the story suggests, Wing Biddlebaum's main distinguishing characteristic is his hands: "Their restless activity, like unto the beating of the wings of an imprisoned bird, had given him his name." The word *hands* occurs more than thirty times in the story and becomes a controlling metaphor for understanding its theme and the conflicted character of the tormented Biddlebaum. As Anderson puts it, "The story of Wing Biddlebaum's hands is worth a book in itself."

Biddlebaum's name was once Adolph Myers, and he was a teacher in Pennsylvania. He was a natural teacher who encouraged the students to dream and use their imaginations to vivify their lives and aspirations: "With the boys of his school, Adolph Myers had walked in the evening or sat talking until dusk upon the schoolhouse steps lost in a kind of dream. Here and there went his hands, caressing the shoulders of the boys, playing about the tousled heads. As he talked his voice became soft and musical. There was a caress in that also. In a way the voice and the hands, the stroking of the shoulders and touching of the hair were a part of the schoolmaster's effort to carry a dream into the young minds. . . . Under the caress of his hands doubt and disbelief went out of the minds of the boys and they also began to dream." Myers was loved and respected as a teacher; yet, the town turns on him when an emotionally disturbed boy has sexual fantasies about him and tells his father that Myers molested him. The teacher was beaten and nearly lynched before being run out of town. He took the name "Biddlebaum" for himself as he fled. He ended up at his aunt's home in Winesburg, Ohio and became a nervous, haunted man, never understanding what had prompted the town's wrath against him in Pennsylvania but suspecting it had something to do with his hands, since the mob had warned him to keep his hands to himself. In the twenty years since, he has frequently hidden them out of shame and guilt, although when he loses himself in conversation they seem possessed with a life of their own, to the fascination of the people in Winesburg: "Winesburg was proud of the hands of Wing Biddlebaum in the same spirit in which it was proud of Banker White's new stone house and Wesley Moyer's bay stallion, Tony Tip, that had won the two-fifteen trot at the fall races in Cleveland." Nevertheless, Biddlebaum lives in a self-imposed exile, "forever frightened and beset by a ghostly band of doubts." George is the only person with whom he has something like a friendship.

As with his students years before, Biddlebaum encourages young George to follow his dreams beyond the emotionally stultifying confines of Winesburg: "And you are afraid to dream. . . . You must begin to dream." When he unconsciously reaches to put his hands encouragingly on George's shoulders, Biddlebaum is suddenly horrified and excuses himself. George intuits that Wing's hands are at the root of his torment (and of his personality) but decides not to pursue his curiosity about them. "'I'll not ask him about his hands,' he thought, touched by the memory of the terror he had seen in the man's eyes. 'There's something wrong, but I don't want to know what it is. His hands have something to do with the fear of me and of everyone.'"

The story closes as it begins, with Biddlebaum waiting at home for a visit from George, "still hunger[ing] for the presence of the boy, who was the medium through which he expressed his love of man." Preparing for bed, he resembles "a priest engaged in some service of his church. The nervous expressive fingers, flashing in and out of the light, might well have been mistaken for the fingers of the devotee going swiftly through decade after decade of his rosary." In his quiet repose he seems to have the dignity of a religious hermit.

"Hands," as with other stories in *Winesburg, Ohio*, has as one of its principal subjects sexuality and particularly sexual frustration. While the story does not suggest that the accusations of molestation against Biddlebaum are true, the intimate nature of his teaching methods seems to have an erotic component. Adolph Myers is described as effeminate, leading his classroom with "a power so gentle that it passes as a lovable weakness." "In their feeling for the boys under their charge," the story continues, such natural teachers "are not unlike the finer sort of women in their love for men." When Biddlebaum approaches that familiar degree of intimacy again, with George, he withdraws in panic. His isolation in Winesburg, it seems, is caused not only by his response to the trauma of nearly being lynched; he separates himself because of his inability to face his desires, desires that are expressed unconsciously by his caressing hands.

Discussion Questions

1. "The story of Wing Biddlebaum is worth a book in itself," Anderson writes. "Sympathetically set forth it would tap many strange, beautiful qualities in obscure men." What sort of qualities does Anderson have in mind? How can Biddlebaum be viewed as a frustrated artist, unable to exercise his talent?

2. What changes come over Biddlebaum when he is with George Willard? What does the change in his composure indicate about his feelings for George?

3. According to the story, Winesburg is proud of Wing Biddlebaum's hands. Why? What does the townspeople's pride in Biddlebaum say about their attitude toward individuality?

—*Patrick Meanor*

HELEN WHITE

Helen White is the daughter of Banker White, one of the most affluent members of the village of Winesburg, and his socially condescending wife in Sherwood Anderson's short-story collection *Winesburg, Ohio*. The most desirable of the young women in Winesburg, Helen is the fantasy love of the young men in the town. Shy and taciturn Seth Richmond in the story "The Thinker" recalls Helen's schoolgirl notes to him, from which he inferred that he had become "the favorite of the richest and most attractive girl in town," and he fantasizes about lying with Helen among fragrant blossoms amid the soft humming of bees. In "Drink" Helen is also the sexual fantasy of young Tom Foster, who "never asserted himself" and avoids personal involvement in order to "escape" the pain and suffering he observes everywhere. During a moment of drunkenness, actually an experiment that Tom says enables him to register experience without causing anyone else to suffer, he imagines himself making love to Helen on the seashore.

Helen's major function in the text is to complement and illuminate the character of her friend George Willard, a young newspaper reporter and aspiring writer who is the central figure of the collection. Helen has grown up in Winesburg, where she, like George, struggles toward maturity among persons whose hopes and dreams have gone unfulfilled. Helen's character is most fully realized in "Sophistication," the penultimate story of the collection, in which she, along with George, walks to the Winesburg Fair Ground the night after the fair has ended and experiences an enlightened moment when, as the narrator says, "the thing that reflects and remembers," a sign she is coming to her "womanhood," overcame her "unthinking" animal nature. Her maturation parallels that of George, and her presence has "renewed and refreshed him." Reflecting upon the people of Winesburg, that stream of humanity of which she is a part, she faces sadness as she sees "the meaninglessness of life" and "at the same instant" acknowledges her love for those townspeople who constitute the life she knows best. She has experienced a necessary awareness for her move to adulthood and a perspective essential to her future. Helen appears for the last time in *Winesburg, Ohio* in George's thoughts as he leaves the village, remembering her as she once looked "standing by a window in the Winesburg post office and putting a stamp on an envelope."

Helen provides the best reference point in *Winesburg, Ohio* by which George's evolving maturity and perspective can be measured. Approximately midway into the text, in "The Thinker," an obtuse and self-absorbed George wants to fall in love with Helen because he needs to know about love to write a love story, revealing a lack of the "understanding" the narrator stresses repeatedly throughout the stories. At the conclusion of "Sophistication,"

George reaches this "understanding," as does Helen. An earlier story, "Death," anticipates this revelatory moment when Dr. Reefy tells George's misunderstood mother, Elizabeth, "You must not try to make love definite. It is the divine accident of life." Helen and George are together in nocturnal silence during their heightened awareness, when each has the same thought: "I have come to this lonely place and here is this other." As critic Edwin Fussell has noted, both perceive that "love is essentially the shared acceptance of two people . . . of their final separateness."

Discussion Questions

1. In the story "Sophistication" the narrator says, "In youth there are always two forces fighting in people. The warm unthinking little animal that struggles against the thing that reflects and remembers, and the older, the more sophisticated thing had possession of George Willard." What do you believe is the implied conflict here? Does either of these two forces ultimately prevail in the lives of Helen and George during the evening at the Fair Ground? Provide evidence from the story to support your conclusion.

2. Critic Malcolm Cowley has observed that Sherwood Anderson's stories in *Winesburg, Ohio* have not plots but "moments" during which "aliveness" comes to a character or characters, "a sudden reaching out through the walls of inarticulateness and misunderstanding." Cite examples from the story that best illustrate Helen's coming alive.

3. The reader gains glimpses of Helen White's mother's character from occasional comments by the narrator. In "Respectability" Mrs. White is reported to have complained to the telegraph company that Wash Williams's telegraph office in Winesburg "smelled abominably." In "The Thinker" she has "a heavy brass knocker" on her door, her "innovation" introduced to the village, and she is reported to have "organized a women's club for the study of poetry." And to one of Helen's young college professors, Mrs. White says of Winesburg, "There is no one here fit to associate with a girl of Helen's breeding." Could Mrs. White possibly be responsible for Helen's suffering alienation just as others have in Winesburg? Is there evidence in the text that Helen is separating herself from the values of her mother?

4. Can the reader cite instances in the text in which Helen's feminine qualities have a specific effect upon George?

—John C. Unrue

GEORGE WILLARD

George Willard is an aspiring young writer and a major character in Sherwood Anderson's *Winesburg, Ohio,* a collection of stories about persons who live in the Winesburg community. A newspaper reporter for the *Winesburg Eagle,* George is regarded by troubled townspeople as the person most likely to express their pent-up feelings that have alienated them from a community with which they would like to be reunited. The first story of the collection, "The Book of the Grotesques," serves as a prologue and identifies the major cause of the suffering of many people in Winesburg. According to an old man, also a writer, they have become "grotesques" because they have taken from hundreds of the truths of the world a single truth by which they choose to live. Their "truth" becomes a falsehood and burden, often manifested as pronounced outward signs of inner despair. In "Hands," Wing Biddlebaum, a former teacher accused of fondling his young students, has hands that have ceased to express his creative enthusiasm and instead move frantically. In "The Philosopher," Dr. Parcival, a victim of betrayal who has withdrawn from society, sees everyone facing personal "crucifixion" and has a drooping or twitching eyelid; and Jesse Bentley, a religious fanatic in "Godliness," "caught in conflict between his religion and his greed," has a frightful look of madness. George learns from each person he observes, especially from those who tell him their experiences with love, sex, marriage, loneliness, betrayal, alienation, death, and disillusionment. Each person's story contributes to the perspective George will need as a writer.

The women in George's life are particularly important to his maturation. Louise Trunnion, about whom there were "whispered tales," gives him his sexual initiation; his mother, Elizabeth Willard, a "defeated wife," nurtures his capacity to dream and protects him against defeat; his teacher, Kate Swift, denied love and professional fulfillment, advises him that as a writer he must get "to know life" and to learn "what people are thinking about, not what they say"; and Helen White, the young woman to whom he is romantically attracted, helps him toward an enlightened understanding of women and love. Throughout most of the text, George is incapable of that understanding. Self-absorbed and insecure, he is initially more concerned with gaining experiences by which he can affirm his manhood and that he believes will prepare him for a writing career that he has idealized. With the death of his mother, when he is ultimately "urged by some impulse outside himself," George begins to understand her as never before. He sees her as "the lovely dear" and acknowledges the beauty of her spirit. Later George becomes even more detached from himself and less self-absorbed. In "Sophistication" he experiences an enlightenment that is the climax of *Winesburg, Ohio.* In the silence and darkness at the Winesburg Fair Ground with Helen, he "reflects and remembers," shedding his egotism, contemplating the meaninglessness of life, and yet feeling "something like reverence" for the people of his town. He wants to love and be loved by Helen, but he does not want to be "confused by her womanhood" or his "manhood," words that imply conventional roles followed in Winesburg and preclude love. Rather, he sees Helen at last as "the other," separate and distinct from himself. George has matured to the point at which he can recognize Helen's separateness, respect it, and feel compassion and love not previously possible. He, along with Helen, has "for a moment taken hold of the thing that makes the mature life of men and women in the modern world possible." In "Departure," the concluding story of the book, George leaves Winesburg, freeing himself from an environment filled with "grotesques" mired in defeat. He is more sensitive, understanding, and compassionate than ever, aware of his limitations and the necessity of facing his own isolation. As he boards a train he carries with him the potential for becoming an artist who might one day give expression to the defeated ones he leaves behind in a town that is "a background on which to paint the dreams of his manhood."

Most critics agree that Sherwood Anderson derived inspiration for *Winesburg, Ohio* from Edgar Lee Masters's *Spoon River Anthology* (1915), a collection of poems in which the secret lives of persons in a small town are revealed. Anderson offers a key to his own intention in his dedication of the book to his mother, Emma Smith Anderson, "whose keen observations on the life about her awoke in me the hunger to see beneath the surface of lives." Although *Winesburg, Ohio* is a short-story collection, Anderson thought of it as something more, observing that not only did all of the stories belong together, but also that "they made something like a novel, a complete story."

Winesburg, Ohio, with its themes of initiation, alienation, and loneliness—unified by the central character, George Willard, in whom an early Anderson critic saw "the real Anderson"—was hailed as a revolutionary approach to the short story. Looking back at the book a half century after its publication, another critic concluded that the collection, "true in its livingness," remains "a classic."

Discussion Questions

1. Critic Malcolm Cowley has suggested that in the stories of *Winesburg, Ohio* one often finds a "single moment of aliveness . . . the sudden reaching out of two characters through walls of inarticulateness and misunderstanding." Other "moments" reveal intense awareness. Cite instances of such "moments" for George and discuss their importance.

2. Love is a major theme in *Winesburg, Ohio*. In part 3 of "Godliness" Louise Bentley writes John Hardy a note saying, "I want someone to love me and I want someone to love," words that are echoed in "Sophistication" when the narrator says that George Willard "wanted to love and he wanted to be loved" by Helen White. Discuss George's changing perception of love throughout the text.

3. Discuss the manner in which George Willard's character functions to bring about unity and coherence in *Winesburg, Ohio*.

4. Near the conclusion of *Winesburg, Ohio* the narrator observes that both Helen White and George Willard find words inadequate. "It seemed to Helen that the world was full of meaningless people saying words," and George regrets his earlier wordiness, in particular his own bragging. George and Helen have their moment of enlightenment in "Sophistication" during "their silent evening." Why do you think silence and darkness were important to their newfound perception?

—*John C. Unrue*

REFERENCES

David Anderson, ed., *Sherwood Anderson: Dimensions of His Literary Art: A Collection of Critical Essays* (East Lansing: Michigan State University Press, 1976);

Mary A. Van Antwerp, ed., *Sherwood Anderson, Willa Cather, John Dos Passos, Theodore Dreiser, F. Scott Fitzgerald, Ernest Hemingway, Sinclair Lewis,* Dictionary of Literary Biography Documentary Series, volume one (Detroit: Gale Research, 1982).

Rex Burbank, *Sherwood Anderson* (New York: Twayne, 1964);

Irving Howe, *Sherwood Anderson* (Stanford, Calif.: Stanford University Press, 1951);

Robert Allen Papinchak, *Sherwood Anderson: A Study in Short Fiction* (New York: Twayne, 1992);

Walter B. Rideout, ed., *Sherwood Anderson: A Collection of Critical Essays* (Englewood Cliffs, N.J.: Prentice-Hall, 1974).

Eugene P. Sheehy and Kenneth A. Lohf, comps., *Sherwood Anderson: A Bibliography* (Los Gatos, Calif.: Talisman, 1960);

Kim Townsend, *Sherwood Anderson* (Boston: Houghton Mifflin, 1987);

Kenny J. Williams, *A Storyteller and a City: Sherwood Anderson's Chicago* (De Kalb: Northern Illinois University Press, 1988).

Harriette Simpson Arnow
(July 7, 1908 – March 22, 1986)

THE DOLLMAKER
(New York: Macmillan, 1954)

GERTIE NEVELS

Gertie Nevels is the female protagonist and title character of Harriette Arnow's novel *The Dollmaker,* as well as the wife of Clovis Nevels and mother of his five children. The Nevels family lives, initially, in a rural Kentucky town on a rented farm that Gertie and her children work while Clovis works as a tinkerer and sometime coal-truck driver. When Clovis leaves to take a job in a Detroit factory instead of joining the military as Gertie believes, she is forced to leave the places she has always known and the land she wanted to buy to enter a different world.

Author Arnow had a similar experience, following her husband from Appalachian Kentucky to Detroit for a job during World War II. In a 1983 interview with Haeja K. Chung, she talked about how Gertie, as a character, grew out of her wartime life: "I wondered how women who had never used a telephone or seen or used any appliance run by electricity . . . how they would . . . 'adjust'—in many ways. And out of all this wondering and thinking, Gertie for some reason was the one I chose." Arnow's comments highlight how common this sort of exodus was for southern and Appalachian people looking for work in the middle twentieth century, as the world modernized around them.

Gertie is introduced in the novel while saving her dying son's life by performing a roadside tracheotomy on him on the way to the doctor in town. She is strong and determined in these early scenes, and these characteristics stay with her throughout the novel. This fact is evidenced at the end of the book by her willingness, when her family needs money, to sacrifice the block of wood from which she plans to carve a figurine of Jesus. She takes this final relic from her life in Kentucky and cuts it into sections to create figurines to sell instead of the single carving she had wanted for herself as a sign of her determination to survive and accept this new life. Gertie's sacrifice of her dream of owning the Tipton Place, however, seems to be more of a surrender than a sign of strength. Gertie believes she has bought the land and paid for it, but Clovis arranges to have the deal broken, taking away the freedom Gertie thought she had.

Arnow herself has noted, as have critics, that Gertie is a silent character who does not express herself well in words, with or without her Kentucky dialect. Arnow has called her "inarticulate" and "incoherent" in interviews, but all acknowledge that Gertie finds expression through Bible references as well as the whittling she does for pleasure. Her spare expression contributes to her isolation in both Kentucky and Detroit, with her own family and with strangers.

Gertie's central role in *The Dollmaker* is as a mother, and her children serve sometimes as her support system and at other times as her link to the outside world. These changing dynamics result in tense and complicated family relationships. Two of the children, like their mother, love and need the land and do not thrive in Detroit. The oldest boy, Reuben, returns to Kentucky without telling anyone, and Gertie responds by trying to make Cassie, the youngest daughter, better able to adapt. She tells the girl that her imaginary friend is not real. Cassie is hit by a train near the Neveleses' home shortly afterward while attempting to hide her continuing interactions with the imaginary Callie Lou.

Gertie's other children—Clytie, Enoch, and Amos—lose the culture Gertie holds onto in order to survive in their new city home, including the accent and speech patterns of Appalachia. Clovis also changes, adopting the attitudes of his work friends about drinking, home life, and his relationship with his wife. Gertie feels this same pressure from her peers, but she remains awkward and uncertain of herself and isolates herself from the Irish, Polish, and other immigrant families that live nearby.

While Gertie idealizes the peace and nature of a Kentucky farm, the novel reveals her difficulties both there and in Detroit. Critics have argued over whether Gertie surrenders or succeeds by the end of the novel, but those arguments establish different goals for Gertie as a character and present differing ideas on what message Arnow is trying to tell with Gertie's story. Arnow has responded to these ideas in several interviews, maintaining that she was frustrated with Gertie's silence and stubbornness throughout the writing process but declining to define what she wants readers to think at the end.

The Dollmaker was the 1955 runner-up for the National Book Award, losing to Faulkner's *A Fable*, and is frequently taught in women's and Appalachian literature classes.

Discussion Questions

1. Arnow once said that Gertie felt more at home with the people in the alley than she ever did in the Kentucky she longed to return to. Which "home" fits Gertie better and why?

2. Gertie's verbal expression comes primarily through the Bible, and this religious feeling finds its way into her artistic expression, whittling. She has a conflict over religious belief with her mother, however, and does not attend church in Detroit when

her children start going. Explore the role of religion and religious expression in Gertie's life.

3. When Gertie arrives at the doctor's office, having shown strength and determination to get there, she hesitates at the door. The driver who brought her says, "Lady, you can't be afraid of nothing. Just walk in." What is Gertie afraid of then? What role does this fear play in the rest of the novel?

4. Near the end of the novel, Gertie begins to change in response to her Detroit environment and lets go of the remnants of "home" for her family, most notably her "Jesus" wood. Is Gertie adapting or surrendering? Will she continue to adapt? Is this a sad or hopeful ending? Why?

5. Mothers are supposed to be models and examples to their children. What do Gertie's children (individually and collectively) see her as a model of? Consider how this changes over the course of the novel.

—*Monica F. Jacobe*

REFERENCES

Duane Carr, "Harriette Arnow: The Dispossessed as Self-Reliant Woman," in *A Question of Class: The Redneck Stereotype in Southern Fiction* (Bowling Green, Ohio: Bowling Green State University Popular Press, 1996), pp. 157–166;

Haeja K. Chung, ed., *Harriette Simpson Arnow: Critical Essays on Her Work* (East Lansing: Michigan State University Press, 1995);

Wilton Eckley, *Harriette Arnow* (New York: Twayne, 1974).

Isaac Asimov

(January 2, 1920 – April 6, 1992)

᷇᷇᷇

FOUNDATION

(New York: Gnome Press, 1951)

HARI SELDON

Hari Seldon, a mathematician who invents psychohistory and establishes the Foundation, is the pivotal and most fully developed character in Isaac Asimov's Foundation Series, which occurs 22,000 years in the future, covers a period of 547 years, and includes seven volumes, beginning with the short-story collection *Foundation* in 1951 and concluding with *Forward the Foundation* in 1993. The Foundation Trilogy, the three central volumes of the series, received a special Hugo Award from the World Science Fiction Society as "the greatest all-time science fiction series" in 1966. Seldon is also the central character in each of the three volumes that comprise the "Second Foundation Trilogy," an homage to Asimov's original work by three other authors, Gregory Benford, Greg Bear, and David Brin.

Seldon initially appears as a frail old man in the first story in *Foundation,* "The Psychohistorians," and dies before its second story, "The Encyclopedists," occurs. Yet, he also appears six times posthumously—as a holographic projection speaking from "the Vault"—in the second and last two stories in *Foundation* ("The Traders" and "The Merchant Princes"), in *Foundation and Empire* (1952), and in *Foundation's Edge* (1982). Psychohistory is a statistical methodology that analyzes a mathematical simulation of the human population of the galaxy to predict its future; Seldon uses it to discover that the impending collapse of the first Galactic Empire will be followed by thirty thousand years of anarchy, but he also foresees that skillful manipulation of the future might reduce this period of barbarism to a single millennium. The Foundation is an academic community Seldon establishes on a remote planet to effect this alteration of the future by serving as the nucleus of a second empire that could arise in only a thousand years. His posthumous appearances in the Vault convey his commentary on crucial future events, the "Seldon crises," to the Foundation's citizens, who know far less about the historical forces shaping their present and their destiny than does Seldon.

In *Foundation* and the first part of *Foundation and Empire* Seldon establishes his infallibility through unerring analysis of a series of four crises. In a fifth instance, however, his analysis is wildly inaccurate because the Mule, a mutant who conquers both the waning Empire and the Foundation, is an anomaly psychohistory could not foresee. Yet, Seldon had also established a secret Second Foundation expressly to deal with such anomalies, and in *Second Foundation* (1953) this foundation defeats the Mule. In *Foundation's Edge,* set nearly two hundred years after *Second Foundation,* Seldon's analysis of another crisis is again uncannily accurate—because an "even-more-secret guardian" to both foundations, the living planet Gaia, has steered galactic history back onto the path Seldon had predicted.

Even though he is little more than a mysterious figure able to predict the future, Seldon is still one of the few memorable characters in the Foundation Series. Asimov develops him into his most fully realized character in the prequels *Prelude to Foundation* (1988) and *Forward the Foundation,* which relate the last fifty years of Seldon's life and thus occur nearly fifty years before the events of *Foundation.* In *Prelude to Foundation* Seldon is an unassuming, thirty-two-year-old scholar who visits the capital planet of the empire, Trantor, and is ruthlessly manipulated into remaining there and devoting the rest of his life to developing psychohistory by Chetter Hummin—who is really the twenty-thousand-year-old R. Daneel Olivaw, the robot protagonist of Asimov's four robot novels, in disguise. (In the Foundation Trilogy Daneel is also, under the name Eto Demerzel, first minister to Emperor Cleon I.) Hummin has been attempting for twenty millennia to fulfill his programming by devising a mechanism for safeguarding humanity. Although initially tricked into remaining on Trantor, Seldon stays because of his altruistic dedication to humanity's future, his love of order, and his fascination with psychohistory itself. Daneel also provides him with a lifelong protector and companion in Dors, a female android. Seldon comes to love Dors and eventually marries her, even though he understands that as a robot she is incapable of returning his feelings. Echoing the thematic concern with bigotry that suffuses nearly all of Asimov's science-fiction novels, Seldon is appalled by the prejudice he encounters on Trantor, which is directed both against himself (as an "Outworlder") and the working-class inhabitants of Dahl Sector—where he meets Raych, who becomes his adopted son, and Yugo Amaryl, who becomes his closest friend and collaborator. Seldon hopes that "there is some sort of psychohistorical solution to the problem of human bigotry," which he believes is universal, but he never finds one.

Forward the Foundation, which begins eight years later, relates the last forty years of Seldon's life and his struggle to establish the foundations. Seldon succeeds Daneel/Demerzel as Cleon I's first minister not out of personal ambition, but because the office enables him to promote and fund his psychohistory project while using psychohistory to forestall the collapse of the empire until the foundations can be established. An able politician who constantly regrets that his ministerial duties prevent him from devoting more time to research, he is happy to return to scholarly life after Cleon is assassinated. Throughout *Forward the Foundation,* Seldon says goodbye to the people important to him and to the Foundation: "One by one through his long life, he had lost his friends and those he had loved." He must sacrifice his only living relative, his granddaughter Wanda, to a secret exile on Trantor, which assures that he will never see her again, so that she can establish the Second Foundation. In the epilogue of the novel, after completing his life's work by recording the Vault's holographic messages, Seldon dies alone but "with the future he created unfolding all around him."

Daneel reveals in *Foundation and Earth* that Gaia is his primary scheme for protecting humanity and that he later "turned to the second-best and helped bring about the development of ... psychohistory," which is ultimately a failure, as backup for Gaia. Thus, Seldon is manipulated into devoting his life to a project that is not only fatally flawed but is also not the mechanism for safeguarding humanity he believes it to be. Asimov, who finished *Forward the Foundation* shortly before his death and identified strongly with its dying protagonist, notes in his memoir *I. Asimov* (1994) that, "like Hari Seldon, I can look at my work around me and I'm comforted. . . . I've . . . imagined . . . many possible futures—it's as if I've been there." While many subsequent science-fiction series—such as Frank Herbert's *Dune* novels, which also feature protagonists who are able to predict the future—have been profoundly influenced by Asimov's Foundation Series, none include a character who closely resembles Hari Seldon.

Discussion Questions

1. While the premise of psychohistory is that individuals and individual acts are irrelevant to the broad movement of historical forces, Hari Seldon is an individual whose life's work, most specifically the development of psychohistory, appears to have the most profound effect on the broad course of history. Discuss this apparent contradiction and its relevance to the question of whether human behavior is predestined or the product of free will. Are these two concepts really mutually exclusive?

2. Compare Hari Seldon's ability to foretell the future with psychohistory to Paul Atreides's prescient ability in Frank Herbert's *Dune*.

3. Compare Hari Seldon's explicit concern with bigotry in *Prelude to Foundation* and *Forward the Foundation* to the more implicit treatment of bigotry found in Asimov's robot novels *The Caves of Steel, Naked Sun, The Robots of Dawn*, and *Robots and Empire* and in the two Empire novels in which it is most prominent, *Pebble in the Sky* and *The Currents of Space*.

—*Donald E. Palumbo*

I, ROBOT
(New York: Gnome, 1950)

SUSAN CALVIN

Dr. Susan Calvin is a robot psychologist in Isaac Asimov's *I, Robot*, a collection of nine short stories published previously and gathered together into a loose novel structure. Calvin appears in six of the nine stories in *I, Robot*—although in "Robbie," she is present only as an unnamed teenage girl. She also appears in stories in other Asimov anthologies: four stories in *The Rest of the Robots* (1964) and the short story "Feminine Intuition" in *Robot Visions* (1990). *I, Robot* falls into a category that Asimov called "social science fiction," meaning that its plot and characters deal with the impact of scientific advances on humans, including their fear of technology and their relationships with increasingly complex robots. She is, according to her "official" biography in the fictional *Encyclopedia Tellurica*, "the first great prac-titioner of a new science," robopsychology. Her job is to analyze the robots, account for anomalies, solve problems, and if necessary, order their destruction when their malfunctions are not repairable.

At age twenty, Calvin is described as a "frosty girl, plain and colorless, who protected herself against a world she disliked by a mask-like expression and a hypertrophy of intellect." She is similarly described throughout the novel by various male colleagues, with an emphasis on her "cold" nature, her "icy, somewhat acid, calm," and her "schooled indifference." Her eyes are described as "sharp" and "cold," her voice as "low and colorless," and her mouth as "thin-lipped." If she smiles, her smile is "frosty." As she grows older, these attributes become more pronounced. Of herself, Calvin admits that she has "been called a robot" for her seemingly cold exterior, but at various points in the narrative she does display emotion, warmth, and enthusiasm, particularly when talking about her robots or about Stephen Byerley, the World Coordinator whom she helped prove was not a robot, but whom she always knew was a robot. Despite her background in psychology, humans and human foibles do not appear to interest Calvin. Any "dilemma" facing one of the robots interests her greatly, however.

Susan must fight continually against the male chauvinism of her colleagues. Thematically, her struggle for professional acceptance and equality is mirrored in the robots' struggle for societal acceptance. At one point, she tells Peter Bogert, a mathematician at U.S. Robot and Mechanical Man, that "all normal life . . . resents domination," and Calvin clearly resents attempts by her male colleagues to thwart her work. Resentment by male colleagues for her abilities are common, and she is often discussed by these colleagues in a derogatory manner. In "Little, Lost Robot," for example, Bogert insists that "she understands robots like a sister," that she hates people, and that she is "an extreme neurotic" with "paranoid tendencies." Yet, in this story and the others in which she figures, Calvin, and not the male scientists, is the one to solve the problems with the robots.

Calvin's role in the novel is to highlight the importance of ethics in a technologically advanced society, and for this reason she has high regard for the Three Laws of Robotics. In "Evidence," Calvin remarks that the Three Laws are merely an outcropping of "the essential guiding principles of a good many of the world's ethical systems," and thus a robot should be indistinguishable from "a very good man." When she finds that the Nestor (NS-2) robots were not fully programmed with the First Law, she is outraged and demands that all sixty-three robots be destroyed if they cannot find the one robot whose adherence to First Law has been weakened.

Calvin's idealistic view of the robots leads her to believe that they will function for the good of society, and she often argues that they are "a cleaner better breed" than the humans. She even goes so far as to regret the possibility that Byerley may be a human rather than a robot, because, "By the Laws of Robotics, he'd be incapable of harming humans, incapable of tyranny, of corruption, of stupidity, of prejudice." For Calvin, the robots are responsible for making the world a kind of utopia. The robots can offer humans a safer, more prosperous, world than the humans can create on their own; in fact, the machines are all that "stand between mankind and destruction." When Byerley argues that this new world order will result in a complete loss of human free will, Calvin counters that the world has "always been at the mercy of economic and sociological forces it did not understand—at the whims of climate and the fortunes of war." Calvin sees the machines as making "all conflicts . . . evitable," that is, wholly anticipated by the robots and resolved before reaching a crisis point.

In his first volume of autobiography, *In Memory Yet Green* (1979), Asimov recalls that Calvin first appeared in his story "Liar!" published in 1941. He describes her as "more intelligent and more capable than any of the men in the story." He was inspired to create a female scientist because of his positive relationship with his graduate adviser, Professor Mary Caldwell; however, he is quick to point out that Calvin is "nothing at all like Professor Caldwell in appearance or behavior."

Between 1940 and 1950, Asimov wrote a series of acclaimed short stories involving robots with positronic brains (a device that served as a central computer for the robots and gave them a form of consciousness). Each story involves a robot malfunction that the human protagonists must explain and correct. When Asimov gathered together the stories

in *I, Robot*, he systematically revised the stories by adding a cohesive link between the stories, in the form of narrative regarding Susan Calvin's preemptive retirement and a fuller explanation and inclusion of his Three Laws of Robotics. *I, Robot* is an important work in its field because of its place in the development of realistic, or hard, science fiction, because of the ethical code embodied in the Three Laws, and because of its support of the benefits of technology. Asimov took exception to the negative attitude of many toward robots, citing the image of Dr. Victor Frankenstein and his monster as a poor antecedent for the kind of highly controlled, thinking machine that he had created. In his introduction to *The Rest of the Robots*, Asimov writes that "As a person of science, I resented the purely Faustian interpretation of science." Susan Calvin functions to reflect Asimov's more sympathetic, enlightened attitude toward robots.

Discussion Questions

1. Is Susan Calvin as "cold" as she appears? What evidence exists in the text to suggest that the perceptions of her male colleagues are sexist? Why is Calvin so distanced from the other humans in the novel?

2. In the final story, "The Evitable Conflict," Calvin proclaims that the robots have established a utopian world. Some critics have argued that in this utopia there is no longer any human free will and that there is no longer anything left for the humans to do—that they no longer have a purpose. What would Calvin's response be to these charges? Is her assessment of the situation plausible?

3. In many critical articles, Asimov's robots are compared to the robots in Karel Capek's 1921 play *R.U.R.* How are Asimov's robots different? Compare and contrast the characters of Susan Calvin and Young Rossum and their separate approaches to the field of robotics.

—*Patricia Donaher*

REFERENCES

Neil Goble, *Asimov Analyzed* (Baltimore: Mirage Press, 1972);

James Gunn, *Isaac Asimov: The Foundations of Science Fiction*, revised edition (Lanham, Md.: Scarecrow Press, 1996);

Miller, Marjorie, *Isaac Asimov: A Checklist of Works Published in the United States* (Kent, Ohio: Kent State University Press, 1972);

Joseph D. Olander and Martin Harry Greenberg, eds., *Isaac Asimov* (New York: Taplinger, 1977);

Donald E. Palumbo, *Chaos Theory, Asimov's Foundations and Robots, and Herbert's Dune: The Fractal Aesthetic of Epic Science Fiction,* Contributions to the Study of Science Fiction and Fantasy, no. 100 (Westport, Conn.: Greenwood Press, 2002);

Joseph F. Patrouch, *The Science Fiction of Isaac Asimov* (Garden City, N.Y.: Doubleday, 1974);

William F. Touponce, *Isaac Asimov* (Woodbridge, Conn.: Twayne, 1991).

Jean M. Auel

(February 18, 1936 –   )

✿

THE CLAN OF THE CAVE BEAR

(New York: Crown, 1980)

AYLA

Ayla, the heroine in *The Clan of the Cave Bear,* is a Cro-Magnon living with a clan of Neanderthals in the last Ice Age, about thirty thousand years ago. Orphaned as the result of an earthquake that killed her mother and separated her from those of her kind, the "Others," five-year-old Ayla is found by the Neanderthals and integrated into their small tribe. Her adopted mother is Iza, the highest-ranking woman in the clan, a healer who refuses to leave Ayla to die on the plains. Iza's brother is Creb, the tribe's Mog-ur (shaman). To the rest of the clan, Iza, a pregnant woman with no husband, and Creb, who is crippled, old, and blind in one eye, which makes him useless as a hunter, are the misfits of the tribe.

While Iza and Creb are different because of their talents, Ayla is initially different because of her looks. Neanderthals, while slightly shorter than Cro-Magnons, had a more compact, denser, muscular body. Ayla is tall, blonde, and blue-eyed; the clan members have low brows and dark eyes and hair. Although both species, as determined by scientific artifacts, were family-oriented, Ayla is the only one who gives physical affection to Creb.

The clan's ability to survive is based on memory drawn from their ancestors; Ayla, as a Cro-Magnon, has no such memory, and her adventures are the result of environmental lessons and self-taught survival skills that utilize thought and reasoning. She is thus better equipped to deal with the future than the clan. The difference between memory and adaptation is shown when Ayla jumps into the water and rescues a drowning clan child. The clan, with no memory of swimming, would have let the child die. In the manner of the obedient, subservient clan women, Ayla is obedient in the clan's presence; secretly, however, she defies their traditions, teaching herself how to use the men's weapons. She also modifies the clan's use of the sling, turning it into a lethal weapon. As a strong woman in a culture where women are viewed as weak, every personal triumph in conquering her environment also creates new dangers for her, particularly in her dealings with one of the clan's future leaders, Broud, the favored son of the current leader. As Ayla matures and circumvents many of the tribe's traditions, she also has to survive their punishments.

Broud, once he becomes the clan's leader, tries to eject Creb from the tribe. Ayla stands up for Creb, forcing a confrontation between herself and Broud, her longtime rival, with detrimental results to both of them.

With meticulous attention to detail, Auel portrays Ayla learning about herbal medicines, creating fire from sticks, hunting for food and clothing, and delivering her own baby. While the clan believes that spirits are responsible for pregnancies, Ayla realizes that it is actually the men who impregnate the women.

Because Auel found little anthropological literature that specifically addresses the lifestyle of the women, she speculates about the details of Paleolithic life between the gaps in scientific knowledge. While the experts still cannot determine why the Neanderthal people died off, Auel shows how the clan bases its experiences on the unchanging past, while Ayla and the Others adapt to their changing environment with new tools and techniques. In defying the clan to become less like the clan women and more like the men, Ayla controls her own destiny.

Discussion Questions

1. In one passage in the novel Ayla goes into the water to swim and then, shortly after, rescues a child who has fallen into the water and is in danger of being swept away by the current. Only later in the novel does she first see her reflection in a pool of water. Since Ayla is clearly not a stranger to bodies of water, why does it take her so long to notice her reflection?

2. Linda S. Bergmann, in *Twentieth-Century Romance and Historical Writers,* observes that "although the series is set in the Stone Age, it raises contemporary feminist concerns about gender roles, and is as much about our own time as about prehistory." Do you believe her statement is true? Explain your answer with specific references from the novel.

3. Early in the book, Ayla's life is at stake when she is stalked by a hungry lioness. She escapes, but not before the lioness claws her left thigh, leaving "four deep parallel gashes." How does this scar affect Ayla's place within the clan? Would you consider it a symbol? If so, of what?

—*Diana Fox*

REFERENCES

Tracy Cochran, "The View from Mount Auel," *Publishers Weekly,* 22 April 2002, pp. 35–37;

Clyde Wilcox, "The Not-So-Failed Feminism of Jean Auel," *Journal of Popular Culture,* 28 (Winter 1994): 63–70;

Diane S. Wood, "Female Heroism in the Ice Age: Jean Auel's Earth Children," *Extrapolation,* 27 (Spring 1986): 33–38.

B

✼

James Baldwin
(August 2, 1924 – December 1, 1987)

✿

ANOTHER COUNTRY
(New York: Dial, 1962)

VIVALDO MOORE

Vivaldo Moore is the main white male character in James Baldwin's *Another Country*. He is the best friend of Rufus, an African American; in a romantic relationship with Rufus's sister, Ida; in artistic competition with Richard, also a novelist and his former teacher; and in a sexual encounter with Eric, which helps both Eric and Vivaldo accept their sexuality. Vivaldo, like Baldwin, is a writer who lives in Greenwich Village. He is also a bohemian, and his point of view informs most of the depictions of the Village and its bohemian subculture, both positive and negative, in the novel.

Vivaldo faces pressure from many directions in the novel: sexual, racial, artistic, and familial. He feels guilt about his relationship with his immediate family. He does not get along with his father, and he knows that his bohemian lifestyle is seen as a rejection of his working-class background. He enjoys the freedoms of the bohemian subculture but worries that his family will never understand his way of life. His family is also racist and unlikely to accept his friendships or relationships with African Americans. "Any writer, I suppose, feels that the world into which he was born is nothing less than a conspiracy against the cultivation of his talent," Baldwin wrote about himself, but the quotation applies to Vivaldo as well.

Vivaldo is a writer and a focal point for the artistic themes in the novel. His teacher and friend, Richard, is also a writer, and has just had his first novel published. The novel is a detective story, and considered by the other characters to be popular, not serious, fiction. After reading Richard's book, Vivaldo feels as if Richard has changed and lost his artistic passion: "He had not liked the book. He could not take it seriously—it would never mean anything to anyone." After Vivaldo reads Richard's detective story, the friendship between the two men starts to deteriorate. The book Vivaldo is writing is serious fiction. Richard fears Vivaldo is the better writer, and Cass, Richard's wife, loses respect for Richard as she gains it for Vivaldo. Through this subplot the issue of highbrow versus popular art is raised. Vivaldo, however, suffers from writer's block throughout most of the novel. This creative block seems to be connected to his unwillingness to deal with the issues of his life: his attraction to African American women, racism, and his own bisexuality.

"It is rare indeed that people give. Most people guard and keep; they suppose that it is they themselves and what they identify with themselves that they are guarding and keeping, whereas what they are actually guarding and keeping is their system of reality and what they assume themselves to be." This comment by Baldwin describes Vivaldo's actions and consciousness. In his relationships with both Rufus and Ida, he avoids confronting and dealing with the issue of their race. He fails to understand that even if he treats Rufus and Ida as equals, much of society does not, and by ignoring that point, he ignores a major part of their experiences.

43

His relationship with Ida forces him to confront the question of race. His sexual relations with white women had always been failures, and he had only been able to achieve intense orgasm with African American women. Until he met Ida, however, his encounters with African American women had been confined to prostitutes. With Ida, Vivaldo tries to ignore the race question and only focus on love. As Ida continuously points out to him, though, their love can be true only if they accept that race is an issue for them. Her affair with Ellis, a white executive who promises to help her career in exchange for sex, forces Vivaldo to face the racism of general society and how it affects Ida.

Rufus's death and Eric's return from France force Vivaldo to confront his bisexuality. He had past experiences with boys, and there is a hidden sexual tension, which he will not admit to, in his friendship with Rufus. Vivaldo wonders if the tension from not admitting his bisexuality contributed to Rufus's suicide. He is able to work through this guilt, and accept his sexuality, only after he has a sexual encounter with Eric: "He felt fantastically protected, liberated by the knowledge that—there was a man in the world who loved him."

Only after Vivaldo confronts these issues and starts to move toward a resolution is he able to resolve his writer's block and move toward artistic credibility and experience true love with Ida, free from racial stereotypes: "a detail that he needed for his novel, for which he had been searching, fell, neatly and vividly, like the tumblers of a lock, into place in his mind." The novel ends with Vivaldo working on his novel while Ida sleeps in bed next to him, calling out his name.

Vivaldo can be compared to Leo Percepied in Jack Kerouac's *The Subterraneans* (1958). Like Vivaldo, Kerouac's narrator is also a bohemian and a writer, and the novel details his relationship with Mardou, an African American woman. Both novels map out the counterculture of the 1950s and 1960s as they explore questions of race and sex, using the more progressive attitudes of this emerging subculture as a starting point for a critical discussion of sexuality and race relations in America.

Discussion Questions

1. Compare Richard and Vivaldo as writers. Take into consideration the issue of popular versus serious fiction/art.

2. Compare Vivaldo to Leo Percepied in Jack Kerouac's *The Subterraneans.*

3. Discuss Vivaldo's writer's block and why the block finally disappears.

—*Frank D. Casale*

IDA SCOTT

Ida Scott, the main African American female character in James Baldwin's *Another Country,* is used by Baldwin to explode the racist stereotypes that surround interracial sexual relationships. Ida is the younger sister of Rufus Scott, a jazz musician, who as the novel opens is driven to suicide by the same sexual stereotypes. Rufus's suicide propels Ida into her two main actions in the novel: her relationship with Rufus's white friend Vivaldo, and her attempt to follow her brother's jazz career by trying to make it as a singer.

Baldwin wrote in "Notes of a Native Son": "I imagine one of the reasons people cling to their hates so stubbornly is because they sense, once hate is gone, they will be forced to deal with pain." This concept applies to Ida. She feels intense hatred for the white world she blames for driving Rufus to commit suicide, and she uses this hatred to help justify her attitude toward whites, especially white men. "I felt that I'd been robbed. And I had been robbed—of the only hope I had. By a group of people too cowardly to even know what they had done." This hatred allows her to mourn for her brother as a victim of racism, but it prevents her from mourning for her brother as a person. Her hatred also allows her to idolize her brother and ignore, the same way the white characters ignore racial issues, Rufus's flaws. Rufus used sexual relations to empower himself and compensate for black men's loss of power because of racism, and this combination prevented him from experiencing the love that could have saved him. Ida, at first, cannot see that Rufus's white lovers might have really loved him, and she uses her hatred to stereotype both Leona and Eric.

At first, Ida cannot see white men as anything else but victimizers; she can conceive of them only as men who see her as a sexual object or who treat all black women as prostitutes. Ida, like Rufus, uses sex as a tool for revenge and empowerment. Just as Rufus acts out myths of black male sexuality, Ida acts out the stereotype of black woman as prostitute in order to take advantage of the white men who are seeking to take advantage of her. "There was only one thing for me to do. . . . I used to see the way white men watched me like dogs. And I thought about what I could do to them. How I hated them, the way they looked. . . . I didn't want to be at their mercy. I wanted them to be at mine." She uses her sexuality in order to get ahead in the world. She uses her hatred of white men to perform this role and remain emotionless during these encounters.

The death of Rufus brings Ida into contact with Vivaldo, which begins to change her attitude toward white men. "But I liked you, and the few times I saw you it was kind of—*relief*—from all those other, horrible people. You were really nice to me. You didn't have that look in your eyes." Vivaldo attempts to treat Ida the same as he would any white woman, to such an extent that he refuses to admit to or even discuss the racial aspect of their relationship or race generally. Ida accuses him of being racially insensitive and reverts to her old attitudes about men. When she comes into contact with Steve Ellis, a powerful entertainment executive who can advance her singing career, Ida uses these resurfaced feelings to justify her affair with Ellis in an attempt to become a success.

The other African American musicians she plays with, who remember her brother, scold her for her actions. This reaction makes Ida question herself. When she faces the possibility of losing Vivaldo after he discovers the affair with Ellis, she truly changes and opens up to the possibility of love crossing the racial divide between them. She will only accept this possibility if Vivaldo will accept the racial question in the first place, which discovering the affair forces him to do.

Ida can be compared to Mardou Fox in Jack Kerouac's *The Subterraneans*. Both are African American women dating white male writers. Both relationships take place in a bohemian setting and within a bohemian circle of artists. In *The Subterraneans,* however, the roles are reversed. Mardou attempts to look beyond the racial component of the relationship, while Leo Percepied, the male character, is haunted by racial stereotypes that prevent him from fully trusting Mardou's intentions, just as Ida is unable to trust Vivaldo's for much of *Another Country*.

Discussion Questions

1. At first Ida believes she will be able to use Ellis the same way she has used men in previous relationships. Why did her affair with Ellis upset her while her previous affairs did not?

2. Why does Ida blame the white characters in the novel, Vivaldo, Leona, Cass, and Eric, for her brother's suicide?

3. Why does Ida first begin to fall in love with Vivaldo?

4. Explain Ida's sudden desire to become a singer. Why does she decide to try this career?

—*Frank D. Casale*

RUFUS SCOTT

Although Rufus Scott kills himself by leaping off the George Washington Bridge at the end of the first chapter of James Baldwin's *Another Country*, the character remains central to an understanding of the rest of the novel. Rufus, an African American jazz musician, is Ida Scott's brother, Vivaldo Moore's friend, a former lover of Eric Jones, and acts as a locus for the major themes of the novel: race, sex, sexual orientation, and artistic credibility. Rufus's memory haunts the other characters for the remainder of the book, driving them toward a resolution of their conflicted desires and relationships.

For Rufus, sex is a tool for power and revenge. In his sexual encounters with white men (Eric) and women (Leona), Rufus seeks to exact revenge for racism and to gain the power he is denied by white society in everyday life. "Rufus had watched him, smiling. He felt a flood of affection for Eric. And he felt his own power." In his sexual encounters, Rufus revels in the myth of the sexuality of the black male, acting out that role in the only arena in which he can feel social or personal power. Baldwin wrote of love and hate: "the object of one's hatred is never, alas, conveniently outside but seated in one's lap, stirring one's bowels and dictating the beat of one's heart." The entire novel plays out this ambivalence between objects of hatred and objects of love, but Baldwin's point is most clearly seen in Rufus's relationships with Eric and Leona.

Sexual power becomes a means for black revenge on white society. Upon first meeting Leona, a white southern woman with whom Rufus forms a violent relationship, he "remembered suddenly his days in boot camp in the South and felt again the shoe of a white officer against his mouth. . . . the white officer with a curse, had vanished, gone forever beyond the reach of vengeance." Rufus and Leona's first sexual encounter follows, and it is clear that passion and racial violence are intertwined in the act: "And shortly, nothing could have stopped him, not the white God himself nor a lynch mob arriving upon wings. Under his breath he cursed the milk white bitch and ground and rode his weapon between her thighs."

At first Leona and Rufus's relationship appears to be a happy one, but it soon cracks under the pressure of societal disapproval of interracial dating. Drinking heavily, the couple retreats from society to live in rundown neighborhoods. They lose their jobs and end contact with family and friends. Rufus reacts violently to this pressure and strikes out at Leona with acts of revenge and power: "It was not love he felt during these acts of love. . . . he began to pick fights with white men . . . the eyes of his friends told him that he was failing. . . . but the air through which he rushed was his prison and he could not even summon the breath to call for help." Rufus's inability to come to terms with either his bisexuality or his ambivalence in his sexual relationships with whites blocks him from experiencing the one thing that could have saved him: love for love's sake.

Rufus acts as a role model for his sister Ida's confidence and career, but more importantly, because they are both African American, he is perhaps her only object of true love. Rufus's relationship with the white Vivaldo is more complex. Vivaldo and Rufus are best friends, yet there are two powerful issues between them: sex and race. Both characters are bisexual, yet neither will admit it to or discuss it with the other. Likewise, the topic of race is never discussed or explored. As a result of the unspoken secrets between them, Vivaldo is unable to help Rufus at his lowest point by giving him the thing he most needed: pure love. Yet, Rufus's death leads Vivaldo to his own experience of true love with Ida, only after he and Ida admit and discuss the question of race.

The setting of the novel is also important. Harlem is a symbol of the repressed and boxed-in desires and aspirations of African Americans, while Greenwich Village is a bohemian space. In the Village artistic values trump commercial ones, and it is also a free zone where the racial and sexual mores of society as a whole do not apply. Interracial and homosexual relationships are tolerated, providing a temporary refuge for the characters in *Another Country*.

Rufus can be considered alongside another Baldwin creation, Sonny, from the short story "Sonny's Blues," which also takes place in Greenwich Village and Harlem. Sonny, like Rufus, is a jazz musician who is driven onto a path of self-destruction by the racism of society. While Rufus goes into a self-destructive cycle of drinking and violence, Sonny gets addicted to heroin. Sonny, however, is able to find redemption in his music, and he uses his music as an expression of his feelings about racism.

Discussion Questions

1. Baldwin's title, *Another Country*, implies that space and place are key elements in the novel. Discuss the significance of Harlem and Greenwich Village to the action of the novel.

2. Discuss the relationship between Rufus and Leona. Why is the relationship so self-destructive?

3. Rufus and Vivaldo are best friends. Why are they unable to discuss the issue of race or racism?

4. Discuss the impact of Rufus's suicide on the other characters.

—Frank D. Casale

❦
GO TELL IT ON THE MOUNTAIN
(New York: Knopf, 1953)

GABRIEL GRIMES

Gabriel Grimes is the father of the protagonist, John Grimes, in James Baldwin's semi-autobiographical novel *Go Tell It on the Mountain.* Gabriel is not John's biological father, though John is unaware of this fact. His mistreatment of John is, at least partially, influenced by the absence of a blood connection between them. The importance Gabriel places on lineage is explained in the section of the novel titled "Gabriel's Prayer." A prayer is a reverent petition to God, and in "Gabriel's Prayer," the reader is witness to Gabriel's plea for, and subsequent attainment and distortion of, salvation.

At the start of "Gabriel's Prayer," he is a young man facing a conflict similar to that John faces on his fourteenth birthday. Gabriel's mother, much like John's family, is desperately pushing him toward salvation. Like John, Gabriel is a sinner, though his sins seem to far outweigh those John commits. He wantonly drinks to excess and carouses with women; thus, he carries the burden of unrepentant sin. The adult, "saved" Gabriel, now a deacon in the Temple of the Fire Baptized, selectively acknowledges these earlier sins and, in retrospect, envisions himself as having actively struggled against those sins even while sinning: "This burden was heavier than the heaviest mountain and he carried it in his heart."

As a young man, Gabriel often stayed away from home, trying desperately to ignore his mother's wishes for him to be saved. After yet another night spent drinking and having sex with a prostitute, he finds himself under a tree that had routinely been witness to his passing in a similar condition. At this tree Gabriel is brought low and raised high. "When at last he lifted up his eyes he saw a new Heaven and a new earth; and he heard a new sound of singing, for a sinner had come home." In this new state of grace, he marries a community outcast, Deborah, in a self-important effort to elevate her status: "so the Lord had sent him to her, to raise her up. . . . Their marriage bed would be holy, and their children would continue the line of the faithful, a royal line." Deborah is unable to bear children, however, thus endangering Gabriel's vision of himself and his future. His state of salvation is thus severely tested by the boldly, sensual advances of Esther—a test he fails. After learning that Esther is pregnant after their liaison, Gabriel sends her away and later denies their son, Royal, even after Esther's death. After Royal dies and Deborah's death soon follows, he seeks renewed redemption by moving north, marrying Elizabeth, and vowing to love her illegitimate son, John, as his own.

One of the interesting aspects of Baldwin's novel is that the frame story about John is far less complex than the secondary story of his father. The reader sees John only on his fourteenth birthday, whereas the novel traces Gabriel's life from early adulthood until the present on John's birthday. Gabriel's existence can be broken into four distinct periods: his young adult life as a sinner; his life after salvation with Deborah; his brief time (nine days) in the company of Esther, which produces Royal; and lastly his life with Elizabeth, John's mother, and their children, Roy, Sarah, and Ruth. During these periods, despite Gabriel's protestations otherwise, he repeatedly falls from a state of grace. One of his greatest failures is his inability to reconcile himself with his flawed human nature. Gabriel sees himself as God's anointed and therefore above sin.

Go Tell It on the Mountain is dominated by binary oppositions, which the novel explores in order to offer the possibility that there can be a middle ground between the two. The adult Gabriel is simultaneously a sinner who privileges his biological son (the rebellious, trouble-making Roy) over his stepson (the bright, well-behaved, and introspective John) and who verbally and physically abuses his family. This tension between righteousness and sin, between damnation and salvation is at the heart of the novel. These pressures are played out through the relationship between father and son, and they beg the question as to whether the sins of the father are inevitably and inescapably visited upon the son.

At the beginning of "Gabriel's Prayer," Gabriel is brought back to a time before his own salvation by the silence that invades the Temple of the Fire Baptized after his sister Florence's cries at the altar. In this moment of silence, it is clear that Gabriel believes that his sins are only distant memories and that they have no bearing on his present. He believes that he has left his mountain, his burden of sin, in the past. Florence's greatest desire is to expose Gabriel's sins: "I'm going to find *some* way—some way, I don't know how—to rise up and tell it, tell *everybody,* about the blood the Lord's anointed is got on his hands."

Though Royal is lost, along with Deborah and Esther, the text suggests that Gabriel's past is carried into the present through Roy's behavior; through Gabriel's ongoing refusal to accept responsibility for the errors he committed in the past and those he continues to commit; and through his excessive pride, which leads him to fear that a child not his biological own might enter the kingdom of salvation instead of one from his "joyful line." "Neither of his sons was here tonight, had ever cried on the threshing-floor. . . . Only the son of the bondwoman [John] stood where the rightful heir should stand." Gabriel is obsessed with his lineage and legacy, and ultimately he is obsessed with an image of himself as one of God's select. These obsessions are wholly detrimental to any positive connection with those around him, most especially John. Gabriel cannot embrace John without facing the guilt of not embracing his own illegitimate son, Royal. He chooses to name his sons Royal and Roy in order to signify the passing of his throne (pulpit). But the "bastard" son John follows Gabriel to the altar before God, not his "legitimate" offspring. John Grimes, though worthy in seemingly every sense, will always be unworthy in Gabriel's eyes only because of his parentage and because of Gabriel's fiercely judgmental ways.

Gabriel Grimes is not an easily defined character. He is at once a hardworking, God-fearing family man and a dictatorial, uncompromising patriarch. Ultimately, his complexity of character echoes the complexity of existence explored throughout the novel.

Discussion Questions

1. Early in the novel, John Grimes innocently asks his mother if his father is a good man. What is your response to this question, keeping in mind the period of American history in which Gabriel Grimes has lived and worked?

2. Gabriel Grimes is a complicated character, at once a God-fearing, hardworking family man and an abusive tyrant. He is also a saint in the Temple of the Fire Baptized. Using his character as a guide, what is Baldwin saying about organized religion in *Go Tell It on the Mountain?*

3. Critics continue to debate Baldwin's position on Christianity. Some critics read *Go Tell It on the Mountain* as an indictment, while others read it as a vindication. How do you read the novel? Can the novel be read as accomplishing both?

4. Gabriel Grimes is the patriarchal head of the Grimes family. How might one characterize Gabriel's relationship to women in the novel? Are these relationships equitable? Do they include elements of dominance and subjugation?

—*Sharon L. Moore*

JOHN GRIMES

John Grimes, the protagonist of James Baldwin's *Go Tell It on the Mountain,* is introduced on the morning of his fourteenth birthday, a Saturday in March 1935. The action of the story is limited to this single day, a day on which John is pushed by himself, his family, and the larger community of his family's Pentecostal church, the Temple of the Fire Baptized, to determine the path of his future. A central concern for John is whether to follow his father's path into the church and the pulpit or to forge his own path, one that will presumably lead him away from piety and into the city and secular concerns. John is drawn to the broad way (education, friends outside of the church, burgeoning sexuality, and the city of New York and all it offers), but he has always been told that the way of the Lord (and his father) is narrow. He envisions this narrow way as being dominated by humiliation, hunger, and toil. The key question, then, surrounding John throughout the novel is which path he will choose to follow.

Three adults are particularly influential in John's life: his aunt Florence; his father, Gabriel (John is unaware that Gabriel is not his biological father); and his mother, Elizabeth. The middle third of Baldwin's novel is dedicated to providing Florence's, Gabriel's, and Elizabeth's individual histories. In these stories the reader comes to understand their present-day relationships to John and to one another. All three adults are sinners. Florence's sin is, in part, the hatred she harbors for her brother Gabriel. Gabriel's sins include adultery and excessive pride. Elizabeth's sin is getting pregnant outside of marriage. Each deals with sin in a unique manner. In telling their individual stories of struggle and sin and their subsequent attempts for redemption and salvation, Baldwin presents the reader with the question of whether the sins of the previous generation are visited upon the child, in this case John. Can John be cleansed, and does that cleansing necessitate leaving his father's house?

There are several struggles present in the frame story: John against his father; John against God, of which Gabriel is representative; John against the expectations of his family and community; and John's potential life in the "shining city" (New York) against his potential life as a "saint," a saved member of the congregation who is baptized in the faith and who possesses the Holy Spirit. The opening of the novel establishes these conflicts: "Everyone had always said that John would be a preacher when he grew up, just like his father. . . . Not until the morning of his fourteenth birthday did he really begin to think about it, and by then it was already too late."

A closer look at the protagonist's name emphasizes these tensions as well: John is one of the twelve apostles of Jesus, and his letters focus on the struggle between a righteous existence and the lure of sin. 1 John 2:15 summarizes the message John Grimes has gotten from his family (in particular, from his father) and his church community: "Do not love the world or the things in the world. If any one loves the world, love for the Father is not in him." The surname Grimes creates an interesting juxtaposition, with its apparent reference to grime as soot, smut, dirt, and filth adhering to or embedded in a surface. In this novel, John fears that he is contaminated with the filth of worldliness.

When John awakens on his birthday, he does so in a state of sin—so his strict upbringing has forced him to feel and believe. The sin that convicts John in his own mind is masturbating while "thinking of the boys, older, bigger, braver." However, this is just one of the many temptations John faces, for he is drawn to the city. In an ironic reversal, this "city upon a hill" is not the shining city envisioned in the Bible but is rather New York City, seemingly far away from religious purity and light.

After completing his weekly chores, John takes the birthday money his mother gives him and heads to Central Park. Here the text introduces the significance of the "mountain" in the title of the novel. In the center of the park lies John's favorite hill and beyond it a world of possibilities he can only imagine: "He did not know why, but there arose in him an exultation and a sense of power, and he ran up the hill like an engine, or a madman, willing to throw himself headlong into the city that glowed before him." In the city, he imagines, he might be a poet, a college professor, or even a movie star. Florence, Gabriel, and Elizabeth have a decidedly different relationship to their own mountains. For John, climbing the mountain is about possibility and hope; however, for the others their mountains are about suffering, guilt, and endurance. Their mountains are to be overcome, ignored, or endured.

John confronts his metaphorical mountain on the evening of his birthday. On this night—related in the last section of the novel, "The Threshing Floor"—John will choose between the narrow way of God and toward salvation (as defined by his family) or the broad way of life outside the Temple of the Fire Baptized. "The Threshing Floor" is an appropriate title for the climax of the novel, for as the word *thresh* implies, it is literally on the floor of the temple that the sinners are separated from the truly saved.

John eventually finds himself on the floor before the altar internally grappling with his demons. "And something moved in John's body which was not John. He was invaded, set at naught, possessed." He is not alone on this threshing floor; he is joined by Florence, Gabriel, and Elizabeth. It is John, however, who does battle throughout the night between the possibility of salvation and an ironic voice insisting "that he rise—and, at once, to leave this temple and go out into the world." In the end, he is presumably saved; however, that salvation seems quite different from what his father experiences in his section of the novel. The novel hints that John will subsequently go out into world, which throughout the text is presented as antithetical to salvation: "no matter what happens to me, where I go, what folks say about me, no matter what *anybody* says, you remember—please remember—I was saved. I was *there*." John's story is greatly influenced by Baldwin's personal experience. Although it is not necessary to know Baldwin's biography in order to understand the novel, having some awareness of that background can enrich the reading. As such, it is tempting to conclude that John will indeed run headlong into New York City and there realize his dreams.

Discussion Questions

1. Robert Frost once wrote that "the best way out is always through." Focusing on John Grimes, what is this character's relationship to Frost's philosophy? Part of your task is to determine what the character is *in* and whether or not the character gets *out*.

2. The possibility of redemption and the notion of salvation are dominant themes in *Go Tell It on the Mountain*. Does John find salvation in Baldwin's novel? In thinking about this question, you should first determine how the characters in the novel define salvation, and ask yourself whether John's notion of salvation is consistent with that working definition.

3. One notable aspect of *Go Tell It on the Mountain* is its ambiguous conclusion. Though John seems to undergo a transition, the novel does not take the reader beyond his fourteenth birthday. Looking at specific evidence in the text, speculate about John's future. The novel closes with the following statement by John: "I'm ready," he says. "I'm coming. I'm on my way." Where is he going, and in what way is he prepared?

4. *Go Tell It on the Mountain* makes extensive reference to both the Old and New Testament. Two ways in which to think about John's character is in relation to the Apostle John and John the Baptist. How do these two biblical figures enrich your understanding of John, and how do they enrich your understanding of the novel as a whole?

—*Sharon L. Moore*

꧁

"SONNY'S BLUES"

Collected in *Going to Meet the Man* (New York: Dial, 1986).

SONNY

Sonny is one of two central characters in James Baldwin's short story "Sonny's Blues." The other is an unnamed first-person narrator, Sonny's older brother, an algebra teacher who has learned that Sonny, from whom he has been estranged, has been convicted for possessing and peddling heroin. Recalling the past, the narrator reveals reasons for his and Sonny's estrangement. Sonny had wanted to be a jazz musician, and his brother did not approve, failing to see that "music was life or death" to Sonny. Sonny had left school and joined the navy. When he returned, he took a room in Greenwich Village and rejected his brother's attempts to get him to change "the way he was living." After Sonny's release from rehabilitation, the brothers reunite, and Sonny moves into his brother and sister-in-law's apartment, but the relationship is fragile. Sonny continues to study *"everything"* that can contribute to his jazz education, especially the music that evolves from the suffering of the "long line" of African American people with whom he feels a shared experience. The brothers' relationship strengthens, and Sonny is able to communicate with his brother, to whom he had said previously, "I hear you. But you never hear anything I say." Sonny finally gains his brother's understanding and acceptance. The story concludes with Sonny's taking his brother to a jazz club where he plays his blues, liberating from anguish himself and all others who truly listen and enabling his brother to comprehend that Sonny's "blues" are both purgation and creation, essential to Sonny's survival.

Sonny's character evolves largely from views Baldwin expresses in two essays that preceded the publication of "Sonny's Blues," "Everybody's Protest Novel" (1949) and "Many Thousands Gone" (1951), in both of which he criticizes Richard Wright's presentation of the character Bigger Thomas in *Native Son* (1940). Stating that "literature and sociology are not one and the same," Baldwin adds that "to tell the Negro's story" one must not leave him in a "social arena" as a statistic among "social realities" that deny him humanity and fail to reveal any "discernible relationship to his own life, to his own people," or to their "shared experience." "Sonny's Blues" begins with Sonny in the "social arena" as a statistic. The narrator learns about Sonny's arrest in the newspaper and repeatedly refers to the news about Sonny as an "it" before Sonny "became real" to him again. From this point Sonny is presented incrementally in ever-more-human terms.

"It is only in his music," Baldwin observed, that "the Negro in America has been able to tell his story," and especially in the blues. Baldwin biographer David Leeming has revealed that seven years after "Sonny's Blues" appeared Baldwin noted in "The Uses of the Blues" that the blues provide a catharsis for anguish and that joy results from one's having faced reality. In the final scene of the story Sonny demonstrates this point to his brother when he plays "Am I Blue" in the jazz club. Sonny's music is what Baldwin regarded as a "history of anguish," or as the narrator suggests, "the tale of how we suffer, and how we are delighted, and how we triumph." Baldwin regarded as paramount the articulation of this struggle. Sonny transcends his suffering and its potentially destructive consequences, developing the story's themes of identity and of survival of the artist as outsider.

The enigmatic "cup of trembling" to which the narrator compares Sonny's drink that sits atop the piano is an allusion to Isaiah 51:22: "Behold I have taken out of thine hand the cup of trembling, even the dregs of the cup of my fury; thou shalt no more drink it again." A metaphor for pain and suffering, Sonny's "cup of trembling," however, is not removed but remains with him, as does the "long line" who have gone before him. It is the source of his blues, his art, and his redemption.

Discussion Questions

1. One critic has noted what he calls "a cultural chasm" between Sonny and the narrator, despite the brothers' having grown up together. What evidence can you cite that a cultural division exists, and what does the narrator's inability to see Sonny as "serious" indicate about their differences?

2. Two scenes in the story include references to family. The first occurs when Sonny and the narrator argue in Sonny's room in Greenwich Village and the narrator observes that Sonny treated other people there "as though they were his family, and I weren't." The second occurs in the jazz club, where the bass player, Creole, says to the narrator, "You got a real musician in *your* family," and the narrator observes when hearing Sonny play that "Sonny was part of the family again." How is *family* a key term in the story, and what do you see as its possible extended meanings?

3. Readers often observe that the narrator has moved from ignorance to understanding, from rejecting Sonny to accepting him, by the time he has heard Sonny play "Am I Blue." What has Sonny enabled the narrator to understand about Sonny and about himself?

4. One reader has seen Sonny as "the artist in exile." Do you believe that this is a valid observation? What evidence can you provide to support this assertion?

—John C. Unrue

TELL ME HOW LONG THE TRAIN'S BEEN GONE
(New York: Dial, 1968)

CALEB PROUDHAMMER
Caleb is the older brother of Leo Proudhammer, the narrator and protagonist of James Baldwin's *Tell Me How Long the Train's Been Gone*. Caleb serves as a negative foil for Leo, the most successful black actor of his time. Whereas Leo manages to rise above his humble beginnings in Harlem and become a positive role model for young blacks, Caleb is depicted as a stereotypical young black man who gets in trouble with the law and whose only chance of advancement is the military. After a conversion on the battlefield, Caleb finds religion and becomes a preacher. His retreat into organized religion is seen by the younger brother as well as the author as a sign of defeat.

According to David Leeming, Baldwin's biographer, the close fraternal bond between Caleb and

Leo mirrors that between Baldwin and his half brothers Sam, who saved James from drowning, and David, who died in prison. Several incidents depicted in the novel, such as the brothers' harassment by white policemen, are taken directly from the author's life. In the first part of *Tell Me How Long the Train's Been Gone*, Caleb takes the place of the father and becomes Leo's teacher, protector, and model. Caleb remains a realist, whereas Leo escapes into the fantasy world of the movies. When the brothers are badgered by two white policemen, Caleb asserts: "All black people are shit to them. You remember that. You black like me and they going to hate you as long as you live just because you're black." Caleb occasionally exhibits a streak of irresponsibility and does not always take his fatherly role seriously. He frequently prefers hanging out with his friends and his girlfriend to babysitting his brother, leaving Leo to his own devices. Caleb has ambition and wants to make something of himself, but he eventually falls into the trap set for many black men his age. He drops out of school and is implicated in a store robbery. Even though he claims that he was not involved, he is arrested and sent to prison. Leo is traumatized by losing his protector and father figure.

Caleb disappears from Leo's life for four years, and when he returns from the prison farm he is a changed man: "He was thinner, much thinner, but harder and tougher. He was beautiful, with a very dangerous, cruel, and ruthless beauty." In an intimate scene at the center of the novel, the brothers' roles are reversed. Leo comforts his older brother, who was beaten at the prison farm and sexually harassed by a white guard. A sexual encounter between the brothers grows out of Leo's need to console Caleb.

Whereas Caleb serves as Leo's model in the first part of the novel, he is presented as a negative foil to his brother in the latter part. Unlike Leo, who refuses to fight in the war, Caleb joins the army and is stationed in Italy, where he becomes intimate with a young Italian woman. When Frederick Hopkins, a white fellow soldier whom Caleb considers his friend, tries to intrude in the relationship, Caleb is driven to violence. Just as Caleb is about to kill his rival on the battlefield, Frederick is shot by the enemy. His death marks the turning point in Caleb's

life, and he turns to religion: "I knew, I knew for the first time that there was a God somewhere. I knew that only God could save me, save *us*, not from death but from that other death, that darkness and death of the spirit which has created this hell." He proclaims "I'm free at last," alluding to Martin Luther King Jr.'s famous "I have a dream" speech of August 28, 1963. Caleb becomes a pastor at the New Dispensation House of God, which is housed in a former theater, and his aggressive attempts to show Leo the path to salvation, which culminate in him slapping his brother repeatedly, drive a wedge between the two. In an act of liberation Leo tells his "no-good, black Holy Roller" brother: "Once, I wanted to be like you. I would have given anything in the world to be like you. Now I'd rather die than be like you." Caleb's influence, however, cannot completely be overcome. While recuperating in the hospital after his heart attack, Leo has a frightening dream, fraught with symbolism, in which Caleb pursues him and strikes him repeatedly with a wooden Bible. Caleb then refuses to rescue his brother, who is drowning in the ocean, in a marked reversal of the drowning incident in Baldwin's life.

Whereas Caleb replaces the father in the first part of the novel, he is in turn replaced by Black Christopher, Leo's lover, in book 3. While Mr. Proudhammer resists Caleb's persistent attempts to convert him and appears to be disappointed in his older son, he treats Christopher like a son. The militant young man, who believes in the need for violent action, is able to rekindle in the disillusioned father the hope for racial progress. Lynn Orilla Scott has pointed out that Baldwin brings the novel full circle by substituting Christopher for Caleb in a passage that repeats an earlier one almost word for word. At the beginning of *Tell Me How Long the Train's Been Gone*, ten-year-old Leo describes his father and brother as follows: "They both looked very much like each other on those days—both big, both black, both laughing." In the last paragraph of the novel, the thirty-nine-year-old actor observes his lover and father, walking through the streets of Harlem: "They looked very much like each other, both big, both black, both laughing." The family unity has been restored, albeit in a different configuration and, according to Carolyn Wedin Sylvander, old-time Negro religion has been replaced by young black militancy.

Discussion Questions

1. Leo Proudhammer states that "the theater began in the church" and that he and his brother "were both performers." How are the roles of the actor and the reverend similar and dissimilar?

2. George-Michel Sarotte states in his book *Like a Brother, Like a Lover* that Caleb is a modern version of LeRoy, the young black man in *Another Country* (1962). Do you agree or disagree with his assessment?

3. The Christian name Caleb means "bold" in Hebrew; Caleb was one of twelve Israelite leaders sent by Moses to explore the Promised Land. Why, in your opinion, did Baldwin choose this name for the older brother?

4. According to David Van Leer, "Caleb's abrupt conversion from rebellious youth to persecuting Minister seems unmotivated." Do you agree or disagree with his assessment?

—*Karl L. Stenger*

LEO PROUDHAMMER

Leo Proudhammer is the first-person narrator of James Baldwin's novel *Tell Me How Long the Train's Been Gone*. As the novel opens, Leo, the most acclaimed black actor of his time, has suffered a heart attack while performing William Shakespeare's *Othello*. He claims that the attack was brought on by "nervous exhaustion and overwork," but it subsequently becomes obvious that his illness is a symptom of the unresolved conflicts in his life. Both the near-death experience and the enforced bed rest that follows cause the actor to reflect on his life. His reminiscence does not progress in a chronologically straightforward manner but is rather characterized by stream-of-consciousness techniques: frequently, one memory elicits another (later or earlier) memory, which in turn flows into an altogether different recollection. Not only does this technique give an accurate picture of the medicated patient's state of mind, but it also points to the conflicts and incongruities in Leo's life, which he calls "that desperately treacherous labyrinth." There are several instances

when the actor's memory is hazy and vague, particularly when he has to deal with unresolved and deeply personal issues. Instead of being a "definite historian," Leo resembles, according to Lynn Orilla Scott, an "archeologist," who "seeks a new wholeness in the discontinuities and division of memory."

In book 1, "The House Nigger," the archeological digging through the layers of the past begins in the hospital, in a scene that employs cinematic techniques: "The light did not fall on me, on me where I lay now. I was left in darkness, my face could not be seen. In that darkness I encountered a scene from another nightmare, a nightmare I had had as a child. In this nightmare there is a book—a great, heavy book with an illustrated cover. The cover shows a dark, squalid alley. . . . The beam of the flashlight shines down the alley, at the end of which I am fleeing, clutching something. The title of the book in my nightmare is, *We Must Not Find Him, For He Is Lost.*" The first third of book 1 depicts Leo's miserable childhood in Harlem and his family's struggle to survive. Whereas Leo's father despairs over the family's dire financial situation and escapes into an alcoholic haze, his mother is embroiled in a continuous war with shop owners and the landlord. Because Leo's parents are preoccupied with the business of daily survival, his older brother, Caleb, takes on the parental role: "Caleb was my touchstone, my model, and my only guide." The brothers experience racism firsthand when they are harassed by the police. Baldwin based this episode as well as others (the family's ongoing struggle with the landlord Rabinowitz and Leo's being lost on the subway and his rescue by a kind black man) on his own life. *Tell Me How Long the Train's Been Gone* is generally considered Baldwin's most autobiographical novel. Baldwin biographer David Leeming states: "Leo Proudhammer *is* James Baldwin, complete with large eyes, 'pigeon toes,' and 'jiggling behind.'"

The only means of Leo's escape from his dire circumstances is the make-believe world of the movies, and he decides to become an actor. Like other Baldwin characters (the musicians and singers in *Another Country*, "Sonny's Blues," *Blues for Mister Charlie*, and *Just Above My Head*; the woodcarver in *If Beale Street Could Talk*), Leo uses art as an escape hatch. He leaves home and spends the next "grimy, frightening, untidy years" as a struggling actor in Greenwich Village. There he meets Barbara King, "a refugee schoolgirl from Kentucky," who escaped her rich and stifling family for a bohemian life in New York.

Book 2, "Is There Anybody There? Said the Traveler," focuses on Leo's intimate relationships with the two most important people in his life, fellow thespian Barbara and his older brother, Caleb. While participating in "The Actors' Means Workshop," which is modeled on Lee Strasberg's Actors Studio, Leo becomes intimate with Barbara. Their relationship is destined to remain that of "incestuous brother and sister," however, because Leo is bisexual. Moreover, racial and, above all, class barriers prevent the two from marrying. As Barbara puts it: "a wife who was both white *and* rich! It would be horrible. We'd soon stop loving each other." Leo's intimate encounter with Barbara is linked with that between the brothers by Leo's need to protect and comfort those he loves. When Caleb returns from a Southern prison farm, where he was sexually harassed and taunted by a white guard, Leo consoles him and initiates sex between them: "More than anything on earth, that night, I wanted Caleb's joy." This pivotal scene, which occurs in the center of the novel, marks, according to Scott, Leo's transition to manhood. It is also an expression of Baldwin's criticism of the inherent homophobia of the black revolutionary movement: "By figuring an incestuous homosexual act as repairing the damage of white homosexual rape (or threatened rape), Baldwin is challenging the homophobia in the Black Nationalist movement that equated all homosexuality with signs of white oppression and internalized self-hatred."

Baldwin's challenge to the Black Nationalist movement is even more direct in book 3, "Black Christopher." After years of struggle Leo has become the most acclaimed black actor of his time and a model for the black community. When he meets the radical activist Christopher Hall, "black in color, black in pride, black in rage," and enters into an intimate relationship with him, Leo is forced to rethink his role as a public celebrity. Christopher's militancy reawakens a younger, more radical Leo: "Not so very long ago, I had stood as he now stood and had hoped as he now hoped. What had my hope come to? It had led me to this moment, here. I heard his cry because it was my own." Leo starts attending political rallies and even considers Christopher's call to arms: "I think you agree that we need us some guns. Right?" "Yes," I said. "I see that." *Tell Me How Long the Train's Been Gone* is also remarkable because it presents the homosexual as an instigator of political change, as Stanley Macebuh has observed: "Homosexuality becomes in fact, and not merely in potential, the authentic well-spring of a burgeoning revolutionary mood." The novel ends on an ambiguous note. Leo, having agreed with Christopher's call for arms, leaves for Europe, alone, where he recuperates from his heart attack in a friend's house in the South of France. He then returns to the United States, where he stars in a movie and a new play. The last lines of the novel take the reader up to the present and reveal the point of origin for Leo's recollections: "I . . . found myself, presently, standing in the wings again, waiting for my cue."

Discussion Questions

1. When Leo Proudhammer's friends present him with replicas of the lions in Trafalgar Square, they include a note referring to his Christian name ("For Leo, the lion. Long may he wail"). Lynn Orilla Scott has pointed out that his last name links him to John Henry, the African American folk hero, who wants to die "with a hammer in my hand." What, in your opinion, is the significance of the protagonist's name?

2. Some critics have claimed that the title of the novel as well as the titles and epigraphs of the individual books are not clearly connected with the content of the novel. Do you agree or disagree? Make your argument citing evidence from the novel.

3. The open-endedness of the novel has baffled many readers and critics. Some believe that Leo has joined Black Christopher's fight, while others think that Leo is as he was before his heart attack. Considering the fact that the ending of the novel is chronologically also its beginning, how do you interpret Leo's waiting in the wings, about to go onstage?

4. James Baldwin stated in an interview with a French critic that he thought of Leo as Rufus Scott, the black jazz drummer in *Another Country* (1962), without Rufus's need to kill himself. What similarities and dissimilarities are there between the two characters?

5. James Baldwin stated in a 1986 interview with Richard Goldstein of the *Village Voice:* "A black gay person who is a sexual conundrum to society is already, long before the question of sexuality comes into it, menaced and marked because he's black or she's black. The sexual question comes after the question of color; it's simply one more aspect of the danger in which all black people live." Is this statement supported by the depiction of Leo in the novel or not?

—*Karl L. Stenger*

REFERENCES

Trudier Harris, ed., *New Essays on Go Tell It on the Mountain* (New York: Cambridge University Press, 1996);

Kenneth Kinnamon, ed., *James Baldwin: A Collection of Critical Essays* (Englewood Cliffs, N.J.: Prentice-Hall, 1974);

David Leeming, *James Baldwin: A Biography* (New York: Knopf, 1994);

Stanley Macebuh, *James Baldwin: A Critical Study* (New York: Third Press, 1973);

Dwight A. McBride, *James Baldwin Now* (New York: New York University Press, 1999);

Therman B. O'Daniel, ed., *James Baldwin: A Critical Valuation* (Washington, D.C.: Howard University Press, 1977);

Horace A. Porter, *Stealing the Fire: The Art and Protest of James Baldwin* (Middletown, Conn.: Wesleyan University Press, 1989);

Louis H. Pratt, *James Baldwin* (Boston: Twayne, 1978);

Lynn Orilla Scott, *James Baldwin's Later Fiction: Witness to the Journey* (East Lansing: Michigan State University Press, 2002);

Fred L. and Nancy V. Standley, *James Baldwin, a Reference Guide* (Boston: G. K. Hall, 1980);

Standley and Standley, eds., *Critical Essays on James Baldwin* (Boston: G. K. Hall, 1998);

Carolyn Wedin Sylvander, *James Baldwin* (New York: Ungar, 1980).

Toni Cade Bambara
(March 25, 1939 – December 9, 1995)

✍

THE SALT EATERS
(New York: Random House, 1980)

VELMA HENRY

Velma Henry is a middle-aged black woman who is fighting for social change in her hometown of Claybourne, Georgia, in Toni Cade Bambara's novel *The Salt Eaters*. Velma is the "border-guard," according to her mother: When she was a child, her responsibility was to "negotiate with the would-be intruders . . . the landlord, the insurance man, the green-grocer, the fishpeddler, to insure Mama Mae one more bit of peace." As she grew older, her responsibilities multiplied to include work as a political activist, her duties as a wife and a mother, and employment at the local chemical plant, where she was suspected of sabotage. Eventually her inability to keep her life separate from her political work causes her to self-destruct. *The Salt Eaters* focuses on her quest for personal wholeness—what made her fall apart and how she might put her life back together.

The title *The Salt Eaters* refers to a specific healing property of salt, its ability to draw the poison of a snake from an open wound: "Helps neutralize the venom . . . to neutralize the serpent is another matter." Minnie Ransom, the healer, explains that there is a "difference between eating salt as an antidote to snakebite and turning into salt, succumbing to the serpent." Velma comes to Minnie with her "face bloated," suggesting that she has too much salt in her body and is therefore "succumbing to the serpent." Salt is the metaphor for Velma's life: She has eaten too much of it, which is to say that she has taken on too much in her life and is now feeling the effects.

The novel begins with Minnie asking Velma if she is ready to be healed: "Are you sure, sweetheart, that you want to be well?" No one can heal her, Minnie is suggesting, if she does not want to be healed. She adds: "just so's you're sure, sweetheart, and ready to be healed, cause wholeness is no trifling matter. A lot of weight when you're well." Minnie's words establish clear boundaries between herself and Velma, emphasizing that Velma has lost the ability to create them for herself. Though the two women keep each other at a distance, they connect at intimate levels throughout Velma's healing process.

The novel portrays Velma as a conglomeration of parts, influences, and experiences as they are perceived by the other characters associated with her. She has lost her connections with her friends and family, just as she has lost her connection with herself, therefore causing her mental and physical breakdown. According to Ruth Elizabeth Burks, "the characters speak little, because they have lost the desire to communicate through words. Their thoughts, as conveyed by Bambara, are more real to them than that that is real." Bambara conveys a sense of Velma mostly through the thoughts, dreams, premonitions, fragmented memories, and visions of the other characters. Her husband, Obie; her godmother, M'Dear Sophie; her sister, Palma; her coworkers and friends; and many other people who have small parts in the story reveal details that link each character together. What they all have in common is their relationship with Velma.

Many of the other characters regard Velma as being "thoughtless, selfish. . . . Velma was always all right, it was the people around her that were kept in a spin." Sophie wonders aloud: "And did you think your life is yours alone to do with as you please? That I, your folks, your family, and all who care for you have no say-so in the matter?" Because Velma is part of a society interconnected by close relationships, she would affect many lives, personally and politically, by committing suicide. The connection between the personal and the political life is essential not only to this novel but also to those of many feminist and black activists writing at the time.

Bambara has said that the novel "came out of a problem-solving impulse." As she writes in "What It Is I'm Doing Anyhow," writing is "one of the ways I participate in struggle." In 1982, in a taped interview with Kay Bonetti, Bambara reflected on her work: "When I look back at my work with any little distance the two characteristics that jump out at me is one, the tremendous capacity for laughter, but also a tremendous capacity for rage." The rage came from the injustices she saw in the treatment of children, the elderly, and the oppressed black community. She embodies these qualities in Velma. Though Velma has little to laugh about throughout the novel, her rage is apparent. She is known to have a temper that could explode at any moment. Her outbursts are described as "the ooze of Velma's Lava threatening any minute to engulf everything." She loses control of her temper because of her inability to control her life. As the strains of her work, her home life, and her rage over injustice reach their pinnacle, she falls into an emotional collapse.

A loud crash of lightning heard by every character in the novel, followed by a downpour of rain, marks the beginning of Velma's healing. "Velma would remember it as the moment she started back toward life, the moment when the healer's hand had touched some vital spot and she was trying to resist." Velma is finally able to return to herself, to find the boundary she needs in order to separate herself from her work.

Discussion Questions

1. Why is it important for the characters to be connected by family ties, friendship, a sense of community, or otherwise? Have they always been connected, or was there some point in the novel that their connection was severed?

2. Describe the relationship between Velma and her godmother, Sophie, at the beginning of the novel, compared to their relationship at the end. How do the changes they undergo affect their relationship?

3. Why does Fred Holt appear in the novel? How is he connected to Velma? What does he learn from her?

4. Speculate what Velma's life will be like after she is healed. How might her relationship with her friends and family change or remain the same?

MINNIE RANSOM

Minnie Ransom is an unmarried, elderly black woman who is a natural healer in Claybourne, Georgia, during the 1980s in Toni Cade Bambara's *The Salt Eaters*. She is an important character to her community because she brings people together and provides spiritual support and healing. Bambara has described Minnie as "the fabled healer of the district, her bright-red flouncy dress drawn in at the waist with two different strips of kenti cloth, up to her elbows in a minor fortune of gold, brass and silver bangles, the silken fringe of the shawl shimmying at her armpits." Minnie's appearance suggests a celebration of her own womanhood, history, and culture. She is a strong woman with a strong connection to nature and freely communicates with the spirit world. Working at the threshold between the physical and spiritual realms, Minnie communes with her patient, Velma Henry, while at the same time "traveling" and conversing with her spirit guide, Old Wife. Minnie's position between the supernatural and the natural enables her to become the boundary that Velma is not able to form between her life and her home life. Minnie remains both separate from and yet an important part of Velma's healing.

Minnie is described in *The Salt Eaters* as "Minnie Ransom herself," meaning that she understands her place in life and is comfortable being what she is meant to be, unlike Velma. Minnie is aware that she, and everyone else, has the ability to make choices. Minnie's first words present Velma a challenge: "Are you sure, sweetheart, that you want to be well?" She wants her patients to understand that they have the power to choose. Minnie gives Velma the choice of health, and as soon as Velma decides that she wants to be well, her healing can begin.

Minnie is in tune with the spirit world. She consults her spirit guide, Old Wife, but often starts an argument with her when Old Wife will not give her the straight answers she is looking for: "Ain't you omniscient yet, Old Wife? Ain't you all knowing?" As a spirit, Old Wife plays an active role in the novel. She floats between the world of the living and the world of the dead. She is crucial to the living characters as a provider of advice and guidance. The fusion of natural and supernatural elements in the novel links the novel to African cultural traditions.

The division between technology and nature can be seen in Velma and Minnie. In contrast to Minnie, Velma is trapped in the technological side of life, actively participating in politics and working in the local chemical plant. Minnie must help Velma reconnect with her spiritual side in order to begin her healing. In *The Salt Eaters* Bambara insists that healing is a form of release from bondage, as Minnie's last name, Ransom, suggests. Minnie encourages Velma to go deep within herself, to find the memories that had once confused her, and to face the ghosts of her past. The reader is able to follow Velma on her journey through memories, bits of conversations, and thoughts. Minnie's relationship with Velma remains detached, yet she is ready to give Velma assistance if she needs it. Velma, sitting on a stool next to Minnie, feels "the warm breath of Minnie Ransom on her, lending her something to work the bellows of her lungs with. Minnie does not attempt to breathe for Velma, but rather loans her breath so that she can relearn how to do it herself. At the end of the novel Minnie realizes that there is "no need of [her] hands," and she "withdraws them, drops them in her lap just as Velma [rises] on steady legs." The "burst cocoon" of her shawl left behind on the floor symbolizes that Velma has broken free from her constraints. She emerges a changed and healed woman.

As Susan Willis notes, Minnie marks a departure from the political activist characters in Bambara's earlier works. Minnie is a different type of independent black woman: a spiritual healer. She has been compared to the character of Mary Rambo, the mother/healer figure in Ralph Ellison's *Invisible Man* (1952). Like Minnie, Mary takes care of the less fortunate with her natural ability to nurture.

Discussion Questions

1. As a spirit guide, Old Wife gives Minnie advice, but she will not give Minnie a straight answer about Velma. Why would Velma be any different than other patients Minnie has taken care of? Use examples from the text to support your answer.

2. Minnie is the natural healer, connected to the earth and the spirit world. Which character in the novel is similar to Minnie but is not considered to be a healer? What is this character's relationship with both Minnie and Velma?

3. In what ways, besides as an antidote to snake venom, is salt talked about in the novel? Cite at least three instances where salt is mentioned and what circumstances it meant to describe.

4. What role does music play in the story? To Velma? To Minnie? To the other characters?

—Anne Bahringer

REFERENCES

Elliott Butler-Evans, *Race, Gender, and Desire: Narrative Strategies in the Fiction of Toni Cade Bambara, Toni Morrison, and Alice Walker* (Philadelphia: Temple University Press, 1989);

Linda Janet Holmes and Cheryl A. Wall, *Savoring the Salt: The Legacy of Toni Cade Bambara* (Philadelphia: Temple University Press, 2007);

Janet Sternburg, ed., *The Writer on Her Work* (New York: Norton, 1980);

Claudia Tate, ed., *Black Women Writers at Work* (New York: Continuum, 1983);

Martha M. Vertreace, "Toni Cade Bambara: The Dance of Character and Community," in *American Women Writing Fiction: Memory, Identity, Family, Space,* edited by Mickey Pearlman (Lexington: University Press of Kentucky, 1989), pp. 155–166.

Russell Banks

(March 28, 1940 –   )

༄

CONTINENTAL DRIFT

(New York: Harper & Row, 1985)

ROBERT DUBOIS

Bob Dubois, the protagonist of Russell Banks's *Continental Drift,* is a working-class, thirty-year-old American male. He is married to Elaine and has two daughters, Ruthie and Emma, and he earns $137.44 per week in 1979 in Catamount, New Hampshire. Banks fills in these details using an omniscient narrator to give the facts of this typical American husband and father in the late twentieth century. In the first chapter of the novel, "Invocation," the author writes that the teller of tales should be a *loa* or wise man evaluating his characters' actions and motivations. In much of the novel, however, he also demonstrates Bob's character, his faults and strengths, by showing him in action and letting the reader judge his mistakes and good intentions.

In one scene, for example, Dubois (pronounced *Du-boys* by the local New Englanders) awkwardly tries to buy a pair of skates for Ruthie in a Sears department store. It is late because he stopped in a bar after work and had an adulterous tryst with his mistress, and the clerk is impatient and rude, making Dubois angry, but quietly so. Finally, in response to the clerk's abruptness he shouts, "Better. I want something better," a comment that foreshadows the search he will make for a better life throughout the novel. With no authorial comment, he walks out without the skates and breaks all the windows in his own car. His treatment of the clerk had been restrained, controlled by his desire not to be noticed, a shyness and lack of assertiveness that drives him to let out his rage in self-destructive ways. He alone is the victim of his outburst. Banks depicts a good man doing harm to himself and family—Ruthie does not get the skates—despite his good intentions. This kind of character portrayal without the author's comment is more effective than an outline of Dubois's traits given by an omniscient narrator. Although the style of the *loa* is effectively used by Banks, his revealing of the character is more satisfying and convincing to the reader when he shows, not tells. In a review in *The Nation,* critic James Marcus lauds Banks's use of narrative voice to develop Dubois's character, saying that the combination of direct description and the revealing of the character through his actions and dialogue make Dubois an "eloquently fleshed-out character."

The physical descriptions of Dubois jibe with his character: he has a friendly face when he is being himself and a closed, hard face when he is putting on an act; he looks brilliant one moment and stupid the next, depending on his mood. "Bob's face is like an intelligent dog's, unable to hide or effectively disguise his emotions, and it's forced him into being fairly honest," Banks says of him. His naiveté and innocence, which get him into deep trouble, are reflected in these looks, and his bulk and strength belie his vulnerability.

Banks likes to use foils in his novels, characters who are direct or approximate opposites of the protagonists. They serve to accentuate some outstanding characteristics of the main character, illustrating faults and virtues more distinctly. In *Continental Drift,* Bob's older brother, Eddie, acts as a foil; his greed and racial hatred emphasize that Bob is the opposite of this kind of man. His character flaw is the reticence to face real problems. He cannot suppress his self-destructive anger. Vanise Dorsinville, a Haitian woman needing desperately to get out of a life of physical danger, imprisonment, and rape, also serves as a contrast to Dubois. Her journey, which alternates chapters with Bob's story in *Continental Drift*, is a vital necessity; Bob's seems more like an internal conflict, an inability to overcome boredom and frustration. He uproots his family to Florida to relieve his boredom and angst and to make more money. Banks uses Vanise's troubles to contrast with Dubois's, making the latter's troubles seem trivial, his ambition more egotistical. Banks said in a symposium published in *The New York Times* that all good writing is travel writing, that it is an account of a journey, a test; he mentions Herman Melville, Nathaniel Hawthorne, and Mark Twain and their treatment of their characters as they are tested by travel. Banks himself left New Hampshire for Florida and the Caribbean when he was young. He asserts in this symposium that the journey taught him more about people than he ever could have learned at home, that it gave him a clearer idea of race and injustice. *Continental Drift*, as the story of Bob's journey, is a tragedy; he loses everything, including his life. His awareness of social and moral problems, which is heightened by his journey, is wiped out by his death.

The incident in the Sears store can be seen as foreshadowing of Dubois's flight from reality to violent self-destruction throughout the novel. His passive acceptance of Elaine's idea of going to Florida to start a new life results in his shooting a robber in his brother's liquor store. Taking a job in Florida with his old friend working on a ship that smuggles aliens and drugs leads to his compliance in drowning a boatload of innocent people to avoid being caught by the Coast Guard, an action that will lead him to even deeper despair. His conscience-driven attempt to give Vanise the money he earned for drowning her fellow aliens leads to his death at the hands of thieves who take the money. The source of the rage that he carries within is never discussed in the novel. Robert Niemi suggests that Bob's passivity, his permitting problems to rule him and never overcoming them, has caused him to be a victim of circumstances.

Discussion Questions

1. What is the difference between Bob's approach to solving his problems and Vanise's? How are they similar and different?

2. Discuss your assessment of Dubois's character: How did Banks lead you to these assessments? Were you led to your judgments by the character's actions and dialogue or the narrator's direct explanation of the character's traits?

3. Since the novel ends with the protagonist's death, what would you give as Dubois's tragic flaw, the main reason for his downfall?

4. Most representative characters in fiction tend to be stereotypical heroes with little individuality. How does Banks make Dubois seem more like a real person with distinctive characteristics?

—*Denis Hennessey*

❦

AFFLICTION
(New York: Harper & Row, 1989)

WADE WHITEHOUSE

Wade Whitehouse is a protagonist much like many of Russell Banks's heroes in prior novels and short stories: he belongs to the struggling working class; he had a troubled family life in childhood; he is intelligent but too sensitive to the challenges that life presents him. *Affliction* is narrated by Wade's younger brother, Rolfe, who acts as a foil to Wade in many respects. Rolfe missed much of the abuse Wade took from their father. He escaped from the small town where they grew up, Lawford, New Hampshire, by going away to college and staying away. From his home in suburban Boston, where he teaches history in a high school, Rolfe tells Wade's story. His narrative covers about two weeks in Wade's life directly, but he alludes to previous incidents in his brother's life, going back to childhood and early adulthood.

Wade is forty-one at the beginning of the story, divorced from Lillian and the father of Jill, who lives with her mother and stepfather outside of town. Wade works as a well digger, a truck driver, and a part-time policeman in Lawford. Wade is taking

Jill to the town's Halloween party as Rolfe begins the story, but he runs late as usual and has to buy Jill's costume hastily, making Jill feel uneasy and disappointed.

Wade's actions reveal a pattern of poor preparation followed by confusion leading to one of his spurts of anger, and Rolfe tells of these incidents with a combination of frustration and contempt for his older brother. Rolfe's language reflects his education and maturity, a contrast to Wade's bullheaded temperament. Several reviewers of *Affliction* comment on Rolfe's narration, which seems to be privy to Wade's inner thoughts and motivations while telling the story from 150 miles away. Banks handles Rolfe's omniscience by having the younger brother take the voice of a storyteller, admitting using his imagination where he feels he needs it, but knowing what his brother is thinking because of having been raised so closely to Wade.

Three major problems face Wade in the two weeks Rolfe chooses to describe. His relationship with his ex-wife and the distance, physical and emotional, from Jill eat away at his conscience and feed his anger, the anger that starts him on his pattern of plodding failure. Secondly, Wade is jealous of Jack, a younger acquaintance who is having a relationship with a young woman Wade admires. The third problem is more general and complex: Wade feels that his boss, LaReviere, is taking advantage of him in ways that are both blatant and subtle. Rolfe never clearly describes whether the pressures of these problems are real or just part of Wade's paranoia.

Banks uses the image of a toothache as a reminder of Wade's pattern of being conscious of an annoyance without taking action to rid himself of it. Instead of taking direct steps to have the tooth treated, Wade drinks to relieve the pain. Only at the very end of the novel does Wade pull the tooth out himself, violently and painfully, with a common pair of pliers. Another image that helps portray Wade's paralysis in solving problems is his anger at having to stop traffic outside the school because of snow. Drivers glower at him for delaying them. As he keeps the traffic halted, Wade holds "his arms straight out, one aimed north and one south, with both hands up. Motionless,

expressionless, he held his post in the middle of the road. . . . He looked like a demented scarecrow. He felt like a statue, however: a man made of stone, unable to bring his arms down or force his legs to work."

Wade is physically a big man with the large strong hands of a man who does heavy work, and he is attractive to women. He and Lillian had met in high school and were married young. Margie Fogg, the girl he has seen since the divorce and sometimes stays with, must see beyond his reticence to the vulnerable and emotional man that he must be. He can talk to her and tell her of his problems, but in a guarded way.

The glimpses Rolfe gives of their early family life tell in some detail of the violent moods of their father, Glenn. Glenn's masculine combativeness and violence are released during his drinking episodes and the targets are his sons, Wade and Rolfe. He teases the boys, parodying their pathetic attempts to defeat him in arm wrestling. One incident involves Wade as a young boy telling Glenn never to hit his mother again. Wade threatens his father with a skillet, and Glenn punches him mercilessly as though he were hitting a grown man. After the beating, Glenn belittles Wade, and "Wade let himself slide slowly down to the floor, where he sat with his legs straight out, his head slumped on one shoulder, his arms flopped across his lap—a marionette with its strings cut."

It is this frustrated and humiliated person, tormented by a father who shows nothing but contempt for him, made narrow in his view of the world by never leaving his small hometown, and victimized by a boss who sees him as just another pawn to use and dismiss, that Banks shows attempting to contend with the ordinary pressures of life. Are the problems Wade encounters real or prompted by paranoia? Banks characterizes Wade so completely that his actions in the last third of the novel are clearly revealed to be results of alcoholic delusions. Wade murders Jack, alienates Margie by showing the violent side of himself, and in a manic rage clubs his father to death and disappears. Rolfe's narration of these events leaves some doubt as to whether or not Wade exaggerated his problems.

Wade is a character who evokes sympathy, not disdain. Robert Niemi suggests that because Wade does not die after his violent actions at the end of the novel but instead fades into anonymity, that he will continue a life of pain and torment caused by his inheritance of violence. This tragic ending illustrates clearly the theme of never-ending violence for Wade Whitehouse, a man caught in the trap of inherited alcoholism and abuse.

Discussion Questions

1. How does Banks characterize his narrator, Rolfe? What hints can be noted showing the younger brother's contempt for Wade, perhaps even jealousy?

2. What evidence does the novel give that there is a caring, loving side of Wade Whitehouse that Lillian and Margie Fogg can see in him?

3. Wade's daughter Jill says that she loves him, but what can be making her anxious to get away from him? How do Jill's reactions show the pattern of failure in Wade's life?

4. Wade's tragic flaw is not pride. What elements of his character inevitably make his life doomed from the start? What could he have done to avoid his patterns of failure?

—*Denis Hennessy*

REFERENCE

Robert Niemi, *Russell Banks* (New York: Twayne, 1997).

Djuna Barnes

(June 12, 1892 – June 18, 1982)

NIGHTWOOD

(London: Faber & Faber, 1936; New York: Harcourt, Brace, 1937)

NORA FLOOD

A large-hearted, passionate weeper of copious tears, Nora Flood is Djuna Barnes's portrait of lovelorn and unrequited yearning in her novel *Nightwood*. A serious-minded hostess of a Bohemian salon turned publicist for a circus, Nora has a face that reminds people of an American pioneer beset upon by Indians "crouched in ambush." She soon comes to have her "singular" equilibrium forever disrupted by her new lover, Robin Vote, a married woman. Habitually trusting, Nora discovers "that to love without criticism is to be betrayed" and, further, that "those who love everything are despised by everything." Unguarded, devoid of cynicism or irony, her disastrous affair with Robin renders her "like a person who looks up to discover that they have coincided with the needs of nature in a bird." Nora is both foolish and superb in the manner of the first Christians. She robs and diminishes herself for others, "carry[ing] her betrayal money in her own pocket." Because there had been "no ignominy in her," no willingness to reproach or accuse and thus no impulse to forgive, she had come to function for others in a manner superior to that of a priest in his confessional, while remaining herself untangled in the painful coils of the world.

When Nora herself is heartsick and in need of consolation, she seeks advice about "the night" from its "watchman," Dr. Matthew O'Connor. Initially, Nora and Robin had been "so 'haunted' of each other that separation was impossible." But Robin eventually flees the oppressive regularity of the home that Nora had convinced herself Robin unconsciously desired as a stay against her instability. Hardly more consciously, Nora had sought to counterbalance Robin's flightiness with compensatory repetition-compulsions. Fearing that Robin's dissolute wanderings will make her "lose the scent of home" or, worse, that she will become the magnetic center of all impending catastrophe, Nora tries to preserve her beloved, her second self, against flux and mortality by entombing her, forever incorruptible, in the life's blood of her own obsessive imagination.

Barnes sketches the stages of the lover's degradation with concise, deft strokes: Nora watches people to see if their gestures "turn up" in Robin's own, and she jealously recognizes in Robin's own inadvertent phrases and gestures a night world of nonchalant debauch that she can never share and to which Robin will inevitably return. Even Robin's capacity for oblivious sleep breeds envy, suspicion, and dread inasmuch as it represents her unreachable otherness, a secret world of remorseless iniquity from which the lover is barred. (O'Connor goads: "When she sleeps, is she not moving her leg aside for an unknown garrison . . . murdering us with an axe? Eating our ear in a pie. . . ?") Awakening from her own recurring nightmares of losing Robin, Nora compulsively dwells upon them, "taking the body of Robin down with her into [them], as the ground things take the corpse, with minute persistence, down into the earth, leaving a pattern of it on the grass, as if they stitched as they descended."

Discovering Robin in the arms of Jenny Petherbridge, Nora experiences both "an awful happiness" that Robin is protected from death by "the successive arms of women" and "a sensation of evil, complete and dismembering." Nora feels Robin like a phantom limb, "an amputation" she cannot "renounce"—and, indeed, O'Connor comes to think of her as "the dismantled." Striving to understand Robin, Nora attempts to imitate her dissipated and debauched life in port-city dives, but to no avail. She comes to see herself as Robin's opposite inasmuch as Robin forgets, while she remembers all too painfully. But, however obsessive it is, Nora's memory is also selective, and this, according to O'Connor, may be her saving grace: "you are the only one strong enough to have listened to the prosecution, your life; and to have built back the amazing defence, your heart!" Preferring the illusion of the mythologizer to the seeker of a truth that does not exist, O'Connor admonishes Nora that while Robin had rightly sought to preserve herself by assimilating Nora into her dream life—from which "you'll never get out"— she, on the other hand, has "been unwise enough" to subject Robin to "a formula" in the attempt to garb "the unknowable in the garments of the known."

O'Connor's sustained critique of both women's personalities also constitutes a remarkable series of caustic insights into the existential origins of erotic longing. O'Connor explains that Robin, seeking self-oblivion, has sought to evade the invasive nature of Nora's love: "She saw in you that fearful eye that would make her a target forever." From O'Connor's perspective, while Robin's new lover is only a "looter" who compensates for feelings of deficiency by "snatching the oats out of love's droppings," Nora and Robin are linked forever, for better or worse:

"though . . . buried at opposite ends of the earth, one dog will find them both." Indeed, all three women have entered into an ongoing dance of death: "you'll all be locked together, like the poor beasts that get their heads fattened with a knowledge of each other they never wanted, having had to contemplate each other, head-on and eye to eye, until death."

Both O'Connor and Nora understand love in terms of death, knowledge of death, and the knowledge that comes as a kind of death. For Nora, "Love is death, come upon with passion. . . . I love her as one condemned to it." Speaking as "Matthew," Barnes's abject saint, O'Connor commiserates, "You have died and arisen for love." More sternly, he tries to make her see that she has been "blood-thirsty with love" and now that love has died, she keeps "'bringing [Robin] up,' as cannons bring up the dead from deep water."

Miserable with guilt that her protective possessiveness has, like a "fixed dismay," intervened between Robin and Robin's own holy mystery, Nora demonstrates her right-minded New Englander's gift for self-recrimination. She wonders whether she has acted demonically in trying to take possession of someone who was otherwise "uninhabited." She speculates that "There's something evil in me that loves evil and degradation—purity's black backside! That loves honesty with a horrid love, or why have I always gone seeking it at the liar's door?" Ashamed of histrionics that have made her "a fine and terrifying spectacle," she remains distraught with the exquisite pain of knowing herself forgotten. It is Nora's sad fate to illustrate one of O'Connor's most poignant aphorisms: "Everything we can't bear in this world, some day we find in one person, and love it all at once."

Perhaps drawing on her own emotional life, Barnes shrewdly links the dynamics of Nora's painful relationship with Robin to an internal psychodynamic characterized by a narcissistic desire for the self. O'Connor helps Nora to recognize that the woman was "yourself, caught as you turn in panic; on her mouth you kiss your own. If she is taken you cry that you have been robbed of yourself." However, to properly reflect the full range of tonalities that the book mobilizes for its portrait of Nora, the pacifying wisdom of self-understanding that O'Connor proffers must be counterbalanced by his rendition of the raging curse of the abandoned homosexual lover, which Nora's nobility keeps her incapable of expressing: "low riding mouth in an empty snarl of the groin! May this be your torment, may this be your damnation."

Discussion Questions

1. The interpretive implications of Barnes's analysis of Nora and Robin's relationship are ambiguous, as exemplified by Nora's repeated references to the doll Robin had "given us—'our child.'" Are details such as these best understood as insightful glimpses contributing to an analysis of a psychological paradigm structuring lesbian love generally or do they only serve to illustrate the aberrant psychological dynamic operating between two idiosyncratic, not to say grotesque, personalities?

2. Perhaps as a kind of shock treatment, and though mitigated by compassionate fellow feeling, O'Connor persistently blames Nora for failing Robin. What are the terms of his indictments? On what criteria does he found his judgments? With which of his judgments does Nora concur?

—*David Brottman*

MATTHEW O'CONNOR

"Dr. Matthew-Mighty-grain of salt-Dante-'Connor," as he calls himself, emerges virtually self-created out of the logos of his own sardonic conceits and lapidary aphorisms. in Djuna Barnes's *Nightwood*. The eccentric O'Connor functions as priestly hub for the emotionally abject denizens of Barnes's netherworld despite the fact (or precisely because) he is a homosexual "fisher of men" haunting the *pissoirs* of Paris, a nocturnal transvestite, and an unlicensed practitioner of abortions whose gynecological "interest" has driven him far from San Francisco's notorious Barbary Coast.

A "vexatious" father confessor and reluctant suffering servant, the put-upon O'Connor appropriates the imagery of Revelation ("Haven't I eaten a book too?") when he protests that too much has been revealed to him by the aggrieved and distraught who come to him demanding he bear witness to their confusion and suffering. Ordained only by sustained degradation, he laments the price he has paid to acquire the sorrowful wisdom that attracts them to him: "I have divorced myself, not only because I was born as ugly as God dared premeditate, but because with propinquity and knowledge of trouble I have damaged my own value." Thus overburdened, he is akin to the generic French priest, described by the narrative voice as "a vessel already filled to overflowing, [giving] pardon because he could no longer hold . . . like a full bladder."

Although O'Connor has an Irish priest's genius for execration and malediction, his "boggish and biting" language is also drawn from his medical practice, which provides an unsentimental materialist foundation for his subtle diagnosis of spiritual yearning and the equally spiritual need for degradation: "You beat the liver out of a goose to get a *pâté;* you pound the muscles of a man's cardia to get a philosopher"; "we do not 'climb' to heights, we are eaten away to them." In "the grave dilemma of his alchemy," O'Connor knows all too well as a doctor that "there is no pure sorrow" since the soul is "a bedfellow to lungs, lights, bones, guts and gall! There are only confusions . . . confusions and defeated anxieties."

O'Connor descries his drinking buddy, a defrocked priest, whose greedy appetite for hearing the secrets of others has made him like the overfed ducks in the park who, too weighted down by feeding on bread crumbs, can no longer fly south when the season turns. Yet, despite claiming that the need to minister to his suppliants' complaints "has made me the liar I am," O'Connor cultivates the "scorned and the ridiculous" for the anecdotal material they provide him. While not lacking empathy, he cannot "forbear scandal, in order to gossip about the 'manifestation of our time' at a later date." He asks, "Why do they all tell me everything, then expect it to lie hushed in me, like a rabbit gone home to die?" But he exonerates himself as a revealer of truths to all who come "down the grim path of 'We know not' to 'We can't guess why.'"

Blessed and accursed in equal measure with a mordantly comic sensibility, O'Connor observes "the mad strip of the inappropriate that runs through creation." This perspective in turn enables him to contemplate the "wonderful unhappiness" that resides in the fact that "the foetus of symmetry nourishes itself on cross purposes." Thus, he can tell a grotesque anecdote about a legless girl who, after being raped and abandoned by a sailor, "had to roll herself back again, weeping something fearful to see, because one is accustomed to see tears falling down to the feet." As a diagnostician of mankind's "universal malady," O'Connor recognizes that, "take away a man's conformity and you take away his remedy"; yet, he also recognizes that even the most monstrously freakish remain joyously transfixed by their own "difference." Thus, he takes pride in being, and knowing himself to be, "a fart in a gale of wind, an humble violet under a cow pad," and he finds consolation in believing that although "the funniest-looking creature on earth," there is nevertheless "beauty in any permanent mistake like me."

Although O'Connor is usually revealed through the medium of his voice, he is occasionally glimpsed through the eyes of others—most memorably when Nora Flood, a suppliant, witnesses the ordinarily scruffy doctor rouged and wearing a woman's flannel nightgown and curly wig. With panache both pitiable and admirable, O'Connor performs a veritable aria on his "most amusing predicament," the fact that God has mistakenly deprived him of being who he really is: "am I to blame if I've turned up this time as I shouldn't have been, when it was a high soprano I wanted, and deep corn curls to my bum, with a womb as big as the king's kettle, and a bosom as high as the bowsprit of a fishing schooner?" Although all he ever wanted was to knit, cook, and bear children for some man, his "only fireside is the outhouse." He must remain "the Old Woman who lives in the closet," "the last woman left in the world" despite being "the bearded lady." As he talks, Nora cannot help but notice an abdominal brace that gives her "the impression that the feminine finery had suffered venery," as well as a swill-pail "brimming with abominations."

O'Connor is existentially committed to squalor ("Man is born as he dies, rebuking cleanliness"). Nora notes with astonishment that his impossibly small room—"as mauled as the last agony"—is disgustingly dirty and cluttered with rusted and broken medical implements. These furnishings function

discursively as fetishistic, partial objects of himself inasmuch as he subsequently declares himself a broken instrument. O'Connor proceeds to lecture Nora on "his favorite topic," "the night." The night is the inversion, in every sense, of the day because it "is unpremeditated," completely permissive beyond the constraints of the will, particularly the American will to hygiene. The Frenchman, he claims, has learned to accommodate the filth of sin and therefore "can trace himself back by his sediment . . . and so find himself in the odour of wine in its two travels, in and out." The American, however, "separates the two for fear of indignities, so that the mystery is cut in every cord."

For his disquisition on "that stupendous and threadbare glomerate compulsion called the soul," O'Connor draws upon his own experience to render a toxic, but not disapproving, vision of erotic love. With Goyaesque rhetoric O'Connor paints a portrait of "that night-fowl that caws against" the spirits of the watchful lover and the sleeping beloved, "dropping between [them] the awful estrangement of his bowels," their tears "the drip of . . . his implacable pulse . . . until both are carrion." He goes on to describe lovers as two rotting apples whose touching accelerates a "suppuration" for which they are both in "dire need." It is typical of O'Connor's acerbic compassion that such exchanges of fluid testify to a helpless aggression latent in the individual's irreducible loneliness—a conviction also encapsulated in his observation that "tears shed by one eye would blind if wept into another's eye."

Discussion Questions

1. Matthew O'Connor says that, "God laughs at me, but his laughter is my love." He also refers to God as " 'she' because of the way she made me; it somehow balances the mistake." Do you find any evidence in O'Connor's theological vocabulary and his biblical allusions that Barnes is using her character to explore the relationship between humor, particularly sacrilegious humor, and salvation—or even beatitude?

2. O'Connor claims that "Even the contemplative life is only an effort—to hide the body so the feet won't stick out"; he also refers, more ambigu-

ously, to the lowly feet left standing when the dead lie prostrate. On the basis of these and other references to the body how would you characterize his subtle conception of the relation between spirit and matter? Which is more lustful for O'Connor, the body or the soul?

3. Is O'Connor's insistence that "all suffering does *not* purify" and that in fact "it moils and blathers some to perjury" sufficient justification for his refusal to mollify Nora? How would you reconcile this bedside manner with his observation that the Irish lie and—like all charlatans, mystics, and great doctors—they have the power to exalt or heal those whom they flatter?

—*David Brottman*

FELIX VOLKBEIN

"Baron" Felix Volkbein in Djuna Barnes's *Nightwood* has inherited from his father, a dandy and poseur with fraudulent pretensions of being noble, the need to offer "remorseless homage" to the aristocratic European past. Anxiety-ridden, melancholy, and socially abject, Felix is the object of Barnes's most sustained satire, although there is some poignancy in her character study as well. Like most satirized characters, he is best understood in terms of his preconscious gestures and habitual preoccupations. Thus, his essential nature reveals itself in "the genuflexion the hunted body makes from muscular contraction, going down before the impending and inaccessible, as before a great heat." Indeed, Felix is said to have hired servants who look like royalty and to have "clung to his title to dazzle his own estrangement."

Felix's veneration of propriety, his pretense and respect for breeding, and his yearning for the stability of a past that is largely fantasized are deeply rooted in his Jewish racial heritage, which has left him, like his father, "heavy with impermissible blood." This blood is in fact an embarrassing "diversity of bloods" that serves to bar him from authentic aristocracy's tacit claim to purity, which is the source of its apparent instinct for "the correct thing." Thus, "with the fury of a fanatic," Felix has "hunted down his own disqualification." Barnes's analysis of the predicament of the acculturated European Jew is often incisively witty; for example, another character

describes Felix as "screaming up against tradition like a bat against a window-pane." Sometimes, however, her analysis seems to reveal ignorance of Jewish cultural tradition, as when incessant geographical displacements are said to have prevented European Jewry "the accumulation of that toughness which produces ribaldry, nor, after the crucifixion of its ideas, enough forgetfulness in twenty centuries to create legend." And sometimes her remarks skirt contemporary racist discourse, as when commenting on the rootless cosmopolitanism that makes "the Jew seem to be everywhere from nowhere," she goes on to refer to "some country that he has devoured rather than resided in."

Felix attempts to "resuscitate" and "mend" the relics of a glorious past by means of a singularly obsessive attentiveness comparable to that of a child drawing. Barnes's portrayal of his vicarious identification with the pageantry of a history not his own demonstrates an intuitive grasp of the psychological dynamic that sometimes characterizes subordinate minorities. His devotional "submission" and his compulsive need to pay tribute, manifest in his habitual bowing down to anyone who might be "someone," paradoxically rehabilitate respect for his own emotions: "he loved that old and documented splendour with something of the love of the lion for its tamer." Hoarding the glories of an aristocratic Christian past in his imagination, he becomes the "'collector' of his own past." The ultimate irony here is that the Jew's history has become "a commodity" by way of "the Christian traffic in retribution."

Despite his fever for correctness, Felix finds momentary respite from loneliness in the demimonde among circus performers who have also appropriated dignity by means of bogus aristocratic titles. A pedant by necessity of his essential instability, Felix has a penchant for collecting "the odd"—be it heretical beliefs or obscure legends "of men who became holy and of beasts that became damned." This accounts for his friendship with the renegade doctor Matthew O'Connor, whom he tries to understand in terms of his own hobbyhorse as "a servant of a defunct noble family, whose movements recall, though in a degraded form, those of a late master." Thus, when he sees the doctor plucking hairs out of his nostrils it seems to Felix "the 'vulgarization' of what was once a thoughtful plucking of the beard." On their first meeting, the audacious O'Connor overstimulates Felix's "humbled hysteria"—a "fury" subdued by a melancholy that has brought his "beast to heel." Through O'Connor he meets and marries his destiny, the dissolute and enigmatically vacant Robin Vote.

"Racially incapable of abandon," Felix needs marriage, by his own testimony, like he needs the past. Both needs reflect his need for eternity—for "a condition that cannot *vary,*" a habit that efficiently vouchsafes safety by obviating unwanted freedom. Delusively trying to give Robin the past he worships, he loses it in her presence, becoming a mere "sightseer." Robin's unformed personality gives him "the most formless loss," instead of fulfilling the promise embodied in marriage of security as a stay against disquiet. Felix later confesses that in his fantasy of conversion, he had mistaken Robin's seeming acquiescence and lack of established personality for an opportunity "to achieve immortality, but be free to choose my own kind."

Robin leaves Felix, but leaves behind a portion of herself, a strange, "maladjusted" child, Guido, that Felix suspects may be mentally unsound because of his mother's own damnation. O'Connor seeks to allay Felix's anxiety that his son might have inherited the moral derangement of his mother, providing a typically sardonic argument that his son is "blessed" inasmuch as he "is what you have always been looking for." O'Connor seems to mean two things by this. He suggests that Guido's apparent madness or idiocy proves him the last in an aristocratic line ("In the king's bed is always found, just before it becomes a museum piece, the droppings of the black sheep"). And he declares that Felix has found the "calamity . . . we are all seeking." Robin can thus be seen to have delivered Felix to the end he had not known he had wanted: a completely absorbing preoccupation. "He knew at the same time that this stricture of acceptance (by which what we must love is made into what we can love) would eventually be a part of himself."

Felix comes to realize through Robin and their son that "the most unendurable is the beginning of the curve of joy." Despite turning to drink, he always carries a pocketful of medicine and hand cream for his son's chapped hands. But details of poignant tenderness blur into the ruthless cruelty of satire. Although he fights his compulsive inclinations, Felix in the end is drunk in a café, gaping at the probably hallucinatory presence of Grand Duke Alexander of Russia. As the man passes by, Felix cannot help but make "a slight bow, his head in his confusion making a complete half-swing, as an animal will turn its head away from a human, as if in mortal shame."

Discussion Questions

1. How would you resolve the seeming paradox that someone so obsessed with aristocratic nobility as Felix Volkbein would seek the company of circus performers and marry a woman he first sees in a drunken stupor amid tawdry decor reminiscent of a brothel?

2. If O'Connor rightly perceives that the mind of Felix's son, Guido, "is not made secure by habit," how might it serve as a hopeful counterbalance to the self-abasing inclinations of his father?

3. To what degree is Barnes's discourse about race and "blood" the product of her time, and does she ever transgress the boundaries beyond which the satirist should not go?

—*David Brottman*

Robin Vote

Robin Vote, the object of Nora Flood's obsession in Djuna Barnes's *Nightwood,* is almost exclusively constructed from the multiple perspectives of those who have been damaged by her. She abandons, betrays, and forgets all who have loved her: her husband, Felix, and their sickly child, Guido; Nora, her first lesbian lover; and Jenny Petherbridge, her second. All the major characters, even Felix and Nora's confidant, Matthew O'Connor, who does not like her, are to greater or lesser degrees Robin's votaries. They are all fascinated and unnerved in equal measure by her enigmatic detachment. Perhaps it is more accurate to say that they are devoted to the impression she has left with them, since—and this is the source of their pain—she is an absence, a vacancy, in their lives. Described as "the eternal momentary," she is no more than image inasmuch as "an image is a stop the mind makes between uncertainties."

Robin is first witnessed sprawled in drunken stupor, immersed in the chirping of birds, and smelling of "earth-flesh, fungi." Further images reiterate her essential passivity while serving to associate her with water made phosphorescent by decaying vegetation. As she lies beneath the gaze of Felix and O'Connor, she seems to have "invaded a sleep incautious and entire . . . as if sleep were a decay fishing her beneath the visible surface." Oblivion, Robin's natural element, facilitates a narcissistic assignation: "as if this girl were the converging halves of a broken fate, setting face, in sleep toward itself in time, as an image and its reflection in a lake seems parted only by the hesitation in the hour." Stupefaction sustains her "luminous deteriorations" against all else; later, despite the pulsations of pregnancy, she maintains "a stubborn cataleptic calm."

Robin is completely self-absorbed in the manner of a somnambulist. She is, in fact, given to listless wandering in "formless meditation," as if "strangely aware of some lost land in herself." Felix observes that she is "like those people who, coming unexpectedly into a room, silence the company because they are looking for someone who is not there." She is estranged and strangely emptied. With thoughts "unpeopled," Robin's mind resides "where reason was inexact with lack of necessity." Though beautiful, in the eyes of O'Connor, Robin has "the face of an incurable yet to be stricken with its malady"; her smile is "the smile of an 'only survivor.'" For her bemused husband she is a figure of weathered endurance that is yet "a figure of doom."

Robin's lassitude has the "density" of an undomesticated animal, to which she is frequently compared. Not fully human, she bears within her "the quality of the 'way back' as animals do." Her eyes are "clear and timeless," with "the long unqualified range in the iris of wild beasts who have not tamed the focus down to meet the human eye." Nora picks up Robin at a zoo, where she gazes at a caged lioness as if gazing at her own remote pain reflected back: "she regarded the girl, as if a river were falling behind impassable heat, her eyes flowed in tears that never reached the surface." O'Connor interbreeds the animal metaphors with other recurring imagery, comparing Robin's temples to "those of young beasts cutting horns, as if they were sleeping eyes." She is

for him a "beast turning human"—an eland wearing a bridal veil, "hoof raised in the economy of fear, stepping in the trepidation of flesh that will become myth." Given this persistent discourse, it is all the more pointed that Jenny Petherbridge describes Robin as the type who "always lets her pets die . . . the way that animals neglect themselves."

Nora thinks of Robin as her child—"incest" being "one of her powers." O'Connor, shrewdly sardonic and savoring bleakness, recognizes her face as one "that will age only under the blows of perpetual childhood." His gift for hyperbole allows him to intuit the exact nature of Robin's relation to Nora; he imagines Nora having found a hypnotic beast-child in Robin's eyes, "as in the eye of a child lost a long while be found the contraction of . . . distance—a child going small in the claws of a beast, coming furiously up the furlongs of the iris." For O'Connor, Robin is both child and beast insofar as she has been "stripped" of "all transactions with knowledge" and left with "a sort of first position in attention."

Robin's paradoxically selfish lack of self, her somnolent "difficulty remembering herself," reduces her husband and her lovers to an attentive disquiet in accord with the principle that "people always fear what requires watching." Thus, living with her, Nora constantly watches with anxiety her desire to escape and her longing to stay for fear "she would be lost again." Nora hears it, too, with equal disquiet, in the "debased and haunting songs" Robin sings, from a past unknown and unshared. Felix also watches as he diligently shepherds Robin among his beloved monuments. He nervously registers an essential disorderliness in the fact that "often her taste, turning from an appreciation of the excellent, would also include the cheaper and debased, with an emotion as real."

Failing conversion to Felix's veneration of the past, Robin converts to Catholicism. As she haunts churches, the nuns regard her flitting presence "as if some inscrutable wish for salvation, something yet more monstrously unfulfilled than they had suffered, had thrown a shadow." They recognize "that they were looking at someone who would never be able to ask for, or receive, mercy." The question of Robin's spiritual condition invariably arises among those who witness her. O'Connor slyly remarks that "too little" sense of identity has given her the unconscious conviction that she "can do no wrong." Developing his insight into Robin's "primitive innocence," he warns Nora that she is "the uninhabited angel . . . you have always been hunting!"

In the grips of their pathos, none of Robin's intimates can do without mythologizing. For this reason they exculpate Robin's compulsive seeking of self-defilement, her desire for "anonymity," and her resistance to the possibility of being touched deeply by another. Nora momentarily disturbs Robin's almost hermetic absence from herself and others by striking her, fittingly, as she sleeps: "I saw her come awake and turn befouled before me, she who had managed in that sleep to keep whole. . . . No rot had touched her until . . . I had struck her sleep away." Mad with regret and loss, Nora is relentlessly forgiving: "she couldn't do anything because she was a long way off and waiting to begin." Felix also comes to a similar recognition, comparing Robin's "undefinable disorder" to that of someone "who has come from some place that we have forgotten and would give our life to recall." Nora comes to recognize that Robin's dreamy passivity is a mode of aggression: "She would kill the world to get at herself if the world were in the way, and it *is* in the way."

The attentiveness and the mythologizing contribute to everyone's pain, Robin's included. Thus, Nora also comes to recognize that Robin "turned bitter because I made her fate colossal. She wanted darkness in her mind—to throw a shadow over what she was powerless to alter—her dissolute life, her life at night."

Discussion Questions

1. How do you judge the willingness of the other characters to tolerate, indulge, or even honor Robin's amorality? Are there sufficient grounds for claiming that Robin lives beyond the categories of good and evil?

2. Arriving home from her round of seedy dives, Robin exclaims to Nora that she wants "everyone to be gay, gay"—"only you, you mustn't be gay or happy, not like that, it's not for you, only for everyone else in the world." How would you characterize this outburst? What are its psychological origins? What kinds of emotions are entailed?

—*David Brottman*

REFERENCES

Phillip Herring, *Djuna: The Life and Work of Djuna Barnes* (New York: Viking, 1995);

AnnKatrin Jonnson, *Relations: Ethics and the Modernist Subject in James Joyce's* Ulysses, *Virginia Woolf's* The Waves, *and Djuana Barnes's* Nightwood (Oxford & New York: Peter Lang, 2006);

Louis F. Kannenstine, *The Art of Djuna Barnes: Duality and Damnation* (New York: New York University Press, 1977);

Douglas Messerli, *Djuna Barnes: A Bibliography* (Rhinebeck, N.Y.: D. Lewis, 1975);

James B. Scott, *Djuna Barnes* (Boston: Twayne, 1976).

Philip Barry
(June 18, 1896 – December 3, 1949)

୬୧

THE ANIMAL KINGDOM
New York, Broadhurst Theatre, January 12, 1932; (New York: S. French, 1932)

TOM COLLIER

The young publisher Tom Collier is the protagonist of Philip Barry's three-act comedy of manners *The Animal Kingdom*. The play is a study of marriage and moral integrity. Barry describes Tom as being "in his early thirties, slim, youthful, with a fine, sensitive humorous face." Tom and his fiancée, Cecelia Henry, have just announced their engagement when Tom learns that Daisy Sage, a painter with whom he has had a three-year intimate relationship, has returned from a long stay abroad. He visits Daisy to inform her of his wedding plans, hoping she will agree to maintain a platonic friendship with him. In the meantime, however, Daisy has realized that she wants to rekindle her romance with Tom, marry him, and have children. When she hears of Tom's engagement to Cecelia, she sends him away. Rather than remaining friends with a married man, Daisy wants to make a "sharp, decent, clean" break. While Tom and Daisy had a partnership that was both physical and spiritual, Tom's relationship with Cecelia is based purely on physical attraction.

As soon as Tom and Cecelia are married, Cecelia begins to assert a transforming influence on Tom. In pursuit of wealth and social status, Cecelia uses her sexuality to manipulate him. She keeps him away from the circle of writers and musicians who were Tom and Daisy's mutual friends and convinces him to publish sensational books for a quick profit instead of the intellectually engaging books that earned him the respect of his peers. Cecelia also presses Tom to fire his quirky boxer-turned-butler, Red Regan, because Red does not fit into the elegant household she would like to run. The scene in act 2 where Tom tries to bring himself to dismiss Red, while Red simultaneously tries to tell him that he plans to quit, is an example of Barry's skilled use of language to convey character and emotion in a moving but humorous way. In his book on Barry, Joseph P. Roppolo discusses this passage, arguing, "The short choppy speeches, which say almost nothing, the hesitancy, the silences—all these serve to underline the high regard each has for the other and the strong emotion which neither can or will put into a blunt statement."

Before long, and in spite of Cecelia's wishes, Tom rehires Red. Tom's rebellion against Cecelia is a sign that he is unhappy in his marriage. Another sign of Tom's dissatisfaction is that he resumes contact with his old friends. After visiting an exhibition of Daisy's paintings (and giving her honest criticism on the poor quality of her work), he also attempts to reestablish his friendship with her. "There never were such friends as you and me," he tells her. "It's wicked to give that up, to lose anything so fine for no good reason." Although she is attracted to Tom, Daisy is conflicted about their relationship and abruptly leaves for another stay abroad. Several months later, Cecelia gives a birthday party for Tom, to which she invites Tom's old friends in an effort to keep her husband happy. At the party, Daisy reviews the proofs for a new magazine Tom is about to publish and expresses her dismay at its shallowness. Expressing her sadness about Tom's loss of his individuality, Daisy tells him, "I pity you with all my heart!" and leaves.

Eager for money, Cecelia has encouraged Tom to sell his small press to a larger, less selective publishing house and urges him to accept a check from his father, Rufus, who hopes to bribe the couple into moving into his house to keep him company during the winter. In a scene that mirrors an earlier moment when Cecelia seduced Tom to keep him away from a concert given by one of his friends, Cecelia attempts to entice Tom sexually into accepting his father's present. Tom pretends to play along, but inwardly feels resentment for his wife and her preoccupation with money. He subtly reveals that Cecelia reminds him of a prostitute and resolves to leave her for Daisy. Before Tom departs, he endorses his father's check to Cecelia and sets it on the mantelpiece. Barry concludes the play with Tom's comment to Red—"I'm going back to my wife"—a statement that shows he regards Daisy, not Cecelia, as his true mate.

Discussing *The Animal Kingdom*, Roppolo suggests that Tom Collier makes a moral decision when he leaves Cecelia for Daisy. He argues that, according to Barry, "A marriage built alone on the appetites of the animal kingdom is no marriage and no ceremony of itself can make it sacred. There must be mutual love and respect, elevating the contract into both the intellectual and the spiritual kingdoms." In Roppolo's analysis, Tom "must reject the dictates of a society which places a high value on marriage; and, ironically, by so doing he finds himself on firm moral ground. His rebellion against social restrictions regains for him his personal integrity." Barry also examines the question of what constitutes a fulfilling marriage in other comedies, such as *Paris Bound* (1927) and *The Philadelphia Story* (1939), and in some of his serious dramas, such as *In a Garden* (1925) and *Tomorrow and Tomorrow* (1931).

Discussion Questions

1. Barry was a writer with a keen interest in the intersection between wealth and morality. How does Tom Collier's relationship to money mirror or contrast that of Johnny Case's in Barry's *Holiday?* What do the characters tell you about Barry's attitude toward wealth?

2. How is Tom's relationship with Cecelia similar to or different from his relationship with Daisy? Did Tom make the right decision in leaving Cecelia for Daisy? Justify your argument with examples from the play.

3. Barry was a devout Catholic, and traces of his religious beliefs can be found in many of his plays. How do Tom's actions in *The Animal Kingdom* reinforce or undermine Catholicism?

—*Claudia Wilsch Case*

༄

HOLIDAY

New York, Plymouth Theatre, November 26, 1928
(New York, Los Angeles & London: S. French,
1929)

JOHNNY CASE

Johnny Case is the protagonist of Philip Barry's three-act comedy of manners *Holiday*. Ben Smith played Johnny on Broadway, where the comedy ran for 229 performances. Brooks Atkinson noted in his *New York Times* review that the actor put "ruggedness as well as freshness into his part." In Barry's satirical attack on American capitalism, Johnny rebels against the conventional idea that people should spend their entire lives working and wait for old age to retire.

Johnny is thirty years old, and Barry describes him as being "medium-tall, slight, attractive-looking, luckily not quite handsome." On a recent vacation at Lake Placid, he met and fell in love with Julia Seton. As the play opens, the couple plans to announce their engagement to Julia's family. Upon arriving at the Setons' house in New York City, Johnny realizes that his fiancée belongs to a wealthy family who occupies a prominent position in society. Julia's siblings, Linda and Ned, prepare him for his conference with their father, financier Edward Seton. "Money is our God here," Linda warns Johnny, and she and Ned suggest that their father, to whom Linda mockingly refers as "Big Business," will be displeased with his lack of wealth and pedigree. While Johnny is not as rich as the Setons, he has been working hard since childhood and has become a successful lawyer and investor. He does not, however, enjoy working for the sole purpose of accumulating wealth. Rather, as Thomas A. Greenfield explains it, Johnny sees work "as a means of purchasing time away from work." His unconventional plan for the future is to use his savings to go on an extended vacation, enjoy his youth, discover himself, and return to work only once his money runs out. As Johnny explains, "it's always been my plan to make a few thousands early in the game, if I could, and then quit for as long as they last, and try to find out who I am and what I am and what goes on and what about it—now, while I'm young, and feel good all the time."

Whereas the free-spirited Linda is sympathetic to Johnny's dream, the conservative Julia and Mr. Seton react to it with shock, and Julia tries to convince Johnny to keep working. "There's no such thrill in the world as making money," she tells him. Mr. Seton considers Johnny's idiosyncratic attitude toward work and money "deliberately un-American," thus revealing that he deems Johnny a threat to the established social order. While Julia accepts and echoes her father's preoccupation with wealth and social status, Linda and Ned revolt against them. Ned expresses his rebellion through heavy drinking, and Linda conveys hers through a desire to distance herself from the spiritually empty life of high society and through her fascination with Johnny. Although Johnny professes his love for Julia, he is simultaneously attracted to Linda.

With Julia and Edward Seton opposing his plan to "retire young, and work old," Johnny leaves town and books a passage to Europe, but he returns to the Seton home just before his ship departs to tell Julia he will postpone his holiday for her sake. Mr. Seton is delighted at Johnny's apparent change of heart and immediately begins to make plans for Johnny and Julia's future. He offers the couple the use of two of his houses and arranges their honeymoon—which is to include several business meetings. Seeing his prospective father-in-law make decisions for him, Johnny recognizes that, should he marry Julia, he would no longer be in control of his own life. As a result, he calls off the wedding and sets out for the port. "I suppose the fact is, I love feeling free inside even better than I love you," Johnny admits to Julia, who accuses him of being an "idler." Once Linda realizes that Julia does not love Johnny, she leaves her father's house to catch up with him and presumably pursue a relationship with him.

Commenting on Barry's depiction of Johnny as an individual who revolts against society's pressure to conform, Ronald H. Wainscott points out in *The Emergence of the Modern American Theater, 1914–1929*, "Johnny's attitude and insistence on quitting are made a bit too easy, since he already made money in the stock market, but at least he does not take excessive pleasure in wealth. It can be argued, nevertheless, that Barry has seriously undercut his use of satire because his hero can be independent of the stifling big-business atmosphere only by having first exploited it."

The rebellion of young people against an older, often wealthy, generation is a recurring theme in Barry's work and appears, for instance, in the comedies *The Youngest* (1924) and *The Animal Kingdom* (1932). Stylistically, *Holiday* is an excellent example of Barry's skilled use of witty and sophisticated dialogue, a trait shared by his other comedies of manners, such as *The Philadelphia Story* (1939), and some of his serious dramas, such as *Hotel Universe* (1930).

Discussion Questions

1. What do you think of Johnny's idea to take several years off from work while he is young and to return to work when he is older? Would this idea be more or less practical or acceptable in today's society than in the 1920s?

2. *Holiday* was written just before the stock market crash of 1929. During the 1920s, American business was booming, but by the 1930s, America had plunged into the Great Depression. How might the reaction of audiences who saw the 1928 premiere of the play have differed from the reaction of audiences who saw productions of the play during the 1930s or later?

3. Both *Holiday* and *The Philadelphia Story* are set in American high society. How does Johnny Case's role as an outsider to society compare to either George or Mike in *The Philadelphia Story?* Which characters have an easier time gaining access to or acceptance by high society? Why?

—*Claudia Wilsch Case*

⋘❦

THE PHILADELPHIA STORY

New York, Shubert Theatre, March 28, 1939 (New York: Coward-McCann, 1939)

TRACY LORD

Tracy Lord is the protagonist of Philip Barry's three-act comedy of manners *The Philadelphia Story*. The play examines the relation between social class and personal integrity and takes a probing look at marriage and divorce by tracing Tracy's transformation from a "virgin goddess," who judges human weakness, into a tolerant human being. Barry wrote the part of Tracy specifically for Katharine Hepburn, who played the role both on Broadway, where *The Philadelphia Story* ran for 417 performances before it toured the United States, and in the 1940 movie version of the play.

Barry describes Tracy as "a strikingly lovely girl of twenty-four." Tracy is a member of a prominent Pennsylvania family who at the outset of the play is preparing for her wedding to George Kittredge. George has worked his way up in the coal industry and covets the prestige that being married to a well-bred and wealthy woman such as Tracy would grant him. He idolizes her and likens her to a goddess. The wedding is going to be Tracy's second; she is divorced from C. K. Dexter Haven, a well-to-do dandy, whom she has known her entire life, but whom she left because she could not tolerate his drinking. Tracy's mother, Margaret, is separated from Tracy's father, Seth Lord, whom Tracy despises for having a liaison with a dancer and whom she does not want present at her wedding. Yet, as Dexter warns Tracy, "you'll never be a first class woman or a first class human being till you have learned to have some regard for human frailty."

On the eve of the festivities, the gossip magazine *Destiny* is planning to publish a revealing article about Seth's affair. In an effort to suppress the piece, Tracy's brother Sandy, a journalist himself, has secretly invited the reporter-photographer team Mike Connor and Liz Imbrie to cover his sister's wedding, which is certain to be a social event of note. Sandy hopes that the editor of *Destiny* will swap the embarrassing exposé about Seth Lord for a detailed story about Tracy's nuptials. The appearance of members of the press motivates Tracy and other members of the family to put on various quirky performances to mislead the journalists about the true nature of life at the Lord house, and incites Tracy to concoct a scheme to prevent the reporters' account of her wedding from being published. She asks Sandy to write a candid article about Sidney Kidd, the publisher of *Destiny* (who is a parody of Henry Luce), and plans to use the article to bribe Kidd not to run the story about her wedding, thus guarding the family's privacy.

During Mike and Liz's visit, Tracy finds herself attracted to the reporter, who mirrors Tracy in that he, too, views the world through a lens of intolerance (which in his case is focused on the upper class). Getting to know Tracy softens Mike's critical attitude toward the rich, and the two have a drunken tryst in the swimming pool the night before Tracy's wedding. Although she does not remember the details in the morning, a vague recollection of her fall from grace makes Tracy recognize her own humanity. When George finds out about his fiancée's misstep, he becomes enraged, but it is Tracy who ultimately breaks off their engagement when confronted with George's intolerance toward her behavior. Realizing that neither George nor Mike is the right partner for her and that she and Dexter may each have faults but were a good match, Tracy agrees to remarry Dexter the same day. Dexter understands that, because of her "slip," Tracy has developed tolerance for human shortcomings, which redeems her as a wife. At the end of the play, Tracy gleefully proclaims that she feels "like a human being" and promises Dexter to be more flexible, or "yare," in the future, like the yacht Dexter once built for her.

Barry's comedy of manners *Paris Bound* (1927) resembles *The Philadelphia Story* structurally. The play also concerns the subject of divorce, and, like the comedies *Holiday* (1928) and *The Animal Kingdom* (1932), deals with the qualities that make spouses compatible and contribute to the success or failure of a marriage. As in his other comedies, Barry employs clever dialogue in *The Philadelphia Story* and both celebrates and mocks the American upper class.

Discussion Questions

1. Discuss the significance of social class in *The Philadelphia Story*. Is Dexter the best match for Tracy because they have the same class background? Are George and Mike unfit to marry Tracy because they come from a lower social class? Justify your answer with examples from the play.

2. When George comments on Tracy's tryst with Mike the night before her wedding, Tracy finishes George's sentence, "But a man expects his wife to—" with the words, "—To behave herself. Naturally," thus anticipating George's demands on a wife. Dexter restates this line: "To behave herself naturally." How does his omission of the period before the word *naturally* alter the meaning of Tracy's line? Explain how these two lines illustrate Philip Barry's characterizations of George and Dexter and the men's relationships to Tracy.

3. In his stage directions, Philip Barry states that *The Philadelphia Story* takes place in 1939, the year it was first performed, which was at the end of the Great Depression. What evidence is present in the text that the play takes place during this desperate time? What is the reaction of the Lord family to the Depression?

—*Claudia Wilsch Case*

REFERENCES

Stanley Cavell, *Pursuits of Happiness: The Hollywood Comedy of Remarriage* (Cambridge, Mass.: Harvard University Press, 1981);

Brendan Gill, "The Dark Advantage," in *States of Grace: Eight Plays by Philip Barry*, edited by Gill (New York: Harcourt Brace Jovanovich, 1975), pp. 3–47;

Brenda Murphy, *American Realism and American Drama, 1880–1940* (Cambridge: Cambridge University Press, 1987);

Joseph P. Roppolo, *Philip Barry* (New York: Twayne, 1965).

Tony J. Stafford, "Philip Barry," in *American Playwrights, 1880–1945: A Research and Production Sourcebook*, edited by William W. Demastes (Westport, Conn.: Greenwood Press, 1995);

Ronald H. Wainscott, *The Emergence of the Modern American Theater, 1914–1929* (New Haven, Conn.: Yale University Press, 1997).

John Barth
(May 27, 1930 –   )

LOST IN THE FUNHOUSE: FICTION FOR PRINT, TAPE, LIVE VOICE
(Garden City, N.Y.: Doubleday, 1968)

AMBROSE

Ambrose is a character in three of the short stories in John Barth's collection *Lost in the Funhouse*. Different stages of Ambrose's childhood are depicted in "Ambrose His Mark," "Water-Message," and probably the best-known story in the collection, "Lost in the Funhouse."

"Ambrose His Mark" tells how Ambrose, a few months old, gets his name when a swarm of bees lands on him, covering the port-wine birthmark on his face. The bees do not harm him, and the family decides to name him after Saint Ambrose, who was also swarmed by bees as an infant. For Saint Ambrose, the swarm of bees was a predictor of his future eloquence, of a "honeyed tongue"; for Barth's Ambrose, this experience foreshadows his future as a writer. As the story unfolds, other poignant details from Ambrose's life are revealed. For example, his father, doubting that he actually is Ambrose's father, has a breakdown at his son's birth and is committed to a hospital, while his mother tries to cope with postpartum depression, experiencing highs and lows that plague her throughout Ambrose's young life.

In "Water-Message," Ambrose, now in the fourth grade, tries desperately to fit in with the neighborhood boys. His older brother, Peter, is a natural leader and starts a secret club. Ambrose comes up with the name ("The Occult Order of the Sphinx") but is deemed too young to join. He struggles to keep up with the older boys, humiliates himself to avoid a beating by a schoolyard bully, and admits shamefully and sadly to his mother that he is a "sissy." When he finds a message in a bottle on the beach, however, he gets an inkling of the grander world beyond his childhood travails. This story of preadolescent angst provides a glimpse of the intelligence and self-awareness that distinguish Ambrose from his peers but become the bane of his existence.

This theme of agonizing self-awareness is brought to fruition in the title story, the most important and oft-cited story in the collection. In "Lost in the Funhouse," Ambrose, Peter, their mother and father, Uncle Karl, and a neighbor girl, Magda, travel to Ocean City, Maryland, to spend the Fourth of July at the seaside. Thirteen-year-old Ambrose has a desperate crush on fourteen-year-old Magda and tries shyly to get closer to her. When he invites her to go through the fun house with him, Peter joins them. Ambrose watches as Peter and Magda run off playfully into the fun house and, while trying to find them, gets increasingly and hopelessly lost.

Ambrose's attempts to attract Magda are thwarted by his excruciating insecurity, a feeling he believes is unique to him. He wonders if he will ever become a "regular person" or if he is doomed always to be odd. His sense of isolation is magnified by a strong intelligence that makes him unable to forget any detail of his life, and an even stronger self-consciousness that forces him constantly to narrate his life to himself: "Strive as he might to be transported, he heard his mind take notes upon the scene: *This is what they call* passion. *I am experiencing it.*" In Ambrose's opinion, this self-consciousness is what keeps him from having direct contact with his life or the people in it. His every experience is filtered through this screen of self-narration, dulling the event, making him feel like a spectator rather than a participant in his own life. Such a person, he concludes, is suited only to be a writer, to chronicle life rather than live it. The story implicitly equates narratives with fun houses, and because Ambrose is not able to enjoy the fun house, to connect directly to his life, he reluctantly resigns himself to becoming a writer of narrative: "Therefore he will construct funhouses for others and be their secret operator—though he would rather be among the lovers for whom funhouses are designed."

Ambrose's self-consciousness is mirrored in the self-consciousness of the story itself, highlighting the form of reflexive metafiction for which Barth is well known. Metafiction is a form of narrative that continually reminds the reader that the story is just that: a story. In this case, the narrator frequently intrudes, posing questions that cast doubt on the realism of the narrative. For example, after making an intricate point, the narrator asks, "Is it likely . . . that a thirteen-year-old boy could make such a sophisticated observation?" Barth uses such metafictional techniques to highlight what he calls in his essay "The Literature of Exhaustion" "the used-upness" of certain forms of literature. Barth means that, by the late twentieth century, traditional narratives are no longer powerful enough to illuminate the reality of contemporary experience. To demonstrate this point, "Lost in the Funhouse" is a story about the failure of stories. Just as Ambrose gets lost in the fun house, this story seems also to lose its way, meandering toward but never quite providing a climactic moment or a clear-cut ending. The narrator bemoans this state of affairs: "We should be much farther along than we are; something has gone wrong." The story is failing to provide the necessary climax and resolution of the plot: "At this rate our hero, at this rate our protagonist will remain in the funhouse forever." If Ambrose cannot find his way out of the fun house, the story cannot end the way it should; the story faces the same fate as its protagonist, as neither is able to come to a proper end. Thus, Barth illustrates his argument that contemporary authors must experiment with form to find a new structure capable of taking the place of older ones.

—*Marjorie Worthington*

Discussion Questions

1. What do the subtle clues in "Ambrose His Mark" indicate about the strife in Ambrose's family? What are the unspoken problems here? Find specific evidence in the story to support your answer.

2. To what extent are Ambrose's fears and insecurities normal childhood anxieties and to what extent is Ambrose more odd than most? Support your answer with evidence both from the stories and from your personal experience.

3. At the end of "Water-Message," after finding the message in the bottle, "Ambrose's spirit bore new and subtle burdens." What does this mean? Why does Ambrose seem less concerned about fitting in with the older boys at the end of the story? How has finding the message changed his outlook on his life?

4. The narrator of "Lost in the Funhouse" claims that this story does not have a proper structure and does not adhere to the diagram of "Freytag's Triangle" that he provides. Is that true? Is there no real climax in this story, or is this story more traditional than it might seem at first?

5. Does Ambrose ever get out of the fun house? How can you tell?

REFERENCES

John Barth, "The Literature of Exhaustion," *Atlantic Monthly,* 220 (August 1967): 29–34;

Max F. Schulz, *The Muses of John Barth: Tradition and Metafiction from* Lost in the Funhouse *to* The Tidewater Tales (Baltimore: Johns Hopkins University Press, 1990);

Joseph J. Waldmeir, ed., *Critical Essays on John Barth* (Boston: Hill, 1980);

Heide Ziegler, *John Barth* (New York: Methuen, 1987).

L. Frank Baum
(May 15, 1856 – May 6, 1919)

❧

THE WONDERFUL WIZARD OF OZ
(Chicago: George M. Hill, 1900)

DOROTHY GALE

Dorothy Gale is the central character in *The Wonderful Wizard of Oz,* the best known of L. Frank Baum's fantasy novels for children, though she also appears in several Oz sequels. Transported to the magical and colorful land of Oz from her drab home in Kansas by a cyclone, Dorothy faces challenges and dangers with the help of her three companions, the Scarecrow, the Tin Man, and the Cowardly Lion. In the end, she defeats evil and finds her way back to Kansas.

Baum's novel was distinctive in its time, in that it was written, as the author said, "solely to please children of today." While many other works for children in the late nineteenth and early twentieth centuries were written with didactic purposes and heavy-handed morals, *The Wonderful Wizard of Oz* was written solely for enjoyment.

Dorothy differs from other protagonists at this time, because she is one of the first heroes of a children's novel to be portrayed as a real child, similar to the children who would read the book. Baum wrote primarily for girls, believing that boys of the time were "surrounded by wonders" from birth. He felt that little girls needed the imaginings and fantasy of fairy tales. The book found a readership of boys as well, though, since Dorothy "asks the right questions. She is not sappy. . . . she is straight and to the point and a little bit aggressive," Gore Vidal writes.

Baum admitted that he was inspired to write about a little-girl character by Lewis Carroll's heroine, Alice, of *Alice's Adventures in Wonderland* (1865). "The secret of Alice's success lay in the fact that she was a real child," he wrote, "and any normal child could sympathize with her all through her adventures." In addition, Baum was impressed by the fact that in the novel, Alice "is doing something every minute, and something strange and marvelous, too; so the child follows her with rapturous delight." Baum set out to accomplish the same result when he wrote of Dorothy's adventures in Oz.

However, Dorothy is very much an American girl: independent, brave, and practical. While Alice is concerned with manners and social status, author Alison Lurie notes that Dorothy "takes for granted her equality with everyone she meets." In addition, Dorothy is clearly a girl of the American West. Baum admitted his preference for women of the West over their eastern sisters because western women "delight in being useful; a young lady's highest ambition is to become a bread-winner." Dorothy demonstrates this no-nonsense western practicality throughout the book. When the Witch of the North advises her to set out along the yellow brick road, Dorothy first washes, changes her clothes and shoes, and packs enough food to start on the journey. She even locks the door of the house and pockets the key. All of these actions show Dorothy's practical view of life; unruffled by her unusual situation, she does what she has been taught to do when starting on a journey. Throughout the book, Dorothy maintains this down-to-earth attitude. The Emerald City is beautiful, but it does not dazzle her; the witch is evil but does not frighten her.

Unlike Alice, Dorothy wastes little time on tears, regardless of how bleak her situation becomes. When the Wizard admonishes her and her companions to kill the Wicked Witch of the West before he will help them, Dorothy does cry, but she quickly dries her tears saying, "I suppose we must try it." Even when she is a prisoner of the witch and forced to be her servant, the little girl never loses heart. She sneaks food to the Cowardly Lion and manages to kill the witch by throwing a bucket of water over her.

Another difference between Dorothy and other protagonists in children's books of the time period is that Dorothy rescues herself from her predicaments. She takes action, whether it is to set bravely off along the road to the Emerald City or to the land of Glinda, the Good Witch of the South, to find a way back to Kansas when the Wizard has left without her. Her friends help her, of course, but in the end, Dorothy herself, using the power of the witch's silver shoes, makes her own way back to Kansas. As Madonna Kolbenschlag writes, Dorothy "doesn't depend on 'snaring' a prince or reconciliation with a father-figure in order to improve her situation. . . . there is always a sense in the narrative that Dorothy will be resourceful enough to triumph over adversity." Unlike the princesses of the fairy tales of Hans Christian Andersen and others, Dorothy never languishes in a tower waiting for help.

Baum offers little physical description of Dorothy in the novel, and Michael Patrick Hearn asserts that Dorothy can consequently be seen as "an Everychild," a protagonist all readers can relate to. In Dorothy, Baum created a realistic American child protagonist. He thus set the stage for the many strong and convincing female protagonists of children's books who followed.

Discussion Questions

1. Baum wrote that western girls have "energy and vitality" and are free of nonsense and self-pride. Using examples from the book, discuss how Dorothy embodies these qualities of a western girl.

2. Baum's novel appeared shortly after Lewis Carroll's *Alice in Wonderland.* Both have strong female protagonists; yet they are very different. Using examples from both texts, show how the two girls are both alike and different from each other.

3. Alison Lurie writes that Dorothy "takes for granted her equality with everyone she meets." Using examples from the text, agree or disagree with this statement and then support your answer. In what ways is this a typical "American" quality?

4. Fantasy novels often center around a change or transformation in the main character. Do you think Dorothy changes between the beginning and the end of *The Wonderful Wizard of Oz?* If so, how does she change? What does that change—or lack of change—suggest about Dorothy's adventures and a possible theme of the book? Use examples from the text to support your argument.

—*Patti J. Kurtz*

THE WIZARD OF OZ

The Wizard of Oz is one of the central characters in L. Frank Baum's fantasy novel *The Wonderful Wizard of Oz*. The Wizard is continually spoken of with anticipation and awe, sometimes referred to as "the great and terrible Oz." Because the Witch of the North tells Dorothy Gale, a young girl carried to Oz from her home in Kansas by a cyclone, that Oz "is more powerful than all the rest of us [witches] together," Dorothy believes that he can fulfill her wish to return home, as well as the wishes of her friends the Scarecrow, the Tin Man, and the Cowardly Lion.

Tales of the Wizard's reputation grows as Dorothy travels closer to the Emerald City, where he resides. The inhabitants of Oz that Dorothy encounters express amazement that she has the nerve to seek an audience with him. Before she leaves the land of the Munchkins, Boq, an important Munchkin who opens his home to Dorothy, tells her, "It is better for people to keep away from Oz, unless they have business with him." When she reaches the outskirts of the Emerald City, one farmer tells her he has never seen Oz, nor does he know of any other living person who has. Thus, rumors about the Wizard's appearance and powers abound. As Dorothy discovers, Oz does exist, though not in the form that his subjects believe.

When Dorothy and her friends finally reach the Emerald City, a soldier with green whiskers tells her that Oz has agreed to see her because she wears the silver shoes, which formerly belonged to the Wicked Witch of the East, killed by Dorothy's falling house, and because she bears the mark of the Good Witch of the North's kiss on her forehead. Suspecting that she might be a witch, he has decided to end his isolation.

When Dorothy and her companions meet Oz, he appears in various shapes: a giant head, a beautiful woman, a ball of fire, and a great beast. He uses such shape-shifting to terrify them and coerce them into killing the Wicked Witch of the West. During Dorothy's second interview with the Wizard, after she and her friends have accomplished their mission, she discovers that Oz is a trickster, a "humbug," to use his own words. Rather than a powerful wizard, he is a middle-aged man from Omaha who was stranded in Oz in much the same way as Dorothy.

He has accomplished his various illusions through trickery, ventriloquism, and mechanical devices. Despite his deception, Oz is not a bad man. Rather, he is a harmless scoundrel who is proud of his trickery, illusions that have in fact benefited the Emerald City by keeping the wicked witches from attacking.

In his preface to *The Wonderful Wizard of Oz*, Baum calls it "a modernized fairy tale," intended to introduce "a series of newer 'wonder tales' in which the stereotyped genie, dwarf and fairy are eliminated." Thus, in creating the Wizard and his other characters, Baum reacted against creatures of pure fantasy, drawing instead on people and objects in the world around him. The character of the Wizard, an ordinary man who uses trickery to make his subjects believe he is god-like, was an innovation in children's literature at the time. There is textual evidence to suggest that Baum put a good deal of himself into the character of the Wizard: he gave the character, for example, his love of stage magic and of puns.

Oz insists that while he may be a fraudulent wizard, he is a good man; however, since people persist in seeing him as a wizard, they never have a chance to know him as a mere mortal. Once his wizardly role has been destroyed by the falling of the screen he hides behind, the man is revealed for what he is. Michael Patrick Hearn notes in his introduction to *The Annotated Wizard of Oz* (2000) that this revelation in the novel can be seen as a metaphor for the changes in American life at the turn of the twentieth century. Technological advances, at once miraculous and frightening, required many people to rethink their lives and their places in the world. Many inventors of the time—Thomas Edison, for example, considered by some critics to be an inspiration for the Wizard—straddled the line between scientist and showman.

While the Wizard lives up to his promises to Dorothy's companions, his efforts to help her return to Kansas are not as successful. Oz builds a huge balloon to cross the desert but forgets to include any means of controlling its flight. When the balloon rises into the air without Dorothy, her hopes of returning to Kansas are momentarily dashed, since Oz cannot return for her. Though Baum writes that "that was the last any of them ever saw of Oz," he brought the character back in *Dorothy and the Wizard in Oz* (1908), in which he decides to live in Oz permanently, and he appears in subsequent books, including *The Emerald City of Oz* (1909), though he no longer rules Oz. In subsequent novels the Wizard becomes an apprentice to Glinda the Good Witch of the North, who teaches him magic so that in the end, the Wizard transforms from humbug to true wizard.

Discussion Questions

1. Many critics have written on the biblical overtones in chapter 11 of *The Wonderful Wizard of Oz*, in which Dorothy and her companions meet the Wizard. Using examples from the text, discuss how Baum's language and description of the Wizard make allusions to biblical descriptions of God. What is the effect of the revelation that the Wizard is a man after all? What might Baum's message here be?

2. *The Wonderful Wizard of Oz* fits nicely into Joseph Campbell's outline of the hero's journey, presented in *The Hero with a Thousand Faces* (1948). Using examples from the text and from Campbell's theory, analyze how the Wizard does or does not fit into this outline. What role does the Wizard appear to play? How does the revelation of Oz's true identity affect the role he plays in Dorothy's heroic journey?

3. Many writers have suggested that Baum saw himself as the Wizard and put a good deal of his own personality into the character of Oz. Using examples from the text and from Baum's own life, agree or disagree with this comparison.

4. For more than half of the text, Oz seems to be a powerful wizard possessed of great magic, who sets a test or challenge for Dorothy and her friends. In J. R. R. Tolkien's *The Hobbit* (1937), Gandalf seems to be a similar character, a powerful and wise magician who sends Bilbo on a journey that will challenge him. Using examples from both texts, compare and contrast the two wizard characters and show how each supports and enhances the theme of the novel.

5. Michael Patrick Hearn notes that many events and descriptions in the novel foreshadow the revelation of the Wizard as a fraud and a humbug. Using examples from the text, point out the ways in which Baum prepares the reader for that revelation.

—*Patti J. Kurtz*

REFERENCES

Brian Attebery, *The Fantasy Tradition in American Literature* (Bloomington: Indiana University Press, 1980);

Douglas G. Greene and Peter E. Hariff, *Bibliographia Oziana: A Concise Checklist of the Oz Books* (Kinderhook, Ill.: International Wizard of Oz Club, 1988);

Michael Patrick Hearn, ed., *The Annotated Wizard of Oz,* Centennial Edition (New York: Norton, 2000);

Raylyn Moore, *Wonderful Wizard, Marvelous Land* (Bowling Green, Ohio: Bowling Green State University Popular Press, 1974);

Michael Riley, *Oz and Beyond: The Fantasy World of L. Frank Baum* (Wichita: University Press of Kansas, 1997);

Katharine M. Rogers, *L. Frank Baum, the Royal Historian of Oz* (New York: St. Martin's Press, 2002).

Edward Bellamy

(March 26, 1850 – May 22, 1898)

ᘓᖬ

LOOKING BACKWARD: 2000–1887

(Boston: Ticknor, 1888)

JULIAN WEST

Julian West is the narrator and protagonist of Edward Bellamy's utopian novel, *Looking Backward: 2000–1887*. The novel was a publishing phenomenon, selling hundreds of thousands of copies in its first year and inspiring hundreds of "Bellamy clubs," where reform-minded Americans met to discuss the problems and possible solutions that the novel posited.

Readers easily identified with the thirty-year-old West, an educated and thoughtful Bostonian who is troubled by social unrest and endemic poverty but feels powerless to effect change. As a member of the upper class, able to live on the interest from inherited wealth, West has, he admits, "a large stake in the existing order of things": "Living in luxury, and occupied only with the pursuit of the pleasures and refinements of life, I derived the means of my support from the labor of others, rendering no sort of service in return." Class divisions into rich and poor, educated and uneducated, seem entirely natural and unalterable. Although he perceives suffering around him, he shares the anxieties of the upper class about possible insurrections, anarchy, and rebellion fomenting in the lower classes. Like many others, he is antagonistic to workers for their proliferation of strikes: his marriage, for example, repeatedly is postponed because strikes hinder the completion of the house in which he plans to live with his bride. Yet, at the same time that he feels resentment, West suffers from a bad conscience because he lives so much better than others; he feels both threatened and isolated.

Suffering from insomnia, West is hypnotized by a mesmerist and falls asleep in a basement bedroom of his Boston home. When the house burns down during the night, friends and neighbors assume that he perished; but he survives to be discovered in the year 2000, when the land on which his house was located is excavated in order to build a laboratory for a physician, Dr. Leete. In a trance, West's bodily functions underwent total arrest, allowing his survival for more than a century.

The Boston in which West awakens has changed dramatically, and the novel traces his encounter with this new society, characterized by political and economic equality, a socialist economy, and a myriad of new inventions. The social, political, and economic problems that plagued America in 1887 have been obliterated, the result of a new spirit of cooperation spanning the western world. Despite his investment in his status and class, West proves to be an ingenuous and curious time traveler. In conversations with Leete and his daughter, Edith—the book consists mainly of conversations—West explains the cause and effect of capitalism, individualism, and competition in nineteenth-century America; his hosts, providing a critique of that system, explain the "industrial evolution" that resulted in profound change.

Growing up in Chicopee, Massachusetts, an industrial town of gristmills, sawmills, and cotton mills, Bellamy witnessed the class divisions between mill owners and their workers, who eked out a living and whose children often were forced to labor in the mills instead of attending school. Trained as a lawyer, he left the profession when he realized that he could not represent a landlord in an eviction case; he became a writer, working as a journalist while he hoped for success as a novelist. By the time *Looking Backward* appeared, he already had published four novels, the most popular of which was *The Duke of Stockbridge,* a fictional account of an eighteenth-century grassroots rebellion in western Massachusetts.

Bellamy believed that poverty and exploitation could be solved by socialism, but he knew that the term itself—closely associated with anarchism in Americans' minds—raised fear. In *Looking Backward* he used instead the term *nationalism,* defined as government ownership of all production; the institution of an industrial army of workers, whose jobs are suited to their abilities and talents; and communal child care and housekeeping, which make it possible for women to contribute in the workplace.

In the true spirit of utopian fiction, the new Boston also offers technological amenities unknown to the nineteenth century: West discovers credit cards, for example, that make money unnecessary; radio broadcasts that bring music and sermons to one's home; and covered cities that protect citizens from rain and snow. In this new society, owning a personal umbrella is a metaphor for selfishness and disregard of others' needs. The nation must protect everyone. Instead of shopping at privately owned stores, consumers request items at a giant state-owned warehouse. With a fair allowance for all, citizens can afford their daily needs and also their occasional indulgences.

West's role in the novel is that of Everyman, countering Leete's explanations with objections to socialism that were familiar to Bellamy's readers: the state cannot be trusted with more power since politicians are essentially corrupt; lack of competition will result in complacency; private wealth is the just reward of those more able than others; happiness derives from the accumulation of goods. Patiently, Leete counters West's arguments until West is thoroughly persuaded that change must come: "I who had lived in those cruel insensate days, what had I done to bring them to an end? I had been every whit as indifferent to the wretchedness of my brothers, as cynically incredulous of better things, as besotted a worshipper of Chaos and Old Night, as any of my fellows." He has seen the light, and as a final reward—the end of the love story that serves as a subplot—he marries Edith. Bellamy created in West a man who comes to believe in the "essential nobleness" of humanity, and who revises his definition of *progress* to include and celebrate brotherhood and *happiness* to include social responsibility.

Discussion Questions

1. What is Julian West's view of human nature? What qualities does he believe are inherent in all human beings?

2. In nineteenth-century America, what does it mean to be a worthy person? How does that view change in the new society?

3. Some scholars have criticized Bellamy's depiction of women in his utopia. Drawing upon West's relationship with Edith Leete, to what extent do you think women's opportunities and roles changed from what they were in the nineteenth century?

4. William Morris wrote *News from Nowhere* (1892) as a critique of *Looking Backward*. Compare the responses of Morris's protagonist William Guest to West's responses to a new society. What assumptions does Guest have about free will, equality, creativity, and happiness?

—*Linda Simon*

REFERENCES

Edward Bellamy, *Looking Backward: 2000–1887,* edited, with an introduction, by Daniel Borus (Boston: St. Martin's Press, 1995);

Sylvia Bowman, *Edward Bellamy* (Boston: Twayne, 1986);

Nancy Snell Griffith, *Edward Bellamy: A Bibliography* (Metuchen, N.J.: Scarecrow Press, 1986);

Daphne Patai, ed., *Looking Backward, 1988–1888: Essays on Edward Bellamy* (Amherst: University of Massachusetts Press, 1988).

Saul Bellow
(June 10, 1915 – April 5, 2005)

THE ADVENTURES OF AUGIE MARCH
(New York: Viking, 1953)

AUGIE MARCH

Augie March is the eponymous main character of Saul Bellow's novel *The Adventures of Augie March.* According to literary critic Leslie Fiedler, Augie "is an image of a man at once totally Jewish . . . and absolutely American—the latest avatar of Huckleberry Finn." Although the novel is not about Augie's life and identity as a Jew, Fiedler is right to point out Augie's ethnicity. He is an urban boy from the working classes only one generation removed from his Eastern European, Jewish ethnic origins. Like Huck Finn, Augie is a free spirit determined to make his own way in the world despite social pressure to settle down and conform to social norms.

Augie is not only the main character of the novel but also its narrator. In the opening paragraph he introduces himself in characteristically brash, buoyant fashion:

> I am an American, Chicago born—Chicago, that somber city—and go at things as I have taught myself, free-style, and will make the record in my own way: first to knock, first admitted; sometimes an innocent knock, sometimes a not so innocent. But a man's character is his fate, says Heraclitus, and in the end there isn't any way to disguise the nature of the knocks by acoustical work on the door or gloving the knuckles.

Augie is proud that he is an American, but he has no interest in conforming to a particular American ideal. He is self-taught, he boasts, and pledges to chart his own course through life. He is endearingly optimistic. Yet, for all of Augie's independence and exuberance, there exists an underlying current of fatalism to his narration, as indicated by his reference to Heraclitus, the ancient Greek philosopher. The novel centers on his search for himself and his attempt to determine his fate according to his own rules.

Augie is often described as a picaresque hero, a character who, like Huck Finn, caroms from adventure to adventure and, along the way, begins to mature from a naive boy to someone more worldly and aware of himself and his surroundings. Augie's adventures begin in the streets of Chicago. Raised by his adoptive grandmother, Grandma Lausch, he navigates the city streets, mixing it up with neighborhood toughs. Later, he comes under the influence of William Einhorn, a local power broker who gives him a job as an errand boy. The novel is marked by transitional moments in Augie's life, typically when he meets and becomes the protégé of a father figure or falls in love with a woman. In each instance he conforms to his newly adopted role. For example, after working a series of dead-end jobs as a teenager, Augie meets Mr. and Mrs. Renling, upper-class Jews who give him a job at their luxury sporting-goods store. To make the scruffy-looking Augie more presentable, the Renlings clothe him in "tweeds, flannels, plaids, foulards, sport shoes, woven shoes Mexican style, and shirts and handkerchiefs," an outfit meant to allow him to blend into upper-crust society.

Augie's adventures take him across the United States and around the globe—from Chicago to Mexico and finally to Europe. Throughout his travels, he harks back to his personal declaration of independence and never allows himself to be settled or captured by anyone or anything. Instead, he seeks adventure. One section of the novel, for example, follows Augie and his girlfriend, Thea, to Mexico, where they go into business hunting giant iguanas with the aid of an eagle named Caligula. Later, Augie is stranded at sea in a small boat with a fanatical philosopher. Throughout the novel, his life continues to take strange twists and turns. Though he does eventually get married to Stella, an actress, he never truly settles down. True to his opening words, he does what he must to remain free and to live according to his own rules.

Augie ends the novel in France. Describing himself as "a sort of Columbus of those near-at-hand," he wonders if he "may well be a flop at this line of endeavor." Like Columbus, he sets out to discover a new world of possibilities and is only partly successful. He reflects: "Columbus too thought he was a flop, probably, when they sent him back in chains." Augie's fate, it seems, is to keep moving and searching for himself and his place in the world.

Discussion Questions

1. In Augie March, Saul Bellow created a passive character who is deeply influenced by the people he encounters. Which of the many characters who affect Augie is the most important? Do you see a particular relationship as pivotal in his development?

2. *The Adventures of Augie March* has been read as a parable that comments on American optimism. What are the references and the reasons that make such a reading of the novel plausible? What does the novel say about America?

3. Bellow later had some reservations about *The Adventures of Augie March*, remarking "I had to tame and restrain the style I developed in *Augie March* in order to write *Henderson* and *Herzog*." Compare *The Adventures of Augie March* to one of these other novels. What evidence of Bellow's restraint can you cite?

4. *The Adventures of Augie March* initiated a phase of Bellow's work that is evident in later novels such as *Henderson the Rain King* (1959), *Herzog* (1964), *Mr. Sammler's Planet* (1970) and *Humboldt's Gift* (1975). Compare Augie to one of Bellow's subsequent protagonists. What are their essential similarities?

—*Jeremy Shere*

DANGLING MAN
(New York: Vanguard, 1944)

JOSEPH

Joseph in Saul Bellow's *Dangling Man* (1944) lives in Chicago in a one-room apartment with his wife, Iva. The novel is set in 1942; with World War II raging abroad, Joseph (whose surname is not revealed in the novel) awaits his call to military service. In the meantime, he seeks a personal definition of freedom and to do so quits the everyday regime of his job at a travel agency. Joseph's experiences are based on Bellow's own, when he lived as an avid but isolated intellectual writer and reader prior to being drafted.

Left alone for much of the day, Joseph creates a journal to record his mundane activities and intellectual musings. These journal entries are the narrative of the novel. At first, Joseph is hesitant about this solipsistic journey that requires his wife's financial support. He records his reservations about being unemployed, finding an authentic self, and publicly admitting these sentiments: "I have thought of going to work, but I am unwilling to admit that I do not know how to use freedom and have to embrace the flunkydom of a job because I have no resources—in a word, no character." Joseph feels estranged by his hollow, directionless existence, most especially from his former self, a balanced and social individual.

Now, each day is indistinguishable from the next. As Joseph notes, unlike in his previous life, when there were "baking days, washing days," in his self-induced isolation and sabbatical from work, "it is difficult to tell Tuesday from Saturday." At times, his mind becomes preoccupied with trivial details. In his growing paranoia, every action is scrutinized for its larger significance. Joseph's constant contemplation of human nature fuels fights and arguments. For example, during an outing, a former acquaintance, "Comrade Jim," fails to greet Joseph properly. According to Joseph, this slight carries grave significance: Jim is unfriendly because he follows the Communist Party's protocol to exclude nonmembers. In Joseph's own words, this slight amounts to Comrade Jim "helping to abolish freedom and begin tyranny." Incensed by this thought, Joseph shares his disdain for his former friend with all within earshot.

Moreover, his obligatory visits and occasional run-ins with family and neighbors also prove disastrous. Most end violently; he compares himself to a "human grenade whose pin has been withdrawn." Much of the mayhem occurs because Joseph adopts a new philosophy. Early on, Joseph writes how he is rejecting the present "code of the hardboiled" that mandates "if you have difficulties, grapple with them silently." He vows to share and express his feelings openly.

Joseph's newfound candor comes at a cost: it ruptures his social ties. In a memorable scene, to the horror of his family, he berates and then spanks his niece, after she misbehaves and calls him a "beggar." Later, he contemplates the origins of these violent, aggressive impulses. He blames the belief of society in the individual's limitless potential. According to Joseph, this philosophy encourages individuals to strive for a greatness that is ultimately unattainable. Consequently, this striving creates an "inner climate of darkness" that produces "a storm of hate and wounding rain out of us."

Joseph's concerns about the nature of violence apply to the global stage. As Malcolm Bradbury comments about *Dangling Man,* "The book has rightly been seen as one of the best American war novels, far as it is from any battlefield." Indeed, Joseph's existential crisis dramatizes the lasting psychological impact of war on the general population. In Joseph's relentless self-scrutiny, he is at war with own inner self. His philosophical questions about destiny, freedom, and violence, inspired by such French existentialists as Jean-Paul Sartre and Albert Camus, are prevalent national anxieties in wartime and postwar America.

Joseph communicates this paramount concern in his second conversation with the "Spirit of Alternatives." This dialogue records Joseph's anxiety about his sequestered existence. He has grown "weary of it," and "its value" seems to be "decreasing day by day. Soon it will become distasteful." At the same time, his ruminations indicate that he has gained a new perspective on the purpose of his existence. He accepts Benedict de Spinoza's philosophy that "no virtue could be considered greater than that of trying to preserve oneself." Moreover, he understands the meaning of the dictum. It is not about prolonging the duration of one's life, but about saving its quality—"our dignity, our freedom." He seems invigorated by a new sense of social responsibility, a theme that reappears in Bellow's novels.

Despite this intellectual epiphany, by the end of the novel Joseph's home life is deteriorating rapidly. There is an obvious change in his temperament; he quarrels with Iva and shouts at his neighbor. As Iva observes, "You never used to be so mean and ugly tempered." In the aftermath of these domestic disputes, aware of his growing insanity, Joseph eagerly enlists in the military. His tone is celebratory as he starts his new life: "Hurray for regular hours! And for the supervision of the spirit! Long live regimentation!" His final hope is that he will now learn what he could not alone. However, since he surrenders to a bureaucracy to do so, his future is uncertain.

Later in his career, Bellow distanced himself from his two early works, calling *Dangling Man* his "M.A." and *The Victim* (1947) his "Ph.D." As evidenced by his later novels such as *Seize the Day* (1956), *Henderson the Rain King* (1959), and *Herzog* (1964), however, Bellow continued to create male protagonists who are at crossroads, searching for a new direction and most especially, for a means to conduct that search.

Discussion Questions

1. Speculate about why Bellow writes *Dangling Man* in the journal form. What would be different if Bellow had not chosen this narrative style?

2. Saul Bellow once remarked, "I cannot exceed what I see. I am bound, in other words, as the historian is bound by the period he writes about, by the situation I live in." Is this also true for Joseph?

3. How do images of Joseph's environment (his apartment, the city) reflect his search for a new identity? How does his urban experience compare with Asa's in *The Victim?* Cite examples from both texts to support your position.

4. Discuss Joseph's enlistment in the army. Does he gain a type of freedom? Interpret this paradox with references to other stages of Joseph's journey.

—*Ilse Schrynemakers*

✑

HERZOG
(New York: Viking, 1964)

MOSES HERZOG

Moses Herzog, a middle-aged professor of history in New York City, is the protagonist of Saul Bellow's novel *Herzog*. At age forty-seven, Herzog is restless and directionless, frightened by the feeling that he is "falling apart." His second marriage has failed, and his grief over the breakup is aggravated by the knowledge that his former wife, Madeleine, has betrayed him with his best friend, Valentine Gersbach.

In the first line of the novel, Herzog thinks: "If I'm out of my mind, it's all right with me." Seeking to reestablish order and confirm his sanity, he is "overcome by the need to explain, to have it out, to justify, to put in perspective, to clarify, to make amends." For the better part of the narrative, he delves into memories that trigger the urge to compose real and imagined letters—most often only fragments—to family, friends and enemies, famous intellectuals, and politicians, both dead and alive. Herzog's contemplations meander, and he conjures up memories of childhood, his two marriages, many friendships, and various affairs with women.

Herzog, an historian of philosophy (his dissertation was *The State of Nature in Seventeenth and Eighteenth Century English and French Political Philosophy*), embarks on actual journeys in the course of the novel, but more important are his many diverse mental expeditions. His general considerations about the meaning of human life are followed by epistolary questions to Martin Heidegger, reflections about the nature and future of modern democracies and Alexis de Tocqueville's beliefs, and observations addressed to Martin Luther King Jr. Herzog thinks about Martin Buber's writings and T. E. Hulme's "definition of Romanticism as 'split religion'" but also refers repeatedly to transcendentalist ideas—Walt Whitman and Ralph Waldo Emerson are quoted or misquoted.

Herzog practices a form of Puritan soul-searching, undergoing a quasi-therapeutic process to understand and overcome the trauma of his divorce. Andre Gordon and others have thus analyzed the novel in the context of "psychological and sociological studies of bereavement, marital separation, and divorce grief," claiming that Herzog's divorce is the ultimate cause of his bereavement and also the overriding topic of the novel. Herzog remembers his childhood days in Montreal, and these descriptions in particular provide to the novel a Jewish American flavor, which many scholars have meticulously analyzed, pigeonholing Bellow with other twentieth-century Jewish American writers such as Philip Roth, Bernard Malamud, and Cynthia Ozick.

Taking stock of his life and career, Herzog comes to the conclusion that he has been a bad husband twice, a bad father to his children, an indifferent citizen, a remote sibling, an egotist, and a lazy lover. He characterizes himself as passive, dull, and elusive. His latest book project has amounted to eight hundred pages stored in a closet, and the marriage to and separation from Madeleine has left him sexually damaged.

The whole narrative is Herzog's personal history; yet, his idiosyncratic suffering extends to a form of *weltschmerz:* "The description might begin with his wild internal disorder, or even with the fact that he was quivering. And why? Because he let the entire world press upon him. For instance? Well, for instance, what it means to be a man. In a city. In a century. In transition. In a mass. Transformed by science. Under organized power. Subject to tremendous controls. In a condition caused by mechanization. After the late failure of radical hopes. In a society that was no community and devalued the person." *Herzog* is thus not only a story about an eccentric individual or about a twentieth-century American Jew; it is also about the state of mankind in the 1960s.

Following the torrent of ideas, thoughts, letters, and scraps, he contemplates murdering Madeleine and Gersbach and ends up in a car accident with his young daughter. He retreats to the Berkshires with broken ribs, finally finding a temporary peace. The novel ends on programmatic lines: "At this time he had no messages for anyone. Nothing. Not a single word."

Margaret M. Gullette has labeled *Herzog* a "progress novel of the middle years," and M. A. Quayam calls it a novel of sin, "suffering, search, and salvation," dubbing Bellow "a neo-transcendental writer, or a latter-day heir to the Emerson-Whitman tradition." Malcolm Bradbury has identified as the major topic of the novel the intellectual hero in search of reality, pointing out that mental dissolution of the "hero as suffering joker" is at its core. For Bradbury, what makes *Herzog* such a "flamboyantly great comic novel of multiplied and maddened ideas" is its "metaphysical and intellectual energy," which creates a "most powerful form of late modern intellectual comedy." Other critics have classified the novel as "Jewish-American" or rooted in the traditions of modernism or English Romanticism. This broad, sometimes mutually exclusive variety of critical perspectives indicates the denseness and vast interpretive potential of Bellow's novel.

Discussion Questions

1. Herzog's full name is Moses Elkanah Herzog. What, if anything, does his name signify about him?

2. Herzog is still in a sense obsessed by his second wife, Madeleine, and her betrayal. How can their relationship be characterized?

3. Discuss what Herzog means by his claim that "we mustn't forget how quickly the visions of genius become the canned goods of the intellectuals."

—*Eva-Sabine Zehelein*

୧ୄ

HUMBOLDT'S GIFT
(New York: Viking, 1975)

CHARLIE CITRINE

Charlie Citrine, the protagonist and narrator of *Humboldt's Gift,* opens the novel recalling his time as a student and an aspiring writer. His story is narrated from a maturity that encompasses literary celebrity, marital and financial failure, and spiritual ambivalence. He distracts himself from his writer's block and his quest to understand the role of the artist in America with his girlfriend, Renata; unlikely and expensive literary projects; and gangland excursions in the company of a small-time hood, Rinaldo Cantabile. The project that Citrine has been wavering over for some years is, significantly, a book he calls "Great Bores of the Modern World." Even he realizes that it is a project that will never come to publication. He is increasingly disengaged with everything and everyone around him. As he says, "People of powerful intellect are never quite sure whether or not it's all a dream." His passivity leads everyone around him to use him, and most of the characters in the novel want to force their viewpoint on him, sue him for what they see as their share of his largely dissipated fortune, or involve him in their own projects. It is a passivity that marks many of Bellow's leading male characters.

In the 1930s an idealistic young Citrine had made the journey east from Chicago to New York to meet Von Humboldt Fleisher, the famous avant-garde author of *Harlequin Ballads.* They began a relationship that spanned Humboldt's decline into poverty, loneliness, and periodic insanity and Citrine's rise to literary celebrity. Over the decades the two men embarked on several more-or-less failed collaborations, one of which, a movie treatment Citrine receives after Humboldt's death (the "gift" referred to in the title of the novel), allows Citrine to triumph over his problems. The gift enables him to find both his backbone and his independence again.

The women in Citrine's life—Renata and her conniving mother, the Senora; Cantabile's wife, Lucy, who is working toward her Ph.D. on the once-celebrated Fleisher; Humboldt's long-suffering wife, Kathleen; Demmie Vonghel, whom Citrine would have married had she not died in the rain forests of South America; Naomi Lutz, his childhood sweetheart who wants him to redeem her good-for-nothing son; and Denise, the grasping socialite wife who is divorcing him as expensively as possible—can all be seen in terms of Bellow's response to his own five marriages, the most recent of which had dissolved as he was writing *Humboldt's Gift.* One of the main themes of *Caldofreddo,* the movie based on Humboldt's bequest, is cannibalism, which also figures as a significant motif in *Humboldt's Gift.* The women in *Humboldt's Gift,* with the exception of Kathleen, begin as partners and helpmates, but they eventually deceive their menfolk and extort from them. Against this feminine conspiracy Citrine attempts to articulate an alternative to the highly macho literary patriarch represented by Fleisher, the writer who "performed all the stormy steps of that routine"—the routine that lies at the heart of the failed modernism of the late twentieth century.

Now in his sixties, Citrine has become interested in "the immortal spirit." He has developed a personal idealistic, even spiritual, existentialism based on the writings of the German anthroposophist Rudolph Steiner. Anthroposophy, Citrine believes, gives him an alienated view of the world. "Other-worldliness tinged it all and every little while my spirit seemed to disassociate itself." He fully realizes that such a belief can make him appear naive, even foolish. Cantabile, in particular, after having Citrine's precious Mercedes-Benz reduced to a pile of battered metal over a gambling debt, adopts

him and looks after him as a kind of idiot savant. *Humboldt's Gift* can be seen to reflect Bellow's own interest in anthroposophy and the rejection of modernism, of Sigmund Freud in particular, as well as his own quest for the place of the "artist in America." In an interview in *The New York Times* in 1975 Bellow said that "Citrine represents my sense of the comic absurdity of American urban life. He is attached to people as a poet would be, but he also perceives the nonsense of the courts and lawyers, the absurdity of ambition and the hilarity of sexual mores."

Citrine, recalling Humboldt and his attempt "simply to live" with Kathleen, says that "we must listen in secret to the sound of the truth that God puts into us." Critics have noted that he is actually a rather dull, reflective character and one who articulates many of Bellow's own concerns at length. Indeed, Citrine can be seen as a portrait of Bellow. Perhaps it is significant that the author named his character after a transparent semiprecious stone.

The novel, as Bellow said in the 1975 interview, "is intended to hold up a mirror to our urban society and to show its noise, its uncertainties, its sense of crisis and despair, its standardization of pleasures." Yet, at the end of the novel, in early spring, after Humboldt's reburial, Citrine and the aged Menasha, who had boarded with his family when Citrine was a child, find two flowers peeping up among the dead leaves. Menasha, who has just sung the "In questa tomba oscura" (In this obscure tomb) aria from *Aida* over Humboldt's grave, asks what the flowers are called. Citrine replies, "Search me . . . I'm a city boy myself. They must be crocuses." In the tradition of floral symbolism the crocus represents the imminent spring and rebirth.

Discussion Questions

1. One of the central themes of *Humboldt's Gift* is a particular kind of betrayal that seems to define Citrine's relationship with women. Does he deliberately seek out those particular relationships or is it something in himself? Is Kathleen, Humboldt's widow, one of those types? What makes her different for Citrine?

2. At the end of *Humboldt's Gift*, Citrine seems aware that the money he makes from *Caldofreddo* will disappear as readily as all his other money, yet

it does not seem to worry him. What is the real significance of Humboldt's gift?

3. Bellow once said that "I don't know what I think until I see what I say. I'm a hostage to my tongue." Similarly, Citrine describes Humboldt as a "nonstop monologuist." How might these two statements apply to Citrine himself?

—*Jim Hall*

VON HUMBOLDT FLEISHER

Von Humboldt Fleisher is a once-famous writer who is recalled by a friend, author and playwright Charlie Citrine, in Saul Bellow's novel *Humboldt's Gift*. "The book of ballads published by Von Humboldt Fleisher in the Thirties was an immediate hit," the first sentence of the novel, describes the high-water mark of Humboldt's literary career. His life and penurious death drive much of what happens to Citrine over the duration of the narrative. The two men fall into a lifelong, almost father-son, friendship when the young Citrine travels to New York to meet the writer after the publication of *Harlequin Ballads*, the book of poems that has so rapidly catapulted the older writer to fame. In his prime Humboldt lived his life with a force that was almost primal. He was, Citrine says, "An avant-garde writer, the first of a new generation, he was handsome, fair, large, serious, witty, he was learned. The guy had it all." Yet, he states later, "I doubt that Humboldt had had a single good day in all his life. . . . Perhaps not so many as two consecutive hours of composure." *Humboldt's Gift* examines the contradictions inherent in the artistic and creative life of America.

For most of the novel Humboldt is depicted as a spent force, a "sublime fool"—one who, for all his raging against a society that constantly disappoints him and friends bent on forgetting or betraying him, is never able to recapture his early brilliance. His frustration leads to anger, attacks upon his friends and family, and eventually madness and isolation. While he still has money, his main obsession is litigation, often directed at old friends and collaborators. Even his wife, the saintly Kathleen, eventually leaves him after he tries to run her down with his car.

The gift of the title refers in part to Humboldt's flawed genius, but it is also the bequest that Humboldt leaves Citrine in his will, which turns out to be the treatment for a movie that both men had worked on at the height of their friendship. The gift is the device around which the novel develops. When Citrine says that Humboldt is "one of my significant dead," he does not merely mean that the poet has died. Citrine is also aware that he has betrayed the doomed older man, cut him out of his life. While writing a *Life* article on Robert Kennedy, and as part of the senator's entourage, he sees the derelict Humboldt near Central Park, "a dying man eating a pretzel stick at the curb, the dirt of the grave already sprinkled on his face. Then I rushed away." That failure haunts Citrine and is the turning point of the novel.

Bellow regularly drew on real friends and acquaintances, and indeed himself, for his work. *Humboldt's Gift* is something of a roman à clef in that Humboldt is obviously based on Bellow's own friend and mentor Delmore Schwartz. In 1952 both men taught briefly in the Creative Arts Program at Princeton University. Schwartz's reviews of Bellow's work first drew the younger man to the public's attention as an important writer. Like Humboldt, who dies "at the Ilscombe . . . sitting on his bed in this decayed place, probably reading," Schwartz died after a protracted period of mental instability, practically penniless and unrecognized, in a cheap New York hotel. On Humboldt's death, the cops "carried him on to the morgue. At the morgue there were no readers of modern poetry. The name Von Humboldt Fleisher meant nothing. So he lay there, another derelict." Bellow once described his Pulitzer Prize–winning novel as a "comic book about death," but it is also about how Citrine, with some assistance from the money that comes from the "gift," ultimately redeems both his old friend and himself. At the end of the novel Citrine has Humboldt exhumed from his pauper's grave and reburied with his mother.

Bellow derived his hero's name from the nineteenth-century naturalist and explorer Baron Alexander von Humboldt. Humboldt spends his life trying to understand nature, to get to its essence. At the end of his life Baron von Humboldt attempted to produce a synthesis of his work, the *Kosmos,* that would unify the sciences;

he was unable, though, to complete the impossible project before he died. In a similar way the poet, according to Citrine, "wanted to drape the world in radiance, but he didn't have enough material. His attempt ended at the belly." He wanted to produce the synoptic work of literature, the elusive "great American novel," that will encapsulate and describe America and the American experience for all time. If any writer could achieve such a feat it seemed that Humboldt could. "His spiel," as Citrine recalls it, "took in Freud, Heine, Wagner, Goethe in Italy, Lenin's dead brother, Wild Bill Hickok's costumes, the New York Giants, Ring Lardner on grand opera, Swinburne on flagellation, and John D. Rockefeller on religion"—all in the journey time of the Christopher Street ferry.

Humboldt's obituary in *The New York Times* reminds Citrine that "Humboldt did what poets in crass America are supposed to do. He chased ruin and death even harder than he chased women. He blew his talent and his health and reached home, the grave, in a dusty slide." One of the themes of the novel follows Citrine's, and indeed Bellow's, flirtation with the philosophy of the anthroposophist Rudolph Steiner. Citrine takes the notion from Steiner that "the educated speak of the disenchanted (a boring) world. But it is not the world, it is my own head that is disenchanted. The world cannot be disenchanted." Humboldt's problem was always that he could never ignore, or even mask, that enchantment. His head was never disenchanted.

Discussion Questions

1. Talking about his belief in the power of art, Humboldt announces, "Remember: we are not natural beings but supernatural beings." What do you think he means by that? Would Citrine agree with him? Would Saul Bellow?

2. How might Humboldt's relationship with Citrine be seen as fatherly? Can you find specific moments in the novel that illustrate this quality? There are other instances when both men quite violently resist that relationship. Can you find some examples? What is it that comes between them?

3. Is Humboldt's decline inevitable? What is it that he wants so badly that he allows it to destroy him?

4. Some critics have seen Rinaldo Cantabile, the mobster who befriends Citrine, as a kind of mirror image of Von Humboldt Fleisher. Compare Cantabile's values and his actions with Humboldt's. Can you find evidence to support the argument?

—*Jim Hall*

MR. SAMMLER'S PLANET
(New York: Viking, 1970)

ARTHUR SAMMLER

Arthur Sammler, the main character of Saul Bellow's *Mr. Sammler's Planet,* is an elderly Polish Jew who has been brought to America after World War II as a displaced person and, incompletely assimilated, has remained displaced, emotionally and intellectually. Like many of the title characters of Bellow's novels, he is "a peculiarly delicate recording system" registering the play of novel ideas. Once an Anglophile and habitué of the Bloomsbury group of artists and intellectuals, he has had enough of "the old European culture game" as a consequence of his experiences during the war. Blinded in the left eye by a German soldier and dumped into a pit along with his wife and hundreds of others, he managed to crawl from beneath the dead bodies. But as a consequence of this resurrection Sammler has been compelled to adopt a beyond-the-grave perspective. He feels himself "a vestige, a visiting consciousness" that has been "severed" from others "by preoccupations too different and remote, disproportionate on the side of the spiritual." The reverence accorded his rectitude and the avuncular role that is forced upon him by everyone he knows are played off against his alienated perspective on contemporary America in a manner that suggests Sammler is wryly conceived by Bellow as an alternative Uncle Sam.

Sammler is detached: "The damaged left eye seemed to turn in another direction, to be preoccupied separately with different matters." Yet, he is also voyeuristic: "If the majority walked about as if under a spell, sleepwalkers, circumscribed by . . . minor neurotic trifling aims, individuals like Sammler were only one stage forward, awakened not to purpose but to aesthetic consumption of the environment. . . . translating heartache into delicate, even piercing observation." His personal intimations, deepened by the writings of the thirteenth-century mystic Meister Eckhardt, tell him that "God Himself was drawn toward the disinterested soul." But because "all postures are mocked by their opposites," Sammler finds himself persistently drawn back to the ordeals of "creatureliness"—"its low tricks, its doggish hind-sniffing charms." He is a reluctant, and for that reason all the more compulsive, witness of the minutiae of the passing scene, which are nonetheless "curious ciphers and portents." Contemplating the mystery of existence, and his own unlikely continued existence, Sammler sees himself, somewhat ruefully, as a man "assigned . . . to condense, in short views, some essence of experience and because of this having a certain wizardry ascribed to him." But while he has come to recognize that metaphysical symbols reside in the common elements of everyday life, his acute awareness often produces knowledge he would just as soon avoid.

Sammler recognizes that the "very harsh surgery" that has severed him from what others take for granted might be affecting his perceptions and judgments insofar as "the shadow of his nerves would always cast stripes." He also suspects that he sometimes views the world with the hardness of the criminal—someone who brutally "brushes aside flimsy ordinary arrangements." His encounter with just such a man, a black pickpocket and mugger, provides one of the few slender threads of plot upon which Bellow strings Sammler's observational pearls. Witnessing the criminal at his work on a bus disrupts Sammler's customs and habits, and that stimulates, indeed revives, his imagination and reckless curiosity: "The air was brighter. . . . The world . . . was wickedly lighted up . . . and this explicitness taunted Mr. Minutely-Observant Arthur Sammler." At the same time that intensified vision vivifies existence, it also exposes the dizzying "fury" of a turbulent world.

While delivering a public lecture, Sammler is shouted down by a campus radical, who accuses him of being irrelevant because of sexual impotence. Surrendering the podium, he muses on his younger contemporaries, their pervasive "tooth-showing, Barbary ape howling . . . like the spider monkeys in the trees . . . defecating into their hands, and shrieking, pelting the explorers below." Soon after, Sammler is again an unwilling witness to a mugging by the black criminal; but this time he is "seen seeing." The man follows him home and, as a silent threat, forces him to look at his genitals. Typically, Sammler receives and reads this as a sign—"a symbol of superlegitimacy or sovereignty . . . unanswerable." By exposing his penis as an instrument of terror, the mugger had revealed "his metaphysical warrant." He had testified by the root of that word *(testes)* to the insight of the philosopher Arthur Schopenhauer, Sammler's namesake, that the "blinding power" of the cosmic Will is not easily constrained by ideas. The fact that the mugger acts in a "barbarous-majestical manner indicative of a mad spirit . . . mad with the idea of *noblesse*" converges major preoccupations of Sammler's thought regarding the unruliness he sees all around him, particularly the covert connection between illicit or licentious conduct and a desperate striving for a transcendent order.

As a reluctant confidant of all who know him, Sammler finds himself a "registrar of madness." Just as he sees things he does not want to see, he hears things he does not want to hear from those who feel compelled to confess their chaos to him. "Declare for normalcy," he muses, "and you will be stormed by aberrancies." Most of his intimates are self-deluded, devising ingenious stratagems for obstructing and complicating theirs and others' lives. His daughter, Shula, an emotionally disjointed bag lady; his great-nephew Wallace, an unremittingly hapless schemer; and Wallace's sexually voracious sister, Angela, all do mischief out of a restlessness dilated with the unbounded contemporary expectation of gratifying "teased, cheated, famished needs." All are undisciplined enthusiasts subject to immoderate whims that represent different forms taken by the neurotic American panic to "keep the wolf of insignificance from the door." Reacting to a desperate need to make the world (and themselves) seem "remarkable" and "interesting," they impulsively display themselves to Sammler—demanding his attention. Psychologically unstable, living in a socially unstable time, they gravitate to Sammler, who seems to embody the "idea of stability." They seem oblivious that war trauma has left their kindly uncle vulnerable to impatience and "fits of rage," perhaps because his "rancor" is constrained by deep, genuine sympathy. Certainly none is aware that toward the end of the war their beloved moral exemplar had shot an enemy soldier as he begged for his life, that he had learned the luxurious, pitiless "bliss," the world-brightening "ecstasy" of murdering with impunity.

Sammler is falsely perceived by others, whose perceptions are shaped and colored to their needs. Thus he recognizes that his daughter needs to think of him as a "superior" being, a maker of "beautiful culture." Shula, a "loony" culture maven, embarrasses and plagues her father with her conviction of his greatness and his obligation to edify the world with written reminiscences of his former intimacy with the writer H. G. Wells. She steals a scientific manuscript about the possibilities of establishing civilization on the moon in the hope of stimulating her father to write. Sammler is thereby confronted with a second example of the lawlessness of a generation whose inclinations have been deformed by too much aestheticism and intellectualism and who consequently think, "For the creative there are no crimes." The theft also stimulates Sammler to contemplate how it is that most forms of contemporary lunacy are produced by the impulse to transcend the self by any means necessary. Sensitive to paradox, Sammler understands that the impulse to go beyond the self constitutes, by a dialectical principle of engendered opposites, the complete triumph of the modern ideology of individualism, which warrants each person's "life-claim," the "right to be whatever—whatever it all came to."

Sammler comes to think that much illicit behavior is a response to boredom and anguish, and that people opt for the "magic of extremes" in order "to obtain the grace of madness." Sammler sees the histrionic antics of his relatives magnified in the carnivalesque spectacle of the late 1960s urban street scene, a grotesque motley of clownishly incoherent styles of dress. The performance on the street of "our modern individuality boom"—its fallacious idolization of originality, its contrived displays of idiosyn-crasy, its self-mythologizing masquerades copied from media images—provides Sammler with ample evidence that contemporary life is characterized by the appalling attempt of "a wretched itching, bleeding" humanity to affirm freedom in the absence of models of truly liberated consciousness.

But Sammler knows that the drive to be unique and extraordinary ends in a criminal assault on the normative and everyday. "Like many people who had seen the world collapse once, Mr. Sammler entertained the possibility it might collapse twice." He reads the signs of "the suicidal impulses of civilization" in the slackness, orgiastic banality, shallowness, and childish distemper that pervade contemporary life. Its glamorization of violence and its tolerance of emotional vehemence and sexual excess, justified in the name of hygienic purging, are manifestations of a universal dissatisfaction produced by desires that cannot possibly be requited. Because there are no cures, only the orchestration of disorders, any thoughtful person might wish "to sue for divorce from all these human states." However, while Sammler cannot turn a blind eye to other people's restive seeking of the extraordinary, his abiding ideal is to establish a relationship with the infinite that allows him to need "nothing but the finite and the usual."

Discussion Questions

1. What are Sammler's objections to those who would provide "the superstructure of explanation," and where in the text does Bellow subvert these objections through his characterization of Sammler himself?

2. Sammler provides extensive analysis of contemporary "sexual madness." According to his diagnosis, what are the causes of the proliferation of sexual obsession, fetishism, and exhibitionism (including the need to verbally recount sexual misadventures)?

3. The moon accrues many meanings in Sammler's internal discourse with himself. How is the moon linked, as a symbol, with the lunacy he witnesses everywhere? Which textual passages best exemplify Sammler's speculation that the moon might function as a utopian site of transcendence—of escape from the baseness, neediness, and sensuality that characterizes the earthbound ordeal?

—*David Brottman*

SEIZE THE DAY

(New York: Viking, 1956)

TOMMY WILHELM

Tommy Wilhelm is the protagonist of Saul Bellow's novella *Seize the Day*. In approximately six hours, his character and fate are revealed. Tommy lives in the Hotel Gloriana in New York, and although his father, Dr. Adler, lives in the same hotel, the two men are alienated from each other. Tommy is separated from his wife and two sons. He has quit his job because he was passed over for a promised promotion in favor of the boss's son-in-law. His girlfriend, Olive, has withdrawn from him because she, a devout Catholic, can no longer bear the ostracism caused by their illicit affair. Tommy is down to his last few dollars. He prays, "Oh, God. . . . Let me out of my trouble. Let me out of my thoughts, and let me do something better with myself. For all the time I have wasted I am very sorry. Let me out of this clutch and into a different life. For I am all balled up. Have mercy."

Now in his mid forties, Tommy keeps reviewing his past life and sees nothing but a series of bad decisions and bad breaks. He lost his mother too soon; he left college too early in order to pursue a career in Hollywood, which never materialized. He married the wrong woman. Choked, congested with negative emotions, he seeks relief. First, he asks his father for money and "other things a father can give to a son . . . one word from you, just a word"; Adler offers nothing in response. Tommy asks his wife, Margaret, for a divorce so that he can marry Olive; Margaret refuses. He gives his last money to Dr. Tamkin, a fraudulent visionary, to speculate in commodities, but Tamkin loses it. But at least Tamkin speaks of essential matters and encourages Tommy to live again. "You have to pick out something that's in the actual, immediate present moment," he says. "And say to yourself here-and-now, here-and-now, here-and-now. . . . Be in the present. Grasp the hour, the moment, the instant." Bellow's choice of title suggests the importance of Tamkin's advice to Tommy.

At the very end, Tommy seizes the instant, or is seized by it. His elderly father and his own recurrent failures have forced him to confront the question of death. At the funeral of a stranger, Tommy's congested heart finally bursts forth in a flood of uncontrollable emotion; he "sank deeper than sorrow, through torn sobs and cries toward the consummation of his heart's ultimate need." He has found a kind of release, but the novella is ambiguous as to whether it is a triumph or a defeat.

Bellow was fond of quoting Walt Whitman's assertion that America needs comedies about death. Yet, the comedic aspect of *Seize the Day* must be carefully balanced against the sympathetic and dignified presentation of the author's typical hero. Tommy is willing "to be the carrier of a load which was his own self, his characteristic self." He accepts his responsibilities and flaws; he longs for connection with others. To maintain this delicate balance between comedy and sympathy, Bellow characteristically employs a third-person, sharp-focus point of view. He concentrates on Tommy's thoughts, feelings, and actions but often rises above them to become impersonal, objective, and ironic. He switches occasionally to Adler's point of view in order to offer a different perspective on Tommy. By moving from inside Tommy to outside and then back again, the reader gains a rounded picture of the protagonist.

Tommy prefigures two of Bellow's best-known protagonists, Moses Herzog of *Herzog* and Charlie Citrine of *Humboldt's Gift*. All three men have money troubles, family troubles, women troubles. They all experience the difficulty of consummating the "heart's ultimate need" in a mass, capitalistic society. They are all presented comically yet sympathetically. In a still broader perspective, Tommy is related to the alienated hero found in much modern American fiction, especially during the conservative 1950s, heroes such as J. D. Salinger's Holden Caulfield, Ralph Ellison's Invisible Man, and John Updike's Rabbit Angstrom.

Discussion Questions

1. Should one like Tommy? How does the sensitive reader react to him? What in the text accounts for those reactions?

2. What is the function of Dr. Tamkin? Why is it that, although Tommy suspects Tamkin is a liar and a charlatan, he is still drawn to him?

3. Examine the instances in which the narrator switches from Tommy's point of view to that of Dr. Adler. How does this narrative strategy enrich and complicate the story?

4. The ending has evoked very different reactions. Some see it as Tommy's triumph; others view it as his ultimate defeat. Did Bellow make it deliberately ambiguous? What do you think, and what is the basis for your reaction?

—*Mark A. Weinstein*

THE VICTIM
(New York: Vanguard, 1947)

ASA LEVENTHAL

Asa Leventhal, the protagonist in Saul Bellow's second novel, *The Victim*, wrestles with the extent of his responsibility for the dire predicaments of others. During one summer, while his wife is temporarily away, Leventhal's existential angst escalates largely because of the unwelcome and constant demands of Kirby Allbee, a Gentile who blames Leventhal for his current unemployment, and Elena, the wife of his brother Max, who nurses a sick child. These present-day hardships are compounded by Leventhal's haunting memories of his insane mother and emotionally distant father. Set amid the streets of New York City, the novel draws upon urban images to depict Leventhal's psychological torment. In one particular scene, in his paranoia he believes the doors of a train intentionally close upon him. Central to Leventhal's paranoia is his felt experience of anti-Semitism exacerbated by the taunts and persecutions of Allbee. Early in the novel, soon after Leventhal begrudgingly assists Elena during his brother's absence, Allbee accosts Leventhal and accuses him of precipitating Allbee's ruin. Apparently, years ago, when Leventhal was unemployed, Allbee arranged an interview for him with his boss, Rudiger. Allbee believes Leventhal's rude banter with Rudiger cost Allbee his job, an outcome Leventhal intentionally plotted because, as Allbee conjectures, "You were sore at something I said about Jews."

Leventhal denies the allegations. His cry of "Why me?" vocalizes a lack of understanding of and his resistance to the persecutions. Allbee only magnifies the charges, later blaming his failed marriage and his wife's death on Leventhal and not on his own drinking problem. Allbee asserts that the cultural attitude of the Jews contributed to this predicament. He tells Leventhal: "You won't assume that it isn't entirely my fault. It is necessary for you to believe that I deserve what I get. . . . It's a Jewish point of view." Concurrently, after his nephew dies, Leventhal feels his brothers-in-law, Roman Catholics, hold him responsible.

At first, Leventhal desires nothing but his solitude, to be free of responsibility for his actions and of the messy, emotional entanglements of relationships. He maligns Allbee for deeming him a catalyst for Allbee's own wrecked state. He believes that Allbee is "Haunted in his mind by wrongs or faults of his own which he turned into wrongs against himself." If Allbee only sees himself as a victim, however, then so does Leventhal. Both are victimized by each other but also victimize each other, since neither accepts responsibility for one's own problems and instead makes the other accountable. Moreover, as novelist J. M. Coetzee notes, the narrative style of the novel, with its lack of an "authorial word," does not dictate which character is the victim or the persecutor. In this way, the book creates one of its central themes, the notion of shared responsibility for the human condition.

The tensions between Leventhal and Albee can be compared to the Jew/Gentile relationship in another post–World War II novel, Bernard Malamud's *The Assistant* (1957). This novel depicts how Morris Bober, a kindhearted Jewish grocery-store owner, transforms the life of a Roman Catholic drifter, Frank Alpine. At first Morris's attacker and then later his assistant, Frank learns from Morris to act with compassion and responsibility. Moreover, in *Leopards in the Temple*, Morris Dickstein deems the focus of *The Victim* on Leventhal's existential angst "prophetic" of the direction of postwar fiction. After World War II, American literature shifted attention "towards metaphysical concerns about identity, morality, and man's place in the larger scheme of the universe," as evidenced by the characters in Ralph Ellison's *Invisible Man* (1952), Richard Wright's *Black Boy* (1945), Robert Penn Warren's *All the King's Men* (1946), and Lionel Trilling's *The Middle of the Journey* (1947).

At the start of chapter 5 of *The Victim*, while on the ferry to Staten Island traveling to see his distressed sister-in-law, Leventhal experiences an epiphany that leads him to connect his ordeals with the larger human condition. He observes that "the light over them, and over the water was akin to the yellow revealed in the slit of the eye of a wild animal, say a lion, something inhuman that didn't care about anything human and yet was implanted in every human being too, one speck of it, and formed a part of him that responded to the heat and the glare." Later, Leventhal accepts some responsibility for Allbee's plight and thus offers Allbee his place to stay. Their feud seems temporarily thawed. Leventhal's altruism invites only more suffering, however. His spiritual journey is comparable to Job's in that others, in particular, his sister-in-law and Albee, "heap their ills and maladjustments" on him; Bellow adapts Job's epic, biblical struggles into modern-day hardships.

Discussion Questions

1. *The Victim* explores a classic philosophical question about human nature: whether an individual's fate is a choice or a destiny. Based upon your reading of the novel, consider how Bellow answers this question. In what instances are Asa's problems beyond his control? In what instances does he cause them?

2. Bellow's *Dangling Man* was published three years before *The Victim*. In both of these early Bellow novels, the protagonists grapple with their search for freedom and an understanding of moral responsibility. How do the two novels capture these themes differently?

3. Many commentators note the relatively small role female characters play in Bellow's novels. How do you view Bellow's portrayal of women in *The Victim*?

4. In an essay about Bellow's characters, Charles Simic argues that "they see their suffering as perhaps the last outpost of the heroic in our day and age." Based upon the novel's portrait of Asa, how does Bellow define "heroic"? Cite examples from the novel to support your position.

5. How do you interpret the ending of the book? Does Asa transcend his struggles or temporarily appease them? Explain.

—*Ilse Schrynemakers*

REFERENCES

James Atlas, *Saul Bellow: A Biography* (New York: Random House, 2000);

Gerhard Bach, *The Critical Response to Saul Bellow* (Westport, Conn.: Greenwood Press, 1995);

Bach, ed., *Saul Bellow at Seventy-Five: A Collection of Critical Essays* (Tübingen: Gunter Narr, 1991);

Malcolm Bradbury, *Saul Bellow* (New York: Methuen, 1982);

Jeanne Braham, *A Sort of Columbus: The American Voyages of Saul Bellow's Fiction* (Athens: University of Georgia Press, 1984);

Gloria L. Cronin and Ben Siegel, eds., *Conversations with Saul Bellow* (Jackson: University Press of Mississippi, 1994);

Robert R. Dutton, *Saul Bellow*, revised edition (New York: Twayne, 1982);

L. H. Goldman, *Saul Bellow's Moral Vision: A Critical Study of the Jewish Experience* (New York: Irvington, 1983);

Eugene Hollahan, ed., *Saul Bellow and the Struggle at the Center* (New York: AMS Press, 1996);

Peter Hyland, *Saul Bellow* (New York: St. Martin's Press, 1992);

Michael P. Kramer, ed., *New Essays on Seize the Day* (Cambridge & New York: Cambridge University Press, 1998);

Joseph F. McCadden, *The Flight from Women in the Fiction of Saul Bellow* (Washington, D.C.: University Press of America, 1981);

Robert G. Noreen, *Saul Bellow: A Reference Guide* (Boston: G. K. Hall, 1978);

Ellen Pifer, *Saul Bellow: Against the Grain* (Philadelphia: University of Pennsylvania Press, 1991);

Stanley Trachtenberg, ed., *Critical Essays on Saul Bellow* (Boston: G. K. Hall, 1979).

Cherie Bennett
(October 6, 1960 –   )

ᘒ

LIFE IN THE FAT LANE
(New York: Delacorte, 1998)

LARA ARDECHE

Lara Ardeche, the protagonist of Cherie Bennett's *Life in the Fat Lane,* is a sixteen-year-old junior at Forest Hills High School in Nashville, Tennessee. As the novel opens, Lara seems to live a charmed life: she is an honor student, a classical pianist, and an athlete; she is also both pretty and popular. Her parents are particularly proud of the many beauty pageants she has won, and Lara embraces the values espoused by the pageants so completely that she tries to live up to an idealized version of this role in her daily life. For instance, she reminds herself when tempted to lose her temper that "Beauty queens are friendly, controlled, sweet, and soft-spoken at all times." Lara believes that she deserves her success: she works hard, is loyal to her friends, and does her best to be kind and gracious to everyone. If she has enjoyed some advantages, such as a rich grandfather who built a gym in her home and paid for a family vacation at a "ritzy resort" on Hilton Head, she does not really give it a thought: she accepts the circumstances of her life as a given.

The highlight of Lara's young life is her election as homecoming queen of her high school. Shortly thereafter her life begins to fall apart, and she is forced to question her most basic assumptions about the world. The first sign of trouble is unexpected weight gain: a month after being crowned homecoming queen, Lara has gained ten pounds. Eventually, she gains one hundred pounds in a single year. As her perfect facade is shattered by this weight gain, at the same time her idealized home life begins to breaks down: her parents begin to quarrel, and her father finds reasons to go away on "business trips" that are later revealed to be visits to a mistress. At first, Lara believes that discipline will solve her weight problem: she will eat sensibly and exercise, and soon she will be her slender self again. She inexplicably continues to gain weight,

however, and her dieting becomes more extreme, until at one point she announces that she will stop eating entirely for five days. Much to her surprise, Lara finds that as she gains weight, people react differently to her than they did when she was the slim and attractive homecoming queen. Her father criticizes her rather than expressing affection; girls she thought were her friends make cruel remarks about her size; her mother accuses her of cheating on her diet; and even complete strangers feel free to make fun of her. Finally, she is diagnosed with a rare condition called Axell-Crowne Syndrome, in which the body hoards calories and thus a person who eats little continues to gain weight.

Lara hates being fat: she feels that she is no longer herself and at one point exclaims to her parents "I'd rather have cancer than this!" Life becomes a series of daily humiliations, and she withdraws from social activities, quits playing the piano, and even breaks up with her boyfriend because she feels he is no longer attracted to her. When her family moves to Detroit and she enters a new high school there, the humiliation continues: students go out of their way to torment her, including one boy who makes a play on her name by calling her "Lard-ass." At one point she takes refuge in the girls' restroom, still mystified by their cruelty: "I sat in that stall and cried. I felt defeated, worthless. I felt like less than nothing. Just because I was fat." Not long after this crisis, several students are kind to her and offer their friendship, but she is not sure she wants it. Lara does not truly want friends; she wants to be at the top of the high-school social structure. She still embraces that value system, within which the people offering her friendship are all losers, and if she accepts their friendship she will be admitting that she is a loser also.

Lara resumes playing the piano, which provides her both with an activity at which she can excel and a means to express herself. Equally importantly, music introduces her to new social contexts where she can meet people who are completely uninterested in the high-school social world. Her piano teacher is a large woman who offers sympathy and friendship, but Lara rejects her at first, still believing that she is superior because she was a slender homecoming queen only a year ago. Gradually, however, she manages to cast off the beauty-pageant value system and to accept herself and other people as they are. She finally concludes that life is unpredictable and that it is alright for her not to be perfect.

Discussion Questions

1. Why do you think Bennett attributes Lara's weight gain to a rare metabolic condition rather than overeating, heredity, or some other more common cause? How does your feeling about Lara change, depending on whether you consider her weight gain to be "her fault" or not?

2. How do the changes in the family dynamics of the Ardeche household mirror the changes in Lara's body (and social standing)?

3. When Lara is in the hospital having tests to see if the reason for her weight gain can be identified, her classmate Patty, who has a weight problem of her own, confronts her with a hard truth about herself. Lara rejects the message as merely a personal attack. By the end of the book does Lara understand what Patty was trying to say to her?

—*Sarah Boslaugh*

REFERENCE

Donna Smith, "*Life in the Fat Lane:* Author Cherie Bennett Tackles the Tough Subject of Kids and Weight," *Teenagers Today.com* <teenagerstoday. com/resources/articles/weight.htm> [accessed June 7, 2006].

Thomas Berger

(June 20, 1924 –   )

⁙
LITTLE BIG MAN

(New York: Dial, 1964)

JACK CRABB

Jack Crabb, the protagonist of Thomas Berger's novel *Little Big Man,* is interned in the Marville Center for Senior Citizens, purported to be 111 years old, and claims to be the only living survivor of the Battle of Little Big Horn. The supposed editor of the novel, Ralph Fielding Snell, suspects that Crabb is "a potential confidence man" but still transcribes Crabb's story. Snell declares that "Crabb seemed to specialize in the art and craft of coincidence," which warns the reader of the astonishing turns of chance that continuously bring Crabb into contact with many famous historical figures and events of the West.

Crabb's story begins with his boyhood as the son of a charlatan preacher. His father's desire to join up with the Mormons brings Crabb and his family west from Missouri and leads to the family's dissolution. After a group of Cheyenne attack Crabb's family and their fellow travelers, he finds himself fatherless. His older sister, Caroline, whose romanticism leads her to insist upon her own capture by the Cheyenne, takes Crabb along with her. Thus begins his seemingly lifelong movement between the white community and the Native American community, primarily the Cheyenne. Soon after entering the Cheyenne camp of Old Lodge Skins, Caroline abandons him and the Cheyenne, and Crabb is adopted by Old Lodge Skins and the tribe, whose name, Crabb relates, translates to "Human Beings." As a Cheyenne he earns the name Little Big Man. His subsequent travels take him back to Missouri, where he is adopted by the Reverend Pendrake. After running away from the Pendrakes, he returns to the Cheyenne, marries a Cheyenne bride, and then watches as George Armstrong Custer and his troops massacre most of his Cheyenne family. After swearing to revenge himself upon Custer, he wanders again, making money in the buffalo trade, adopting a prostitute as a daughter, and learning how to shoot from Wild Bill Hickok. Later, the Cheyenne kidnaps his white wife, Olga, a Scandinavian immigrant he meets while seeking his fortune out West, leading Crabb to return once more to Old Lodge Skins's tribe, only to find his wife and child have become the family of Younger Bear, his main rival among the Cheyenne. Eventually, he convinces Custer to allow him to serve as a scout at the Battle of Little Big Horn.

One of the central roles Crabb fulfills in the novel is giving the reader a firsthand witness to the history of the American West. Although Crabb's accounts often differ with popular accounts of the West, Berger did extensive research in order to, as he told interviewer Andrew Ward, "verify Jack's narrative." In discussing the unlikely sequence of events that

Crabb describes, Berger invoked his sense of fiction as "a magical means of overcoming the limitations of time, space, and physical possibility"; nonetheless, as others have suggested, it is actually possible for Crabb to have done and seen all that he claims.

Crabb, while the protagonist of this novel, cannot really be considered a hero. Rather, his character owes more to the venerable tradition of the traveling rogue or the more modern conception of the anti-hero. During Old Lodge Skins's initial attack on his family, Crabb responds not with heroic action, but by hiding and wetting himself in fear. Throughout the rest of the novel, he uses his intelligence to get himself out of situations, such as the deception he practices upon Hickok in order to survive a shootout with the legendary gunfighter.

Crabb struggles to understand exactly who he is. He begins the novel asserting, "I am a white man and never forgot it, but I was brought up by the Cheyenne Indians from the age of ten." However, the greater kindness shown to him by the Native Americans and particularly Old Lodge Skins makes readers wonder why Crabb continuously asserts his racial identity. He vacillates between a desire to live among the Indians and a desire to live among whites and supposed civilization, seemingly unable to be satisfied in either space—at least not for long. He often finds himself swept up by idealists and romantics, figures with what he calls a "positive vision," including his sister, Custer, and Old Lodge Skins. In contrast, Crabb sees himself as a realist, and in many ways he is. For example, his encounter with Hickok does not lead Crabb to romanticize gunfighting but instead to question the value of killing another man in a fight: "what did you establish when you found the better man?" Nevertheless, he concedes his weakness for romantics, and his interactions with Mrs. Pendrake and his adopted daughter, Amelia, and his last moments with Custer make evident his own romanticism. Crabb's contradictory positions surface when he discovers Mrs. Pendrake having an affair with a soda jerk, which leads him to declare, "I was finished with golden chalices that might get turned into slop jars." However, one page later, Crabb admits that "I love her still, for if you know anything about that kind of feeling, you know how close it is connected to hopelessness and thus is about the only thing in civilization that don't degenerate with time."

Crabb's movements throughout American history serve several purposes in the novel. First of all, he leads the reader to question the assumptions he or she has about life in the West. (In Snell's foreword, a nurse discredits Jack's tale by his absence from a movie about the Battle of Little Big Horn. This anecdote prefigures Crabb's tale, which questions the representations of history the reader has received and accepted as fact and truth.) Because Crabb's tale is episodic, because he explores a large section of America while calling into consideration racial prejudice, and because he frequently criticizes and becomes dissatisfied with civilization, he descends from a tradition of American literary heroes including James Fenimore Cooper's Natty Bumppo and Mark Twain's Huck Finn. Like Bumppo, Crabb lives among the Native Americans while also fighting against them. He also praises many aspects of their culture while insisting upon his whiteness. However, Berger seems much more intent on revealing the problems inherent in Crabb's judgments than Cooper was. Although Crabb shares many commonalities with Huck Finn—including his mixture of realism and sentimentality—Crabb grows up in the novel, or at least must join the adult world. In addition to these American antecedents, Crabb resembles other protagonists of satires, such as Jonathan Swift's Lemuel Gulliver, especially in that, like Gulliver, Crabb is both the vehicle for and the subject of satire.

Discussion Questions

1. In the first line of the novel proper, Crabb insists that "I am a white man and never forgot it, but I was brought up by the Cheyenne Indians from the age of ten." What is the significance of Crabb's immediate insistence upon his race? To what extent does he repeat this pattern of reiterating his race throughout the novel? Is the novel offering a critique of Crabb's conception of race and racial difference?

2. Throughout the novel, there are doubts cast upon Crabb's reliability as a narrator and whether the story he is telling is true. First, try to account for these instances when Crabb's veracity and honesty are called into question. Then, consider why Berger repeatedly includes such references in the novel. Is Berger offering a commentary on how history is recorded, or how accurate historical accounts can be? If so, what is the nature of that commentary?

3. In the chapter "My Niece Amelia," Crabb adopts a young prostitute who falsely claims to be related to Crabb. What motivates Crabb to adopt Amelia? What is the significance of her transformation? Why, once she changes, must they part ways? To what extent does this episode in the novel reveal many of the issues and ideas regarding family discussed elsewhere in the text?

4. How would you characterize Crabb's relationship with General Custer? Why does his attitude toward Custer change? Why is Crabb unable to kill Custer? Why does Crabb wish Old Lodge Skins to respect Custer? What is the significance of Old Lodge Skins's explanation to Crabb as to why Custer was not scalped during the Battle of Little Big Horn?

—*Michael Leigh Sinowitz*

OLD LODGE SKINS

Cheyenne Indian Old Lodge Skins is one of the central characters in Thomas Berger's novel *Little Big Man*. Throughout the novel, he is described through the perspective of Jack Crabb, named Little Big Man by Old Lodge Skins, the chief of his tribe, who adopts Crabb as a son. The novel comprises mostly the centenarian Crabb's narrative of his own life from roughly the age of ten through the death of Old Lodge Skins following the Battle of Little Big Horn.

Old Lodge Skins is introduced in a scene that mixes startling violence and black comedy. He and several fellow Cheyenne come across a band of white travelers, including Crabb and his family, as they head out west from Missouri seeking the Mormons. Looking for coffee, they are instead offered alcohol, which intoxicates them and precipitates a minor massacre, during which Crabb's father is killed. Old Lodge Skins returns with horses he wishes to offer as a form of reparation. In a parody of traditional captivity narratives, Crabb's sister, Caroline, runs away with the Cheyenne—Jack in tow—claiming they have demanded she accompany them to their camp. Caroline's romantic notion of Cheyenne life soon crumbles, and she abandons Jack, who thus becomes a part of Old Lodge Skins's family.

From this moment onward, Old Lodge Skins plays a central role in raising Crabb, and though Crabb frequently leaves his company over the course of his life, Old Lodge Skins always accepts his return without judgment. In an interview with Andrew Ward, Thomas Berger discusses the role Old Lodge Skins plays in Jack's life: "Having at a tender age lost his father, who was bonkers anyway, and getting small emotional benefit from his foster dad, the gluttonous gasbag Reverend Pendrake, young Jack would have been in grievous need of virile guidance had he not early acquired the protection of Old Lodge Skins." Early in his reminiscences, Crabb says that "in later years I grew greatly fond of Old Lodge Skins," in part because "he had more bad luck than any human being I have ever known, red or white, and you can't beat that for making a man likable." Old Lodge Skins's bad luck is symbolized by the jackrabbits that Crabb says appeared in large numbers whenever the chief ventured from his camp. The similarity between *jackrabbit* and *Jack Crabb* underscores that Crabb, too, reenters Old Lodge Skins's life at some of its worst moments, including Custer's massacre of the Cheyenne at the Washita River, an attack that leaves much of Old Lodge Skins's immediate family dead.

Old Lodge Skins reappears at the close of the novel after Custer dies (with Crabb by his side). Crabb takes Old Lodge Skins to visit the body of Custer, and he asks Jack to accompany him as he goes to the top of a vast hill and then passes away. Despite his initial appearance in the novel as a part of a massacre of settlers, Old Lodge Skins's position in the novel changes radically by the end. Through the character of Old Lodge Skins, Berger calls into question traditional portrayals of the American West, showing how Native Americans have been victimized by the European settlers' perception of them as noble savages. Perhaps the best-known literary examples of this stereotype are the Native American characters in James Fenimore Cooper's *The Last of the Mohicans* (1826), the noble and stoic Chingachgook and Uncas and the villainous Magua. Old Lodge Skins, according to Crabb, "started out as a buffoon," but that "was only around white men"—"Among the Cheyenne he was a sort of genius." Old Lodge Skins calls himself and the rest of the Cheyenne—as opposed to the white people—"human beings."

Crabb claims—with varying degrees of skepticism—that Old Lodge Skins actually possesses some of the fantastic or mystic powers he is said to practice. In one sequence he appears to summon a herd of pronghorn antelope so that they can be used to feed the Cheyenne, and after he loses his ability to see, he is able to still "see" in a figurative and spiritual sense and thus can be guided safely away from the Washita massacre. In this way, Old Lodge Skins is yet another of the figures with a "positive vision" to which Crabb has a "weakness." He offers Crabb a sense of what it means to support a family, to see that family is not tied up simply in notions of blood but, as Crabb later says, can be chosen by a kind of elective affinity. Old Lodge Skins's principal characteristic in the novel is his spirit of generosity and his profound gratefulness simply to have had a chance to live in the world. Despite the many setbacks he has faced and even his belief that the Cheyenne have lost the larger battle with the white men, he maintains a positive outlook on the world (as opposed to the white "civilization," often connected with destruction and extermination throughout the novel). In his dying speech he thanks "the Everywhere Spirit" for all of the good *and* the bad in his life: "Thank you for all of my victories and for all of my defeats. Thank you for my vision, and for the blindness in which I saw further."

Discussion Questions

1. Berger introduces Old Lodge Skins in a scene that, in part, reenacts the greatest fears of savagery associated with Native Americans, particularly during the time of the settlement of the West. Why do you think he places Old Lodge Skins in this role? To what extent—and through what deeds—is Old Lodge Skins rehabilitated for the reader later in the novel?

2. Examine the scene in which Crabb and Old Lodge Skins reunite following the Battle of Little Big Horn. Old Lodge Skins now believes that white men actually do know "how to die properly." What does he mean by this? How do these ideas about how to die properly represent competing views of the world and cultural differences between the Cheyenne and the white community?

3. What is the symbolic significance of Old Lodge Skins's loss of vision? Is Berger trying to suggest that Old Lodge Skins is unable to properly perceive the situation that he and the Cheyenne

find themselves in? What is the significance of Crabb guiding the blind Old Lodge Skins away from the massacre at the Washita River?

4. Old Lodge Skins's final words in the novel and in his life are addressed to the Everywhere Spirit and concern Jack Crabb: "Take care of my son . . . and see that he does not go crazy." What does this prayer suggest about Old Lodge Skins? Does it suggest that the reader should reevaluate Crabb's relationship with Old Lodge Skins?

—*Michael Leigh Sinowitz*

REFERENCES

Sherrill E. Grace, "Western Myth and Northern History: The Plains Indians of Berger and Wiebe," *Great Plains Quarterly*, 3 (1983): 146–156;

Brooks Landon, *Thomas Berger* (Boston: Twayne, 1989);

David W. Madden, *Critical Essays on Thomas Berger* (New York: G. K. Hall, 1995);

Leo E. Oliva, "Thomas Berger's Little Big Man as History," *Western American Literature*, 8 (1973): 33–54;

Michael Leigh Sinowitz, "The Western as Postmodern Satiric History: Thomas Berger's Little Big Man," *Clio*, 28 (1999): 129–148.

Alfred Bester
(December 18, 1913 – September 30, 1987)

THE STARS MY DESTINATION
(New York: New American Library, 1956)

GULLY FOYLE

Gulliver (Gully) Foyle is both the hero and the villain in Alfred Bester's novel *The Stars My Destination*. Foyle, a man of few skills and even less motivation, has drifted through life as a mechanic's mate third-class on a merchant marine spaceship. In the first few pages of the novel, he is the lone survivor of a mysterious accident that leaves his ship, the *Nomad*, crippled and drifting in space halfway between Mars and Jupiter. For nearly six months, he is forced to live inside a small storage locker on the oxygen-starved wreck. The defining moment in his life comes when he believes he has finally been rescued: the ship *Vorga* approaches his wreck. Even though he signals to them, they pass by without rescuing him. Dismayed, Foyle feels as if he has finally died and loses all hope. Yet, the abandonment saves him. To this point, he had shown no ambition, no drive. Now, motivated by rage, he dedicates his life to avenging himself against the crew of the *Vorga*. It is the first time that he "dies" and is figuratively reborn. The death and rebirth of Foyle is a theme that will be repeated throughout the novel. He begins his new life recovering from his ordeal on an inhabited asteroid. The people there tattoo onto his face a tiger pattern, which later becomes a powerful symbol of Foyle's inner conflict.

Back on Earth, Foyle attempts a direct confrontation with the owner of the *Vorga*, corporate magnate Presteign. When Foyle's attempts at violent retribution fail, he is jailed in a maximum security prison deep underground in France. There, he encounters a woman named Jizbella McQueen, who teaches him to think for the first time in his life, to solve problems using reason instead of strength. Together they escape through a dark, water-filled tunnel—another kind of rebirth. Jizbella helps him to arrange plastic surgery to disguise himself, but the surgery only partly succeeds. When his emotions run high, the invisible tiger-striped scars become clearly visible on his face. Nevertheless, Foyle reinvents himself once again as the outrageous Geoffrey Fourmyle of Ceres: ridiculous socialite, circus owner, and performer. In this disguise, he pursues his retribution, eluding both corporate and government power along the way. They wish to capture Foyle for another reason, as well: on board the *Nomad* was a secret weapon of incredible power, PyrE. Only Foyle knows where the wreck of the *Nomad* is hidden and can lead the competing interests to the weapon.

One by one, Foyle confronts the crew members of the *Vorga*, searching for the identity of the commander of the ship. He ruthlessly interrogates, tortures, and murders them in a single-minded pursuit of revenge. When he discovers the identity

of the commander of the *Vorga*—a woman whom he loves—he loses the desire to kill. Foyle gains, for the first time, some perspective on his life of empty violence and destruction: "I've come to my senses.... I've realized that I've been behaving like an animal." This realization is yet another figurative rebirth. Foyle takes the PyrE, which he had hidden in the basement of St. Patrick's Cathedral, and distributes the powerful explosive randomly to common people all over the world, thus depriving both corporate and government powers of exclusive access to the weapon. In this way, he states, "I've handed life and death back to the people who do the living and the dying. The common man's been whipped and led long enough by driven men like us."

Critical attention to the character of Foyle has brought new perspectives to the study of Bester's novel. Critic Adam Roberts places him within a long tradition of characters motivated solely by revenge. He likens *The Stars My Destination* to Jacobean revenge dramas such as Thomas Middleton's *The Revenger's Tragedy* (ca. 1607) and John Webster's *The Duchess of Malfi* (1614). Moreover, Roberts draws a parallel between Foyle and William Shakespeare's Othello and Hamlet. Not only Foyle, but the novel as a whole is "truly Shakespearean in scope, energy, vitality and character." Critic Donald Palumbo labels him as representative of the "monomyth," enacting the age-old story of the quest. In Palumbo's estimation, Foyle is an archetype for a questing character: thrust into an adventure he does not ask for, he faces and overcomes great difficulties. In the process, he defeats a nemesis. Then he returns to his world with a gift for the rest of humanity. Indeed, the trajectory of Foyle's character seems to include all of the human experience, from helplessness and rage to, finally, altruism and contentment. He is a character writ large, acting out on a stage much larger than life.

Foyle's intellectual and emotional growth is obvious. Indeed, his transformations are dramatic from the moment the *Vorga* abandons him and he decides to repair his ship and fly it somewhere to rescue himself. He begins life in the novel with no skills, no friends, no future, and no prospects. By overcoming each obstacle he faces, he gradually learns how to survive in the world, how to use all of his strengths—intellectual, spiritual, and physical—to cure the pain in his life. Not only that, the main conflict for Foyle changes significantly throughout the course of the novel. He mistakenly believes the conflict is an external one, him versus the crew and, especially, the commander of the *Vorga*. But he realizes gradually that he is battling against himself, his inner animal, symbolized by the tiger-mask scarring that appears when he lets his animalistic emotions run away from him. By overcoming his rage, by abandoning his revenge quest when it reaches the climax, he is able to develop that "rare disease called conscience" and fully come into his own, ready to return to his people and claim his destiny.

Discussion Questions

1. One important encounter Foyle has is with Jizbella McQueen. How does their relationship, which begins in the Geoffrey Martel prison, contribute to the growth and development of Foyle's character?

2. Foyle's most drastic emotional and physical change occurs when he transforms from Gully Foyle into Fourmyle of Ceres, the owner of Fourmyle Circus and a worldwide celebrity. Discuss this transformation. Does the earlier version of Foyle hint that a transformation to a person like Fourmyle is possible? What was it about Foyle's situation that led him to choose such an outlandish disguise?

3. It is easy to see Foyle as a Christ-like figure near the end of the novel, especially as he undergoes a kind of death in the lower levels of St. Patrick's Cathedral that is followed by a descent into a version of hell. After his resurrection on the other side of that death, Foyle emerges seemingly unencumbered even by the laws of physics: He can now psychically teleport across space and time. On the final page of the book, Foyle sleeps while his people "await the awakening." What message will Foyle bring to his people? Will he have anything profound to say? If so, what?

4. Foyle's grand gesture at the end of the story consists of distributing the power to destroy the world to the common people of the world. Foyle sees this act as one of empowerment. The government and military authorities see his act as irrespon-sible and incredibly dangerous. Who is correct? Will Foyle's act offer the world a better future?

—*William Gillard*

REFERENCES

Alfred Bester, *The Stars My Destination*, introduction by Paul Williams (Boston: Gregg, 1975);

Fiona Kelleghan, "Hell's My Destination: Imprisonment in the Works of Alfred Bester," *Science Fiction Studies*, 21, no. 3 (1994): 351–364;

Patrick A. McCarthy, "Science Fiction as Creative Revisionism: The Example of Alfred Bester's *The Stars My Destination*," *Science Fiction Studies*, 10, no. 1 (1983): 58–69;

Donald E. Palumbo, "The Monomyth in Alfred Bester's *The Stars My Destination*," *Journal of Popular Culture*, 38, no. 2 (2004): 333–368;

Carolyn Wendell, *Alfred Bester* (San Bernadino, Calif.: Borgo Press, 1982).

Ambrose Bierce
(June 24, 1842 – January 11, 1914)

ᦉ

"AN OCCURRENCE AT OWL CREEK BRIDGE"

Collected in *Tales of Soldiers and Civilians* (San Francisco: E. L. G. Steel, 1891).

PEYTON FARQUHAR

Peyton Farquhar, the main character of Ambrose Bierce's short story "An Occurrence at Owl Creek Bridge," is at the beginning of the story identified only as a man standing upon a railroad bridge in northern Alabama. His name is not given; he is isolated from the other members of the group of men on the bridge. With formal and objective description, the story indicates that Farquhar is about to be hanged. His hands are tied behind his back and a noose is draped around his neck. The tone remains unemotional, and the narrative focuses only on what seem to be the objective details of the process of hanging. The condemned man, apparently a gentleman, appraises coolly the mechanics of his hanging:

"The arrangement commended itself to his judgement as simple and effective."

Farquhar wishes to spend the last moments of his life thinking about his wife and children and closes his eyes. At this point his perceptions begin to become distorted. He hears a noise like the stroke of a blacksmith's hammer. It seems as slow as the tolling of a death knell, and it progressively gets slower and slower—"What he heard was the ticking of his watch."

Section 2 of the story provides a limited amount of background information concerning Farquhar. He is a member of an old and distinguished Alabama family, supports the Southern side in the Civil War, and looks for an opportunity to aid the cause. That opportunity seemed to come when a person who was apparently a Confederate soldier told him of Owl Creek Bridge. Farquhar resolves to burn the bridge, but the soldier is really a Union scout, and Farquhar is captured.

In section 3 of the story Farquhar believes that he has escaped from the people who were trying to hang him. In reality, he is hanged and is dying. His dying hallucinations are related to the reader without the story revealing them as such until the end. Bierce provides hints throughout the section that cast doubt on Farquhar's point of view. The light that he follows after he thinks the rope has broken, for example, can be compared to the light described by people who have undergone a near-death experience. He feels the pain in his neck, the irregular beating of his heart, and the swelling of his tongue but does not recognize it as a result of the hanging.

Bierce saves the reality of Farquhar's death for the surprise ending of the story, but prior to that he tries to provide a real sense of the hanged man as a person. He is depicted as a devoted family man, a quality emphasized in the final section of the story; Farquhar's fantasy of escape climaxes with his return to his wife and children. His neck snaps just as he imagines embracing them.

Discussion Questions

1. Besides those mentioned, what other hints do you see that Peyton Farquhar is not really free?

2. Why would a Union scout want to encourage Farquhar to try to burn the bridge at Owl Creek?

3. In what ways is Farquhar a victim of his social beliefs?

4. One of the major themes of literature is the disparity between appearances and reality. Besides those differences mentioned, what additional ones do you perceive in this story?

5. Ambrose Bierce's stories are known for their sardonic and cynical tone. Some argue that this story is typical of those attitudes. Others argue that this story is an exception. Based on his characterization of Farquhar, which do you think is the case?

—*Robert Dodge*

REFERENCES

Cathy N. Davidson, *Critical Essays on Ambrose Bierce* (Boston: G. K. Hall, 1982);

Robert C. Evans, ed., *Ambrose Bierce's "An Occurrence at Owl Creek Bridge": An Annotated Critical Edition* (West Cornwall, Conn.: Locust Hill Press, 2003);

Roy Morris, *Ambrose Bierce: Alone in Bad Company* (New York: Oxford University Press, 1999).

Earl Derr Biggers
(August 24, 1884 – April 5, 1933)

THE HOUSE WITHOUT A KEY
(Indianapolis: Bobbs-Merrill, 1925)

CHARLIE CHAN

Charlie Chan is a Chinese American police detective with the rank of sergeant who works for the Honolulu Police Department in Hawaii. He first appeared in 1925 in Earl Derr Biggers's novel *The House without a Key*. He was the main character in five more novels, the last of which, *Keeper of the Keys*, was published in 1932, before Biggers's death the following year. By this last novel, Chan had been promoted to inspector and had occasionally traveled far from Honolulu to investigate cases.

Biggers, an accomplished journalist and playwright, had once read about the exploits of a real Chinese detective in Hawaii, Chang Apana, and Apana's real-life example served as part of the inspiration for the character of Chan. Biggers, in creating his sleuth, wanted to work against a stereotype of the evil Chinese villain that had prevailed since the nineteenth century in mystery and sensational fiction.

In contrast to evil geniuses such as Sax Rohmer's Dr. Fu Manchu, Charlie Chan is a happily married father of eleven children. A traditionalist torn by the often-conflicting values of East and West, Chan is generally bemused, if not alarmed, by the habits and activities of his Americanized children. He talks in pidgin English, with convoluted syntax, and his speech is peppered with Confucian-style aphorisms, such as "The fool in a hurry drinks his tea with the fork." Chan's slightly exotic manner, which sometimes exposes him to prejudice and ridicule, leads many to underestimate his keen intelligence. In *The House without a Key*, elderly spinster Miss Minerva Winterslip, member of a proud Boston family, tells Chan she does not approve of Confucius's "do-nothing doctrine." Chan responds in typical fashion: "Humbly asking pardon to mention it, I detect in your eyes slight flame of hostility. Quench it, if you will be so kind. Friendly cooperation are essential between us." From that point on, Chan quickly wins the respect and trust of Miss Winterslip and a young scion of her family. Through Chan, Biggers demonstrated that a Chinese detective could become a hero.

Though he is a member of a police department, Chan generally functions as a one-man force. He is cast in the mold of detectives such as Hercule Poirot or Sherlock Holmes. The six Charlie Chan books are not police procedurals. Chan operates by such activities as gathering evidence from the crime scene, watching suspects and finding clues to their motivations, and reading through newspapers for information. From this data, he isolates the essential clue that leads him to the identity of the murderer. Though he deals with other crimes, such as jewel thefts and robberies, it is murder that arouses Charlie's fiercest desires to see justice done. He often interprets crimes as personal affronts, particularly if he perceives that he has "lost face" because of something that has happened during his investigation. For example, in *The Black Camel*, when he has been tricked by the killer, he tells those touched by the crime, "I give you my word . . . the person who struck that blow will pay. I am in no mood that turns the other cheek tonight." He is often philosophical, however, over the tribulations he faces as a policeman in the course of his duty. As he explains at the end of *The Black Camel*, "as you know, my friend, a gem is not polished without rubbing nor a man perfected without trials."

Interactions with his family bring to the fore Chan's often wry humor. In *Charlie Chan Carries On*, when son Henry cheekily asks to use his father's car while Chan is away, he replies, "Yes, you may use my car, but please treat it with unusual kindness. Do not continually demand more than it has to give, like speed-mad young people you imitate."

Biggers wrote only six Charlie Chan novels, but they were successful. The character has remained in the popular imagination thanks primarily to the movies that have featured him.

Discussion Questions

1. How does Earl Derr Biggers's portrayal of Charlie Chan differ from depictions of Chinese characters in mysteries prior to 1925? Characters from other works you may consider include Ernest Bramah's Kai Lung and Sax Rohmer's Fu Manchu.

2. Choose a specific book in the series. Contrast Charlie Chan's detective methods with those of sleuths such as Sherlock Holmes and Hercule Poirot—does Chan function more as a policeman or as a private detective?

3. How does Charlie Chan use his own culture to his advantage as a detective? For example, does he use anti-Asian prejudice to make suspects discount his intelligence?

—*Dean James*

REFERENCE

T. J. Binyon, *Murder Will Out: The Detective in Fiction* (Oxford: Oxford University Press, 1989), pp. 99–100.

Francesca Lia Block

(December 3, 1962 –   )

༄

WEETZIE BAT

(New York: Harper & Row, 1989)

WEETZIE BAT

Weetzie Bat is the free-spirited central character in Francesca Lia Block's novel *Weetzie Bat,* which has been augmented by three sequels about Weetzie and her extended family: *Witch Baby* (1991), *Cherokee Bat and the Goat Guys* (1992), and *Missing Angel Juan* (1993)—and a prequel, *Baby-Bop* (1995), in the collection *Dangerous Angels: The Weetzie Bat Books* (1998). In 2005 Block returned to Weetzie in an adult novel, *Necklace of Kisses,* which depicts the character at age forty.

When asked about the origin of Weetzie, Block responded in an interview in the *School Library Journal* that as a teenager she saw a "bubblegum pink" Ford Pinto with the license plate WEETZIE on the freeway in the San Fernando Valley: "And there's this bleach-blond head of this girl in this car. All of a sudden she was just this person—a name and an image can just inspire you to *create.* So I started writing these little stories, and she eventually became my alter ego." Weetzie is also a product of her setting, Los Angeles, which the characters alternately call "Shangri-LA" and "Hell-A." Weetzie discovers who she is and what matters to her against a backdrop of Los Angeles freeways, old Hollywood landmarks, punk clubs, and many varied eateries (food is also an important connector of individuals in the novels). *Weetzie Bat* is episodic, more a set of linked short stories than a single narrative.

Weetzie initially is an outsider. She befriends Dirk because he, with his towering black Mohawk and red 1955 Pontiac, is the only one in their school who understands her, a girl with bleached blond hair who wears pink harlequin sunglasses, a feathered headdress, and 1950s taffeta dresses on which she has written poetry in glitter. Weetzie's parents are divorced. Her father, a former screenwriter and a drug addict, has moved to New York.

Weetzie lives with her mother, a fading starlet who does not understand or accept Weetzie's interests any more than Weetzie's peers at school do. Although she appears flamboyant and unconcerned with others' perceptions of her, Weetzie, like many characters in coming-of-age fiction, is nonetheless seeking love and acceptance without having to sacrifice her independence. After learning that Dirk is gay, Weetzie, in a nod to the story of Aladdin and his magic lamp, wishes on an old lamp for them both to find love.

Block has been compared to S. E. Hinton and Robert Cormier for her willingness to write about controversial subjects. The family eventually formed by Dirk, Weetzie, their lovers, and their children certainly qualifies as unconventional. After Weetzie makes her wish, Dirk finds a blond surfer named Duck, and Weetzie finds Max, whom she calls My Secret Agent Lover Man. Weetzie has a child that could have been fathered by any of the three men, and the family also chooses to raise Max's child by another woman, Vixanne Wigg. Weetzie, with her optimism and love, holds the family together. As she thinks at the end of the novel, "I don't know about happily ever after . . . but I know about happily." Block told the *School Library Journal:* "My ultimate fantasy was to find my own family, to create a nonjudgmental, very loving, unusual, beautiful little family in a perfect little environment, where we could live in that alter-ego world, where everything was full of magic."

Many critics read *Weetzie Bat* as fantasy. There is certainly an element of wish fulfillment, as Weetzie reconciles with both her parents, finds the family she has always wanted, and lives a creative, stimulating life without the need to work at any kind of regular job. She and her family live in a cottage inherited by Dirk from his grandmother. Not surprisingly, some have called the book a literary fairy tale. Block has acknowledged in interviews that she was inspired by reading the magic realist novel *One Hundred Years of Solitude* (1967; translated 1970), by Gabriel García Márquez, to blend magic with realism in her work. Since *Weetzie Bat,* other young adult writers have used magic realism; however, none has matched Block's edgy, urban setting and characters.

Not only is the setting true to Los Angeles in the early 1980s, but for all its fantastic and even comic elements the book does not avoid difficult issues. Weetzie does get her wishes, but she still has to cope with her father's death, her mother's alcoholism, her lover's depression, and the anxieties of modern urban life. Her beloved Hollywood is changing; pollution is destroying the environment; and people are dying from a new and terrible disease, AIDS. Weetzie may be funny at times and talk in a high-pitched, squeaky voice, but she is not a cartoon character, nor is her life a comic strip.

Weetzie is a distinctive character in young adult literature. She inhabits a magical world of alternative popular culture and challenges mainstream cultural boundaries in her lifestyle. Nonetheless, she also represents strong positive values in her capacity for love, forgiveness, and tolerance. She creates a circle of friends, lovers, adults, and children from different cultures who honor and respect one another, forming an artistic community and a nontraditional extended family. Despite the inevitable challenges of loss and sorrow, Weetzie maintains her ability to see wonder in everyday life. Looking at her family gathered around the kitchen table after Dirk and Duck have returned from a trip to deal with the death of Duck's former lover from AIDS, she sees them full of love, "lit up and golden like a wreath of lights." Weetzie acknowledges that life can be frightening but stresses that people can and must choose love over fear.

—*Terri Doughty*

Discussion Questions

1. Francesca Lia Block has said that she is inspired by fairy tales in her writing. Can you find references to fairy tales in *Weetzie Bat* (for example, when Weetzie is grieving her father's death, she is described as "the girl in the fairy tale sleeping in a prison of thorns and roses"). How do these references add meaning to the novel? Is Weetzie a typical fairy-tale heroine?

2. Weetzie's parents are divorced and she does not have a happy family life as a child. How does this affect her views on family? How is her nontraditional family with Dirk, Duck, and My Secret Agent Lover Man a response to her childhood family?

3. Francesca Lia Block says that she was inspired to write stories about Weetzie after seeing a girl in a pink car on the freeway. Clearly, Weetzie develops as a product of Los Angeles, which the characters call both "Shangri-LA" and "Hell-A." How is the city both of these things, and how does each affect Weetzie?

4. At different points in the novel, Weetzie confronts the loss, or near loss, of a loved one: My Secret Agent Lover Man gives in to depression and leaves Weetzie for a while; her father dies; and Dirk leaves to find Duck, who has run away after finding out a former lover is dying of AIDS. How do these events affect Weetzie's understanding of love?

REFERENCES

Patricia Campbell, "People are Talking About . . . Francesca Lia Block," *Horn Book,* 69 (January/ February 1993): 57–63;

Dangerous Angels: The Weetzie Bat Books (New York: HarperCollins, 1998);

David Levithan, "Wild Thing," *School Library Journal,* 51, no. 6 (June 2005): 44–47.

Edward Bloor
(October 12, 1950 –   )

ఴ

TANGERINE
(San Diego: Harcourt Brace, 1997)

PAUL FISHER

Paul Fisher, the first-person narrator of Edward Bloor's first novel, *Tangerine,* begins his story as he and his family (father, mother, and brother Erik) are moving to Tangerine County, Florida. Paul is visually impaired, but as Bloor has noted, he "struggles mightily to lead a normal life and to see things as they really are despite the thick-framed glasses that cover his injured eyes." The ability to see truly marks a key distinction between characters. Paul claims early in the novel that "I can see things that mom and dad can't. Or won't." Paul is afraid of his bullying older brother and alienated from his father, who is obsessed with his older son's potential as a star football player and has no time for his younger son. Paul is an athlete as well, a soccer player, and he is angry that his father never notices his achievements. Paul is closer to his mother, though she refuses to acknowledge the tensions in the family and is not always aware of Paul's emotions and needs.

Paul's story is a combination of genres: school fiction, sports fiction, and the coming-of-age novel. Paul attends two schools—first, the affluent Lake Windsor High School, where he is not allowed to play soccer because of his disability and where he classifies himself a "freak" and second, after a sinkhole damages Lake Windsor, Tangerine Middle School, a school with a mostly lower-income Hispanic student body, where, so he can play soccer, he ensures no one knows about his disability. Paul, who sees so clearly the differences between his parents' reality and his own, also sees the differences in class and ethnicity between himself and his classmates; yet, he does not allow these differences to interfere with forming friendships with them. Persevering through their initial suspicion of him, Paul creates a place for himself, finding a substitute family in Luis, Tino, and Theresa Cruz; helping on the Cruz family citrus farm, Paul earns the respect and affection he wants from his own family. In an interview, Bloor stated that he found inspiration in the transition Florida was undergoing between the old citrus economy and a new, more diversified economy: *Tangerine* "is about both the people who are moving out and the people who are moving in." Paul is the only character "moving in" who comes to understand those already long established in Tangerine County.

In the same interview, Bloor reports that his favorite reading as a child was sports stories. Paul is clearly in the tradition of the underdog: like another popular boy character of the 1990s, J. K. Rowling's Harry Potter, Paul has his moments of triumph on the playing field, proving his worth by helping his team achieve victory. In Paul's conflict with his father and brother, Bloor appears to critique sports celebrities who get away with criminal behavior: Erik embodies a link between sports and violence. Paul too seems implicated in this association, as his soccer team is called the War Eagles; he likens one of their games to a war, and he proves himself to his team by fighting an opponent. The War Eagles are

an unusual team in the league, however, not only because they are from a lower-income school, but also because they are the only team with female players and a female coach. Despite these progressive elements, Paul clearly enjoys the thrill of belonging to a team that inspires fear in its opponents, instead of being afraid, as he usually is around his brother. Above all, he enjoys his acceptance as a "brother" to his teammates.

Paul's journey in the book is one toward self-knowledge and self-respect. His successes in Tangerine County give him the confidence to stand up for himself. Paul's ultimate defiance of Erik triggers his memory of how his eyes were damaged, leading to a cathartic confrontation with his parents in which he releases his rage at them and lets go of his self-hatred. As he tells a friend, "I *am* all right. I'm more than all right. Finally." Paul is the sole witness to his brother planning an attack on Luis that kills him. His finding the courage to tell everyone what he has seen signifies Paul's maturity. An older athlete tells Paul that "the truth shall set you free," and so it does. Although the novel ends with him expelled from school and his family's facade of middle-class success shattered, he is ultimately optimistic. As his father drives him to his third school of the year, Paul sees in the citrus groves along the roadside "a golden dawn."

Ever since J. D. Salinger introduced Holden Caulfield in *The Catcher in the Rye* (1951), the high-school student who struggles to reconcile his or her view of the world with that of adults has been a staple in young adult fiction. Another popular topic in young adult fiction is the protagonist who must find courage to assert his or her belief in what is right and wrong despite opposition. *Tangerine* can be seen as a more positive take on themes addressed in Robert Cormier's *The Chocolate War* (1974). Unlike Cormier's Jerry Renault, Paul triumphs, for everyone accepts his version of events and their meaning as the "real truth."

Discussion Questions

1. On several occasions, Paul challenges his father's eyesight and that of other adults in the novel. Why is Paul the only one who can see the truth about his brother?

2. Paul discovers that his parents knew the truth about his eye injury and yet they allowed him to blame himself for it, as they did not want him to hate his brother. Was their concern justified?

3. Lake Windsor Downs is built over the top of old citrus groves, and decaying vegetable matter leads to muck fires, mosquito infestations, and sinkholes; even the landscape seems to reject the newcomers to Florida. How does Paul, an alien figure to the students at Tangerine Middle School, find acceptance there?

4. Compare Paul's soccer career to Erik's football career. Would Paul like to be in Erik's place?

5. In his second novel, *Crusader,* Bloor's Roberta, like Paul, confronts racial and ethnic prejudice in her community, as well as crime in her family. Do both books display similar attitudes toward these issues? Do both protagonists play similar roles in resolving the issues?

—*Terri Doughty*

REFERENCES

Holly Atkins, "Enjoy this Tangerine," *St. Petersburg Times,* February 18, 2002, D6;

Terri Doughty, "Locating Harry Potter in the 'Boy's Book' Market," in *The Ivory Tower and Harry Potter,* edited by Lana Whited (Columbia: University of Missouri Press, 2002), pp. 243–257.

Judy Blume

(February 12, 1938 –   )

❦
ARE YOU THERE, GOD? IT'S ME, MARGARET

(Englewood Cliffs, N.J.: Bradbury, 1970)

MARGARET SIMON

Margaret Simon, the first-person narrator of Judy Blume's novel *Are You There, God? It's Me, Margaret,* has remained a favorite of preteen girls since the book was published in 1970. Margaret's heartfelt and realistic coming-of-age questions about making friends, fitting in, and understanding the equally confusing issues of puberty and religion still ring true. The much-loved

only child of a Jewish father and a mother whose fundamentalist parents wrote their daughter off when she married, Margaret lives in a home where religion is a banned topic. "Margaret doesn't even go to Sunday school—or Hebrew school," her new friends marvel. But she does confide in her personal God about the things sixth-grade girls think about: boys, breasts, and menstruation.

Moose Freed, the older boy who cuts the Simons's grass, captures Margaret's attention completely: "I liked the way he sang as he worked. I also liked his teeth. I saw them when he smiled at me. They were very clean and white and one in the front was a little crooked." Margaret's absorption in Moose's work is so intense that she almost refuses when her mother invites her to shop for her first "Gro-Bra," a Dacron contraption designed for those who "are not quite ready for a double A," as the Lord and Taylor saleswoman suggests. Later, at home in the privacy of her closet, Margaret tests out the "gro" theory by stuffing socks in each side of the bra, and she discovers she "liked the way it looked." The final obsession, menstruation, is one Margaret shares with her new friends, the PTS's, or Pre-Teen Sensations. They are pitted against one another to see who will be the first to begin her period. Conspicuously absent from the clique is Laura Danker, the beautiful and buxom sixth grader who is so well developed that she has no need for the exercises the PTS's do, in unison, while chanting "We must, we must, we must increase our busts."

Margaret is a good girl, with a highly developed conscience, but she is not a goody-goody. When her classmates decide to torture Mr. Benedict, their first-year teacher, by refusing to put their names on their history tests, Margaret goes along with the crowd but fumes inwardly. She empathizes with Mr. Benedict's newcomer status, and when he assigns all sixth graders to do a yearlong independent study, she obeys willingly. While her classmates groan loudly about the additional work, Margaret cheerfully decides her topic will be religion, reasoning that "if I could figure out which religion to be I'd know if I wanted to join the Y or the Jewish Community Center." After asking God for his opinion, declaring, "I won't make any decisions without asking you first," she makes plans to research Judaism by accompanying her beloved Grandma Simon to temple on Rosh Hashannah. She promises, "I'll look for you God. I've never been inside a temple or a church." Margaret's intensity and dedication are highlighted by her focus on this religious research, which also takes her to a Methodist service as well as a Catholic Mass and confessional.

Margaret is a careful observer, one who notices everything and cares deeply about others' feelings. She is tolerant of her mother, Barbara, who dabbles in art in her lonely suburban home just like all the others on the block. When her mother is in a hurry to drive the group home too early from a long-awaited square dance, Margaret understands that she is "in the middle of a painting . . . a lot of different fruits in honor of Thanksgiving." She notes that although her mother gives paintings away every Christmas, her father thinks "they wind up in other people's attics." At Margaret's first "supper party" during the holidays, when she ends up in the closed-door kissing game with the dreaded Norman Fishbein, she is too careful of his feelings to tell him how appalled she is by the situation. When he pleads, "I really like you Margaret. How do you want me to kiss you?" she answers simply, "On the cheek and fast."

Margaret's sensitivity gets a strong challenge when her maternal grandparents, the evangelical Hutchins from Ohio, decide to reacquaint themselves with their daughter and her family during a visit over spring break. Margaret, who had been anticipating a vacation visit to Florida with Grandma Simon, has to forfeit the trip. As her maternal grandparents walk down the airplane stairs, clutching each other, Margaret astutely takes stock of their appearance and her father's pressed lips and difficulty talking; she thinks, "This is harder on my father than it is on me."

During a strained family dinner—"really fancy . . . the kind mother usually has when I'm sent to bed early and there are flowers on the table and a hired lady to wash dishes"—Margaret hears her mother apologize that they will not be able to use the living room. Barbara makes the excuse that the room is empty because she has just ordered new furniture. Although Margaret knows that this boast is not true, she intuits her mother's need to emphasize the Simons's happiness and material wealth, thinking, "I knew she hadn't ordered anything. But I didn't tell." Margaret's newfound grandparents totally lack sensitivity, however, and when they persist in ignoring her feelings by talking about her as if she were not present, Margaret reverts to more-typical preteen behavior: shouting and storming up to her own room.

Margaret is memorable and lovable because of this realism, because of her believable and serious thoughts about issues that all twelve-year-olds consider earthshaking. A good girl who strives to find God and to be a good friend, daughter, and granddaughter, Margaret makes an excellent companion for young readers who are perplexed by their families, their bodies, and their entry into adolescence.

Discussion Questions

1. Many libraries have experienced challenges to Blume's books, primarily because of her candor in discussing bodily functions. Do you agree that Blume is too direct in describing physical details? Why do you think she does include these details?

2. Most of the time Margaret is quite sensitive and kind. However, there are several moments in which she is hurtful to others. Describe these moments and explain what you believe causes her to lash out.

—*Harriett S. Williams*

FOREVER . . .

(Scarsdale, N.Y.: Bradbury, 1975)

KATHERINE DANZIGER

Katherine Danziger is the seventeen-year-old protagonist of Judy Blume's *Forever . . .*, one of the earliest and most widely read young adult novels. During her senior year of high school, Katherine falls in love with Michael Wagner and the two become inseparable, but during the summer before college, their relationship falters and then painfully dissolves. Blume's willingness to narrate not only the thrill of young romance but also the curiosity, ambivalence, joy, and frustration experienced by teenagers as they initiate and grow comfortable in a sexual relationship broke new ground when the novel was published.

One of the most inviting aspects of Katherine is her honesty. *Forever . . .* is told primarily in

Katherine's first-person, present-tense narration, though letters are used late in the novel as well. The reader's sense that Katherine is telling the full truth when she describes her relationships with friends and family makes her a compelling narrator as she moves into emotionally difficult terrain regarding her own sexuality. Early in the novel she admits that she might be a bit insecure and prone to sarcasm when she first meets an interesting guy, but her self-awareness only makes her seem more reliable.

Katherine is also responsible and confident about her decisions and abilities. She ended her previous relationship with a boy named Tommy Aronson because he tried to pressure her into having sex. Yet, after she does become sexually active with Michael, she makes an appointment at Planned Parenthood to ensure that her activity does not result in an unwanted pregnancy or venereal disease. Two of Katherine's friends serve as foils in the novel. Her best friend, Erica, wavers between an eagerness to lose her virginity and a desire to abstain until she is in a strong relationship. Erica's involvement with Artie, a young man unsure about his own sexual orientation, complicates matters for her. Katherine also cannot help but compare herself to Sybil, an acquaintance with a high IQ, a variety of sexual partners, and an unwanted pregnancy.

In addition to the often-taboo topic of teenage sexuality, Blume briefly touches on alcohol and drug use. In these areas, Katherine is conservative. In one episode she demonstrates her maturity when Michael and Erica attempt to ease their distress over Artie's suicide attempt by getting drunk, and she carefully remains sober in order to drive them home safely.

Throughout the novel, Blume emphasizes Katherine's utter normalcy. Unlike her younger sister, Jamie, she has no special talents or career aspirations. She does well in school without particularly excelling. She has no conflicts with classmates or teachers. She gets along easily with her parents, and they even like Michael; they are merely skeptical of the growing insularity between the two of them. The only crises that mar Katherine's world are Artie's suicide attempt, which results in his finally getting help, and the death of her ailing grandfather, which is sad but neither unexpected nor tragic. Consequently,

the focal point of Katherine becomes her sexuality, as a healthy, untroubled part of her life. *Forever . . .* acknowledges the existence of venereal disease, pregnancy, and peer pressure, but these dangers do not define Katherine's experience of sexuality. Instead, the book focuses upon her curiosity, her thoughtfulness, her passion, and her somewhat uncomfortable discovery that physical attraction and romantic love are complex and dynamic experiences.

Discussion Questions

1. Is Katherine a good friend? Consider her relationship to and treatment of Erica, Michael, Artie, and Nan as you formulate an answer.

2. Censors opposed to Blume's novel have described it as a how-to manual for teenagers interested in sex. Is this a fair evaluation of the novel? How important is sex in Katherine's relationship with Michael?

3. *Forever . . .* was written before AIDS was named as a disease. The devastating consequences of HIV and AIDS changed how people, including teenagers, think and act in regard to sex. Compare Katherine's attitudes about sexual health and responsibility with those of a teenage character in a novel set in the present day, such as Sarah Dessen's *The Truth about Forever* (2004) or Megan McCafferty's *Sloppy Firsts* (2001).

4. Are Katherine's parents right or wrong to make her accept the job at Foxy's summer camp? Why?

5. Blume has been both lauded and attacked for being nonjudgmental in her portrait of teenage life. Generally, this means she does not foist her own opinions about moral and ethical behavior on her readers. *Forever . . .* includes scenes with drugs and alcohol in addition to sex, and both adoption and abortion are discussed. How would you describe the moral beliefs of Katherine?

—*Megan Lynn Isaac*

REFERENCES

Diana Gleasner, "Judy Blume," in *Breakthrough: Women in Writing* (New York: Walker, 1980), pp. 15–41;

John Gough, "Reconsidering Judy Blume's Young Adult Novel *Forever . . . ,*" *Use of English*, 36 (Spring 1985): 29–36;

Jen Jones, *Judy Blume: Fearless Storyteller for Teens* (Berkeley Heights, N.J.: Enslow, 2008);

Mark Oppenheimer, "Why Judy Blume Endures," *New York Times Book Review*, p. 16;

Susan Thompson, "Images of Adolescence: Part 1," *Signal*, 34 (January 1981): 37–59;

Maryann N. Weidt, *Presenting Judy Blume* (New York: Twayne, 1990).

Paul Bowles

(December 30, 1910 – November 18, 1999)

〰️

THE SHELTERING SKY

(London: Lehmann, 1949; New York: New Directions, 1949)

KIT MORESBY

Kit Moresby, along with her husband, Port, and their companion, Tunner, are American travelers in the North African Sahara in Paul Bowles's novel *The Sheltering Sky*. Gena Dagel Caponi suggests that *The Sheltering Sky* is "the first 'road novel' of the 1950s, a period in America when travel was, once again, synonymous with self-discovery." But as Paul Fussell has written, travel after World War II was problematic, a time of "post-tourism," when the disillusionment of travel, devoid of romantic transcendence, was all that could be expected in the nuclear age. Port and Kit have managed to avoid the war by staying on the move. This trip to the interior of the North African Sahara is a last-ditch effort to penetrate some geographical and psychological interior. Instead, what they find is the limitless nothingness behind the paradox of a "sheltering sky."

Even though Port considers himself "the protagonist, Kit the spectator" in their lives, his death from meningitis or cholera—two-thirds of the way through the novel and deep in the desert—allows Kit to emerge as the true center of consciousness in the novel. The centrality of her point of view is hinted at early on in the vivid description of her eyes, especially "the intensity of her gaze," around which "the rest of her face grew vague," suggesting perhaps that her identity will be lost in the intensity of her search, with "only the piercing, questioning violence of the wide eyes" remaining.

Despite a deep connection on the level of consciousness, Port and Kit seem incapable of connecting physically. Kit relies on Port for direction, so when he refuses to direct her, Tunner is there to offer his assistance and seduces her. Tunner is handsome but shallow, although he likes being around Kit and Port because they are "beings who dealt almost exclusively with ideas, sacred things." Like many events in the novel that seem inevitable, their inclusion of Tunner in their travel plans seems calculated to keep the couple at a distance from each other. They sleep in separate rooms, and Port seeks out prostitutes. On a bike ride to the top of a mountain in chapter 13, Port presses her hand, but that is as close as they come to a passionate sexual connection.

Kit constantly relies on others—especially men—to help her navigate the world and to define her. After Port's death, she bathes in a fountain, a sort of moonlight baptism before she disappears into the emptiness of the desert, where she can bury her old self and invent a new one. At times she is aware of playing a "game" of willful amnesia, as though now she can make her own omens, "*be* them," implying some "further possibility in existence." Taken up by a Bedouin caravan, Kit is shared by Belqassim and his partner, which is reminiscent of how Port in effect shared her with Tunner. Belqassim treats her increasingly like a piece of property, especially after she becomes one of his many wives. Like the other women of Belqassim's harem, she knows that all decisions about their future are "being made far beyond them," so nothing much has changed from the beginning of the novel where she realized that "Other people rule my life."

On her return to civilization, Kit is picked up by a consular officer, Miss Ferry, who assures her that her luggage is not lost, since nothing really disappears in the desert. Yet Kit insists: "Everything's lost." Kit herself is lost, but she is not sure she wants to be found. So when Miss Ferry says that Tunner is waiting for her, she hops a streetcar that goes to "the end of the line," on which note the novel ominously ends.

Bowles admitted that Port and Kit "began as painfully close representations" of himself and his wife, Jane, herself a successful writer, who felt that her depiction in the novel was "cruel." Later, however, the characters "acquired autonomous identities," providing "the emotional tension" rather than the plot providing it. Part of this emotional tension might be attributed to Paul and Jane's sexuality (Paul was homosexual, Jane bisexual). As Bowles told interviewer Paul Evans, however, the true protagonist of the novel is the desert.

The title is ironic. The sky provides no shelter from the nothingness that, in Port's view, the sky conceals and reveals. Late in the novel, Amar, a policeman who first helps Kit and then steals from her, says: "The head is like the sky," always turning and going too fast. Thinking too much about the past drives one crazy: "life is a cliff, and you must never turn around and look back when you're climbing. It makes you sick." Kit recalls that someone once said "the sky hides the night behind it, shelters the person beneath from the horror that lies above." Port made this statement, but Kit seems to be following Amar's advice in forgetting. Post-touristic travel, it seems, causes the traveler who penetrates to the interior to see through romantic illusions into the "severe clear" of reality, without the "sheltering sky."

—*Richard Collins*

Discussion Questions

1. Since Port Moresby dies long before the end of the book, Kit emerges as the true protagonist of the novel. Locate the point at which Kit takes over as the center of the novel. Look up the literary term *chiasmus* and explain how it applies to this novel.

2. In chapter 13, when Port and Kit ride bicycles to the top of a ridge, they come as close as they ever will to connecting. They talk about the sky, what is behind it, and what it is protecting them from. The chapter ends with Port's pressing her hand. In the Bernardo Bertolucci movie version of Bowles's novel, Port and Kit make love. How does this addition alter the meaning of the scene?

3. Alice B. Toklas wrote to Bowles that no novel since *The Great Gatsby* (1925) had impressed her so much, and that with a limited number of characters

he had portrayed "an epoch." But she wished that he had "compressed" the section she called "Kit in the Sahara," presumably the last third of the novel, and wanted him to explain to her its inclusion. Explain its inclusion.

REFERENCES

Gena Dagel Caponi, *Paul Bowles* (New York: Twayne, 1998);

Jeffrey Miller, *Paul Bowles: A Descriptive Bibliography* (Santa Barbara, Calif.: Black Sparrow, 1986);

Richard F. Patteson, *A World Outside: The Fiction of Paul Bowles* (Austin: University of Texas Press, 1987);

Wayne Pounds, *Paul Bowles: The Inner Geography* (New York: Peter Lang, 1985);

Lawrence D. Stewart, *Paul Bowles: The Illumination of North Africa* (Carbondale: Southern Illinois University Press, 1974).

Kay Boyle
(February 19, 1902 – December 27, 1992)

"THE WHITE HORSES OF VIENNA"
Collected in *The White Horses of Vienna and Other Stories* (New York: Harcourt, Brace, 1936).

DR. HEINE

Dr. Heine is one of three central characters in Kay Boyle's story "The White Horses of Vienna," which depicts the rise of Nazism in Austria. The seeds for the story can be found in the compendium *365 Days,* a collection of sketches by various authors, which Boyle edited and published in 1936 while living in Austria. In Boyle's piece for January 29, "Austrian Nazis Continue to Demonstrate Despite Warning by Pocket Chancellor," she slips into the role of a Nazi sympathizer who lights candles in the shape of a swastika. Boyle expanded this material significantly in "The White Horses of Vienna" by adding the figure of Dr. Heine, a young Jewish student doctor, who is sent by a Viennese hospital to a small Alpine village in order to temporarily replace the ailing village physician. In the first three pages of the tripartite story, which is told in the third-person from a limited omniscient point of view, the stage is set and the village doctor and his wife are introduced. The unnamed doctor has sought refuge in the remote Alpine region, because he, unlike Heine, feels uncomfortable in the cities he has lived in. His face is described as "split in two, with one side of it given to resolve and the other to compassion," which suggests his complicated personality.

When Heine arrives, he is met by animosity. As the wife observes his dark, alien face, the quality of his skin, and the arch of his nose, her prejudices about Jews come to the surface: "So much had she heard about Jews that the joints of his tall, elegant frame seemed oiled with some special, suave lubricant that was evil, as a thing come out of the Orient, to their clean, Nordic hearts." Recalling the myth of Ahasverus, the Jewish shoemaker who insulted Jesus and who was doomed to wander the length and breadth of the earth, never to find peace, until the Day of Judgment, Heine is regarded as "a wanderer whose people had wandered from country to country and whose sons must wander, having no land to return to in the end." The wife shows some humanity toward him when his coat catches fire—she smothers the fire with a rug and even offers to mend the coat. However, the racial prejudice inculcated in her eventually surfaces: "And then she bit her lip suddenly and stood back, as if she had remembered the evil thing that stood between them." The village doctor, on the other hand, does not exhibit racial prejudice even though he is a Nazi sympathizer. When his wife objects to Heine's presence because of his race, the husband responds that it was not a good thing for the young man being sent to their village: "It's harder on him than us." According to Joan Mellen, Boyle's purpose in the depiction of the doctor's treatment of Heine may have been to show that "it wasn't always anti-Semitism which drew Austrians to Nazism, that indeed many fascist movements became racist only as they collaborated with their Nazi occupiers."

Whereas the doctor and his wife and their reaction to Heine are the focus of the first section of the story, Heine gains prominence in the second and third parts, and the reader increasingly sees the world though his eyes. It is established that Heine is apolitical and does not recognize the signs of danger surrounding him. He complains repeatedly that everything is politics and finds escape from the dire economic and political situation in art and card playing: "In Vienna we play cards, always play cards, no matter what is happening." Heine's view stands in marked contrast to that of the village doctor, who recognizes the need for action. He responds to Heine that there was a time for cards, but there is something else to do now. It is eventually revealed to Heine and to the reader that the doctor injured his leg while helping to light swastika fires on the mountainside. Heine's naiveté is signaled not only by the constant smile he sports even in the face of danger, but also by the story of the royal, white horses in Vienna, with which he entertains the family during a meal. In the story, the famous Lippizzaner horses still perform their amazing feats despite the fact that there is no royalty left to perform for. When one of the horses is sold, the horse's groom tries to prevent its departure by inflicting cuts on its legs. The injuries, however, result in the death of the horse, and the groom commits suicide because he cannot bear being separated from it. It is obvious that Heine sees the story as a parable for fierce loyalty and that he completely ignores its political dimension. In contrast to Heine's story stands the puppet play that the doctor puts on for his family, Heine, and some villagers. It features a monstrously handsome grasshopper called "The Leader" and a ridiculous, dwarfed clown called "Chancellor." When Heine realizes the political implications of the play—the beautiful grasshopper represents Adolf Hitler, while the absurd clown stands for Engelbert Dollfuss, the ineffectual Austrian chancellor, who was responsible for the massacre of members of the Social Democratic opposition—his initial enthusiasm for the grasshopper, whose graceful dance reminds him of the white horses in Vienna, wanes, and he begins to recognize the danger the developing political situation is putting him in: "Dr. Heine found he was not laughing as loudly as before." Heine's growing political awareness can also be seen in the scene in which he apprehensively watches the swastika fires on the mountain: "He felt himself sitting defenseless there by the window, surrounded by these strong, long-burning fires of disaster. They were all about him, inexplicable signals given from one mountain to another in some secret gathering of power that cast him and his people out, forever out upon the waters of despair."

The story ends on an ambiguous note when in the last paragraph Heine's gradually developing awareness of the political situation seems to give way to a renewed retreat into an idyllic past. When the Heimwehr, a paramilitary right-wing group, arrests the village doctor, Heine thinks "in anguish of the snow-white horses, the Lippizzaners, the relics of pride, the still unbroken vestiges of beauty bending their knees to the empty loge of royalty where there was no royalty any more."

Discussion Questions

1. Whereas the doctor and his wife remain nameless, Boyle names the young student doctor from Vienna after the famous Jewish nineteenth-century poet Heinrich Heine. What, in your opinion, is the significance of this character's name?

2. Considering that animal symbolism plays a crucial role in Boyle's story, how do you interpret the significance of the young fox that is caught by the doctor and lives with the family without shyness or fear and even watches the puppet play "in fascination, his bright, unwild eyes shining like points of fire in the dark?"

3. Both Dr. Heine and the village doctor are portrayed as wanderers, and both are depicted smiling frequently. What are the similarities and dissimilarities between the two characters, and what are their functions in the story?

4. Although the story revolves around Heine, Boyle did not choose him for the title but rather the Lippizzaner horses. Do you agree or disagree with her choice?

5. It was Boyle's aim to explore the rise of Nazism in Austria. How does Heine's character contribute to this theme?

—*Karl L. Stenger*

REFERENCES

Elizabeth S. Bell, *Kay Boyle: A Study of the Short Fiction* (New York: Twayne, 1992);

M. Clark Chambers, *Kay Boyle: A Bibliography* (New Castle, Del.: Oak Knoll Press, 2002);

Zofia P. Lesinska, *Perspectives of Four Women Writers on the Second World War: Gertrude Stein, Janet Flanner, Kay Boyle, and Rebecca West* (New York: Peter Lang, 2002);

Joan Mellen, *Kay Boyle: Author of Herself* (New York: Farrar, Straus & Giroux, 1994);

Sandra Whipple Spanier, *Kay Boyle: Artist and Activist* (Carbondale & Edwardsville: Southern Illinois University Press, 1986).

T. Coraghessan Boyle
(December 2, 1948 –   )

THE TORTILLA CURTAIN
(New York: Viking, 1995)

DELANEY MOSSBACHER

Delaney Mossbacher is one of the four main characters in T. Coraghessan Boyle's novel *The Tortilla Curtain*. Delaney lives with his second wife, Kyra, a successful real-estate agent, and six-year-old stepson, Jordan, in Arroyo Blanco Estates, an affluent and exclusive community located in Topanga Canyon on the outskirts of Los Angeles, California. A native New Yorker, environmentalist, and self-proclaimed "liberal humanist," Delaney is a forty-something member of the baby-boom generation and former participant in antinuclear demonstrations. He writes a column, "Pilgrim at Topanga Creek," for an environmentalist magazine, *Wide Open Spaces,* and serves as househusband for Kyra and Jordan.

At the opening of *The Tortilla Curtain,* Delaney accidentally hits a Mexican migrant worker, Cándido Rincón, with his brand-new Acura. This incident is the first in a series of encounters between the Mexican workers and the wealthy inhabitants of Southern California that Boyle uses to examine the racial tensions resulting from the problems of Mexican poverty and illegal immigration. Throughout the novel, Boyle explores the extent to which these racial tensions impact Delaney's liberal values and, by extension, the idealism of baby boomers.

Boyle positions Delaney and the other three main characters of the novel in a dialectical narrative that recalls nineteenth-century novels such as George Eliot's *Middlemarch* (1871–1872) and Leo Tolstoy's *Anna Karenina* (1875–1877; translated 1886). *The Tortilla Curtain* comprises two intertwining plotlines that follow the experiences of two married couples: Delaney and Kyra and Cándido and his pregnant wife, América. These correspondences demonstrate Delaney's and Cándido's common humanity. They shop at the same Chinese grocery store, are both married to independent and strong women, enjoy drinking beer, cook a turkey on Thanksgiving, and live in Topanga Canyon. But despite these mutual characteristics, Delaney and Cándido are separated by poverty and race. While the affluent Delaney chooses to live in an elegant home in Arroyo Blanco because of its proximity to the unspoiled nature of Topanga Canyon, the poor Cándido is forced to live in a hidden camp at the bottom of the canyon. While Delaney sees nature as a benign but theoretically dangerous inspiration for his magazine column and a place for him to hike at his convenience, Cándido's poverty compels him to live in nature and to know the reality of searching for water and food in the unforgiving weather of a Southern California summer. While Delaney's race makes him free to walk the streets of his community, Cándido's race obliges him to look out constantly for the American authorities who threaten to arrest him as an illegal immigrant. While Delaney, as the recipient of a considerable inheritance from his parents, only works because he wants to, Cándido must work to survive. And while Delaney routinely retreats to his study for a few hours a day to write his column, Cándido seeks work every day as a menial laborer just so he can have enough money to feed his wife and himself and possibly save for an apartment.

By revealing the key similarities and differences in Delaney's and Cándido's experiences, Boyle's dialectical narrative discloses the hollowness of Delaney's liberal idealism. For example, Delaney criticizes the racism inherent in the push by some members of his community to construct a gate and, eventually, a wall in Arroyo Blanco to deter crime. But when he witnesses Cándido being assaulted by a white truck driver, he does nothing to intervene. In addition, when Delaney sees in Arroyo Blanco the same mysterious Mexican with the San Diego Padres baseball cap who bothered him on one of his hikes, the man the reader knows as José Navidad, Delaney confronts him for being in his neighborhood, only to discover that Navidad has been hired to deliver fliers.

While Boyle uses the reprehensible actions of Navidad, who harasses Delaney and Kyra and rapes América, to add complexity to his exploration of poverty and illegal immigration, he ultimately traces the process by which Delaney loses his liberal values and becomes a racist. As Boyle has suggested in an interview, Delaney's actions become "an anatomy of what racism and scapegoating are." Near the midpoint of the novel, his car is stolen while he is hiking. After Delaney obtains a new Acura, Boyle writes, "That was the American way. Buy something. Feel good. But he didn't feel good, not at all. He felt like a victim." As the novel progresses, Delaney's feelings of victimization cause him to become irrational and angry in his thoughts about and behavior toward the Mexicans. He first demonstrates his irrationality and anger when he confronts Navidad, and he continues this behavior later in the novel, when he stakes out a section of the newly constructed wall in the hope of taking photographs of the vandal who has spray-painted slurs. Assuming that this vandal is Navidad, Delaney reviews the photographic evidence and is dismayed to find a picture of Cándido. Even though the evidence does not reveal Cándido as the perpetrator of the crime Delaney makes Cándido the scapegoat and tries to use a gun to apprehend him. Delaney's action is particularly disturbing because it reveals how he has rejected his realization earlier in the novel that he himself "was the hater . . . the redneck, the racist, the abuser."

Boyle sets Delaney's final confrontation of Cándido against the backdrop of an actual historical event: the Old Topanga Fire of November 1993. In the novel, Cándido starts the fire when he attempts to roast a frozen turkey at his camp. After the fire, when Delaney arrives at the camp with his gun, a mudslide occurs that threatens to destroy everything in its path. At the conclusion of the novel, Cándido saves Delaney from drowning in a river, conclusively demonstrating the common humanity that transcends race and class.

Delaney and *The Tortilla Curtain* not only fit into the tradition of the nineteenth-century dialectical novels of Eliot and Tolstoy, but also into the tradition of the social protest fiction of Charles Dickens and John Steinbeck. Boyle's resolution to write a novel on illegal immigration recalls Dickens's decision in *Hard Times* (1854) to write a novel on the devastating social impact of utilitarianism, with Delaney functioning as a modern-day Gradgrind or Bounderby, one whose racism and wealth contribute to poverty and suffering. In addition, taken from *The Grapes of Wrath* (1939), Boyle's epigraph for the novel—"They ain't human. A human being wouldn't live like they do. A human being couldn't stand it to be so dirty and miserable"—makes an immediate parallel between the suffering of Steinbeck's Joad family and that of Cándido, América, and other poor Mexicans living in America in the 1990s. Read in the context of *The Grapes of Wrath*, Delaney illustrates Boyle's opinion that the problems of social inequality that Steinbeck addressed in the 1930s have not been solved.

Discussion Questions

1. What problems does nature cause for Delaney and Cándido in the novel? What do the ways in which they deal with these problems suggest about their economic class?

2. Do Delaney's actions in the novel reflect his "liberal humanist" values? Focus on his attitudes about race, gender, class, and the environment.

3. How does Boyle use Delaney and *The Tortilla Curtain* as a whole to reflect contemporary debates about Mexican poverty and illegal immigration?

4. Does Delaney resemble the chief male protagonists of other Boyle novels: Tierwater in *A Friend of the Earth* (2000), Marco in *Drop City* (2003), or Kinsey in *The Inner Circle* (2004)? Discuss the relationship between the characters' idealistic beliefs and their actions. Do they practice what they preach?

5. Imagine that Delaney is a character in John Steinbeck's *The Grapes of Wrath*. How would he react to the plight of the Joad family?

—*Paul Gleason*

REFERENCES

Peter Cotes, "Eastenders Go West: English Sparrows, Immigrants, and the Nature of Fear," *Journal of American Studies*, 39 (2005): 431–462;

Heather Hicks, "On Whiteness in T. Coraghessan Boyle's *The Tortilla Curtain*," *Critique*, 45 (2003): 43–64.

Ray Bradbury
(August 22, 1920 –   )

෴

FAHRENHEIT 451
(New York: Ballantine, 1953)

GUY MONTAG

Guy Montag is the central character of Ray Bradbury's dystopian novel *Fahrenheit 451*. Like Winston Smith in George Orwell's *Nineteen Eighty-Four* (1949) and Bernard Marx in Aldous Huxley's *Brave New World* (1932), Montag struggles to assert his individuality in a world where books, along with genuine thought and social interaction, are strictly forbidden. Montag is a complex character who undergoes significant changes during the course of the novel, and the other major characters in the book, Clarisse, Beatty, and Faber, serve to highlight those transformations.

At the beginning of the novel, Montag is an extension of the government, performing his duty as a fireman: burning books. Montag takes pleasure in his work; his hands are described as "the hands of some amazing conductor playing all the symphonies of blazing and burning to bring down the tatters and charcoal ruins of history." He performs his task mechanically, "with his symbolic helmet numbered 451 (the temperature at which book paper catches fire and burns) on his head." On his way home from work, he meets a young girl, Clarisse McClellan, who avoids the "parlor walls" of the television and instead engages in conversation and roams the city in the middle of the night: "I like to smell things and look at things, and sometimes stay up all night, walking, and watch the sun rise." Clarisse is associated with life and the natural world; she tells Montag about the man in the moon, rubs a dandelion under his chin to find out if he is in love, and leaves "a bouquet of late flowers on his porch, or a handful of chestnuts in a little sack, or some autumn leaves neatly pinned to a sheet of white paper and thumbtacked to his door."

The character of Clarisse provides a contrast to Montag's character and way of life. Unlike her natural world, Montag's world is dominated by mechanical creatures, including the "Electronic-Eyed Snake" that saves his wife, Mildred, from an overdose, and the firemen's "Mechanical Hound" that searches out and destroys any citizens who have broken the law. Montag's home is devoid of life or personality; his bedroom is described as "the cold marbled room of a mausoleum," and his wife is "covered and cold, like a body displayed on the lid of a tomb." Both Montag and Mildred have lost any sense of identity or history. He asks her, "When did we meet? And *where?*" She answers: "It's been so long. . . . It doesn't matter." Clarisse's disappearance, and presumed death, compels Montag to evaluate his own life—"How do you get so empty?" he asks himself—and to begin secretly reading books.

The two other significant characters in *Fahrenheit 451* are Faber, a former professor and book lover, and Montag's boss, Captain Beatty. While Faber possesses an intellectual authority, Beatty possesses the authority associated with power, law, and conformity. Montag seeks out Faber as a guide; he says, "I want you to teach me to understand what I read." Faber, like Clarisse, equates books with life: "This book has *pores.* . . . This book can go under the microscope. You'd find life under the glass, streaming past in infinite profusion. . . . The good writers touch life often." Throughout the novel Faber provides Montag with courage, strength, and advice. The characters' names suggest a kinship between them: Bradbury claimed in an afterword to *Fahrenheit 451: The 50th Anniversary Edition* (2003) that "Montag is named after a paper manufacturing company. And Faber, of course, is a maker of pencils!"

Beatty, on the other hand, represents the world Montag is struggling to escape. Though Beatty admits that he once read books, he lost faith in them. He claims, "What traitors books can be! You think they're backing you up, and they turn

on you." Beatty is unable to tolerate the ambiguity or uncertainty that comes with reading and reflection, and he says the "real beauty" of fire "is that it destroys responsibility and consequences." In "A Conversation with Ray Bradbury," published in the fiftieth-anniversary edition of the novel, Bradbury explains Beatty's motivations: "You have to understand how Beatty became a burner of books. He has a history. He was a book reader, but after various crises in his life—his mother died of cancer, his father committed suicide, his love affair fell apart—when he opened the books, they were empty. They couldn't help him. So he turned on the books and burned them."

Perhaps the most important scene in the novel occurs at the beginning of the third section, "Burning Bright," where Montag is commanded to burn down his own house and then turn himself in as a traitor. When Montag kills Beatty, who turns into "a shrieking blaze, a jumping, sprawling gibbering manikin, no longer human or known, all writhing flame in the lawn," he embraces his own humanity, at the same time destroying his old identity.

Montag's transformation is complete when he escapes the city and the clutches of the Mechanical Hound and finds himself floating down a river. Like Clarisse, he finds beauty in his surroundings, noticing the stars and the smell of hay and flowers. For the first time, his life begins to have meaning: "The more he breathed the land in, the more he was filled up with the details of the land. He was not empty. There was more than enough here to fill him." After meeting the book people (ones who memorize books such as Jonathan Swift's *Gulliver's Travels*, 1726) in the woods and witnessing the bombing of the city, Montag suddenly exclaims: "I remember. Chicago. Chicago a long time ago. Millie and I. *That's* where we met!" He then begins to recall passages from Ecclesiastes. It is finally the gesture of memory that makes Montag fully alive and human.

Discussion Questions

1. Why does Montag show his books to Mildred's friends?

2. Is Montag angry at his wife for betraying him? Why does he think about her at the end of the novel?

3. How does Montag think books will help him?

4. Would Montag have been able to escape without Faber's help?

5. Watch François Truffaut's motion-picture adaptation of the novel. What differences do you see between the novel and the movie? How is Montag's character portrayed in each?

—*Liz Beasley*

SOMETHING WICKED THIS WAY COMES
(New York: Simon & Schuster, 1962)

CHARLES HALLOWAY

Charles Halloway is the adult protagonist of Ray Bradbury's novel *Something Wicked This Way Comes*. He is the janitor at the local library. The father of thirteen-year-old Will Halloway in the novel, Halloway is based on Bradbury's own father. Throughout *Something Wicked This Way Comes*, Bradbury accentuates the differences between Halloway— who views himself as an old man at the age of fifty-four, believing that he has lived out his usefulness without really experiencing life—and Will and his best friend, Jim Nightshade, who have their whole lives before them. Halloway and the two boys are forced to confront their fears as well as their dreams when a carnival, "Cooger and Dark's Pandemonium Shadow Show," comes to town one October a few days before Halloween. For Halloway, the carnival becomes a metaphor for life and leads him to acknowledge that each individual has to make life-changing choices along the way.

When Will sees his father pushing his broom among the library shelves, he thinks, "That's Charles William Halloway . . . not grandfather, not far-wandering ancient uncle, as some might think, but . . . *my father*." Halloway loves his son, but they have never really been close. Charles feels that eons have passed since he was a boy himself but well remembers running "like the leaves down the sidewalk autumn nights." He envies Will and Jim, who are still young enough to run on autumn nights.

In Green Town, Halloway is considered an upstanding family man. Each night he allows himself a single drink at the saloon to help fill the empty place inside him. As he leaves the library on the night the carnival comes to town, he hears a man in a dark suit—Mr. Dark, the owner of the carnival—whistling the carol "I Heard the Bells on Christmas Day," a song that always makes Charles sad. He thinks of all the innocents of the world whom life had "hit without warning, ran, hit, came back and hit again."

As Will and Jim learn the secrets of the carnival and Mr. Dark, they are initially unable to convince anyone of what they have seen. Halloway, however, believes them instinctively, just as he instinctively knows when he comes face to face with Dark that he is corrupt and has a hidden propensity for violence. When he learns that Dark is intent on harming Will and Jim, Charles sets out to protect his son. For the first time, Will sees his father as someone to look up to. While Will and Jim hide, Charles researches the carnival, discovering that it is run by supernatural figures, the "Autumn People," that feed on human disappointment and discontent. They have appeared every few decades since 1846, bringing with them a carousel that can age a person or restore him to his lost youth.

The prospect of turning back the clock has appeal for Halloway, but he rejects Dark's offer of a ride on the carousel to protect Will. When Dark uses his magic to locate the boys hiding in the library shelves, he takes them away, leaving Halloway behind to die from a heart attack at the hands of the Dust Witch, another of the Autumn People. In the face of death, Halloway embraces life and realizes that laughter can counteract the Autumn People's evil power. Armed with this knowledge, he breaks Dark's spell over the boys and brings the carnival crashing down through generosity and laughter. He falters momentarily when confronted with fun-house mirrors showing his advancing age, but Will cries: "Oh Dad, I don't care how old you are, ever! . . . I love you." Halloway literally kills Dark with kindness; realizing that the carnival owner has become a boy in order to escape, Halloway embraces him, telling him that "you can't stand being near people like me," and Dark dies from exposure to his love of life. Having accepted his life and connected with his son, Halloway can run home with Will and Jim as a companion.

Discussion Questions

1. When Charles Halloway first encounters Mr. Dark, the carnival owner is whistling "I Heard the Bells on Christmas Day." What is the significance of this carol to Halloway, particularly as it relates to his understanding of good and evil?

2. Discuss the effectiveness of Bradbury's use of the carnival as a metaphor for life in symbolizing Halloway's acceptance of the circumstances of his own life.

3. Discuss how Charles Halloway's desire to be young again affects his relationship with Will and Jim. How does Halloway imagine that children would react if they were instantly made adult, or adults if they were instantly made children?

—*Elizabeth R. Purdy*

WILL HALLOWAY

Will Halloway is one of two thirteen-year-old protagonists in Ray Bradbury's *Something Wicked This Way Comes.* The other is Will's best friend and next-door neighbor, Jim Nightshade. Will is the son of Charles Halloway, a janitor at the local library. *Something Wicked This Way Comes* is a novel about good and evil and the life choices that determine the path each individual may take.

Bradbury opens *Something Wicked This Way Comes* with the nostalgic acknowledgment that "October was a rare month for boys," a time when "it seems Halloween will never come in a fall of broomsticks and a soft flap of bed sheets around corners." Although Will and Jim engage in the same normal activities that have entranced boy characters since Tom Sawyer and Huckleberry Finn, the title of the book leaves no doubt that dark forces are at work.

Bradbury uses the names of the major characters to illustrate this dichotomy of good and evil in all human beings. For instance, Will Halloway's name, with its suggestion of "holy way," denotes light and innocence. He is described as having "hair as blond white as milk thistle" and eyes as "bright and clear as a drop of summer rain." Jim's surname suggests that he has a dark quality that is antithetical to Will's

character. Will has been protected from the harsh realities of life that Jim has been forced to confront on a daily basis, and Charles knows intuitively that Will is likely to be "hit, hurt, cut, [and] bruised" by life without ever understanding how it could happen. Conversely, Jim expects life to be full of adversities.

Will recognizes that he and Jim are different in both personality and circumstance, thinking: "I climb hills. Jim yells off church steeples. I get a bank account. Jim's got the hair on his head, the yell in his mouth, the shirt on his back, and tennis shoes on his feet." Even so, Will understands that Jim has something he will never have and envies him. Will's strength comes from the love he feels for his father and his friend and from his ability to live in the moment. He is thus less vulnerable than either Charles or Jim to the enticements of evil.

With the natural curiosity of young boys, Will and Jim discover the secrets of "Cooger and Dark's Pandemonium Shadow Show." They watch in secret as a forty-year-old carnival owner turns himself into a twelve-year-old boy. While Will's attraction to the carousel is tempered by fear, Jim realizes that his life would be far easier if he were old enough to take care of himself and his mother. This reaction frightens Will even further, and he accuses Jim of wanting to "just go away and leave me here." Because of the stability in his home, Will is able to resist the lure of cheating fate by adding years to his life.

Confronted by the first real evil he has ever witnessed and aware that his life is in danger, Will seeks reassurance from his father, wanting to be told that good will always triumph over evil. From his perspective as an adult, Charles understands that sometimes being good is not enough and that evil may flourish unchecked. When Will asks his father whether or not he is a good man, Charles's response forces both of them to examine the meaning of being good. This conversation is significant for both father and son because it allows Will to see his father as a human being separate from his role as father and husband.

The events surrounding the arrival of the Autumn People in Green Town serve to break down the barriers between Will and his father, enabling them to realize how much they love one another. When Dark offers Charles the chance to be young again, he realizes that the dream comes at too high a price. Charles's love for Will is so encompassing that he is able to resist Dark's attempt to lure him into evil. Will is ultimately able to free himself when his father's love reaches out and summons him from Dark's spell. Will decides that his father is a hero after Charles causes the carnival to destroy itself.

Despite the Halloways' victory over evil, a barely conscious Jim remains in danger as he rides the carousel. The ensuing scene in which Charles commands his son to make faces and dance around is bizarre but oddly appropriate. Even though Will is devastated at the apparent loss of his best friend, his love for his father motivates him to join in Charles's antics. Once Jim is released from the spell of the carousel, he, too, is drawn into the dance. The dance serves the dual purpose of celebrating the triumph of good over evil and honoring the strength of the renewed bond among the three protagonists.

When Will tells his father, "Oh Dad, I never knew you," it is clear that all three protagonists have come to a greater understanding of themselves and of one another. Will has been changed less by the events of that October week than either Charles or Jim, but he has grown in his ability to understand both his father and his friend and in his awareness of his own strengths.

Discussion Questions

1. Name three aspects of Charles Halloway's character that Will changes his mind about as the story progresses.

2. Will and Jim are described as opposites in terms of appearance, character, and background. What is the basis for their friendship?

3. What is Will's role in defeating the evil forces of Mr. Dark's carnival?

—*Elizabeth R. Purdy*

JIM NIGHTSHADE

Jim Nightshade is one of two thirteen-year-old protagonists in Ray Bradbury's *Something Wicked This Way Comes.* Jim lives next door to his best friend, Will Halloway. Since Jim does not know

his own father, Will's father, Charles, feels a responsibility to look out for Jim as well as for his own son. Bradbury uses Jim's surname to suggest darkness and secrecy within the novel. These characteristics are present in Jim not because he is evil but because events in his life have made him vulnerable to evil.

Jim's mother has lost two other children, and Jim tells her that he knows he will never have children because there is "no use making more people" that might die. The loss of his father and siblings has caused Jim to distrust life. He feels that if he were older, he could make life easier for his mother. Bradbury depicts the friends in such a way that Jim appears more mature and aggressive than Will, who trusts life and those around him.

Jim and Will are different in looks as well as in personality and circumstance. Born on the same Halloween night only "seconds apart, one light, one dark," the boys are almost the same size. However, Jim's hair is wild and thick, "the glossy color of waxed chestnuts," and his eyes are "mint rock-crystal green." The boys also differ in their reading habits. Will loves to read Jules Verne, while Jim prefers reading about "water cures, death-of-a-thousand-slices or pouring white-hot lava off castle walls on trolls and mountebanks." The boys' choice of reading matter is indicative of Jim's tendency to confront life and of Will's preference for observing it. As the story evolves, however, the stability of Will's life proves to have equipped him for action in ways that neither boy can predict.

Bradbury's love of symbolism is also evident in his naming of Tom Fury, a wanderer who has dedicated himself to protecting others from the wrath of nature. Fury convinces Jim that the Nightshade house needs a lightning rod for protection. Subsequently, Jim removes the lightning rod, opting to take his chance with a potential lightning strike. Will realizes that such behavior is typical of Jim, who perceives fear as "a new electric power" that he "must try for size." Jim's greatest fear is that he will not be able to stand up to whatever life throws at him. Consequently, he takes the initiative, believing that by action he can control the events of his life. This tendency comes into play later in the novel when Jim allows himself to believe that he can become an adult by riding a magic carousel without facing the consequences of his actions.

The events that place Jim under the spell of evil forces begin when an unexpected carnival, "Cooger and Dark's Pandemonium Shadow Show," arrives in Green Town the week before Halloween. After hearing the music of the carousel on the wind, the boys set out to trace the source. In the middle of an isolated meadow, they witness the arrival of a mysterious train, which appears to be without passengers. The eerie scene quickly comes to life when Mr. Dark, a tall man in a dark suit, appears.

After the boys witness one of the carnival owners turning into a twelve-year-old boy by riding a magic carousel backward, Jim begins to imagine that his life would improve if he were able to ride the carousel forward to become an adult. Because the losses in Jim's life have created emptiness, he convinces himself that riding the carousel would fill the void. During the night the boys discover that the Dust Witch, the carnival's fortune-teller, has marked a "silver ribbon" on the shingles of Jim's house. This then, is the "lightning strike" that Tom Fury had predicted. Contrary to what might be expected from their personalities, it is Will rather than Jim who succeeds in seeking out and confronting the Dust Witch. In this sequence of events, Jim serves as a motivating force for Will to uncover hidden strengths in himself in order to protect his friend.

After hiding out for several hours, Jim and Will flee to the library and the protection of Charles Halloway, the custodian there. When Mr. Dark uses his magic to make it appear that Charles is having a heart attack, Jim takes it as evidence that adults cannot protect him from life. Seeing Jim and Mr. Dark standing together, Will is struck by the fact that each examined the other "as if he were a reflection in a shop window late at night." Bradbury uses this scene to illustrate Jim's vulnerability to evil and to his potential for turning out like Mr. Dark. Without trust, Jim is unable to consider how his life choices affect the choices of those around him, and his dissatisfaction with his circumstances makes him susceptible to the same evil that shapes Mr. Dark.

Although Jim's attraction to the carousel is strong, so is the bond that he and Will share. Jim believes that they will remain friends even if he magically ages a few years and hopes to preserve "their friendship for other times of loss." Their relationship, which shapes the personalities of both boys, is integral to the final showdown between good and evil, in which Jim recognizes Will as a stabilizing force in his life. Like Will, Charles Halloway is committed to saving Jim from himself. As Jim rides the carousel toward magical adulthood and its inherent evil, his love for Will causes him to put out his hand to his friend, who has obeyed Charles's order to grab Jim "so we can finish the fight for him."

Discussion Questions

1. What does Charles Halloway mean when he describes the friendship between his son and Jim Nightshade as a situation in which each plays "the potter to see what shapes [they] can make of the other"?

2. Why does the carousel exert such a strong attraction for Jim Nightshade?

3. How are Jim and Will different in their approaches to life?

—*Elizabeth R. Purdy*

REFERENCES

Ray Bradbury, *Fahrenheit 451: The 50th Anniversary Edition* (New York: Random House, 2003);

Katie De Koster, *Readings on Fahrenheit 451* (San Diego: Greenhaven, 2000);

Steven Dimeo, "Man and Apollo: A Look at Religion in the Science Fantasies of Ray Bradbury," *Journal of Popular Culture*, 5 (Spring 1972): 970–978;

Jonathan R. Eller and William F. Touponce, *Ray Bradbury: The Life of Fiction* (Kent & London: Kent State University Press, 2004);

Russell Kirk, *Enemies of the Permanent Things: Observations of Abnormality in Literature and Politics* (New Rochelle, N.Y.: Arlington House, 1969);

David Morgan, *Ray Bradbury* (New York: G. K. Hall, 1999);

William F. Touponce, *American Writers Supplement 4* (New York: Scribners, 1996);

Jerry Weist, *Bradbury, An Illustrated Life: A Journey to Far Metaphor* (New York: Morrow, 2002);

Sam Weller, *The Bradbury Chronicles: The Life of Ray Bradbury* (New York: Morrow, 2005).

Bruce Brooks
(September 23, 1950 –   )

༄

THE MOVES MAKE
THE MAN
(New York: Harper & Row, 1984)

JEROME FOXWORTHY

Jerome Foxworthy, the seventh-grade protagonist of the 1985 Newbery Honor book, Bruce Brooks's *The Moves Make the Man,* has the task of integrating Chestnut Street Junior High School, the largest white junior high in Wilmington, North Carolina. Disappointed that the move will not allow him to play basketball for the high school his older brothers attend, Jerome focuses on excelling academically at Chestnut as much as he excelled at his former school. Basketball is his passion, but he also develops an interest in Bix, a boy he first observes playing shortstop for a local white baseball team. Though amazed at Bix's precision and passion for the sport, Jerome pities the shortstop when his well-dressed and attractive but apparently crazy mother walks onto the baseball diamond and screams his name nonstop. The juxtaposition between the confident athlete Jerome observes on the field and the shy, downtrodden, and somewhat emotionally disturbed kid who becomes his partner in home economics class at school puzzles and intrigues Jerome enough to prompt him to get to know Bix better.

Though set during the integration struggle, racism serves more as a backdrop than as a primary issue within the novel. Jerome makes racially charged comments such as "Nobody ever thought to make the jigaboos let little crackers into their schools. Always it was them that did the keeping out and letting in"; but given that he is integrating a school, he deals with surprisingly few incidents of racism. He does discover that both the coach and many of the players on the Chestnut basketball team are racist, and not even his skill on the court can get him past these obstacles and onto the team. Later in the novel, Jerome enters a seg-

regated country store with Bix and his stepfather, and Jeb, the owner, spits on his grill to show his hostility toward serving blacks, then throws all three of them out of the store, labeling Bix a "nigger lover." Jerome deflects both of these conflicts, considering the racist behavior the problem of the aggressor, not his own. Except for these two incidents and the ongoing misunderstandings between Bix and Jerome that partially stem from a lack of cross-cultural exposure and understanding, Brooks does not focus on racial conflicts.

The book does explore many difficult relationship conflicts, however, and for these, Brooks offers no easy answers and no resolution. Jerome and his siblings learn to take responsibility for running the house after their mother is injured in an elevator accident, but even prior to this incident he enjoys the closeness between himself and his widowed mother and older brothers, Maurice and Henri. In contrast, Bix fights with his stepfather, who refuses to allow him to see his mother after she has been sent to a mental institution for shock treatment. Jerome feels empathy for Bix, given the contrasts in their family lives, but this relationship is far from simple. On several occasions, Jerome witnesses Bix's out-of-control emotional outbursts that frighten him as well as anyone else who witnesses them. Despite Bix's unpredictability, Jerome takes on the challenge of teaching him to play basketball, a sport that Bix initially despises because of an ongoing conflict with his stepfather. In time, Bix becomes an excellent basketball player, but despite Jerome's insistence that he learn how to fake, Bix refuses to learn Jerome's "moves," considering faking synonymous with lying. And lying or any form of untruth is anathema to Bix.

The Moves Make the Man is a frame novel, and the story begins and ends with Jerome acquiring Bix's notebook that he used as a journal in an effort to try to understand why he ran away and where he might have gone. Jerome is particularly concerned about Bix because of the circumstances under which he ran away. After begging his stepfather to be allowed to see his mother, Bix finally challenges him to a basketball game. If he loses, he agrees to stop asking to see his mother; if he wins, his stepfather must take him to see his mother. Thanks to the training Jerome has given him, Bix does win, but when he finally sees his mother and she initially does not recognize him, he pulls the "fastest and completest fake possible . . . and . . . on thirty people instead of the usual one." Bix embraces the old woman in the bed next to his mother's; sobs uncontrollably, calling out, "MOTHER MOTHER MOTHER"; then exits the building, never to be seen again. Since Brooks leaves Bix's situation unresolved at the end of the novel, both Jerome and the reader can only speculate about his whereabouts, his motivation for running away, and how he manages to elude all of those searching for him. Worse, before Bix's stepfather puts Jerome on a bus back home, he blames Jerome for Bix's running away, telling him, "Don't think I don't understand you, boy, and don't think you did Bix any good at all with all of your black-cat basketball and your black-cat fakes. See where faking got him?" As Jerome struggles to understand Bix and his dysfunctional family, he begins to examine himself and particularly his perspective on faking, seeing finally that any time he fakes, someone will be on the receiving end of that fake, since "There are no moves you truly make alone."

Discussion Questions

1. Jerome's family life starkly contrasts with Bix's. Discuss the messages that this novel conveys about the relationship between (or the lack thereof) race and family life.

2. The incident in which Bix brings a fake apple pie to dinner at the Foxworthys' home seems to be an important scene for several reasons. Discuss its significance to Jerome, to Bix, and to Mrs. Foxworthy.

3. Despite Jerome's level of education and high educational standards, he narrates the novel in an informal, colloquial dialect and also often uses the word *nigger*. How do these linguistic choices on Brooks's part impact the story?

REFERENCE

Christine McDonnell, "New Voices, New Visions: Bruce Brooks," *Horn Book,* 63 (1987): 188–191.

Gwendolyn Brooks
(June 7, 1917 – December 3, 2000)

‿◖

MAUD MARTHA
(New York: Harper, 1953)

MAUD MARTHA BROWN

Maud Martha Brown is the protagonist of Pulitzer Prize–winning poet Gwendolyn Brooks's sole novel, *Maud Martha.* She is a young African American woman growing up in the segregated South Side of Chicago during the 1930s and 1940s. The novel presents her life in thirty-four vignettes or short impressionist sketches as she deals with the problems of racism, poverty, and intraracial conflict in pre– and post–World War II America. The introduction of the feisty dark-skinned Maud Martha marks an important juncture in American and African American literature; she is one of the earliest African American female protagonists in literature who is not a tragic mulatta or a mammy figure. She is characterized by her ordinariness—she is not beautiful, rich, or glamorous—yet her life is rich in common everyday experiences. Over the course of the novel Maud Martha goes through rites of passage such as sibling rivalry, intergenerational conflict with her parents, courtship, the challenges of a new marriage, and childbirth.

Maud Martha's story may be seen as a revision of the Cinderella myth. She has humble beginnings; yet, she struggles to find ways to define her life without a fairy-tale ending. Maud Martha is sensitive and intelligent, and she possesses an inherent curiosity about the world around her. As Brooks indicates in the opening chapter of the novel, "What she liked was candy buttons, and books, and painted music . . . and the west sky, so altered viewed from the steps of the back porch; and dandelions." Yet, she is often not given sufficient outlets for her talents and is metaphorically and socially often relegated to the "back porch" of life, as evidenced through second-class treatment and limited economic opportunities.

Maud Martha feels the sting of rejection because of the intraracial prejudice for Eurocentric beauty and light complexions over Afrocentric features and dark skin. Even in her courtship with her future husband, Paul, she feels that her dark skin is a barrier that will prevent him from appreciating her inner beauty. She agonizes over feelings of inferiority and doubt because she possesses African features and believes that she will not be loved. She views her color as a barrier: "But he keeps looking at my color, which is like a wall. He has to jump over it in order to meet and touch what I've got for him. He has to jump away up high in order to see it. He gets awful tired of all that jumping." Nevertheless, the two lovers are able to overlook societal definitions of beauty, and they marry and start a life together.

Married life in South Side is difficult for Maud Martha. Because there is only limited housing available in a real-estate market driven by discriminatory housing practices and inflationary rents for African Americans, she and her husband are forced to live in a small, one-room kitchenette apartment. In this cramped abode she fights roaches and mice to make a place for her to establish her new family. Maud Martha also enters the domestic force as a maid in order to make ends meet and support her family financially. She finds the work demeaning and becomes the object of ridicule from her employer, Mrs. Burns-Cooper, who belittles Maud Martha's meager living quarters and brags of her own largesse. Maud Martha feels the need to retaliate in response to this abuse and decides to quit without notice, reflecting, "What difference did it make whether the firing squad understood or did not understand the manner of one's retaliation or why one had to retaliate?" In this scene she makes a strong claim for shared respect and humanity in all people, saying: "Why, one was a human being. One wore clean nightgowns. One loved one's baby. One drank cocoa by the fire—or the gas range—come the evening, in the wintertime."

An important scene occurs near the end of the novel when Maud Martha encounters a racist Santa Claus who refuses to talk to her daughter Paulette. She tries to downplay the situation and save Paulette from the pain of the rebuff. Projecting her anger onto her sister Helen, Maud Martha imagines that Helen "would not have twitched, back there. Would not have yearned to jerk trimming scissors from the purse and jab jab jab that evading eye. Would have gathered her fires, patted them, rolled them, and blown on them." In this stream-of-consciousness passage, Maud Martha's frustration at her inability to protect her daughter, or even herself, from racist slights and discrimination is painfully clear.

Brooks, in her 1972 memoir *Report from Part One*, acknowledges that *Maud Martha* is in many ways autobiographical, saying "much of the 'story' was taken out of my own life, and twisted, highlighted or dulled, dressed up or down." The novel did not receive much critical attention when it was first published, perhaps because of the subtle, lyrical style of its prose and because the popularity of other novels of the day centered on more overt social protest, such as Richard Wright's *Native Son* (1940), Ann Petry's *The Street* (1946), and James Baldwin's *Go Tell It On the Mountain* (1953). A few writers, such as Paule Marshall, author of *Brown Girl, Brownstones* (1959), however, recognized the groundbreaking qualities of *Maud Martha*. She called it the best portrayal of a black woman up to that time and identified the character of Maud Martha as a significant model for her own protagonist.

In the decades since its publication *Maud Martha* has been recognized as an important part of the American and African American canons and as a telling portrait of urban life for African Americans in the mid twentieth century.

Discussion Questions

1. In what ways is *Maud Martha* a bildungsroman or coming-of-age story?

2. Compare Maud Martha to Paule Marshall's heroine Selina Boyce of *Brown Girl, Brownstones*, considering how both characters deal with the challenges of growing up in an urban environment.

3. What is life like for Maud Martha as a young woman growing up in Chicago in the 1930s and 1940s?

4. What are some of the ways in which Martha shows her independence throughout the novel?

5. How would you describe Maud Martha's relationships with her family members—sister, parents, husband, and child?

—*Valerie D. Frazier*

REFERENCES

Gwendolyn Brooks, *Maud Martha,* in *Blacks* (Chicago: David, 1987);

Jacqueline Bryant, ed., *Gwendolyn Brooks'* Maud Martha: *A Critical Collection* (Chicago: Third World Press, 2002);

George Kent, *A Life of Gwendolyn Brooks* (Chicago: Third World Press, 1990);

R. Baxter Miller, *Langston Hughes and Gwendolyn Brooks: A Reference Guide* (Boston: G. K. Hall, 1978).

Charles Brockden Brown

(January 17, 1771 – February 21, 1810)

ARTHUR MERVYN; OR, MEMOIRS OF THE YEAR 1793, PART 1

(Philadelphia: Printed and published by H. Maxwell, 1799); part 2 (New York: Printed and sold by George F. Hopkins, 1800)

ARTHUR MERVYN

Arthur Mervyn, the central character of Charles Brockden Brown's novel *Arthur Mervyn,* appears to personify the national story during a transitional period in the early American republic. Having grown up on a farm near Philadelphia, a countrified Arthur leaves home and makes his way to the city in search of his fortune. Arthur attempts to find his way in the world, rising from rural roots to a broader engagement with a more cosmopolitan society and economy. But far from any successful conclusion to this transition, Arthur's first appearance in the novel, narrated at the beginning by the kindly Dr. Stevens, finds him leaning against a wall and suffering from the yellow fever that ravaged Philadelphia from August to November 1793. Stevens takes Arthur in, treats him and, in turn, is treated to the young man's story.

When Sawny Mervyn, Arthur's widowed father, marries a "milk-maid and market woman," a hireling with whom the son has previously dallied, Arthur is forced to leave the farm that should have been his patrimony. In Philadelphia, he finds an economy and society in a difficult period of transformation; economic optimism is inspiring risky financial speculation, and an expanding population is stressing the ability of the city to meet the needs of its citizens, especially as the devastating plague takes hold. Because of the unpredictability of such a fluid economy and the increasing competition for individual resources, Arthur experiences difficulties finding a suitable position from which to begin his rise in the world. He soon finds employment, however, as a copyist in the service of an unscrupulous man named Thomas Welbeck, who involves him in both murder and conspiracy.

Like the United States in the 1790s, Arthur exists between an older authoritarian system, governed at various times by England, by the church, by republican virtues of decorum and deference, and by a nascent market economy and democratic political and social systems. On the one hand, the former cultural system is manifested in the novel through Arthur's continuing to seek employment and direction in roles that make him subservient to older authority figures—the criminal Welbeck, the Quaker farmer William Hadwin, Dr. Stevens, and even the widow Achsa Fielding, who becomes Arthur's wife. These relationships represent traditional connections of kinship and apprenticeship that had been the economic mainstay of the culture but were beginning to break down across early American society as a whole, especially in mercantile centers such as Philadelphia.

On the other hand, Arthur often displays flashes of self-reliance and independence. Even in his early act of accepting the copyist position Welbeck offers, the line that comes to Arthur's mind when asked for a sample of his penmanship is from William Shakespeare's *Romeo and Juliet:* "My poverty, but not my will consents." While authority figures dictate much that happens in Arthur's adventures, he still develops an understanding of the value of active engagement with the world around him: "Books and inanimate nature were cold and lifeless instructors. Men, and the world of men, were the objects of rational study, and our own eyes only could communicate just conceptions of human performances. The influence of manners, professions and social institutions, could be thoroughly known only by direct inspection." Although he is most often in situations requiring him to attend to advice from authority figures, Arthur, when in a position to give advice himself, tends to promote individual independence. To Eliza Hadwin, the farmer's daughter to whom he becomes, young as he is, something of a father figure, he says, "Consult your own understanding, and act according to its dictates. Nothing more is wanting to make you useful and happy."

Arthur's wrestling with ideas and experiences of dependence and independence, the tension between his often self-seeking actions and his admirable ideals, reflects the chaos inherent in the setting of the novel. Like many Americans trying to make the transition from royal subject to free citizen, like the nation itself, Arthur does not always act in accordance with his professed beliefs. He often acts out of selfishness and ignorance, hoping that all will work out well in the end: he says, "I am incapable of any purpose that is not beneficent; but, in the means that I use and in the evidence on which I proceed, I am liable to a thousand mistakes. Point out to me the road by which I can do you good, and I will cheerfully pursue it." Brown saw the yellow-fever crisis that struck Philadelphia in the autumn of 1793 as the perfect backdrop against which such individual struggles might be portrayed: "The evils of pestilence," he writes in the preface to *Arthur Mervyn*, ". . . have already supplied new and copious materials for reflection to the physician and the political economist. They have not been less fertile of instruction to the moral observer, to whom they have furnished new displays of the influence of human passions and motives." Brown is the "moral observer" here, and in this novel he "depicts, in lively colours, the evils of disease and poverty" as these and other difficulties buffet the lives of Arthur Mervyn, the city of Philadelphia and the young United States.

Charles Brockden Brown clearly influenced both American and British authors: Nathaniel Hawthorne, Edgar Allan Poe, and the Shelleys, to name a few. Hawthorne, in the fictional sketch "The Hall of Fantasy," describes a hall in which "stood the statues or busts of men, who, in every age, have been rulers and demi-gods in the realms of imagination, and its kindred regions. . . . In an obscure and shadowy niche was reposited the bust of our countryman, the author of Arthur Mervyn." Arthur Mervyn's literary descen-dants in Hawthorne's stories include, among others, Robin in "My Kinsman, Major Molineux" and the title character in "Young Goodman Brown."

Discussion Questions

1. Arthur grows up in the countryside near Philadelphia. How does this upbringing—in all its details—influence his behavior and choices throughout the novel? Francis Carwin, antagonist in Brown's *Wieland*, has a similar rural upbringing. Explain the differences in the two lives and characters.

2. Good intentions generally seem to drive Arthur Mervyn's actions. How, then, does he so often seem to find his morals compromised and himself in physical danger?

3. Arthur has been seeking his own independent place in the world. As the novel nears its conclusion, however, he finds himself on the verge of marriage to an older woman, a woman regarding whom he says, ". . . I was wax in her hand. Without design or effort, I was always that form she wished me to assume" and "Was she not the substitute of my lost mamma." What complications and implications regarding Arthur's desire for independence and security arise out of his marriage to Achsa Fielding?

4. Brown's Arthur Mervyn and Hawthorne's Robin Molineux are both innocents migrating from the country to the city in early America. How are their experiences similar? How are they different? How can these similarities and differences be explained?

—*Michael Cody*

EDGAR HUNTLY, OR, MEMOIRS OF A SLEEPWALKER

(3 volumes; Philadelphia: Printed by H. Maxwell, 1799)

CLITHERO EDNY

Clithero Edny is the antagonist in Charles Brockden Brown's early American Gothic novel *Edgar Huntly*. A mournful character suffering from both fanaticism and somnambulism, Edny becomes the unwilling recipient of Edgar Huntly's misguided compassion. His guilt over past crimes has left Edny without hope of redemption, but Huntly, to disastrous effect, still tries to redeem him.

A native of County Armagh in Northern Ireland, Edny is raised among "the better sort of peasants" before being taken under the protection of Euphemia Lorimer, who intends that he eventually become her son's "most faithful and intelligent" servant. Once the boys grow to adulthood, however, Lorimer's impatience with having a "monitor" leads to their friendly separation and Edny's return to Mrs. Lorimer's household, where he advances as a trusted servant and ultimately becomes the fiancé of Clarice Wiatte, niece of his patroness. This engagement, however, places Edny in a social quandary. "I was habituated," he later tells Huntly, "to consider the distinctions of rank as indelible. The obstructions that existed, to any wish that I might form, were like those of time and space, and as, in their own nature, insuperable." Much of Edny's anxiety, then, arises from his understanding of the clear and insurmountable distinction between himself as a peasant and the aristocratic woman he desires. Even though he is assured that Clarice's affection for him is genuine, he remains uneasy with the differences between his social status and hers.

To Edny's misfortune, Mrs. Lorimer's twin brother, Arthur Wiatte, Clarice's father, is a wicked man to whose life and fate Mrs. Lorimer believes her own to be bound. Wiatte attacks Edny in an alley one night, attempting to rob him, and Edny, unaware of his attacker's identity, kills him with a pistol. With this event, he begins a downward slide toward madness. Believing Mrs. Lorimer when she says that "the stroke that deprives [my brother] of life will . . . have the same effect on me," Edny concludes that to spare her suffering he must murder her, as well. His killing of Wiatte was accidental; his decision to take Mrs. Lorimer's life misguided and impulsive. He fails in his attempt on Mrs. Lorimer, almost killing Clarice instead, and escapes to America, to an area of Pennsylvania known as Solebury. Having found employment at a Solebury farm near the edge of a wilderness known as Norwalk, Edny's state of mind leads him into somnambulism, and it is in the midst of his unconscious actions that Huntly first sees him and immediately considers him the prime suspect in a brutal local murder.

Edny's somnambulistic behavior includes running half naked through the countryside at night, repeatedly digging a hole beneath the elm that was the scene of the recent murder and plunging into the wilds of Norwalk. Huntly watches and follows, certain that Edny murdered Huntly's friend. Once he confronts the Irishman and hears his story, however, his interest in revenge becomes lost in a blindly compassionate desire to restore himself to the good graces of Mrs. Lorimer.

Edny's fanaticism is in part religious. For example, Huntly fears for the fugitive's life in the wilderness of Norwalk and takes him food. He finds Edny asleep in a cave and, instead of waking him, leaves the food there for him to discover later, not knowing that the sleeper intends to commit suicide by starving himself. When Edny awakes, he eats, believing that divine providence has left the food to sustain him until such time, as Edny puts it, when "my God should summon me to retribution." Until death comes, Edny determines to remain apart from human society and takes up residence in a hut that, earlier in the novel, had been the scene of Huntly's destruction of a raiding band of the displaced Delaware tribe.

Still, Huntly cannot allow Edny to fade into the wilderness. When he learns that Mrs. Lorimer is alive and well, now happily remarried to a man named Sarsefield and expecting a child, he believes that this news will heal Edny's mind and restore him to the past and the social world from which his actions have apparently separated him. Huntly locates Edny and tells him that his patroness lives and is presently in New York City. Edny leaves immediately, promising to kill her as he failed to do in Ireland or return to kill Huntly if he has lied. At last, Edny's violent madness manifests itself with such force that even Huntly can see it.

"Clithero is a maniac," Huntly finally admits in a letter to Sarsefield that appears near the end of the novel. Edny is found and stopped before he accomplishes his murderous mission; during transport by boat to "the hospital," he jumps overboard and drowns himself, preferring death to the social separation of prison or asylum. In Edny, Brown presents a study of mental illness decades before psychology became established as a discipline. His anxieties over social status, his inability to deal with guilt, and his religious fanaticism join together to make him a character of powerful and unsettling obsessions. In Brown's canon, Edny is strongly connected with Francis Carwin of *Wieland,* another outsider who wreaks havoc among those dwelling on the American borderland between civilization and wilderness. Three writers of fiction in the American Renaissance—Nathaniel Hawthorne, Edgar Allan Poe, and Herman Melville—wrestled with ideas and characters similar to those inhabiting Brown's fiction. Thus Clithero Edny's various psychoses seem present to some extent in Hawthorne's Roger Chillingworth; in characters from Poe's "William Wilson" and "The Tell-Tale Heart," among many others; and in Melville's Ahab.

Discussion Questions

1. How do strict class structures in Old World Ireland influence Clithero Edny's understanding of who he is and his behavior? How do Edgar Huntly's more democratic ideas come in conflict with Edny's social background?

2. Both Clithero Edny and Edgar Huntly are somnambulists. Both experience separation from the young women to whom they are engaged. Both have looked up to Sarsefield as their mentor. Considering these and other commonalities existing between them, discuss Brown's use of such doubling and what it might contribute to an understanding of the novel. Although the story is Huntly's, how might Edny be seen as the original and Huntly as the double?

3. "How imperfect are the grounds of all our decisions!" Huntly writes in response to Edny's story of his life before coming to Pennsylvania. Yet, this is not the kind of thinking expected from someone who grew up during the eighteenth-century Enlightenment. Still, in spite of this realization, Huntly seems to believe that reasonable dialogue with Edny will cure the Irishman's ills. Why might he think this, and why does it not work?

4. Huntly often encounters panthers in places where he is pursuing or seeking Edny. At one point Huntly describes Edny's "arms, bosom and cheek" as "overgrown and half-concealed by hair." What might such incidents and descriptions suggest about Edny? About a human in the wilderness?

—*Michael Cody*

EDGAR HUNTLY

Edgar Huntly, title figure of Charles Brockden Brown's 1799 novel *Edgar Huntly,* narrates his disturbing story, set in the year 1787, via a long memoir written for Mary Waldegrave, his fiancée and the sister of his recently murdered best friend. In his attempt to discover Waldegrave's murderer, Huntly travels—both consciously and unconsciously—deep into the wilderness of Norwalk, Pennsylvania, a fictional place north of Philadelphia. This trackless wild becomes the scene of his pursuit of Clithero Edny, his prime suspect in Waldegrave's murder, as well as of dangerous experiences with precipices and panthers, a raiding party of the displaced Lenni Lenape Delaware tribe, and his own psychological limits.

Huntly, a young man without wealth or property, is passionate and impulsive. Once his suspicions land on Irish immigrant Edny as Waldegrave's murderer, he determines to discover the truth. But when he realizes that Edny is a sleepwalker and that this condition arises out of a mind troubled by past events over which the Irishman seemingly had little or no control, Huntly's compassion rises above his desire for revenge: "He, indeed, said I, is the murderer of excellence, and yet it shall be my province to emulate a father's clemency, and restore this unhappy man to purity, and to peace." Huntly's own abnormal psychological state—resulting largely from Waldegrave's death, Edny's story of misfortunes, and his own precarious social status—leads him to become the second sleepwalker in the novel.

Huntly's somnambulism involves him in shocking savagery. Coming out of one sleepwalking episode, he finds himself at the bottom of a pit inside a lightless cave. His desperation to escape and to slake his ravenous hunger lead to a confrontation with a panther, which he kills and then eats raw. When he finally finds the mouth of the cave, he finds it sheltering a band of marauding Lenni Lenape and a young girl they have taken captive in one of their raids. Huntly, in a violent series of events, kills all the war party and rescues the girl.

He and the girl are soon discovered by a posse, and although the girl is taken back into the protection of the community, Huntly, not seriously hurt but bloody and unconscious, is mistaken—and left—for dead. After awaking and recovering his strength he struggles back toward his uncle's farm. At the same time Huntly learns that his uncle has died at the hands of the Lenni Lenape, he also learns that among those who left him for dead was his longtime friend and mentor, Sarsefield, who had recently returned to America from Ireland, "inspired" by "parental affection" for Huntly, "with fortune and a better gift than fortune in my hand." Given that the death of Huntly's uncle represents the end of protection for Huntly, as he, along with his sisters, is to be turned out of the house by his cousin, Sarsefield's offer seems to be salvation. Huntly's blend of compassion and impulse, however, seals his fates when he, for what he considers good reason, sets in motion a chain of events that, at the end of the novel, causes Sarsefield to withdraw his offer of fortune and protection. With his last words in the novel, a letter to Sarsefield, Huntly identifies in himself the motivation behind many of his actions throughout the story: "I have erred, not through sinister or malignant intentions, but from the impulse of misguided, indeed, but powerful benevolence."

Charles Brockden Brown once described *Edgar Huntly* as "doleful" in tone, referring to its "gloominess and out-of-nature incidents." Much of this assessment must be based on the character and actions of its protagonist and title figure. Huntly comes to ruin while attempting to pursue the best course of action regarding the care of his sisters; his hope of marrying Mary; his attempt to discover Waldegrave's murderer; and his efforts first to restore Edny to the good graces of Mrs. Sarsefield and then, finally, to warn her husband that Edny, who Huntly now realizes is a "maniac," is on the loose and intent on killing her. When conscious, Huntly represents, at least in part, both the rational mind of the eighteenth century and the interest in sensibility of the

period. His character seems generally known and admired in the largely rural region surrounding Norwalk. Sleepwalking, however, pushes him into a state of lawless and violent savagery reflective of the American frontier condition. He loses the social controls imposed by republican notions of decorum and civic virtue and acts, instead, in radical and unexpected ways.

Brown created Huntly's story as an attempt to define the Gothic for American authors and readers. He claims in the preface "To the Public" that he intends to stir his readers' imaginations and inspire their sympathy "by means hitherto unemployed by preceding authors. Puerile superstition and exploded manners; Gothic castles and chimeras, are the materials usually employed for this end. The incidents of Indian hostility, and the perils of the western wilderness, are far more suitable" materials for the creation of an American Gothic. *Edgar Huntly*, with its use of clearly American settings and historical events, of character doubling (Huntly and Edny) and of abnormal psychological states, can easily be seen as having influenced the work of the generation of American writers that followed Brown—James Fenimore Cooper, Nathaniel Hawthorne, Edgar Allan Poe, and Herman Melville. Brown's Edgar Huntly, as a character, serves in some ways as literary forefather of such figures as Hawthorne's Goodman Brown from his story "Young Goodman Brown"; the title character of Harold Frederic's *The Damnation of Theron Ware;* the nameless protagonist of Ralph Ellison's novel *Invisible Man;* and Inman of Charles Frazier's *Cold Mountain*.

Discussion Questions

1. In Brown's preface "To the Public," he claims that "America has opened new views to the naturalist and politician, but has seldom furnished themes to the moral painter." What does he mean by this? If he is making claims to have done the work of a "moral painter" in *Edgar Huntly*, how might this shape Huntly's character and govern his actions? What morals are discovered and how are they revealed?

2. M. H. Abrams describes the most successful of early Gothic novels as having "opened up to fiction the realm of the irrational mind and of the

perverse impulses and the nightmarish terrors that lie beneath the orderly surface of the civilized mind." Explain how Brown goes about cracking the "surface" of Edgar Huntly's "civilized mind" to explore what lies beneath.

3. Huntly has already experienced the events he relates in the novel before he takes up the pen to record them. These experiences have left him shaken, and he is not certain he can commit them to paper "with order and coherence." As he begins his narrative, however, he describes himself as "melancholy" because of the violent death of his friend Waldegrave, but he is also alive with curiosity about what happened to his friend and interested in investigating the murder. From this state of relative balance, what events in Huntly's pursuit of Clithero Edny reveal either positive or negative developments in Huntly's character?

4. Huntly experiences two main somnambulistic events in the novel. How do these events affect Huntly? What might these represent to the reader attempting to understand the young man?

5. Edgar Huntly enters the wilderness on a mission to find the truth about Waldegrave's murder. Hawthorne's Goodman Brown enters the wilderness to test himself. Both characters emerge from the wilderness changed in identifiable ways. How is Edgar Huntly's wilderness experience similar to and different from that of the title figure in Nathaniel Hawthorne's "Young Goodman Brown"?

—*Michael Cody*

◖◗
WIELAND; OR THE TRANSFORMATION

(New York: Printed by T. J. Swords for H. Caritat, 1798)

FRANCIS CARWIN

Francis Carwin is an important character in Charles Brockden Brown's *Wieland; or the Transformation* and the narrator and protagonist of *Memoirs of Carwin the Biloquist*. In *Wieland,* after he happens upon Mettingen, the pastoral, isolated Wieland estate, and becomes involved in the lives

of its inhabitants, Carwin sets into motion events that lead to tragedies in the Wieland family. With his gift for mimicking and projecting voices (biloquism), Carwin first reproduces the voice of Catharine, Theodore Wieland's young wife and the mother of his four children, in a place from which she is absent. Having injected only perplexity into the rational, idealistic family, he progresses to a trick that has a far more serious consequence. Mimicking the voice of Clara, Wieland's sister, he constructs a sexually explicit dialogue with himself that convinces Henry Pleyel, Catharine's brother who secretly loves Clara, that Clara is impure. Clara, who loves Henry in return, becomes unbalanced with anguish and bewilderment. Carwin's most catastrophic hoax, however, is reserved for Wieland and his family. Pretending to be the voice of God, Carwin directs Wieland to kill his wife and children. After carrying out the order and being subsequently imprisoned, he escapes with the intention of killing Clara. Carwin, hiding in the darkness of Clara's room and again feigning the voice of God, commands Wieland to "Hold!" He addresses Wieland, "Man of errors! cease to cherish thy delusion," converting Wieland from a madman to a "man of sorrows" who kills himself rather than live with the truth of his horrendous actions.

When Carwin intervenes in Wieland's mad attempt to kill his sister, he has come to Clara with the intention of confessing his role in the tragic events and justifying his actions. He explains to Clara that he is an American like her but spent years in Europe and the British Isles, under the influence of a man who proved to be an enemy, before returning to his native land and wandering the Pennsylvania countryside. It was coincidental, he says, that he arrived at Mettingen, and he claims to have toyed with the Wieland family "without malignant intentions." He has indulged his talent for biloquism out of curiosity about their reactions. He concedes, however, that his actions "possibly effected more than I designed."

Despite his explanation, Carwin remains an ambiguous character. Pleyel discovers a newspaper account of an escape from Newgate Prison in Dublin by a prisoner convicted of murder and robbery who surely is Carwin. Is Carwin then a common criminal? Or is he "in league with some infernal spirit," as a distant kinsman of the Wielands is told? Is he "ruffian or devil, black as hell or bright as angels?" Clara asks. The question of Carwin's wickedness is left unanswered as he denies his guilt in the crimes of which he was accused. What is certain is that he is the catalyst for discoveries made by the main characters about the unreliability of their senses and, despite the rationality on which they have prided themselves, about the irrationality at the core of their psyches. Clara comes close to exonerating Carwin when she admits that he could not have brought about the vile events if the Wielands had not been vulnerable and thus complicit. "If I had been gifted with ordinary equanimity or foresight," she says, "the double-tongued deceiver would have been baffled and repelled."

After Brown completed *Wieland; or the Transformation*, he apparently thought the character of Carwin begged for further development. He began *Memoirs of Carwin, the Biloquist*, which details the life of Carwin, but he never completed it. He nevertheless published a substantial fragment serially in the *Literary Magazine*. The narrator of his own story, Carwin recounts how he was born the second son of a Pennsylvania farmer who was unsympathetic to Carwin's thirst for knowledge and dislike of farming. When he was fourteen years old he discovered his talent for biloquism: he was sent to fetch the cows and learned that he could throw his voice off the rocky cliffs in the shrill tones of "a Mohock savage." Eventually using his gift to escape his father and the farm, Carwin encounters a man named Ludloe, who presents himself as Carwin's benefactor, takes him to Europe, and makes wide experience available to him. Although Ludloe initially appears to Carwin as a kindly mentor, he proves to be a cynic and an exploiter. He sets up Carwin's false imprisonment, and it is as much from Ludloe as from the prison that Carwin escapes to America.

Whether one accepts or rejects Carwin's explanation for his wrongdoing and his account of his own history, he clearly is an example of the stock character the mysterious stranger, as in the title of Mark Twain's posthumously published novella, the

interloper who reveals to individual members of the group he invades the secret recesses of their hearts and minds and the chink in the armor of their rationalism or virtue. Despite his devotion to Enlightenment values, Wieland is susceptible to religious fanaticism and ready to believe that like Abraham he is being asked by God to prove his obedience. Clara is subconsciously attracted to Carwin (and perhaps to her brother) despite her belief that she is in rational control of all her instincts, whether regarding sexuality or violence. Carwin, a protean character who changes appearances regularly, has something for everyone. With his deceptions, meddling, and imposition of will on others, he anticipates Henry James's Madame Merle in *The Portrait of a Lady* (1881) and Nathaniel Hawthorne's Roger Chillingworth in *The Scarlet Letter* (1850).

At the end of the eighteenth century Brown not only created Carwin as a functional character in his novel but he also used him to deliver warnings to the young American nation and to explore some of the most serious social and political issues of the day. The question of whether the United States should follow an isolationist policy is partially answered by Brown as he shows the dangers of insularity and perhaps even the impossibility of maintaining it. He also reveals the flaws in the extremes of religious fervor and rationality. The first can lead to madness and destruction, and the other fails in the face of untrustworthy senses. What people think they hear and see is not always true. Through Carwin, Brown introduced a dose of intellectual skepticism into the American dialogue.

Discussion Questions

1. Evaluate the evidence that Carwin is a satanic agent bent on corrupting the Wieland family. To what extent does Brown undercut the evidence?

2. How do you account for the fact that Carwin changes appearances often? Once seen in the garb of a clown, he is later seen as a monster with sunken eyes and the face of an inverted cone; at the same time, according to Clara, he had a radiance inexpressibly serene and potent. Do these different descriptions tell more about Carwin or Clara?

3. Ludloe is a complex character whose intentions and apparent philosophy seem to shift. To what

extent is he responsible for Carwin's later actions in America? What did Carwin learn from him?

4. Both *Wieland; or the Transformation* and *Memoirs of Carwin, the Biloquist* contain allusions to many different religions besides Christianity. How does that multiplicity contribute to one of Brown's dominant themes?

—*Darlene H. Unrue*

CLARA WIELAND

Clara Wieland is the narrator of Charles Brockden Brown's epistolary novel *Wieland; or The Transformation*. Clara's narrative unfolds in the form of two letters, one long (comprising chapters 1 through 26 of the novel) and one short (chapter 27), written to unnamed friends. She begins her story with accounts of her paternal grandfather, a German musician and playwright, and her father, who developed an evangelical Protestant fervor that drove him from Europe to North America to convert the Indians to Christianity. Establishing in Pennsylvania an estate, Mettingen, he became wealthy and married a mild-mannered woman who produced two children, Clara and her brother, Theodore. When Clara was six years old, her father, who had become increasingly melancholy and mystical, was the apparent victim of fatal spontaneous combustion, a scientific phenomenon widely discussed in the late eighteenth century. Clara's mother died a few months afterward, and Clara and Theodore spent the remainder of their childhood under the protection of a maiden aunt and an uncle. When Theodore reached adulthood, he married Catherine Pleyel, a childhood friend of his and Clara's, and for several years the insular society at Mettingen thrived as a rational utopia. "Our education had been modeled by no religious standard," Clara says. "We were left to the guidance of our own understanding."

All of their lives change dramatically when Theodore Wieland is persuaded by a voice he believes to be God's to kill his wife and four children. Imprisoned for murder, he escapes and attempts to kill Clara before the voice commands him to stop and tells him his senses have deluded him. Unable to bear the truth, Wieland commits suicide. The voice has been the work of Francis Carwin, a mysterious stranger whose talent for ventriloquism and mimicry (biloquism) directed Wieland's tragic actions. By mimicking the

voice of Clara, Carwin also has convinced Henry Pleyel, Catherine's brother, who secretly loves Clara, that she is engaged in a sexual affair with Carwin. Clara, bereft and haunted by nightmares, looks forward only to death. When she nearly dies in a fire, however, she develops a new appreciation for life and settles in France with her uncle. After Carwin confesses to Pleyel that he mimicked Clara's voice in a sexually explicit dialogue, Pleyel declares his love for Clara, who returns it. As the novel closes, Clara is living happily with Pleyel in France.

Throughout the long letter Clara's tone is somber as she explains all that has befallen her and her family. The short letter, written three years after the first, ties together the plot and subplot (a melodramatic tale of seduction and betrayal involving persons outside the Wieland family), explains the events that led to her newfound happiness, and includes moral observations for the sake of the reader.

Clara's story, set between the end of the French and Indian War and the beginning of the American Revolution, is filled with both neoclassical elements and the trappings of Gothic romance. Clara is on the one hand a representative woman of the Enlightenment who admires the classics and takes pride in her rationality. But she is also a typical heroine of Gothic romance (a genre at its peak of popularity when Brown was writing the novel), a beautiful, virtuous woman living in a many-compartmented manor house on a remote estate in the wilderness, witnessing vile deeds and seemingly supernatural occurrences, and confronting an enigmatic villain. The opposition between the classical and the romantic in the novel reflects the conflict in Clara's mind between a Christian theological premise that the supernatural intervenes miraculously in human lives and the eighteenth-century reliance on science and reason.

As a narrator Clara is thorough and analytical as she reveals her thoughts, feelings, and the steps in her emerging awareness. The styles in which she writes the segments of her history reflect the stages of her emotional and mental development. As she moves toward a breakdown as a result of her horrifying experiences, the syntax of her sentences breaks down as well. She is among eighteenth-century American literary characters, such as the titular heroine of Hannah Webster Foster's *The Coquette; or, The History of Eliza Wharton*

(1797), who anticipate later stream-of-consciousness protagonists. Clara's early declarations that her story "will exemplify the force of early impressions" and that her act of recording her history is a form of "therapy" anticipate Edgar Allan Poe's deranged narrators and the theories of Sigmund Freud.

The title has multiple meanings. *Wieland* refers simultaneously to Clara's father, her brother, and to the Wieland family collectively. The second part of the title—*The Transformation*—is relevant to each family member. The elder Wieland was transformed from one kind of physical matter to another. The younger Wieland was transformed into a murdering madman. Wieland the American family is transformed into nothingness. Clara is transformed from a completely rational woman to one who has learned that evidence derived from the senses can be deceptive. She also concedes that powerful emotions escape rational control, and her limited view of life enlarges significantly. Her hard-won perspective at the conclusion of her story constitutes an initiation.

Discussion Questions

1. The subtitle of *Wieland; or The Transformation* is *An American Tale*. Taking into consideration Clara's European ancestry, the roots of Protestantism in her father's fanaticism, and the isolation of the Wieland estate, consider the ways Clara's story is "an American tale." In Clara's experience do you find warnings Brown is directing to his fellow Americans in the fledgling new nation?

2. Some readers have seen Clara as a recasting of William Shakespeare's Desdemona and Ophelia. How is she similar to those characters? In what ways is she different? How do the differences help define her character and the themes of the novel?

3. In the novel Clara is the center of the issue of free will and moral responsibility. She fluctuates between blaming her brother for his tragic actions and blaming Carwin. What, finally, is the conclusion she draws about individual accountability?

4. Brown was influenced by his Quaker schoolmaster Robert Proud, who saw history as a repetition of an endless search for new Edens that inevitably collapse in imperfection. How does Clara's story embody Proud's theory?

—*Darlene H. Unrue*

THEODORE WIELAND

Theodore Wieland is a central character in Charles Brockden Brown's *Wieland; or The Transformation,* a novel set in the period of the Paxton Riots of 1763–1764 (a massacre provoked by religious zealotry) and inspired by an actual family tragedy in 1781 when a New York farmer murdered his wife and four children as a result of religious delusion. In the "Advertisement" for the novel, Brown reminds readers that there had recently appeared "an authentic case, remarkably similar to that of Wieland." Brown also incorporated in *Wieland* elements of the contemporary Gothic romances of Ann Radcliffe and William Godwin and anticipated the nineteenth-century tales and romances of Edgar Allan Poe and Nathaniel Hawthorne. The novel reveals Brown's personal struggle to find common ground between Jean-Jacques Rousseau's idealism, to which he subscribed, and the Scottish common-sense philosophy he thought underlay the economic self-interest of the new nation.

Early in the novel brief histories of Wieland's father and grandfather are provided by his sister, Clara, the narrator, and help explain Wieland's character and fate as well as the subtitle of the novel, *An American Tale*. The grandfather Wieland, a musician and founder of the German theater, was the son of a nobleman who disowned him when he married the daughter of a merchant. The only son of that union, Wieland and Clara's father, expressed his inherited artistic sensibility in Protestant fundamentalism, which led him to North America to convert the Indians to a radical form of Christianity. Settling in Pennsylvania, he established an estate he named Mettingen, married a kind woman, and fathered two children, Theodore and Clara. Through thrift and shrewd purchases of land and slaves, he became prosperous. He also became increasingly melancholy, reclusive, and fanatically religious, building near the main house an open-sided summerhouse that served as a temple to which he repaired twice a day to practice his singular form of religion.

When Wieland was a child, his father was the apparent victim of a fatal spontaneous combustion while meditating in his temple. An intensely bright light suffusing the scene was followed by "a loud report, like the explosion of a mine" and incessant "piercing shrieks." His mother soon died as a result of the shock, and the orphans Theodore and Clara were reared to adulthood by kind relatives who provided tranquillity and instruction "in most branches of useful knowledge." Wieland married Catharine Pleyel, a childhood friend, and within six years they had four children. By the time the main action of the novel begins, Wieland's family is the center of an insular Mettingen society that includes Clara, Henry Pleyel (Catharine's brother), servants, several relatives, and a few external persons who make up a minor subplot. The small, self-contained group seems to constitute a utopia founded on reason and an appreciation of the arts.

Wieland, described by Clara as "grave, considerate, and thoughtful," apparently inherited his father's melancholy. "I scarcely ever knew him to laugh," she says. Perhaps as a defense against emotions barely under the surface, Wieland clings to reason and the intellect. An "indefatigable student" who reads many authors, he admires Cicero above all. Indeed, he is so much obsessed with Cicero that he places a marble bust of him in the temple, collects all editions of his works, and attempts to discover the gestures and cadences with which the Latin in Cicero's texts ought to be declaimed. In Wieland, Brown has created a caricature of the eighteenth-century man who takes neoclassical veneration of the ancients to the point of absurdity, a tendency dramatically revealed in a scene between Wieland and Henry Pleyel, whom Clara describes as "the champion of intellectual liberty" and one who rejects "all guidance but that of his reason." The two rationalists, Wieland and Pleyel, who enjoy "bandying quotations and syllogisms," descend into an extensive and ridiculous argument over the mood of a Latin verb.

The melancholy that coexists with Wieland's rationality derives from his curiosity about his father's death. Was it the result of a scientifically explicable spontaneous combustion, or was it a supernatural act? The conflicting questions represent the paradox of revealed religion and reason within Wieland and at the heart of American eighteenth-century thought. Although Brown points out in a footnote that the phenomenon of spontaneous combustion had been validated in a medical journal (the apparent source for an essential element in the plot), Wieland is not so certain. With an uneasy suspicion that a supernatural agent might have been responsible for his father's death, he is susceptible to the machinations of the biloquist (ventriloquist and mimic) Francis Carwin, who, out of curiosity about the effect his biloquism will have on the Wielands, wreaks havoc on the family. Creating voices that seem to be Catharine, then Clara, and finally God, Carwin stirs up general confusion and perplexity: he causes Pleyel, who secretly loves Clara, to conclude that she is engaged in a sexual liaison with Carwin, and leads Wieland to murder Catharine and his four children and to attempt to kill Clara. Wieland, imprisoned for the murder of his wife and children, admits to the murders but describes the voice of God that ordered him, in words reminiscent of the story of Abraham and Isaac, "In proof of thy faith, render me thy wife." After the hideous crime was committed, he explains, the voice of God spoke again: "Thou hast done well; but all is not done. . . . the sacrifice is incomplete. . . . thy children must be offered. . . . they must perish with their mother!" In preventing the murder of Clara, Carwin, again as the voice of God, tells Wieland that his senses have deluded him. Wieland finally cannot live with the knowledge of his terrible deeds, and he commits suicide.

Although Wieland has been deceived, and later disillusioned, by Carwin, his actions raise broad questions about the reliability of the senses, free will and responsibility, and the relative strengths of supernatural belief and rationality. Through the character of Wieland, Brown focused attention on central philosophical issues in the young American nation at the end of the eighteenth century and the dawn of the nineteenth. Brown pointed out the tragedy that ensues in a too-credulous acceptance of what people think they see and, in particular, what they think they hear.

Discussion Questions

1. Trace the evolution of Theodore Wieland's madness from his grandfather's artistic sensibility through his father's religious bent and finally to his own dedication to reason and the classics. What was Brown saying about each way of looking at the world?

2. In Wieland's story, what is Brown's point about utopian societies? What political advice was Brown offering his countrymen?

3. Because Clara tells her brother's story, the reader has greater insight into her mind than into Wieland's. What significant differences do you infer between the two of them that accounts for Clara's survival and Wieland's destruction? How much can be accounted for by chance?

4. Some critics have seen Brown's account of Theodore Wieland's "transformation" as an anatomy of madness that anticipates some of Edgar Allan Poe's characters such as Roderick Usher and William Wilson. Discuss Wieland's traits that Poe might have drawn upon.

5. Discuss the theme of science versus art in the story of Theodore Wieland's life and death.

—*Darlene H. Unrue*

REFERENCES

Philip Barnard and Stephen Shapiro, Introduction to *Edgar Huntly; or, Memoirs of a Sleep-Walker* (Indianapolis: Hackett, 2006);

David Lee Clark, *Charles Brockden Brown: Pioneer Voice of America* (Durham, N.C.: Duke University Press, 1952);

Emory Elliott, Introduction to *Wieland; or the Transformation, and Memoirs of Carwin, the Biloquist* (Oxford: Oxford University Press, 1994);

Norman S. Grabo, *The Coincidental Art of Charles Brockden Brown* (Chapel Hill: University of North Carolina Press, 1981);

Patricia L. Parker, *Charles Brockden Brown, a Reference Guide* (Boston: G. K. Hall, 1980);

Donald A. Ringe, *American Gothic: Imagination and Reason in Nineteenth-Century Fiction* (Lexington: University Press of Kentucky, 1982): 36–57;

Ringe, *Charles Brockden Brown* (Boston: Twayne, 1991);

Bernard Rosenthal, ed., *Critical Essays on Charles Brockden Brown* (Boston: G. K. Hall, 1981);

Harry R. Warfel, *Charles Brockden Brown, American Gothic Novelist* (Gainesville: University of Florida Press, 1949);

Wieland; or, The Transformation: An American Tale, and Other Stories, introduction by Caleb Crain (New York: Modern Library, 2002).

William Wells Brown
(March 1815 – November 6, 1884)

꘎

CLOTEL; OR, THE PRESIDENT'S DAUGHTER

(London: Partridge & Oakey, 1853); revised as *Clotelle: A Tale of the Southern States* (Boston: Redpath / New York: Dexter, Hamilton, 1864)

CLOTEL

Clotel is the central character in William Wells Brown's novel, *Clotel; or, The President's Daughter. Clotel*, the first novel written by an African American male, was inspired by rumors that Thomas Jefferson had engaged in sexual relations with one of his female slaves and had children born to that slave. Clotel is Brown's fictional rendering of Jefferson's daughter. In writing the novel, he asked himself: What would happen to a daughter of Jefferson born to a slave mother? Since the laws designated a child to the status of its mother and not its father, any children born to slave mothers were automatically slaves. In his characterization of Clotel, Brown opens the door to discussing slavery, race, gender, politics, and other issues pertinent to pre–Civil War America. At the forefront of the novel is the question of love: Can love exist between couples when one individual owns the other? Clotel is the product of such a relationship, and she later finds herself in a similar position with Horatio, the young, wealthy, white Southerner who purchases her.

From the beginning of the novel, the narrator establishes that Clotel's situation is not an anomaly. The novel opens with the assertion that "there is a fearful increase of half whites, most of whose fathers are slaveowners, and their mothers are slaves." Even more significantly, the opening of the novel acknowledges that American society at this time tolerates this behavior: "Society does not frown upon the man who sits with his mulatto child upon his knee, whilst its mother stands a slave behind his chair." This image automatically combats any desire to see the relationship as one in which both individuals participate willingly. Thus, when Jefferson upon his death fails to free either the slave mother or the child, both are left to the wishes of society, and society places them on the auction block. The narrator calls into question the moral status of a society that fails to protect its women and children. Throughout the first chapter of the novel, accurately titled "The Negro Sale," the narrator balances a discussion of Clotel's status with the inability of African Americans to marry, bringing attention to their morally degraded position of being forced into sexual relations in which they have no power. Clotel's mother, Currer, is not protected by her relationship with Jefferson, and thus, like her daughter, her future after Jefferson's death lies on the auction block.

Clotel's experience at auction is significant as it places direct emphasis on the values society places on the purity and innocence of the female. Clotel is sold to Horatio for a high price because she is healthy, sweet-tempered, of moral character, and intelligent. The importance placed on these characteristics points to the hypocrisy of American society, which praises the innocence and purity of women while forcing these women to engage in sexual relationships outside of marriage. Horatio insists that he loves Clotel, but his words are contradicted by his behavior. He sets her up in a cottage in the woods well away from polite society. Clotel desires to have a life with Horatio and asks that he take her away to Europe, where they can live together as man and wife. Horatio, however, is motivated by his need for social status in the American South and is unwilling to stand against the laws of the time. He instead marries a young white female, Gertrude, whose familial relationships provide him with the political opportunities he is pursuing. Clotel thus becomes susceptible not only to Horatio but also to the whims of his wife. Gertrude comes to represent the sentiment of many white women in the South, who are unable to control their husband's wandering desires and therefore take out their frustrations on the female slave. Gertrude has Clotel sold to the lower South, where she is destined to a life of hardship. Horatio's daughter, Mary, is forced to work as a slave in her father's home. Horatio is impotent as a father, unable and unwilling to come to Mary's aide. Gertrude's disgust with Mary is not limited to her status as Horatio's daughter with a slave, but to her physical being. She turns Mary outdoors to do labor so that

her skin will be darkened and her status as a slave will not go unnoticed by the community around her.

In his introduction to the Bedford Critical Edition of the novel, Robert S. Levine discusses Brown's use of pastiche, borrowing from or imitating other works or styles, in his writing of *Clotel*. One of the texts that Brown imitates is Lydia Maria Child's short story "The Quadroons." In retelling this story, Brown depicts Clotel as a character who exercises control over her life despite her enslavement. When she is sold south, she concocts a plan to escape that replays the escape of William and Ellen Craft, a fugitive slave couple who escaped to Boston from Macon, Georgia; Clotel uses the advantage of her light complexion to pass as white and escapes to the North aboard a train. Clotel's ability to pass for white highlights the problem of using biological features, such as skin color, as signifiers of race. It also allows her momentarily to gain some control over a society that had rendered her inferior. After achieving her freedom in the North, Clotel returns to the South to save her daughter. As she is about to be captured, she looks to heaven and begs that she would find the compassion there that she did not receive on Earth, and then leaps into the Potomac River. The chapter depicting Clotel's death is titled "Death Is Freedom." It also evokes the belief of African Americans that death was a blessing as it not only allowed them to escape from the system of slavery but also to return, at least spiritually, to Africa. The irony of Clotel's death lies in the location of her demise, on the doorstep of the nation's capitol. Thus, her death further links her to her father, Thomas Jefferson, and the promise of American freedom.

Discussion Questions

1. In the novel Clotel's sister Althesa meets a slave woman named Salome. Salome is a young German immigrant who is sold into slavery despite the fact that she is white. How do Salome's and Clotel's experiences complicate the way that status in American society at that time was determined?

2. An important theme in the novel is the role that color plays in American society. How does Clotel's success at passing as white undermine the biological racism that was prevalent in nineteenth-century scholarship?

3. The novel *Clotel* tells not only Clotel's story but also her family's. Her family seems destined for unhappiness in America. The only African American character in the text to achieve happiness does so in France. Agree or disagree with the assertion that Brown's novel suggests that the only hope for African Americans during the nineteenth century was either in death or abroad.

—*J. A. Brown-Rose*

REFERENCES

Curtis W. Ellison and E. W. Metcalf Jr., *William Wells Brown and Martin R. Delaney: A Reference Guide* (Boston: G. K. Hall, 1978);

M. Giulia Fabi, *Passing and the Rise of the African American Novel* (Urbana: University of Illinois Press, 2001), pp. 8–29, 147–151;

William Edward Farrison, *William Wells Brown: Author and Reformer* (Chicago: University of Chicago Press, 1969);

J. Noel Heermance, *William Wells Brown and Clotelle: A Portrait of the Artist in the First Negro Novel* (Hamden, Conn.: Archon, 1969);

Robert S. Levine, "'Whiskey, Blacking, and All': Temperance and Race in William Wells Brown's *Clotel*," in *The Serpent and the Cup: Temperance in American Literature,* edited by David S. Reynolds and Debra Rosenthal (Amherst: University of Massachusetts Press, 1997), pp. 93–114.

Pearl S. Buck
(June 26, 1892 – March 6, 1973)

❦

THE GOOD EARTH
(New York: Day, 1931)

O-LAN

O-lan first appears in Pearl Buck's Pulitzer Prize–winning novel, *The Good Earth*, when she is sold out of slavery in the great House of Hwang to become wife to the farmer Wang Lung. Like Ma Joad in John Steinbeck's *The Grapes of Wrath* (1939), she is the real strength in the family, although she does not share Ma's dominance in the narrative. With the experience she has gained as a slave in the House of Hwang, O-lan provides the worldly knowledge that propels Wang Lung from a humble farmer to master of the same great house.

Buck's belief that "the basic discovery about any people is the discovery of the relationship between its men and its women" is borne out in her works and especially in *The Good Earth*. Although women were subservient to men in China at the time, O-lan and Wang Lung form a kind of partnership and in much of the novel have a solid, if in no way romantic, relationship. Without being asked, she appears beside him to toil in the fields in addition to caring for the house and his ancient father. She is not a stereotypical character, although in Western eyes she became a model of the Chinese farmwife. The reader learns much about her from her silences and the expression in her eyes. She speaks little and "in a flat plain voice." Refusing any help, she bears her children alone behind a closed door, often returning to the fields the same day. One of her girl children, who is seriously retarded, becomes a favorite of their father and is referred to throughout the novel as their "poor fool." Buck herself had a retarded child and was sympathetic to the condition in a way unusual for the time. During the famine, O-lan bears another girl, whom she smothers, as there is no way for her to either feed or flee with an additional child. Throughout she manages the household effectively, having learned everything from economics to food preservation through observation in the kitchen of the great house.

When her and Wang's initial prosperity is interrupted by drought and famine, O-lan makes the decision that they flee to the south, where she begs for food while Wang pulls a rickshaw, seeing white faces for the first time. Soldiers are everywhere, and the rich, threatened by the military, flee for their lives, leaving many of their treasures behind. Finally, in an uprising of the poor, O-lan steals jewels from a house abandoned by a rich family—her upbringing as a slave having taught her where the rich hide their treasures—while Wang steals cash. With their loot they are able to return to their home and buy even more land. Some critics have questioned the morality of their thievery, despite the couple's dire circumstances.

Even though she and Wang become successful, O-lan's life is a sad one. She is not beautiful and neither expects nor receives love from Wang, although it is clear that this lovelessness grieves her. Obviously ill after their return from the south, apparently from a cancer of some sort, she does not take to her bed until she is unable to walk. During her life she asks for only three things. The first is to take her firstborn son to the great house to show to her old mistress her new status as wife and mother; the second, to keep two pearls for herself from the stash of jewels that she steals to save the family; and the last, to see her oldest son married before she dies so that she can rest assured that their house will continue. Although her first and third wishes are realized, the second is not.

She is forced to accept the humiliation of Wang's bringing home a second wife, Lotus, a pretty, not-so-young concubine on whom he dotes. To add further insult, he demands O-lan's only beautiful possession, her two precious pearls, to give to Lotus. When she protests that she wants them for her youngest daughter, he replies, "Why should that one wear pearls with her skin as black as earth? Pearls are for fair women!" In addition, he brings into their home as Lotus's servant Cuckoo, once a concubine in the great house, who had abused O-lan when she was a slave there. In her grief O-lan moans over and over, "I have borne you sons—I have borne you sons."

In her final days Wang realizes how important O-lan has been to him, tries to comfort her by spending hours at her bedside, and feels grief; but it is not the grief that a man feels for his beloved. Rather it is what he might feel for a partner or a faithful animal companion. He can never accept her big feet, flat face, and dark skin.

Buck's novels provided many Americans with their only knowledge of China in the 1930s, and it was primarily for *The Good Earth* that she received the Nobel Prize in 1938. She was the first American woman to win the prize.

Discussion Questions

1. Is it wrong for O-lan to steal the jewels that enabled her family to become so prosperous? Why or why not?

2. Although O-lan is uneducated, she is clearly intelligent. Explain how her intelligence manifests itself throughout the novel.

3. O-lan is not beautiful. Explain how this fact influences her relationship with Wang Lung and her own self-concept.

4. Explain why the two pearls O-lan kept for herself were so important to her.

—*Felicia F. Campbell*

WANG LUNG

Wang Lung is the protagonist of Pearl Buck's 1931 Pulitzer Prize–winning novel, *The Good Earth*. The novel begins with his marriage and follows him throughout his long life, in the process defining rural Chinese life before the Chinese Civil War of 1927–1949, which led to the Communist Revolution, as well as the complex relationships between men and women and among different social classes, subjects Buck, who considered China her first home, knew well. Of her characters she said, "It is people who have always afforded me my greatest pleasure and interest, and as I live among the Chinese, it has been the Chinese people. . . . They are people. I can no more define them than I can define my own relatives and kinsmen."

Wang Lung begins as an unlettered, unsophisticated farmer (the term *peasant* was not used in China at this time), tied to the land through inclination as well as necessity. His marriage to the slave O-lan is fortunate for him: having grown up and served in the kitchens of the wealthy House of Hwang and observing their ways, she has the sophistication that he lacks in the ways of the larger world. Wang Lung is kind to O-lan, but he never displays affection or questions why she speaks only when it is essential. He felt that "it should be enough that she fulfilled her duty" and was ashamed of his curiosity about her. "She was, after all, only a woman."

During a period of drought and famine, they flee to the south, where Wang Lung pulls a rickshaw and O-lan begs. Here Wang Lung encounters western missionaries for the first time and is both appalled and frightened by the missionary with eyes "as blue as ice" and a big nose. He is equally horrified by the picture of the crucifixion that the missionary gives him, wondering what the crucified man could have done to merit such a punishment and whether the missionary is seeking vengeance for what had happened to the man. He finally uses the picture as insulation in his shoe. This experience illustrates Buck's dim view of the missionary cause developed through her own growing up in a missionary home in China.

Wang Lung and O-lan's flight to the south may be compared to the Joads' flight to California in John Steinbeck's *The Grapes of Wrath* (1939). Both families see the extreme wealth of the capitalists contrasted with their own extreme poverty. One difference, however, is that Wang Lung has managed to hang onto his land, while the bank has seized the Joads'.

Wang Lung and O-lan are saved when the city is invaded; they join the looters, stealing enough money, gold, and jewels to return to their home. The morality of their stealing from the fleeing rich in the south is often debated by critics and in classrooms, but Buck shows their circumstances to be so dire that they have little choice. During the next few years, Wang Lung prospers enough to hire help, making his trusted neighbor Ching his overseer, and to continue to buy up the lands of the bankrupt House of Hwang.

At this point the only thing marring Wang Lung's happiness is his lazy, dishonest uncle, who moves himself and his family into Wang Lung's house. Wang Lung allows this invasion because he hews to the ancient tradition that one must respect one's elders, and because once the uncle has moved in Wang Lung finds that he cannot throw him out since his uncle has influence with the group of roving bandits terrorizing the neighborhood and thus provides him with protection.

With prosperity comes restlessness, and Wang Lung begins to spend time at a local teahouse frequented by the wealthy. There he falls in love with a prostitute named Lotus, whom he takes home as his concubine, a culturally acceptable action. He dotes on her, giving her everything she demands, even bringing Cuckoo, once the concubine of the master of the House of Hwang, into his household as Lotus's servant, even though he knows that Cuckoo had abused O-lan during her years of slavery in that house. Lotus is shallow and demanding, and Wang Lung spends large amounts of money attempting to make her happy. The depth of his infatuation can be seen when he aggrieves O-lan by demanding the two pearls—her only beautiful possessions, which she was saving to leave to her daughter upon her death—to give to Lotus. O-lan, who also suffers from a fatal illness, is heartbroken and keeps saying, "But I have borne you sons." When her illness reaches its terminal stages and she is bedridden, Wang Lung is kind to her, although he realizes that he has never loved her because she was not beautiful. He buries her with respect on their old land, where he himself will be buried.

Finally Wang Lung is prosperous enough to buy the House of Hwang and, persuaded by his sons, moves into it, leaving his uncle in the old house. He does not find peace, however, and lives in the midst of family quarrels and disappointments, his only respite coming with Pear Blossom, a young slave he takes as his concubine and treats much as a daughter.

Only when he returns to his original house and land to die does he once more experience the peace that he had known during the time he was working the land. Yet, it is a new era, and the reader knows from the conclusion that his sons do not share his passion for the land and will undoubtedly sell it on his death.

In his presentation speech awarding the Nobel Prize to Pearl Buck in 1938, Per Hallstom described Wang Lung as "created from the same stuff as the yellow-brown earth in the fields, and with a kind of pious joy he bestows upon it every ounce of his energy. The two belong to each other in origin, and they will become one again with the death he will meet in tranquility." To understand Wang Lung is to see him as human first and Chinese second, as eternal as "the good earth."

Discussion Questions

1. What does it say about Wang Lung that he cares so much for his "poor fool," as he calls his mentally retarded daughter?

2. Was it wrong for Wang Lung to participate in the looting of the city, thus gaining enough money rebuild his life and begin to build his fortune? Why or why not?

3. Does Buck suggest that Wang Lung would have been happier had he not made a fortune and had he kept farming the land? Explain.

—*Felicia F. Campbell*

REFERENCES

Pearl S. Buck, *My Several Worlds* (New York: Day, 1954);

Peter Conn, *Pearl S. Buck: A Cultural Biography* (Cambridge: Cambridge University Press, 1996);

Paul A. Doyle, *Pearl S. Buck* (New York: Twayne, 1965);

Kang Liao, *Pearl S. Buck: A Cultural Bridge across the Pacific* (Westport, Conn.: Greenwood Press, 1997).

Edgar Rice Burroughs

(September 1, 1875 – March 19, 1950)

◖◖◖

TARZAN OF THE APES

(Chicago: McClurg, 1914)

JANE PORTER

Jane Porter is the love interest of the noble savage Tarzan in the adventure-fantasy series written by Edgar Rice Burroughs, which begins with *Tarzan of the Apes*. In almost all of the twenty-six novels that comprise the series, there is a juxtaposition of the primitive and the civilized, the struggle between basic human instincts and the veneer of culture, which is represented in the characters of Tarzan and Jane. At least in this first novel in the series, this basic tension is never resolved.

While Tarzan is raised by apes, Jane is raised in "my own dear South," as she calls it. In *Tarzan of the Apes* she is viewed as a commodity: she must be possessed either as the object of physical desire or as an object of barter. When Jane rejects Tarzan in favor of William Clayton, the current Lord Greystoke, Tarzan, rather than announcing he has undeniable proof he is the real Lord Greystoke, remains silent. He does not want to take away Clayton's "title and his lands and his castles" because "it would take them away from Jane Porter also."

"Jane was not coldly calculating by nature," Burroughs writes, "but training, environment and heredity had all combined to teach her to reason in matters of the heart"; the influences of civilization, breeding, and heredity lead her to decide in favor of Clayton over Tarzan because Clayton is the man who most epitomizes civilization: "Did not her best judgment point to this young English nobleman, whose love she knew to be of the sort a civilized woman should crave, as the logical mate for such as herself?" She thus rejects Tarzan and chooses Clayton, who stands for everything civilized. The use of the word *mate* instead of *wife*, however, is a telling reminder of what Jane experienced in the "impenetrable blackness of the jungle" when she and Tarzan were alone.

In the jungle Jane is attracted to "this god-like man" because of his virile presence. When she is carried off by the rogue ape Terkoz, Tarzan arrives in time to save her. She watches, "her eyes wide with mingled horror, fascination, fear, and admiration[,] . . . the primordial ape battle with the primeval man for possession of a woman—for her." While he fights, she notices Tarzan's "great muscles of back and shoulders knotted beneath the tension of his efforts. . . . the veil of centuries of civilization and culture was swept from the blurred vision of the Baltimore girl." When Tarzan kills Terkoz, Jane rushes to him as "a primeval woman who sprang forward with outstretched arms toward the primeval man who had fought for her and won her." Tarzan "took his woman in his arms and smothered her upturned, panting lips with kisses." At this moment, according to Burroughs, Jane "knew the meaning of love." Suddenly she comes to herself: "an outraged conscience suffused her face with its scarlet mantle, and a mortified woman thrust Tarzan of the Apes from her." Tarzan is not put off, however, and carries her off into the jungle. Civilization drops away, and Jane responds only with emotion and instinct to her "forest lover."

Returning to "prosaic Wisconsin," Jane reflects on what has happened to her: "She had been carried off her feet by the strength of the young giant when his great arms were about her in the distant African forest"; but today she sees the incident as "a temporary mental reversion . . . to the psychological appeal of the primeval man to the primeval woman in her nature."

Discussion Questions

1. Compare and contrast the characterization of Jane in the novels to her portrayal in any of the Tarzan movies.

2. Several times throughout the novel Tarzan saves Jane just as she is about to succumb to a series of perils. Find at least three of these moments and discuss how they reflect the central theme of the novel.

3. In the novel, Jane is described as being but nineteen years old. Are her actions those of a nineteen-year-old? Give examples from the text to demonstrate your position.

4. Compare and contrast the way Jane acts in Africa with the way she acts in Wisconsin. What kind of demands are made of her in the jungle and at the cabin in Wisconsin?

5. Throughout the early part of Jane's experiences it is mentioned that she is in need of protection from the males around her. Do her actions show that she is a "helpless female," or something else? Use examples to prove your position.

—*Bob Bell*

TARZAN

Tarzan, who was introduced in Edgar Rice Burroughs's novel *Tarzan of the Apes* and appeared in twenty-three subsequent works, is the most popular character created by the prolific Burroughs. In a 1927 letter, the author wrote: "I liked to speculate as to the relative values of heredity, environment, and training in the mental, moral, and physical development of . . . a child, and so in Tarzan I was playing with this idea." The conflict between Tarzan's heredity and the jungle environment in which he is raised provides much of the narrative tension in Burroughs's story. Throughout *Tarzan of the Apes* Tarzan is portrayed as gradually realizing the limitations of his "savage" upbringing. By the end of the story aristocratic heredity triumphs over the impulses of the ape: Tarzan sacrifices his happiness for Jane's by not revealing his true identity as Lord Greystoke, effectively relinquishing his title to Jane's fiancé, William Clayton.

Tarzan's progression from "white ape" to gentleman is represented in several stages: from ape to human, to a more specific identification with white humanity, and finally to gentleman. Throughout his childhood Tarzan does not distinguish between himself and the apes who raise him. Even after he encounters humans from a nearby tribe, he compares their brutality and love of violence for its own sake unfavorably with the ethics of the animal kingdom, in which killing is done only in self-defense or for food. After Tarzan wins the kingship of the tribe through his intelligence and the use of a tool, his father's knife, he quickly realizes that these human attributes set him apart from his tribe: "he found that he had grown away from his people. Their interests and his were far removed. They had not kept pace with him, nor could they understand . . . the many strange and wonderful dreams that passed through [Tarzan's] active brain." He is not an ape but a man. However, he quickly moves from identification with all of humanity to identification with whites: he is not as cruel as the African tribesmen are portrayed as being, and he is not black.

Tarzan finds the white society he craves through his interaction with the Porter party. It is Jane Porter who first evokes his aristocratic heritage. When he gives Jane his mother's locket, she curtsies and he responds by bowing to her and kissing the locket. This gesture "was the hall-mark of his aristocratic birth, the natural outcropping of many generations of fine breeding, and hereditary instinct of graciousness. . . . Now, in every fiber of his being, heredity spoke louder than training." During the climactic final scenes of the novel, however, Tarzan contemplates killing Canler to free Jane from her obligation to him. She rebukes him, telling him, "You are no longer a savage beast. You are a gentleman, and gentlemen do not kill in cold blood." Tarzan silently replies, "I am still a wild beast at heart." Yet, when Canler's threat has been removed by other means, Tarzan, realizing that he is, in fact, a gentleman, chooses to allow Clayton to keep the title Lord Greystoke and to marry Jane. Tarzan's final statement to Clayton—"I was born [in the jungle]. . . . My mother was an Ape. . . . I never knew who my father was"—implies that this now-refined British gentleman will return to the jungle, where he feels most at home.

Along with his idealization of aristocratic manhood, Burroughs's acceptance of the related ideas of imperialism, racism, and social evolution (the belief, popular at the turn of the twentieth century, that northern Europeans and the wealthy were the most advanced people) has bothered many critics of the novel. Ruth Mayer, for instance, argues that the continuous upward progression from ape to gentleman that Tarzan experiences represents Burroughs's notion of the ideal training for a civilized white man. She writes, "Burroughs makes [civilization] out as a complicated mixture of heredity and training that has to be protected and cultivated, and is much too unique to be passed on," and she concludes that "to become truly white and truly male, his novel argues, you have to go to Africa and become an ape." In 1932 Burroughs argued, "It pleased me . . . to draw comparisons between the manner of men and the manner of beasts and seldom to the advantage of men. . . . I wanted my readers to realize that man alone of all the creatures . . . derives pleasure from inflicting pain on other creatures, even his own kind." Yet, in his novel Burroughs depicts Tarzan's terrorizing of African "cannibals" neutrally, without comment or censure. The stranded whites, at the mercy of Africans and mutinous sailors, are portrayed as the true victims of man's cruelty.

Tarzan of the Apes is frequently compared with other literary works. Burroughs drew one comparison himself when, in a 1938 interview, he commented upon the inspiration for Tarzan. "As a boy I loved . . . the boy Mowgli in Kipling's 'Jungle Books.' I suppose Tarzan was the result of those early loves." In Rudyard Kipling's book, the orphan Mowgli is raised by wolves and other animals until he becomes a man. However, in his introduction to the Penguin Books edition of *Tarzan of the Apes*, critic John Seelye argues that "the *Jungle [Books]* emphasiz[e] the need for community, while *Tarzan* is absolutely bloody-minded and celebrates the ascendancy of superior individuals."

Despite such criticisms, the continuing popularity of the character of Tarzan through twenty-three sequels, which chronicle the ape-man's marriage with Jane and the adventures of the couple and their son, and in the numerous motion-picture and television versions testifies to the public's persistent appetite for such entertainment.

Discussion Questions

1. Some critics have argued that the plot of *Tarzan of the Apes* is implausible. Even Burroughs recognized this. In 1927 he wrote, "I do not believe that any human infant or child, unprotected by adults of its own species, could survive a fortnight in such an African environment as I describe in the Tarzan stories." Yet, many readers of the novel are able to suspend their disbelief. Is there any element in *Tarzan of the Apes* that is believable? What are the differences between those portions of the novel that are believable and those that are not?

2. John Seelye claimed that Mowgli and the animals he lived with formed a community, while Tarzan was self-reliant. Is there evidence in Burroughs's novel that contradicts this claim? For example, where and how does Tarzan acquire his weapons? While Tarzan may not be part of a supportive group such as Mowgli's, is he solely responsible for his survival in the jungle?

3. The fans of the original 1912 magazine version of *Tarzan of the Apes* did not approve of Tarzan's renunciation of civilization at the end of the novel and complained to the publisher until Burroughs produced a sequel. Are the final scenes (Tarzan's relinquishing of his birthright and his implicit return to the jungle) an appropriate ending to the novel? What could Tarzan (or Burroughs) have done differently that would be more satisfying to a reader? If Tarzan had accepted his heritage and was somehow able to marry Jane, would this fit Burroughs's notion of the actions of an aristocrat? How could all these elements be reconciled into an appropriate narrative conclusion?

4. In thinking about the ending of *Tarzan of the Apes*, Burroughs's biographer Irwin Porges found Tarzan's ease in acclimatizing to civilization more significant than his apparent rejection of his aristocratic heritage. Porges argues that "Tarzan and his circumstances [while in the jungle] represent abnormality: within this strange situation nature's irresistible pressure for a righting, a balance, forces heredity to assume its proper place." Is this a convincing reading of Tarzan's circumstances and char-

acter? Does Tarzan's heredity lead him irresistibly to the resumption of his place in society?

—*Christopher M. Sutch*

REFERENCES

Leslie Fielder, "Mythicizing the Unspeakable," *Journal of American Folklore,* 103 (October 1990): 390–399;

Eling B. Holtsmark, *Edgar Rice Burroughs* (Boston: Twayne, 1986);

David Leverenz, "The Last Real Man in America: From Natty Bumppo to Batman," *American Literary History,* 3 (Winter 1991): 753–781;

Richard A. Lupoff, *Edgar Rice Burroughs: Master of Adventure* (New York: Ace, 1968);

Ruth Mayer, "The White Hunter: Edgar Rice Burroughs, Ernest Hemingway, Clint Eastwood, and the Art of Acting Male in Africa," in *Subverting Masculinity: Hegemonic and Alternative Versions of Masculinity in Contemporary Culture,* edited by Russell West and Frank Lay (Amsterdam & Atlanta: Rodopi, 2000), pp. 247–265;

Irwin Porges, *Edgar Rice Burroughs: The Man Who Created Tarzan* (Provo, Utah: Brigham Young University Press, 1975);

John Taliaferro, *Tarzan Forever: The Life of Edgar Rice Burroughs* (New York: Scribner, 1999);

Tarzan of the Apes, edited, with an introduction, by Maura Spiegal (New York: Barnes & Noble, 2006).

William S. Burroughs

(February 5, 1914 – August 2, 1997)

༄

NAKED LUNCH

(Paris: Olympia, 1959; New York: Grove, 1962)

Dr. Benway

Dr. Benway conducts sadistically "disinterested" medical experiments in William S. Burroughs's *Naked Lunch.* Despite Benway's protest that he is "a reputable scientist, not a charlatan, a lunatic, or a pretended worker of miracles," he is a prime example of Burroughs's characteristic appropriation of iconographic figures from pulp fiction and B movies. Burroughs makes no attempt to create Benway as realistic: he provides little biographical background and establishes no psychological or emotional inner life for him. He, rather, relies on the reader's familiarity with prototypes of the mad doctor. More than just the central figure of Burroughs's most memorable "routines," farcical skits and vignettes, Benway functions as a reference point situating the need to control, generally, and representing, more specifically, the crypto-fascistic medical establishment that tortures junkies and "queers" hygienically in the name of therapy.

Benway, like Burroughs, "is a manipulator and coordinator of symbol systems"; but he uses his expertise for the purpose of "interrogation, brainwashing and control." His objective is to get his wards to internalize the mechanisms of control by making them feel secretly complicit in the indulgence of illicit desires that he has in fact instigated. Deviously applying the principles of reconditioning, Benway and his colleagues seek to achieve complete control of body and will through the coordination of humiliation and deprivation: the prevention of the relief of tension stimulated by suggestions, erotic or otherwise, that appeal to latent inclinations. Benway repudiates the traditional control procedures of totalitarianism: mass arrest, incarceration, and torture in its more overtly brutal forms. His specialty is the inculcation of anxiety and guilt rather than terror, on the principle that the "subject must not realize that the mistreatment is a deliberate attack of an antihuman enemy on his personal identity. He must be made to feel that he deserves *any* treatment he receives because there is something (never specified) horribly wrong with him." While the infliction of pain can be salubrious once the subject is brought to feel that such punishment is deserved, the withholding of threatened torture produces "the appropriate feeling of helplessness and gratitude" toward the interrogator.

Benway has worked toward "Total Demoralization" in order to establish "a beachhead of homogeneity" out of the "shambles of potentials." Yet, he is designated a possible "double agent." If he does in fact subvert other agents, it is less because of a shift of allegiance than the virtuoso's enthusiastic need to show off. He describes with relish how he uses his techniques to exploit the confusion that sometimes develops in narcotics agents between their true identity and the identity they assume for their undercover work. He convinces the rival agent that his cover story—for example, that he is a queer addict—is his true identity, so that "his agent identity becomes unconscious . . . out of his control." Punctuating his speech with "limp-wristed" gestures, Benway articulates his belief that heterosexual agents are "frustrate latent queer." Extrapolated, this notion would further insinuate that those who become narcs are latent junkies, for whom control substitutes for dope. Within the terms of this devious logic of substitution, Benway's duplicitous agency can also be recognized in the fact that he has experiential knowledge of how cocaine activates the pleasure receptors of the brain and that he also refers to having had "a *yagé* [liana] hangover" when he got into a scalpel fight with a medical colleague.

Most fundamentally, the designation of double agent could refer to the fact that Benway and his colleagues need a steady supply of the socially disreputable needs they are commissioned to extirpate in order to maintain their own status and power. By this convoluted logic, Benway, control addict and co-opter of others' needs, comes to personify the totality of unlimited need that Burroughs designates "a basic formula of evil." Although Benway is an agent of control, he has anarchic impulses as great as agent William Lee's. He is said to be "concocting a serum" whose purpose is a mystery; but a telepathic trace has been put on him because he is an "Arty type"—which is to say, he has "no principles" and "Might do anything . . . Turn a massacre into a sex orgy . . . Or a joke." These attributions might help to explain why Burroughs uses Benway to express some of his own cherished etiological theories about the brain chemistry produced by different drugs and the mutual incompatibility of addiction and schizophrenic psychosis. It is also Benway who voices both Burroughs's convictions regarding the link between psychosis and literacy, advertising, and the media, and his suspicions regarding the sinister, counter-evolutionary consequences of essentially matriarchal welfare states.

Discussion Questions

1. Benway guides William Lee and the reader through his hellish institution, pointing out its various denizens and making acidic comments on them out of the side of his mouth in a manner reminiscent of Burroughs himself. Which thematic preoccupations found elsewhere in *Naked Lunch* are developed further by Benway's anecdotal commentary on the INDs and the Latah?

2. Benway's anecdote about a man with a talking anus is one of Burroughs's most critically analyzed "routines." How does the general pattern of events and the specific details of each stage of the transformation serve as a parable regarding the atrophying, usurping, and occluding nature of addiction; the comparability of homosexuality and addiction; and the need to control the instability of the body?

3. By what logic does Burroughs link the jelly of "Undifferentiated Tissue," which covers the man's (facial) mouth and leads to the amputation of his head, to the cancerous growth of bureaucratic agencies and to "the basic American rottenness"? And what, exactly, is "the basic American rottenness"?

—*David Brottman*

WILLIAM LEE

William Lee is a drug addict living "in a permanent third-day kick" in William S. Burroughs's *Naked Lunch*. The oblique, fragmented description of his attempts to score drugs and evade narcotics agents provides a loose frame and minimal foundation for Burroughs's fusion of scurrilous sadistic reverie and phantasmagoric slapstick farce. These elements are sometimes shaped into satirical vignettes of degradation, which depict "deplorable conditions like vaudeville skits." But it is not always easy to determine where Lee's "routines" leave off and Burroughs's "cut-ups" (a technique where passages are cut-up and randomly reorganized) take over. This difficulty has many sources: narrative time shifts that disrupt the reader's sense of linear progression, the mutations of characters that subvert assumptions about the demarcations of self, the grotesque objectification of fleeting subjective impressions, and certain similarities between the character's experiences and the author's biography. ("William Lee" was the pseudonymous author of Burroughs's first book, the semi-autobiographical *Junky*.)

Lee describes himself in the declining stages of his addiction, going from "white tendrils of fungus curled round . . . naked bones" to a "transparency" that makes him so difficult to see that people have to cover him "with a project" in order to see him as anything other than a trick of the light. However, despite the provision of such evocative descriptive detail, Burroughs adamantly insisted that *Naked Lunch* should be read not as a novel but as "a blueprint, a How-To Book" demonstrating "How-to extend levels of experience." Thus, what seems hallucinatory is also revelatory inasmuch as it objectifies the addict's experience of addiction. For example, Lee describes himself on the run from narcs that are tracking him, not with bloodhounds but with an addict, Willy the Disk, who, hypersensitized by need, is "feeling for the silent frequency of junk" with an ectoplasmic mouth.

Lee himself is an "agent" of "the narcotics industry"—a term Burroughs uses to describe the tacit organization of mutual need that exists between junkies, pushers, narcs, and the medical establishment. The porous, unstable demarcation between users and narcs is made explicit when Lee is listed as one of the "defecting agents" from whom "the danger, as always, comes. . . . Because all Agents defect and all Resisters sell out." Reference is also made to the apparently not-uncommon case of an undercover agent "who forgot her real identity and merged with her cover story." A similar idea, expressed in more comically extravagant terms, appears early in Lee's sketch of the junkie life, when he describes Bradley the Buyer, the "best narcotics agent in the industry," who, after becoming a typical junkie—a gray, spectral, "earthbound ghost" of "rancid ectoplasm"—developed a "yen" so huge that, like some monster out of science fiction, he began to absorb others into the green, slimy jelly of his need. This enveloping slime seems to be linked by a logic of association with seminal fluid, which flows in copious amounts during the many fantasies of sadistic sex in the book, and with "Undifferentiated Tissue," a cancerous substance with an immoderate, protean capacity for growth that Burroughs identifies with the junkie's loss of individuality to his amorphous need.

Lee is a "double agent" working for the Factualists, subversives who battle other totalitarian factions vying for supremacy in the Interzone, a vast hive-like city humming with "sex and commerce," where "all human potentials are spread out in a vast silent market" of past and future illicit goods and services. The designation given to Lee's group seems to identify them with the same intent to expose reality that is indicated by Burroughs's retrospective comment on the implication of the title of the book: "a frozen moment when everyone sees what is on the end of every fork." The Factualists are at odds with groups representing different methods of reducing multifarious human difference into uniformity by establishing control over the body-psyche interface. Lee and the other Factualists seek to evade and subvert the program of the Divisionists, who clone themselves from amputated bits of themselves. Given the inexorable process of self-replication, "there will be only one replica of one sex . . . one person in the world with millions of separate bodies," because "every replica but your own is eventually an 'Undesirable.'" The Liquefactionist program, evidently derived by Burroughs from Josef Stalin's campaign of terror, "involves the eventual merging of everyone into One Man by a process of protoplasmic absorption." However, since "you can never be sure of anyone in the industry," it must remain unclear to the end of this process who that man will be and who has been whose "dupe." What is clearer is that "there is one Mark" no hustler can beat: "The Mark inside."

In the last section of the book, Lee describes killing two narcs, Hauser and O'Brien, only to realize that this episode has been a paranoid fantasy, that the cops do not actually exist and that he has been "occluded from space-time like an eel's ass occludes when he stops eating on the way to Sargasso." The puzzling fact that Lee feels himself "moving into the past . . . clawing at a not-yet of Telepathic Bureaucracies, Time Monopolies, Control Drugs" is illuminated in a subsequent section titled "Atrophied Preface," which, in keeping with the temporal disjunctions of the book, appears at the end. Lee has been "taking the junk cure," a process in which "cures past and future shuttle pictures through his spectral substance vibrating in silent winds of accelerated Time."

Discussion Questions

1. How are both incarnation (possessing a body) and incarceration (a mechanism of control) implicated in Lee's understanding of Time?

2. Lee is said to "live in perpetual quarantine," and he is required by the bureaucracy "to file an immediate affidavit that he is suffering from bubonic plague." How do these and other descriptions illuminate Burroughs's analyses of the nature of disease and the nature of bureaucracy?

—*David Brottman*

REFERENCES

Michael B. Goodman, *William S. Burroughs: An Annotated Bibliography of his Works and Criticism* (New York: Garland, 1975);

Frank D. McConnell, "William Burroughs and the Literature of Addiction," *Massachusetts Review*, 8 (Autumn 1967): 665–680;

Ted Morgan, *Literary Outlaw: The Life and Times of William S. Burroughs* (New York: Holt, 1988);

Timothy S. Murphy, "Intersection Points: Teaching William S. Burroughs's *Naked Lunch*," *College Literature*, 27 (Winter 2000): 84–102;

Jennie Skerl, *William S. Burroughs* (Boston: Twayne, 1985).

Octavia E. Butler

(June 22, 1947 – February 24 2006)

❧

KINDRED

(Garden City, N.Y.: Doubleday, 1979)

EDANA FRANKLIN

Edana Franklin, who calls herself Dana, is the protagonist and first-person narrator of Octavia E. Butler's novel *Kindred*. The twenty-six-year-old African American writer is married to a white man, Kevin. She must confront the past of her own family when she vanishes repeatedly from 1976 Los Angeles and reappears on an antebellum Maryland plantation. There she must rescue her ancestor Rufus Weylin, the master's son, each time she arrives. Dana has no control over this unexplained form of time travel: whenever Rufus is in danger, she is summoned to save him. By contrast, she can only return to the present if her own life is threatened.

Dana guides the reader through an era that threatens her health and life. She also must fight for her own existence in the twentieth century: she must make sure Rufus lives long enough to father her ancestor Hagar with a black woman, Alice. Commenting on the realistic and graphic depictions of Dana's experiences, Butler explained to interviewer Joshunda Sanders: "The idea was always to make the time emotionally real to people." *Kindred* is a neo-slave narrative, an attempt by a contemporary African American novelist to revisit (and rewrite) the past from the perspective of black history.

Dana must learn to remember that which she never knew and which has not been preserved in the official historical records: the neglected and traumatic history of slavery. In the process of uncovering her family's secret history, she becomes deeply traumatized. While Dana must learn to safeguard a forgotten history, she must also struggle to keep herself safe from it. Angelyn Mitchell notes about Butler's work and other neo-slave narratives that they "give witness to what has been historically unspeakable and, in some ways, unimaginable." Butler asks her readers to recognize the shortcomings of the official historical records and to honor the stories of those who remain lost forever. As Dana puts it: "Hagar Weylin Blake had died in 1880. . . . No doubt most information about her life had died with her. . . . So many relatives that I had never known, would never know."

The beginning and ending of the novel reflect on Dana's responsibility as an historical witness. Returning to the present after killing Rufus, Dana finds her arm fused to a wall at "the exact spot Rufus's fingers had grasped it" as he was dying. The past holds on to Dana, even after her last trip, and she in turn will forever reach out to the past. Her amputated arm also makes her kindred to those slaves who were punished with the amputation of a limb because they had run away.

Dana's ancestor Alice functions as her double. Like Dana, Alice was once free but is enslaved by Rufus. The two also resemble each other physically, and after Alice's death, Rufus remarks, " 'You were one woman,' he said. '. . . Two halves of a whole.'" Alice represents a frightening variation of Dana's possible fate on the Weylin plantation, were she not able to travel back to 1976. As Dana concludes about her own possible fate in the antebellum South: "A slave was a slave. Anything could be done to her."

Dana's last name and the time frame of her journeys to the past comment on the bicentennial of the Declaration of Independence. While in 1976 America officially celebrated two hundred years of freedom and independence, Dana—and the reader—is reminded that African American history had not recorded two hundred years of freedom yet. Thus, much like founding father Benjamin Franklin, Dana must declare her own independence by liberating herself from Rufus's rule.

Dana may also be compared to Lilith, the protagonist of Butler's science-fiction trilogy *Lilith's Brood.* Both Lilith and Dana are subjugated by someone who holds power over them. Yet, they show compassion for others, are industrious and intelligent, assess situations objectively and quickly, and consider all consequences of their actions carefully. Both strive for their goals continuously, even if the chances of succeeding seem remote.

Discussion Questions

1. The title of the novel *Kindred* can be understood in several different ways. What does the term mean to Dana?

2. Alice can be seen as Dana's double. Explain how the two characters mirror, contradict, or complement each other. How does Rufus see each woman?

3. In the beginning, Dana and Kevin think they are just playing a role on the antebellum plantation. Does this change? Explain in what ways they remain outsiders and in what ways they become part of the antebellum social system.

4. Critics have noted that Dana begins to see similarities between Kevin and the Weylin men. What are these similarities? Why does the novel draw a parallel between these men?

—*Éva Tettenborn*

REFERENCES

Christine Levecq, "Power and Repetition: Philosophies of (Literary) History in Octavia E. Butler's *Kindred,*" *Contemporary Literature,* 41, no. 3 (2000): 525–553;

Lisa A. Long, "A Relative Pain: The Rape of History in Octavia Butler's *Kindred* and Phyllis Alesia Perry's *Stigmata,*" *College English,* 64, no. 4 (2002): 459–483;

Angelyn Mitchell, *The Freedom to Remember: Narrative, Slavery, and Gender in Contemporary Black Women's Fiction* (New Brunswick, N.J.: Rutgers University Press, 2002), pp. 6–21;

Joshunda Sanders, "Interview with Octavia Butler," *In Motion Magazine* (14 March 2004) <http://www.inmotionmagazine.com/ac04/obutler.html> [accessed November 13, 2007];

Marc Steinberg, "Inverting History in Octavia Butler's Postmodern Slave Narrative," *African American Review,* 38, no. 3 (2004): 467–476.

James Branch Cabell
(April 14, 1879 – May 5, 1958)

JURGEN: A COMEDY OF JUSTICE
(New York: McBride, 1919)

JURGEN

Jurgen—a retired poet and now a pawnbroker—is the central figure in James Branch Cabell's *Jurgen: A Comedy of Justice*, a novel that begins in the fictional, medieval kingdom of Poictesme and moves rapidly into a fantasy world of myth, symbol, and legend. That Jurgen has forsaken poetry for pawnbroking suggests that he is a failed artist who has lost the drive to create his own imagery; he has turned to a profession in which he can make money on the secondhand images that others pawn from necessity. For all Jurgen's creativity, there seems to be something lacking in his character.

One evening, on the way home from his pawnshop, Jurgen (a trickster, always ready with an ingenious argument, often based on sources that he himself has manufactured) hears a Cistercian monk curse the devil and puts in a good word for evil in the universe. He asks the monk to think of Satan's "fine artistry, as evidenced in all the perilous and lovely snares of this world, which it is your business to combat, and mine to lend money upon." Immediately ,Jurgen meets a man dressed in black, who grants Jurgen an unspoken wish: when Jurgen arrives home, his wife, Dame Lisa, has disappeared. After several days, Jurgen goes in quest of her, a quest that he quickly turns into a search for "justice, over the grave of a dream and through the malice of time."

Jurgen all but forgets his wife, until he meets a woman who resembles her down to her "twisted little finger" but who may (or may not) be an evil magician. At the urging of Princess Guenevere, he cuts off this woman's head and is only slightly taken aback when the headless woman does not change into the magician. "At all events," says Jurgen, "I have done that which seems equitable; and I have found no comfort in the doing of it." His response seems strangely muted, without strong regret or elation.

As a quest hero, Jurgen claims to be in search of justice, rationality, and meaning in the universe. His search, rather haphazard and intellectually unmotivated, leads him to a series of women who symbolize ways of giving meaning to a nonrational universe. Guenevere, for example, stands for chivalry, Anaitis for sexuality, and Helen for beauty. Jurgen's relationships with these women, however, are, with the possible exception of Helen, almost entirely sexual. Jurgen is a comic character, a figure of fun, and his sexualized quest is presented not seriously but comically.

Jurgen's most traumatic encounter is with a brown man with queer feet—the great god Pan, who promises to show Jurgen "All." Cabell does not describe Pan's vision of the universe, but Jurgen is devastated. The universe does not care at all about him. Jurgen responds: "I tell you quite candidly, you brown man, there is something in Jurgen far too admirable for any intelligent arbiter ever to fling into the dustheap. I am, if nothing else, a monstrous clever fellow: and I think I shall endure, somehow. . . . I believe I can contrive some trick to cheat oblivion when the need arises." No matter what, Jurgen must maintain his illusions, and he flees to the closest cathedral, looking for the reassurance of Christianity, a reassurance that he does not receive.

In the first Modern Library edition of *Jurgen*, Cabell added an "Epistle to a Pawnbroker," an open letter to the character Jurgen. In this letter, Cabell admits that the fictional Jurgen is modeled on "a flesh-and-blood" person (probably Schuyler Otis Bland, Cabell's mentor at the College of William and Mary). Cabell prefers to remember this "dark and nimble and sleek-headed and impudent-eyed boy" as "young and untamed and rather wonderful," before he "dwindled away into sedate mediocrity— and thence to a well-tended plot in a cemetery." As Cabell puts it, "So must the young male who is worth his salt delight to jaunt abroad; to see and to admire the world's strangeness." But the middle-aged pawnbroker seeks the stability that youth eschews. For Jurgen "illusions are necessary," and the illusion of stability remains. After "testing a sufficient number of pleasures and palaces," Cabell tells the fictional Jurgen, you were "again safely caught in the talons of a virtuous female: and you liked it. It was a situation as nearly permanent as any man may hope to attain upon this side of the grave." Cabell presents Jurgen as an Everyman figure who willy-nilly must follow the pattern that Cabell describes in his epistle.

Jurgen, to use Henry Fielding's phrase, is a "comic epic in prose," and Jurgen and Fielding's *Tom Jones* share certain character traits, including sexual exuberance and the lack of a strict conscience. But Jurgen and Homer's Odysseus are perhaps closer to each other in shared traits: each is a trickster and a womanizer, and each, after a long quest, returns to his wife. At bottom Jurgen and Odysseus are quite different, however, and the contrast between the two may tell readers more than the comparison, especially in their attitudes toward immortality and identity. Further, Jurgen is related to the questing heroes in medieval and Renaissance romances such as *Amadis of Gaul* and Sir Philip Sidney's *Arcadia,* but most closely to the comic romance *Orlando Furioso* by Ariosto. The questing allegorical heroes of Edmund Spenser's *The Faerie Queene* may be seen as the serious counterparts of Jurgen. Miguel de Cervantes's Don Quixote is also a comic, questing knight in a realistic world. Finally, Jurgen has certain affinities to Johann Wolfgang von Goethe's Faust.

Discussion Questions

1. F. Scott Fitzgerald sent Cabell a copy of *The Great Gatsby* (1925) with this inscription: "I hope that parts of this will please you half as much as every story of yours pleases me." Compare and contrast Jurgen and Gatsby.

2. *Jurgen* is filled with strange references, anagrams, verbal playing, and puzzles. In what ways do those reflect Jurgen's character?

3. At the end of chapter 1, Jurgen must take off the cross that "had once belonged to his mother" before he can enter the cave. What is the importance of leaving the cross on a barberry bush?

4. Jurgen enters the cave three times. What do these three entrances tell us about Jurgen?

5. Do all the female characters in the novel embody values that Jurgen considers and tests? How many value systems does he reject and why?

—*W. L. Godshalk*

REFERENCES

Frances Joan Brewer, *James Branch Cabell: A Bibliography of His Writings, Biography, and Criticism* (Charlottesville: University of Virginia Press, 1957);

Joe Lee Davis, *James Branch Cabell* (New York: Twayne, 1962);

W. L. Godshalk, *In Quest of Cabell: Five Exploratory Essays* (New York: Revisionist Press, 1975);

Edgar MacDonald, *James Branch Cabell and Richmond-in-Virginia* (Jackson: University Press of Mississippi, 1993).

George Washington Cable
(October 12, 1844 – January 31, 1925)

ᐧᐧ

THE GRANDISSIMES
(New York: Scribners, 1880)

HONORÉ GRANDISSIME
Although the German American immigrant and apothecary Joseph Frowenfeld is the protagonist of George Washington Cable's *The Grandissimes,* Honoré Grandissime is by every measure the hero of

the novel. A Creole gentleman and a New Orleans merchant, Honoré is confronted with an ethical (and financial) dilemma when he inherits his family's landholdings and discovers that the solvency of the Grandissimes depends upon a single prosperous plantation that the family does not rightfully own. If he returns the plantation to its proper heirs, Honoré will most likely bankrupt his entire family, but if he does nothing, he will certainly perpetuate the poverty of the rightful owners of the property, Aurora and Clotilde Nancanou. To complicate matters, the Nancanous are direct descendants of the de Grapions, longtime archrivals of the Grandissimes, and Honoré is in love with Aurora.

To come to grips with this situation and act in accordance with his emerging social conscience, Honoré must first overcome the laissez-faire tendencies that signal his complicity in the class inequities and racial injustices of his community. For example, when he first meets Frowenfeld, he tells the immigrant that he will soon be participating in all the local vices in spite of his convictions: "They all do it—all those who come," Honoré says. "They hold out a little while—a very little; then they open their stores on Sunday, they import cargoes of Africans, they bribe the officials, they smuggle goods." But when Frowenfeld asks why Honoré does not condemn such activities but instead silently endorses them, he replies, "Mr. Frowenfeld, my habit is to buy cheap and sell at a profit. My condemnation? My-de'-seh, there is no sa-a-ale for it! it spoils the sale of other goods, my-de'-seh. It is not to condemn that you want; you want to *suc-ceed*. Ha, ha, ha! you see I am a merchant, eh? My-de'-seh, can *you* afford not to succeed?"

Aside from demonstrating how economics and ethics are often at odds, Honoré stands in for post-Reconstruction Southerners who, as Cable later argued in his essay "The Silent South" (1885), could no longer allow their reticence to be construed as support for practices that denied African Americans their civil rights or as a quiet endorsement of the caste system and sectionalist alienation such practices perpetuated. Instead, citizens of the New South had to join the rest of the nation in discussing the common future of its citizens, black and white, Northern and Southern. This theme of breaking

silence runs throughout *The Grandissimes* and is firmly connected to Honoré's development as a character. Over the course of the novel, he gradually learns to take responsibility for his inaction and implicates himself as an accomplice in crimes he could have prevented if only he had spoken up. One such crime is the brutal torture and death of Bras-Coupé, an African prince turned chattel slave. Another is the relegation of Honoré's quadroon half brother, Honoré Grandissime f.m.c.—short for "free man of color"—to the status of a second-class citizen on account of his "mixed blood." In learning how to speak out against such crimes instead of saying nothing, Honoré lends his voice to the "silent majority" of Southerners who were weary of such crimes and serves as a role model for Cable's Southern contemporaries. In "The Silent South," Cable wrote that in order "to go forward we must cure one of our old time habits—the habit of letting error go uncontradicted because it is ours." Honoré lives up to this principle by doing what he knows in his heart to be right even though it goes against his ingrained habit of doing nothing simply because it is socially, politically, or economically expedient.

Honoré rises above the fray where Frowenfeld often falls short because, unlike Frowenfeld, who invites the scorn of the Creole community by incessantly lecturing its members about what they should and should not do, Honoré leads by the examples his words and actions set for others. He thus exemplifies Cable's political philosophy as well as his rhetorical strategy in *The Grandissimes*. Cable believed that the novel does best "that teaches without telling," as he explained in a letter to novelist and literature professor Hjalmar Hjorth Boyesen. Recognizing that Southern society was "sore to the touch," to use Honoré's words, Cable used *The Grandissimes,* and in particular Honoré's transformation, to teach his fellow Southerners how to become better citizens of the reunified nation without telling them what to do. Cable hoped, by so doing, to avoid the kind of backlash against his democratic idealism that Frowenfeld suffers from throughout the novel.

At the time Cable was writing *The Grandissimes,* the conventions of American literature were undergoing a sea change. The romantic sensibilities that characterized American fiction prior to the Civil

War had given way to a nascent American realism. This conventional transition is exemplified by Cable's novel, which juxtaposes realistic depictions of real-life social ills with the fictional romantic subplot of the narrative. This juxtaposition, and Honoré Grandissime's role in it, is the key to understanding how Cable uses the conventions of romance to offer a realist critique of the politics of the New South. Honoré is a romantic hero of a romantic love story, but the sanguine optimism of the romance in which he figures is undercut by the starkly realistic depicting of torture and disfigurement included in the centerpiece of the novel, "The Story of Bras-Coupé." As Honoré comes to realize that he was an unwitting accomplice to the death of Bras-Coupé, Cable shows the reader how romanticized portrayals of a slave-owning society (for example, the narratives of the plantation tradition) enable crimes against humanity such as those depicted in "The Story of Bras-Coupé." Honoré is therefore not only a role model for Southerners after Reconstruction, he is also an object lesson in what romantic literature conceals beneath its fictional facade.

Discussion Questions

1. When Frowenfeld first encounters Honoré Grandissime, the reader is told that Honoré's "whole appearance was a dazzling contradiction of the notion that a Creole is a person of mixed blood." Why does Honoré's race matter in the context of the narrative?

2. The narrator, along with the rest of Creole society, is shocked and appalled to see Honoré riding his horse side by side with the American governor in chapter 15. What does this scene represent? Why is Honoré vilified for conversing with a "Yankee"?

3. In "The Silent South," Cable makes a fine distinction between civil rights and social equality. Cable advocated for the former, but called the latter "a fool's dream." How do Honoré's beliefs resemble Cable's? Whose political platform more closely resembles Cable's, Honoré's or Frowenfeld's?

4. When Frowenfeld accuses Honoré of allowing the torture of Bras-Coupé to take place, Honoré exclaims, "they lied to me—said they would not harm him!" Do you believe Honoré's excuse? Why or why not?

5. In chapter 45 the two Honoré Grandissimes team up to form the mercantile house Grandissime Brothers. But just three chapters later Honoré admits "he had come out the beneficiary of this restitution, extricated from bankruptcy by an agreement which gave the f.m.c. only a public recognition of kinship which had always been his due." Why does this partnership fail to make the two Honorés equals in the eyes of society? Can just one person, in this case Honoré, make a difference when it comes to remedying widespread social ills such as slavery?

—*Michael Germana*

REFERENCES

John Cleman, *George Washington Cable Revisited* (New York: Twayne/Simon & Schuster, 1996);

Michael Germana, "Real Change: George Washington Cable's *The Grandissimes* and the Crime of '73," *Arizona Quarterly*, 61, no. 3 (2005): 75–108;

Louis D. Rubin Jr., *George W. Cable: The Life and Times of a Southern Heretic* (New York: Pegasus, 1969);

Arlin Turner, *Critical Essays on George W. Cable* (Boston: G. K. Hall, 1980);

Turner, *George W. Cable: A Biography* (Durham, N.C.: Duke University Press, 1956).

Abraham Cahan
(June 6, 1860 – August 31, 1951)

‹۵

THE RISE OF DAVID LEVINSKY
(New York: Harper, 1917)

DAVID LEVINSKY

David Levinsky is the first-person narrator of *The Rise of David Levinsky,* by Abraham Cahan. He relates the story of his life beginning with his youth as an Orthodox Jew in Russia, living among Christians. Levinsky spends his time studying the the Talmud with various rabbis and other Orthodox students. At first, he is a pious, intelligent, and promising religious student. This early academic career provides a contrast with his later career as a capitalist. Two pivotal scenes occur in the Russia sections of the novel. The first is the death of Levinsky's mother, who is killed by a Christian mob during anti-Jewish riots. The second major action is Levinsky's first unsuccessful encounter with a female, Matilda (the pattern is repeated throughout the novel). The encounter confuses him but also propels him to leave Russia for America.

The process of socialization from green immigrant to American citizen is also captured in the novel. Levinsky is forced to confront the pressures of immigration and socialization to a new culture as soon as he arrives in America. He learns the difference between a secular, business-oriented culture and the traditional and religious culture he left behind. Part of Levinsky's rise is his forsaking traditional Jewish and Russian garb and manners for modern American ones. He cuts his beard and gives up his Talmud studies, exchanging his heritage and early dreams for a chance at success. Levinsky learns one of the hard lessons of immigration: an immigrant must fit in in American society in order to rise in status. When he interacts with Americans, he is always conscious of his appearance: "I never did so without being conscious of my gestures and trying to make them as American as possible." He learns that to fit in means to imitate: "I was forever watching and striving to imitate the dress and the ways of the well bred American merchants with whom I was, or trying to be, thrown. All this I felt was an essential element in achieving business success."

The Rise of David Levinsky is an example of the American novel of upward mobility, which entails some version of the rags-to-riches story of the American Dream. Cahan's novel can be compared to William Dean Howells's *The Rise of Silas Lapham* (1885). In fact, Howells served as a mentor to Cahan, and Cahan adhered to Howells's faith in realism and wrote a defense of the approach: "Is it not a time for sincerity here? Will it not be well for this Nation if strong, new, American writers arise who will give us life—real life, with its comedy and its tragedy mingled—give us what in my Russian day we called the *thrill of truth?*" Both title characters, Levinsky and Lapham, experience a rise to wealth and the moral choices and compromises that rise entails. Levinsky works, hustles, and schemes his

way to the top with a combination of entrepreneurialism and corruption.

One reason Levinsky is so successful is that his Americanization is also a process of being socialized to a capitalist system. Levinsky learns the nature of commodification, that everything has a value and can be bought or sold. One of the first things that Levinsky learns to sell is the story of his mother's death. He is able to get money and favorable treatment by telling the story. Levinsky's tale is also a tale of loneliness and failures with women. He is never able to hold a normal relationship. Women are treated as another commodity, or as a proper trophy. Conquests denote acumen, not love.

Cahan uses Levinsky's rise as an opportunity to criticize capitalism. Levinsky succeeds not just as a result of hard work but also of capitalist competition and dirty tricks. He breaks unions, takes advantage of immigrant workers, cheats his creditors and partners, and sees business as a war. Although at the end of the novel he is a titan of industry, powerful and wealthy, he also ends up lonely and depressed. He is an empty millionaire, who chased material over human goals. As he says, "I feel that if I had my life to live over again I should never think of a business career. . . . David, the poor lad swinging over a Talmud volume . . . seems to have more in common with my inner identity than David Levinsky, the well known cloak manufacturer."

Discussion Questions

1. Discuss why the novel can be read as a critique of capitalism or entrepreneurialism.

2. Compare Levinsky to Silas Lapham in William Dean Howells's *The Rise of Silas Lapham.*

3. Discuss Levinsky's relationships with women. How does he view women? Why does he end up alone?

4. The term *green* is used in the text to describe immigrants. What does the term connote, and how does Levinsky get rid of his "green-ness"?

—*Frank D. Casale*

REFERENCES

Jules Chametzky, *From the Ghetto: The Fiction of Abraham Cahan* (Amherst: University of Massachusetts Press, 1977);

Sanford E. Marovitz, *Abraham Cahan* (Boston: Twayne, 1996);

The Rise of David Levinsky, introduction by Seth Lipsky, notes by Katrina Irving (New York: Modern Library, 2001).

James M. Cain
(July 1, 1892 – October 27, 1977)

‹‹☙

MILDRED PIERCE
(New York: Knopf, 1941)

MILDRED PIERCE

Mildred Pierce is the main character in James M. Cain's novel titled for her. Born Mildred Ridgely in 1903, she grows up in Southern California. In 1920, at the age of seventeen, she is seduced by Bert Pierce, a novice real estate tycoon in his mid twenties; she is "excited by him," Cain reports, "mainly on account of his dashing ways." She feels "a-tingle and grown-up" when he takes her out in his "sports roadster." Bert makes an honest woman of his underage girlfriend "a month later, she quitting school two days before the ceremony." When Bert's financial empire collapses in 1929 (all his money is invested in AT&T), things change quickly. "In September he had been rich, and Mildred picked out the mink coat she would buy when the weather grew cooler. In November, with the weather not a bit cooler, he had had to sell the spare car to pay current bills." Bert takes the financial losses philosophically. The blows to his self-respect and his self-image are something else again. "He had become so used to crediting himself with vast acumen that he could not bring himself to admit that his success was all luck, due to the location of his land rather than to his own personal qualities." He makes no effort to find work, preferring to live "in a world of dreams, lolling by the river, watching the clouds go by." Mildred finds this unacceptable. She needs to know where the money is coming from to meet the interest payments on the house, and to put food in her two children's mouths. She unceremoniously dumps Bert and sets about finding a solution to her family's problems on her own.

Others, however, view the events in question differently than does Mildred. Her daughter Veda, for example, tells her: "you got yourself knocked up . . . for the money." In those days, she reminds her mother, Bert "was quite rich, and I'm sure you knew it. When the money was gone you kicked him out. And when you divorced him, and he was so down and out . . . you quite generously stripped him of the only thing he had left, meaning this lovely, incomparable, palatial hovel that we live in." Veda omits only one item in her indictment—Mildred also stripped Bert of his car, not long after she threw him out of the house. Cain stated that he conceived *Mildred Pierce* as "the story . . . of a woman who uses men to gain her end," the story of "a venal American housewife . . . who didn't know she was using men, but imagined herself quite noble."

There is some question about exactly how Mildred manages to go on imagining herself "quite noble" in the face of the mounting evidence to the contrary—her use of Wally Burgan to get her restaurant, for example, and her conscious and deliberate use of Monty Beragon to keep Veda in her life. (The similarities in the names given to these to men by the author suggest that in Mildred's mind they are interchangeable tools of her advancement toward her goals.) Cain suggested that the explanation might lie in Mildred's defective intelligence: "She was a peculiar study to me. I never could make up my mind if she had any brains." Joyce Carol Oates takes no position on that issue but does refer wonderingly to Mildred's "profound ignorance," which, she says, "is matched perfectly by the characters who surround her." Often, of course, a lack of knowledge can lead to the same behavior as a lack of intelligence. In Mildred's case (as with Bert's), it may be a deficiency in self-knowledge that has prevented her from realizing the extent to which her success results from her skill at manipulating men.

Such skill is not the only reason for Mildred's success, though she usually has to be led to see the value of a new idea and seldom has one herself: it is Wally who suggests the location for Mildred's first restaurant and who encourages her to offer free parking; it is Mrs. Gessler, Mildred's eccentric next-door neighbor, who suggests adding a bar once

Prohibition ends. But whatever Mildred is, she is practical, and once she has been persuaded of the value of a new idea, she can be counted upon to find and tirelessly implement the most efficient possible plan for making it a reality.

There is an important sense, however, in which building Mildred Pierce, Inc., is never any part of Mildred's purpose. It merely happens while she is working to achieve her one true goal: the approval, acceptance, and love of her older daughter, Veda. In this, she is oddly reminiscent of Isabel Amberson, the main female character in Booth Tarkington's novel *The Magnificent Ambersons*. Both Mildred and Isabel are enslaved by their firstborn children. Mildred is bled dry, then discarded, her business in ruins, by her arrogant, snobbish daughter. Isabel watches helplessly as her arrogant, autocratic, snobbish son, George, tosses aside her only chance for happiness in a life already cut short by a congenital heart defect. Neither has the self-respect to do without the good opinion of her uncaring, thankless offspring. Mildred, whatever her defects of intelligence or self-knowledge may be, is a woman of genuine ability and solid accomplishment, a woman who has plenty of basis for a healthy self-esteem, a woman who should not have to live at second hand through her daughter. Nevertheless, her insatiable desire for the love and approval of her daughter Veda leads Mildred to marry Monty Beragon, whom she knows to be a wastrel; to buy his decaying mansion in Pasadena; to restore it to its former splendor; and to pick up the tab for the lavish parties Monty and Veda throw there. To meet these expenses, she is forced to drain the corporation of funds to such an extent that she eventually finds herself unable to pay her creditors. Her company goes into receivership, and she loses control of her business, though it goes on operating in her name. As the novel ends, she is back where she began, married once again to Bert Pierce, living in Glendale, uncertain where her next dollar is coming from.

Discussion Questions

1. Joyce Carol Oates remarks that in James M. Cain's novels, life is merely "a bungling process." As a result, she argues, the characters in Cain's novels experience "no education . . . in moral terms at all. *Mildred Pierce* points out the all-too-human predicament in the series of confrontations and exposures of the daughter Veda's hatefulness and the constant failure of Mildred Pierce to understand." Do you agree? At the end of the novel Mildred tells Veda, as she leaves for New York, "this time, don't come back." Will Mildred take Veda back again? Use evidence from the text to support your answer.

2. Isabel Amberson Minafer, in Booth Tarkington's novel *The Magnificent Ambersons,* is said to see an "angel" when she looks at her son, George. That is, she sees only his best qualities, even though those qualities are usually hidden from view. Does the same theory apply to Mildred Pierce when she looks at Veda? Support your answer with evidence from the novel.

3. After building and losing her business, Mildred remarries Herbert Pierce, her former husband and the father of her daughters. Why does she do this? Use evidence from the text to support your answer.

4. When, at the beginning of the novel, Mildred is first forced to fall back on her own resources, she turns down a housekeeping job and refuses even to consider a job as a waitress, despite her desperate need for money. Later, after she has taken a position as a waitress, she hides the fact from her children and almost everyone else she knows; also, she "held aloof from the restaurant itself, and the people connected with it," in part because of "her ideas of social superiority." Attitudes like these did in fact prevail among the American upper and middle classes during the years in which Cain's novel is set. Do you think they still prevail? Do they still exist in contemporary society at all? To what extent?

—Jeff Riggenbach

REFERENCES

Roy Hoopes, *Cain: The Biography of James M. Cain* (New York: Holt, Rinehart & Winston, 1982);

David Madden, *James M. Cain* (New York: Twayne, 1970);

Joyce Carol Oates, "Man under Sentence of Death: The Novels of James M. Cain," in *Tough Guy Writers of the Thirties,* edited by Madden (Carbondale: Southern Illinois University Press, 1968), pp. 110–128.

Truman Capote
(September 30, 1924 – August 25, 1984)

◦◦

BREAKFAST AT TIFFANY'S: A SHORT NOVEL AND THREE STORIES
(New York: Random House, 1958)

HOLLY GOLIGHTLY

Holly Golightly, the main character of Truman Capote's 1958 novella *Breakfast at Tiffany's,* was Capote's favorite of the characters he created. Though there are quite a few male characters in the book, including the mafia boss Sally Tomato; Holly's husband, Doc Golightly; and various boyfriends, including Sid Arbuck, Rusty Trawler, and Jose Ybarra-Jaegar, the only other major character is the narrator, Fred, but he is essentially a vehicle for conveying Holly's story.

Fred establishes Holly as a character who is difficult to categorize; he mentions the "ragbag colors of her boy's hair" and her face that is "beyond childhood, yet this side of belonging to a woman." He guesses her age at "anywhere between sixteen and thirty." Holly is both male and female, child and adult. Although she is obsessed with men and even asks the narrator to "get a list of the fifty richest men in Brazil," she admits her own bisexuality: "Of course people couldn't help but think I must be a bit of a dyke myself. And of course I am. Everyone is: a bit."

The question of Holly's authenticity intrigues Fred throughout the book. Although she is an aspiring actress who is "well groomed" and conveys "good taste," he observes another side of Holly, one that is rough, lonely, and vulnerable. As he listens to her singing and playing guitar, he comments, "But there were moments when she played songs that made you wonder where she learned them, where indeed she came from. Harsh-tender wandering tunes with words that smacked of pineywoods or prairie. One went: *Don't wanna sleep, Don't wanna die, Just wanna go a-travelin' through the pastures of the sky.*" Other characters hint at Holly's enigmatic character: O. J. Berman, the Hollywood actor's agent who first discovered Holly, calls her "a *real* phony" because "she believes all this crap she believes." He says, "My

guess, nobody'll ever know where she came from. She's such a goddamn liar, maybe she don't know herself any more."

Names are important in *Breakfast at Tiffany's,* especially in understanding the complexity of Holly's identity. The card on her mailbox reads "Miss Holiday Golightly, Traveling"; the name has a musical quality that implies the spirit of the traveler—or one who literally goes lightly through the world. When Holly's husband, Doc, appears, he says, "Her name's not Holly. She was a Lulamae Barnes." Holly refuses to return to Doc, claiming that she is no longer a "child-wife from Tulip, Texas." She has reinvented herself as a well-dressed New Yorker, a "playgirl," "a fragile eyeful," and a "beautiful movie starlet and café society celebrity." Holly has mixed feelings, though, and when she tells Doc "I'm not Lulamae," she realizes that "the terrible part is . . . I am. I'm still stealing turkey eggs and running through a brier patch. Only now I call it having the mean reds."

Near the end of *Breakfast at Tiffany's,* when Holly leaves her cat in Spanish Harlem, she has a revelation: "Oh, Jesus God. We did belong to each other. He was mine." The scene is significant because what Holly wants most is a sense of belonging. She frequently thinks about the comfort of family and home, and she even calls the narrator "Fred" because he reminds her of her brother: "Like my brother Fred. We used to sleep four in a bed, and he was the only one that ever let me hug him on a cold night. By the way, do you mind if I call you Fred?" When Holly learns that her brother has been killed in the war, she becomes obsessed with domestic life. She is gripped by a "keen sudden un-Holly-like enthusiasm for homemaking" and tries to turn her apartment into a home, buying furniture, appliances, books, and records.

The title *Breakfast at Tiffany's* points to Holly's dreams of safety and home. Tiffany's, a famous high-end jewelry store in New York, represents an ideal world for her; she says, "If I could find a real-life place that made me feel like Tiffany's, then I'd buy some furniture and give the cat a name. I've thought maybe after the war, Fred and I—." When Fred is killed, and when Holly's fiancé, Jose Ybarra-Jaegar, breaks their engagement, her dreams go unrealized. Her apartment retains a "camping-out atmosphere; crates and suitcases, everything packed and ready to go." Holly herself claims that "home is where you feel at home. I'm still looking."

Holly's homeless quality is both a gift and a burden, and this quality makes the tone of Capote's book both sweet and sad. Holly is able to reinvent herself, throw wild parties, and enjoy the company of wealthy, important men. She is a free spirit who drinks, dances, and rides horses through Central Park. She is naive as well, regularly visiting the "darling old man" Sally Tomato in Sing Sing prison and giving him "weather reports," which turn out to be coded messages about illegal activities. The narrator is captivated by Holly's light and magical presence; he notices her one evening dancing with a group of army officers, saying she "floated round in their arms as light as a scarf." Even though the narrator recognizes that Holly is an "utter fake," he too is charmed and invigorated by her facade. When he and Holly decide to steal Halloween masks from Woolworth's, he says, "successful theft exhilarates. . . . We wore the masks all the way home."

In the end, Holly's masks reveal a devastating loneliness. When she is prosecuted for her dealings with Tomato, her former roommate, Mag Wildwood, wants nothing to do with her. Holly justifies going to Brazil at the end of the book by saying, "I don't think anyone will miss me. I have no friends." The most telling description of Holly's character comes from her own words: "Never love a wild thing. . . . It's better to look at the sky than live there. Such an empty place; so vague. Just a country where the thunder goes and things disappear."

Discussion Questions

1. Why does the book begin with the rumor that Holly has been in Africa? Does the opening scene contradict or affirm the last lines of the novella, or the narrator's hope that Holly has found a place where she belongs?

2. In the 1961 film adaptation of *Breakfast at Tiffany's,* a romance blossoms between Fred and Holly Golightly. Does the relationship between Holly and the narrator in the book seem like a romantic one? Why or why not?

3. Explain what Berman means by a "real phony." Do you agree with his assessment of Holly?

4. Holly says, "Be anything but a coward, a pretender, an emotional crook, a whore: I'd rather have cancer than a dishonest heart." Do you think that Holly has lived an "honest" life?

—*Liz Beasley*

❧

"A CHRISTMAS MEMORY"
Collected in *Selected Writings* (New York: Random House, 1963).

BUDDY
Buddy is one of two central characters in Truman Capote's short story "A Christmas Memory." His real name and surname are unknown; he has been given his nickname by the other central character, his elderly female cousin, whom Buddy refers to throughout as "my friend." While the story focuses on an episode involving the seven-year-old Buddy and his cousin, it is Buddy's role as narrator, looking back after more than twenty years, that heightens the emotional impact of the story.

"I often use 'real' people in my work, and then create a story around them," Capote wrote. "My story, 'A Christmas Memory' is entirely autobiographical." The story is based on the young Capote's friendship with his cousin, Miss Sook Faulk, with whom he lived in the late 1920s and early 1930s. The two formed a close bond, primarily because they were ignored by other family members. Capote's mother sent him to live with her relations in Monroeville, Alabama, when he was two years old. Sook, who—like Buddy's friend—was "still a child" despite being in her sixties, became the center of the boy's life. Capote has commented, "I had an elderly cousin, the woman in my story *A Christmas Memory,* who was a genius; she certainly didn't know it, nor did anyone else: most people thought she was an eccentric, simple minded lady with an unusual talent for making scrapquilts."

Critics have commented on the fairy-tale quality of "A Christmas Memory": in the first line Buddy invites the reader to "Imagine a morning in late November." The details he supplies often resemble stage directions, specific yet general, allowing the reader to imagine this timeless paradise: "Consider the kitchen of a spreading old house in a country town." Buddy relates that "Just today the fireplace commenced its seasonal roar" and proceeds to use only present-tense verbs to create a sense of immediacy. Having guided the reader into this fairy-tale world, Buddy introduces his seemingly ageless cousin, who offers him refuge from the "[o]ther people" who "inhabit the house." These nameless others represent for him the presence of evil, "Potent with eyes that scold, tongues that scald." He assures his reader that "though they have power over us, and frequently make us cry, we are not, on the whole, too much aware of them. We are each other's best friend."

Buddy relishes the beauty, simplicity, and spontaneity of this timeless world fixed in his memory. "It's always the same," he comments; one fall morning his cousin will stare out the kitchen window and then announce: "It's fruitcake weather!" These words fill Buddy with the promise of wonderful days, when he and his friend will conspire to obtain the ingredients—including bootleg whiskey—for baking fruitcakes. The drama is heightened for Buddy when he must retrieve the "Fruitcake Fund," which is "hidden in an ancient bead purse under a loose board under the floor under a chamber pot under my friend's bed."

Through Buddy's eyes readers come to understand his love for this woman whom the older relatives scold or ignore. He conveys her combination of humility and vivacity by explaining that she has never "worn cosmetics, cursed, wished someone harm, told a lie on purpose, let a hungry dog go hungry." What she "does do" is "dip snuff . . . tame hummingbirds . . . know the recipe for every sort of old-time Indian cure," and she even killed "the biggest rattlesnake ever seen in this county." Though she is chastised for sharing the leftover fruitcake whiskey with Buddy, she serves as his model of virtue, particularly through her unconditional charity. In such· a charitable spirit she assures Buddy that they will "put an extra cup of raisins" in a fruitcake for Mr. Ha-Ha Jones, the fearsome bootlegger who gives them the whiskey for free.

Having successfully delivered thirty-one fruitcakes to people they barely know, the two embark on a journey to chop down a Christmas tree, and Buddy's description of the pastoral setting is Edenic: "Always, the path unwinds through lemony sun pools and pitch vine tunnels. Another creek to cross: a disturbed armada of speckled trout froths the water round us, and frogs the size of plates practice belly flops." When a "rich mill owner's lazy wife" asks to purchase the tree the pair of "triumphant huntsmen" are dragging home—insisting they can get another one—Buddy's friend reflects that "There's never two of anything." This line foreshadows the pain of their inevitable parting, which Buddy's friend anticipates the next day: "I guess I hate to see you grow up. When you're grown up, will we still be friends?"

Buddy signals the end of their lives together, stating: "This is our last Christmas together. . . . Those who Know Best decide that I belong in a military school." On this final Christmas his friend shares with him perhaps her most valuable lesson. While the two sit in the pasture preparing to fly the homemade kites they have given each other for Christmas, Buddy's friend explains that one should not think he has to wait for death before he can see God: "I'll wager at the very end a body realizes the Lord has already shown Himself. That things as they are . . . just what they've always been, was seeing Him." When one December morning Buddy learns of her passing, he remarks that the news "sever[s] from me an irreplaceable part of myself, letting it loose like a kite on a broken string." He looks at the sky as if expecting to see "rather like hearts, a lost pair of kites hurrying toward heaven."

Buddy has parallels in other autobiographical fiction in which the author recollects powerful childhood memories that have instilled lasting values in his or her narrator. Examples of such narrators include Thea Kronborg in *The Song of the Lark* (1915) by Willa Cather, a major influence on Capote, and Scout Finch of *To Kill a Mockingbird* (1960) by Harper Lee, who portrays Capote—her childhood friend in Monroeville—as Dill Harris in her novel.

Discussion Questions

1. Compare Buddy to Dill Harris in *To Kill a Mockingbird*. What traits suggest that the two characters are based on the same person?

2. Near the end of Buddy's narrative his tone becomes elegiac. What rhetorical devices does he use to soften the news of his friend's impending death and the death of their dog, Queenie?

3. "A Christmas Memory" is basically free of symbolism until the final line. Why might Capote choose to introduce a symbol at this point, and what does the symbolism convey regarding Buddy?

4. How does point of view affect the telling of "A Christmas Memory"? How might the story change if it were told by the seven-year-old Buddy, by his friend, or by one of the other relatives?

5. Buddy's recollection uses irony as a means of conveying meaning indirectly. Find at least three examples of this technique in the story, and explain what unstated meaning Buddy conveys with each.

—*John Cusatis*

OTHER VOICES, OTHER ROOMS
(New York: Random House, 1948)

JOEL HARRISON KNOX

Joel Harrison Knox is the main character in Truman Capote's 1948 novel, *Other Voices, Other Rooms*. Joel is a different kind of young protagonist, a clever boy finding his way in the Deep South; he is not necessarily gay by contemporary standards, but he is definitely unconventional, not particularly masculine, and could be considered effeminate by readers. Joel is thirteen, on the verge of transforming from boy to adolescent.

He is slight, slumped, not tall, with soft brown eyes, and light-brown hair. He is described with language that makes the reader picture a feminized boy, drawing upon the author's own description by his aunts who took care of him at a similar age. Joel's lack of traditional boyishness does not go unnoticed. Radclif is "a balding six-footer with a rough, manly face," and he looks over Joel with a skeptical eye. Radclif "had notions of what a 'real' boy should look like," and Joel appears very different to him: "He was too pretty, too delicate . . . each of his features was shaped with a sensitive accuracy, and a girlish tenderness softened his eyes . . . and there was an

unyouthful sag about his shoulders." Capote signals to the reader that Joel is a young man who embodies some kind of homosexual implications.

Nonetheless, Joel is perceived as exceptionally bright by the first characters he meets. Sydney Katz, the owner of the Star Café, speaking to Radclif who will soon take Joel to Skully's Landing, remarks that Joel is "smart as a whip. Knows words you and me never heard of." It is Joel's intelligence, his ability to see, to observe that contributes to the developments in his character: by witnessing in detail, Joel relays the social issues that the novel depicts. Joel begins his journey as a coming-of-age hero, and as the novel unfolds, Joel's discoveries around the landing, of the house, of his parentage, of the people around him, black and white, lead him to a stronger sense of himself and his particular differences, emphasizing the rite of passage that marks the end of the novel. Capote has explained that Joel served as a kind of autobiographical exorcism: "*Other Voices* was my way of finding metaphors for what I knew but couldn't understand . . . and *Other Voices* was my way of . . . giving myself up in order to *be* myself" (Brinnin 121–122). Despite this admission of an autobiographic foundation, Capote did contest the early reception of the novel that attempted to label it as a homosexual novel.

Joel's journey reflects a particular identity discovery as he tries to make a new home for himself. The settings of Noon City and Skully's Landing epitomize Capote's vision of the rural South. Joel sees the South as a slow-paced rural location, without any form of modern life, as the Landing in its antiquated state exhibits. In this setting, many observations are made by Joel, causing the novel to reveal a fluid social commentary. Joel learns to see people as people, not as colors or genders, for example; the novel thereby stresses the importance of abolishing racism and gender norms.

Joel encounters many characters, and all of them are remarkably unconventional. These characters allow Joel to see a particular reflection of his own self, and through Joel's interactions with his new friends, he can observe and question the world as he discovers his true self. Through his friendships with the masculine Miss Roberta, the campy Miss Wisteria, the opposing twins prissy Florabel and her tomboy sister Idabel, or the African American characters Zoo and Little Sunshine, Joel's story reflects a world in transition, a world not separate from a segregated past, and a world that is, in some ways, a microcosm of Capote's South. Joel, as the main character, is the cornerstone of anticipated social change.

Moreover, Joel, via his experiences, reflects social or cultural change. As Joel chooses his friends, he learns to exist in a much wider picture of the world. Capote critiques the Old South as he satirizes aspects of the novel's setting. The irony is politically charged, as Zoo's rape implies toward the end of the novel. The novel's gentle ease, the way Capote unfolds the story almost seamlessly, is countered by a heavy ending, where rape, a bedridden invalid, and gender-masquerade change the lighter rite-of-passage (or coming-of-age) theme prevalent throughout most of the novel. An acute social consciousness is marked by the end of the novel. Joel's literary significance lies in the observations he makes about the South, race, gender, and sexuality—observations that come through dramatic situations, such as Zoo's journey north, or Joel's discovery about his father and cousin Randolph. Through his father, who remains absent, and through the ending of the story, Joel understands his own sexual orientation, as he sees two adults who clearly defy gender norms.

Abandoned, seemingly, at the start of the story, he meets characters who reflect his own developing characteristics. As Joel is not a typical boy, he is paired with Idabel, his foil character. Roberta boots them out of her diner, detecting her own lesbianism in Idabel's boyishness, almost foreshadowing the way that the younger characters detect their sexual diversity in older ones (Idabel will discover this later on with Miss Wisteria, as Joel realizes his in cousin Randolph). At Skully's Landing, however, Joel comes face to face with his own lack of traditional masculinity: his absent father and effeminate, quirky cousin Randolph prove his best mirrors of reflection at the very end of the novel: "Gradually the blinding sunset drained from the glass [of Randolph's window . . .]: a face trembled like a white beautiful moth, smiled. She beckoned to him, shining and silver, and he knew he must go: unafraid, not hesitating, he paused only at the garden's edge where, as though he'd forgotten something, he stopped and looked back at the bloomless, descending blue, at the boy he had left behind" (231).

Joel sees a reflection of himself in this version of his cousin who is masquerading as a woman. In such an image, Joel sheds his past, the boy he once was, to become a new boy, even as a young homosexual or drag queen. Joel will, presumably, step away from any previous image of himself and become someone different. Part of the strength of this novel and its leading character is the embodiment of a voice for sexual diversity, characterized by a youngster. Capote reveals that sexuality is not always conventional, in more than one case; and through Joel's queerness, Idabel's boyishness, Miss Roberta's butch mannerisms, and Miss Wisteria's questionable pedophilia, Capote depicts aspects of desire that society, at the time the novel was published, would simply not touch. This portrayal of taboo subjects links Capote to contemporaries such as Tennessee Williams and Carson McCullers. Joel's character reflects a series of beliefs about social change. Joel represents not only a young man on the verge of discovering his own homosexuality but also a character who finds beauty in his eclectic, nonconventional new friends. He also portrays the importance of personal difference, social change, and related ideas about freedom.

Joel Harrison Knox has been deemed autobiographical in several ways. The displaced childhood, solo travel, and observational qualities that accompany Joel throughout *Other Voices* have biographical associations with Capote's own childhood. Joel, in many ways, remains a coming-of-age character with a unique series of experiences, situations, and a rather exceptional environment—not unlike the young Capote's. Capote, during his childhood and like Joel, was seen as an "outsider." It should be noted that the greatest strength in Joel's characterization is that he allows the reader to see and question limited ways of thinking and being.

Discussion Questions

1. Think about Joel and his close friendship with Idabel. Examine the differences in traditional gender norms that are associated with each character. Why does Capote create characters who challenge such conventions?

2. Evaluate the success of the coming-of-age theme or rite-of-passage theme in this novel. Explain the theme and analyze the level of success that Capote achieves.

3. What kinds of social issues are important in this novel? How does Joel serve as a method for relaying important social issues to the reader? (Think about the roles of women in the novel and the African American characters.)

—*Brian M. Peters*

REFERENCES

Steven Adams, *The Homosexual as Hero in Contemporary Fiction* (New York: Barnes & Noble, 1980);

John Malcolm Brinnin, *Truman Capote: A Memoir* (New York: Delacorte/Seymour Lawrence, 1986);

Gerald Clarke, *Capote: A Biography* (New York: Simon & Schuster, 1988);

Helen S. Garson, *Truman Capote: A Study of the Short Fiction* (Boston: Twayne, 1992);

Lawrence Grobel, *Conversations with Capote* (New York: New American Library, 1985);

William Nance, *The Worlds of Truman Capote* (New York: Stein & Day, 1970);

Kenneth T. Reed, *Truman Capote* (Boston: Twayne, 1981).

Raymond Carver
(May 23, 1938 – August 2, 1988)

✎

"A SMALL, GOOD THING"
Collected in *Cathedral* (New York: Knopf, 1983).

HOWARD WEISS

Howard Weiss is a father whose family life is disrupted when his son is seriously injured in a hit-and-run accident in Raymond Carver's story "A Small, Good Thing." Carver revised the story from an earlier one, "The Bath," keeping the same premise but fleshing out the story and giving the characters names and particular personalities. In the story, Howard's wife, Ann, orders a birthday cake for the couple's son, Scotty. Before they can pick up the cake, however, Scotty is hit by a car and falls into a coma. He revives briefly two days later but then dies suddenly. Meanwhile, the baker from whom Ann ordered the cake leaves increasingly angry messages for them to come and pick it up. To the distraught couple, the calls seem to be the work of a cruel prankster.

In the wake of the accident Howard begins to evaluate his life and finds that he looks upon himself as a reasonably satisfied husband and father. He had performed well in college and attained an advanced degree in business; he had also attained a junior partnership in an investment firm. He is grateful for his happiness and "so, so lucky—and he knew that." He is conscious that he has avoided "any real harm, from those forces he knew existed and that could cripple or bring down a man if the luck went bad, if things suddenly turned." Howard maintains a qualified optimism as he tries to evaluate objectively the facts of Scotty's accident.

Details in the story indicate that Howard is a supportive husband. He rubs the back of Ann's neck and constantly assures her that Scotty is going to be fine. Carver describes acts of simple intimacy that emphasize the couple's love for each other: "He took her hand and put it in his lap, and this made him feel better, her hand being there. He picked up her hand and squeezed it. Then he just held her hand." They admit, after this show of compassion, that they have both prayed over Scotty's disaster. When Scotty unexpectedly dies as Ann and Howard are celebrating his regaining consciousness, Howard responds with an outpouring of grief.

Back at home, Howard and Ann finally make the connection about the birthday cake and are furious at the baker for his seeming callousness. They drive to the bakery to confront him. Though the initial confrontation is angry and even threatening, once the baker understands that Scotty is dead and that the entire situation was an enormous failure of communication, he repeatedly apologizes and asks the couple to forgive him. Carver portrays the scene in the bakery as a form of communion. The baker's table becomes an altar of reconciliation, and he exhorts Howard and Ann to eat the cinnamon rolls he has just prepared: "You have to eat and keep going. Eating is a small, good thing in a time like this." Admitting his own profound loneliness and feelings of doubt and inadequacy, the baker, through his conciliatory offer of sustenance, finds self-acceptance: "He was a baker. He was glad he wasn't a florist. It was better to be feeding people."

Discussion Questions

1. How does Howard's sensitivity to his wife's emotional fragility reveal itself throughout the story? What specific attitudes and actions of Ann evoke Howard's empathetic responses?

2. What is it in the baker's manner that convinces Howard to relinquish his anger and bitterness?

3. What is the symbolic significance of the title "A Small, Good Thing"? How does it relate to Howard's acceptance of the death of his son? Originally the story was titled "The Bath." What significance does bathing have on Howard's overwhelming sorrow? How does it help him?

4. A mystical transformation seems to take place at the end of "A Small, Good Thing." Compare the similar transformation—or revelation—that takes place at the conclusion of Carver's story "Cathedral."

—*Patrick Meanor*

"WHAT WE TALK ABOUT WHEN WE TALK ABOUT LOVE"

Collected in *What We Talk about When We Talk about Love* (New York: Knopf, 1981).

MEL MCGINNIS

Mel McGinnis is the major character in Raymond Carver's "What We Talk about When We Talk about Love." The story takes place in a kitchen in Albuquerque, New Mexico, where four characters are engaged in a sometimes heated discussion on the general topic of love. The four characters are drinking heavily, and by the conclusion of the story, they are all intoxicated. Critic Warren Carlin, along with three other Carver commentators, suggests that Carver based this story on Plato's *Symposium*, which is also a serious discussion on love during a drinking bout. The difference between Carver's story and Plato's is that the host in the Platonic symposium waters down the wine so the participants do not get too intoxicated. Mel, on the other hand, keeps plying his guests and himself with gin. By the end of the afternoon, the four have consumed two entire bottles before dinner.

Mel is a cardiologist and cardiac surgeon, and he has initiated a long conversation with Terri, his second wife, and a younger married couple about love and its various manifestations. He controls the discussion firmly, an indication that he is obsessed with the topic. Mel insists that the conversation be directed at one point: the definition and nature of love.

Before Mel attended medical school, he had gone to a seminary for five years, an influence that surfaces in his philosophical discussions of love. Because of his theological training, he firmly believes in absolutes. He tells the story of Terri and Ed, whom she lived with before marrying Mel. Ed said he loved Terri so much that he tried to kill her. Mel cannot understand his action as an act of love. Love cannot coexist with hatred in his dogmatic mind. Both his seminary education and his later scientific training will not allow him to accept philosophical ambiguities.

The remainder of the discussion focuses on Mel's attempt to define the nature of love in narrow terms. He does not understand Terri's loyalty to Ed even after Ed's second failed suicide attempt; he drank rat poison and shot himself in the mouth. He died of the gunshot wound before Terri explains that she stayed with Ed at the hospital for three days because "He didn't have anyone else" and after the poison failed to kill him. Laura, Nick's wife, explains Ed's actions to Mel as romantic, even heroic, love: he died for Terri's love. Mel continues his attempt—with the assistance of one gin and tonic after another—to categorize love. He insists that physical love includes "carnal love" or "sentimental love, the day-to-day caring about the other person." When his comments turn cynical, Terri lightheartedly accuses him of being drunk, a charge she repeats two other times during the course of the story. Mel becomes angry—even threatening—and advises her to shut up.

Continuing his drinking, Mel demonstrates his admiration for medieval courtly love. Searching for modern examples, he points to an old couple—patients of his—who had been critically injured in a near-fatal automobile accident. What convinced Mel of the sincerity of their depthless love was the elderly husband's depression when he could not see his wife: "Can you imagine? I'm telling you, the man's heart was breaking because he couldn't turn his goddamn head and *see* his goddamn wife." The essence of the courtly love tradition, Mel dimly recalls, is that the greatest act of love was platonic, beholding the beloved without any sexual contact. At the conclusion of the story he imagines himself not in a knight's armor but in a beekeeper's bonnet, in a fantasy in which he imagines killing his first wife, who was allergic to bee stings: "I'll knock on the door and let loose a hive of bees in the house." By the end of the story, his discussion, paradoxically, has moved from definitions of love to murder; and his three companions are as drunk as he.

After Terri's offer to spread out some cheese and crackers—which she does not do—the story concludes in quiet but slightly frightening paralysis. Mel aggressively announces that he has spilled the last of the gin. Carver suggests that, along with the gin, any attempt to define the nature of love has gone as well. The discussion ends in drunken stupor. No new definition, knowledge, or understanding has emerged about love when the quartet—with Mel as moderator and principal commentator—talks about love. Love remains, more than ever, mysterious and indefinable at the conclusion of the story. Though the conversation begins in daylight, it concludes in darkness, paralysis, and quiet desperation. Laura asks: "Now what?"

Discussion Questions

1. How does Mel McGinnis's alcohol consumption derail his logical thinking? Give at least three specific examples.

2. What evidence of Mel McGinnis's intellectual background surfaces during his pronouncements on the definition and nature of love?

3. Compare and contrast Plato's *Symposium* to Carver's story in terms of theme, techniques, and narrators.

—*Patrick Meanor*

REFERENCES

Ewing Campbell, *Raymond Carver: A Study of the Short Fiction* (New York: Twayne, 1998);

Adam Meyer, *Raymond Carver* (New York: Twayne, 1995);

Randolph Runyon, *Reading Raymond Carver* (Syracuse, N.Y.: Syracuse University Press, 1992);

Arthur M. Saltzman, *Understanding Raymond Carver* (Columbia: University of South Carolina Press, 1988).

Ana Castillo

(June 15, 1953 –   )

≈

THE MIXQUIAHUALA LETTERS

(Binghamton, N.Y.: Bilingual Press/Editorial Bilingüe, 1986)

TERESA

Teresa, or Tere, is one of two main characters in Ana Castillo's epistolary novel, *The Mixquiahuala Letters.* Castillo's first attempt at fiction, it won the Before Columbus Foundation's American Book Award in 1987. The novel consists of a series of letters written by Teresa to her best friend, Alicia (whose surnames are not given in the novel). The title refers to a small town in rural Mexico visited by the two young women as they travel together after meeting as students at a summer language institute in Mexico City. Some of the letters are written immediately after the events of that first summer, while others deal with the women's lives in the years following their return to the United States. The letters chronicle Teresa's attempts to make sense of the relationship she and Alicia forge through the loves, tragedies, and adventures they share in Mexico.

Like Castillo herself, Teresa is a Mexican American poet from a poverty-stricken, working-class background, eager to explore her heritage and caught up in the counterculture movements of the 1960s and 1970s. Tere even uses the lowercase *i* for the personal pronoun, as Castillo does in her poetry. Some critics suggest the novel is at least partially autobiographical, drawn from Castillo's own travels in Mexico during her early twenties with her friend and fellow author Cherríe Moraga.

Initially, Tere is suspicious of the pale-skinned artist Alicia, whom she immediately identifies as white, wealthy, and privileged. They soon become close friends, however, drawn to each other's loneliness, creativity, and hunger for life. While the friendship they build in Mexico is clearly a touchstone for both women in the ensuing years, the plot of their story is anything but clear. As in her second novel, *Sapogonia: An Anti-Romance in 3/8 Meter* (1990), Castillo utilizes such postmodern elements as shifting narrative time lines and multiple endings. Teresa's letters are numbered but not dated. As the book begins, Castillo tells readers that they may read the letters in three possible orders, laid out in three different tables of contents. The story is further complicated by Teresa's admission that what is written in the letters is not necessarily the facts but merely her memories of them—events she suggests Alicia may remember differently.

Once she arrives at the language institute, Teresa discovers that the feeling of alienation she experiences in the United States as a dark-skinned Chicana too Mexican to fit into American culture is reversed in Mexico, where she is often regarded as a *gringa* (white girl) too American to fit into Mexican culture. She describes herself as undeniably Mexican-looking, with dark Indian features and a Spanish surname, and she is at once proud and ashamed of her obvious resemblance to the exotic, foreign Mexicans that the other students, all white, are at the institute to encounter. Her discomfort and sense of always being on the wrong side of the border are exacerbated by the lone Mexican instructor at the school. He dislikes her, she speculates, because she does not look like the pretty, blonde American girls, but rather "like the daughter of someone like him, except that he'd made the wade to the other side." At the same time, her occasionally awkward Spanish and American attitudes are a source of contempt for many Mexicans she meets.

The difficulties of living within and between two cultures haunt Teresa's quest for a heritage she can celebrate both as a Mexican American and as a woman. The battle between competing racial, cultural, and class identities plays out in Tere and Alicia's friendship and is epitomized in their differing physical appearances. Teresa's ancestors include Mexican Indians and Spanish conquistadors—she is a living symbol of European conquest of the indigenous peoples of the Americas.

Tall, slim, and light-skinned, Alicia seems to embody perfect Anglo femininity to Tere (despite the fact that Alicia's grandmother was from Spain), but Alicia sees herself as merely thin and pale compared to Teresa's voluptuous figure and dark beauty. When a handsome young Mexican artist praises Alicia's sketches but asks Tere for a date, Alicia is crushed. That night, in their hotel room, Alicia weeps at her image in a mirror while Teresa pretends not to know why her friend feels humiliated. Years later, however, when Alicia is on the verge of suicide over a failed love affair, Tere writes that if they were back in that hotel "i wouldn't deny to you again that i understand why you hated yourself. . . . you had been angry that i never had problems attracting men. You pointed out the obvious, the big breasts, full hips. . . . Underlining the superficial attraction men felt toward me is what you did not recognize. i was docile."

This docile "Mexican" part of her identity is ironically what Tere hopes to lose in Mexico, even while recognizing that her modern, feminist consciousness is largely a reflection of a white, middle-class women's movement that generally ignored nonwhite, working-class women like herself. Many of Teresa's clashes with Mexican culture are over its traditional and strongly patriarchal attitudes toward women, especially young women traveling alone. Nonetheless, Tere finds herself continually drawn to Mexico, delighting in the landscape, art, architecture, music, and deep passion for life she finds there.

Such an open exploration of the continuing legacy of conquest and colonization, racial and ethnic mixing, sexism and sexuality through an empowered female character was groundbreaking, especially in the field of Chicano literature. Tere was something new on the landscape of American literature. Although many subsequent writers, Latina and non-Latina, have created strong young women, few have been as willing as Castillo to wrestle with such taboo subjects as illegal immigration, racial mixing, and homosexuality.

In the end, the story of what finally happens to Teresa and Alicia, what they learn or do not learn from their experiences, is up to the reader to decide. The version Castillo offers in the first table of contents, "For the Conformist," concludes with Alicia's triumphant one-woman show at a fashionable art gallery and Tere's return to Mexico to stay with the parents of her baby's father. "For the Cynic" leaves Teresa raising her baby alone and shaking her head over what she sees as yet another of Alicia's doomed love affairs. "For the Quixotic" ends with the two friends, now in their thirties, eagerly planning another trip to Mixquiahuala.

Discussion Questions

1. One of the contradictions Teresa struggles with in Mexico is her uneasy awareness that as a relatively well-off American she may be romanticizing and colonizing Mexicans as much as she feels romanticized and colonized by white culture north of the border. Can you find examples of episodes in which Teresa turns Mexican culture into a tourist spectacle?

2. Many critics have written about the erotic undercurrents in Tere and Alicia's relationship, and some argue that it is their unresolved desire for each other that drives them to seek out a series of male lovers who use and desert them. Can you find evidence to support this argument?

3. Mexico can be seen as a sort of third main character in this novel, far more than simply a setting or backdrop. Analyze the role played by Mexico in shaping Teresa's identity as a Latina in America and her relationship to the history, cultures, and religions of Mexico.

4. Why do you think Castillo chose to offer multiple endings for her readers? Do all three of the options seem equally believable to you? How did you feel being given the responsibility of deciding what finally happens to Tere and Alicia?

—*Sara L. Spurgeon*

REFERENCES

Norma Alarcón, "The Sardonic Powers of the Erotic in the Work of Ana Castillo," in *Breaking Boundaries: Latina Writing and Critical Readings* (Amherst, Mass.: Amherst University Press, 1989), pp. 268–273;

Tanya Long Bennett, "No Country to Call Home: A Study of Ana Castillo's *Mixquiahuala Letters*," *Style*, 30 (Fall 1996): 462–479;

Alvina E. Quintana, "Ana Castillo's *The Mixquiahuala Letters*: The Novelist as Ethnographer," in *Criticism in the Borderlands: Studies in Chicano Literature, Culture, and Ideology*, edited by Hector Calderon and José David Saldivar (Durham, N.C.: Duke University Press, 1991), pp. 72–83;

Sara L. Spurgeon, *Ana Castillo*, Western Writers Series, no. 163 (Boise, Idaho: Boise State University, 2004).

Willa Cather

(December 7, 1873 – April 24, 1947)

DEATH COMES FOR THE ARCHBISHOP

(New York: Knopf, 1927)

JEAN MARIE LATOUR

Father Jean Marie Latour is the Catholic priest referred to in the title of Willa Cather's novel *Death Comes for the Archbishop*. He is patterned on an actual person, Father Jean Baptiste Lamy, the first bishop, and then archbishop, of Santa Fe after New Mexico was ceded to the United States in the Treaty of Guadalupe Hidalgo, which ended the Mexican War. Since this redistribution of land had split the Diocese of Durango (Mexico) between two national governments, it was necessary to have a church authority in each. Lamy, who was then already serving in missionary work in Ohio, was consecrated as bishop and appointed to this responsibility in 1850.

Death Comes for the Archbishop is an episodic novel. Even so, a rather full characterization of Father Latour emerges, since his presence is central in almost every chapter. Even in episodes that center on Father Vaillant, it is clear that Latour is the controlling presence. For example, in the chapter when Vaillant obtains the two white mules that he and Latour then ride about their vast diocese for many years, there is still an emphasis on the importance of providing a suitable mount for the bishop. Thus,

Vaillant, though in some ways the more interesting of the two characters, always remains subordinate to Latour, in keeping with their relative ecclesiastical ranks.

Throughout, Latour is presented as a spiritual intellectual. He is devout, certainly, but is less ready to believe in miracles, for instance, than his friend Vaillant. In the opening chapter, when the reader first meets Latour directly after he is referred to in the prologue (where, in a pleasant meeting of church officials at a villa overlooking Rome, he is chosen to be vicar apostolic to New Mexico), he is seen riding through arid central New Mexico, lost and without water, on his arduous return trip from having presented his credentials to the Bishop of Durango. A Frenchman only recently arrived in the American Southwest and confused in the alien landscape, he sees a juniper tree that appears to him to have the form of a cross, dismounts, and spends half an hour in prayer. Almost at once his horse smells water, and man and beast, near death from thirst, arrive at a small Mexican settlement called Agua Secreta, meaning Hidden Water. The episode is in the style of a legend. An almost miraculous event happens, and it is told simply, directly, and with its meaning made absolutely clear.

This opening incident when Latour finds water in the desert sets up motifs that resonate throughout the novel. It also sets up a beautiful but little-noticed demonstration of Cather's care in structuring this book, since near the end, as he lies dying, Latour recalls a legend involving another juniper, in which a priest named Father Junípero also finds miraculous refreshment in the desert. The two legends are almost perfectly balanced in their placement.

Latour is not always presented as a perfectly serene man. One episode, "December Night," finds him undergoing a period of spiritual "coldness and doubt." Significantly, Father Vaillant has been away on missionary travel for several months when this episode opens. Their friendship has been perhaps the most treasured aspect of Latour's life, after his religious commitment, and Vaillant has often provided the hearty, simple faith that Lamy needs to warm his life. On his deathbed Lamy remembers the moving scene when he persuaded Vaillant to leave his home in France and go with him to America

as a missionary priest. For the most part, however, Lamy is shown not only as a serene but as a reserved and diplomatic church leader, fully in control of his emotions and manner as he deals with difficult situations. He does not shrink from confrontations when they are necessary but prefers to wait until the time is right and meanwhile, throughout his ministry, draws strength from quiet reading and solitude or moments shared only with Vaillant. This habitual serenity and restraint prevails even when he feels distressed over U.S. treatment of the Navajo Indians, who were (as the novel shows in a summary fashion) starved out of their lands in 1863 and sent on a three-hundred-mile trek on foot to a prison camp near Fort Sumner in the eastern part of New Mexico.

Another difficulty faced by Latour, and faced as well by the historical Lamy, was the opposition of Catholic priests who had been in New Mexico before the Mexican War and who persisted in following practices that had grown up over long years of distance from any close supervision by the authorities at Rome. The leader among these was Padre Antonio José Martínez at Taos. Martínez appears in *Death Comes for the Archbishop* under his own name (as does the Western scout Kit Carson) in a negative portrait that has long rankled with New Mexicans. It is by no means clear that the historical Lamy was as perfectly right in this conflict as Cather presents Latour as being.

Cather stated, in her published commentary on this novel, that part of her inspiration came from a famous woodcut by the Dutch artist Hans Holbein, the Younger, in a series of emblematic pictures called *Dance of Death* (1538). In the picture showing death coming for a bishop, the skeletal figure of Death holds by the hand an old, stooped man in ecclesiastical robes and leads him gently away. In the background scene, a flock of sheep has become scattered, and the shepherds are in postures of grief. It is an appropriate visual emblem for *Death Comes for the Archbishop* and one that recalls how significantly Cather has revised the conventions of the Western novel, in writing this work centered on the peaceful and spiritual presence—not without its adventures—of Father Latour in the rugged Southwest.

Discussion Questions

1. Try to find prints of Holbein's *Dance of Death,* which Cather cited in explaining her intentions in *Death Comes for the Archbishop.* How much understanding does Holbein's woodcut of the bishop help in interpreting her treatment of Father Latour?

2. Why do you think Cather changed the name of Father Lamy in creating her fictional character, when she retained the actual names of Kit Carson and Padre Martínez? How ethical or appropriate do you think it was for her to write about them as she did under their actual names?

3. *Death Comes for the Archbishop* takes place in an area that is often the setting of Westerns. In what ways does Father Latour resemble, or differ from, a conventional Western hero? (Consider the fact that he draws a gun on Buck Scales, for example.)

4. Cather once said in a letter that *Death Comes for the Archbishop* is a novel without a single woman character except the Virgin Mary. That is not literally true. How does Latour relate to the women characters in the novel?

5. In saying that *Death Comes for the Archbishop* had no women characters, Cather likened it in that respect to Joseph Conrad's *The Nigger of the "Narcissus."* You might look into Conrad's novel for reasons of gender but also might compare its treatment of race to Cather's treatment of racial differences in *Death Comes for the Archbishop.* How do you assess Latour's interactions with people of different races than his?

—*Janis P. Stout*

JOSEPH VAILLANT

Father Joseph Vaillant is one of the two main characters, both of them Catholic priests, in Willa Cather's novel *Death Comes for the Archbishop.* He is the vicar and longtime friend to Bishop Jean Marie Latour, who later becomes the archbishop of the title. Like Latour, Vaillant was based on an actual figure; in his case, Father Joseph Projectus Machebeuf. Machebeuf was born, educated, and ordained in France before coming to the United States as a missionary. He served in Ohio and then came to New Mexico to shape the newly independent Diocese of Santa Fe after New Mexico and other territories were ceded to the United States by Mexico under force of arms

in 1848. The life of the fictional Vaillant follows these same outlines.

In her characterization of Vaillant (perhaps named because she saw him as being valiant in his service to the church), Cather emphasized contrasts between him and Father Latour. Vaillant is more simple and direct, less intellectual. Born into a family of lower social class than Latour's, he first met Latour when they went to seminary at Montferrand, France. There he had been, as Cather describes him through Latour's eyes, a "lively, ugly boy" of an outstanding "fervour of his faith" though undistinguished scholarly ability. In New Mexico as well, he is fervent in his devotion, especially to the Virgin Mary. Latour thinks and plans; Vaillant acts. He travels relentlessly around the huge diocese on mule or horseback, bringing the sacraments and religious instruction to his parishioners. Latour's emphasis is on the church as an institution and on the beautiful accoutrements of life, especially the material embodiment of the church in the cathedral he envisions. Vaillant's emphasis is on his ministry to the people of the diocese. Latour is aristocratic, Vaillant humble. He is not above going into the kitchen and cooking his own mutton in order to have it done just so, when he visits parishioners—to their astonishment. At one point he is even described trimming his toenails and corns, the better to walk his path of service. He relates with ease and directness to the poor and generally uneducated Mexican people to whom he ministers.

Readers may think that the ways Vaillant speaks of his Mexican parishioners, while affectionate, are condescending. He describes them as dear but ignorant children, who are superstitious and have "foolish ways." At the same time, it is clearly Cather's intention to show what a virtuous man he is, especially in that as a Frenchman he is happy to serve among these uneducated people. "I have almost become a Mexican!" Vaillant claims, emphasizing to Latour his wish to be left in his missionary position, not called back to Santa Fe. "I am *their man!*" It is an indication of Vaillant's common touch that he is given a nickname in the novel—Blanchet, or Whitey—while Latour is always called by his formal name. Father Vaillant is also a good cook, a skill Latour greatly appreciates.

Some of the most moving episodes in the novel relate to the friendship between the two priests. The first of these is the moment of their first meeting, when they were in seminary. More poignant is the moment when, as young priests, they leave their home in France to come to America. Vaillant is so torn between his wish to go and his love for his home and family that he almost misses the coach that takes them to their ship. The novel gives many scenes of their talking together as friends as well as ministerial colleagues. Latour relies on Vaillant's companionship, and Vaillant in turn enjoys cooking traditional French food for Latour on special occasions. The scene of their departure from France is balanced, near the end of the book, by a scene when Vaillant departs from Santa Fe to serve, once again, as a missionary priest in the rough mining camps of Colorado. The two are advanced in years now, and, doubting that they will ever meet again, each in turn kneels to receive the other's blessing.

In the novel, Vaillant dies before Latour does, after suffering various injuries in traveling over the undeveloped mountain roads. Latour's sorrow for his old friend darkens his later days, though he accepts the loss with a serene resignation as he does other problems. In reality, Archbishop Lamy died before Machebeuf. Apparently, Cather reversed the order for dramatic effect, to keep the spotlight on the archbishop and on his dying thoughts, which include thoughts about Vaillant. She seems to have conceived the character of Vaillant as a kind of complement, or completion, of her rather distant and austere main character. The virtues of one compensate for weaknesses of the other, as if the two together would comprise one perfect priest. Part of her intention may have been to show the complexity of the life of the church and how its historic strength has come from drawing together into unity a great variety of devout people.

Discussion Questions

1. Cather said that the writing of *Death Comes for the Archbishop* was like a "happy vacation from life, a return to childhood." In turning away from the issues of her time, is she being escapist, or is she choosing to confront deeper issues?

2. Which of the two priests do you find more interesting? more congenial? Why?

3. Latour and Vaillant have different conceptions of what miracles are. Explain their ideas. Is this difference a key to understanding the two characters more generally?

4. How do you evaluate Vaillant's and Latour's attitudes toward other cultures and ethnic groups? How do they differ in this respect?

—*Janis P. Stout*

A LOST LADY
(New York: Knopf, 1923)

MARIAN FORRESTER

Marian Forrester, the title character of Willa Cather's *A Lost Lady* (who is sometimes referred to by critics as the "American Emma Bovary"), has a deeply ambiguous character, both admirable and limited. She married a titan of industry of late-nineteenth- and early-twentieth-century America, Captain Daniel Forrester, who was one of the railroad builders who helped tie America together. Marian is his second wife and twenty-five years his junior, and through much of the novel she serves as Captain Forrester's companion and nurse as much as his wife.

Forrester won his wife with some physical derring-do in California, but their life in a declining Nebraska town, where the novel takes place, is circumscribed by the injuries he suffered in a fall from a horse and, later, by a stroke. Marian is genuinely devoted to her husband, admires his stalwart character, and tends conscientiously to his physical needs; but it is clear from nearly the beginning of the story that theirs is a marriage that cannot satisfy her more youthful nature. In an act of gratuitous cruelty, Ivy Peters, a coarse local youth, blinds a woodpecker and watches it in its distress, and Cather's description of the bird can also apply to Marian: "There was something wild and desperate about the way the darkened creature beat its wings in the branches, whirling in the sunlight and never seeking it, always thrusting its head up and shaking it, as a bird does when it is drinking."

Although Marian seems to have her life under control in the beginning of the novel, as the story progresses she, too, becomes "wild and desperate."

As long as her husband has financial security, Marian is a bewitching figure in the little town of Sweet Water, where they live after the captain's injury. She is sparkling and vivacious, possessed of both fragility and grace, with eyes that were at once "lively, laughing, intimate, nearly always a little mocking." She is surrounded largely by bumpkins and rough young men and nosy housewives but does not bemoan her situation and brings elegance and a sense of the larger world to her woebegone small town. She is an enthusiastic hostess to her husband's important business friends whom she helps attract to Sweet Water to see Captain Forrester. She does not, while she is "up" in the world, attract the animosity to be expected from those who are clearly her social inferiors, which is a tribute to her own native courtesy and grace. Niel Herbert, nephew to the town judge and the character through whose eyes much of the action of the novel unfolds, is a particular admirer of Marian and says that in her glance there was something "that made one's blood tingle."

Marian is usually referred to in the novel as "Mrs. Forrester," and it is as a wife that her downfall takes place. As sensitive as he is to her provocative yet decorous feminine nature, Niel admires her most for the relationship she has with her husband. He is especially disappointed, then, to discover that she is having an affair with Frank Ellinger when her husband is away, which shows the dark side of Marian's character, always suspected by the reader but not overtly seen until about halfway through the novel. The decline in her character is also accelerated by her husband's loss of wealth because of the failure of one of his banks—Marian is the kind of person that "needed" money, the novel makes clear—and his eventual death. Although Marian is able to maintain appearances after a fashion during these hardships, sympathy for her character is also undercut by Niel's deep disappointment with her infidelity. Although she never entirely loses her capacity to dazzle and captivate others, especially Niel, the symbol of her decline in the second half of the novel is her growing friendship with Peters, who has grown up to be a shady lawyer who makes money for Marian with

questionable business dealings: "Mrs. Forrester, rascality isn't the only thing that succeeds in business," says Niel, to which she replies, "It succeeds faster than anything else, though." Marian ends up having intimate relations with Peters, too, as a result of her financial dependency and the loss of her previous lover, Ellinger, through marriage to another woman. Yet, for all her weaknesses, Niel realizes that her husband "knew his wife better even than she knew herself; and that, knowing her, he,—to use one of his own expressions,—valued her." Niel himself cannot forget that Marian was not "willing to immolate herself," as did other widows of the "great men" who had settled the West, and "die with the pioneer period to which she belonged"; instead, she "preferred life on any terms." The novel itself is by no means as critical as Niel is in this regard.

Willa Cather often drew her characters from life, and Marian's was drawn from that of Lyra Garber, the widow of Silas Garber, the founder of Red Cloud, Nebraska (where Cather grew up), and a two-term governor of the state. As a child Cather "loved" Lyra Garber, and "her lovely hair and laugh . . . made me happy clear down to my toes." The author said the story of *A Lost Lady* came to her within an hour of hearing of Mrs. Garber's death. There is something elusive about Marian; Cather did not intend her as a character study so much as a portrayal of the effect she had on others. Thus, the novel ends with Niel receiving news of Marian's death and that "she was well cared for, to the very end," for which he is grateful.

Discussion Questions

1. To what extent is Marian Forrester a sympathetic character? What are the factors, positive or negative, which enter into your opinion?

2. What evidence is there that Mrs. Forrester is a good wife?

3. Is Mrs. Forrester manipulative of other persons in the novel? If so, is there any justification for such actions? If not, what word would you use to describe her influence on others?

4. Does what Niel hear of Mrs. Forrester's fate at the end of the novel seem an appropriate end to her life? Why or why not?

—Richard L. Harp

NIEL HERBERT

Niel Herbert is the youthful observer of events in Willa Cather's *A Lost Lady* and a loyal friend to Marian Forrester, the title character of the novel. As such he foreshadows other, better-known observer characters such as Nick Carraway in F. Scott Fitzgerald's *The Great Gatsby,* a novel influenced by *A Lost Lady,* as Fitzgerald acknowledged. Niel is the nephew of Judge Pommeroy, an important figure in the dusty Nebraska plains town named Sweet Water, where the events of the book take place.

Niel is handsome, studious, and a loner; these qualities make him a counterpoint to Mrs. Forrester, who is drawn to and dependent on men—she was someone who needed to be married, Niel concludes. He is not, though, without empathy and a certain natural nobility that make his role as the moral voice of the novel not inappropriate. Niel can never approve of Marian's sometime dependence on unsuitable men, but he is also far from absolutely condemning her, as he always remains appreciative of the vivaciousness and elegance she brings to their backwater town.

Niel's character is described as being reserved, which derives not from "embarrassment or vanity, but from a critical habit of mind, [which] made him seem older than he was." These traits of personality were reinforced by his father's having to leave Sweet Water because of financial reverses and Niel's remaining behind to a kind of monastic routine, "resolved to remain a bachelor." Yet, the charm of the house that Mrs. Forrester keeps slowly draws him out of his penchant for solitariness, and as he grows older and "dull and tired of everything, he used to think that if he could hear that long-lost lady laugh again, he could be gay." It is a measure of the complexity of the novel that neither Mrs. Forrester, the "lost lady," nor Niel, the upright but sometimes dull young man, are one-dimensional characters. Marian's strength of character is shown in the care she gives her elderly husband after his financial failure. Niel, even after he becomes aware of her faults, remains gallant and chivalrous toward her, wishing when he sees her after a lengthy absence that he could "carry her off . . . the earth of sad, inevitable periods, away from age, weariness, adverse fortune!"

This same chivalrousness makes Niel always wish to care for Mrs. Forrester and to protect her, for example, from the familiarity and unscrupulous business schemes of Ivy Peters, a coarse local youth who grows up to be a lawyer of questionable principles. But the novel makes clear that the efficaciousness of such behavior, while charming and appreciated by Marian, is no longer a match for the "new men" of the West. Still, Niel does what he can, such as preventing Marian's indiscreet and angry conversation with Frank Ellinger, a former lover, from becoming too great a subject of the town gossipmongers. At one point Mrs. Forrester hints that as a widow she would find Niel a more appealing intimate friend than Ivy, but the thought is repugnant to Niel, and this incapacity on his part, this inability to be more than a sympathetic friend after the death of Captain Forrester, is perhaps a limitation in his character, as there is no sign that he has any other important human connections.

Around the time this novel was being written Cather said she drew characters for her novels from life, making them "composites of three or four persons. I do not quite understand it, but certain persons seem to coalesce naturally when one is working up a story."

Niel's experience and understanding of life comes not only from his society with Mrs. Forrester but also from his reading of a set of classic literature that he finds in Judge Pommeroy's library. He especially admires the Roman poet Ovid's work on love, the *Heroides,* which he read over and over and "felt they were the most glowing love stories ever told," and reading such works influences his life more than his formal education, which involved training to be an architect. Niel's "admiration and loyalty" to Mrs. Forrester comes to an end when he discovers she is having an affair with the coarsely attractive Ellinger—a discovery that occurs in the same chapter that describes his reading of similar literary liaisons in Ovid.

Niel is also an observer in the novel of the passing of the West that had been settled by the tough pioneers and railroad entrepreneurs that he greatly admired. The combination of opposites he especially admires in the Forresters' union—Captain Forrester, the rough-and-ready builder of railroads with unshakable integrity, and Marian, the enchanting hostess who provided the social setting that gave point and elegance to such conquests—proves to be a fragile one. In the second half of the novel Niel observes, after the Captain becomes an invalid, that the consolidation of the railroad men's accomplishments was falling to lesser men such as Peters, who lacks "the princely carelessness of the pioneer" and would "destroy and cut up into profitable bits" the great spaces of land that his predecessors had tamed. *A Lost Lady* speaks movingly and with love not only of the decline of a grand lady but also of a Western way of life not to be recaptured.

Discussion Questions

1. How would you describe the change in Niel's attitude toward Mrs. Forrester after he learns that she has broken her marriage vows?

2. What adjective would best describe Niel's overall attitude toward Mrs. Forrester?

3. Cather seems not to regard Niel's vocation or intellectual interests as particularly important to his character in this novel. Do you agree with this presentation of his character—or do you think the novel should tell more about his other interests besides those concerning the Forrester family?

4. Does Niel have any particularly serious faults?

—Richard L. Harp

༄

LUCY GAYHEART
(New York: Knopf, 1935)

LUCY GAYHEART

The title character of Willa Cather's novel *Lucy Gayheart* is a young woman from a small Midwestern town who wishes to be a concert pianist but never goes further than being a fairly good accompanist. Readers often compare her unfavorably to Thea Kronborg, the heroic central character of Cather's *The Song of the Lark,* and find her wanting in stamina and determination.

While Cather was writing *Lucy Gayheart,* she wrote a letter to a friend, the playwright Zoë Akins, in which she said that her new heroine was a foolish or shallow young girl. Nevertheless, the author

treats seriously Lucy's desire for a career in music. The way in which she presents Lucy's longing for beauty, when she sees the first emerging star of the night during a frosty evening of ice-skating, while she is home for Christmas vacation from her piano studies in Chicago, seems to indicate that she is not entirely lacking in depth. Certainly, Lucy's place in the memories of her townspeople, after her death, shows that she has been a person of significance in their minds. Readers may wonder, then, what Cather meant by her disparaging remark.

The answer seems, at least in part, to have something to do with Lucy's relationships with men. While in Chicago, she takes a job as rehearsal accompanist for a famous singer, Clement Sebastian, and falls in love with him—or at least, falls into a romantic fantasy about him. When her friend and possible sweetheart from her hometown, Harry Gordon, comes to Chicago and proposes to her, she tells him that she has "gone all the way" with Sebastian. She means that she has adopted Sebastian's total commitment to art, but she realizes that Harry will think that she has had a sexual relationship with the older man. She knows that he will then stop pursuing her. Later, when she has returned home in apparent failure, Harry still nurses a grudge against her. Her foolish and untrue words ultimately lead to her death: when the aloof and resentful Harry refuses to stop and give her a ride on a freezing cold day, she trudges on to the Platte River to go ice-skating and falls through the ice.

As in *The Song of the Lark,* Cather has written a story about a girl from a small town modeled on Red Cloud, Nebraska, who goes away to the city to become an artist and becomes to some degree estranged from her family. This time the artist-heroine does not succeed. Yet, at the point of her death Lucy had decided to go back to Chicago and renew her efforts, no longer as an accompanist for Sebastian, who has died, but independently. She has been inspired by the commitment to musical quality she has seen in the performance of a touring singer at the local opera house, who "strove after excellence" even while singing to people at a place far from the urban centers of musical culture. Lucy resolves that she, too, will strive for excellence even if she never reaches the rarefied levels of musical stardom. The ending of the novel leaves open whether she would have succeeded.

After her death Lucy becomes associated with two images in the minds of those who remember her. One is the "bright winter stars" Harry sees through a window as he thinks of her, which he associates with eternity. The name *Lucy* means "light," and her association with sparkling light is established in the exhilarating ice-skating scene at the start of the novel. Seeing the first star of the evening, Lucy experiences what she feels is a "flash of understanding" between herself and the star and salutes this "point of silver light," much as Thea Kronborg salutes a soaring eagle with which she identifies. The second image with which her memory is associated is the imprint of her feet in a stretch of concrete sidewalk she had run across, as a child, when it was still soft. This image may recall what Cather once wrote in an essay about the writer Katherine Mansfield, that in even the most "harmonious" families every person is always "escaping, running away, trying to break the net which circumstances and his own affections have woven about him."

Lucy has indeed tried to escape her humdrum family life and the prospect of a dull marriage to Harry. Instead, the branches of a submerged tree entrap her when she falls through the ice, almost like a net snarled around her skates. But although her story is tragic, her life serves a redemptive purpose for the townspeople, for whom her memory shines out as an emblem of beauty and joy beyond the everyday world.

Discussion Questions

1. Is Lucy Gayheart's urge to leave home unusual? Should it be attributed to her musical vocation, or is it true that most people feel an urge to leave home—even if they later come back?

2. Clement Sebastian's valet says at one point that "plumbers and brewers and bank clerks and dressmakers" who sing in a choral society find "something to help them through their lives." What does he mean? Does this statement sufficiently account for the meaning of music to Lucy, or does her love of music belong to another category?

3. Explain fully and clearly the significance of the imagery of light and stars to the characterization of Lucy Gayheart. What does the initial ice-skating

scene tell us about Lucy? How does it, then, contribute to irony in the novel?

4. Compare the function of the song "I Dreamt I Dwelt in Marble Halls" in *Lucy Gayheart* (book 2, chapter 7) and in James Joyce's story "Clay" (from *Dubliners*). How can the song be significant in both works?

—*Janis P. Stout*

MY ÁNTONIA
(Boston & New York: Houghton Mifflin, 1918)

JIM BURDEN

Jim Burden, the first-person narrator of Willa Cather's *My Ántonia,* arrives in Nebraska from Virginia at around nine years old, much in the same way that Cather came to Nebraska with her parents as a child. An orphan, Jim is being sent to his grandparents' farm, with only a farmhand accompanying him on the train west. Riding to his new home in a jolting wagon, after alighting from the train, he feels that "the world was left behind, that we had got over the edge of it, and were outside man's jurisdiction. I had never before looked up at the sky when there was not a familiar mountain ridge against it. . . . I felt erased, blotted out."

Jim is to a great extent Cather herself, transformed into a boy. Records of the author's life make it clear that the graciousness of her grandparents' home is much the same as that of Jim's grandparents'; the Burdens' move into Black Hawk parallels Cather's parents' move into Red Cloud; and Jim goes off to the University of Nebraska, where he reads the Latin classics, much as Cather did.

At various points in the novel, however, Cather distances herself from Jim, almost as if her personality, which she had remade into his, was then being split. This splitting is most obvious in the introduction to the novel, where a first-person speaker who seems to represent Cather herself speaks about an encounter with Jim, her childhood friend. They mention a special girl they had known in Nebraska named Ántonia Shimerda, a Bohemian immigrant who seems to both of them to embody their best memories of childhood and the fertility of the land itself. Both agree to write down their reminiscences about Ántonia, but the narrator of the introduction never does. The manuscript Jim writes is the novel that follows. Jim first titles it "Ántonia," then adds the prefatory *My*.

What Jim means by "*my* Ántonia" has been the subject of critical debate. Is he saying that this account of Ántonia is only his and may not describe her as others see her? Or is he revealing an urge to possess and control her? If so, he may be showing himself to be a classic manipulative male, and thus is setting up a feminist reading of the novel. Or if, as the introduction seems to indicate, Jim's life is not entirely happy, especially with respect to his marriage, his addition of the word *my* may indicate his need to hold close to someone who makes him feel secure.

These uncertainties as to Jim's motivations continue throughout the novel. He meets the Shimerda family on the train as he is coming to Nebraska from Virginia. Like many immigrants who came directly from their homes in Europe to farm country in the Midwest, they are just completing their journey from Bohemia, lured by a kinsman who schemed to sell them his farm at an inflated price. When Jim's grandparents visit their new neighbors as a matter of course and help them through various hardships, Jim and Ántonia become fast friends. The early sections of the book are an account of their life of freely rambling on the prairie, their acquaintance with various other immigrant neighbors, and their adventures, such as Jim's killing of a large rattlesnake, much to Ántonia's admiration. But they also reveal the beginnings of a certain hypocrisy in Jim.

Readers soon realize that they cannot entirely rely on Jim's interpretations. In the episode of the rattlesnake, for example, he expresses his pleasure that Ántonia will now respect him more. He regards it as fitting that she should, despite the fact that she is older than he; after all, he is a boy and she only a girl. One element that remains tacit in his thinking is that she is also of far less social status than he. Later, Jim's distaste for what he regards as Ántonia's coarseness when she has to work in the fields "like mans," as she says, may strike readers as unsympathetic, and when he refuses to have anything further

to do with her after she bears a child out of wedlock, he clearly seems judgmental and harsh. When he later tells her that he would have liked to have had her for his sweetheart (implying that the possibility is now closed), his honesty with himself, as well as with others, is further called into question. When he apparently tries, in the last chapter, to position himself as one of Ántonia's little boys and to define her as an icon of motherhood, he seems to display a regressive urge.

What to make of Jim Burden—whether Cather means for her readers to be skeptical of him, or if he is intended to serve as her spokesman—is one of the central questions of *My Ántonia*. It is hard to find a satisfactory answer, but in any event Jim does become an excellent case study in narrative point of view. For all his seeming naiveté in much of the novel and the seeming simplicity and wholesomeness of life on the prairie, the development of Jim as an unreliable narrator places *My Ántonia* squarely within the tradition of modernism.

Discussion Questions

1. Compare Jim Burden to Jake Barnes, the narrator of Ernest Hemingway's novel of the same time, *The Sun Also Rises*. The two are obviously very different. In what ways do the authors use similar techniques in developing their characters as centers of consciousness?

2. What is the symbolic importance of Jim's name? In what ways are Jim's memories a *burden* to him?

3. The epigraph to *My Ántonia* is a Latin quotation from the Roman poet Virgil, "Optima dies . . . prima fugit." Look up the meaning of this line and explore ways in which it is a key to the character of Jim Burden and his presentation of Ántonia.

4. To what extent does Jim's idealization of Ántonia resemble Gatsby's idealization of the "fresh, green breast of the new world" in F. Scott Fitzgerald's *The Great Gatsby?*

—*Janis P. Stout*

LENA LINGARD

Lena Lingard, one of the main characters of Willa Cather's *My Ántonia*, is a career woman who boldly announces that "I've seen a good deal of married life, and I don't care for it. I want to be so I can help my mother and the children at home, and not have to ask lief of anybody." Lena's determination not to place herself under the control of a man and to avoid a life of domestic drudgery makes her a foil for Ántonia Shimerda, the Bohemian immigrant who is idealized by Jim Burden, the narrator of the novel, for her maternal fecundity. To some extent Lena seems to represent the author, herself a career woman firmly in control of her own life, also interested in fashion and consciously dressing the part of the New Woman. Lena's presence in the novel complicates its portrayal of women and their social roles.

Lena is one of the "hired girls" whose company Jim enjoys after his grandparents move to the town of Black Hawk, Nebraska. Daughters of immigrant farmers, they are placed by their fathers in jobs in town where they do domestic work so that they can contribute to their families' incomes. Lena, a Norwegian, is a helper to a dressmaker, who decides that she has a knack and teaches her to sew. Lena's friend Tiny Soderball, a Swede, works as a waitress at a local hotel where traveling salesmen stay. Other hired girls are Bohemian or Danish. They bring vitality and ethnic richness to the staid town, and their work helps the immigrant families to rise economically; but as Jim observes, they are regarded as lower-class by the natives of Black Hawk, whose sons enjoy dancing and laughing with the immigrant girls but choose local girls when they marry. Often the hired girls return to their rural homes, having found themselves pregnant by their employers or employers' sons.

Lena exudes an aura of sexuality. She is physically beautiful and is regularly pursued by men. Before she hired out in town, while she was still tending cattle on her father's farm, her beauty intoxicated a neighboring farmer and led his jealous wife to come after her with a knife. Increasingly, she becomes a preoccupation for Jim, as well. In book 3 of the novel, which is called "Lena Lingard," they have an affair in Lincoln while Jim is a student at the University of Nebraska and Lena is operating her own dressmaking business. They attend plays and eat breakfast together, and Jim congratulates himself on the maturity of their relationship: "Lena was at least a woman, and I was a man." They talk about marriage desultorily, but Lena maintains her inten-

tion to "be accountable to nobody," and Jim plans to leave Lincoln for Boston to continue his studies.

Lena's business in Lincoln flourishes to the point that she can have a house built and furnished for her mother. Later, in California, her business expertise leads her to even greater success. She is in a prosperous business partnership with Tiny Soderball, who has also made a lot of money as a hotel keeper and now manages Lena's financial affairs. Tiny is described as caring for nothing but money anymore and as having lost her capacity for enjoyment of life. Lena, on the other hand, remains caring and generous. It is she, in fact, who suggests that Jim go visit Ántonia after she is settled in her role as farmwife and mother.

Discussion Questions

1. Is the story of Lena and Ole Benson, the married farmer who becomes infatuated with her, portrayed as comic? Use details from the novel to support your answer. What aspects of the incident suggest that it is not intended to be funny?

2. What is the significance of Lena's suggestion that her brother have their mother's name embroidered on the handkerchief he is giving her, rather than the word *Mother?*

3. In what ways does Lena resemble, or differ from, Alexandra Bergson in Cather's novel *O Pioneers!?*

4. One of the plays Lena and Jim attend together is *Camille,* by Alexandre Dumas *fils,* about a Paris courtesan who is dying of consumption. (The play was famously adapted by Giuseppe Verdi for his opera *La Traviata.*) In what ways is Lena like Camille, the heroine of the play? How is she different?

5. Does *My Ántonia* argue that women must make a choice between careers and satisfying home lives? If so, does Cather seem to approve of one choice over the other? If not, why doesn't Lena opt for both work and marriage?

—*Janis P. Stout*

ÁNTONIA SHIMERDA

Ántonia Shimerda, the title character of Willa Cather's novel *My Ántonia,* is probably Cather's best-known creation. Ántonia is a lively and charming youngster in the early chapters of the novel, with flashing brown eyes and an eagerness to learn everything her new friend, Jim Burden, can teach her about America and the English language. As she matures, she demonstrates strength and perseverance in times of hardship and an inclination to nurture those around her. When she has a baby by a railroad man who lured her away to Denver with promises of marriage, Jim is judgmental and repelled, but when he reluctantly consents to see her, he is surprised to find that she is proud of her baby daughter and has no wish to hide her. She later marries a Czech farmer named Anton Cuzak, bears many children, and manages a prosperous farming household. Jim, who narrates the novel, calls her "a rich mine of life, like the founders of early races."

On one level, the novel may be considered a celebration of motherhood, with Ántonia an uncomplicated farm woman whose claim to heroism is located in her fertility. Jim is an unreliable narrator, however, who tends to gloss over what he calls her "battered" appearance. Motherhood and childbearing have been a strain on her. When Jim visits Ántonia and her family after his long estrangement from her, he learns that she has higher aspirations for her daughters. She is glad they will not have to "work out"—that is, work as maids or housekeepers—as she did, and she holds up a successful local businesswoman as a "heroine in the family legend."

Cather based Ántonia on a Bohemian immigrant girl, Annie Sadilek, whose family lived near the Cather family farm in Red Cloud, Nebraska. Annie was one of the first people Cather met when she moved to Nebraska as a child in 1883. As in the novel, Annie's first daughter was born out of wedlock, but rather than hiding the fact, she proudly displayed a portrait of the baby in the photographer's shop window in Red Cloud. In a 1921 interview Cather acknowledged the real-life basis of the character of Ántonia. She continued her friendship with Annie (whose married name was Pavelka) throughout her life and often sent gifts to the Pavelka family.

As seen through Jim's perspective, Ántonia represents some of the conflicting ideas of the early twentieth century as to women's proper roles. As a boy, Jim finds it disappointing that Ántonia becomes muscular and rough from having to work in the fields. He wants her to be more dainty and feminine. At the end, however, when he returns to his hometown as a disillusioned adult and sees her surrounded by her children and by the evidence of her hard work, he prefers to idealize the past and her role in his own childhood. In a sense, Jim never sees the complexity in Ántonia's character that Cather makes evident to the reader through his narration.

Discussion Questions

1. What specific qualities does Ántonia teach her daughters to admire about Frances Harling? Does Ántonia demonstrate those qualities herself as a young woman? What does her delight in going to dances while she is working in town for the Harlings say about her character? Is it consistent with her characterization that she refuses to stop attending dances when Mrs. Harling tells her to?

2. Compare Ántonia and the other main female character in *My Ántonia*, Lena Lingard. Are there any similarities between the two, in addition to the obvious differences? Does the novel seem to support the choices one of them makes more than the other one?

—*Janis P. Stout*

꒰꒱

"NEIGHBOUR ROSICKY"

Collected in *Obscure Destinies* (New York: Knopf, 1932).

ANTON ROSICKY

Anton Rosicky is the central character of Willa Cather's story "Neighbour Rosicky," set in Nebraska. Readers felt that with these stories she was returning to her own place after years of setting her works in a great variety of places such as New Mexico, New York, San Francisco, Chicago, and Quebec. What may be less obvious is that she was also coming back to the focus on ordinary people (frequently immigrants) and everyday happenings that had characterized novels such as *My Ántonia* more than a decade earlier.

Rosicky, an aging man with a bad heart when the story opens, is an immigrant from Bohemia, which at the time Cather wrote was a region of Czechoslovakia. He and his wife, Mary, speak Czech in private, and Cather's spelling of the dialogue in the story indicates that their English is spoken with an accent. They belong, then, to a group in whom she took great interest throughout her career, immigrants from Europe who came to the American agricultural heartland to make a new life.

Rosicky was modeled on John Pavelka, the husband of Annie Sadilek Pavelka, a Bohemian woman Cather met when she came to Nebraska as a child and for whom she had retained particular affection. (She was the model for the title character in *My Ántonia*.) Like Pavelka, and also like Frank Shabata of *O Pioneers!*, Anton Rosicky was essentially a city man before he came to the Great Plains to be a farmer. In London, where he lived for two years as a teenager, and then in New York, where he lived until the age of thirty-five, he worked as a tailor. As he thinks back over his life, he remembers how he enjoyed the advantages of city life, particularly the opportunity to attend operas in New York. The fond tone in which he remembers these things shows that he is a man who takes pleasure in life.

At the same time Rosicky also remembers, as he sits reminiscing during the long winter while his doctor has cautioned him to refrain from outdoor work, the dissatisfaction he felt in the city as he came to feel more and more restless. Ultimately, he wished to be closer to the life of the soil. He had spent part of his youth in Bohemia on the farm his grandparents rented, and especially in springtime, as he walked around New York on quiet Sundays, those long-ago "ties with the earth and the farm animals and growing things" kept calling him. For that reason he decided to join one of the Czech communities in the Midwest that he had read about in newspapers. He never dreamed that he might prosper sufficiently to own his own land, but at the time of the story he is indeed an independent farmer of modest but sufficient means.

The warm, pleasure-loving aspect of Rosicky's character is evident in his and Mary's willingness to put good food on the table rather than skimp in order to save money. She is shown making *kolache* (a traditional fruit-filled pastry that requires attentive, skilled handling) and serving coffee, and he regularly buys her candy with his spare change. He refuses to sell the cream from his cows' milk even though it would bring a good price, agreeing with Mary that it is better to feed it to their children. His readiness to take pleasure in life is particularly seen when he insists on having a lavish Fourth of July picnic after he has just discovered that he has lost all his corn for the year. "We might as well enjoy what we got," he explains. Another incident involving food demonstrates this pleasure. When he was working in London and was poor, some people speaking Czech whom he encountered on the street gave him money for food, and he used it to buy the makings of a big Christmas dinner for his indigent landlady and her underfed children. From all these details readers see Rosicky as a generous person and one naturally allied with what might be called a life principle that is represented by food, the essential sustainer of life.

For Rosicky, loving life does not mean clinging to it in desperation as death approaches. Rather, he matter-of-factly sees the nearby graveyard as a comfortable place for a man to "lie down in the long grass." He takes comfort in thinking that in death he will not have to go farther than the edge of his own field. Before that time arrives, however, he feels a need to arrange for happiness in his children's future. Knowing that his son's wife, Polly, who had been a town girl, is lonely and dissatisfied on their farm, and knowing that his son will not be happy if they move to town, he is at pains to show them the wisdom of taking such pleasures as they can afford, in order to achieve balance in life. He goes to their house unasked, lends them his car to go to town to the movies, provides money for the tickets, and even washes the supper dishes and thoroughly cleans the kitchen so Polly will feel free to go. During his few minutes alone with her, he shares some of his memories of city life.

When Rosicky suffers a heart attack, the previously cold and distant Polly cares for him and tells him, before she has told anyone else, that she is going to have a baby. He feels happy in thinking that she will be a more nurturing woman than she previously seemed. His death soon afterward is juxtaposed with the prospect of ongoing life, both in the form of the expected baby and in the form of his fertile fields. As the doctor looks at the graveyard where Rosicky now lies buried, he thinks of something "complete and beautiful," a phrase that invokes the idea of a complete natural cycle.

Discussion Questions

1. What insights into Anton Rosicky's characterization are provided by the title of the book in which the story appeared, *Obscure Destinies?*

2. Rosicky is seen performing two kinds of work that were at the time the story is set usually considered women's work: sewing and washing dishes. What does his willingness, or even gladness, to do these things indicate about his character?

3. What commonalities do you see between Anton Rosicky and Ántonia of the novel *My Ántonia,* who is also Bohemian?

4. Explore some ways in which the doctor's phrase "complete and beautiful" seems appropriate to the character of Rosicky as it is developed in the story.

5. Another major work in American literature that deals with immigrants from Europe who engage in agricultural work on the Great Plains is *Giants in the Earth* by O. E. Rölvaag. What comparisons and contrasts do you see between Rosicky and the central male character of Rölvaag's novel?

—*Janis P. Stout*

꩜

O PIONEERS!
(Boston & New York: Houghton Mifflin, 1913)

ALEXANDRA BERGSON

Alexandra Bergson is the "Amazonian" daughter of a Swedish immigrant who dies without reaching success in his struggle to make a productive farm on Nebraska's plains in Willa Cather's novel *O Pioneers!* On his deathbed the farmer tells his two older sons that they are to stay on the land and be guided by Alexandra. He thus sets her up both for extraordinary success, since a woman would not customarily have been allowed to take control, and for her brothers' resentment. Over the years they grumblingly do what she says, even when they would rather give up and sell out. Alexandra's story is one of long struggle and ultimate success and wealth, though at the cost

of remaining unmarried and often lonely until long past the age when most women marry.

O Pioneers! is the story of a woman's determination and love for the land. Rather than choosing between suitors, as she would in a conventional plot involving a woman protagonist, Alexandra decides how to raise pigs, what kind of hay to plant (she chooses alfalfa, an innovative crop), and whether to stretch family resources by buying more land during a recession. Cather shows such decisions as being important not only in themselves but also in relation to Alexandra's emergence as a heroic figure in her own right, not in relation to a stronger male. Indeed, the only strong male in the book is her fantasy of a gigantic figure, perhaps representing the land itself, who comes and carries her off over the pastures when she is tired.

The sweetheart Alexandra marries late in life is a weak but loyal friend from childhood. Having moved away and become an artist (actually, a lithographer, someone who translates others' paintings into reproducible form) after his family sold their farm during a recession, Carl returns when Alexandra is forty years old and successful. They discuss the possibility of marrying, but he leaves again in search of greater independent success when her brothers become openly hostile. They imply that Carl is only after Alexandra's money and land (now separate from theirs), that she is too old to marry anyway, and that the land ought by rights to belong to the men of the family. Her boldness and strength show in her reply: that they can ask their lawyers whose land it is. Only when she is plunged into grief over the death of her younger brother, Emil, does Carl come back, and they then enter into a marriage less of passion than of long-tried friendship. Readers differ over how much satisfaction to take in this ending, though it is clear that Cather intends it as a fulfillment. The last words of the novel, "Fortunate country, that is one day to receive heart like Alexandra's into its bosom . . . ," celebrate her as a hero.

O Pioneers! can be considered innovative, then, in the nature of its heroine, in the way it resists the conventional love plot, in its choice of a setting and way of life not generally regarded as exciting, and in treating immigrant characters seriously and respectfully. Cather called the novel a "two-part pastoral," which treats rural life in an idealized way while paying tribute to beauty and art. Alexandra is portrayed as an artist, her medium being the land itself. The second part of the novel intertwines a love story involving Emil and his illicit love for Marie Shabata, the discontented and somewhat frivolous wife of a neighboring farmer. In a melodramatic climax Marie's husband finds them together and kills them both. Although Alexandra does not have a central role in this second part of the two-part pastoral, it is she who links the two parts and thereby remains central to the novel as a whole. Moreover, the ensuing moral issue is hers, as she must decide how to accept the tragic event. She does so, not by understanding the power of sex and how irresistibly her restless brother and this vibrant but discontented young woman were drawn together, but by blaming Marie for enticing Emil into the affair. Instead of forgiving the two young people, she chooses to forgive Marie's frustrated and surly husband for killing them. In an act that may be either curiously misguided or genuinely saint-like, she visits Frank Shabata in prison and promises to try to help him get out. But it is clear that she will never recover from her grief over Emil. Partly for this reason, the end of the novel, when Carl comes back after reading about the murder in the newspaper and he and Alexandra decide to marry, has a mood of somberness rather than joy.

Discussion Questions

1. Unlike Theodore Dreiser's *Sister Carrie* (1900), which takes its female central character from a Midwestern farm to the city, Cather keeps Alexandra on the farm. Compare the two characters and the effects of these authorial choices. Does this basic fact of the plot affect the meaning of the books for today's readers?

2. In celebrating Alexandra's connection with the land, Cather writes that "for the first time, perhaps, since that land emerged from the waters of geologic ages, a human face was set toward it with love." Is there an element of unfairness in that statement, since people had made their home there before Alexandra?

3. In *A Room of One's Own*, Virginia Woolf writes that the traditional novel has no room for genuine human interaction between women, since it pits them as rivals for a hero's affection. Discuss the importance of female friendship in *O Pioneers!*

4. By the time she wrote *O Pioneers!* Cather had come to reject her own first novel, *Alexander's Bridge*. Why do you suppose she adopted the same name, in its female form, for the central figure of her second novel?

—*Janis P. Stout*

ONE OF OURS
(New York: Knopf, 1922)

CLAUDE WHEELER

Claude Wheeler, the main character of Willa Cather's Pulitzer Prize–winning novel *One of Ours*, is a dissatisfied Nebraska farm boy who goes off to fight in World War I as a means of escape. To him the war is a glorious thing, and he relishes the opportunity to become acquainted with French culture. The novel is ambiguous as to whether his starry-eyed view of the catastrophic war should be read straightforwardly or ironically, as an indication of his naiveté.

Cather noted in letters that Claude was based on her cousin Grosvenor (G. R.) Cather. Upon seeing a newspaper report of his death at Cantigny, one of the first battles in which the U.S. Expeditionary Force was involved, she knew immediately that she would write a novel based on him. She also told friends that she felt a strong identification with Claude, especially his feeling of being trapped on the farm and his wish to experience the wider world. Similarly, when Cather finished college and had trouble finding a way to leave home and begin a career, she feared "dying in a cornfield" far from the satisfactions of art and music. Although the prototype for Claude was Cather's cousin, his characterization is also autobiographical.

The early parts of the novel show Claude as a sensitive young person often at odds with his coarse father and crass older brother but favored by his gentle mother. When he goes to college in Lincoln, the pious Mrs. Wheeler, hoping to protect him from irreligious ideas, insists that he attend a small church college rather than the university. Claude realizes he is not getting any breadth or depth of education. But his time in Lincoln does give him a wider vision of life, partly through his acquaintance with a lively German American family whose home is enriched by books and good conversation and partly through a history course he is able to take at the university.

When Claude's studies are cut short by his father's decision to put him in charge of the family farm, he tries to settle down by marrying Enid, a girl he has known since childhood. What he does not know is how rigid she is in her religious ideas or how averse she is to sex. His frustration in his marriage only adds to his restlessness. When Enid goes to China to join her missionary sister, he feels free to get away as well.

Claude announces his intention to enlist in the army on 8 April 1917, a week before the United States declared war on the Central Powers. Book 3 of the novel portrays the early months of that year, when many people in Nebraska were keen to enter the war, while others, represented in the novel by Claude's brother Bayliss, believed the United States should stay out of it. Claude's father supports the war for financial reasons, and Mrs. Wheeler wants America to help beleaguered France. Claude gains his father's favor for the first time in his life when he expresses his intention to enlist.

Book 4 of the novel, "The Voyage of the *Anchises*," follows Claude's voyage to France following his training as a second lieutenant. In this section *One of Ours* touches realistically on the flu pandemic that ravaged the world in 1918 and 1919, which took a heavy toll in the close quarters of troopships. Book 4 is also of interest in showing how Claude's character develops a feminine, nurturing side when he is called on to help nurse sick and dying soldiers.

Book 5, "Bidding the Eagles of the West Fly On," named from a line appropriated from the poet Vachel Lindsay, portrays Claude's time in France as a soldier before he is killed in battle. Even his death is in a sense idealized, as he dies cleanly of a shot through the heart when he leaps onto the rampart of a trench, leading his men in a charge. Readers'

impressions of this part of the novel are usually that it is unrealistic, partly because of the heavy emphasis on Claude's admiration for the French way of life as he gets to know it. Yet, Cather does show decaying bodies and displaced people. Moreover, it is through Claude's point of view, and not necessarily Cather's, that the war is affirmed as a noble effort. When Claude looks out from his trench over a devastated wasteland and feels glad that he can see some of the scenery of Europe, the novel is limited to his perspective. Claude never faces the grim facts of the destructiveness of the war.

The last part of the novel, then, can be read as unrealistic idealization or as an exercise in narrative irony. Even the ending, when Claude's mother and the faithful family servant grieve his death, may or may not be ironic. Certainly, it recognizes that many soldiers are coming back disillusioned, even suicidal. Mrs. Wheeler is right that her son never suffered such disillusionment, but it is hard to accept her statement that it was better for him to die as he did.

Cather began *One of Ours* soon after the end of the war, before an attitude of disillusionment became prevalent, but by the time it was published the war was four years in the past and such attitudes were spreading. Even though it was a popular success, many reviewers and critics pronounced it ill-informed and overly glorified. Some thought it foolish to try to write a battle scene if one had not been in battle. Ernest Hemingway, for example, wrote in a personal letter that Cather probably got her knowledge of war by watching the movie *The Birth of a Nation*. The reputation of *One of Ours* has no doubt suffered by its having been judged according to the disaffected or even cynical views that became established conventions of war writing later in the 1920s. Its characterization of Claude lacks depth only if one reads the book solely as a war novel, neglecting the first half.

Discussion Questions

1. Read Ernest Hemingway's *The Sun Also Rises* or John Dos Passos's *Three Soldiers* and compare their responses to World War I with Cather's.

2. Why is an allusion to Virgil's *Aeneid* (Claude's troopship named for Aeneas's father, Anchises)

significant to Cather's treatment of her character's participation in the war?

3. Claude Wheeler is not the only example of Cather's depicting herself, in her novels, in the guise of a male. What are other examples? What might have motivated her to portray herself this way in *One of Ours?* How successful is she in this practice?

4. Is Claude Wheeler overly sensitive and too idealistic, or do you sympathize with him? Why?

5. Claude's wife, Enid, is depicted negatively in *One of Ours.* Is it possible that Claude's dissatisfaction with her is in some ways a criticism of Claude himself? Write a consideration of the novel that takes Enid's perspective.

—*Janis P. Stout*

"PAUL'S CASE"

Collected in *The Troll Garden* (New York: McClure, Phillips, 1905).

PAUL

Paul is the protagonist of Willa Cather's "Paul's Case," a story set in early-twentieth-century Pittsburgh. He is still in high school when the story opens, though he has been suspended for a week, with the official reason given as "Disorder and impertinence." Paul's story covers an unspecified time during the fall and winter, likely no more than a few weeks. He requests a meeting with the faculty to petition to be allowed to return to school. He arrives wearing a red carnation in his lapel. This flower strikes the faculty as "not properly significant of the contrite spirit befitting a boy under the ban of suspension."

After the meeting, Paul runs off to his job as an usher at Pittsburgh's Carnegie Hall. Once there, he is transported: "He felt a sudden zest for life; the lights danced before his eyes and the concert hall blazed into unimaginable splendour." When the concert is over, Paul waits outside to catch sight of the featured soprano of the evening. As she enters her hotel, which is just across the street, in his imagination Paul enters it with her and, once there,

forgets he is standing outside in the snow, cold and wet. He arrives home late, sneaks inside through a basement window, and spends the night huddled there in the cold and dark.

The next day, Sunday, Paul is forced to spend on the front stoop of the family's row house with his father and his sisters. The picture of that life emphasizes Paul's unwillingness to be trapped in its boundaries. He wants the life of the captains of business he hears about, not the life of those who labor for those captains. As things are, he feels trapped. In an essay on Katherine Mansfield, Cather once wrote of families that "Always in his mind each member of these social units is escaping, running away, trying to break the net which circumstances and his own affections have woven about him." Certainly, this contention applies to Paul.

That night, Paul feigns going to a friend's to study, but instead goes downtown to a theater. "It was at the theatre and at Carnegie Hall that Paul really lived; the rest was but a sleep and a forgetting." "Perhaps," the narrative voice says, "it was because, in Paul's world, the natural nearly always wore the guise of ugliness, that a certain element of artificiality seemed to him necessary in beauty. Perhaps it was because his experience of life elsewhere was so full of Sabbath-school picnics, petty economies, wholesome advice as to how to succeed in life, and the unescapable odours of cooking, that he found this existence so alluring, these smartly-clad men and women so attractive, that he was so moved by these starry apple orchards that bloomed perennially under the lime-light."

Things get steadily worse for Paul. His father takes him out of school, makes him quit his usher's job, and gets him a beginning clerk's job in an office. Six weeks later, Paul is on a train to New York City. He has stolen $1,000 and has absconded. Once in New York, he first buys new clothes. He then takes a cab to the Waldorf, where he registers without difficulty, because he pays in advance. His stay is marked by both flowers and snow, which, taken together, might be thought of as symbolizing Paul and the drab world from which he has, for a little while, escaped.

The first afternoon, Paul takes a nap. Inside it is warm and fragrant from flowers he has had brought up. Outside it is snowy and cold. When he awakens, it is three o'clock in the afternoon, "half of one of his precious days gone already." Nonetheless, he takes over an hour to dress, perfectly. Then he takes a cab to Central Park, noting not just the snow, but all the wonderful people, and all the flowers in covered stands on the street corners.

He returns to the Waldorf and, as he goes down to dinner, is so affected by the environment—the music from the orchestra rising through the elevator shaft, the throngs of people in the corridor—that he has to sink into one of the chairs there "to get his breath."

As beautiful as it is downstairs, however, his room is so entrancing to him that he finds it difficult to leave it. What the stolen money has provided is so delightful to him that he wonders "that there were honest men in the world at all."

He does, however, join up with "a wild San Francisco boy, a freshman at Yale, who said he had run down for a little 'flyer' over Sunday." Their evening together is not detailed, but in the morning, "their parting in the elevator was singularly cool."

Paul's embezzlement soon catches up with him: "On the eighth day after his arrival in New York, he found the whole affair exploited in the Pittsburgh papers." He knew from the start that there would be an end to his escape into what seems to him his proper life. Even though he tells himself of his adventure "that it had paid . . . . Ah, it had paid indeed!" he has, nonetheless, bought a revolver as a "way to snap the thread." He is reluctant to use it, however. Instead, suffering from a hangover, he leaves his hotel, takes a cab to the ferry, a train to Newark, and finally another cab to "the Pennsylvania tracks out of town." Once there, he stations himself with those tracks "some twenty feet below him."

He notices the carnations in his lapel "were drooping with the cold, . . . their red glory all over." He realizes that all the flowers he had seen in the glass cases that first night must have by now also wilted. "It was only one splendid breath they had, in spite of their brave mockery at the winter outside the glass; and it was a losing game in the end, it seemed, this revolt against the homilies by which the world is run." He scoops a little hole in the snow and drops one of his carnations into it, then covers it over with snow, indicating symbolically his intention with his own life.

He dozes for a while, until he hears the sound of a train approaching. "When the right moment came, he jumped. As he fell, the folly of his haste occurred to him with merciless clearness, the vastness of what he had left undone." He feels something strike his chest, his body flying through the air, "on and on, immeasurably far and fast, while his limbs were gently relaxed." The story ends: "Then, because the picture making mechanism was crushed, the disturbing visions flashed into black, and Paul dropped back into the immense design of things." "Paul's Case" is often identified as a naturalistic story in that Paul is born into an environment for which his temperament is not suited, and in the conflict that necessarily follows, the environment wins: flowers do not belong in the snow.

Discussion Questions

1. Why do you think Cather referred in the title to Paul's story as Paul's "Case"? What do you make of the subtitle of the story—"A Study in Temperament"?

2. What is the significance of Paul's living on "Cordelia Street"?

3. What do you make of the uses of the adjective *hysterical* and the adverb *hysterically* in the third paragraph of the story?

4. What is belladonna? Why is it significant in the story?

5. What significance do you make of the references to pictures of George Washington and John Calvin in Paul's room?

—*John H. Irsfeld*

THE PROFESSOR'S HOUSE
(New York: Knopf, 1925)

TOM OUTLAND

Tom Outland is the alter ego of Professor Godfrey St. Peter, the other main character in Willa Cather's *The Professor's House.* Outland appears suddenly on the Midwestern campus where St. Peter teaches, raw and untutored but with a youthfulness and candor that the professor and his family find attractive. Outland did not grow up in a conventional family, and the St. Peters become his substitute family; he spends many evenings with them, eventually falling in love with the eldest daughter, Rosamund, whose temperament, however, subsequent events show to be much different than his own. There is a mystery to Tom's past that the St. Peter family is careful not to be too curious about but that Tom eventually reveals to them, which forms the second part of *The Professor's House.*

About a year before coming to Hamilton where the St. Peters lived, Tom had been herding cattle in New Mexico with his good friend Roddy Blake. Sometimes the cattle would cross over a large river and disappear into the canyons and high mesa on the other side, but Outland and Blake were told not to pursue them—the difficulties getting them back across the river were too great. Tom nonetheless eventually does pursue them. He climbs high up the great mesa—it is about one thousand feet tall—where he discovers cliff dwellings used by an Indian tribe that, by all discernible evidence, had not been there for a long time. Tom is thus initiated into a life-changing experience. Blake seems to share his generous enthusiasm, and the two of them arrange to spend several months up on the mesa when their work as hired hands is over. Outland takes copious notes about the pottery, architecture, and natural landscape within which these mysterious people lived. He has a mixture of religious and aesthetic awe and fascination, amounting to a kind of reverence, for these well-preserved remnants of a civilization that he and Blake were the first to disturb. In an interview in 1925, the year in which *The Professor's House* was published, Cather said that "when I was a little girl nothing in the world gave me such a moment as the idea of the cliff dwellers, of whole civilizations before ours linking me to the soil."

Outland and Blake agree that they need expert opinion about the significance of what they have found, so Tom agrees to go to Washington, D.C., to contact officials at the Bureau of Indian Affairs and the Smithsonian Institute and inform them of their discovery. But in descending from his aerie utopian civilization to the plains of the political and self-seeking world of Washington, Tom encounters

disillusion. First, he cannot even get in to see the most relevant officials; when he finally does do so, he discovers that they are either ignorant of the importance of his find or subordinate it to more-immediate budgetary concerns. Only in the friendship of a young secretary who helps Tom make appointments does he encounter the disinterested friendship and help that he expected would surround him in Washington and that Cather in general presents as the ideal of her novel. There is a naiveté about Tom's understanding of the way the business and political worlds really work, but this quality is more than counterbalanced with an appealing freshness in his character. He leaves Washington wanting no more than to "live a free life and breathe free air, and never, never again to see hundreds of little black-coated men pouring out of white buildings."

In a way Outland is Cather's picture of a grown-up Huckleberry Finn. Like Huck, Outland was orphaned at a young age; grew up to know the loveliness of life in the desert, as Huck had discovered the pleasures of life on a raft; and saw enough of the ways of sophisticated, civilized men to know that he wanted no part of them. But because Outland is older than Huck, Cather is able to depict what happens to such a person when they do grow up.

After his disillusioning experience in Washington, Tom, like Huck at the end of *Huckleberry Finn,* "lights out for the territory"—back to the Southwest—but when he arrives there, he finds more disillusionment. He learns, shockingly, that his friend Blake had sold all the items they discovered on the mesa to a German buyer for $4,000. He indignantly tells Blake that they "belonged to boys like you and me, that have no other ancestors to inherit from," and he is so angry with his friend that he drives him away from their camp. He never sees Blake again. This confrontation again shows both the admirable and the limited side of Tom's character: neither utilitarian nor greedy, he genuinely appreciates valuable cultural artifacts for their own sake and has the imagination also to visualize a way of life that had not existed for hundreds of years. Further, in addition to the patriotic motives for preserving the mesa's artifacts Tom had also experienced religious emotions; "I had read," he says, "of filial piety in the Latin poets and I knew that was what I felt for this place." But he does not see that others are not bad persons if they do not share his vision.

Tom Outland dies on the battlefields of World War I. There was an incomplete, even tragic, quality to his life. He was a talented inventor who was unable to profit, with either fortune or fame, from his major invention; instead, the wealth from that engineering creation went to Godfrey St. Peter's daughter, Rosamund (to whom Tom was once engaged), and her husband, Louie, neither of whom has the idealism or imagination of Tom. But even though Tom never marries and is not recognized while alive for his engineering brilliance, the influence of his character lives on in the life of Godfrey St. Peter. St. Peter shared many interests with Tom, not least a mutual passion for the Southwest, which Tom had explored and about which St. Peter, an historian, wrote the multivolume *Spanish Adventures in North America.*

Discussion Questions

1. Is Tom too idealistic about the archaeological remains he finds on Blue Mesa? Or is his reaction entirely admirable in its rejection of seeking any financial gain from the artifacts there?

2. What connections are there between the two halves of Tom's life that are presented in the novel: the discoveries on Blue Mesa, and his later career, mainly reported by the narrator of the novel, as an inventor and then as a soldier killed in action in World War I?

3. What is the attitude of the St. Peter family (apart from the professor) toward Tom?

4. Is Tom's character strong enough to tie together the two halves—the depiction of the life of a middle-aged Godfrey St. Peter and that of the discovery of the remains of the vanished civilization on Blue Mesa—of the novel?

—*Richard L. Harp*

GODFREY ST. PETER

Godfrey St. Peter is a professor who finds that his interest in life and particularly in his marriage has waned in Willa Cather's *The Professor's House.* One of Willa Cather's most complex characters, St. Peter is at a crossroads in his life at the beginning of the novel. His marriage to Lillian has lost the passion of its earlier decades, even to the extent of his not

wanting to live in the same house with her. He does not dislike her but finds that their interests are irretrievably separate. Lillian is interested in a social life of status and popularity, similar to the desires of their daughter Rosamund, and St. Peter does not share this interest. He recognizes the justice of his wife's complaints about his lukewarmness toward the family's interests but seemingly has no power to recapture past energies: "I've lived pretty hard," he tells her. "I wasn't willing to slight anything—you, or my desk, or my students. And now I seem to be tremendously tired. One pays, coming or going." The extent of this divide between husband and wife is revealed most pointedly at the end when St. Peter is disappointed at the prospect of his wife's returning to their home after she has been away several months in Europe with their son-in-law and their daughter. No particular blame is attached to his wife by St. Peter for this alienation, as he feels, basically, that it is simply his own life force that is ebbing away. He does not have a physical ailment—the doctor he consults at the end of the novel can find nothing wrong with him—but rather a vague malaise.

James Woodress has noted that psychologically *The Professor's House* is the most autobiographical novel that Cather ever wrote. St. Peter, for example, is like Cather in believing that art and religion are closely connected. One day he uncharacteristically lectures passionately to a class about European art and religion, a lecture that his wife overhears; she subsequently tells him that he is getting too involved in his subject: it is not dignified, she thinks, to let students know too much of what one really thinks. St. Peter earlier in his life had been able to divide his intellectual interests from his family ones, but now such compartmentalizing has become impossible, and the resulting lassitude almost causes his death. At the end of the novel he goes to sleep in the comfortable attic room of the old family home, where he went to work and escape from his wife; a windy storm blows out the gas flame of his heater and slams shut his window, thus raising gas levels in the study to potentially fatal levels. St. Peter had been warned about this danger, and it is unclear whether or not he is fatalistically courting death. He is, however, saved from asphyxiation by the unexpected arrival of the family's seamstress, Agatha, who has come to help the professor get ready for the rest of the family's return from Europe.

St. Peter's study in the house had been, he thought, "a shelter one could hide behind . . . a hole one could creep into," not unlike what the vanished Indian civilization on the top of Blue Mesa meant for the other major character of the novel, Tom Outland. It is one of many similarities between the middle-aged professor and Outland, the young protégé who unconsciously influenced St. Peter to reevaluate his life. Outland had been an explorer of the same lands, the American Southwest, that are the focus of St. Peter's lifelong work of scholarship, *Spanish Adventurers in North America.* Outland, the idealist, taught St. Peter that worthwhile pursuits, such as the artifacts Outland had discovered on top of Blue Mesa (a place modeled in Cather's novel upon the lost Anasazi civilization at Mesa Verde, Colorado), are satisfying for their own sake, for the love and wonder that they arouse. To financially or in some other utilitarian manner benefit from such pursuits is anathema to Outland, and as a result St. Peter recognizes how surrounded with practical affairs his own life has become. To compound his weariness, Rosamund and her husband, Louie, have become rich through an engineering invention of Outland, which brought him no financial benefit, as he died in World War I while still a young man. Rosamund, who was engaged to Outland, wants her father to have some of the money from his invention as well, but St. Peter is adamant: "my friendship with Outland is the one thing I will not have translated into the vulgar tongue."

St. Peter had lived the conventional life of the college professor and family man, with the conventional satisfactions. The novel is about his discovering the inadequacies of those satisfactions. To be a successful author and teacher, an outwardly—and genuinely—loving husband and father are not enough to sustain his life fully. He is closer to his younger daughter, Kitty—he can share memories with her of the "real" Outland, the one who had been a romantic explorer of the Southwest—but knows that she, too, will seek out his advice and companionship only sporadically now that she is grown and married. Why, St. Peter wonders in his melancholy musings, "when a man

had lovely children in his house, fragrant and happy, full of pretty fancies and generous impulses, why couldn't he keep them? Was there no way but Medea's, he wondered." His reference is to the classical witch who sacrificed her own children to keep them from dying at the hand of another. At the end of the novel St. Peter finds it oddly bracing that, having now no thought of suicide, he will have to learn "to live without delight."

Discussion Questions

1. Do you think St. Peter is justified in leading a life basically apart from the rest of his family?

2. What are the factors that cause Tom Outland to have such a profound influence on St. Peter? Is this influence attributable more to Outland's character or to St. Peter's?

3. In what ways are the two houses in which St. Peter lives appropriate or inappropriate symbols for his character?

4. In what ways does St. Peter's professional work as an historian, the kinds of scholarly works that he writes, affect his relationship with his family and with Tom Outland?

—*Richard Harp*

꩜

THE SONG OF THE LARK
(Boston & New York: Houghton Mifflin, 1915)

THEA KRONBORG

Thea Kronborg, the central character in Willa Cather's third novel, *The Song of the Lark,* is an opera singer from a fictional small town in eastern Colorado, called Moonstone, which closely resembles the town where Cather grew up, Red Cloud, Nebraska. After long years of study and struggle that seem not to be leading Thea to success, she withdraws to mountainous northern Arizona for a period of rest and serious thinking, as Cather did in 1912, when she was editor of *McClure's Magazine* in New York but was not making much progress as a writer. After her time in the Southwest, Thea returns to her musical training with new commitment and ultimately achieves star status in New York, much as

Cather herself did. In many ways, then, the story of Thea is autobiographical, even though she is a singer rather than a writer and the daughter of Swedish immigrants rather than a long-settled American family like the Cathers.

In addition to the parallels with her own life, Cather also modeled Thea on the famous opera star Olive Fremstad, whom she met in 1913. Fremstad was also Swedish by descent and had also grown up in the Midwest. She was a strong, vigorous woman. In a letter to her friend Elizabeth Shepley Sergeant in June 1914, Cather wrote that she had visited Fremstad at her vacation home in the Maine woods and been astonished at her energetic fishing, rowing, and hiking. Thea, too, exhibits a similar level of physical energy and strength during her time in Panther Canyon (modeled on the actual Walnut Canyon in Arizona). After she becomes a star, she so immerses herself in her roles that after singing the role of Elsa, in Richard Wagner's opera *Lohengrin,* she is exhausted, even haggard—just as Cather said Fremstad was after singing another major Wagnerian role in April 1913.

Despite these many parallels, and despite the fact that Cather went so far as to seek Fremstad's reaction when the novel was published, she flatly denied the connection and told her editor that he should take care not to give credence to rumors that her character was based on the opera star. She was always reluctant to let her working methods or the sources of her books be known. But in this case there can be no doubt. She even prepared for the novel by writing an article about Fremstad for *McClure's,* where she had worked as an editor from 1906 to 1912. Not a singer or musician herself, she attended rehearsals and carefully studied the working lives of singers to make the novel believable, and when it was in proofs, she had it read by a music critic she knew in Pittsburgh to ensure its accuracy.

Most of *The Song of the Lark* is spent in following Thea's early life and preparation for her career. The years of her success are only briefly glimpsed at the end. The point that is emphasized in this brief concluding view is that in order to reach such a level of achievement, it has been necessary for her to center her life almost solely on her art, to the exclusion of human ties. She has become emotionally hard and withdrawn from ordinary human life. As a story of the growth and maturation of a person searching for identity and a mission in life, the novel can be said to belong to the genre of the bildungsroman. More specifically, as a story of the growth and development of an artist it is properly designated a *kunstlerroman* (from the German word for artist, *kunstler*).

The discipline of art is not the only thematic interest of the novel, however. Cather's use of the Arizona setting is of great significance in relation to her long interest in the Southwest, culminating in the novel that is often thought to be her greatest achievement, *Death Comes for the Archbishop.* At the time Cather wrote, the characteristics of Western fiction (and art) were well established as a genre centered on adventure, ruggedness, and conflict, in which the appropriate hero had to be masculine. One of Cather's lasting effects on American literature was to develop alternative ways of thinking about the West.

The Song of the Lark is of great importance in relation to the emergence of strong, self-reliant women characters who have the freedom to shape their own lives, on their own terms. Clearly, Thea rejects any expectation that she will be a conventional wife and mother. When wealthy Fred Ottenburg mentions the possibility of their getting married and having a conventional life of financial comfort with a nice apartment and a family, she says it sounds "perfectly hideous." Instead, her aspirations are indicated in her response to an eagle she sees flying above the canyon: "O eagle of eagles! Endeavour, achievement, desire, glorious striving of human art!" She does agree to go away with Fred to Mexico in the expectation that they will later be married—but without her giving up her career, which Fred wants for her almost as much as she wants it herself. Later, she finds out that he is already married with no possibility of a divorce. At the time the novel was published, Cather's readers were shocked by the implications of their traveling together in this unconventional way, unmarried but apparently in intimacy.

In 1921, in an interview for the *Lincoln Sunday Star,* Cather asked the rhetorical question, "As for the choice between a woman's home and her career, is there any reason why she cannot have both?" Perhaps she had been thinking along those lines for some time. At the end of *The Song of the Lark* Thea seemingly has the best of both worlds, professional success and also marriage to Fred. But her success comes first, and the marriage is presented in such a secondary way that some readers do not even notice that it has occurred.

Discussion Questions

1. Why would Thea Kronborg have been considered an unusual heroine for a novel in 1915? Are readers today still likely to think she is strange or unwomanly? If not, what has changed in the meantime to affect readers' expectations?

2. What are the distinctive elements of the Western setting as Cather presents it in part 4 of *The Song of the Lark*? In what ways is this section important in the novel?

3. Alexandra, the central character of Willa Cather's novel *O Pioneers!*, is also the daughter of Swedish immigrants. In what ways are she and Thea Kronborg similar? In what ways are they different?

4. Another woman writer of Cather's time who was successful then, though her name is not well known today, was Mary Austin. Explore the similarities and differences between *The Song of the Lark* and Austin's novel *A Woman of Genius*.

5. Is art worth the sacrifices Thea makes?

—*Janis P. Stout*

❧

"A WAGNER MATINÉE"

Collected in *Youth and the Bright Medusa* (New York: Knopf, 1920).

GEORGIANA CARPENTER

The story of Georgiana Carpenter, the central figure in Willa Cather's story "A Wagner Matinée," is narrated by her nephew Clark, a student in Boston who lived with Georgiana and her family on the Nebraska plains when he was a boy. Clark meets Georgiana's train after she travels from Red Willow County, Nebraska, to Boston for the settling of the estate of an uncle who left her a small legacy. Clark remembers his aunt's love of music and takes her to hear a symphony orchestra perform a program of Richard Wagner.

Thirty years earlier Georgiana, a music teacher at the Boston Conservatory, met and fell in love with a shiftless farm boy, Howard Carpenter, when she spent a summer vacation in his village in the Green Mountains. Despite strong opposition from her family and friends, she eloped with him to establish a homestead on the primitive Nebraska frontier. For many years she has endured the hard life of a farm woman, giving birth to six children and spending most of her waking hours cooking, ironing, milking, sewing, and otherwise tending to her children, husband, and farmhands. The only expression of her love of the arts and letters in all those years has been found in her occasional opportunities to teach and encourage others. Clark recalls that she introduced him to the works of William Shakespeare and taught him Latin and music.

When Georgiana returns to Boston, she is like an alien in the city in which she spent her youth and developed her love of the arts. Clark observes her "queer, country clothes" and her timidity about going to lunch at a stylish restaurant. "She was chiefly concerned that she had forgotten to leave instructions about feeding half-skimmed milk to a certain weakling calf" and "was further troubled because she had neglected to tell her daughter about the freshly-opened kit of mackerel in the cellar, which would spoil if it were not used directly." Clark fears that the "little pleasure" he planned for his aunt has been a mistake, that she has been gone from the city too long to reenter a world to which she was dead. He also wonders if it might be cruel to let her see again all that she gave up: "I began to think it would be best to get her back to Red Willow County without waking her." But when the musicians begin the first number, the *Tannhäuser* overture, Georgiana clutches Clark's sleeve, and he knows that for her a thirty-year silence has been broken.

The question Clark implicitly raises—whether it is kinder to let the person adjusted to life without art remain in her darkness—is not answered in the story. Georgiana has such a powerful awakening and rapturous afternoon that she wants to stay in Boston. After the concert she bursts into tears and sobs, "I don't want to go, Clark, I don't want to go!" Clark is sympathetic to her dilemma. Like her, he has seen the difference between the hard life on the prairies and life nourished by art in the city. "For her, just outside the concert hall, lay the black pond with the cattle-tracked bluffs; the tall, unpainted house, with weather-curled boards, naked as a tower; the crook-backed ash seedlings where the dish-cloths hung to dry; the gaunt, moulting turkeys picking up refuse about the kitchen door."

A question answered clearly in the story is whether the artistic soul can be destroyed by long starvation. When Clark sees Georgiana weeping during the "Prize Song," he thinks, "It never really died, then, the soul which can suffer so excruciatingly and so interminably; it withers to the outward eye only; like that strange moss which can lie on a dusty shelf half a century and yet, if placed in water, grows green again." Her emotional reaction is a counter to her own warning to Clark when as a boy he was persistently trying to learn a passage from an old score of *Euryanthe* he had found among her music books. "Don't love it so well, Clark, or it may be taken from you." Many years later Clark concludes that though artistic fulfillment might be lost, it can be found again.

"The Wagner Matinée" is one of Cather's many treatments of the conflict between rural and city life and the relative merits of the two ways of living. She is said to have revised the story many times in order to soften Georgiana's thoughts about her Nebraska life; nevertheless, there seems little doubt in this story that Cather's sympathies lie with the city dwellers. In other works, such as *My Ántonia* and "Neighbour Rosicky," Cather makes a stronger case for life on the prairie, especially if there are compensations for the harshness. Often the European immigrants who have brought to the prairies a love of music and the other arts are able to find a balance between living close to the soil and retaining an appreciation of cultural traditions. In "The Wagner Matinée," as in "Paul's Case," Cather also is examining the struggle of an artistic soul to survive in a discouraging environment.

Discussion Questions

1. How much responsibility does Howard Carpenter bear for his wife's unfulfilled life? What kind of husband would have made her life in Nebraska happier?

2. What do you infer to have been the good in Georgiana's life in the past thirty years? How does it balance what she has lost?

3. Clark alludes to John Keats's poem "On First Looking into Chapman's Homer" to describe

Georgiana's reaction to the concert. Why is that an appropriate reference?

4. To what does Cather contrast Georgiana's linen duster "black with soot" and the black bonnet "grey with dust"? How do the images represent the opposition of prairie life and city life?

5. Clark guesses what is in Georgiana's mind as she looks back toward Nebraska. What convinces the reader that he interprets Georgiana's thoughts accurately?

—*Darlene Unrue*

REFERENCES

Marilyn Arnold, "The Integrating Vision of Bishop Latour in Willa Cather's *Death Comes for the Archbishop*," *Literature and Belief,* 8 (1988): 39–57;

Arnold, *Willa Cather's Short Fiction* (Athens: Ohio University Press, 1984);

Willa Cather, *A Lost Lady*, includes historical essay by Susan J. Rosowski, with Kari A. Ronning (Lincoln: University of Nebraska Press, 1997);

Cather, *The Professor's House*, includes historical essay by James Woodress (Lincoln: University of Nebraska Press, 2002);

Philip Gerber, *Willa Cather*, revised edition (New York: Twayne, 1955);

David Harrell, *From Mesa Verde to The Professor's House* (Albuquerque: University of New Mexico Press, 1992);

Hermione Lee, *Willa Cather: Double Lives* (New York: Pantheon, 1989);

John J. Murphy, ed., *Willa Cather: Family, Community, and History* (Provo, Utah: Brigham Young University Humanities Publications Center, 1990);

Sharon O'Brien, *Willa Cather: The Emerging Voice* (New York: Oxford University Press, 1987).

O'Brien, ed., *New Essays on My Ántonia* (Cambridge: Cambridge University Press, 1999);

Guy Reynolds, *Willa Cather in Context: Progress, Race, Empire* (New York: St. Martin's Press, 1996);

Rosowski, *The Voyage Perilous: Willa Cather's Romanticism* (Lincoln: University of Nebraska Press, 1986);

Merrill Maquire Skaggs, *After the World Broke in Two: The Later Novels of Willa Cather* (Charlottesville: University Press of Virginia, 1990);

Janis P. Stout, "Willa Cather and the Performing Arts," in *The Cambridge Companion to Willa Cather,* edited by Marilee Lindemann (Cambridge: Cambridge University Press, 2005), pp. 101–115;

Steven Trout, *Memorial Fictions: Willa Cather and the First World War* (Lincoln: University of Nebraska Press, 2002);

Loretta Wasserman, *Willa Cather: A Study of the Short Fiction* (Boston: Twayne, 1991);

James Woodress, *Willa Cather: A Literary Life* (Lincoln: University of Nebraska Press, 1987).

Raymond Chandler

(July 23, 1888 – March 26, 1959)

&

THE BIG SLEEP

(New York: Knopf, 1939)

PHILIP MARLOWE

Philip Marlowe is the hard-boiled but chivalrous private detective who is the protagonist of Raymond Chandler's seven mystery novels—*The Big Sleep* (1939), *Farewell, My Lovely* (1940), *The High Window* (1942), *The Lady in the Lake* (1943), *The Little Sister* (1949), *The Long Good-Bye* (1953), and *Playback* (1958). Marlowe narrates each of these novels, providing commentaries on the action that are peppered with the similes for which Chandler is famous: "I belonged in Idle Valley like a pearl onion on a banana split" and "It was a blonde. A blonde to make a bishop kick a hole in a stained glass window."

Marlowe is perhaps unusually well educated for a private eye, making casual references to authors such as Marcel Proust, T. S. Eliot, and Ernest Hemingway. Marlowe refuses to take detective work that he feels is beneath him (such as divorce cases). He rarely gets along with the police or the other official branches of law enforcement, having been fired for insubordination from his job as an investigator for the district attorney's office.

Marlowe's role as a modern-day knight affects all of his personal relationships. He is intensely loyal to those whom he has chosen to serve (whether for reasons of friendship or professional duty). A prime instance of this loyalty is provided in *The Big Sleep,* where Marlowe seeks to serve client General Sternwood dutifully. Marlowe refuses the sexual advances of Sternwood's younger daughter, Carmen. Late in the novel, Sternwood is angry with Marlowe because Marlowe has investigated aspects of the family's personal affairs that Sternwood wanted left alone. Marlowe tells Sternwood, "I'd like to offer you your money back. It may mean nothing to you. It might mean something to me." Sternwood is impressed by Marlowe's sense of honor and actually hires him to look into the same bit of family business about which he was intitially angry. The novel closes with Marlowe compromising his moral code in order to protect General Sternwood (by hiding from Sternwood the fact that Carmen is a psychotic killer); Marklowe is willing to become "a part of the nastiness" to protect a dying old man.

Another example of Marlowe's loyalty is his relationship with Moose Malloy in *Farewell, My Lovely.* Malloy is a rather stupid ex-con who wants nothing more than to find his lost love Velma, and the only thing Marlowe has in common with Malloy is a penchant for futile loyalty. *The Long Goodbye* provides the most extended examination of Marlowe's loyalty. Terry Lennox is both friend and client, and Marlowe could not serve him with more fidelity. Marlowe does not understand Lennox's code, but he recognizes that Lennox does indeed have one, saying, "Whatever his rules were he played by them." Marlowe suffers greatly for his friendship with Lennox; when the police suspect that the missing Lennox murdered his wife, Marlowe goes to jail rather than tell police that he drove Lennox to Tijuana.

In his essay "The Simple Art of Murder," Raymond Chandler defines the role of the ideal hard-boiled detective:

> . . . down these mean streets a man must go who is not himself mean, who is neither tarnished nor afraid. The detective in this kind of story must be such a man. He is the hero, he is everything. He must be a complete man and a common man and yet an unusual man. He must be, to use a rather weathered phrase, a man of honor, by instinct, by inevitability, without thought of it, and certainly

without saying it. He must be the best man in his world and a good enough man for any world.

Marlowe fits this description well. He is a man with an anachronistic code of honor wandering the "mean streets" of Los Angeles from the late 1930s to the late 1950s; W. H. Auden calls Chandler's novelistic setting "the Great Wrong Place." Marlowe is loyal, educated, tough, and intelligent. He knows that he is different from the fictional detectives that preceded him, saying in *The Big Sleep*, "I'm not Sherlock Holmes or Philo Vance. I don't expect to go over ground the police have covered and pick up a broken pen point and build a case from it."

Chandler makes chivalry an extended metaphor in all of his novels. For example, Marlowe explicitly comments upon his role as a knightly detective in *The Big Sleep* when he finds his client's adult daughter naked and waiting for him in his apartment. He turns away and toward his chessboard: "There was a problem laid out on the board, a six-mover. I couldn't solve it, like a lot of my problems. I reached down and moved a knight, then pulled my hat and coat off and threw them somewhere." After rejecting the daughter's advances, Marlowe looks down at the chessboard and tells the reader, "The move with the knight was wrong. I put it back where I had moved it from. Knights had no meaning in this game." Critic Paul Ferguson argues that Marlowe is a disillusioned romantic "aware of and concerned with the disillusion of the modern world," providing "a lens through which we may view the world." This lens colors the world that the readers see; Marlowe's world is a modern wasteland, viewed through the eyes of a disillusioned knight. A perspective of honor serves to emphasize angst felt at the loss of that same honor within the corrupted culture.

In 1958 Chandler began a Marlowe novel called *Poodle Springs*, which he set aside after completing only the first four chapters (prior to his death in 1959). Perhaps he was unable or unwilling to complete *Poodle Springs* because he had domesticated Marlowe a bit too much, allowing him to marry the wealthy Linda Loring (from *The Long Good-Bye*). Chandler explained why he abandoned the book in a letter to Maurice Guinness,

[A] fellow of Marlowe's type shouldn't get married, because he is a lonely man, a poor man, a dangerous man, and yet a sympathetic man, and somehow none of this goes with marriage. I think he will always have a fairly shabby office, a lonely house, a number of affairs, but no permanent connection. . . . It seems to me that this is his destiny—possibly not the best destiny in the world, but it belongs to him. No one will ever beat him, because by his nature he is unbeatable. No one will ever make him rich, because he is destined to be poor. . . . I see him in a lonely street, in lonely rooms, puzzled but never quite defeated.

Discussion Questions

1. How is Chandler's Philip Marlowe similar to or different from the detective characters of Chandler's predecessor Dashiell Hammett (such as Sam Spade, the Continental Op, and Nick Charles)?

2. Some critics have accused Philip Marlowe of misogyny. Based upon a careful reading of one or more of Chandler's novels, do such charges seem justified? Why or why not?

3. Several critics have observed that Philip Marlowe is a knightly hero. Analyze this theme in one or more of Chandler's novels. What is accomplished by setting a chivalrous detective in the mean streets of Los Angeles?

—*Marc Seals*

THE LONG GOODBYE
(London: Hamilton, 1953)

TERRY LENNOX

Terry Lennox is the friend of detective Philip Marlowe in Raymond Chandler's *The Long Goodbye*. Lennox provides the main motivation for the plot of the novel, and the title refers to Marlowe's relationship with Lennox.

The novel opens with Marlowe's first encounter with Lennox, "The first time I laid eyes on Terry Lennox he was drunk in a Rolls-Royce Silver Wraith outside the terrace of The Dancers." As

Marlowe kindly takes the unconscious Lennox to his house, he notes the scars that cover one side of Lennox's face (indicating extensive cosmetic reconstructive surgery). Over the ensuing months, Marlowe and Lennox form a friendship, based mostly upon Marlowe's rescue of the drunk Lennox. Perhaps Marlowe is compelled to help this drunken stranger because Lennox has exceptional manners, which Marlowe approves. Marlowe tells the parking attendant, "He's the politest drunk I ever met." Lennox reveals several details of his life to Marlowe, including his friendship with a Las Vegas racketeer and the fact that he married his ex-wife Sylvia for her wealth. A month after Marlowe lends Lennox money to get to Las Vegas, he discovers that Lennox has remarried Sylvia. Lennox and Marlowe become periodic drinking buddies. Lennox shows up early one morning carrying a gun and asking for a ride to the Tijuana airport. Though Lennox makes it clear that his wife is dead, Marlowe insists that he not be told any details (giving Marlowe plausible deniability). After dropping Lennox off in Tijuana, Marlowe returns to his house to find the police waiting for him. Marlowe is taken to jail, where he remains for three days, for aiding a suspected murderer. He is released when it is reported that Lennox has been found dead in Mexico with a suicide note and full written confession by his side. Marlowe neither believes that Lennox killed his wife nor that his death was a suicide. Marlowe returns home to find a rambling letter from Lennox; Lennox has also enclosed a $5,000 bill. Sylvia was actually killed by a woman named Eileen Wade. Eileen's first husband was Paul Marston, who was presumed dead in World War II. Marlowe learns that Lennox and Marston are the same person. Eileen Wade commits suicide, leaving a full confession. At the close of the novel, Marlowe is visited by a man who identifies himself as Señor Cisco Maioranos. Maioranos volunteers to tell Marlowe of Lennox's "last scene." Marlowe recognizes Maioranos as Lennox, who has been altered by cosmetic surgery. Marlowe notes, "Nobody can change the color of a man's eyes."

Chandler's friend Natasha Spender has correctly observed that Chandler presents, through the novel's three main male characters, "three distinct self-portraits." Spender explains,

Raymond was [like Terry Lennox] a young ex-soldier in the early twenties, battle-scarred and scared, whose pride was that 'of a man who has nothing else.'. . . Like that of Roger Wade, the successful, middle-aged, alcoholic and egocentric writer, Raymond's drunken stream of consciousness could also at bad moments be full of self-hatred, writer's angst and sarcastic hostility. . . . Marlowe, of course, represents Chandler's ideal self. . . .

The novel examines the tenuous (and often nonexistent) relationship between law and justice. In an early conversation with Terry Lennox, Marlowe says that he does not like hoodlums. Lennox replies, "That's just a word, Marlowe. We have that kind of world. Two wars gave it to us and we are going to keep it."

People, especially men, who adhere to *any* code are respected by Marlowe. After one of their earliest encounters, Marlowe says of Lennox, "Whatever his rules were he played by them." Lennox's rules differ greatly from those of Marlowe, but Lennox lives by them.

In the final scene of the novel, Terry Lennox returns, having adopted a new nationality and a new face to accompany his new identity. He has changed his name to Señor Cisco Maioranos. Lennox tells Marlowe, "An act is all there is. There isn't anything else. In here [he says tapping his chest] . . . there isn't anything. I've had it, Marlowe. I had it long ago." They shake hands, and Marlowe replies, "So Long, Señor Maioranos. Nice to have known you—however briefly." Marlowe tells the reader that he never saw Lennox again.

Discussion Questions

1. Lennox has at least three identities—Terry Lennox, Paul Marston, and Cisco Maioranos. Which is his *true* identity (or does he even have one)? Use Lennox and his other identities to discuss the concept of the instability of identity.

2. Why does Marlowe risk so much to protect Terry Lennox, a man he barely knows? Is there something about Lennox, or is it more a function of Marlowe's character?

3. Compare and/or contrast Terry Lennox with Moose Malloy (from Chandler's *Farewell, My*

Lovely). What similarities or differences do you find with regard to these characters' relationships with Philip Marlowe?

—*Marc Seals*

REFERENCES

Matthew J. Bruccoli, *Raymond Chandler: A Descriptive Bibliography* (Pittsburgh: University of Pittsburgh Press, 1979);

Bruccoli and Richard Layman, eds., *Hardboiled Mystery Writers: Raymond Chandler, Dashiell Hammett, Ross Macdonald,* Dictionary of Literary Biography Documentary Series (Detroit: Gale Research, 1989);

Philip Durham, *Down These Mean Streets a Man Must Go: Raymond Chandler's Knight* (Chapel Hill: University of North Carolina Press, 1963);

G. A. Finch, "Marlowe's Long Goodbye," *Armchair Detective,* 6 (1972): 7–11;

Tom Hiney, *Raymond Chandler: A Biography* (New York: Atlantic Monthly Press, 1997);

Frank MacShane, *The Life of Raymond Chandler* (New York: Dutton, 1976);

William Marling, *Raymond Chandler* (Boston: Twayne, 1986);

Robert F. Moss, *Raymond Chandler,* Dictionary of Literary Biography Series (Detroit: Gale, 2002);

Natasha Spender, "His Own Long Goodbye," *The World of Raymond Chandler,* edited by Miriam Gross (New York: A & W, 1978), pp. 27–158.

Denise Chávez

(August 15, 1948 –   )

❦

THE LAST OF THE MENU GIRLS

(Houston: Arte Público, 1986)

ROCÍO ESQUIBEL

Rocío Esquibel is the primary narrator of *The Last of the Menu Girls,* Denise Chávez's collection of seven interconnected coming-of-age stories. She grows up in the 1950s and 1960s in a southern New Mexico town, where she lives with her mother, Nieves, and younger sister, Merced. In a predominantly feminine environment, Rocío tries to figure out what it means to be a woman, how to relate to her Chicano community, and who she wants to grow up to be. This process often appears difficult and challenging but is represented with tenderness and humor.

In *The Last of the Menu Girls* many first-time experiences are reported: Rocío depicts her first job, mentions her first sexual emotions, and recounts her initial dealings with death and illness; she also grows familiar with her shortcomings and learns how to consider them as positive qualities. Starting a new summer job as a menu girl, Rocío's function is to gather lunch and dinner orders from hospital patients, but as her insatiable curiosity, energy, and empathy are promptly recognized, she is promoted to nurse's aide. Yet, from the first lines of the book, Rocío claims "I never wanted to be a nurse," a statement she repeats three times in the course of the novel. Moreover, she is repulsed by the physical consequences of illness. Soon her apprehensions are overcome by a growing awareness that in all the hospital beds lie human beings, not merely anonymous patients. After this realization, she becomes so dedicated that she takes on double shifts: "My heart reached out to every person, dragged itself through the hallways with the patient, cried when they did, laughed when they did."

As summer ends, Rocío realizes that her empathy can be a precious tool in life. She grows conscious of how her compassion may help her to find a place in a world that traditionally gives little agency to women and, because of pervasive racism, even less to women of Mexican American origin who come from a barrio. Rocío resists limiting her life to being a lowly menu girl, a nurse's aide, or a teacher like her mother; she wishes to steer clear of "traditional serving roles which society has prescribed for women," as Rudolfo Anaya states in the foreword to the *The Last of Menu Girls.* Rocío finally chooses to become a writer and to nurse through writing. Indeed, she aims to give a voice to people who are seldom listened to or taken into consideration: not only ill people from the hospital or people living in poverty, but most especially, individuals of her community. In various interviews, Chávez reveals her commitment to people who share the same legacy with her: "I've always been very loyal to my community, my state, and the people I grew up with." She adds, "It's a grace to voice the many inarticulate cries that not only belong to you but to others as well." Rocío also seems driven by such dedication when she promises herself never to forget people she has been close to: "To remember. It seemed right."

Commitment and difficulties in relating to one's community are paramount issues in the novel. Rocío struggles with the question of how to relate to her absent father, who, when he does come home, confuses her with her sister. She also ponders how to form relationships with people whom she constantly wants to criticize. Notable in the longest story of *The Last of the Menu Girls,* "Compadre," is the list of values shared by *compadres*—lifelong friends bound by "a union truer than family, higher than marriage." According to Nieves, despite all the flaws of the person one chooses as a lifelong friend, one must care for him or her for better or worse. Having a *compadre* means always retaining a connection to a "living soul." The worst possible predicament in life, according to her, is being "disconnected from any living soul." Rocío sees many flaws in this idea of *compadres;* she considers her extended family to be annoying at times and criticizes them harshly. In spite of these feelings, though, she perceives the significance of such ties: how they make life interesting and endurable. By allowing Regino, her mother's *compadre,* to take over the narration in the sixth section of the last story, Rocío gives him a place of choice in her story and her heart (just as when she lets her boyfriend, Loudon, or her friend Kari Lee narrate). Regino voices one of the final questions of the novel, thus giving direction to many of Rocío's worries: "What is living without love?"

Discussion Questions

1. Can you determine Rocío's approximate age in each story? Does it remain the same in each section? Citing evidence from the narrative, can you find at least two examples per chapter to sustain your estimation of her age?

2. Identify instances of characters switching back and forth between Spanish and English in *The Last*

of the Menu Girls. In which stories in particular is this common? What do such language choices reveal about Rocío's coming-of-age process?

3. Try to find evidence to support an argument that Rocío will not follow her mother's path. What hints are there that she will succeed in escaping a life filled with disappointments and "deep hurts, deep distresses"?

4. What do you think leads Rocío to depression in the story "Space Is Solid," and what allows her to recover?

—*Erika Lynn Scheidegger*

REFERENCES

Annie O. Eysturoy, *Daughters of Self-Creation: The Contemporary Chicana Novel* (Albuquerque: University of New Mexico Press, 1996), pp. 113–132;

Bridget A. Kevane and Juanita Heredia, *Latina Self-Portraits: Interviews with Contemporary Women Writers* (Albuquerque: University of New Mexico Press, 2000): 33–44;

Deborah L. Madsen, *Understanding Contemporary Chicana Literature* (Columbia: University of South Carolina Press, 2000) pp. 135–165.

John Cheever
(May 27, 1912 – June 18, 1982)

"THE COUNTRY HUSBAND"
Collected in *The Housebreaker of Shady Hill and Other Stories* (New York: Harper, 1958).

FRANCIS WEED

Francis Weed, the main character of John Cheever's story "The Country Husband," is a middle-aged New York businessman whose life is thrown into disarray by his encounters with a teenage babysitter and a woman he recognizes from his military service during World War II. "The Country Husband" is, next to "The Swimmer," the best-known and longest story in John Cheever's collection *The Housebreaker of Shady Hill* (1958). It has been highly praised by Cheever critics as his most accomplished story; Vladimir Nabokov labeled it "a miniature novel beautifully traced." The story won the O. Henry Award for 1956.

Francis lives in a northern suburb of New York City called Shady Hill, a subtle allusion to the ancient Greek mythological underworld, which was a place of shadows and shade. Even his name helps identify some of his major character traits, at times ironically. The name *Francis* means "free, open, and candid," qualities that he certainly lacks, at least in the beginning of the story. He is neither emotionally nor socially free during the first third of the story. He learns painfully that neither he nor his wife in any way controls the social lives of the young people of Shady Hill when he observes, with shock, that he must pay respect to Mrs. Wrightson, the actual social arbiter of which youngsters get invited to the desirable dances in their small, wealthy village. He also discovers that he is, generally speaking, quite uncomfortable in expressing his deepest feelings and that his senses do not vivify his everyday experiences in any sort of meaningful way: "Wood smoke, lilac and other such perfumes did not stir him, and his memory was something like his appendix—a vestigial repository."

His surname, Weed—one of the most common and universal of natural materials—ironically defines him as one who does not enjoy nature. Francis is the essence of the conventional, middle-class, WASP stereotype until he encounters two very different females: Ann Murchison, the teenage babysitter for his children, with whom he immediately falls in love; and a nameless French maid at a friend's cocktail party, whom he recognizes from a French village when he was in World War II. The epiphanic effect of meeting Ann opens up Francis's stultified emotional life and releases him from his puritanical moral and emotional restraints in a life-altering way: She is "beauty and perfection . . . and he experiences in his consciousness that moment when music breaks glass, and felt a pang of recognition as strange, deep, and wonderful as anything in his life."

The Frenchwoman is the same woman Francis had observed being vilified as a Nazi collaborator. She was "the woman being punished at the crossroads. . . . One woman spat on her, but some inviolable grandeur in her nakedness lasted through the ordeal." His memory of her terrible suffering and his presumption that she did not survive awakens

in Francis their shared humanity: "the encounter left Francis feeling languid; it had opened and left them dilated." In this vulnerable condition Francis first gazes upon the innocent radiance of Ann. His boring and predictable life in Shady Hill has been radically transformed by both memory and desire. In this state he imagines taking Ann to France on his old troopship and living with her in Paris. His newly recognized romantic idealism propels Francis to risk changing into one who is more than willing to recognize his feelings and act on them. The experiences with both women has made him conscious of "the miraculous physicality of everything."

It becomes fairly obvious as the story progresses that he, Ann, and the Frenchwoman have become mythic figures rather than merely characters in a story. Cheever told his creative-writing students at Barnard College that their function in constructing fictions was to "mythologize the commonplace." One of the major developments in Francis's character is that he begins consciously to observe daily events and people in mythological terms. As he waits for the morning train to the city, he observes on a passing train a naked woman combing her hair: "A wonderful feeling enveloped him, as if light were being shaken about him, and he thought again of Venus combing and combing her hair as she drifted through the Bronx." Weed clearly understands the change that is taking place in his consciousness: he is seeing the common life around him as "plainly a paradise." Finding a new emotional and spiritual power within himself, he boldly approaches Mrs. Wrightson and blatantly insults her, thus potentially damaging his children's future ascent up the societal rungs of their small community.

One of the possible damaging effects of Francis's newly discovered emotional freedom is that he begins to perform actions that are morally reprehensible. Once he discovers that Ann is engaged to Clayton Thomas, a homely, awkward, highly intelligent but slightly priggish young man, Francis immediately spreads lies and harmful gossip about him. When Francis's secretary storms out of the office in response to his cruel lies concerning Clayton, Francis realizes that he has sinned, that he is capable of genuine wickedness: "He was in trouble. . . . The feeling of bleakness was intolerable, and he saw clearly that he had reached the point where he would have to make a choice." Like Dante in *The Inferno,* Francis finds that he has lost his way "in the gathering dark."

Because Francis has discovered his true humanity—his weakness and vulnerability—in the memory of the still-living Nazi collaborator and his adolescent passion for the teenage babysitter, he has also found that he is capable of functioning as a free, human being making moral choices. He chooses from among five possible paths: psychological help; religion and confession; seducing Ann; a visit to a Danish massage parlor; or drunkenness. He chooses to seek counsel from his secretary's psychiatrist, Dr. Herzog, who advises him to take up woodworking—which he does—so that he may distract himself from his sexual obsession with Ann and, thus, his midlife crisis.

Cheever, as in many of his stories and novels, proposes nature as a redemptive agent for his confused and troubled characters: "Francis finds some true consolation in the simple arithmetic involved and in the holy smell of wood." In a classic romantic solution, Francis Weed finds himself made whole through his engagement with nature.

Discussion Questions

1. What are the major contributing factors that transform Francis into a romantic idealist?

2. When and why does Francis descend into deep despair and depression?

3. What is it that brings Weed to the sure knowledge that he has been truly wicked?

4. What effect does observing the Nazi collaborator French maid at a neighborhood cocktail party have on Francis?

—*Patrick Meanor*

"THE ENORMOUS RADIO"

Collected in *The Enormous Radio and Other Stories* (New York: Funk & Wagnalls, 1953).

IRENE WESTCOTT

Irene Westcott and her husband, Jim, are literary versions of Adam and Eve in the Garden of Eden in John Cheever's story "The Enormous Radio."

Irene discovers a source of hidden knowledge and lures her naive husband into irresistible temptation. This story was one of the first to depart from Cheever's earlier naturalism by combining elements of realism and fantasy, grounded as it is in the myth of mankind's fall into sin. Cheever's practice of "mythologizing the commonplace," one of his primary creative techniques, here deepens the significance of the story.

Since the Westcotts' old radio has quit working, Jim has purchased a new, large, and expensive one. Irene immediately notices its serpentine qualities, its "malevolent green dials," and the "violent forces that were snarled in the ugly gumwood cabinet," the gumwood suggesting its power to entrap objects and animals, including human beings. The initial sound of the new radio is so powerful that "it knocked a china ornament from the table to the floor." As Irene and Jim learn to control the power of the radio and begin listening to chamber music by Mozart and Schubert, they are deeply disturbed by hearing the actual lives of some of the neighbors in their apartment building: "The Westcotts overheard a monologue on salmon fishing in Canada, a bridge game and a bitter family quarrel about an overdraft at the bank. They turned off their radio at midnight and went to bed weak with laughter." Jim decides that listening in on the lives of their neighbors is both dangerous and unethical, but Irene insists on listening at all hours of the day and night: "She overheard demonstrations of indigestion, carnal love, abysmal vanity, faith and despair." She begins to understand that she has led a sheltered life, and some of the sadness and tragedy she overhears "astonished and troubled her." Irene cannot control her morbid curiosity about the lives in her building, however, and continues to listen, though not without some guilt.

When Jim recognizes that Irene's personality seems to be changing, Irene confesses that she has become obsessed with eavesdropping via the radio: "Oh, it's so horrible, it's so dreadful . . . I've been listening all day and it's so depressing." Having learned that all of her seemingly normal neighbors hide secrets of money problems, sickness and imminent death, and sexual infidelity, she begins to doubt the validity of her own happiness. "Life is too terrible, too sordid and awful," she tells Jim. "But we've never been like that, have we darling? We're happy, aren't we, darling? We are happy, aren't we?"

Irene begins to understand that her and Jim's feelings of superiority to the common crowd may be illusory. The naiveté has been exposed by the radio that, like the serpent in the Garden of Eden, invades their idyllic existence as "an aggressive intruder . . . the dials flooded with a malevolent green light." Like Adam and Eve, the Westcotts' newly acquired knowledge creates—within Irene especially—a deep sense of shame, and they begin to attack and blame each other for their past failures and weaknesses. To Irene's horror, Jim confesses that beneath the surface of their seemingly happy lives, they are experiencing serious financial problems. He admonishes Irene, rather harshly, to cut down on her expensive tastes. He also accuses her of lying to him about her failure to pay their bills on time. Further, Jim proceeds to enumerate Irene's past transgressions—the sordidness of her earlier life: "You stole your mother's jewelry before they probated her will. You never gave your sister a cent of that money . . . not even when she needed it." The final paragraph of the story indicates the full impact of Irene's devastating fall into self-knowledge: "Irene stood for a minute before the hideous cabinet, disgraced and sickened, but she held her hand on the switch before she extinguished the music and the voices."

Irene Westcott is one of Cheever's first characters whose dilemma is not strictly a moral one, concerned with making a good or evil choice. Her real dilemma is that she has misunderstood her own life. She discovers that the reality she has been living is one that she has unconsciously created, and that reality has protected her from the real sufferings of others, the cruelty of time, and the injustice of life for many people. She also realizes, vaguely, that she, like the mythic Eve, is a fallen woman in a fallen world, a wasteland of illusion and disappointment.

Discussion Questions

1. How does the discovery of the reality of the lives of her neighbors affect Irene Westcott's ability to reevaluate her own past ?

2. What elements of the story does Cheever use to convince the reader that the Westcotts are living in a sort of paradise?

3. What do Irene's opinions of her neighbors' lives show her about her own life? And what forces her to change her opinions?

—*Patrick Meanor*

FALCONER
(New York: Knopf, 1977)

EZEKIEL FARRAGUT

Ezekiel Farragut, the main character of John Cheever's novel *Falconer*, is a forty-eight-year-old college professor and drug addict (formerly heroin, now methadone) who has been brought to Falconer Prison for killing his brother Eben. Husband of Marcia, Farragut is one in a long line of emasculated males in Cheever's fiction. His name connects him to the two spheres that Cheever tried to join together in his writing and in his life, the spiritual and the mundane, the faraway and the close at hand, in what the novel calls "the mystery of the bonded spirit and the flesh." Ezekiel is one of the books of the Old Testament, and Farragut is a parkway, named for the American admiral, near Cheever's home in Ossining, New York. Farragut's prison sentence also connects him to Cheever's career-long interest in various forms of confinement: bad families, bad marriages, small-town and suburban life, alcoholism, and addiction. Falconer Prison is thus not simply the place where Farragut is confined; it is a metaphor for his inner spiritual and psychological state. Drawing on the two years he taught writing at Sing Sing Prison and the month he spent in 1974 at Smithers Rehabilitation Institute in New York City, where he had gone when his alcoholism took a suicidal turn, Cheever began *Falconer* knowing only one thing: that "Farragut had to get out."

Farragut, like Cheever, is strongly drawn to the natural world from which he is now almost entirely separated, reduced to a glimpse of blue sky, the turning of the leaves, the smell of grass, the sound of birds. Farragut will not be free to enjoy nature and all it represents in Cheever's fiction until he is able "to leach self-pity from his emotional spectrum," and that means he must think about something other than his dose of methadone and about someone other than himself. "You got cellblock F," a guard tells him. "F stands for fucks, freaks, fools, fruits, fat-asses like me, phantoms, funnies, fanatics, feebies, fences and farts. There's more, but I forget it. The guy who made it up is dead." Farragut is also dead, figuratively speaking. Although his background makes him an anomaly on cellblock F, he is no less self-deluded and self-pitying than the others, only much more keenly drawn to the light. His initial breakthrough occurs when he and Jody, a fellow inmate, become lovers. More important than the previously straight Farragut's questioning what his loving another man means is the fact that this love lies beyond self-interest. Farragut keenly feels his loss when Jody escapes Falconer but is pleased that Jody is free. From his recurrent dream involving a beautiful woman, a sea island, and a nursery rhyme, he works his way back to reality by seizing on "the details of the moment. They were not particularly sweet, but they were useful and durable": as useful and durable in their way as the vista seen from the abandoned water tower Jody took him to, which became their trysting place.

A riot at another prison, Amana (also known as "the Wall"), affords Farragut a different kind of opportunity to connect with his fellow prisoners and with the outside world by passing along information and by attempting to assemble a contraband radio. (The Amana riot is based on the September 1971 riot at Attica Prison in Upstate New York, which occurred while Cheever taught at Sing Sing.) The fact that the riot fails to bring about meaningful prison reform, resulting only in a change in the color of the prisoners' clothing from gray to "a noncommittal green," underscores Cheever's emphasis on individual guilt and individual salvation. It is a preference that makes Cheever a characteristically American writer in the Puritan tradition. Farragut does selflessly care for a dying fellow prisoner, Chicken #2, whose deathbed interest in the afterlife mirrors rather than cynically undermines Farragut's own hopefulness. (Farragut is not only based on Cheever generally and on his own spiritual striving in particular; he comes to embody the cardinal Christian virtues of faith, hope, and charity and to experience *caritas* as well as *eros* on his way to personal redemption.) Prompted by Chicken #2, Farragut finally begins to confront the murder of Eben. In suddenly striking his brother "eighteen to twenty times" with a fire iron, Farragut sought to murder not just his abusive, alcoholic, and self-pitying older brother but the corresponding part of himself as well. Realizing that "cunning and courage" are needed, the often passive Farragut acts to effect his salvation in the form of an escape plan lifted from Alexandre Dumas *fils*'s novel *The Count of Monte Cristo* (1844–1845). Taking the place of Chicken #2's corpse, he is carried out of Falconer Prison in a body bag. Having undergone this symbolic death, he emerges from his dark night of the soul as one reborn, having "lost his fear of falling and all other fears of that nature." "Rejoice, he thought, rejoice," the novel ends.

Farragut's journey is far more a spiritual quest than either a prison or recovery narrative, even though it clearly has affinities with both. Although Cheever denied it at the time the novel was published (especially in an interview with his daughter, Susan), Farragut is also connected with the author by virtue of his bisexuality. Cheever's being able to write about Farragut's rejoicing in his love for Jody eventually freed the author to become much more open about his love for other men.

Discussion Questions

1. Although educated (a professor) and mature (forty-eight), Farragut seems surprisingly naive and (like many Cheever protagonists) youthful. Where is his naiveté most apparent? Where is his youthfulness most apparent?

2. Farragut's long recollection of his brother's murder (and the events leading up to it) comes near the end of the novel. Why can he face what he has done only at that point in the story?

3. Farragut's love for Jody and his selflessly caring for Chicken #2 stand in striking contrast to his relationship with his wife, Marcia (loosely based on Cheever's fractious relationship with his wife,

Mary). What is it about Marcia that makes her the archetypal American shrew? And what is it about Farragut that may have helped make her so?

4. Compare Farragut's progress from darkness to light in *Falconer* with Neddy Merrill's seemingly opposite movement in Cheever's 1964 story "The Swimmer."

—*Robert A. Morace*

◖◗
"GOODBYE, MY BROTHER"

Collected in *The Enormous Radio and Other Stories* (New York: Funk & Wagnalls, 1953).

LAWRENCE POMMEROY

Lawrence Pommeroy is the main character of John Cheever's short story "Goodbye, My Brother," which was first published in 1951. When *The Stories of John Cheever* was published in 1978, Cheever insisted that "Goodbye, My Brother" appear first in the collection even though the other stories were arranged chronologically, because its central conflict, between two brothers, is a major theme that recurs throughout Cheever's stories and novels. The author himself acknowledged on many occasions that the Cain and Abel story was most important to his entire body of work.

Other characters that play significant roles in the story are Lawrence's brother, the unnamed narrator, who is a secondary-school teacher, and his wife, Helen. Lawrence's divorced sister, Diana, lives in France but returns home for part of the summer at the family summerhouse called Laud's Head. A third brother, Chaddy, and his wife, Odette, are also attending this family reunion. Lawrence's wife, Ruth, keeps a keen eye on their timid and easily frightened children. Mother Pommeroy is the focus of the yearly family get-together. Many of the proper names in the story symbolize or reflect the characters' traits; that is, their strengths, weaknesses, or other personal attributes. The family name, Pommeroy, is French for "king of the apples," and apples are the most important recurring symbol throughout Cheever's stories and novels. Apples embody a paradisal innocence and child-like happiness that the Pommeroys celebrate during these summer days at the Atlantic Ocean shore, not far from Boston.

The setting is bright and sunny until Lawrence arrives late to the celebratory family gathering. He is consistently associated in the story with darkness, the sinister, and the east. When the other family members are enjoying themselves, the narrator describes Lawrence's depressing attitude: "He looked at us all bleakly. The wind and the sea had risen, and I thought that if he heard the waves, he must hear them only as a dark answer to all his dark questions." The narrator seems to suggest that Lawrence has a mystical connection with nature when he relates that "the easterly fog seemed to play into my misanthropic brother's hands." Lawrence is a lawyer and is overly concerned with obeying the law and with not overindulging bodily pleasures. He is adamantly against drinking; he accuses his mother of being an alcoholic, refuses to play card games, condemns dancing, and generally looks upon his family as frivolous and shallow. He denounces them for wasting time. As the story progresses, it is clear that Lawrence is a modern-day version of the joyless Puritans of New England, a group that Cheever frequently attacked for their fear and abhorrence of enjoying the common pleasures of life.

The setting of the story, the fictional setting of Laud's Head, reinforces that the Puritans are Cheever's satiric targets in the story. Archbishop William Laud was the most famous Anglican archbishop beheaded by the Puritans in 1645 for attempting to bring back into the church ritual, music, the Communion table, and the sacramental system that the Puritans had banned. Lawrence's reason for attending the family reunion is in part religiously based: out of the thirteen reasons he lists for why he is parting company with the family for good, one of them is that he is saying "goodbye to the Protestant Episcopal Church." Lawrence becomes, then, the representation of Cheever's rejection of the Puritan ethos. At the conclusion of the story the unnamed brother tries to kill Lawrence by smashing him over the head with a root—a symbolic beheading after Lawrence has just called him a fool.

When Lawrence leaves Laud's Head because of the violent incident, the setting brightens up significantly, and paradise is regained. The narrator states: "I got up and went to the window and what a morning that was! The wind was northerly. The air was clear. In the early heat, the roses in the garden smelled like strawberry jam." He observes "the grace of the light" that unifies the sun, the sea, and the earth. In the concluding image of the story, the narrator watches as his wife and his sister emerge naked from a morning swim, "unshy, beautiful, and full of grace." The image seems to suggest the triumph of naturalness over the dark denial of Lawrence's puritanical, joyless hatred of the body.

Discussion Questions

1. How can Lawrence Pommeroy be viewed as a modern-day version of the Prodigal Son from the Bible?

2. Point out and explain at least three past events that Lawrence has returned home to say goodbye to.

3. What were the three nicknames that the Pommeroy family gave to Lawrence, and why?

4. Point out and explain three instances in "Goodbye, My Brother" in which Lawrence is associated with dark or darkness.

—*Patrick Meanor*

O WHAT A PARADISE IT SEEMS
(New York: Knopf, 1982)

LEMUEL SEARS

Lemuel Sears is the protagonist of John Cheever's ecological novel *O What a Paradise It Seems*. Sears is a wealthy New York City businessman in his sixties who, upon visiting his daughter's home in upstate New York, becomes deeply disturbed by the contamination through pollution of Beasley's Pond, his favorite skating location. The pollution is so severe that it is unfit for skating or any other activity. Sears observes "the shell of a ten-year-old automobile and . . . a dead dog. He thought his heart would break." Sears has been married twice before—both of his wives died—and carries on a passionate affair with a younger woman, Renée Herndon. He also has temporary affair with Eduardo, the elevator operator at Renée's Manhattan apartment building, a middle-aged married man and father of two sons.

From the time he becomes aware of the fall of Beasley's Pond into a wasteland—that it has become sterile and even dangerous—Sears is transformed into a crusader for the ecological survival of the whole area. He is connected to nature and the environment by his highly attuned sensual appreciation for the pleasures that the natural environment offers him and the inhabitants of Janice, New York, an idyllic town. He reveres nature as holy and feels a strong sense of obligation to preserve its pristine condition. Beasley's Pond embodies for him "the sacred grove." Cheever himself comments on his protagonist's accomplishment in the novel: "Sears means to succeed in loving usefulness, and actually he is quite useful. He purified a large body of water."

After rising to the defense of Beasley's Pond, Sears becomes a devoted enemy of pollution in general. He is the last of Cheever's several protagonists who lament and actively battle the damaging encroachments of so-called technological progress. Sears's most dangerous opponents are those corrupt officials who finance the systematic destruction of the pond through the Salazzos, next-door neighbors of Betsey and Henry Logan, Sears's most outspoken supporters in Janice.

Sears hires a professional environmentalist, Horace Chisholm, to gather the scientific evidence documenting the ecological damage that the pond has sustained. Before Sears can present the damaging evidence to the town council of Janice, though, Chisholm is killed by a hit-and-run driver. Betsey Logan devises a plan to get the polluters to stop contaminating the pond. She plants a bottle of teriyaki sauce laced with rat poison in a local supermarket with a warning that the practice will continue unless the pollution stops. Her plan works: the pollution ceases, and the Salazzos promptly leave town. Sears summarizes what he and Betsey have accomplished: "The liveliness of the landscape has been restored. It was in no way distinguished, but it could, a century earlier, have served as a background for Eden, or even the fields of Eleusis if you added some naked goddesses and satyrs." Cheever's biographer, Scott Donaldson, comments: "More than anything Cheever ever wrote, it rejects celebration of an historical past in favor of the present. He was as aware in 1982 as in 1962 of the depredations that nomadism and money-grubbing were causing . . . but he recognizes the futility of looking to an idealized past for relief. If miracles are to be worked, they must come through love, and through a love for the creation and all those who inhabit it."

O What a Paradise It Seems is a novella, slightly longer than a hundred pages. Cheever had originally intended it to be nearly three times as long but discovered as he was writing it that he had terminal bone cancer. He was able to complete the shortened version of the novella before his death in 1982. It ends with Sears in Renée's loving embrace, reflecting on the connection between Beasley's Pond and the cosmos.

Discussion Questions

1. How does human greed contribute to the ongoing pollution taking place at Beasley's Pond?

2. What are the philosophical beliefs that Lemuel Sears tries to put forth in attempting to prevent further pollution to the environment?

3. What has Lemuel's evolving sexual openness have to do with the theme of the novel?

—*Patrick Meanor*

"THE SWIMMER"

Collected in *The Brigadier and the Golf Widow* (New York: Harper & Row, 1964).

NEDDY MERRILL

Neddy Merrill is the protagonist of John Cheever's short story "The Swimmer." The story begins with Merrill and his wife, Lucinda, at a Sunday gathering around a neighbor's pool in one of the fashionable bedroom communities north of New York City. All in attendance are hungover, and Neddy decides to swim across the glamorous and affluent eight miles back to his own home in Bullett Park through the swimming pools of a dozen or so of his acquaintances. It is midsummer when he begins his journey:

"It was a fine day. In the west there was a massive stand of cumulus cloud so like a city seen from a distance—from the bow of an approaching ship—that it might have had a name. Lisbon. Hackensack." The reference to Lisbon, as David J. Piwinski points out in his essay "Lisbon and Hackensack in Cheever's 'The Swimmer,'" links Neddy to the archetypical traveler, Odysseus: the original name of that city, Olisipo, is a variation of Ulyssipo. Neddy, in his less mythic journey home, is bound for Hackensack, New Jersey.

Neddy's journey begins well enough. He is welcomed warmly by the Grahams, who are glad to see him because they have been trying to get him on the phone all morning. He stays for a drink. He understands, as did Odysseus, "that the hospitable customs and traditions of the natives would have to be handled with diplomacy if he was ever going to reach his destination." Next, Mrs. Hammer sees him swim her pool but is not quite certain who he is. The Lears hear him splashing by, and the Howlands and the Crosscups are away. At the Bunkers' pool there is a party. "Prosperous men and women gathered by the sapphire-colored waters while caterer's men in white coats passed them gin." This scene is characteristic in Cheever's upper-middle-class suburban world, but it is often shadowed in his work by disillusion and decline. At this point in the story the Merrills are still both socially desired and usually aloof. As he exits the Bunkers' estate, Neddy suffers his first hint of misfortune: "The gravel cut his feet but this was the only unpleasantness." It is just the beginning of his downward spiral. The Levys are not at home, but he pours himself a drink. "It was his fourth or fifth and he had swum nearly half the length of the Lucinda River"—Neddy's name for the waters he swims home on. He wonders what time it is: "Four? Five?"

It suddenly begins to be dark. A storm passes, and Neddy is surprised that a maple tree is shedding red and yellow leaves. He thinks the tree is "blighted," failing to recognize, in his obstinate blindness, that time has passed and that it is now autumn. This is the first indication that time is passing through the seasons and that he is oblivious to his circumstances. "Was his memory failing," he wonders, "or had he so disciplined it in the repression of unpleasant facts that he had damaged his sense of truth?" He comes to Route 424, and as he tries to cross, "barefoot in the deposits of the highway—beer cans, rags, and blowout patches— exposed to all kinds of ridicule, he seemed pitiful . . . and he had no dignity or humor to bring to the occasion." No longer a member of an elite subur-ban set, he now swims across the public pool at the Lancaster Recreation Center, "and as soon as he entered the crowded enclosure he was confronted with regimentation." The "murk" and "reek" of the "stagnant" pool indicates that he has made a pre-cipitous descent from the glamorous party he had attended months before.

The next neighbors Neddy encounters are the Hallorans, who are suspected of being Com-munists and like to sunbathe in the nude. Mrs. Halloran tells Neddy, "We've been terribly sorry to hear of all your misfortunes," to which Neddy responds: "My misfortunes? I don't know what you mean." She has also heard that he has sold his house and wonders about his "poor" children. Neddy swims on, thinking, "Was he losing his memory, had his gift for concealing painful facts let him forget that he had sold his house, that his children were in trouble?" Near the end of his journey he is amazed to see the autumn constel-lations of Andromeda, Cepheus, and Cassiopeia. His next shock is the rude reception he gets at the Biswangers, a couple that invited him and his wife to dinner four times a year and were always refused. But the tables are turned now. During his swim, the Merrills have fallen from the top of the social ladder to the bottom. Neddy cannot grasp that fact. He is reminded that he had come drunk one Sunday and asked the Biswangers for a five-thousand-dollar loan—which the swimmer seems to have conveniently forgotten. His last poolside disaster occurs at the house of his former mistress, Shirley Adams. She asks him "Will you ever grow up?" and says, "If you've come here for money, I won't give you another cent." Neddy swims across her pool, has trouble climbing out, and begins to cry, "the first time in his life that he had ever felt so miserable, cold, tired, and bewildered." At the Gilmartins' pool the water is wintry "icy," and at

the Clydes' he "paddled the length of their pool, stopping again and again with his hand on the curb to rest." He has gone from exaltation to despair, from affluence to penury as he swims across the miles and the seasons. Only at the end, when he finds his home locked and empty, does he perhaps begin to understand the reality of his decline, the fact that his self-destructive behavior—drinking, carelessness with money, and womanizing—have doomed him.

Discussion Questions

1. Do Cheever's references to the seasonal changes work well enough to give the reader a sense of the passage of time?

2. As Neddy falls from grace, what are the telling instances that most clearly define that fall?

3. Is it believable that Neddy can be so obliv-ous to the fact that his life, as he swims on, is on a downward path?

4. What are the causes of Neddy's material, physical, and social decline?

THE WAPSHOT CHRONICLE
(New York: Harper, 1957)

THE WAPSHOT FAMILY

Leander Wapshot is the main character in John Cheever's first novel, *The Wapshot Chronicle*, pub-lished in 1957. Reviews of the novel were mixed because its structure is episodic and, seemingly, nonlinear. The main reason for its cyclical structure is that the story emerges from the memory of Lean-der, the paterfamilias and chronicler of the history of the Wapshot family. The novel appears fragmented because of the way Leander brings together the journals and legal and historical documents that make up the history of the family. To the surprise of the literary world, the novel won the National Book Award in 1958.

The history of the Wapshot family bears a close resemblance to that of Cheever's own family. Leander, Cheever acknowledged, is modeled closely on Ezekiel Cheever, an early ancestor, who also kept accurate documentation of the Cheever family, though Cheever claimed that he lost much of his ancestor's genealogical materials. The Wapshot family, like the Cheevers, are descendants of sea captains, but Leander is the last in that line when he finds himself as the captain of the *Topaze,* a tourist boat, which was accidentally sunk in a storm. Sarah, Leander's enterprising wife, salvages it and transforms it into a highly successful floating gift shop.

Leander, as opposed to the moralistic Sarah and his puritanical cousin Honora, is an unapologetic celebrant of life's bodily pleasures; he relishes food, drink, history, literature, beautiful women, and amorous desires. But he loves his sons, Moses and Coverly, deeply and tries to guide them into lives that will make them happy and fulfilled. Most importantly, Leander's journals not only record his family's adventures—past and present—but also create a coherent and accurate chronicle of the family that will help Moses and Coverly understand their lives within a familial context. Realizing that his life has been completely dominated by the powerful wills of his wife and the relentless Honora—who controls the family fortunes—Leander decides to honorably drown himself, just as his namesake, Leander (from Christopher Marlowe's "Hero and Leander") does.

Honora Wapshot is the exact opposite of Leander in every way. She is the moral arbiter of the family and condemns immoral behavior of any kind—especially sexual behavior. She is an unrelenting puritanical zealot. Though she has given up trying to control the life-celebrating behavior of Leander, she successfully and rigidly dictates the lives of Moses and Coverly throughout the novel. She pressures them both (by threatening to cut off their rightful inheritance) to leave the Wapshot home, West Farm, and go into the world to seek proper wives and respectable positions. Indeed, after overhearing Moses enjoying a passionate escapade with Rosalie, the daughter of the local Anglican minister, she blackmails both Leander and Sarah to expel Moses from the town of St. Botolph's.

After Honora forces Moses off the family estate, he falls in love with Melissa, whom he eventually marries; though Moses must undergo several quasi-medieval obstacles at cousin Justina's estate, where any sexual activity was strictly forbidden. He is forced to climb naked over the rooftop of Justina's minicastle to meet with the virginal Melissa.

Coverly, Moses's younger brother, leaves with Moses after his expulsion from West Farm. Coverly is gentler and more vulnerable than his older brother and worries about his attraction toward other men. Leander hears about Coverly's sexual doubts and writes him a letter honestly admitting his own youthful homosexual feelings toward some of his male friends. His courageous letter to Coverly assuages his son's doubts about how heterosexual he is, and it also enables him to fall in love with Betsey MacCaffrey, with whom he moves to the sterile suburb of Remsen Park. Betsey, because of the atmosphere of Remsen Park, temporarily loses any erotic interest in Coverly. Leander's letter to Coverly has the residual effect of energizing his sexual allure, however, melting Betsey's temporarily frozen erotic desires.

Because Moses and Coverly have successfully fulfilled the family obligations imposed on them by Honora, they are given their rightful benefices. The first thing they want to do is buy Leander a new boat, though he drowns himself before they are able to do so.

Sarah Wapshot bears a strong affinity to John Cheever's mother, Mary Devereaux Liley, who, after Cheever's father lost the family home during the Depression, restored the family fortunes somewhat when she created a gift shop in Quincy, Massachusetts. Mrs. Cheever called it "The Only Floating Gift Shoppe in New England"; like Sarah, she transformed a boat into her own successful business.

Even though Leander commits suicide at the conclusion of the novel, his journal—and his instructions to Coverly to read from Prospero's speech at the conclusion of William Shakespeare's *The Tempest*—identifies Leander with that magician, the king of an enchanted island. Cheever's chronicle makes Leander the permanent, reigning spirit of the saga of the Wapshot family.

Discussion Questions

1. How does the organization of the novel mirror the evolution of the Wapshot family?

2. How are Leander and Honora Wapshot exact opposites emotionally and spiritually?

3. How does Moses Wapshot's life mirror the life and career of Moses from the Old Testament?

4. What do Cousins Honora and Justina fear most about the moral lives of Moses and Coverly?

5. In what ways is Leander Wapshot a kind of mirror image of the Leander of Christopher Marlowe's poem "Hero and Leander"?

—*Patrick Meanor*

REFERENCES

Samuel Coale, *John Cheever* (New York: Ungar, 1977);

Robert G. Collins, ed., *Critical Essays on John Cheever* (Boston: G. K. Hall, 1982);

Scott Donaldson, ed., *Conversations with John Cheever* (Jackson: University of Mississippi Press, 1987);

Donaldson, *John Cheever: A Biography* (New York: Bantam Doubleday, 1988;

Patrick Meanor, *John Cheever Revisited* (New York: Twayne, 1995);

Robert A. Morace, "The Religious Experience and the 'Mystery of Imprisonment' in John Cheever's *Falconer*," *Cithara: Essays in the Judaeo-Christian Tradition*, 20, no. 1 (1980): 44–53;

David J. Piwinski, "Lisbon and Hackensack in Cheever's 'The Swimmer,'" *Studies in Short Fiction*, 33 (Spring 1996): 273–274.

Charles W. Chesnutt
(June 20, 1858 – November 15, 1932)

THE CONJURE WOMAN
(Boston: Houghton Mifflin, 1899)

AUN' PEGGY

Aun' Peggy is the conjure woman of the title of Charles W. Chesnutt's first book, and she is a character in five of the seven stories in that volume. As a freed slave, a conjure woman, and a witch who "went out ridin' the niggers at night," she works charms for both blacks and whites. For instance, in the first story, "The Goophered Grapevine," the white slave owner asks her to put a "goopher," a charm, on his grapevines because the slaves are eat-

ing too many of the grapes. A new slave eats some grapes, and his health begins to echo the seasons: in the spring and summer he is vigorous, and in the winter he turns into an old man. Once his master recognizes this pattern, he sells him every spring and buys him back, cheaply, in the fall. This first story represents Peggy as "a dangerous and amoral ally, not as some sort of just rescuer," as Charles Duncan points out. While other critics, such as Eric Selinger, have seen her as a character who compensates for the slaves' overall powerlessness and who is concerned with "maintaining relationships, with holding things together," Aun' Peggy's behavior is more complicated morally.

Although in several of the stories Aun' Peggy helps slaves, she never does so gratuitously. She always has an economic motive, and the effects of her conjuration can be both positive and negative. In "Sis' Becky's Pickaninny," she helps to reunite a mother who has been sold away from her baby, while in "Mars' Jeems's Nightmare" she uses her powers to turn a white man into a black one. In this case she does hold things together, because the master, after he becomes white again, becomes kinder and allows the slaves to marry (something he had previously forbidden). The story ends with a celebration: "dey all tuk ter sweethea'tin' en juneseyin' en singin' dancin', en eight er ten couples got married." Aun' Peggy's powers are limited, though, and she realizes that she has "ter be kinder keerful 'bout cunj'in' white folks," because while her status as a free woman somewhat protects her, she still has to be careful not to provoke retaliation from the slave owners, who resent and fear her powers. For instance, in "Hot-Foot Hannibal," the master is upset at her conjuring, but the narrator, Uncle Julius McAdoo, says, "Fer Mars' Dugal' had warned de han's befo' 'bout foolin' wid cunju'ation; fac', he had los' one er two niggers hisse'f, fum dey bein' goophered, en he would 'a' had ole Aun' Peggy whip' long ago, on'y Aun' Peggy wuz a free 'oman, en he wuz 'feard she'd cunjuh him. En w'iles Mars' Dugal' say he did n' b'liebe in cunj'in'. . . he 'peared ter 'low it wuz bes' ter be on de safe side, en let Aun' Peggy alone."

In other stories, Aun' Peggy uses conjuring as a weapon against others in the slave community. For instance, in "Hot-Foot Hannibal" Peggy is asked to intervene in the plans of the master who has decided to "give" Chloe to a new house slave, Hannibal. The plan results in her true love, Jeff, being sent down the river and Chloe dying of a broken heart. Thus, an effort on Peggy's part to undermine the power of the master and to support the slaves in "maintaining relationships" ends up having the opposite effect and destroying relationships and community.

In the end, Peggy is less a character than an artfully deployed stereotype. While her freedom and her ability to conjure give her a certain degree of power, the effects of her activities are often unpredictable both within the white and African American communities.

Discussion Questions

1. Discuss the different representations of the conjure women and the conjure men in *The Conjure Woman,* particularly in "Hot-Foot Hannibal."

2. How does Aun' Peggy give the slaves a sense of their own power (however limited) in the response to the general powerlessness they usually experience?

3. Aun' Peggy is not a fully realized character in *The Conjure Woman.* She certainly is not as "rounded" a character as Julius McAdoo. Why did Chesnutt choose to depict her in this way?

4. Why do you think Chesnutt chose to represent Aun' Peggy only in the pre–Civil War period? Why doesn't he represent her in the present of the telling of the stories?

—*Matthew T. Wilson*

JULIUS MCADOO

Julius McAdoo (Uncle Julius) is one of the two narrators of Charles W. Chesnutt's stories collected under the title *The Conjure Woman.* Chesnutt wrote in the genre of the plantation tale, invented by white writers to express nostalgia for the era of slavery. In the plantation tale, a white narrator encounters an old former slave who tells him a story of slavery days; so there is always a frame tale narrated by the white character and an embedded tale with a black narrator. The African American narrators of the embedded tales almost always express regret for the passing of slavery, as does the slave in Thomas Nelson Page's story "Mars Chan": "Dem wuz good ole times, marster—the bes' Sam ever see! Dem wuz, in fac'! Niggers didn' hed nothin' 't all to do. . . ." Chesnutt detested this kind of ahistorical plantation nostalgia, and his depiction of Julius must be seen as revision of the ex-slave character invented by white writers. These characters, Chesnutt said in a letter, were distinguished by "their dog-like fidelity and devotion to their old masters. . . . I don't care to write about these people. . . ." His representation of Julius is an attempt to take what had become a highly stereotypical character and to show that character from an African American perspective.

One of the elements of the nostalgia of the plantation tale is the rootlessness and powerlessness of the ex-slave narrator; he feels unmoored in the present, in the view of these white writers, without the "civilizing" effects of slavery. With Julius, Chesnutt consciously reverses that powerlessness: Julius is a kind of trickster, and he uses the stories that he tells to the Northern narrator and his wife as a way of manipulating them to achieve certain instrumental goals. In all of the stories except one, Julius gains something from the telling of the tale. For example, in "The Goophered Grapevine" he is hired by the narrator as a coachman, while in "Poor Sandy" he prevents the narrator from disassembling an old cabin that Julius wants to use as a place for his church to meet. Julius's intentions, though, go well beyond manipulating the narrator for some material gain; he recognizes that he has a dual audience, the narrator and his wife, who stand in for Chesnutt's largely white readership. On one hand, the narrator, John, tends to dismiss Julius's tales as mere superstition, as evidence of the backwardness of the freed slaves: "your people," he says, "will never rise in the world until they throw off those childish superstitions and learn to live by the light of reason and common sense." On the other hand, his wife, Annie, is of a "very sympathetic turn of mind," and while she too dismisses as improbable all the magical transformations that Julius relates, she understands their emotional import. She clearly sees how Julius's tales are about the horrors of slavery—not the horrors of physical torture, but the psychological torture endured by slave families through forced separation of wives from husbands or mothers from children.

Julius tells his stories when the Northern narrator comes South and buys a vineyard some years after the Civil War, and while the Northern couple sees him as a relic of a bygone time, Julius never allows them to have a romanticized or nostalgic view of slavery. As an aspect of what he is trying to teach them about slavery and its consequences, he attempts, in "Mars' Jeems's Nightmare," to alert them to the difficulties faced by freedmen in the post–Civil War period by telling a story that is a plea for his grandson, a plea that the narrator make allowances for someone "w'at aint had no chanst ter l'arn."

Uncle Julius is more than just a storyteller, however. He actually has a role in the action of the central story of the volume, "Sis Becky's Pickaninny." At the beginning of that story the narrator's wife is suffering from the kind of nervous condition experienced by the main character in Charlotte Perkins Gilman's "The Yellow Wallpaper." Annie, the narrator's wife, "became the victim of a settled melancholy, attended with vague forebodings of impending misfortune." When Julius speaks to her, she does not answer; she "was apparently without energy enough to speak for herself." Julius tells a story of a separated slave mother and child, and how that separation was healed by a conjure woman, Aun' Peggy. At the end of the story, Annie is not only speaking again, but speaking with "delightful animation." Thus, as Julius tells the story of conjuring, he becomes something of a conjurer himself. He conjures within his readers a recognition of the struggles of the black family to maintain its integrity in a system designed to brutalize and debase.

Discussion Questions

1. Discuss how Julius functions as a trickster in the tales of *The Conjure Woman*.

2. Many works of the late nineteenth century end with a North/South marriage, a sign of the attempts to reconcile the two regions of this country in this period. The final story, "Hot-Foot Hannibal," ends with such a marriage—Annie's sister and a local man, Malcolm Murchison. What does it mean that Julius seems to be instrumental in bringing off this marriage?

3. As a young man, Chesnutt wrote in his journal that one of his ambitions as a writer would be the enlightenment of white people: "I shall write for a purpose, a high, holy purpose . . . The object of my writings would be not so much the elevation of the colored people as the elevation of the whites." Do you think he fulfills this ambition with the stories published in *The Conjure Woman?*

4. In these stories there are actually three time frames. One is created by the frame tale (some time after the Civil War), and one is created by Julius's tale, set before the Civil War. Yet, there is another time period that one needs to take into consideration: the 1890s, when four of these stories first appeared in magazines and then when they appeared together as a volume. How might these stories comment on the time of their publication?

—*Matthew T. Wilson*

THE HOUSE BEHIND THE CEDARS
(Boston & New York: Houghton, Mifflin, 1900)

RENA WALDEN

Rena Walden is one of the four main characters in Charles W. Chesnutt's first novel, *The House behind the Cedars*. "Rena Walden" was Chesnutt's working title for the novel during the long period of its composition; just before it was published, he wrote to his publisher to say that he had not "slept with that story for ten years without falling in love with it, and believing in it," while later in his life, he wrote another correspondent that the novel was "in a way, my favorite child, for Rena was of 'mine own people.'" Chesnutt was referring to people of mixed-race ancestry who were light-skinned enough to pass for white. Indeed, Chesnutt himself could have easily passed but chose, he once said, to be a "voluntary negro." In *The House behind the Cedars* Chesnutt explores these issues of racial identity and passing, focusing especially on the consequences for those who chose to attempt to pass as white.

In *The House behind the Cedars*, Chesnutt focuses on the dilemma of Rena and her brother, John, who is already living in the white world, where his mixed-race ancestry is unknown. John convinces Rena to come with him to his plantation and to pass herself off as a white woman. Unlike her brother, however, Rena never fully overcomes her scruples about posing as white. John, from the time he is a boy, relies on the evidence of the color of his skin: " 'I am white,' replied the lad, turning back his sleeve and holding out his arm. . . ." And he proceeds to live his life according to the "principles of abstract right and reason." On the other hand, Rena, early in the novel, seems to have no convictions about race, and she yields to her brother out of her feelings for him and her nephew and out of a desire to escape "the narrow walls that hemmed her in."

When Rena is introduced to the white world, she is immediately noticed by George Tryon, a young white Southerner who falls in love with her and quickly asks her to marry him, never suspecting that she is of mixed-race ancestry. Rena's doubts come to the fore once she has agreed to marry Tryon. In a conversation with her brother, she says, "If he should find out afterwards, he might cast me off, or cease to love me," and she worries that she could not go through her life without knowing how he would have reacted to her "race," to her "blackness." While her brother does convince her not to tell their secret to Tryon, Tryon discovers the truth through a series of coincidences. When Rena looks at his face, instead of love, she sees "horror." As she says later to her brother: "He looked at me as though I were not even a human being."

Once rejected by Tryon, Rena then becomes aware of race in a way that she had never been before. "Her early training had not directed her thoughts to the darker people with whose fate her own was bound up so closely, but rather away from them. She had been taught to despise them because they were not so white as she was. . . ." Once she decides to cast her lot with her "own people," she resolves to become a teacher in an all-black school. Having made that decision, though, she realizes how she is caught between the black and white worlds, and the sign of that betweenness is the two characters who pursue her: Tryon returns, at the end of the novel, convinced that he will marry her despite all the social and legal prohibitions against mixed-race marriage, while at the same time she is pursued by a stereotypically villainous mulatto character, Jeff Wain. The novel concludes with her death of shock and exposure after being caught in the woods in a storm and with the realization of Tryon that he "had

ruthlessly spurned and spoiled the image of God in this fair creature."

In *The House behind the Cedars*, Chesnutt explores the consequences of passing for Rena and her brother. Although some critics have said that the author completely approves of the brother's decision to pass over into the white world, Chesnutt is clearly critical of him. The cost to John has been nearly permanent separation from his mother and sister (when the novel opens he has not seen them in ten years), and after the events of the novel, it is clear that he will never see them again. In contrast, Rena cannot sever the ties to her community and to her mother. Like Chesnutt himself, she refuses to renounce communal and familial ties, and like Chesnutt, she tries to devote herself to the uplift of the African American community. One could argue, though, that Chesnutt stacks the deck against her in trying to show how she is at home in neither white nor black worlds. Even though Tryon believes he can and will marry her, she cannot recover from the shock of seeing that as a "black" woman she was "not even a human being" to him. Her other suitor, Wain, is a fraud with a living wife who apparently deserted him because of his abusiveness. In the end of the novel, before Rena's death, Chesnutt presents an image of how Rena is trapped. She is at the crossing of a trail with Wain approaching from one side while Tryon approaches from the other. At home in neither world and, in her mind, not a marriage partner for either man, Rena must die so that the reader, along with Tryon, can mourn her loss. In the end Rena becomes a symbol of the apparently unresolvable problem of race in the United States.

Discussion Questions

1. Discuss the differences between Rena and her brother, John. Why has Chesnutt chosen to depict him as almost rigidly rational and her as almost exclusively emotional?

2. Discuss Rena's reservations about passing. How do those reservations contrast with her brother's arguments about passing?

3. As a young man, in his journal Chesnutt wrote that one of his ambitions as a writer would be the enlightenment of white people: "I shall write for a purpose, a high, holy purpose . . . The object of my

writings would be not so much the elevation of the colored people as the elevation of the whites." Do you think that he fulfilled this purpose with the character of Rena Walden?

4. In a series of newspaper articles written a year after the publication of *The Conjure Woman*, Chesnutt argued that the best way to solve the racial problem in the United States was through a thorough race mixing that would leave no trace of distinct races. The critic Sally Ann Ferguson has charged that Rena dies because she is finally unable to marry a white man, and that Chesnutt thoroughly approves of her brother, John. Do you agree?

—*Matthew T. Wilson*

"THE SHERIFF'S CHILDREN"

Collected in *The Wife of His Youth and Other Stories* (Boston & New York: Houghton, Mifflin, 1899).

SHERIFF CAMPBELL

Sheriff Campbell, the main character of Charles W. Chesnutt's story "The Sheriff's Children," is a man with two contrasting personalities. He is respected in his town as a hero of the Civil War, and he also hides a secret that emerges as he comes face to face with a less honorable past he cannot leave behind. The story illustrates the personal and the political fallout of slavery in the post–Civil War South.

Campbell is described as "a tall, muscular man, of a ruddier complexion than is usual among Southerners." He comes from a privileged background, and his history shows some weakness of character. He was "at first an ardent supporter of the Union" and was against the movement for his state to secede. Then, when war became inevitable, he changed his philosophical outlook and enlisted in the Confederate army. After the Civil War he "took the oath of allegiance" to the newly reunited country.

When an elderly war hero is brutally murdered in the peaceful town in which Campbell is the sheriff and witnesses put a "strange mulatto" at the scene of the crime, a search party brings a black man, Tom, to the jail as a suspect. A lynch mob forms, claiming that "Hangin' air too good fer the murderer." The

sheriff is "far above the average of the community in wealth, education, and social position" and counts on the fact that he is "universally popular with his constituents" to keep both him and his prisoner safe from the mob. When addressing the violent group, he is careful not "to recognize anybody in particular" so that he will not be responsible for identifying them with the mob. The sheriff unlocks the fetters on the prisoner's hands and feet so "if I can't hold the jail, you'll have to make the best fight you can."

When the men say "We want to have a talk with the nigger that killed Cap'n Walker," the sheriff tells them they can see him "when he's brought out for trial." "I'm a white man outside," he says, "but in this jail I'm sheriff; and if this nigger's to be hung in this county, I propose to do the hanging." Faced with Campbell's "determined resistance," the mob temporarily retreats; someone among them fires a shot, and the sheriff fires a warning shot after them.

Taking advantage of the distraction, Tom is able to take one of the sheriff's guns and turn the tables on him. "The sheriff mentally cursed his own carelessness," for he had "relied on the negro's cowardice and subordination in the presence of an armed white man." "Good God," Campbell says to the prisoner, "you would not kill the man to whom you owe your own life." He is righter than he realizes: Tom, it turns out, is his son by a slave, Cicely, that Campbell owned before the war.

Campbell "had been sorry . . . many a time since" for his treatment of Cicely and Tom but justified himself in his own mind because he had quarreled with Cicely just before selling her. He desperately needed the money offered for the two slaves to maintain his farm and his position in the community. He tries to reason with Tom that the young man has his freedom and an education, to which Tom responds that he is "Free in name, but despised and scorned": "I learned to feel that no degree of learning or wisdom will change the color of my skin." Tom moves to kill Campbell, but he is shot in the arm by the sheriff's daughter, Polly. Campbell had given her a gun to defend herself when he left her at home to go and face the lynch mob.

Having regained control of the situation, Campbell is a changed man. He binds Tom's arm, locks him in his cell, and returns to the house. He tosses and turns all night, thinking that, had he been more dutiful, he could have given "this son of his the poor simulacrum of liberty which men of his caste could possess." He resolves to compensate Tom for the unfairness shown him and his mother years ago: he will "investigate the circumstances of the murder, and move Heaven and earth to discover the real criminal, for he no longer doubted the prisoner's innocence." He will hire a good lawyer and "atone for his crime against this son of his—against society—against God." At the jail the next morning, however, he discovers that Tom "had torn the bandage from his wound and bled to death during the night." Sheriff Campbell's resolution to atone for his sins against humanity can never be achieved. He has missed his opportunity twice.

Discussion Questions

1. How does the sheriff's attitude toward the prisoner change during the course of the story?

2. Many American authors present "mulattoes" as tragic characters. Compare Tom in "The Sheriff's Children" with other racially conflicted characters in Mark Twain's *Pudd'nhead Wilson*, Edna Ferber's *Show Boat*, and/or Nella Larson's *Passing*.

3. Chesnutt often employs water imagery in "The Sheriff's Children." For example, he describes the town of Troy as having survived "the fierce tide of war" and Tom as having experienced the "slough of slavery." Explicate the author's use of this image pattern as it illustrates the role of environment on character.

4. Compare the sheriff's interaction with the lynch mob with a similar confrontation in Chapter 22 of Mark Twain's *The Adventures of Huckleberry Finn*. How do the two sheriffs interact differently with their respective communities?

—*Clare Gerlach*

REFERENCES

William L. Andrews, *The Literary Career of Charles W. Chesnutt* (Baton Rouge: Louisiana State University Press, 1980);

Richard E. Baldwin, "The Art of *The Conjure Woman*," in *Critical Essays on Charles Chesnutt,* edited by Joseph McElrath Jr. (New York: G. K. Hall, 1999), pp. 170–180;

Charles Duncan, *The Absent Man: The Narrative Craft of Charles W. Chesnutt* (Athens: Ohio University Press, 1998);

Sally Ann Ferguson, "Rena Walden: Chesnutt's Failed 'Future American,'" in *Critical Essays on Charles W. Chesnutt,* edited by McElrath (New York: G. K. Hall, 1999), pp. 198–205;

Otto Heim, "Time and Mobility in the Writing of Charles W. Chesnutt," *Comparative American Studies: An International Journal,* 1 (June 2003): 222–246;

Dean McWilliams, *Charles W. Chesnutt and the Fictions of Race* (Athens: University of Georgia Press, 2002);

Robert Nowatzki, "Passing in a White Genre: Charles W. Chesnutt's Negotiations of the Plantation Tradition in *The Conjure Woman*," *American Literary Realism,* 27 (1995): 20–36;

Matthew Wilson, *Whiteness in the Novels of Charles W. Chesnutt* (Jackson: University Press of Mississippi, 2004);

Henry Wonham, *Charles W. Chesnutt: A Study of the Short Fiction* (Boston: Twayne, 1998).

Tracy Chevalier
(October 19, 1962 –   )

GIRL WITH A PEARL EARRING
(New York: Dutton, 1999)

GRIET

Griet is the main character for Tracy Chevalier's second novel, *Girl with a Pearl Earring*. Inspired by the artist Johannes Vermeer's painting of the same title, Chevalier provides a fictional account of the unknown subject of the work, positing that the young woman depicted is Griet, a sixteen-year-old maid in the Vermeer household.

Griet becomes a maid for Vermeer after her father, a tile painter, is injured in a kiln explosion and can no longer support the family. Her primary responsibility is to clean Vermeer's studio without moving the objects that he is painting. Once Griet proves her abilities as a maid, Vermeer expands her duties to include purchasing supplies and grinding the raw materials used in his paints, tasks that he had previously refused to delegate to others. Griet is, for all purposes, Vermeer's apprentice. Virginia Woolf, in *A Room of One's Own*, describes a fictional character, Judith Shakespeare, the sister of William Shakespeare, who had the same talent as her brother but is limited by the lack of opportunity available to her gender. Similar to Judith, Griet is also limited, both by gender and social class.

Griet's brother, Frans, provides a foil for Griet. Frans is sent by his parents to be an apprentice at a tile-painting factory, where he resents the drudgery of his position, seduces the owner's wife and thus incurs the wrath of the owner, and finally leaves his position, despite the fact that his impoverished parents paid a great deal of money for his apprenticeship. Griet, on the other hand, is sent by her parents to be a maid but fills the role of informal apprentice to Vermeer and, despite her exhaustion, takes great pleasure in her work. Though Griet is attracted to Vermeer, she does not act on her impulses. Their relationship is more a meeting of the minds: "Sometimes we stood side by side in the small room, me grinding white lead, him washing lapis or burning ochers in the fire. He said little to me. He was a quiet man. I did not speak either. It was peaceful then, with the light coming in through the window. When we were done we poured water from a pitcher over each other's hands and scrubbed ourselves clean." Nevertheless, Vermeer's wife, Catharina, views Griet with suspicion. "She was not happy about my being in the attic—it meant I was closer to him, to the place she was not allowed in but where I could wander freely." Catharina's jealousy ultimately forces Griet to leave her position, but instead of leaving town, she marries her young suitor, Pieter, as her parents had encouraged.

Griet has an innate talent that, with proper guidance, might have been great. When Vermeer first meets her, he observes how she has laid out the vegetables that she has chopped, asking why she has separated the whites from one another. Griet responds: "The colors fight when they are side by side, sir." Her sensitivity to color and form is developed as she works with Vermeer. After Vermeer explains the subtle color variations in clouds, Griet can no longer look at colors the same way: "When the light shone on the wall, I discovered, it was not white, but many colors. . . . After that I could not stop looking at things." Griet benefits from the lessons she learns from Vermeer, as would any gifted apprentice. She even boldly changes the drape of a tablecloth in a scene Vermeer plans to paint: "I made a few adjustments to the lines of the folds, then stepped back. It echoed the shape of van Ruijven's wife's arm as she held the quill. Yes, I thought, and pressed my lips together. He may send me away for changing it, but it is better now." She then defends her decision to Vermeer, who paints the scene with the alteration she has made. Finally, Griet anticipates a change needed in a painting and arrives at the solution before Vermeer does: "He was right—the painting might satisfy van Ruijven, but something was missing from it. I knew before he did." The reader is left to imagine what might have happened had Griet been given the opportunity to pick up a paintbrush.

Griet does not, as Deborah H. Cibelli points out, "overturn stereotypes or transcend social class"; she is, however, able to assert some degree of independence within the limited parameters of the cultural expectations of the time. For example, she refuses to show her hair when requested by Vermeer. Instead she wraps her hair like the older woman in the painting *The Procuress*: "My eyes fell on the painting of The Procuress—the young woman's head was bare, her hair held back with ribbons, but the old woman wore a piece of cloth wrapped around her head, crisscrossing in and out of itself. . . . Perhaps that is what women who are neither ladies nor maids nor the other do with their hair." In choosing to wrap her hair in this manner, Griet casts herself in the more active role as the procuress rather than as the younger woman, who is simply an object for exchange. When Griet leaves the Vermeer household, it is she who decides which direction she should take: "When I made my choice, the choice I knew I had to make, I set my feet carefully along the edge of the point and went the way it told me, walking steadily." In the end, Griet sells the pearl earrings that Vermeer had left to her in his will, giving Pieter the fifteen guilders that the Vermeers owed him and keeping the remaining five coins for herself. Pieter had always joked, "It's the price I have paid for you.... Now I know what a maid is worth." Griet ends by observing, "I would not have cost him anything. A maid came free."

Discussion Questions

1. Griet is insistent about hiding all of her hair when other women do not. What does her hair represent to Griet?

2. Van Leeuwenhoek counsels Griet that she should make sure she is able to remain herself around Vermeer, saying, "The women in his painting—he traps them in his world. You can get lost there." Does Griet follow this advice?

3. After Griet leaves her position as maid at the Vermeer house, she arrives at the center of town, where there is a circle with an eight-pointed star in the middle. Griet observes, "Each point indicated a direction I could take." To what extent is Griet free to choose a direction other than the one she ultimately decides upon?

—*Mary Lou Vredenburg*

REFERENCES

Barbara Baker, "Tracy Chevalier," in *The Way We Write: Interviews with Award-Winning Writers,* edited by Baker (London: Continuum, 2006), pp. 35–48;

Deborah H. Cibelli, "'Girl with a Pearl Earring': Painting, Reality, Fiction," *Journal of Popular Culture,* 37, no. 4 (2004): 583–592.

Frank Chin

(February 25, 1940 –   )

꿈

DONALD DUK

(Minneapolis: Coffee House, 1991)

Donald Duk

Donald Duk is the reluctant protagonist of Frank Chin's 1991 novel *Donald Duk,* in which the author explores the Chinese heroic tradition and uses this mythology in order to restore more-powerful images of Chinese masculinity. Through the character of Donald, Chin informs readers of the value of accurate cultural histories and stresses the importance of strong male role models for the Asian community.

Donald Duk takes place during the fifteen-day period of the Chinese New Year, during which time Donald's family, who live in Chinatown, are joined by their relatives for the upcoming celebration. Acutely aware of how this ritual marks him as different from his many white classmates, Donald despises the holiday: "It is Donald Duk's worst time of the year. Here come the stupid questions about the funny things Chinese believe in. The funny things Chinese do. The funny things Chinese eat." Rather than embrace his Chinese identity, Donald would rather be Fred Astaire, a white icon whom he loves to watch on late-night television.

Donald's understanding of what it means to be Chinese comes largely from those outside the Chinese community, including from authorities who publicize mistaken ideas about Chinese American history. Donald's history teacher, Mr. Meanwright, for example, tells Donald's seventh-grade class that the Chinese were a timid, introverted people, victims who could not compete against the "aggressive, highly competitive Americans." Meanwright's misunderstandings represent what Chin sees as mainstream white ideologies and negatively impact Donald's already suspicious position toward his cultural heritage.

Donald is also exposed to more-prideful histories, such as from his father, King Duk, and his namesake, Uncle Donald, a Cantonese opera performer. Uncle Donald introduces Donald to the mythical Water Margin tale, detailing how 108 rebels fought against a corrupt government during the Song Dynasty. Yet, before learning this legend, Donald destroys the model airplane his father built to commemorate the exploits of Lee Kuey, the most famous of the Water Margin's rebel soldiers. Caught by his uncle after he destroys the plane, Donald learns that his original surname is not Duk but Lee, and he realizes that he shares a name with Lee Kuey and with his great-great-grandfather, who worked as a builder on the Central Pacific Railway during the mid nineteenth century.

During the process of rebuilding the damaged plane, Donald experiences a recurring dream that he too is a builder on the railroad. This experience offers him an unparalleled opportunity to connect with his ancestors and to rediscover the heroes of Chinese mythology such as Kwan Kung, the god of literature and war. Kwan appears in the dream as the tracklayer's foreman and also looks suspiciously like Donald's own father. Chin uses the dream as a pedagogical vehicle to help Donald establish a more emotional connection to his cultural past, which results in Donald's tracing his own identity through a long line of courageous men, both real and mythological.

As Donald gets more interested in his dream, he also develops an increasingly politicized awareness of the inaccuracies surrounding historical accounts of Chinese contributions to the American railroad. After dreaming that the Chinese workers won a tracklaying competition in 1869, laying ten miles of track in one day, a feat for which they are not publicly recognized, Donald verifies this story and presents his findings to his history class in a triumphant moment of historical recuperation. As he tells his father: "Everything I dream is true. Or was true. I dreamed we set a world record, and it's true. I dreamed we laid the last crosstie, and it's true." These discoveries, and his newfound pride in his heritage, also help Donald to restore his damaged relationship with his father, who reminds Donald that, "You gotta keep the history yourself, or lose it forever, boy. That's the mandate of heaven."

Donald comes to realize the value of honor, courage, and tenacity, and in this regard serves as a mouthpiece for Chin's ideas about how the next generation of Chinese Americans should regard their cultural inheritance. Chin encourages not a reversion to the past, but rather a recognition of how ancient traditions continue to impact everyday life. As his dream becomes more vivid, Donald begins, for example, to view his everyday surroundings in a new light: "Donald Duk lives all his life at the same Chinatown address on Grant, walks by these shops every day, eats in most of the restaurants in the course of a year, yet doesn't remember seeing all the Kwan Kung statues and posters in the shrines everywhere." Chin's historical project is thus meant as a negotiation between past and present, so that

the past informs the present as a source of connection and community.

As his work in *Donald Duk* suggests, Chin views writing as a form of social education, and he does not shy away from the jarring or explosive nature of this confrontation. As he writes in "Come All Ye Asian Writers," "We are born to fight to maintain our personal integrity. All art is martial art. Writing is fighting." In creating a hero such as Donald, one with a reluctant relationship to his cultural past, Chin is able to show this struggle as being waged both within individuals, and against a larger community inclined to put forth demeaning and stereotypical representations of Asian culture. Donald's triumph in the novel is that he is no longer plagued by self-hate and comes to see his Chinese identity as a source of pride, not shame.

Discussion Questions

1. *Donald Duk* could perhaps be considered a bildungsroman, a story of education and growth. What are the most important lessons that Donald learns? What evidence does the novel provide of his newfound maturity?

2. Donald begins the novel preoccupied with white movie stars, and especially Fred Astaire, whom he idolizes. Why does the author switch Donald's identifications, so that they begin to focus more on Chinese models of masculinity rather than on white icons?

3. The railroad is a recurring trope in Frank Chin's novels and plays, and his work often spotlights that Chinese men were integral to the creation of this national system of transportation. After learning of his ancestors' participation in this project, what alterations occur in Donald's perceptions of them?

4. One of the confusing aspects of Chin's novel is that he has criticized American popular culture for portraying Asians as stereotypical figures of menace, passivity, or stupidity, and yet he names his hero Donald Duk, like the famous Disney icon. How does Donald learn to differentiate himself from the cartoon duck? How is this effort related to his larger project of learning the difference between stereotypical images and realistic representations?

5. Donald is initially a cynical and dismissive adolescent, although that perspective shifts considerably throughout the novel. How would you compare Donald's story to other coming-of-age tales that feature bitter young men, such as J. D. Salinger's *Catcher in the Rye?*

—*Suzanne Leonard*

REFERENCES

King-Kok Cheung, "Of Mice and Men: Reconstructing Chinese American Masculinity," in *Other Sisterhoods: Literary Theory and U.S. Women of Color,* edited by Sandra Kumamoto Stanley (Urbana: University of Illinois Press, 1998);

Patricia Chu, "Tripmaster Monkey, Frank Chin, and the Chinese Heroic Tradition," *Arizona Quarterly,* 53, no. 3 (1997): 117–139;

Robert Murray Davis, "Frank Chin: An Interview with Robert Murray Davis," *Amerasia,* 14, no. 2 (1988): 81–95;

Jinqi Ling, "Identity Crisis and Gender Politics: Reappropriating Asian American Masculinity," in *An Interethnic Companion to Asian American Literature,* edited by Cheung (New York: Cambridge University Press, 1997), pp. 312–337.

Kate Chopin
(February 8, 1851 – August 22, 1904)

༒

THE AWAKENING
(Chicago & New York: Herbert S. Stone, 1899)

EDNA PONTELLIER

Edna Pontellier is the "American woman" whose defiance of social conventions in Kate Chopin's second novel, *The Awakening,* brought infamy and later fame to her creator. Although Chopin came from St. Louis, Missouri, she established herself as a leading Louisiana local colorist for her descriptions of the Creoles and Acadians (Cajuns) among whom she resided when she moved to Oscar Chopin's home in New Orleans and later Natchitoches Parish, Louisiana.

The Awakening, originally titled "A Solitary Soul," marked a significant departure from Chopin's early work. While Chopin's first novel, *At Fault* (1890), and some of her stories betray a somber edge and anticipate elements of her second novel, they nonetheless largely conform to nineteenth-century American mores. In *The Awakening* Chopin turns away from tradition to create a female character modeled after the New Woman emerging at the end of the nineteenth century and motivated by instincts as described by Charles Darwin in *The Descent of Man* (1871). Although Edna never fully awakens, her failed quest for sexual and artistic liberation highlights the ways the male-dominated culture of the South could and did turn women into sleeping beauties.

Edna's transformation begins at a resort on Grand Isle off the coast of Louisiana to which she, her husband, Léonce, and their two young sons have traveled to escape the heat and pestilence of New Orleans. The reserved woman of Mississippi and Kentucky Presbyterian roots is an outsider among the French Catholic Creoles, whose relaxed relationships and frank talk of sexuality initially shock Edna. She nonetheless becomes close friends with the maternal Adèle Ratignolle, who encourages the younger woman to reassess her childhood, which had been dominated by her Bible-thumping but toddy-drinking father.

Although Adèle prompts Edna's ruminations on her past, it is Robert, the son of Madame Lebrun, the proprietor of the resort, who entices Edna away from the prescribed female role she has assumed. Despite Adèle's warning that Edna "is not one of us" and might misunderstand his attentions, Robert engages in a flirtation that quickly becomes an infatuation dictating Edna's subsequent choices and actions in the novel. During a late-night swim he has orchestrated, Edna imagines herself reborn and begins a physical, spiritual, and psychological journey that takes her from the house she shares with her husband in New Orleans and into an affair with a notorious rake, Alcée Arobin. Robert, however, remains an obsession for Edna, even after he deliberately removes himself from her sphere.

Edna's infatuation with Robert as well as her burgeoning artistic aspirations are fueled by the malcontent of the novel, the pianist Mademoiselle

Reisz, whose music at Grande Isle and later in New Orleans produces an emotional tempest in Edna. The recipient of letters from Robert, Mademoiselle Reisz is a conduit through which Edna remains connected to her beloved. At the same time she regards the pianist as the representative female artist who, in Mademoiselle Reisz's own words, "must possess the courageous soul" to reject the traditional roles of women. Edna's assessment does not seem reliable, for Chopin repeatedly emphasizes the diminutive stature and, perhaps, status of the pianist. At the dinner that supposedly marks Edna's final break from her old life, Mademoiselle Reisz must be "elevated upon cushions, as small children are." Her reference to Edna as *reine* (queen) suggests that she, no less than Edna, clings to fairy tales that, far from fostering independence and individuality in women, only perpetuate an unrealistic sense of themselves and the world around them.

With Lebrun's return to New Orleans, Edna imagines her fairy tale is nearly complete as she plans her life with her lover. Reality intrudes when Adèle, in labor with her fourth child, asks Edna to come to her. Throughout the novel Edna has denied the human frailty of herself and others and has distanced herself from her own children, so she naturally regards Adèle's labor as "torture"; however, she cannot drown out Adèle's admonition to "think of the children." Moreover, when she returns to her cottage to find Robert's note announcing his departure "because I love you," Edna realizes that he is not the prince she had imagined. Unable to transcend the world in which she lives or to integrate her conflicting roles and desires, she returns to the sea from which she emerged at the beginning of the novel. Chopin leaves Edna adrift with her memories, but the image of an injured bird plummeting into the gulf suggests that she, too, will soon sink into oblivion.

Edna's implied death was not sufficient for critics of the novel, who admired the skill with which Chopin crafted her work but felt the author was too kind to a character who so flagrantly violated the moral code of her time. Chopin's response—"I never dreamed of Mrs. Pontellier making such a mess of things and working out her own damnation as she did"—failed to redeem the author in the estimation of the literary establishment of the time. Only with the rise of feminism in the 1970s did the novel begin to acquire critical acclaim; today it is the most widely read and discussed of Chopin's works.

The vehemence with which critics attacked *The Awakening* is surprising, because the subject of the novel was not unusual. Works by other women writers, such as Charlotte Perkins Gilman's "The Yellow Wallpaper," anticipate Chopin's assault in *The Awakening* on the paternalistic social order. Henrik Ibsen's *Hedda Gabler* and Gustave Flaubert's *Emma Bovary* are kindred souls to Edna. Chopin, however, identified a different French influence, Guy de Maupassant, whom she felt "had escaped from tradition and authority." In Maupassant, she found a writer willing to suspend moral judgment while he created shocking characters in disturbing circumstances.

Discussion Questions

1. Critics are divided in their opinions regarding Edna's efforts to become a visual artist. Some see her endeavors as indicating real artistic growth. Others think Edna lacks the "courageous soul" and never develops as an artist. Which position do you think is the stronger? To support your argument, consider the details with which Chopin describes Edna's separate attempts to draw or paint as well as the response of other characters to her work.

2. The image of birth informs much of Chopin's novel. How does Edna's progression from beginning to end parallel the gestation and birth of a child? Do you agree with critics who, like Edna herself, think she has truly been reborn? Why or why not? If she is reborn, what is she born into?

3. A refrain that plays through the text is the line Robert Lebrun sang to Edna: "*Si tu savais.*" What does the phrase mean? Why does Edna become upset with Victor Lebrun when he sings it and an added line at Edna's dinner party? What significance do the lyrics have for the work as a whole?

4. In recent years critics have focused on the interaction (or lack thereof) between the races in *The Awakening*. How does Edna respond to people of color in the text? How do the interactions reflect on Edna's supposed evolution? Consider especially the role of the quadroon who watches over the Pontellier boys.

—*Karen Roop*

✍

"DÉSIRÉE'S BABY"

Collected in *Bayou Folk* (Boston & New York: Houghton, Mifflin, 1894).

DÉSIRÉE

Désirée is the mother of an infant whose unexpected and undesired African features generate the central conflict of Kate Chopin's story "Désirée's Baby." An enigma herself, Désirée enters the tale as a toddler abandoned at the Valmondé plantation in Louisiana. The childless Monsieur and Madame Valmondé take in the girl and rear her as their own daughter, whom Madame Valmondé decides "beneficent Providence" sent them. Désirée becomes a "beautiful and gentle, affectionate and sincere" woman, the embodiment of traits that temporarily work their magic on Armand Aubigny, the young owner of the neighboring plantation L'Abri. Aubigny falls in love "as if struck by a pistol shot" and weds the young woman. Although their marriage and the birth of their son briefly temper Aubigny's passion and violence, the reform is short-lived, for as African traits manifest themselves in the infant, Aubigny realizes his son is part black and banishes both his wife and child. Désirée exits the story as mysteriously as she entered it, trudging through rough grass and weeds as she carries her baby toward the bayou.

First published in *Vogue*, "Désirée's Baby" was later included in the 1894 collection *Bayou Folk*. A child of slaveholders, defender of the Confederacy as a teenager, and wife of the son of a former Louisiana slaveholder, Chopin seems an unlikely critic of racism; at times her depiction of African Americans is problematic. In her portrayal of Désirée, however, she resembles her fellow Louisiana writer and critic of Southern racism, George Washington Cable. At the same time, Chopin recognized that "a commonplace theme" must be "handled artistically or with originality" if a story is to succeed. Unlike many of the other stories in *Bayou Folk*, "Désirée's Baby" neither conforms to formulas of popular Southern fiction nor remains rooted in the realism by which Chopin earned her fame. Although Lydia Maria Child's literary creation, the "tragic mulatta," influenced Chopin's story, Désirée is never limited to this type. Instead,

she and her baby assume an allegorical significance through their obvious ties to the foundlings and changelings of fairy tales. Naming the character Désirée, which means "desire," transforms the story's main character into an abstraction akin to Nathaniel Hawthorne's character Faith in "Young Goodman Brown," while the nameless infant is distinguished solely by the fact that his African features become increasingly apparent as he grows. Mother and son are the means by which Chopin exposes the hypocritical racial and sexual division of antebellum Louisiana.

As the baby matures, the failure of the South to evolve becomes increasingly apparent. People Désirée have rarely seen come to stare at the baby. Madame Valmondé, who never wavers in her love for Désirée and the infant, cannot hide her shock at the changes in the child's appearance. Even Désirée momentarily becomes speechless when she finally sees that her child resembles the mulatto boy fanning him. Moreover, Aubigny is compelled to face anew aspects of his own parentage that he has repressed his entire life. As he attempts to exorcize the memory of Désirée and the child by burning their belongings, he pauses to read a letter written by his mother to his father that reveals a surprising source of the black blood running through the veins of Désirée's baby: Aubigny's mother, who died in Paris when he was eight and wrote of her gratitude that he would never know his mother was of "the race . . . cursed with the brand of slavery." Chopin's text never makes clear whether Aubigny knew of the letter and his African heritage all along, but scholars have speculated that he remembers the dark features of his mother. Désirée's race remains a mystery.

The ambiguity, typical of Chopin's fiction, contributes to the continued appeal of the story for a modern audience. Ultimately, neither Désirée nor Aubigny escapes the constraints of society. Although Désirée is a sympathetic character, she is naive and incapable of defining herself apart from her husband. She cannot heed Madame Valmondé's call: "Come home to Valmondé; back to your mother who loves you." Instead, she simply vanishes and thus ensures that she will always be an "idol" rather than a fully developed person. Aubigny, ostensibly in a position of power, must deny a large part of who he is. By concentrating the African blood in the white male whose name is "one of the oldest and proudest in Louisiana," Chopin introduces a Darwinian irony to the theme of miscegenation.

Discussion Questions

1. The first word Monsieur Valmondé hears from Désirée is "Dada." Besides defining Monsieur Valmondé's role in the story, what significance does the utterance have? How does it relate to the theme(s) of the story?

2. La Blanche is only mentioned a few times in the story, but she has a significant parallel to Désirée, especially when the young mother realizes her infant is part black. What is La Blanche's role? Consider especially the symbolism inherent in her name.

3. Madame Valmonde believes "Providence" has sent Désirée to her and her husband. What does this detail suggest about Madame Valmonde's character? What other religious suggestions are embedded in the story? Why has Chopin included them?

4. A key issue regarding the story is whether or not Armand Aubigny knows before he reads his mother's letter that his mother was part black. What does the evidence in the story suggest? What effect does his knowledge, or at least remembrance of the fact, have on your interpretation of the story? How does the story change if Aubigny only learns of his mother's race through his reading of the letter at the end?

5. *Abri* means shelter or refuge. Why has Kate Chopin named Aubigny's plantation L'Abri? How is it a shelter? In your response, consider the details in Chopin's description of L'Abri.

—Karen Roop

REFERENCES

Kate Chopin, *The Awakening: Complete, Authoritative Text with Biographical, Historical, and Cultural Contexts, Critical History, and Essays from Contemporary Critical Perspectives*, edited by Nancy A. Walker (Boston & New York: Bedford/St. Martin's Press, 2000);

Joyce Dyer, *The Awakening: A Novel of Beginnings* (New York: Twayne / Toronto: Macmillan / New York: Macmillan, 1993);

Anna Shannon Elfenbein, *Women on the Color Line: Evolving Stereotypes and the Writings of George Washington Cable, Grace King, Kate Chopin* (Charlottesville: University Press of Virginia, 1989);

Emily Toth, *Unveiling Kate Chopin* (Jackson: University Press of Mississippi, 1999);

Nancy A. Walker, *Kate Chopin: A Literary Life* (Houndmills, U.K. & New York: Palgrave, 2001).

Louis Chu

(October 1, 1915 – February 27, 1970)

EAT A BOWL OF TEA

(New York: Stuart, 1961)

WANG BEN LOY

Wang Ben Loy is the male protagonist in Louis Chu's 1961 novel *Eat a Bowl of Tea*. Ben Loy's personal circumstances are similar to what is known of Chu's own life. Like his creator, Ben Loy was born in China, comes to maturity largely among the Chinese immigrant community in New York, and marries a woman from China with no previous experience in America. If Ben Loy is a self-portrait, however, it is remarkable that he is unidealized. Even though he is the victim of his wife's infidelity, the reader is given to understand why Mei Oi, his bride brought from China, might have found marriage to Ben Loy frustrating. His sexual impotence is a physiological malady, but it also reflects his psychological disorientation, the way his idea of masculinity simply cannot accommodate marriage. Ben Loy, though his identity is deeply rooted in his Chinese immigrant community, is a "rogue male" (one who cannot be assimilated into a domestic situation), such as James Fenimore Cooper's Natty Bumppo, Mark Twain's Huckleberry Finn, and Ernest Hemingway's Nick Adams.

Ben Loy has lived without a wife for his entire adulthood but is young enough (in his early thirties) to be seen as a viable candidate for starting a family. When he meets the bride his father has chosen for him, Mei Oi, at the New York airport, he is dazzled by her beauty. But his life is so centered on the male-oriented world of the "bachelor society" of New York's Chinatown—its gambling, business dealing, and macho posturing—that he finds it hard to pay attention to his new bride in the way that her romantic expectations, as well as her genuine need for personal relationships, require. Ben Loy has been used to consorting with prostitutes.

When Ben Loy finds out about his wife's adultery, he is outraged. Yet, he also remains curiously passive as the actual revenge against his wife's lover, Ah Son, is taken by his father and his father-in-law. What on the one hand is a kind of imperviousness in Ben Loy also has, as its obverse complement, a mental toughness that assists him in enduring difficult situations in life. Ben Loy realizes that he cannot compel his wife's loyalty merely by exerting discipline. Ben Loy semiconsciously undertakes the difficult feat of trying to transfer the sense of community and camaraderie he has felt with his male social network to his relationship with Mei Oi. He makes the sacrifice of leaving the New York area, where he has lived all the time he has been in America, and moves with Mei Oi to San Francisco, where they can make a new beginning.

Ben Loy makes a greater sacrifice, though, in accepting Mei Oi's son as his own, even though the boy was most likely fathered by Ah Son. He does so, to a degree, out of repentance for his earlier neglect. The fact that he assumes the burden of a child for which he was not responsible is also a sign of his ability to exercise authority. He becomes his own man, as he is able to recenter his emotional energies away from the senior men in his social circle and toward his wife. The folk-medical, herbal remedy, the bowl of tea denoted by the title, cures Ben Loy's impotence, meaning that the solution to Ben Loy's problem has come from his own community, his own tradition. Yet, at this moment he becomes most "American," as the head of his own nuclear family, detached from a larger social network that he first felt to be sustaining. His marital problems make him realize that the network was, in part, paralytic for him. By the end of the book, he is, paradoxically, less self-centered and more self-assertive.

Ben Loy is an ordinary man, possessed of no special gifts. But in muddling and managing his way through difficult human situations, he earns the reader's respect. Chu created a Chinese male character able to operate in a more "realistic" or "naturalistic" way in fiction, able to be a part of the fictional terrain and not an eccentric exception, such as Earl Der Biggers's Charlie Chan. Later depictions of Chinese American men, in novels written by both men and women (Gus Lee and Maxine Hong Kingston are two examples), owe a considerable amount to Ben Loy's example.

Discussion Questions

1. Is Wang Ben Loy's sense of his masculinity typically American, typically Chinese, or does it stem from his own personality? How much of the problems Ben Loy has in his marriage to Mei Oi stem from his innate personality, and how much from cultural factors?

2. Because of restrictive immigration policies, Chinese men living in the United States were compelled to live in a "bachelor society." What are the keystones of this society as it is depicted in the novel? What are its good and bad points? Does Chu show the Chinese men as primarily happy or unhappy in their bachelor situation? What is the function of gambling in promoting social ties among the male characters?

3. What symbolic role does Ben Loy's impotence play in the novel? What does its folk-medical cure say about the presence of traditional Chinese culture in the world of the characters?

4. Does the geographical move to the West Coast give the married couple a new start, or does it stem from the adjustments in attitude and expectations that both Ben Loy and Mei Oi have made in their marriage?

—*Nicholas Birns*

REFERENCES

Ruth Y. Hsiao, "Facing the Incurable: Patriarchy in *Eat a Bowl of Tea*," in *Reading the Literatures of Asian America,* edited by Shirley Geok-lin Lim and Amy Ling (Philadelphia: Temple University Press, 1992), pp. 151–162;

Shu-yan Li, "Otherness and Transformation in *Eat a Bowl of Tea* and *Crossings*," *International Migration Review,* 26, no. 4 (1992): 94–110;

Jinqi Ling, "Reading for Historical Specificities: Gender Negotiations in Louis Chu's *Eat a Bowl of Tea*," *MELUS,* 20, no. 1 (1995): 35–51;

Alison Taufer, "Memory and Desire: The Search for Community in Louis Chu's *Eat a Bowl of Tea* and Bienvenido Santos' *The Scent of Apples*," *Asian America: Journal of Culture and the Arts,* 2 (1993): 64–81.

Walter Van Tilburg Clark
(August 3, 1909 – November 10, 1971)

ꞏꞏꞏ

THE OX-BOW INCIDENT
(New York: Random House, 1940)

ARTHUR DAVIES

Arthur Davies runs a general store in Bridger's Wells, Nevada, the setting for Walter Van Tilburg Clark's Western novel *The Ox-Bow Incident*. An elderly, unassuming man, Davies distinguishes himself in the novel primarily for two reasons: he is the most convincing voice of opposition to the vigilante hanging that is to occur; and his remorseful reflection after the hanging helps provide the essential dialogue and context for insight into the significant themes of the novel. Clark creates Davies's role in the novel as an effective means to depart from the classic Western formula. In this novel no magnanimous hero overcomes evil by his physical prowess to restore order and provide justice. Major Tetley subverts the formula. He assumes the role of hero, but in the end his actions only contribute to chaos and guilt. The citizens of Bridger's Wells are left to their limited imaginations concerning law and order. The tension between Davies and Tetley magnifies and universalizes the conflicts of the novel, demonstrating the important themes the author intends.

Readers and critics often notice parallels in the novel embodied by Major Tetley to Adolf Hitler and Nazism: evil tyrants will have their way in the world until good people are courageous enough to oppose them, with violence, if necessary. Clark did not deny a parallel, but he had something closer to home in mind. In an afterword to the novel, first published in the 1960 New American Library edition, historian Walter Prescott Webb quotes Clark concerning his intentions: "It was a kind of American Naziism that I was talking about. . . . what I was most afraid of was not the German Nazis, . . . but that ever-present element in any society which can always be led to act the same way, to use authoritarian methods to oppose authoritarian methods. . . . It can happen here. It has happened here."

The "authoritarian methods" of the novel include Tetley's impelling a vigilante rush to judgment by haphazardly deputizing the participants because the law is said to be too slow. This posturing gives tacit permission to citizens to act on their incomplete notions of justice. Eventually, a so-called democratic process occurs in which a majority vote determines that the hanging is justifiable, despite good reasons to wait for absolute proof. Davies argues against these processes before finally submitting to the vote at last resort (only he and four others finally vote against the hanging). His voice of reason resists the irrational attitudes of the others who spuriously cling to circumstantial evidence. The more Davies argues that a calm, patient, reasoned, and legal approach should be followed to find justice, the more his fellow citizens turn on him in anger and insult. Clark's novel seems to suggest that it is only when the law is used appropriately by rational citizens that the pack mentality driven by fear and greed may be kept in check.

Davies's protests against forming the vigilante posse and against the hanging anticipate his deeply felt remorse demonstrated after the hanging. In the concluding chapter of Clark's five-act tragedy, Davies agonizes over his involvement and lack of effectiveness in preventing the miscarriage of justice. In Clark's rough Western world, most other participants crudely acknowledge their mistake, but in some kind of misplaced stoicism, they seem to want to get on with life, putting the unfortunate deed behind them. But Davies's conscience is not so easily subdued. Though he has less to feel guilty about than anyone else in the novel, he voices the profoundest guilt. In his introspection, he confesses that he is guilty of a "sin of omission" because he failed to do all that he possibly could to prevent the hangings. The participant-narrator, Art Croft, argues that "We're all to blame, and nobody's to blame. It just happened." This view sharply contrasts with that of Davies, who says he knew the men were innocent and that he lacked the courage to use a gun to stand up to Tetley, who leads the hanging. Davies had hoped someone else would finally resist Tetley. By attributing primary blame to Tetley for the incident, however, each participant can potentially alleviate himself of his individual responsibility.

Davies's anxiety expressed in the last chapter of the novel must also be understood in light of the suicide of Tetley's son, Gerald. Gerald says that man is the "worst animal," who hides weakness and evil desires within the pack. He believes humans hunt their "own kind" because of a perverse desire for power. Eventually, he says that it is "better to kill yourself than to kill somebody else." Young Tetley's pessimistic view of humanity contrasts with Croft's view that some things cannot be helped. Davies, however, tries to hold a more enlightened view than either of these positions. He believes in the processes of law and that such processes, when followed appropriately, are the best means for civilizing the unruly nature of humanity and for guaranteeing justice.

Clark's use of Davies's confession in chapter 5 significantly alters the typical Western formula in which a hero often does the necessary dirty work on behalf of admiring citizens. In *The Ox-Bow Incident* there are no heroes in the formulaic sense, and Davies's claims remind readers that the dirty work of finding true justice in a democracy really is the business of each citizen but that citizens dare not act foolishly, giving in to rash desires for blood without full consideration of all possible facts. Though the bitter view of humanity offered by Gerald and the indifferent view of society voiced by Croft may be unsatisfactory, readers must also recognize the emotional cost that accompanies Davies's view. His belief in fairness and equal justice under the law requires emotional investment. The primary lasting message of Clark's novel, then, would thus seem to be that justice is not cheap, and that individuals standing up for what is right is the essence of morality, regardless of the legality, regardless of the outcome.

Discussion Questions

1. Initially, the preacher, Osgood, also speaks against forming the vigilante posse. Why is ridicule directed toward Osgood while Davies's arguments are more respectfully received?

2. Davies claims to be guilty of a sin of omission. How are sins of omission related to sins of commission? Are sins of omission really as problematic as Davies claims?

3. Many of the characters in the novel have secrets that are hinted at and/or only partially revealed throughout the story. Compare and contrast the interior lives of several other characters with that of Davies. How do the others live with their secrets, and where does the novel provide glimpses of their truest, innermost feelings?

—*Kenneth Hada*

MAJOR TETLEY

Major Tetley is the primary ringleader of the hanging in Walter Van Tilburg Clark's *The Ox-Bow Incident*. His first name is not given. Others in the town and the posse simply refer to him as Tetley, or Major Tetley, suggesting his distance from them. He is referred to as the second "biggest man in the valley," arriving in the West "the year after the Civil War." He is reclusive, living in a Southern-style mansion, "quiet and fenced away." Others respect his authority but feel uncomfortable in his presence. More than once he is grudgingly referred to as "God-Almighty-Tetley." The narrator of the novel, Art Croft, says of Tetley: "Irony was the constant expression of [his] eyes, dark and maliciously ardent under his thick black eyebrows." Tetley's manners and methods demand respect but keep him suspiciously at an emotional distance from his neighbors. Nonetheless, he assumes command of the hastily formed posse, directs the criminal investigation, and conducts the hanging procedure.

Concerning the investigation and hanging, Tetley posits himself to be just and fair, allowing for things to be done "regular" in accordance with what a judge would approve. He prides himself on his ability to cross-examine the three accused men. In a methodological manner, he considers the defendants' claims before dismissing each one based on his understanding of contrary evidence. His matter-of-fact method frustrates the defendants and even irks the members of the posse who had been eager to hang the men. Some feel that his manner is evil, believing that he is merely toying with the accused men facing death. Nonetheless, he successfully argues that as leader of the posse he is doing what the community desires and that his manner protects them all. The dialogue in the trial scene suggests that in Tetley's direction of due process and hanging, neither the end nor the means is justifiable. One's manner, as well as one's actions, may be evil, despite surface appearances.

Among Tetley's several flaws, the most grievous is his harsh relationship with his son, Gerald. He forces Gerald not only to ride with the posse but also to actively participate in the details of executing the men. Whenever Gerald falters, Tetley is quick to insult his son in front of the other men. He futilely attempts to make his son into a masculine authority figure and to eradicate what he believes to be Gerald's weak, feminine traits. Gerald's suicide reveals the extent to which Tetley has sacrificed his son to protect his own public image. Devastated, Tetley also kills himself, suggesting that his public demeanor of strength belied a desperation deep within. His public posturing, effective for controlling the others who also shared his limited view of masculine authority in the social pecking order, finally is recognized as a sham: Gerald, who knew him best, refused to live under the tyranny of his father's abuse and maniacal attempts to control others under the pretense of honor and justice.

In the final message of the novel, Tetley's failure undermines the representative notion of a self-made man who overcomes his enemies by masculine prowess and who keeps his neighbors at a distance. His character, and its ultimate demise, suggests the limits of rugged American individualism and the desperate need for community. A residual Southern character from the Civil War era, Tetley wants to transplant his hierarchical views onto the new Western frontier. Yet, Clark's vision seems to suggest that such days are over, and the need for true community and a true understanding of human identity is more important than playing soldier. Tetley's character represents a false dichotomy, pitting a skewed view of masculinity against anything that does not fit the prototype, such as women, minorities, and men who are physically weaker or who lack the major's seeming taste for blood. Tetley erroneously considers willfulness to be virtue, and he refuses to acknowledge fully the rights of others. He mistakes neighbors for subordinates and is apparently blind to the extent of his hubris, all the while suppressing his self-destructive inclinations or transferring them onto other weaker victims—like the three men unjustly hanged or his son.

Tetley must be considered alongside Arthur Davies, his chief opposition in the process of trying and hanging the three innocent men. Tetley is cool and calculating while Davies is emotional. Both men appeal to their fellow riders as a jury, each trying to convince the others of the rightness of his position. Finally, in a gesture toward democracy, Tetley allows a majority vote, but as he rightly predicted, most of the riders are too intimidated to vote against him, despite their growing uncertainty about the ugly business before them.

Tetley's character is in line with other bully characters in American literature who keep family and neighbors in submission. Faulkner's short story "Barn Burning" depicts a criminal father, Abner Snopes, who justifies his activities by blaming others. Both Faulkner and Clark suggest that tragedy results when willful men coerce others. These stories recognize the malignant desperation hiding within these characters, who parade their secret inadequacies before others masked as honor and heroism, which they lack. However, Clark's novel, in particular, argues that Tetley obtains his power because others yield to him, refusing to oppose his tyranny. Perhaps such willful acquiescence suggests that others riding with Tetley may also secretly fear their own inner deficiencies, preferring that someone like Tetley act on their behalf.

Discussion Questions

1. Tetley uses a rational, calm, logical, democratic due process to determine the apparent guilt of the accused. Contrast this approach with the standard Western genre of gunslinging action. Why does Clark depict violence and injustice in this manner?

2. Tetley's logical approach, on the surface, is similar to the approach of Davies, his primary opposing character. Trace the arguments and actions of both Tetley and Davies to determine their similarities and subtle differences. Why is Tetley's view acceptable to the men, especially in light of Davies's logical persistence?

3. Captain Ahab in *Moby-Dick* and Sargent Croft in *The Naked and the Dead* are examples of obsessive strong-willed characters who drove others and themselves to devastating consequences. Compare and contrast Tetley with either of these characters.

—Kenneth Hada

REFERENCES

Kenneth Anderson, "Character Portrayal in *The Ox-Bow Incident*," *Western American Literature*, 4 (1970): 287–298;

Anderson, "Form in Walter Van Tilburg Clark's *The Ox-Bow Incident*," *Western Review: A Journal of the Humanities*, 6, no. 1 (1969): 19–25;

Barclay W. Bates, "Clark's Man for All Seasons: The Achievement of Wholeness in *The Ox-Bow Incident*," *Western American Literature*, 3 (1968): 37–49;

Jackson J. Benson, *The Ox-Bow Man: A Biography of Walter Van Tilburg Clark* (Reno: University of Nevada Press, 2004);

Frederic Carpenter, "The West of Walter Van Tilburg Clark," *College English*, 13 (February 1952): 243–248;

Walter Van Tilburg Clark, *The Ox-Bow Incident*, with an afterword by Walter Prescott Webb (New York: New American Library, 1960);

Richard Etulain, "Walter Van Tilburg Clark: A Bibliography," *South Dakota Review*, 3 (Autumn 1965): 73–77;

A. H. Walle, "Walter Van Tilburg Clark's *Ox-Bow Incident:* Prototype for the Antiheroic Western," *Platte Valley Review*, 23 (Winter 1995): 50–67;

Max Westbrook, *Walter Van Tilburg Clark* (New York: Twayne, 1969).

Evan S. Connell

(August 17, 1924 –   )

《◎

MRS. BRIDGE

(New York: Viking, 1959); *Mr. Bridge* (New York: Knopf, 1969)

INDIA BRIDGE

India Bridge is the title character of Evan S. Connell's first novel, *Mrs. Bridge,* and also a principal character in his subsequent work *Mr. Bridge.* Both novels are set in suburban Kansas City, beginning in the 1930s. They are written in a third-person narrative form, observing incidents in their marriage—in some cases the same events—from the perspectives of each title character. Both novels begin with the title character reflecting on their marriage and end near the time of Walter's death. For India the marriage and her values around that are the driving force of her life. This is true whether she is living out her assigned role without question or, occasionally, having a slight question or an impulse of her own that is not defined by the role as she understands it.

Mrs. Bridge begins "Her first name was India—she was never able to get used to it." In some ways the insecurity and the questions of identity posed to her by this exotic name parallel those of her later life. India is never able to enthusiastically embrace her life, though she believes herself to be happy. She experiences moments of questioning and insight but rarely pursues or acts upon them. Her passivity is reinforced when her few early efforts to exert her own modest needs are unsuccessful in achieving the desired outcome. A poignant scene in the opening episode describes her becoming aware of her own physical desire, after she and her husband have been married for some time and his desire has become less urgent: "She turned to him then, contentedly, expectantly, and secure. However nothing else happened, and in a few minutes he had gone to sleep."

This incident hints at possibilities that, after having been aroused, are squelched and then pushed into a remote corner of her awareness. Such repression occurs not only in this realm but in all areas of her life. India takes her life as it is for granted. Her values are simple and deal with surfaces. Referring to her three children, "She hoped that when they were spoken of it would be in connection with their nice manners, their pleasant dispositions, and their cleanliness, for these were qualities she valued above all others." The events and actions that break through these surfaces upset her. She does not know how to deal with them or grow from them. The distance between her and her children develops based on her use of these superficial values, rather than any deeper moral or ethical ones, to push them toward how they should be. When her son, Douglas, uses the guest towels to dry his hands, for example, India takes him to task, not understanding how he would do such a thing: "Nobody touched them because they looked too nice; guests always did as she herself did in their homes—she would dry her hands on a piece of Kleenex."

Nonconformists outside the family also cause her discomfort. The Van Metres are an older couple with whom she and Walter occasionally dine. They "were given to reading literary magazines no one had ever heard of and attending such things as the opera, whenever a company stopped in Kansas City." Her friend and fellow women's club member, Grace Barron, is in the same age and socioeconomic group as India but has different worldviews. Grace questions her life and values. India does not understand her and cannot grasp what Grace means when she asks, in expressing her dissatisfaction with her limited experience of the world and other people, "Are we right? Do we believe the right things?" Once, when shopping together, they find tiny silver bells revolving around a candlestick. "I feel like those bells," says Grace. "Why are they turning around, India? Why? Because the candle has been lighted. What I want to say is—oh, I don't know. It's just that the orbit is so small." Grace's observations awaken vague thoughts in India, but her tentative efforts at including some of these thoughts into her conversations with her husband are greeted dismissively or with affectionate amusement. Without support or other models, her efforts flounder and die.

The trip to Europe, promised by Walter when they are first together and finally realized twenty-five years later, is like the opening of a door for India. The dramatic change in scene and experiences allows her to enjoy and assert herself more freely. At the Louvre, Walter waits outside while she tours the museum. When she sees the statue *Winged Victory of Samothrace,* it reminds her of an acquaintance from home who was raped. The mood of the trip changes after that, and when she observes Walter looking at a window display of exotic lingerie she wonders: "Why had he stood there looking? What had he been thinking? His expression had been so serious. Were there things he had never told her about himself? Who was he, really? From all the recesses of her being came the questions, questions which had never occurred to her, and there on the foreign street she felt lost and forsaken, and with great longing she began to think of Kansas City."

Despite the fleeting insights of both Walter and India during their trip, when they return home, life resumes its old patterns. India struggles with the inevitable changes resulting from her children becoming adults and making choices that are not necessarily consistent with her vision. Carolyn marries a man who turns out to be abusive and comes and goes from her parents' home periodically. Douglas volunteers for the army as America moves closer to war. Then Walter dies unexpectedly of a heart attack while in the midst of dictating a memo regarding one of his law cases. Life goes on for India, though she finds herself looking at old photograph albums, even imposing those of the European trip on guests to her home. "But the pictures to which she returned most often for her own pleasure were those of her family: they evoke what she had known most intimately, and she had loved most profoundly."

Discussion Questions

1. At the end of the book, Mrs. Bridge is stuck in her car, waiting for someone to find her. Was this an effective way for Connell to end? How would you write the ending? Why?

2. India has a strong sense of proper behavior that seems frozen in time and not responsive to the changing times and the aging of her children. Using Douglas as an example, give examples of how his reaction to India, and his understanding of her, changes over time, ending with his letter to her after Walter's death.

3. The theme of individual conformity and emptiness was a common one in reference to the period and socioeconomic class outlined in *Mrs. Bridge.* However, it has also been addressed in other novels. One example is Virginia Woolf's *Mrs. Dalloway,* which describes an English woman in similar circumstances, who commits suicide. Compare Mrs. Dalloway to India Bridge, and also to Grace Barron. How is she similar to and different from each?

—Nancy Fowler

WALTER BRIDGE

Walter Bridge is the title character of Evan S. Connell's novel *Mr. Bridge,* and was also a principal character in his novel *Mrs. Bridge,* published ten years earlier. Both novels are written in a third-person-narrative form, observing incidents from the perspectives of the respective title characters. The first line of *Mr. Bridge* is "Often he thought: My life did not begin until I knew her," though the book hints that Walter does indeed have a life outside of his marriage.

Both *Mrs. Bridge* and *Mr. Bridge* are structured in a series of short episodes or anecdotes rather than in extended chapters. *Mr. Bridge* is principally set in suburban Kansas City, during the period extending from the 1930s to sometime after the beginning of World War II. Connell, according to the interview with Dan Tooker and Roger Hofheins, used his own family as the basis for the Bridges. "In the two Bridge books, how much came from my own parents, from friends and people I knew, and from my imagination, I really don't know. . . . In one sense they were easy books to write because I could remember what that kind of life was like. I had my own childhood perceptions to fall back on."

Though often cited as an exemplar of emotional repression and single-minded pursuit of financial success, Walter Bridge is much more. He has deep feelings for India, though he is unable to convey them. He considers "I love you" an inadequate statement of "how deeply he felt her presence while they were lying together during the night, as well as each morning when they awoke and in the evening when he came home." At work, a family photograph is strategically placed on his desk so that he can look at it in the course of the day. Walter is driven to succeed in order to provide for his family during the Depression. He is determined not to repeat the mistakes of his father, who has lost several thousand dollars on "penny gold mines, on the schemes of inventors, and similar speculations." He periodically reviews his own stock portfolio, spending "tranquil moments in the basement of the bank examining the handsomely engraved certificates (of reliable stocks in which he had invested) and contemplating the satisfaction they would give after his death."

Though he values financial security, Walter also appreciates the more intangible treasures of life. As he tells his son, Douglas, "no court of law has yet existed which is capable of restoring to us those properties which we consider genuinely valuable." He recounts the story of his grandfather, who was killed by a train robber when he fought back to keep his money. "What is important is that by attempt-ing to save some money he lost his life." Though he seeks to impress this lesson on Douglas, he refuses to give up his own money when he is similarly threatened by a robber: "'Don't be ridiculous,' said Mr. Bridge, and walked away.'" Stunned, the robber does not pursue him further.

Although Walter is removed from their everyday lives, his relationship with his children is a positive one, although how it is expressed varies among his two daughters, Ruth and Carolyn, and his son, Douglas. The family turns to him to resolve complicated or serious situations. When Douglas finds Walter's unloaded pistol under his father's mattress, for example, India panics; but Walter sits down with his son, explains the history of the gun and its proper use, and shows him where the bullets are kept. When Walter's daughter Ruth wants to move to New York, she comes to Walter for approval. He develops a plan that gives her a sum of money on which to live while she establishes herself, but with the agreement that if she has not done so by the time the funds are gone that she will come back to Kansas City. Ruth does not return.

The development of Walter's character over time is most apparent in his relationship with India. He recognizes her role in the accomplishment of his goals and her success in caring for her family: "He had provided the money and he had made decisions, but these things appeared insignificant when he compared them to what she had done." Over time, however, his love and devotion have become as much a habit as a reality. He comes to accept his inability to express his feelings—"After all he was an attorney, not a poet." But he also accepts the distance between him and his wife as normal. Her halfhearted attempts to express interests in his work are met with superficial responses. He accepts her lack of understanding because "he himself did not care what happened at the house during the day." On the surface all is well, but when India finally bursts out with desperate pleas to be assured of his feelings for her, he struggles to respond. Years later, when the two of them take a long-promised trip to Europe, he comes to recognize that although she generally seemed a pleasant backdrop to his life and even though he has real affection for her, in fact she may have been unhappy or at least discontented.

He realizes that his own life is not as much as he would have hoped for. He watches India sleeping, thinking of "her affectionate embrace, which was invariably the same, and he felt resentful, for something which rightfully belonged to every man had been denied him." The book ends on a poignant note with Walter reflecting on his life as he sings "Joy to the World" at a Christmas service. "If he had once known joy it must have been a long time ago. . . . He remembered enthusiasm, hope, and a kind of jubilation or exultation. Cheerfulness, yes, and joviality, and the brief gratification of sex. . . . But not joy. No that belonged to simpler minds."

Discussion Questions

1. *Mr. Bridge* is set in a particular location (Kansas City) and time (the 1930s and 1940s). That period in American history, following the Depression, is commonly considered as an era typified by emotional repression and the drive for financial success and stability. Do you think Walter is a good representative of these themes?

2. There are certain scenes that appear in both *Mr. Bridge* and *Mrs. Bridge*. Find one example. How would you describe the differences in terms of the characters' viewpoint? Does one account seem more accurate than the other?

—*Nancy Fowler*

REFERENCE

Dan Tooker and Roger Hofheins, *Fiction! Interviews with Northern California Novelists* (New York: Harcourt Brace Jovanovich, 1972), pp. 55–69.

Pat Conroy
(October 26, 1945 –   )

BEACH MUSIC
(New York: Nan A. Talese, 1995)

JACK MCCALL

Jack McCall is the narrator and protagonist of Pat Conroy's novel *Beach Music*. Like other of Conroy's works, *Beach Music* is based in large measure on the author's own personal experiences; McCall is the Conroy figure in the novel. Conroy wrote *Beach Music* following his divorce and during the fatal illness of his mother and the nervous breakdown of his brother; these family matters play a central role in the novel.

McCall also shares a significant characteristic with other Conroy protagonists: he is a survivor. A native of South Carolina, McCall, aged thirty-seven, is living in Rome at the opening of the novel with his young daughter, Leah, trying to forget the suicide of his wife and other unhappy events of his past. "I wanted to disappear out of my own life," he says. He has become a writer of travel and recipe books, explaining, "I like writing about strange cities and cuisines because it keeps me at arm's length from the subjects that are too close to me." A loving, gentle father, he is also determined to shield Leah from the craziness of his own experience. But the serious illness of his mother draws him back home—and into a chain of surprising events that force him to reexamine not only his own life and values but also those of the twentieth-century Western world. One of his biggest surprises is to learn that, contrary to what Thomas Wolfe, Conroy's favorite author, had claimed, one can go home again.

As the reader learns through a series of flashbacks, McCall grew up in the small and beautiful low-country town of Waterford with an alcoholic and abusive father, an anxious mother desperately seeking to conceal personal and family secrets, and four conflicted brothers, one of whom is schizophrenic and dangerously close to suicidal. As a youngster, Jack found a partial antidote to his unhappy family situation in an intimate friendship with five schoolmates: Capers Middleton, the spoiled son of a wealthy, aristocratic, old South Carolina family; Mike Hess, a Jewish friend who dreams of a career in theater and movies; Jordan Elliott, the adventurous, free-spirited son of a military officer; Ledare Ashley, who loves Jack but marries (and then divorces) Middleton; and Shyla Fox, the beautiful but deeply troubled girl next door, whom Jack marries. Chaos and the desire for order are the warring oppositions of Jack's existence from an early age; and what will become his lifelong quest for a stable, secure center in the midst of uncertainty and turmoil is symbolized at the opening of the novel by the music that the high-school friends dance to in an old condemned beach house that is collapsing under their feet and being washed out to sea by a heavy storm.

As a student at the University of South Carolina during the Vietnam War era, Jack becomes involved in antiwar efforts largely because of his love for Shyla, who with Capers is a leader of the protest movement. Capers, however, is actually an undercover agent working with the FBI to identify and arrest activists; and his testimony against Jack and Jordan lead to their expulsion from school—and an estrangement of the friends that continues for several years.

Jack's own personal disasters and his struggle for healing and wholeness are intensified by the experiences of his family and friends. His mother, Lucy, dying of leukemia, finally tells him the story of her past—which includes the murder of her abusive father by her mother, the subsequent suicide of her mother, Lucy's girlhood rape by the head of an orphanage, and her brother's avenging murder of the rapist. Jack's Jewish in-laws, who had never accepted his marriage to Shyla and who had bitterly opposed his being granted custody of Leah, reveal the terrible atrocities they had experienced during the Holocaust—atrocities that come to haunt Shyla and eventually drive her to kill herself by leaping off a bridge. Jordan, Jack's alter ego, rebels against his domineering father, aligns himself with a radical student group, and flees to Europe following his accidental killing of two people during an act of protest. Capers, who had betrayed Jack, Jordan, and his other friends because of their involvement in the antiwar movement, now, in the present of the novel, seeks their forgiveness and support for his candidacy for governor.

Several reviewers and critics have argued that the detailed stories of these other characters shift the focus away from McCall and thus destroy the overall unity of *Beach Music*. Such a reading, however, ignores the fact that McCall is representative of modern man, and his angst is historical and cultural as well as personal. Though McCall says, "I carried Waterford around with me the way a box turtle conveys its own bur-

densome shell," it becomes quickly evident that the source of his problem is far greater than a small South Carolina town. He suffers not merely from a dysfunctional family, the betrayal of friendship, and a failed marriage; he also carries in his collective memory the residual and disorienting effects of the Holocaust, the Vietnam War, and global terrorism. The fragmentation of the book, therefore, parallels the fragmentation of McCall's psyche.

Not all of the experiences of McCall, his family, and his friends, however, prove tragic. Interwoven with the sad, dark histories are incidents that dramatize the possibility of rebirth, reconciliation, and redemption. *Felix culpa*—the notion that good can evolve out of evil—is a familiar theme in all of Conroy's work; and that theme is evidenced by the various counternarratives in *Beach Music:* the story of "the Great Jew" Max Rusoff, who escapes pogroms in Europe to become a successful businessman and mayor of Waterford—and then ransoms a young Ruth Graubart (who becomes Shyla's mother) from certain death; the survival of Jack and his teenage friends after being lost at sea for fifteen days; Jack's "resurrection" after nearly being killed in the random shooting by terrorists at the Rome airport; the reconciliation of the childhood friends and their respective families at the end of the novel; Jordan's returning home to accept his just punishment—and then becoming a ministering priest for prison inmates; Jack's marriage to Ledare; and the promise held as possible throughout the novel that Leah—innocent, beautiful, precocious, and loving—might be able to escape the personal and cultural madness that claimed her mother's life. All such encouraging resolutions funnel into the recurring image of the young loggerhead turtles, a symbol of hopeful and ongoing life, breaking from their eggshells, marching across the sand, and swimming into the deep, nurturing ocean. And all of these stories parallel the heroic efforts of Jack McCall to transform the difficulties of his past into a happy present and a hopeful future.

Discussion Questions

1. All of Conroy's novels are "initiation" stories, describing the movement of the protagonist from innocence to experience. In relation to this theme,

trace the character development of Jack McCall from childhood to midlife.

2. Briefly describe what each of the following characters contribute to Jack McCall's understanding and insight: Shyla Fox, Leah McCall, Lucy McCall, Jordan Elliott, Mike Hess, Capers Middleton, and Ledare Ashley.

3. Discuss the relationship of Jack McCall's memory of personal experiences and his knowledge of global terrorism, including the Holocaust and the Vietnam War.

4. What is the symbolic relationship of the descriptions of the loggerhead turtles to Jack McCall's life and experience?

5. Identify a few of the literary allusions and parallels in the novel. How do these function in relation to the character development of Jack McCall?

—*Robert W. Hamblin*

୰୧

THE GREAT SANTINI
(Boston: Houghton Mifflin, 1976)

Meecham Family

The Meechams are a military family and the central characters in Pat Conroy's novel *The Great Santini*. The family comprises the father, Lieutenant Colonel W. P. "Bull" Meecham, a forty-one-year-old, highly decorated marine fighter pilot who commands a squadron of flyers stationed in South Carolina during the 1962 Cuban missile crisis; the mother, Lillian, a vain and beautiful southern woman of lower-class background but with aristocratic notions and ideals; and four children: Ben, a high-school senior; Mary Anne, an eleventh grader; and two younger children, Karen, a seventh grader, and Matthew, whose age seems to be around ten. The story, narrated from a third-person viewpoint, revolves around the ambivalent, strained relationship between the egotistical, domineering, alcoholic, and abusive Bull, modeled on Conroy's own father, and the rest of the family, particularly Ben. A key scene late in the novel describes the four children physically attacking their drunken father, who is beating and choking their mother.

Meecham's chauvinistic love of the United States and the Marine Corps and his reputation as an outstanding fighter pilot lead him to portray himself as "The Great Santini," a self-invented, larger-than-life hero who demands, and enforces, complete obedience and loyalty from his family. To his children, who live in constant anticipation and fear of his violent eruptions of temper, he is also known as "Godzilla" and "King Kong." Meecham commands his family the same way he does his unit of flyers: holding periodic inspections of their rooms, screaming when he is angry or displeased, dishing out psychological and physical abuse, and demanding perfection. "A Meecham," Bull explains, "gets the best grades, wins the most awards, excels in sports, is the most popular, and is always found near the top no matter what endeavor he undertakes." Bull's bravado, as well as his alcoholism and violence, actually veils a deep-seated fear of death that he, like every pilot, confronts each time he climbs into the cockpit of his jet fighter.

Lillian, who is four years younger than her husband, is an intelligent, sensitive, passionate Southerner who feels superior to the single-minded, arrogant, Chicago-born Bull. This regional difference becomes a major point of contention between the couple, as Bull engages in "inveterate assaults on the trellised escutcheons of the Old South" while Lillian defends her native region "as though it were a private garden deeded to her in a last heroic proclamation by the Confederate Congress." Lillian also disagrees with her husband about the marines. "The ego is bloated into something monstrous when a man decides to make the Marine Corps a career," she tells Ben. Lillian loves her husband but fears him, respects him as a military hero but loathes him as a parent. Contented and safe only when Bull is away on a tour of duty, she lives in denial when he is present. "What ever gave you the idea that your father hits me?" she says to Ben. "He never hits me." She clings to the illusion that one day she and Bull will live in a "dream house" in which "no one will be allowed to lose their temper or to be ugly or to make scenes."

With nearly the same resolve and ferocity with which he has engaged the country's enemies in aerial dogfights, Bull wages war with Lillian for the hearts and minds of their children. Ben, as the oldest child and a male, bears the brunt of this assault. "You got too much of your mother in you and not enough of Santini. Not enough man," Bull says. He worries that he has failed Ben by not being able "to drive the natural softness of Lillian Meecham out of him, to root out and expel the gentleness that was his wife's enduring legacy to her children." Such reasoning, to Bull's mind, provides ample justification for the physical abuse of his son, as for Bull's other expressions of tough, masculine love: his taking Ben to observe a drill sergeant's harsh treatment of a group of marine recruits; his encouraging Ben to get drunk on his eighteenth birthday; his disparaging of Ben's favorite teacher ("Any man who teaches a girls' course like English is bound to be a pansy"); his demanding that Ben avenge himself upon a basketball player who has flagrantly fouled him.

Despite the physical and verbal punishment he receives from Bull, Ben loves his father and desperately strives to please him. Mr. Dacus, the school principal, seeks to help Ben understand his ambivalent feelings. "There's something profound about boys and their fathers," Dacus says. "There's bad blood, it seems, almost always and yet there's this inevitable tenderness that neither of them recognizes when it's present. But over a lifetime it's hard to hate the seed that fathered you." Ben realizes the full truth of this statement only after his father's death in a plane crash, but it is a subtext throughout the entire novel. The hostility and hatred that Ben often feels for Bull, as in the violent encounter between the two after Ben beats Bull for the first time in a one-on-one basketball game, are somewhat ameliorated by the scenes, infrequent though they are, of togetherness and tenderness, as when Bull teams with Ben to whip the town bullies, or when Ben goes to look for his drunken father to bring him home, or when they cooperate to give Mary Anne a memorable prom. But the tempestuous relationship with his father is not the only source of Ben's unhappiness: another is his sense of rootlessness. The Meechams are military nomads, and Ben "longed for a sense of place, of belonging, and of permanence. He wanted to live in one house, grow old in one neighborhood, and wanted friends whose faces did not change yearly."

Mary Anne—articulate, witty, and sad—is in some ways the most tragic figure in the book. Severely criticized by her mother because she cares little for her feminine image and greatly undervalued by her father because she is a girl, Mary Anne reads, broods, makes no friends, and fantasizes to an unhealthy degree about her own death and funeral. Unlike Ben, with his involvement in basketball, she has no active outlet for her unhappiness and can express her rage and frustration only in clever, though often vicious, banter with her brother. These sibling arguments epitomize the dysfunction of the Meecham family—and the devastating effects the family's division has upon the individual members.

While *The Great Santini* is sometimes uproariously funny, it is grounded in sad reality: the abuse that Conroy received at the hands of his own military father. "My father's violence is the central fact of my art and my life," Conroy has stated. In a larger context Bull Meecham may be linked with other domineering father figures, such as Mark Twain's Pap Finn, Henry James's Austin Sloper, and William Faulkner's Thomas Sutpen.

—*Robert W. Hamblin*

Discussion Questions

1. Describe Conroy's view of the life of American military families, as depicted in *The Great Santini*. Compare and contrast Conroy's novel with other books treating life in the American military: for example, Mary Edwards Wertsch's *Military Brats*, Sarah Bird's *The Yokota Officers Club*, Anthony Swofford's *Exit A*, or Elizabeth Berg's *Durable Goods*.

2. Like all of Conroy's novels, *The Great Santini* is an "initiation" or "coming-of-age" story. Trace Ben's or Mary Anne's character development in relation to this theme.

3. Trace the behavioral and psychological effects of Bull's violence on the other members of the family.

4. Characterize Lillian. Identify the negative and positive aspects of her relationship with her children.

5. Identify ways the novel both reflects and refutes gender stereotyping. Consider, for example, the traditional views of masculine and feminine behavior, as well as such specific types as the Southern belle, the military father, the soldier, the athlete, the bookworm, and the homosexual.

⚓

THE LORDS OF DISCIPLINE
(Boston: Houghton Mifflin, 1980)

WILL MCLEAN

Will McLean, the narrator and protagonist of Pat Conroy's *The Lords of Discipline,* is a young man struggling to balance the paradoxical realities of freedom and discipline, individuality and group loyalty, personal honor and responsibility to others. A student at Carolina Military Institute (modeled in part on the Citadel, Conroy's alma mater), Will is, by his own definition, a "rebel," a skeptic who first questions and later seeks to eradicate the cruel, inhuman harassment and abuse of first-year students that is intentionally designed to be "the toughest plebe system in the world." McLean is not at all a rebel, however, when he first enrolls in the Institute; on the contrary, he is eager to follow in the footsteps of his father, a graduate of the school and a marine captain decorated for heroism during World War II. Will is confident that the Institute will make him simultaneously a southern gentleman and a loyal American patriot.

This illusion is shattered during an initiation ritual known as Hell Night, when all new cadets are subjected to a vicious hazing that includes both physical and psychological torture. Most of the cadets, even those being victimized by the cruel punishment, accept the process as a necessary rite of passage, a means of turning them from innocent boys into Institute men. But Will sees Hell Night as the beginning of a long process of "indoctrination . . . designed to make us malleable, unimaginative, uninquisitive citizens of the republic, impregnable to ideas—or thought—unsanctioned by authority." In succeeding weeks, throughout the phase of initiation called "The Taming," upperclassmen, especially a secret group of vigilantes known as The Ten, use every means available to force any cadet deemed unworthy or undesirable to withdraw from school. According to Will, such actions are designed to promote the Institute's belief that the individual pronoun *I* is "the one unforgivable obscenity."

Drawing upon his own personal integrity and inner strength, McLean survives the indignities and abuses of both Hell Night and the Taming; but while he is determined one day to "wear the ring" that identifies graduates of the Institute, he vows that he "will not be like them" and initiates a personal assault upon the plebe system. In this regard he sees himself as a guerrilla fighter, "the single voice in my sad country who says 'no,'" an individualist who will henceforward protest and oppose any and all dictatorial powers that seek to control him. What he has learned from his plebe year, he states, is that "I would always be a better hater of things and institutions than a lover of them."

To survive in the Institute's tyrannical, demeaning environment, Will must develop coping mechanisms. Principal among these is a philosophical skepticism expressed in a savage, irreverent sense of humor directed not merely at the Institute and its militaristic goals but at all individuals and topics. Observing the egotism of General Durrell, the president of the school, Will comments: "This runaway megalomania marked him as a blood member of the fraternity of generals." Concerning the system of military rank, Will remarks: "If I ever attend a convention of generals, I hope to control the Chapstick concession to offer some small relief to the obsequious legions of asskissers who spend their days pandering to the egos of generals." To become a member of the Charleston aristocracy, Will insists, one "should have a frontal lobotomy, . . . become a hopeless alcoholic, chain a maiden aunt in an attic, engage in deviant sexual behavior with polo ponies, and talk like [he] was part British and part Negro." Others criticize Will for his constant joking, but he understands that his use of humor is a survival technique: "If I couldn't have found this place hilarious then I would have done something silly like trying to jump off the fourth division."

Another way that Will manages to cope with the Institute's nefarious system is through his involvement in athletics. The point guard on the school's varsity basketball team, he finds in sport a joyous counterpoint to his unhappy, regimented life as a cadet. Significantly, although basketball is a consummate team sport, it also allows for a considerable degree of individualistic style and performance. On the court McLean experiences what he calls "the full abandoned divinity of flight"; there he is in charge of his own destiny, "controlling the flow of games with the unstealable dribble" and thus becoming "truly alive." It is not at all coincidental that during his final showdown with The Ten, he imagines himself again as the athlete, "a running, jiving, fast-talking, quick-handed guard," heroic and triumphant over his enemies.

McLean expresses his independence and rebellion in a variety of actions. He flaunts the immaculate, "spit polish" image of the military cadet by dressing slovenly and mocking inspections—an attitude and practice that prevent him from rising above the lowly rank of private even as a senior cadet. He opposes the racist stance of the Institute by defending the first African American student to attend the school. He resists the sexist attitudes of his fellow cadets to befriend a Charleston woman who is pregnant with another cadet's child. He challenges the homophobic prejudice of the corps of cadets by rooming with a cadet who is suspected of being gay. He defies the stereotype of the "jock" by being an English major and a writer. And he rejects the southern aristocratic bias by choosing two Yankee cadets—one who is middle-class and the other who is poor—among his best friends. At the end of the book he boldly severs his close relationship with the St. Croixs, the prominent Charleston and Institute family that has betrayed him.

It would be a mistake, however, to view McLean's rebellion against authority and idealistic quest for freedom as an endorsement of license or anarchy. He recognizes the need for order and discipline in every individual's life, and he subscribes to the principles of honor, integrity, and loyalty that the Institute espouses. But Will's experiences as an Institute cadet lead him to understand that these qualities must be defined in individual and personal, not institutional, terms. As he concludes at the end of the book, "I wanted to live life passionately, in luxurious free form, without squads, without uniforms or ranks. Freedom was the only thing I had never known, and it was time to walk with abandon, immune from the battalions, answerable only to myself." As a protester against authority and institutions, McLean belongs with other young rebels in American literature, such as Mark Twain's Huckleberry Finn, William Faulkner's Ike McCaslin, J. D. Salinger's Holden Caulfield, and Jack Kerouac's Dean Moriarity.

Discussion Questions

1. *The Lords of Discipline* is a good example of the "initiation" or "coming-of-age" story, a genre that traces the movement of the protagonist from innocence to experience. Trace the character development of Will McLean in relation to this theme.

2. Pat Conroy uses autobiographical elements extensively in his novels. Identify and discuss these elements in *The Lords of Discipline.*

3. This novel is set during the 1960s, a decade characterized by youthful revolt against the authority and traditions of the older generation. How does the novel effectively mirror this time period?

4. Compare and contrast Will McLean with one or more of the protagonists in other Conroy novels.

5. Compare and contrast Will McLean with other young rebels in American literature.

—*Robert W. Hamblin*

THE PRINCE OF TIDES
(Boston: Houghton Mifflin, 1986)

WINGO FAMILY

The Wingo family, which consists of parents Henry and Lila and their three children, Luke and twins Tom and Savannah, is the focus of Pat Conroy's novel *The Prince of Tides.* Like all of Conroy's novels, *The Prince of Tides* is semi-autobiographical. Most of the story takes place on Melrose Island, a South Carolina sea island near the town of Colleton, which Conroy based on Beaufort, South Carolina, his home for much of his life.

Tom Wingo serves as the narrator and protagonist of *The Prince of Tides.* An adult living in Charleston, he travels to New York City after the attempted suicide of Savannah. Because she has blocked out events in her traumatic past, Tom serves as her "memory," recalling events that led to her destructive behavior. Tom's memories, related in flashbacks during sessions with Savannah's psychiatrist, Dr. Susan Lowenstein, cover a span of forty years, beginning with his and Savannah's birth during a raging hurricane and continuing to the present, in which Tom is a failed coach and English teacher.

Through the sessions with Dr. Lowenstein and the romantic relationship that develops between them, Tom is able to admit to himself and to her that the events buried deep in his own memory have prevented him from having an open and loving relationship with his wife, Sally, who is considering leaving him for a fellow doctor.

The other members of the family mostly appear during Tom's flashbacks. His father, Henry, is a thinly disguised version of Pat Conroy's own father. Unlike Don Conroy, a career military man, Henry Wingo is a shrimper. Tom asserts that if Henry "had not been a violent man, . . . he would have made a splendid father." A fighter pilot during World War II (like Don Conroy), Henry committed atrocities in order to survive after being shot down in Germany. When Henry is recalled to duty during the Korean War, his children pray not for his safe return but for his death, which would prevent him from returning to the home where he was "always a stranger" with a "gift for tyranny." By the time his children are grown, Henry has mellowed, developing a loving relationship with Tom's three daughters.

Lila Wingo, who was based on Conroy's recently deceased mother, seems to her children, when they are small, to be the most wonderful mother in the world, the kind who teaches her children to believe "in the dreams of flowers and animals" and who "could turn a walk around the island into a voyage of purest discovery." Tom describes her as "word-struck." Although her children are aware that Lila is a manipulative woman with ambitions to become a member of the social elite of Colleton, they are oblivious to the fact that she is "a liar of the first order" whose ambitions will eventually tear the family apart. After thirty years of marriage, Lila divorces Henry and marries widowed Reese Newbury, a member of Colleton's elite. Tom responds to her decisions with contempt, which Lila recognizes but blames on her marriage to Reese.

It is clear that from the time she was a small girl, Savannah has exhibited signs of mental illness

and that she had developed the ability to bury horrific events so far in her memory that she does not have to acknowledge them. After the birth of Lila and Henry's fourth stillborn child, Rose Aster, Tom discovers that Savannah has removed the baby from the freezer where her father has placed her to await burial. Savannah tells Tom, "I think these little kids are the lucky ones."

After Lila forbids Savannah to write because she is afraid the family's secrets will be recorded, Savannah commits her words to the sand, where they are washed away. Upon high-school graduation, she escapes to New York to become a respected poet and a militant feminist. There, her periods of creativity are interspersed with psychotic episodes in which she sees monsters and hears voices that tell her to injure herself. In their ritualistic greeting after long absences, Tom asks Savannah about her childhood, which Savannah compares to the Holocaust and Hiroshima.

Coming out of the coma that follows her third suicide attempt, Savannah keeps repeating the word *Callanwolde*, which is the Atlanta estate of the Candler family, who created the Coca-Cola Company. It is only after Tom begins to trust Dr. Lowenstein that he tells her about Callanwolde. Its significance to the Wingo family begins when the children encounter a "giant" on the estate grounds, where they are playing during a visit with their paternal grandmother while their father is in Korea. The man becomes infatuated with Lila and follows her to Melrose Island, where he and two friends rape Lila, Savannah, and Tom.

Luke sets the family's pet tiger on the intruders, who are killed. After burying the "evidence," Lila forbids the children to tell anyone, even their father, of the rapes. The revelation of this secret during Tom's sessions with Lowenstein marks a turning point in the recovery of both Savannah and Tom.

Although he is only a year older than the twins, Luke is the hero of Tom's childhood. Unlike Tom, who is an observer, Luke is a man of action. He openly challenges Henry's abuse and engineers a daring attempt to save a white porpoise that has been captured from the South Carolina coast and taken to a Florida aquarium. Luke leaves his beloved home to fight in Vietnam, and upon his return he discovers that his mother, who has been awarded Melrose Island in the divorce settlement, has sold the land to the Atomic Energy Commission to be used in the "production of nuclear weapons."

Luke is unwilling to give up his home and decides to take a stand against what he sees as federal encroachment. Although he knows he will not win, Luke engages in a series of skirmishes with authorities after telling Tom that he is doing it so that he can live with himself. While he succeeds in becoming a "worthy opponent," Luke loses his life after failing to give himself up at a meeting that Tom and Savannah arrange with a federal agent. Fittingly, his siblings bury the "Prince of Tides" at sea.

Discussion Questions

1. Compare Henry Wingo of *The Prince of Tides* with Bull Meecham of *The Great Santini* and explain the impact that Pat Conroy's father, Don, had on the development of both characters.

2. Discuss whether or not it would have made a difference to the mental health and adult lives of the Wingo children if they had disobeyed their mother and told their father, their grandparents, or an official about the rape.

3. Discuss the ethical issues involved in the romance between Tom Wingo and his sister's psychiatrist, Dr. Susan Lowenstein.

4. Choose any poem of Savannah Wingo's in *The Prince of Tides* and relate it to her life.

5. Take a position and defend it concerning whether Luke or Tom Wingo could most accurately be described as the "Prince of Tides."

—*Elizabeth R. Purdy*

REFERENCES

Robert E. Burkholder, "The Use of Myth in Pat Conroy's *The Great Santini*," *Critique*, 21 (1979): 31–37;

Landon C. Burns, *Pat Conroy: A Critical Companion* (Westport, Conn.: Greenwood Press, 1996);

Robert Hamblin, "Sports Imagery in Pat Conroy's Novels," *Aethlon: The Journal of Sport Literature*, 11 (1993): 49–59;

Dannye Romine Powell, *Parting the Curtains: Interviews with Southern Writers* (Winston-Salem, N.C.: Blair, 1994);

David Toolan, "The Unfinished Boy and His Pain: Rescuing the Young Hero with Pat Conroy," *Commonweal*, 118 (1991): 127–131;

Lamar York, "Pat Conroy's Portrait of the Artist as a Young Southerner," *Southern Literary Journal*, 19 (1987): 34–46.

James Fenimore Cooper
(September 15, 1789 – September 14, 1851)

THE LAST OF THE MOHICANS: A NARRATIVE OF 1757
2 volumes (Philadelphia: Carey & Lea, 1826)

NATTY BUMPPO

Natty Bumppo is the white woodsman hero of James Fenimore Cooper's *The Last of the Mohicans*. Though he first appears as a secondary character in Cooper's *The Pioneers* (1823), *The Last of the Mohicans* secured Bumppo's place as a formative American literary hero. In this novel he is also called "Leatherstocking," "Hawk-eye," "Deerslayer," and "La Longue Carabine." The novel takes place in 1757 during the French and Indian War in what is now Upstate New York. Bumppo is called upon to help two sisters, Cora and Alice Munro, together with their companions, Major Duncan Heyward and David Gamut, travel through the dangerous forest. Their destination is the besieged Fort William Henry, where the girls' father, a general in the British army, is warding off attacks by the French and the Huron Indians. Pursuing the group through the forest is Magua, a Huron leader who is in league with the French. When Magua captures both girls and their companions, Bumppo comes to their rescue. When the girls are captured a second time along with Gamut, however, Cora and the noble Native American Uncas are both killed in the final battle. At the end of the novel, Bumppo and Uncas's father, Chingachgook (whose son's death makes him the "last of the Mohicans"), "two sturdy and intrepid woodsmen," are "watering the grave of Uncas" with their tears.

With *The Last of the Mohicans,* Cooper tried to achieve popular and commercial success by catering to, as he called it in an 1822 letter to English publisher John Murray, "the present taste . . . for action and strong excitement." By setting the action of the story in 1757, Cooper was able to write retroactively the myth of national founding and succeeded in combining a melodramatic love story with a violent fantasy about national origins. By transferring the responsibility for Indian removal from the United States onto the British and French, Cooper portrays the noble Native American as nearly extinct through no fault of the United States.

Cooper wrote three more novels featuring Natty Bumppo. These five works together became known as "The Leather-Stocking Tales." Often considered the first American novelist, Cooper was aware of the effect these novels had upon his readers and upon national mythology more generally. In the preface to the collected 1850 edition of the novels he writes, "If anything from the pen of the writer of these romances is at all to outlive himself, it is, unquestionably, the series of 'The Leather-Stocking Tales.'" For Cooper, and for subsequent readers, the character of Bumppo is more than a man: he is the archetypical American hero.

Bumppo, Cooper acknowledged, is a beau ideal whose nature combines the best of two worlds—those of the Native American Indian and of white civilizations. In chapter 12, Bumppo's proud acknowledgment that in his lifetime he has read only the book of nature—"and the words that are written there are too simple and too plain to need much schooling"—emphasizes the importance of aboriginal forms of knowledge and culture. Bumppo is also at pains to communicate his sympathy for Native Americans wronged by the British, French, and Dutch. Yet, at the same time he often mentions his white blood, "uncrossed" by the burden of Indian ancestry and so protected from the temptation of "savagery" offered by the wilderness.

Bumppo's agility is not only physical but also mental and moral. He easily reads the signs of the forest, able to deduce "the truth" of a situation from a muddy footprint or bent branch. He alone among the whites can converse in the native Delaware tongue and so is "the link" between the whites and the alternately helpful and persecuting native tribes they encounter. Perhaps most important, he refuses the fixed morality of doctrine, religious or otherwise, and is always willing to consider other points of view in the course of reconsidering his own. In this way he bears a striking resemblance to another archetypical American hero, Mark Twain's Huckleberry Finn, who in the course of his own journey turns his back on accepted morality.

Though Bumppo's qualities of resourcefulness, radical individualism, and romantic dispossession are seen in a multitude of literary heroes throughout the nineteenth century, other nineteenth-century writers had varied reactions to Cooper's invention. Herman Melville, for example, credited Cooper's works as "producing a vivid, and awakening power upon my mind," while Twain, in his essay "Fenimore Cooper's Literary Offenses," humorously catalogues what he felt were inconsistencies in tone and setting in Cooper's novels and pokes fun at Cooper's somewhat archaic and turgid language. Yet, throughout the nineteenth century, some of the most celebrated American literary characters might be considered direct descendants of Cooper's hero. Like Bumppo, Melville's Ishmael and Twain's Huckleberry Finn are each allied with the natural world, trying to do right in the face of an encroaching, increasingly corrupt civilization. Cooper's works have been faulted in the late twentieth and early twenty-first centuries as insufficiently attentive to the vicious Indian removal policies of the 1820s. Though one of the final images of *The Last of the Mohicans* is of the clasped hands of Bumppo and Chingachgook, and Cooper seemed to sincerely mourn the plight of the Native American, he did so passively and with the view that this planned extinction was inevitable.

Discussion Questions

1. In chapter 3 of *The Last of the Mohicans,* Cooper provides a thorough physical description of Natty Bumppo. Itemize the details of this description and explain what each relates to the reader about Bumppo's character.

2. David Gamut urges Bumppo not to take revenge if David happens to be killed during the journey. Bumppo thinks about this request and concludes:

"There is principle in that . . . different from the law of the woods! And yet it is fair and noble to reflect upon!" What are the characteristics of "the law of the woods"? In which situations does Bumppo follow this law and in which does he depart from it?

3. Bumppo goes by many names. What is the significance of each of these different names? Remember to consider who bestowed each name upon Bumppo.

4. Referring to Uncas, Bumppo reassures Chingachgook that "The boy has left us for a time, but, Sagamore, you are not alone!" Discuss the significance of the relationship between Bumppo and Chingachgook.

—*Sarah Blackwood*

CHINGACHGOOK

Chingachgook is the stalwart Mohican companion to Natty Bumppo (also known as "Leatherstocking" and "Hawk-eye") in the first two novels of the series commonly referred to as *The Leather-Stocking Tales*. Chingachgook is also known as "Le Gros Serpent" and "Indian John." First introduced as an old man in *The Pioneers* (1823), in *The Last of the Mohicans* (a novel set before *The Pioneers*) Chingachgook is more central to the action, and his role is more emotionally compelling than in the earlier novel. In the midst of the French and Indian War, Chingachgook helps Bumppo lead Alice and Cora Munro, Duncan Heyward, and David Gamut through the forest to Fort William Henry. The sisters and Gamut are kidnapped following the historical 1757 massacre at the fort. Chingachgook; his son, Uncas; and Bumppo are again called upon to rescue them. Uncas, ostensibly "the last of the Mohicans," is killed along with Cora in a final battle with Magua, the enemy Huron leader.

Cooper's characterization of Chingachgook received some criticism in the author's lifetime. In the 1850 preface to the collected edition of *The Leather-Stocking Tales*, he notes that "it has been objected to these books that they give a more favorable picture of the red man than he deserves." Cooper goes on to confirm that it was his intention in creating this character to show "the good of the red man," to "see . . . in him one who had the soul, reason, and characteristics of a fellow-being." He follows this defense, however, with an assertion that, in reality, "the red man" is often given over to "evil passions" and a "degraded moral state that certainly more or less belongs to his condition."

It is in these two stark contrasts—the "good" and the "degraded"—that Cooper casts the Native Americans in his novel. The original 1826 preface opens the novel with a summary of which Indians are "good" and which are "bad," and the novel does not hesitate to paint its native characters in broad strokes. The action of the novel is dependent upon the relentless savagery exhibited by the Hurons, who are allied with the French against the British. The pursuing Hurons are characterized as subhuman "lolling savages" given to eating raw meat, simultaneously lazy and passionately violent. Chingachgook, on the other hand, is an idealized and sentimental figure untainted by European civilization. His actions are always selfless and pure, as when he calmly readies himself for almost certain death while protecting the whites huddled together in a cave at Glenn's Falls.

Though Chingachgook is not a fully drawn character depicted as having a flawed humanity, he nevertheless occupies an important place in this novel. He is the fixed moral center of the novel, always adhering to a rigid code of ethics and behavior. When the warrior is introduced in chapter 3, he voices many of the central themes of the novel. Refusing to accept Bumppo's suggestion that there are two sides to every story, he insists that there is a "difference, Hawk-eye, between the stone-headed arrow of the warrior, and the leaden bullet with which you kill!" He then goes on to declare that Native Americans equate saying with doing: "'Tis what my fathers have said, and what the Mohicans have done." Chingachgook's assertion that the Mohican way is an honest and noble one may certainly be understood as being in keeping with the white fantasy of a "noble-savage." By asking Bumppo to accept that the fight over Indian land was never a fair one, however, Chingachgook voices an ethical challenge.

Chingachgook's character is best understood as the perfect foil for Bumppo's agile ethics. Bumppo emerges from this novel as an American literary hero because he continually reevaluates his moral code and his place in the world. His flexibility of mind means that he is never locked into any action that is not pragmatic or the best for the whole. Chingachgook's rigid moral code, on the other hand, values honor, ritual, and tradition and is portrayed in the novel as unsuited for a democracy. The characters of Queequeg from Herman Melville's *Moby-Dick* (1851) and Dirk Peters from Edgar Allan Poe's *A Narrative of Arthur Gordon Pym* (1838) are both variations on the noble-savage companion, troubling in their one-dimensionality yet central to an understanding of the American literary tradition.

Discussion Questions

1. The novel opens and closes with Chingachgook speaking eloquently. Read his dialogue carefully and analyze why such a reticent character is given language at these key moments.

2. Natty Bumppo interrupts Chingachgook's final speech at Uncas's grave. How do you interpret this interruption in light of the pair's close friendship?

3. List, specifically, the characteristics exhibited by Chingachgook that show him to be a literary "noble savage." Note any characteristics that you think allow him to break free of that one-dimensional stereotype.

4. Chingachgook often "speaks" with his hands (see, for example, chapter 22). What is the significance of his sign language?

—*Sarah Blackwood*

✎

THE PILOT: A TALE OF THE SEA
2 volumes (New York: Charles Wiley, 1823)

LONG TOM COFFIN

Long Tom Coffin is one of the minor heroes in James Fenimore Cooper's first sea novel, *The Pilot* (1824). He is from two humble, hardworking Nantucket whaling families: his father is "a Coffin and my mother was a Joy; and the two names can count more flukes than all the rest of the island together." By making Tom representative of the best whalers

in Nantucket, the center of whaling in America, Cooper makes him representative of the best of American seamen. Many critics regard him as the first significant hero in American fiction who was a common sailor rather than an officer. Though Long Tom is clearly the best seaman on the schooner *Ariel*—on which he serves under Lt. Richard Barnstable, the man he has taught to skipper the ship—he remains one of "the people," as common sailors before the mast were called.

The Pilot was published in 1824 as a direct response to Sir Walter Scott's novel *The Pirate* (1821); in the preface to the 1849 edition of his novel, Cooper addresses Scott, stating his intent "to produce a work which, if it had no other merit, might present truer pictures of the ocean and ships than any to be found in *The Pirate*." Indeed, in Scott's novel, ships and the sea figure only peripherally, and there are few characters who are actually sailors. In writing a novel with many extended scenes at sea and allowing Long Tom to rise to a place of prominence in the social order of the ship on which he serves, Cooper Americanizes the sea novel.

Cooper is widely regarded as the father of the American Western; he is also the father of the American sea novel. *The Pilot* drew considerable response from other writers, English and American. Much of the American response to the novel focused on Cooper's Nantucket whaler, Long Tom Coffin. Not all of that response was positive: Nathaniel Ames, a writer contemporary of Cooper's, called Long Tom "a *caricature* (and not a very good one) of an 'old salt.'" But after Cooper, many American writers seemed to take from him that the real heroes of American sea fiction must be like Long Tom.

Long Tom plays a heroic role in most of the key scenes of *The Pilot*. In the absence of Mr. Gray—the title character, a skilled pilot who is a fictional version of American Revolutionary War hero John Paul Jones—Lt. Barnstable consults Long Tom on conducting the *Ariel* safely to anchor. Barnstable values Tom's experience at sea over the rank of those technically superior to him. "I would sooner trust Tom Coffin and his harpoon to back me," he asserts, "than the best broadside that ever rattled out of the three decks of a ninety-gun ship." When the *Ariel* is engaged by a more heavily armed English cutter, the lieutenant's faith in Long Tom is rewarded: throwing his harpoon with deadly precision, Coffin pins the captain of the English vessel to the mast of his ship and thus wins the battle. Later, when the *Ariel* ultimately sinks in a storm, he sacrifices his life to keep Barnstable from going down with the ship.

The year before he published *The Pilot*, Cooper introduced his best-known character, Natty Bumppo, in the novel *The Pioneers* (1823). Coffin and Bumppo, seventy years old in *The Pioneers*, are clearly cut from the same cloth. Bumppo, known also as "Hawkeye," is famous for his sharp powers of vision, as Long Tom is, and both men are associated with weapons that they use both to defend themselves and to provide sustenance: Coffin with his harpoon and Bumppo with his rifle, Killdeer. Each character represents a fierce American individualism that can also pull toward a collective aim.

Long Tom Coffin points to something fundamental about the American experience and about Cooper's Americanization of the sea-novel tradition he claims. Long Tom is a people's hero. He is not only of "the people" on the ship, he is representative of the people on the shore, an embodiment of the American ideal that what one does determine one's character. In the novel, the people, as represented by Long Tom, fight, die, and rise to heroic action, and it is upon their ultimate sacrifice that America moves forward. Though Long Tom dies, he lives on in the sense that all of Nantucket is made up of men like him. Indeed, from the people, Long Tom's example suggests, will always rise up the next generation of American heroes.

Discussion Questions

1. Critics have made much of the fact that Long Tom represents a people's hero because he remains in the forecastle with "the people" of the ship. If Long Tom really embodies Jefferson's notion of a meritocracy, however, shouldn't he be promoted beyond this? Perhaps even to captain?

2. Nathaniel Ames was one of Cooper's contemporaries who considered Long Tom a "caricature."

Are his objections to Long Tom well founded? Use specific details about the character to support your answer.

3. In the sea fiction that follows Cooper by a couple of decades, American writers, particularly Richard Henry Dana and Herman Melville, begin making their ordinary sailor characters the narrators of their books. Are there moments in *The Pilot* where Cooper allows Long Tom to tell his own story? How does Long Tom's own story relate to the main story?

4. Like Natty Bumppo of the Leather-Stocking novels, Tom is proud of his parentage; yet, both of these characters die childless. What is Cooper suggesting about the older generation of American heroes these two represent?

—*Matthew D. Brown*

REFERENCES

Martin Barker and Roger Sabin, *The Lasting of the Mohicans: History of an American Myth* (Jackson: University Press of Mississippi, 1995);

Nina Baym, "How Men and Women Wrote Indian Stories," in *New Essays on* The Last of the Mohicans, edited by H. Daniel Peck (Cambridge: Cambridge University Press, 1992);

Hugh Egan, "Cooper and His Contemporaries," in *America and the Sea: A Literary History,* edited by Haskell Springer (Athens: University of Georgia Press, 1995);

Leslie Fiedler, "Natty Bumppo and Chingachgook," in *James Fenimore Cooper: A Collection of Critical Essays,* edited by Wayne Fields (Englewood Cliffs, N.J.: Prentice-Hall, 1979), pp. 53–58;

William P. Kelly, *Plotting America's Past: Fenimore Cooper and the Leatherstocking Tales* (Carbondale: Southern Illinois University Press, 1983);

John McWilliams, The Last of the Mohicans: *Civil Savagery and Savage Civility* (New York: Twayne, 1995);

H. Daniel Peck, ed., *New Essays on* The Last of the Mohicans (Cambridge: Cambridge University Press, 1992);

Thomas Philbrick, *James Fenimore Cooper and the Development of American Sea Fiction* (Cambridge, Mass.: Harvard University Press, 1961).

Robert Coover

(February 4, 1932 –   )

ॐ

THE UNIVERSAL BASEBALL
ASSOCIATION, INC.

(New York: Random House, 1968)

J. HENRY WAUGH

J. Henry Waugh is the protagonist of Robert Coover's second novel, *The Universal Baseball Association, Inc., J. Henry Waugh, Prop.* Like Walter Mitty in James Thurber's story "The Secret Life of Walter Mitty," Waugh leads both an actual, tangible life and an imaginary life. In the former, he is a lonely, fifty-six-year-old man who holds down a job as an accountant at a small firm. His chief joy in life is the Universal Baseball Association, a fantasy baseball league that he has created that allows him to play out games by throwing dice. He takes these games very seriously; he gives names to both the players and teams, keeps track of their seasons, fleshes out their lives, and keeps aging players on as team managers.

This game is the key to Henry's other life. In his real life, Henry is bored and powerless, a third-rate nobody leading a fourth-rate existence. When he plays his dice game, however, he is in control of an exciting, dynamic world. He is the god of this world, potentially in control of everything that happens within it. As the novel progresses, the game becomes more and more real to Henry, and he resents his "real" life for taking time away from his game. He begins to live more and more within the world of the game. Although through most of the novel he rigidly runs the game according to the results of the dice, once his favorite player, Damon Rutherford, is killed by a freak series of rolls, he begins to actively interfere with the results of the dice, making baseball into a kind of religious ritual and further slipping into his imaginary world, coming to believe more and more strongly both in his role as a god and in the reality of his players.

Henry Waugh first appeared in 1963 in Coover's story "The Second Son," published in the *Evergreen Review.* That story, which was revised to become the second chapter of the novel, ends with Damon Rutherford being killed and Henry suffering a mental breakdown. Coover told interviewer Frank Gado that he "hadn't gotten everything out of the metaphor," however, so he spent several years reworking and expanding the story, "searching out the structure that seemed to be hidden in it." The structure of the novel is drawn from the Bible: "seven chapters corresponding to the seven days of the creation." This structure emphasizes Henry's role as the creator and god of the universal baseball world, "and this in turn naturally implied an eighth, the apocalyptic day." Henry melds two different characters from Coover's first novel, *The Origin of the Brunists:* journalist Justin "Tiger" Miller and lawyer Ralph Himebaugh. Like Miller, games are what keep Henry going. Like Himebaugh, Henry is obsessed with numbers and statistics. Himebaugh's inability to live either wholly in the world of numbers or in the real world lead to his death; Henry's own fate by the end of the novel is similar: he seems to have fallen between worlds.

In the novel Henry identifies strongly with rookie player Rutherford, who he thinks of as "the greatest pitcher in the history of baseball." Damon is everything that Henry is not: young, beloved, a brilliant player. Henry notes that he and Damon's father, Brock, are the same age, thinking of Damon as his son. But he also thinks of himself as being Damon. Indeed, he goes so far as to ask a one-night stand to call him Damon in bed, his game world informing his sexual fantasies. Thus, when Damon is killed, Henry feels like he has both lost a son and died himself.

Waugh's humanity is evidenced in his floundering attempts to live his day-to-day life: going to work, eating a sandwich at the deli downstairs, going to the local bar, and rolling the dice of his game. Lois Gordon points out that "his initials, J. H. W., suggest the Old Testament Yahweh, just as his name sounds like Jehovah," but his divinity is expressed less in his own words than in the speculations of his baseball players about their creator. Though some come to believe that "God exists and he is a nut," others develop elaborate systems of trying to interpret the world of baseball to sense the god behind it. Another still has developed his own dice game, but none can actually guess at Henry's day-to-day reality.

In the final apocalyptic chapter of the novel, Henry's day-to-day reality and Henry himself are no longer visible, leaving only the world of the baseball players and their speculation on the nature of the god controlling their lives. For Jackson I. Cope, this disappearance suggests the way an author is spread out and dispersed into his characters when he or she writes a novel: "There is no interaction now between Henry and his players—they have absorbed his consciousness both in narrative style and in literal fact." Henry has ceased being a differentiated character and now exists only in his creation, the Universal Baseball Association. This creation, which at first was enclosed within the larger world of the novel (Henry's world), now has replaced that larger world. Thus, by the end of the novel, Henry is a character who has ceased to be perceptible, having instead dissolved into the world that he has created.

Discussion Questions

1. Why does Henry, in chapter 6, bring his bumbling friend Lou home to play the Universal Baseball Association Game with him? Is it his friend's reaction to the game that convinces him to cheat, or is it something else? Why does Henry decide to break his own rules?

2. What do you think has happened to Henry in the last chapter? Some critics have argued that he's gone mad and now only lives in the world of his baseball game. Others argue that now that he has created the game it continues to run by itself. What is your opinion? What support can you give for either hypothesis?

3. Coover is often described as writing metafiction, meaning that he is a writer whose books are about writing, or about the process of artistic creation. Is Henry an artist of sorts? How is his creation of the UBA analogous to writing a novel?

—*Brian Evenson*

REFERENCES

Jackson I. Cope, *Robert Coover's Fictions* (Baltimore: Johns Hopkins University Press, 1986);

Brian Evenson, *Understanding Robert Coover* (Columbia: University of South Carolina Press, 2003);

Frank Gado, "Robert Coover," in *First Person: Conversation on Writers and Writing* (Schenectady, N.Y.: Union College Press, 1973), pp. 142–159;

Lois Gordon, *Robert Coover: The Universal Fiction-making Process* (Carbondale: Southern Illinois University Press, 1983).

Robert Cormier
(January 17, 1925 –   )

THE CHOCOLATE WAR
(New York: Pantheon, 1974)

JERRY RENAULT

Jerry Renault, the protagonist of Robert Cormier's *The Chocolate War*, is a freshman at Trinity High School, a Catholic school for boys. Jerry is in many ways alone in the world: his mother is dead, his father distracted and distant, and he has only one close friend at school. He is not distinguished for athletic or academic brilliance, but he has a poster in his locker that suggests that there may be more to him than is immediately obvious. The poster shows a man walking on the beach: "a small solitary figure in all that immensity. At the bottom of the poster these words appeared—*"Do I dare disturb the universe?"* The principal events in *The Chocolate War* stem from Jerry's making a decision that "disturbs the universe" of Trinity: he refuses to take part in the annual school fund-raising project, selling chocolates. This refusal sets in motion a series of actions that eventually lay bare the corruption of both layers of authority at Trinity: the official governance of the Brothers (members of a Catholic teaching order, who comprise the faculty and administration at Trinity) and the unofficial governance of the Vigils, a secret society led by Archie Costello that controls the students through fear and intimidation.

Although participation in the sale is theoretically voluntary, it is clearly expected that each student will sell their quota of chocolates, and social pressure discourages any student from refusing to take part. The chocolate sale is particularly important in Jerry's freshman year, because Brother Leon desperately needs the proceeds from the sale to pay back money he has "borrowed" from the school treasury. To raise the necessary funds, he doubles the price of each box of chocolates and doubles the number of boxes each boy is expected to sell. Brother Leon is so desperate to ensure that the chocolate sale will succeed that he takes the unprecedented step of enlisting the help of Archie and the Vigils.

The Vigils express their power partly through giving students "assignments" that they are required to fulfill. One boy, for instance, is assigned to loosen the screws on all the desks in one classroom so they will collapse when the students sit down. Jerry's assignment is to refuse to join in the chocolate sale for ten days, which the Vigils know will incur the wrath of Brother Leon. Jerry carries out his assignment as expected, but when the eleventh day comes he surprises everyone by continuing to refuse to take part in the sale, thus defying the authority of both the Brothers and the Vigils.

Jerry has to repeat his refusal every day, because Brother Leon holds a daily roll call during which each boy has to state how many boxes of chocolates he has sold. He is not sure why he decides not to sell the chocolates and why he sticks with that decision but feels it has something to do with rejecting Brother Leon and his false values and with expressing himself as an individual. Brother Leon is sufficiently disturbed by Jerry's refusal to ask the Vigils to pressure him into taking part in the sale: they do so by giving him a new assignment, which is to stop his daily refusals and instead agree to sell his quota of chocolates. His simple refusal to take part in this activity has threatened both power structures in the school: even Archie's assistant, Obie, realizes that Archie knows he cannot make Jerry do anything Jerry does not choose to do.

Jerry's continued refusal has increasingly severe consequences: his possessions are vandalized; intimidating phone calls are made to his house in the middle of the night; his art project is stolen; and he is attacked by a gang of boys. The final showdown is a staged fight between himself and the school bully, Emile Janza, during which Jerry is seriously beaten. As he is waiting to be taken to the hospital, Jerry tells his friend, Goober, that his resistance was in vain, that one person cannot defy entrenched power:

"They tell you to do your thing but they don't mean it. They don't want you to do your thing, not unless it happens to be their thing, too. It's a laugh, Goober, a fake. Don't disturb the universe, Goober, no matter what the posters say."

Discussion Questions

1. Jerry twice refuses to sell chocolates: the first time as an assignment from The Vigils, the second time as an expression of his own free will. What is the difference in meaning and consequences between these two refusals?

2. How does Jerry feel about his father and his father's life, and how does that influence his choice to "disturb the universe"?

3. Jerry does not enjoy physical violence and knows he is no match for Emil Janza, the school bully. Why does Jerry agree to meet Janza in a fight that he knows he will lose?

—*Sarah Boslaugh*

REFERENCES
Robert Cormier, *The Chocolate War*, introduction by the author (New York: Knopf, 1997);
Patricia J. Campbell, *Presenting Robert Cormier* (Boston: Twayne, 1985).

Patricia Cornwell
(June 9, 1956 –   )

SERIES
(1990–2003)

KAY SCARPETTA
Dr. Kay Scarpetta is the protagonist and, until *Blow Fly* (2003), the narrator of a series of crime thrillers by Patricia Cornwell. From the first novel, *Postmortem* (1990), through the eleventh novel in the series, *The Last Precinct* (2000), Scarpetta is the chief medical examiner of the Commonwealth of Virginia. In subsequent novels she works as a consultant and for the FBI. In *Predator* (2005), the fourteenth novel of the series, Scarpetta becomes associated with the National Forensic Academy, a

private institute in Florida that maintains its own labs, investigators, and "special ops" staff. This new employer allows Scarpetta greater mobility and eliminates the tensions, explored in the earlier novels, between her and the institutions of which she is a part. Scarpetta is both doctor and lawyer, and her cases involve her in following the physical evidence, especially that related to the bodies of the victims, which leads to an understanding of the crime: what horrors were perpetrated, how, and, ultimately, by whom. As Cornwell has said in an interview in *The Fatal Art of Entertainment: Interviews with Mystery Writers* (1994), edited by Rosemary Herbert, Scarpetta is dealing with the reality of violence: "a horrific, epidemic, plague, almost, that has been visited upon a city." Perhaps the most interesting aspect of this series is its attention to the scientific processes by which physical evidence is collected, examined, and interpreted. Scarpetta sees her role as speaking for the dead, silenced, and powerless: "no one respects the dead more than those of us who work with them and hear their silent stories," as she says in *The Body Farm* (1994).

Like most detectives in the hard-boiled tradition, Scarpetta—at least in the early novels—is an outsider. Living and working in Richmond, a city defined by its Confederate traditions, she was born and grew up in Miami and educated in the North. She is also an ethnic outsider, Italian and Catholic and of working-class origins in a world defined by WASP privilege. Even that ethnicity is marked by difference: though Italian, she is blonde and blue-eyed, from a Northern Italian stock that claims pure bloodlines, though in *From Potter's Field* (1995) she acknowledges that she suspects genetic "cause for some of my more Teutonic traits."

The most significant characteristic of her status as an outsider is her gender. Scarpetta operates as "a woman in a man's world," she notes in *Postmortem*, and that gender difference is often—especially in the early novels—responsible for the threats she faces. While her male predecessor "went hunting with cops . . . [and] to barbecues with the judges," she continues, "the only hunts and barbecues I was invited to were courtrooms and conferences in which targets were drawn on me and fires lit beneath my feet." There are times when male authority—as embodied in her old teachers or in her superiors within the state government—makes Scarpetta feel powerless and defensive. Her desire to devote her career to the dead is defined by some as unnatural; she is seen by others as cold, professional, and clinical. She sees herself, however, as androgynous, as she suggests in *The Body Farm*, "I was a woman who was not a woman. I was the body and sensibilities of a woman with the power and drive of a man."

Power becomes a major issue for Scarpetta and for the series as a whole. Her Mercedes, her houses, and her jewelry, for example, are not only evidence of her good taste and high standards but also ways of controlling, or attempting to control, her environment. Threats to her power become the greatest challenges she faces. Often these threats come not merely from the criminals she faces but from within the system itself. In *Black Notice* (1999) she worries that her enemies are trying to "steal my fire. . . . I use my power for good. . . . And whoever is trying to hurt me wants to appropriate my power for his own selfish use." In *Blow Fly* she finds "unbearable" the notion that she might have lost that power, but her niece, Lucy, argues that it is internally derived rather than externally bestowed. Scarpetta has a difficult time believing this message. The victims with whom she identifies are often, as in the cases of Abby Turnbull and Pat Harvey in *All That Remains* (1992), powerful women threatened by the institutions within which they work.

Increasingly, the villains also often mirror Scarpetta: strong, professional women such as Carrie Grethen in *The Body Farm*, *From Potter's Field*, and *Point of Origin* (1998); microbiologist Phyllis Crowder in *Unnatural Exposure* (1997); and Deputy Chief of Police Diane Bray in *Black Notice*. Through these portraits of women who use their sexuality to get what they want and/or who strike back against the institutions that have disregarded them, the series examines Scarpetta's insecurities and resentments.

Like other contemporary detective writers, Cornwell invokes the traditional isolation of the detective but also modifies it. Kay Scarpetta is divorced and lives alone (except for a dog that appears in *Blow Fly*). She is detached from her immediate family. Her father's death during her girlhood has marked her, both in terms of her relationships with men (whom she expects will leave her) and her commitment to excavating pain: "Sometimes when one is touched by tragedy he becomes its student," she says in *From Potter's Field,* and the masculine pronoun in this conversation between two women suggests her difficulty dealing with that loss. Her mother is a nagging presence in the first few novels but later is simply dismissed as being in ill health. Her sister, Dorothy, is a vocal and negative foil: obsessed with men, a bad mother, jealous of Scarpetta's brains and body.

There are, however, some strong though vexed attachments. Lucy, who ages from ten years old to her early thirties over the course of the series, becomes the character with whom she has the most significant and complex relationship: Scarpetta is mother, mentor, model, and friend to Lucy, but Lucy also protects, saves, and even employs her aunt. Lucy's sexuality (she comes out as a lesbian in *The Body Farm*) also seems to be a safe way of displacing Scarpetta's own sexual ambiguities. Not only does Scarpetta's continuing relationship with Lucy take on a professional dimension, but her other significant relationships—with Pete Marino (initially of the Richmond police) and Benton Wesley (at the beginning of the series a profiler for the FBI)—are defined first in professional terms. Although the dynamics of these relationships change over the course of the series, these characters function as a team whose features seem to reflect those of a dysfunctional family. One of Cornwell's means of defining the positive aspects of family relationship is in Scarpetta's passion for food, which also inspired two cookbooks by Cornwell related to the series: *Scarpetta's Winter Table* (1998) and *Food to Die For: Secrets from Kay Scarpetta's Kitchen* (2001). In this series, however, meals—like Scarpetta's personal relationships and the communities they would affirm—are often disrupted by murder and its consequences.

Cornwell has described Scarpetta in an interview with John Monk (*The Washingtonian* [28 June 1993]) as "in my heart of hearts what I would like to be. . . . A very moral person . . . a child of light, so to speak, who is doing battle with . . . irrationality, inhumanity, and evil." The Scarpetta series tracks the effects of evil on all its victims, including those like the detective who would speak on their behalf.

Discussion Questions

1. How does Kay Scarpetta compare to a female detective such as Sara Paretsky's V. I. Warshawski or Sue Grafton's Kinsey Millhone? (You might consider family history, professional relationships, and ethnic identity, for example.)

2. Is Kay Scarpetta a feminist hero? What aspects of her character—in particular her relationships with other female characters or her relationships with law enforcement institutions—complicate that definition?

3. Choose a particular book in the series. In what ways (if at all) does the victim serve as a foil for Scarpetta? How (if at all) does understanding what has happened to the victim lead to some realization about herself or her own situation?

4. In *The Last Precinct* Scarpetta's friend Anna quotes Friedrich Nietschze: "Be careful who you choose for an enemy because that is who you become most like." Look closely at a particular villain (or group of villains) that one of Scarpetta's investigations pursues. Are there ways in which Anna's warning is valid?

5. With *Blow Fly,* Cornwell shifts the point of view from first person (with Scarpetta as narrator) to third. Examine two novels in the series, one earlier and the other more recent. What difference does the shift make to Cornwell's presentation of Kay Scarpetta?

—Susan Allen Ford

REFERENCES

George Beahm, *The Unofficial Patricia Cornwell Companion* (New York: St. Martin's Minotaur, 2002);

Ann Sanders Cargill, "Chief Medical Examiner Kay Scarpetta," *Clues,* 22, no. 2 (2001): 35–48;

Susan Allen Ford, "Tracing the Other in Patricia D. Cornwell: Costs and Accommodations," *Clues,* 20, no. 2 (1999): 27–34;

Rosemary Herbert, *The Fatal Art of Entertainment: Interviews with Mystery Writers* (New York: G. K. Hall, 1994), pp. 136–261.

John Russell Coryell
(1851 – 1924)

ᥫᦰ
SERIES
(1886–1936)

NICK CARTER

Nick Carter is a private detective featured for fifty years in a series of dime novels and pulp magazines, including *Detective Story Magazine, Magnet Library, New Magnet Library, Nick Carter Weekly,* and the *New Nick Carter Weekly*. The dime novel was a cheaply printed, paper-wrapped format that offered sensationalistic adventure stories and melodramas tailored to the tastes of the increasing number of literate Americans in the latter half of the nineteenth century; like their twentieth-century successors, the pulp magazines, dime novels were enormously popular but considered by some to be disreputable. Carter appeared in more than three thousand stories, written by several dozen authors, from 1886 to 1936, beginning with *The Old Detective's Pupil; or, The Mysterious Crime of Madison Square*. In his first appearance he is a young private detective in New York City. He ages slowly over the course of the dime novels, and in the later stories marries twice and watches his adopted son grow to adulthood and marry. In the pulp-magazine stories he does not age and is not married.

Carter's background is described in his first appearance. He was raised by his father, the famous private detective Old Sim Carter, to be as great a man and crime solver as possible. Toward this end, Sim began training Nick when he was a boy, putting him through a series of physical and mental tests so that Nick is not only capable of lifting "a horse with ease . . . while a heavy man is seated in the saddle," but also is knowledgeable in every area that might conceivably have to do with crime fighting, from the sciences to various languages to art to physiology. Carter is 5'4" tall but is well-muscled, tanned, gray-eyed, and handsome. He lives in a mansion on Madison Avenue in New York City and uses a variety of vehicles, including automobiles, monoplanes, and his yacht, the *Gull,* to travel while on the job.

As an adult Carter is acclaimed as the greatest private detective in the country. He is respected and consulted by the police and enjoys the admiration of the public. His cases often require him to travel around the United States and the world, but he maintains a healthy set of relationships with his family and assistants. He marries Ethel Dalton in his first adventure, and she remains a semiregular character in the series until she is killed in 1904. Carter's first assistant is Patsy Murphy, a bootblack who becomes a full-fledged detective and eventually marries a beautiful South American woman, Adelina de Mendoza, who in turn becomes one of Carter's most valuable agents. Murphy was eventually phased out in favor of Carter's permanent sidekick, Chickering Valentine, a teenage Nevada ranch hand who is a physical double for Carter. Valentine, later named "Chick Carter," begins helping his adoptive father solve crimes while working on his own as a detective. Carter's cast of supporting characters changes and evolves over time, and ranges from the brilliant schoolgirl Ida Jones to "Talika the Geisha Girl," a Japanese detective; Ah Toon, the private bodyguard and royal detective to the emperor of China; and Ten-Ichi, "the son of the Mikado."

Although Carter's enemies are often ordinary blackmailers, kidnappers, Black Hand/Mafia thugs, and murderers, he also has a rogues' gallery of unusual opponents—including the sociopathic vivisector Dr. Quartz; the beautiful Russian princess and deranged criminal mastermind Dazaar the Arch Fiend; the cyborg Paraxtel of the Iron Arm; and Princess Olga, the tiger chief of the Russian Nihilists. Although most of Carter's stories involve ordinary crime, some venture into more fantastic territory. In one story he encounters in the Andes a lost race of mixed native and Viking descent. In another he discovers a hidden city in the Tibetan Himalayas whose inhabitants are masters of "vibrational science" and can channel vibrations to kill others.

The passing of time was slowly acknowledged in the Carter stories. Characters grew older, married, and had children. The children of enemies Carter defeated appeared as adults to fight him. And Carter himself aged incrementally, from twenty-four during his debut to mid thirties by the end of the series.

Carter's character evolved to match the changing literary environment. When he debuted, he was a standard dime-novel detective who was described as brilliant but whose crime solving relied as much on brawn as brain. Within a decade, after Sherlock Holmes had become popular in the United States, Carter changed and became, like Holmes, a brilliant consulting detective whose conclusions were the result of his intellect. In the 1920s and 1930s he became a typical pulp private detective, losing most of his supporting cast, wealth, and history and relying more on his fists than his brain to solve crimes.

Carter's longevity and popularity made him influential on other detective characters. Many dime-novel detectives were modeled on him, and aspects of his character were models for later pulp heroes.

Although Carter is a working private detective and charges for his services, he is primarily motivated by a desire to see justice triumph over evil; his stated goal is to "aim for the right and for righting wrongs." He is resolutely honest and moral and never gives in to temptation; his only vices are beer and the occasional cigar. But while Carter's sympathies are always with the victim, he is not interested in any social restructuring or sustained critique of the establishment. Members of the establishment are occasionally portrayed as criminals, including corrupt bankers and politicians, but generally the resolution of a story leads to a restoration of the social status quo, with the criminal members of the establishment portrayed as aberrations rather than the products of their environment. Crime, in the Nick Carter stories, is usually an individual and isolated event, rather than an indication of a social problem, and in this regard Carter, although a crime fighter, is a defender of the establishment rather than the individual.

Discussion Questions

1. How does the portrayal of Nick Carter compare to Arthur Conan Doyle's portrayal of Sherlock Holmes, Raymond Chandler's portrayal of Philip Marlowe, or Robert Parker's portrayal of Spenser?

2. In what ways is Nick Carter a particularly American character?

3. What statements can be made about the Nick Carter stories based on the ethnic identities of his friends and his enemies?

4. How do the Nick Carter stories compare to modern serial popular culture, such as detective television shows?

—*Jess Nevins*

REFERENCES

J. Randolph Cox, "The Nick Carter Stories," in *Mystery and Suspense Writers: The Literature of Crime, Detection, and Espionage,* 2 volumes, edited by Robin W. Winks (New York: Scribners, 1998): 131–142;

Michael Denning, *Mechanic Accents: Dime Novels and Working-Class Culture in America* (New York: Verso, 1987);

Jess Nevins, *The Encyclopedia of Fantastic Victoriana* (Austin, Tex.: MonkeyBrain, 2005).

James Gould Cozzens
(August 19, 1903 – August 9, 1978)

&❧

BY LOVE POSSESSED
(New York: Harcourt, Brace, 1957)

HELEN DETWEILER

Near the end of *By Love Possessed,* James Gould Cozzens's protagonist, Arthur Winner, observes of Helen Detweiler: "If not tragedy's, Helen was unhappiness's own child! Some fatal sign must be on her. . . . mistake and misadventure knew whom to dog." Thirteen years before the forty-nine-hour "present" of the novel, Helen Detweiler, then age sixteen, was bereaved of both parents by a canoeing accident. After a cheerful shopping errand with the daughters of a lakeside summer neighbor, she returned to learn that her parents had drowned and to witness, with her friends, the death by heart attack of the exhausted would-be rescuer, their father.

The effects on Helen are revealed through the observations and perceptions of Arthur Winner, whose second wife, Clarissa, was the elder of Helen's two companions on that evening. Helen's security, emotional and financial, have been destroyed. Her age, the loss of both parents, and the immediate shift from upper-middle-class comfort to working-girl necessity have affected her temperament and her future. (Her father, a banker, had planned his future carefully; he had intended to die rich, but he "had not intended to die that night; nor this year; nor for many a year.") The responsibility Helen has assumed for the welfare and happiness of her five-year-old brother, Ralph, has motivated her and has required of her stamina and monastic self-renunciation. Did she suppose that her parents died in punishment for their—or perhaps for her own emerging—sexuality? Arthur Winner asks himself. It is evident to him that the care of Ralph has provided Helen with a defense against any importunities from possible suitors. From neurosis she has forged strength of character.

Young Arthur Winner was initially appalled at her sixteen-year-old's resolution, mistrusting the sentimentality of his senior law partner, Noah Tuttle: "Helen was a good girl and a brave girl, and Noah . . . revered goodness and bravery." Arthur Winner's then-living father, also a law partner, concurred with Noah's opinion but rejected his sentimentality: "It's what Helen wants to do," he reminded his son, having "identified that type of true resolve whose force is as nearly inflexible as any human force can be."

Helen has kept her family's mortgaged in-town house by taking boarders. She has trained as a legal secretary and is still employed by Tuttle, now aged. She as bookkeeper has followed Tuttle's instructions without error and without question. Industrious and honest, she has neither personal ambition nor curiosity. Her life and her future, established at sixteen, have been given meaning and purpose through her devotion to her brother.

"Everything frightens me," she tells Arthur Winner, as he tries to reassure her that her strength and courage, which have been tested repeatedly, are extraordinary. In the forty-nine-hour "present" of the novel, Ralph, who ought to be on the point of fulfilling his sister's hopes by starting college, is resistant. Squeamish as to sexual matters, Helen is otherwise clear-sighted about Ralph. Knowing that he is weak, selfish, and without integrity does not make her love

him less; but her unconditional love and her habits of indulging and excusing him have made her powerless to control him. When things get really bad for Ralph (his high-school girlfriend pregnant; another girl bullied into bringing a charge of rape against him; armed pursuit—however ineffectual—by the enraged father of the first girl), he sees no solution but—defying a court order—to flee the state with stolen money, one hundred dollars that he knows to be at hand in his sister's boardinghouse. The sum is adequate only for immediate flight. Helen's solution to her own despair (the money having been scrupulously repaid by her) is not altogether dissimilar from Ralph's. She too seeks immediate escape and drinks cleaning fluid. Unlike Ralph's, however, her escape is permanent.

Helen's suicide results in Arthur Winner's accidental discovery, almost at the end of the novel, that for decades Tuttle's trust payments have been juggled, always with Helen's unsuspicious compliance. The dilemma confronting Arthur Winner submerges the sorrow and regret that he ought to feel: had he been less busy and less preoccupied on the last day of Helen's life, he could have given her reassurance and hope. "Evils that a timely worry . . . could have prevented or eased, befell you as a rule without warning," he reflects, as he talks over the day's events with Clarissa on the night of Helen's suicide. The clues to Helen's sense of deprivation and despair are there for him, as they are for the reader. Commenting on Helen's act of suicide, Julius Penrose says to Arthur Winner, "The sentence, of course, is on the act, not the person. I pity the person. I take her to be mad, possessed by love."

Discussion Questions

1. Why does Helen dedicate her life to providing for Ralph?

2. Clarissa Winner has grown up with Helen. In what ways do they contrast in character and experience?

3. Helen clearly knows how worthless Ralph is. Why does she refuse to acknowledge and act on her understanding?

4. What does Julius Penrose mean when he says of Helen, "I take her to be mad, possessed by love"?

—Arlyn Bruccoli

JULIUS PENROSE

The protagonist and point-of-view character in James Gould Cozzens's *By Love Possessed* is Arthur Winner Jr., but the hero of the novel is Julius Penrose. Intelligent and independent of mind, without illusion, realistic in his expectations and therefore unsurprised by the whims and follies of others, Julius affects an uncompromising manner and speaks to Arthur Winner, at least, in a tone that is formal, measured, sometimes humorous, and always ironic: "the finished phrases, in their level precision almost rehearsed-sounding, the familiar deliberately mincing tones that mocked themselves with their own affectation." His manner of speaking to other people is not knowable: he appears in person in only two scenes, two days apart and both tête-a-tête with Arthur Winner, on the Friday night and the Sunday afternoon of the novel's forty-nine-hour "present," in their shared law offices. He is otherwise seen through the reflections, recollections, and conversations of Arthur Winner.

"By common consent, I'm a hard man, . . . easily put out of patience," Julius says, in explanation of his concurrence in his wife's wish that she have a consultation with Arthur Winner before her formal conversion to Roman Catholicism. "That Julius had such a picture of himself, and that many people who knew Julius Penrose slightly thought of him as a hard man were both doubtless true; yet an acquaintance of years inclined Arthur Winner to say that both Julius and common consent erred. . . . Could Arthur Winner pick from his recollection one instance of the self-denominated hard man acting (though he might often seem to speak it) a hard man's regardless, ruthless part?" Julius suggests that Marjorie, his wife, may have a hope that churchgoing Episcopalian Arthur Winner will successfully argue for a less extreme religious alternative. If Julius is misled by wish (the alternative would indeed be preferable to *him*), it is the only instance in the novel of his self-deception; more probably, he wants to make the promised consultation palatable to the willing but reluctant Arthur Winner. The consultation does not occur as planned; Marjorie incapacitates herself with alcohol, and her spokeswoman and religious mentor, Polly Pratt, comes alone.

Marjorie—through Mrs. Pratt—in fact hopes for Arthur Winner's "forgiveness" for her sin in having induced him, with careful planning and timing, into a brief sexual affair with her during his period of widowhood a few years earlier. The adultery, which becomes known to the reader during the interview, is the interview's real subject. That the adultery has been long known and forgiven by Julius is revealed to the reader and to Arthur Winner at the end of the novel. "Total, the exposure; . . . yet who condemned him, who scorned him, who triumphed over him? . . . Julius's gaze . . . rested on him, as though without use of words to say: . . . you had nothing to fear. Don't you see, I've known all along. Our pact is: As I am, you accept me; as you are, I accept you."

Marjorie's lust for Arthur Winner, her infidelity, and Julius's forgiveness are explained to the reader through oblique allusion to the impotence that resulted from Julius's contracting infantile paralysis ten years before the present of the novel. That his legs are useless is an observable condition: the laborious, assisted entrance he makes into the law office is the reader's first view of him. "Julius lived with pain—not acute; but never in his waking hours wholly relieved." He was married ("I think I could say that Marjorie as maenad [his term for her compelling sexuality] was served no worse by me than she would have been by most men") and the father of two children at the time of his illness. His impotence is alluded to in private conversation by Arthur Winner's wife, Clarissa, the unwilling recipient of Marjorie's confidential revelations, which Clarissa half believes.

Julius is possessed of a quality that enables him to transcend pain and affliction: a sense of humor. He is witty, and because his attitude to himself is also uncompromising, his humor sometimes works as social commentary and not merely as a matter of characterization. Speaking of Marjorie's "project" (her religious conversion): ". . . so many of the news-making converts fell in categories to me naturally suspect. A fancy or high-brow author or two. Sentimental newspaper columnists. Inmates of the theater. Figures of flamboyance in politics. Quondam leading Reds or professional atheists. Uneasy Episcopalian ministers. In short, men and women who must long have been ill-balanced."

A joke that is just funny can nevertheless be understood to portray the self-mockery of the afflicted man: his conversation with Arthur Winner over, and having retrieved the folder he stopped by for, Julius moves again to the chauffeur-driven car that will take him back to his legal business in Washington. The car owner's poodle greets him with a bark. "'What enchanting intelligence! What a ravishing creature!' Julius Penrose said. 'Were I younger, sound, and a single man, I'd ask her to marry me.'"

The second of their meetings occurs in the same place and almost at the end of the novel. Having learned of Helen Detweiler's suicide, Julius anticipates that Arthur Winner will have happened to glance at her current bookkeeping and will therefore have made the discovery that senior partner Noah Tuttle's accounts are seriously short. Julius himself has known and said nothing since he first joined the firm thirteen years earlier. ("My turn of mind, while not I think inquisitive, was and is investigative. . . . From my standpoint, the business was strictly Noah's; and he was . . . handling it ably." Noah's motive—unique in financial history, Julius surmises—was to artificially endow a trust he oversaw that would otherwise have been bankrupt.) As incoming partner after the time of the initial malfeasance (not the case with Arthur Winner), Julius has no legal responsibility for repayment. His observations of Noah Tuttle's personal frugality and systematic increments of repayment have therefore been disinterested. He is able to overcome Arthur Winner's horrified opposition to their continued silence by insisting on otherwise sharing his financial burden: "I, also, am . . . not without human weakness of vanity and self regard . . . if you're resolved to ruin yourself, I'll have to join you." Finally, to the departing Arthur Winner, Julius says, "Be of good cheer, my friend. In this business, we're not licked. . . . We'll come through this. I have decided that we will. I now get to work. I now see where we stand."

Discussion Questions

1. Julius claims to be a misanthrope, but he is devoted to Arthur Winner Jr. What is the basis of Julian's feelings about Arthur? Are Julius's feelings for Arthur stronger than Arthur's for him?

2. Julius is an accomplished ironist. Can the reader be sure whether Julius is indulging in bitter humor or in truth telling in such passages as "the whole national horde of nuts and queers"?

3. *By Love Possessed* outraged liberal critics, and much of the outrage was generated by Julius. Is he a spokesman for Cozzens?

4. Cozzens denounced John Steinbeck's work as sentimental. Is *By Love Possessed* antisentimental?

—*Arlyn Bruccoli*

MARJORIE PENROSE

Marjorie Penrose is the pivotal female character in James Gould Cozzens's *By Love Possessed:* the sleeping nymph for whom Cupid's arrow will strike the peeping shepherd of the ornamental clock described at the beginning and at the end of the novel. But she appears in person very seldom and is seen in the present chiefly through the eyes of Arthur Winner's wife, Clarissa, whose dislike would be even greater than it is if she knew—or credited—Marjorie's whole history. How much Marjorie has actually confided to Clarissa is unclear. In any case, Clarissa regards Marjorie as a compulsive liar.

Observing the awkwardness of Priscilla, Marjorie's teenage daughter, Clarissa comments to her husband, "They move the same way—all over themselves. You even begin to see that expression of Marjorie's—you know; that really odd slant-eyed look, with her mouth open just a little. . . . It's a pity the children didn't take after Julius more." Marjorie's twelve-year-old son, Stuart, is clear-sighted and contemptuous of his mother's reliance on alcohol. She drinks sometimes for courage, sometimes to free herself from the restraints of decorum, and sometimes as a means to avoid confrontation. Clarissa cautions her husband to avoid becoming an intermediary in Marjorie's latest crisis, a conversion to Roman Catholicism: "She works herself up. Then she tries to get everyone around her worked up, too." Keeping Marjorie offstage, described and accounted for through Clarissa, is a useful narrative device: the history of her romantic entanglements is delayed, and neither author nor reader succumbs to her allure by accepting that her sexual magnetism gives her importance.

When Marjorie first appears in person, she is tipsy, somewhat maudlin, and full of generalized confession and remorse. She secretly awaits Arthur Winner's delayed return home on the night following Clarissa's description of her earlier appearance. He notices that Marjorie is wearing what must be the same slacks and sweater that Clarissa had described (omitting his wife's addition that they were "all too evidently" all she was wearing). He observes that "though this pain of Marjorie's was real, and hurt her, she still found in it . . . some sort of harrowing enjoyment." She alludes to her adoration of his dead first wife, Hope; he believes in the reality of her tears, "but that picture of what friends they had been was one of later emotional fancy." His behavior is kind, but he simply wants her to go home, across the road, so that he can enter his house.

Although Marjorie is not loved by author or reader, she is enduringly loved by the most intelligent and clear-sighted character in the novel, her husband, Julius Penrose. ("I know he loves me. . . . It's a love I'm not worthy of," she says to Arthur Winner. But even when Marjorie tells the truth, her emotions are exaggerated and therefore false.) Having been the lawyer who represented her in her divorce, Julius knows the sordid and violent history of her first marriage. Once he succumbs to her, he knows the effect she must have on any man she desires: "of Marjorie's hair of gold, of Marjorie's adorable face, of the sweet disorder, the pretty confusion of Marjorie's ways." (His description of her is spoken in irony, as he explains the college-girl crush of Mrs. Pratt, Marjorie's Roman Catholic confidante and intercessor.) Julius has been crippled and rendered impotent by polio ten years prior to the forty-nine-hour "present" of the novel. His love is therefore pure, now purged of lust. His understanding of her nature—compulsive, self-dramatizing, penitential—is complete, and, despite his habitually ironic tone, full of tenderness. Of Marjorie's manner, he says to Arthur Winner, "She's preordained to fumble; she's fated always to confound confusion." Of her planned conversion, he says, "Let her be happy. I'd no more argue with her than I'd take . . . a blindman's coppers. This, assure her, is how I *really* feel."

Explaining Marjorie's nature to Arthur Winner—for many years his law partner and closest friend—Julius says, "the need[s] uppermost . . . in the conscious Marjorie . . . [are] little-girl needs; pettings, treats, playtimes. . . . Inside the little girl [is] . . . the principle of passion . . . something like a maenad. . . . that Fatal Woman of story and history. . . . One sees Circe; one sees swine. What was in that cup? . . . Her feeling sufficiently penetrated, the principle of passion . . . is made to stir. The stir is electrifying . . . rage answer rage . . . few men of normal potency prove able to refrain their foot from that path."

The reader does not yet know that Arthur Winner, after the death of his first wife and before his engagement to Clarissa, had an affair with Marjorie. And even when the affair is forced upon Arthur Winner's memory during his interview with Mrs. Pratt, he does not suspect that Julius has long known. At the end of the novel, after Helen Detweiler's suicide has made necessary the partners' collusion in concealing Noah Tuttle's misappropriations, Julius says, "If you knew of something . . . you thought it better I should not know, I'm persuaded you'd . . . try every way to keep it from me. . . . Let me be more explicit. I'm persuaded, Arthur, that you *have* done as much for me. And, if unknown to you, I've always thanked you for it."

Discussion Questions

1. *By Love Possessed* fueled charges that Cozzens was anti-Catholic. Does his characterization of Marjorie Penrose support this claim?

2. Marjorie is an agent of disorder in the novel. Does she have any redeeming qualities?

3. Julius and Marjorie Penrose are an ill-suited couple. Why did he marry her? Why does he remain married to her?

4. Marjorie is primarily defined through the points of view of other characters in the novel. How do the scenes in which she actually appears enlarge the reader's perceptions of her?

—*Arlyn Bruccoli*

ARTHUR WINNER JR.

Arthur Winner Jr. is the character through whom all the events of *By Love Possessed*—the past as well as the forty-nine-hour "present"—are perceived. The novel is told in the third person, but the point of view is always Arthur Winner's. Thoughtful, reflective, clear-sighted about the world and about himself, he has a lawyer's realistic attitude toward human nature and does not spend his emotional capital on useless regrets. His scrupulous attention to duty and wish to behave with personal as well as perceived honor are accompanied by tact. His habitual kindness is remarked upon by other characters. It is therefore interesting that fifty-four-year-old Arthur Winner (he is always referred to by both names) is so little likable.

In the novel's first scene he visits his mother in her house and treats her with courtesy and patience, but without real love. He frequently gives thought to his late father, "the Man of Reason," whose law firm he joined when he finished law school at Harvard. Though without his father's mechanical ability or passion for gardening, he is, his mother insists, very like him. "Was he also like *her?*" he wonders later. "Like her, did he determinedly protect himself against unwelcome and disturbing thoughts . . . ? Such ugly concepts . . . threatened his equanimity. He said: Let them not be! One firm exercise of disbelief—there they weren't!" His feelings for his children are similarly detached. For his lawless "warrior" elder son, a pilot who died in a reckless airplane stunt during World War II, his chief emotion had been anxiety that his wife be kept from knowing the details. His second son, now also a lawyer, has disappointed him by choosing the prestige of a Washington, D.C., practice instead of joining the family firm. Arthur Winner is in general content to leave the upbringing of his teenage daughter to her capable stepmother.

During the forty-nine-hour "present" of *By Love Possessed,* Arthur Winner is partly occupied by a legal matter assumed, without expectation of payment, on behalf of his senior partner's secretary, Helen Detweiler. He represents her eighteen-year-old brother, Ralph, who has been accused of rape. The charge is false, and the accusation is soon dropped, but Ralph's problems escalate: the father of his pregnant high-school girlfriend comes looking for him with a gun, and he steals enough money to flee the state, in violation of a court order. ("When someone's scared's when you really can't trust him," Noah Tuttle says to Arthur Winner.) The situation

is too much for Ralph's anguished sister, who takes her own life. Arthur Winner could have prevented Helen's death had he been less busy and less otherwise preoccupied. He acknowledges as much to himself with regret but without self-blame; even the regret is soon swallowed up in personal anxieties.

Arthur Winner's first marriage, which ended with the death of his sweet, rather child-like, sexually frigid wife as a result of complications in an unsuspected pregnancy, was dutifully mourned—but his second wife suits him much better: *"the best break you ever got!"* he acknowledges to himself. Clarissa is an excellent wife: younger but not inappropriately so, ardent, handsome, and athletic (once a talented tennis player with national aspirations), of Arthur Winner's social circle and known to him since childhood, and fond of his teenage daughter. She is also utterly convinced of her great good fortune in marrying Arthur Winner. Clarissa is given to sententious declarations of "we women" wisdom, and her defect is a smugness that would, in fact, be shattered by more complete knowledge of her husband. Arthur Winner's adultery with Marjorie Penrose, his best friend's wife—occurring as it did before her marriage—she would probably forgive. The financial ruin that would result from his responsibility for his senior partner's misappropriations, were they made known, would be devastating to both Winners.

Those misappropriations, committed by Noah Tuttle, the father of Arthur Winner's first wife, are not suspected by Arthur Winner until, at the end of the novel, the suicide of Helen Detweiler results in his accidental discovery "that Noah Tuttle, this paragon of honesty, this soul of all honor, blameless of life and pure of crime . . . had—for years?—been helping himself to, now repaying, now taking again, money that was not his. . . . [Arthur Winner] said aloud: "I am a man alone.""

His moment of melodrama subsides in dramatic irony. His *physical* solitude is immediately relieved by the arrival of Julius Penrose, his law partner and closest friend. The intensity of horror he feels, succeeded by fear that the legally mandated action of exposure will ruin him financially, is mitigated by Julius's revelation that he had made the discovery himself thirteen years earlier and that Noah, given more time, may yet finish repaying the supposedly solvent trust. (Noah's motive in the original misappropriation was to fund a bankrupt trust that he also oversaw.) Julius has remained silent about Noah's actions. Why, Julius asks without bitterness, should Arthur imagine that he must expose the truth; has he not kept another secret? Arthur Winner understands for the first time that his friend has known about and forgiven his adultery. The great irony in *By Love Possessed* is that the presumed misanthrope Julius Penrose is capable of stronger love than anyone else in the novel.

Discussion Questions

1. Arthur Winner is the principal character in *By Love Possessed,* but Julius Penrose is its hero. Discuss ways in which the novel supports this distinction.

2. Cozzens wrote about the social structure of a community and the men who maintain it. What is Arthur Winner's role in Brocton?

3. The plot of *By Love Possessed* ultimately turns on Arthur Winner's affair with his partner's wife. Is Arthur's conduct credible?

4. Community is a key element in James Gould Cozzens's novels. Compare his portrait of Brocton with Sinclair Lewis's portrait of Gopher Prairie in *Main Street* or Zenith in *Babbitt.*

—Arlyn Bruccoli

GUARD OF HONOR
(New York: Harcourt, Brace, 1948)

COLONEL NORMAN ROSS AND CAPTAIN NATHANIEL HICKS

Colonel Norman Ross and Captain Nathaniel Hicks are important characters in James Gould Cozzens's *Guard of Honor.* The novel has a traditional omniscient-third-person narrative; no character is always present or even usually present. Nevertheless, although there are many scenes in which neither appears, the omniscient author relies heavily on the perceptions of Ross and Hicks. They are together rarely: in the first episode, on an airplane flying back to Ocanara Air Force in Florida, where the rest of

the action of the novel takes place; briefly in a scene at the airfield near the end of the novel; and in a key scene mid-novel, in which a potential crisis of racism in the army is resolved (Ross being an active participant in the resolution, Hicks present by accident and only as a witness).

Although their personalities, ages, and situations are not alike, Ross and Hicks are similarly intelligent, observant, and clear-sighted. Each perceives himself as emotionally detached, though circumstances affect Hicks in ways he does not expect. Neither is a professional soldier, though they are in the air force for the duration of the war. Both understand and submit to rules of military hierarchy, and their egos are not tormented or inflated by gradations of rank. Necessary background information on other key characters is given as part of their reflections: the histories of General Bus Beal, who is in charge of the air force base, and of his former wingman, Lieutenant Colonel Benny Carricker—both present in the first scene—are given through Colonel Ross's recollections. Similarly, the histories of Captains Donald Andrews and Clarence Duchemin are recollected by Hicks. (Andrews is self-effacing and mathematically phonemenal; Duchemin is a sensualist with similarities to Dr. Bull in *The Last Adam* but younger, smarter, better educated, and funnier.)

Guard of Honor takes place on three consecutive days in early September 1943. On the flight to Ocanara are Beal; Carricker; Ross; and Beal's crew chief, Master Sergeant Dominic Pellerino; Hicks, a magazine editor in civilian life; Second Lieutenant Amanda Turck; and T/5 Mortimer McIntyre, whose return from furlough would have been AWOL but for Hicks's kindly intercession. All of these characters are of importance in the novel except McIntyre, whose race—African American—prefigures the potential crisis and mutiny.

Ross is a judge in civilian life. His wife, Cora—one of Cozzens's wise and devoted women—has accompanied him to Ocanara: " . . . a normal woman must wholly and heartily hate men for their folly and hypocrisy . . . who would want him, who would mind losing him? . . . She could not, or did not want to, live without this stupid old man." Cora does not fear losing her husband in combat, but her three sons—all of her children—have enlisted, and her real anguish is for the youngest, a college student who might have applied for a deferment and whose joining up was therefore unnecessary.

As their plane comes in to land, another plane suddenly appears in front of them. Though General Beal is a heroic flyer, it is Carricker who aborts the landing and saves them. That experience and the next day's news that Colonel Woodman of Sellers Field (years ago Beal's Squadron Commander, now disappointed in his career and drunk much of the time) has killed himself are unsettling to Beal. He is deprived of Carricker's companionship: Carricker in his anger has punched the pilot of the other plane hard enough to send him to the hospital and is put under arrest in quarters. That the injured pilot, Lieutenant Stanley Willis, is Negro has nothing to do with Carricker's antagonism. As Ross explains later to his wife, "Racial prejudice may be low and infantile; but it is a form of social consciousness. Any form of social consciousness is too advanced for Benny."

Both Willis's injury and a subsequent officers' club incident are misunderstood and manipulated by the self-righteous, defiantly liberal Lieutenant Jim Edsell (a writer in civilian life), who hopes to foment a racial incident that will embarrass the air force and cause trouble with their Floridian hosts. Beal, whose frustration is compounded by his longing to return to combat, leaves his responsibilities in Ross's hands. (Beal has taken a plane and gone flying; the experience is restorative.) Ross is up to the job, aided by the circumstance that Lieutenant Willis has saved the air force three bombers and is scheduled to receive a medal. General Jo-Jo Nichols—smooth, powerful, and missing nothing—has arrived from Washington with the Distinguished Flying Cross, and Ross defeats Edsell's scheme of making Willis's father a witness to his son's humiliation; instead, the Willises share a triumph. "Nathaniel Hicks . . . began to see, not sorry, that though Edsell might be right in his often displayed assumption that there was no fool like an old fool; yet, as well as old fools, there were smart old men."

Cora Ross understands that a wife should be with her husband if possible and is privately severe when her husband tells her that Hicks's wife has stayed home rather than move their children out of school. With regard to Hicks, her criticism proves prophetic. Without any scheme of infidelity

and without falling in love, though Amanda Turck is an appealing and intelligent woman—just the woman for Hicks if he were free—Hicks does make love to her. His unexpectedly empty apartment, the mistaken cancellation of her off-base weekend hotel reservation, and a drink or two too many contribute to his misunderstanding of himself. He has also been chafing under a professional disappointment: he knows that the training manual on which he has been at work will be, if published, valueless (the pilots he interviews tell him so); a scheme to supervise an article about General Beal for publication in a national magazine has begun to excite him, but Beal, during his period of gloom, calls it off. The telephone call that rouses both Hicks and Amanda Turck tells him that the interview is revived, that he must come at once to the airfield to catch the plane (with General Nichols, as it happens) to Washington. It is clear that Amanda Turck expects nothing from him and that she will therefore not be disappointed.

Discussion Questions

1. Ross and Hicks are both point-of-view characters. Do they represent different viewpoints? Are they both spokesmen for Cozzens?

2. What is Cozzens's attitude toward professional officers? Compare with attitudes toward officers expressed in works by James Jones or Norman Mailer or Joseph Heller.

3. Hostile critics charge Cozzens with coldness. Are Ross and Hicks deficient in emotion?

—*Arlyn Bruccoli*

❧

THE JUST AND THE UNJUST
(New York: Harcourt, Brace, 1942)

ABNER COATES

James Gould Cozzens's *The Just and the Unjust* is structured around the week-long death-penalty trial of three men for kidnapping and murder. It begins with a two-and-a-half-page prologue, titled "DOCKET," that ends with the introduction of the novel's overly scrupulous, uptight, unheroic hero: "*Eo die,* the Assistant District Attorney, Abner

Coates, Esq., at 10:40 A.M. opens the Case for the Commonwealth." Because of the unusual and sensational nature of the trial—the drug-dealer victim and kidnap-murder conspirators are all outsiders—the courtroom is packed with onlookers. Abner has taken pains with his speech, writing it out and rehearsing in secret before a mirror, and he is rewarded with surprising praise from his boss, District Attorney Martin Bunting. "I didn't know whether anyone could hear me," says Abner, who has been speaking for his audience. Bunting's reassurance naturally takes Abner's "they" to mean the jury, and Abner recognizes the unintended reprimand: why should the spectators matter?

The trial concludes with what is acknowledged as a defeat for the prosecution—the men are convicted of second-degree murder, and their sentences will be shorter than that of the conspirator who pleaded guilty and testified for the Commonwealth. Abner is aware that Bunting injured his case with his unadorned summing-up, and believes that he himself, less unwilling to stoop to oratorical persuasion, might have been successful.

The crime and trial are minutely detailed, but the novel is not a detective story, though it ends just twenty-six pages after the jury is discharged. Besides the conspirators, their hangers-on, and their victim, a cross-section of the town's inhabitants is presented and characterized: Abner and his boss, Bunting; Abner's father, Linus Coates, a retired judge recently incapacitated by stroke; Abner's close friend from childhood and from law school, now his professional antagonist, Harry Wurtz; Abner's deservedly beloved longtime girlfriend, Bonnie Drummond; her lazy, semidishonest, once-widowed and once-abandoned mother and her appalling half siblings; the overworked and overly powerful head of the Republican Party in a one-party community, Jesse Gearhart; Judge Vredenburg, the presiding judge, and his flirtatious eighteen-year-old daughter, Annette, who has set her sights on Wurtz; and so many other people—courthouse personnel, additional lawyers, partygoers, domestics—that the reader has an illusion of knowing the community.

Abner Coates carries integrity to a fault, and his self-knowledge is such that he is aware of it. In a district where nomination by the Republican Party is

tantamount to election, he initially rebuffs an overture to run for district attorney—a job he wants and is uniquely qualified for, with a salary he needs—because he resents the power of the party boss and dislikes appearing to belong to him. That he wants to marry but can hardly do so on an income from independent law practice makes him the more suspicious of his own motives. Though not passionate, he is not a reluctant wooer; there is doubt neither as to the rightness of his intended nor of his fidelity or hers. His marriage will mean Bonnie's quitting work (not an unreasonable stipulation on his part in 1939) and, therefore, his assuming financial responsibility for her selfish, ethically careless mother and three young half brothers. Reflection that Bunting, who recommended Abner and will think himself obligated to remain in the job rather than move up if Abner declines it, causes him to reconsider—a decision-reversal aided by a better understanding of the powers and personality of Jesse Gearhart. And having committed himself to Jesse, Abner understands that he has lost the freedom of open criticism; that now "he himself was part of how things were." Similarly, committing himself to Bonnie, "suddenly he remembered what he had forgotten—that if he suffered losses, he would have inestimable gains."

Abner's self-knowledge includes awareness of his intellectual limitations. (His dislike of Jesse arose from Jesse's compliments: "If Jesse really thought so, Jesse was a fool; if Jesse did not really think so, he must imagine Abner was a fool.") "The innocent supposition, entertained by most people, that even if they are not brilliant, they are not dumb, is correct only in a very relative sense." Abner learned in law school that the abilities "that got him, without distinction but also without much exertion, through all previous lessons and examinations, were not first rate abilities handicapped by laziness, but second rate." A newspaper report that the fellow student whose example taught him that lesson has been made partner in an important law firm causes Abner no resentment, but he observes that Harry, "reporting the item, looked disconsolate." "A petty triumph of grinds and pedants!" Harry recalls of a law-school competition that he, unlike Abner—who came in last—did not enter. "Few if any people have more brains that I have" is Harry's self-assessment. That he is wrong is understood by the reader, who trusts Abner's attitude—but Harry is persuasive before a jury.

In the novel's last scene, Abner recounts to his ailing father the events of the day: the jury's disappointing verdicts, his own personal and political commitments, the uncertainty of the future augmented by the looming war in Europe. "Nobody promises you a good time or an easy time. . . . when we think of the past we regret and when we think of the future we fear," his father says.

> "Abner said, 'What do you want of me?'"
>
> "'We just want you to do the impossible,' Judge Coates said."

Discussion Questions

1. Abner is dull. Does Cozzens admire him? Is the reader expected to admire him?

2. What does Judge Coates mean when he tells Abner that "in the present every day is a miracle"?

3. Bonnie has the approval of an author who did not approve of most of his female characters. What are her admirable qualities? Is she presented as a model for female conduct?

4. Cozzens often created male characters who are shaped by their professions. How do two of Cozzens's protagonists—Abner Coates and Arthur Winner Jr.—embody lawyers?

—*Arlyn Bruccoli*

✎

THE LAST ADAM
(New York: Harcourt, Brace, 1933)

Dr. George Bull

Dr. George Bull is the physician for a small Connecticut town, New Winton, in James Gould Cozzens's *The Last Adam*. Although the title (not Cozzens's first choice) ironically connects Dr. Bull to both Christ and Adam, the character shares few similarities with either of these biblical figures. Nor is he the beloved, dedicated country doctor who has become a cliché in fiction. At the age of sixty-seven, he is hefty, stubborn, libidinous, and fierce when cornered, much like the animal that shares his name.

Dr. Bull is a character more primal than social, and his professional responsibility to people as the town's sole doctor seems incongruous with his nature.

The novel revolves around a typhoid epidemic in New Winton (based on Kent, Connecticut), for which Dr. Bull, as the town's health officer, is held personally responsible (he neglected to inspect a construction camp where the workers' latrines emptied into the town reservoir). Dr. Bull's presumed carelessness regularly enrages New Winton's citizens; they resent the doctor's unreliability and his tendency to spend hours at his mistress's farm. His ethics seem questionable, and the doctor says of himself, "An old horse doctor like me looks at [his patients] and all he can see is that medical science is perfectly useless in ninety-five out of every hundred cases." When the epidemic strikes, Dr. Bull knows that a doctor, even the prominent Dr. Verney in nearby Stansbury, cannot save all of his patients. Days into the crisis, Dr. Bull considers facts: with forty-three cases and the illness's proven mortality rate of seventeen percent, he can realistically expect seven or eight more deaths in his community. He knows that according to the laws of modern medical science, he cannot save this handful of victims ("'Only question is, who'll they be?'"). He understands it is not a matter of whether those seven or eight will die but of who will die. This attitude is mistaken for indifference by Dr. Bull's patients.

Ultimately, the novel addresses the structure of community, and events culminate in a town meeting where New Winton's citizens try to terminate Dr. Bull for incompetence. The attack is driven by the upper-class Mrs. Banning and others who misconstrue Dr. Bull's actions or blame him for the deaths of loved ones. But most of the accusations spring from the community's puritanical self-righteousness; people seem more concerned with the morality of Dr. Bull's personal life and his twenty-eight-year relationship with Janet Cardmaker than with his performance as a doctor. When Dr. Bull storms into the meeting, he responds to the slander with threats of physical violence and roars, "What I have to say to you is, you . . . can go to blazes. I'll see you all in hell before I'll oblige you by resigning! If you can get me out, if you have any case, and the sense to handle it, why, God damn you, do it!"

Since Cozzens drew on Kent, his New England hometown, for the fictional New Winton, acquaintances looked for themselves in *The Last Adam*. He wrote to his mother on 27 December 1932, shortly before the novel came out: "The avidity with which people try to see themselves in books is amazing, especially as they work hardest to see themselves in unflattering roles. . . . People do themselves too much honor, really; not one in a thousand is intrinsically interesting enough to hold anyone's attention as he stands. He has to be fixed up until he becomes an entirely different person; just as, if you like, I fixed up Dr. T. [Turrell] until, as Dr. Bull, with everything about him drastically changed, he became somebody worth reading about (or I hope he did)."

George Bull answers to no one, including the New Winton community. He eats, sleeps, and drinks when he wants and will not be bothered by the apparent trivialities with which others occupy themselves. He finds refuge on the Cardmaker farm, which is removed from society and its complications. Janet remains indifferent to and George disdainful of town gossip regarding their relationship. The novel closes with Janet's perception of the doctor as he relaxes with her after the meeting, whiskey in hand:

> "There was an immortality about him, she thought; her regard fixed and critical. Something unkillable. Something here when the first men walked erect; here now. The last man would twitch with it when the earth expired. A good greedy vitality, surely the very vitality of the world and the flesh, it survived all blunders and injuries, all attacks and misfortunes, never quite fed full. She shook her head a little, the smile half derisive in contemptuous affection. Her lips parted enough to say: 'The old bastard!'"

Discussion Questions

1. There appear to be various degrees of modernity in the novel—for instance, Dr. Verney's modern office, the village of New Winton itself, and the farms on Cold Hill and near the Cobble. Where does Dr. Bull feel most comfortable? How does modernity function in the story?

2. Are citizens right to be concerned with the morality of the town's physician? Does his private behavior affect his proficiency as a doctor?

3. What classical and biblical myths does Cozzens make use of in the story? (Look especially at the rattlesnake-hunting scene and at Janet Cardmaker's farm.)

4. Cozzens is concerned with the structure of community and the interrelationships among townspeople. How do the relationships among major characters help define both the town and the novel?

—*Jill Jividen*

MEN AND BRETHREN
(New York: Harcourt, Brace, 1936)

ERNEST CUDLIPP

Episcopal clergyman Ernest Cudlipp, the protagonist of James Gould Cozzens's *Men and Brethren*, is an unusual hero: practical, sensible, intelligent, a solver—to the extent that they can be solved—of complex human problems; a fully adult man, who has already come to terms with the realities of professional disappointment. An earlier ministry among Greenwich Village artistic types earned him a reputation as a maverick, and he owes his present Manhattan parish to its being undesirable in the eyes of careerists. Ernest Cudlipp's commitment is to his church and to his working-class parishioners, with digressions of assistance to people—variously connected to him—who are not his parishioners but whom he is able to help because he has become good at it, and whom he helps because there is no one else to take responsibility.

His celibacy, now habitual, is not required by his faith; an Episcopal priest might have been expected to marry. His antagonism to the romance between his seminarian assistant and a worthwhile young woman is based not on her politics (she is a fervid 1930s Communist) but on the fact that she has no money. "Wilbur, if you must marry, marry someone with money. There isn't any reason why the Church should have to support a wife and family for you. As long as you haven't any, you can get along on what would be offered you anywhere." (That Wilbur Quinn is unlikely to follow Cudlipp's advice is evident but not part of the three-day framework of the novel. In any case, Cudlipp wastes no time in useless anxiety.)

The nearest thing to a romantic interest of his own arrives in the person of a longtime friend, Alice Breen, a still-pretty woman, not old but old enough to have given up a never-successful career as an actress. She has for some time been the wife of a successful actor, also Cudlipp's old friend. Lee Breen is toying self-dramatically with the notion of a conversion to Roman Catholicism. His consulting Cudlipp as a pretext for lecturing him about religious faith, and Cudlipp's dismissal of his nonsense, are both comic and highly serious. Cudlipp's religious faith is never in question, and his point of view is that of the novel.

Alice's marriage has been a disappointment, and it is her hope that Cudlipp's interest in her can be aroused by friendly and affectionate compassion. She exerts time and skill in an absurd attempt to demonstrate her potential suitability as a clergyman's wife, but her premarital history and—especially—the fact of her being married are sufficient barriers. "Why should she want me!" he wonders. "A middle-aged little runt of an unsuccessful clergyman with a trying disposition, no money, no future; and,—the insult on the injury, no chance of being caught, which she knows perfectly well." (Alice remains a woman of considerable appeal to both Cudlipp and the reader.)

Cudlipp's church receives necessary charitable support from another, wealthy church, and Cudlipp cannot defy the interference of that church's rector, Dr. Lamb—a man as realistic as himself, but smoother and far more successful, having married a woman with money. The greatest threat to Cudlipp's ministry results from his receiving as a guest in his vicarage an old friend, Carl Willever. Once extraordinarily handsome and still a well-known, compelling preacher, Willever has left his High Church religious order after an unpublicized but sordid homosexual advance to an undercover policeman. Dr. Lamb visits Cudlipp to instruct him that, although the church will not abandon Willever, he cannot remain where he is as Cudlipp's guest. Cudlipp's Bohemian reputation makes him suffi-

ciently suspect already, and the church will not stand for it. Says Dr. Lamb, ". . . neither [Willever] nor anyone else is entitled to anything which is given to him at the expense of your good name and reputation. The parish you serve has first claim on both."

A recipient of Cudlipp's charity appears at his door in need of food and lodging: Lulu Merrick, once the wife of a gifted painter, was—in her young widowhood—proprietress of a busy tearoom in New York. After it failed, Cudlipp and another old friend and tearoom patron, Edna Stone, arranged and have been paying for Lulu's residency in a boardinghouse in New Jersey. But Lulu, unhappy and irrational, has fled the boardinghouse. Persuaded at length to return, she eludes her escort, Wilbur Quinn, and, perhaps by accident, falls between the dock and a moving New York–bound ferry. "Ernie, how horrible!" says Edna Stone when he tells her. "Do you think so?" is Cudlipp's reply.

John Wade, a personable, impecunious, gifted young poet just out of college, for whom Cudlipp has taken some responsibility, giving him a room in his vicarage and putting up with the unauthorized borrowing of small sums of money, is away for the three-day present of the novel wooing a young woman who works for his publisher, but he has left behind a mess for Cudlipp to deal with. Geraldine Binney, a well-to-do young matron and mother recently vacationing with her sister, became besotted with John and is now pregnant with his child and, unable to reach him, making half-serious preparations for suicide. Having made her understand that she was not "seduced" and that she has no future with John, that the romance was an aberration, Cudlipp arranges—through Alice Breen—for her (then illegal) abortion at an expensive private hospital. Visiting her there, he explains himself: "A great obligation has been laid on me to do or be whatever good thing I have learned I ought to be, or know I can do. . . . One like it is laid on you . . . go home and do what your life has prepared you to do. . . . Take your talent and employ it—."

Discussion Questions

1. Ernest Cudlipp is not what readers expect from a clergyman. Discuss ways in which he departs from reader expectations.

2. Compare Ernest Cudlipp with another clergyman in American fiction, such as Sinclair Lewis's Elmer Gantry or Harold Frederic's Theron Ware.

3. Does Cudlipp believe in God?

—*Arlyn Bruccoli*

REFERENCES

Frederick Bracher, *The Novels of James Gould Cozzens* (New York: Harcourt, Brace, 1959);

Matthew J. Bruccoli, *James Gould Cozzens: A Life Apart* (San Diego: Harcourt Brace Jovanovich, 1983);

Bruccoli, ed. *James Gould Cozzens*, Dictionary of Literary Biography Documentary Series (Detroit: Bruccoli Clark Layman/Thomson/Gale, 2004);

Louis O. Coxe, "The Complex World of James Gould Cozzens," *American Literary,* 27 (May 1955): 157–171;

Granville Hicks, *James Gould Cozzens* (Minneapolis: University of Minnesota Press, 1966);

James Gould Cozzens: New Acquist of True Experience, edited by Bruccoli (Carbondale: Southern Illinois University Press, 1979);

Just Representations: A James Gould Cozzens Reader, edited by Bruccoli (Carbondale: Southern Illinois University Press / New York: Harcourt Brace Jovanovich, 1978);

John William Ward, "James Gould Cozzens and the Condition of Modern Man," *American Scholar,* 27 (Winter 1957/1958): 92–99.

Stephen Crane

(November 1, 1871 – June 5, 1900)

ꞏꞏꞏ

"THE BLUE HOTEL"

Collected in *The Monster and Other Stories* (New York & London: Harper, 1899).

THE SWEDE

The Swede is a traveler from the East whose irrational behavior and paranoia unsettle the other guests at a small-town Nebraska hotel in Stephen Crane's short story "The Blue Hotel." The story was first published in *Collier's Weekly* in 1896, when Crane was twenty-five years old. It has a biographical basis—Crane's trip through the West while he was working as a journalist, during which he saw a blue hotel in Lincoln, Nebraska.

The story opens in the fictional town of Fort Romper, where Scully, the proprietor of the blue Palace Hotel, meets a train in order to secure paying guests for his establishment. He succeeds with three passengers from the train, a "shaky and quick-eyed Swede," a cowboy, and "a little silent man from the East." Though at first the Swede seems quiet and furtive, that evening at dinner he behaves almost normally, mentioning that "he had come from New York, where for ten years he had worked as a tailor." Soon, however, it is apparent to all that the Swede is acting oddly, laughing loudly and inappropriately and causing the others to look "at him wondering and in silence."

As a blizzard blows outside, the travelers become more focused on indoor activity, and the Swede and the Easterner form a team, playing cards against Johnnie, the proprietor's son, and the cowboy. Suddenly, the Swede interrupts the flow of the game, and the possibility of concentration, by saying to Johnnie: "I suppose there have been a good many men killed in this room." When others question what he means, stare at him, and assess him to be crazy, the Swede predicts that he himself will be "killed before [he] can leave this house." The introduction of his unfounded and accusatory statements changes the atmosphere into one of heightened anxiety and belligerence.

Though protesting that he will never leave the blue hotel alive, the Swede goes to his room to pack his bags. Scully follows him there and asks if he is crazy. The Swede responds, "There are people in this world who know pretty nearly as much as you do—understand?" In trying to deny that he is insane, the Swede only manages to sound more paranoid and incoherent. Scully continues to try to put him at ease and gives him some whiskey. While drinking, "The Swede laughed wildly. . . . he kept his glance, burning with hatred, upon the old man." While Scully tries to assuage the man's fears and anxiety, the others remain downstairs discussing the Swede's behavior. The Easterner insists: "Why, he's frightened! . . . this man has been reading dime-novels, and he thinks he's right out in the middle of it—the shootin' and the stabbin' and all." "It's awful funny," Johnnie says in response. Scully tries to restore peace around the stove by saying "It was only that he was from the East and he thought this was a tough place. . . . He's all right now."

At dinner, the Swede "domineered the whole feast." After dinner, he insists on another card game, and others reluctantly agree to play with the same partners as before. Soon, the Swede accuses Johnnie of cheating at cards, an allegation that Johnnie responds to by attempting to throw himself on the Swede to fight. Taking the fight outside, "The two combatants leaped forward and crashed together like bullocks." Though the cowboy cheers Johnnie on with cries of "Go it, Johnnie; go it! Kill him! Kill him!" the size and vigor of the Swede ultimately prevails, and Johnnie is forced to give up. The entire party returns indoors, where Johnnie's sisters dress his wounds, and the Swede retreats to his room.

The Swede leaves the blue hotel and finds a saloon, where he violently insists that patrons and barkeeper drink with him, though they repeatedly refuse. A gambler is present, and the Swede makes the fatal mistake of touching him. A brief fight ensues in which the gambler stabs the Swede and he falls dead. "The corpse of the Swede, alone in the saloon, had its eyes fixed upon a dreadful legend that dwelt atop of the cash-machine: 'This registers the amount of your purchase.'" Months later, discussing the light prison sentence the gambler gets for killing the Swede, the Easterner reveals to the cowboy that Johnnie really had been cheating that fateful night at the blue hotel. By abetting and even encouraging the fight between the two men, he concludes, everyone there that night shared a measure of guilt in the Swede's death.

Discussion Questions

1. How do descriptive names like "The Swede" and "The Easterner" change the reader's empathy with the characters?

2. Is the death of the Swede inevitable?

3. How does the early response to the Swede's behavior differ from the response later in the story?

4. How does the Easterner's revelation at the end of the story change the reader's attitude toward the incident at the blue hotel?

—*Clare Gerlach*

"THE BRIDE COMES TO YELLOW SKY"
Collected in *The Open Boat and Other Stories* (London: Heinemann, 1898).

SCRATCHY WILSON
Scratchy Wilson is a frontiersman who drunkenly provokes a confrontation with Marshal Jack Potter in Stephen Crane's short story "The Bride Comes to Yellow Sky." The story is a parody of other writers' stories of bravery and romance in the Old West. In "The Bride Comes to Yellow Sky," the marshal is not heroic but reasonable; the heroine is not beautiful but embarrassed; and the villain, Scratchy Wilson, is not dangerous and sinister, merely drunk and disorderly.

The story opens on a train as Potter returns home to Yellow Sky with his new bride. He is not used to the splendid train environment and lacks the citified manners to interact acceptably with waiters. His embarrassment at the opulent surroundings in the dining car causes him to "appear ridiculous to the Negro porter." After being served by a waiter who "viewed them with the manner of a fatherly pilot," they feel "a sense of escape" to return to their compartment. Potter feels guilty about bringing his bride home to Yellow Sky because he had failed to inform the townspeople that he was going to San Antonio to get married. He avoided telling the townsfolk of his intentions out of shyness, too. "He knew full well that his marriage was an important thing to his town . . . exceeded only by the burning of the new hotel." At last they arrive at Yellow Sky, and he guides his bride home from the station through the streets of the town.

Potter does not realize that trouble had been brewing in Yellow Sky just prior to his return with his new bride. At the Weary Gentleman saloon, the peace is interrupted when a young man "suddenly appeared at the open door. He cried: 'Scratchy Wilson's drunk, and has turned loose with both hands.'" This news of a drunken rampage frightens some saloon customers into fleeing. A stranger in town, a traveling salesman, asks what the excitement is about and is told: "It means, my friend, that for the next two hours this town won't be a health resort." As the townspeople in the saloon answer the salesman's questions about Scratchy's background, it becomes clear that Scratchy's drink-induced rampages are familiar to the locals. "When he comes, you'd better lay down on the floor, stranger," the salesman is told. "This here Scratchy Wilson is a wonder with a gun—a perfect wonder." The barkeeper forcibly moves the salesman to a safe spot behind the bar where they cower together, waiting for Scratchy's violent appearance on the scene. The description of Scratchy is a mixture of humorous and foreboding details. He wears a "maroon-colored flannel shirt," and "In either hand, [he] held a long, heavy, blue-black revolver." His face "flamed in a rage begot of whisky," but this drunkenness seems at odds with his gracefulness, which is described as "the creeping movement of the midnight cat." He shouts out "terrible invitations" to fight, challenging anyone in earshot, but there are no responses from the fearful townspeople. Finally, not getting any satisfaction from the cringing saloon patrons, Scratchy remembers "his ancient antagonist," Potter, and heads to Potter's house.

Potter is just walking down the street with his bride when Scratchy approaches them, reloading his revolver. He pulls another weapon from his holster and aims it at Potter, and the bride's face "had gone yellow as an old cloth." Scratchy, still spoiling for a fight, accuses Potter: "Tried to sneak up on me!" He then warns the marshal, "Don't you move a finger toward a gun just yet. Don't you move an eyelash." Potter says that he does not have a gun on him, and Scratchy doubts his word until he explains: "I ain't got a gun because I've just come from San Anton' with my wife. I'm married."

Scratchy's fun has been derailed. He says, "Well, I s'pose it's all off now." Potter agrees, and the mystified Scratchy puts his guns in his holsters and leaves. Scratchy is as easily confused as the sheriff, and he is just as shy. He is not able to be drunk and disorderly in the presence of the marshal's new wife. The marshal's domesticity signals the end of the Old West.

Discussion Questions

1. How does drunken and belligerent Scratchy's behavior change when he learns that the marshal, Potter, is married?

2. Why are other townspeople's efforts to subdue Scratchy ineffective?

3. Why is Scratchy's clothing described in such detail?

—*Clare Gerlach*

MAGGIE: A GIRL OF THE STREETS
(New York: Appleton, 1896)

MAGGIE JOHNSON

Maggie Johnson, the protagonist of Stephen Crane's *Maggie: A Girl of the Streets,* is a victim of the deterministic interplay between her Bowery environment and her nature. Her fate is to a degree determined by the familial and social conditions in which she is raised. A drunken father, a bellicose mother, a bullying brother, and a poverty-ridden family life create a sordid and violent domestic milieu that is reproduced in the squalid, brutish conditions of the Bowery (a New York City slum), which produces forces that overmaster Maggie's "theatrical, romantic illusions" of an ideal lover who will sweep to her rescue and lead her to a home in the country. This universe of deterministic forces is institutionalized in the factory where she is forced to work to cope with the effects of poverty. Her melodramatic illusions leave her susceptible to the exploitive lust of her brother's friend, Petey, who seduces and then abandons her. Even her developing beauty works to her ruin, prompting her to quit the factory and, under pressure from her brother, to "go on d' toif" as a prostitute. Prostitution accelerates her decline, leaving her socially ostracized from family and church and dependent on the business of men "progressively lower in the social scale, until the final encounter with a 'huge fat man in torn and greasy garments'" brings her career to its catastrophic, if ambiguous, close, either by murder or suicide.

In *Maggie,* the narrative evidences the effects of social determinism, which adapts Charles Darwin's evolutionary theories (natural selection, survival of the fittest, inherited adaptive capacity) to the social realm, positing them as the mechanisms by which human destiny is shaped. If the first chapters establish the hostile environment of the Bowery, succeeding chapters contrast Pete's adaptation to the Bowery with Maggie's desire to escape from it. Chapters 6 and 7 chronicle her attempts to realize this dream of escape. Ensuing chapters document the moral backlash and rejection of the main characters, with a consequential narrowing of Maggie's possibilities, ending in her death. Crane's story is a classic example of the deterministic plot of decline, leading to catastrophic closure for the protagonist—in this instance a young girl of the streets.

Maggie's fate is also shaped by the environment of the Bowery, a harsh and sordid milieu of violent characters, a "dark region where a dozen gruesome doorways gave up loads of babies to the street." Crane underscores the influence of the environment in his oft-quoted inscription in a copy of *Maggie:* "it tries to show that the environment is a tremendous thing in the world and frequently shapes lives regardless. If one proves that theory, one makes room in Heaven for all sorts of souls (notably an occasional street girl) who are not confidently expected to be there by many excellent people." Lacking any positive role models, Maggie turns to stage melodramas and popular romances for her ideals. These two genres spawn not only her dream of escape from the Bowery but also her dream of a perfect lover who will provide the means for this escape: a twofold dream that will prove fatal in the end.

The governing influence of social determinism is evident in Maggie's nature as well. She is susceptible to the illusory values of melodrama, longing to "be where the little hills sing together" and a lover always walked "under the tree of her dream garden." Her idealizing nature is underscored by the imagery with which Crane associates her: images that depict her as being fatally at odds with her environment. She not only "blossomed in a mud puddle," but "none of the dirt of Rum Alley seemed to be in her veins." It is not until Maggie tries to realize her dream, however, that the destructive forces of social determinism are triggered.

Maggie's attempt to realize her dreams for the perfect lover and a home in the country are met by a series of rejections that lead to her early death. Rejected by Pete for another woman, she is forced to pursue a life of prostitution and is subsequently rejected by her mother, who condemns her thankless disobedience. Finally, she is rejected by her brother, Jimmie, who claims that "dis ting queers us." Maggie turns next to the church, only to be rejected by the priest: "the girl had heard of the Grace of God . . . but as she timidly accosted the priest . . . he saved his respectability by a vigorous sidestep. He did not risk it to save a soul." Yet, because moral posturing is a necessary survival trait in the Bowery, as are amoral behaviors, none of these characters can be blamed for Maggie's death. That harsh judgment is reserved for the society that rewards brutality and hypocrisy, while victimizing those who pursue the chimera of its romantic idealism. As evidenced by the events of the novel, the inner nature of the protagonist, the fateful influence of the environment in which she lives, and its attack on false values, *Maggie: A Girl of the Streets* is a cautionary tale, whose heroine is destroyed by collected forces.

Discussion Questions

1. Define what is meant by "social determinism" or "social Darwinism." What specific social forces keep Maggie from realizing her dreams of escape? Is she simply a passive victim of these forces, or does she struggle against them?

2. What role does Maggie's "given nature" play in determining her fate?

3. Why do you think Crane wrote *Maggie: A Girl of the Streets?*

—*Stephen Brown*

"THE OPEN BOAT"

Collected in *The Open Boat and Other Stories* (London: Heinemann, 1898).

THE CORRESPONDENT

"The correspondent" is one of four men adrift in a lifeboat in Stephen Crane's story "The Open Boat." Crane based "The Open Boat" on his own experience as a survivor of the steamship *Commodore*, which sank on January 2, 1897. The *Commodore* was carrying men and arms from Jacksonville, Florida, to Cuba to aid insurgents, and Crane, a newspaper correspondent, went along to cover the uprising. After the mysterious sinking of the ship, Crane and three others spent thirty hours fighting menacing waves in a ten-foot lifeboat off the Florida coast. Within days of reaching shore, Crane submitted his account of the sinking to the *New York Press,* which published the article, "Stephen Crane's Own Story," on January 7. Crane devoted only the last two paragraphs to his experience on the lifeboat, but he anticipated his fictional account, stating, "The history of life in an open boat for thirty hours would no doubt be very instructive for the young, but none is to be told here now."

That Crane's experience was "instructive" to *him* is evident in "The Open Boat," published in *Scribner's Magazine* in June 1897, with the subtitle "A Tale Intended to Be after the Fact: Being the Experience of Four Men from the Sunk Steamer *Commodore.*" As the title indicates, Crane's story shifts the emphasis from the objective facts of the sinking to the subjective experience of the men on the lifeboat. Crane tells his tale through an omniscient-third-person point of view, which often reflects the men's thoughts collectively to emphasize their shared experience. "None of them knew the color of the sky," he begins, initiating two of the major themes of the story: the men's narrow, human-centered vision of the world and the "brotherhood" that their struggle engenders. Crane begins to limit the point of view to that of the correspondent, emphasizing the essential isolation of each character in a universe indifferent to his suffering—another major theme.

The action in "The Open Boat" is tense but limited. While the men face unrelenting physical challenges, the more significant conflict of the story is psychological, as they struggle to reevaluate their place in the universe. This struggle is most pronounced in the correspondent, as Crane indicates in his initial description of the men. All four deal desperately with the practical matter of staying afloat—rowing, bailing, or giving advice—but the correspondent "watched the waves and wondered why he was there."

In trying to understand the meaning of his situation, the correspondent reveals his prior assumption that the universe is beneficent, that men are rewarded for worthy actions. He is, therefore, incredulous when his struggles seem fruitless. Crane states that perhaps the sentiments of all the men "might be formulated thus: 'If I am going to be drowned . . . why . . . was I allowed to come thus far and contemplate sand and trees.'" The men begin to view the world as cruel, cursing its injustice toward humanity, but soon conclude that their cursing, like their actions, is of no consequence, as no one is paying attention: "When it occurs to a man that nature does not regard him as important, and that she feels she would not maim the universe by disposing of him, he at first wishes to throw bricks at the temple, and he hates deeply the fact that there are no bricks and no temples." A man finally understands "the pathos of his situation," Crane continues, when he looks into the sky: "A high cold star on a winter's night is the word he feels that she says to him." Here the point of view shifts exclusively to that of the correspondent, who suddenly becomes aware of his own insensitivity to the suffering of others and subsequently accepts that the universe itself is neither cruel nor beneficent: "she was indifferent, flatly indifferent."

This epiphany occurs after "a verse mysteriously entered the correspondent's head." The words, which he memorized as a child, are about a dying soldier in Algiers who laments that he will never see his native land again. Suddenly these words, which once meant "less to him then the breaking of a pencil's point," represent "a human, living, thing. . . . an actuality—stern, mournful, and fine." Crane writes "The correspondent . . . was moved by a profound and perfectly impersonal comprehension. He was sorry for the soldier of the Legion who lay dying in Algiers."

In the final section of the story "the correspondent again opened his eyes" to find "the sea and the sky were each of the gray hue of the dawning." He finally knows "the color of the sky"; it is neutral, like the universe it symbolizes. In the afternoon, however, "in its splendor" it is "of pure blue"—impersonal, perhaps, but beautiful. The correspondent, "impressed with the unconcern of the universe," recognizes that he must redefine his sense of "right and wrong"; it must come from within. Instead of stripping him of hope, the tacit revelation that he reads in the "high cold star" awakens in him a sense of oneness with the world and a renewed moral consciousness. Having boarded the *Commodore* "cynical of men," the correspondent undergoes a change in perspective "not probable to the average experience, which is never at sea in a dinghy." For this reason, Crane notes, the correspondent knew he was partaking in "the best experience of his life." When the boat finally capsizes, the hardy oiler dies; the physically exhausted correspondent, however, survives through a combination of skill, luck, and the help of others. Comfortable again on shore, the three survivors hear "the great sea's voice" and feel "they could then be interpreters."

In the correspondent, Crane captures the developing turn-of-the-century intellectual climate, which challenged traditional assumptions of man's distinctiveness among the rest of creation. He provides a link between Henry Fleming of Crane's realist novel *The Red Badge of Courage* (1895), who learns of the importance of chance and circumstance in a man's life, and Jack London's nameless protagonist in "To Build a Fire" (1908)—a more typically naturalist work—who has no time "to meditate upon his frailty as a creature of temperature."

Discussion Questions

1. How is the correspondent's new understanding of an impersonal universe symbolized in the man waving his coat on the shore? Consider the comments the characters make regarding this man.

2. Compare the correspondent's observations about the natural world with those of Henry Fleming in *The Red Badge of Courage*. What similar lessons do the two characters learn regarding man and nature?

3. In what ways does the protagonist of "To Build a Fire" take a more extreme view of his place in the world than the correspondent does? In what ways do both characters, with their awareness of an indifferent universe, anticipate such existential characters as Mersault in Albert Camus's *The Stranger*?

4. Consider Crane's description near the beginning of Part V: "As darkness settled finally, the shine of the light, lifting from the sea in the south, changed to full gold." How might the words "full gold" be a play on words, the irony of which further conveys the correspondent's new understanding of nature?

5. Cite examples of figurative language—particularly similes, metaphors, and the use of understatement—as well as other references drawn from the characters' domestic lives on land. How do these references heighten the irony of the men's situation? What purpose do they serve in one's understanding of the correspondent's new perspective?

—*John Cusatis*

⟁

THE RED BADGE OF COURAGE
(New York: Appleton, 1895)

HENRY FLEMING

Henry Fleming, the teenage protagonist of Stephen Crane's realist novel *The Red Badge of Courage,* has had dreams of battlefield heroics that have led him to enlist in the Union army during the American Civil War. While Crane based his descriptions of combat on the Battle of Chancellorsville, which occurred in 1863 along Virginia's Rappahannock River, the fighting serves primarily as a vehicle for the author's more essential concern: the battle that takes place within the mind of Henry Fleming. Crane once remarked, "Between two great armies battling against each other the interesting thing is the mental attitude of the men." Fleming's internal conflict, which concerns the value of bravery, is ultimately resolved on the battlefield, when his self-absorption is displaced by a powerful sense of duty, marking his initiation into manhood.

Crane foreshadows Henry's journey from ignorance to understanding with the opening images of the novel. Henry awakens on a spring morning as the "retiring fogs" unveil a green landscape and an "amber-tinted" river. In contrast to this Edenic setting, however, he observes "the red, eyelike gleam of hostile campfires set in the low brows of distant hills." Later, Henry imagines these "red eyes across the river . . . to be growing larger, as the orbs of a row of dragons advancing." The elusive enemy comes to represent the unknown evil forces Henry had underestimated in his naive eagerness for glory. "In visions he had seen himself in many struggles," Crane writes. "He had imagined peoples secure in the shadows of his eagle-eyed prowess."

The first sign of Henry's impending disillusionment Crane recalls during a flashback occurred during his leave-taking from his mother. Against her will, Henry chose to abandon the safety of the family farm to undertake "breathless deeds" on the battlefield. Anticipating a dramatic, emotional departure, Henry was disappointed by his mother's "saying nothing whatever about returning with his shield or on it." Instead, she peeled potatoes while lecturing him about keeping quiet, doing what he is told, and being sure his clothes are mended. Crane writes, "He bowed his head and went on, feeling suddenly ashamed of his purposes."

Shame, however, is soon replaced by self-doubt and fear, as his valor is about to be tested. "He tried to mathematically prove to himself that he would not run from a battle," Crane writes. He recognizes that "as far as war was concerned he knew nothing of himself." Like the correspondent in Crane's "The Open Boat" (1897), whose sense of self-importance and security is crushed amid the towering ocean waves that swamp his lifeboat, Henry feels "that in this crisis his laws of life were useless. Whatever he had learned of himself was here of no avail." Henry feels like a "mental outcast" among his seemingly fearless comrades. "No one seemed to be wrestling with such a terrific personal problem," Crane explains. Scorning the "merciless government" who "were taking him out to be slaughtered," he longs to be home milking the cows he used to curse. He enters his first skirmish, however, hoping it is true that "a man became another thing in a battle." As he watches many of his comrades flee, he stands his ground. Crane notes, "He suddenly lost concern for himself." Again, Henry calls to mind Crane's correspondent, whose crisis at sea spawns a sense of kinship with his fellow strugglers. Henry becomes part of "a mysterious fraternity born of the smoke and danger of death."

Crane's battlefield, like the ocean in "The Open Boat," becomes a microcosm of the world, governed largely by chance and circumstance and stripped of the illusion of beneficence. When the fighting has settled, Henry is amazed "that Nature has gone tranquilly on with her golden process in the midst of so much devilment." For Crane, living with the awareness that the universe is indifferent to one's fate requires the courage of a steadfast soldier. Henry has passed his "supreme trial" on the battlefield, Crane implies, by earnestly engaging himself in the job he has been summoned to perform, despite daunting odds. "He was at a task," Crane writes. In his essay "War Memories" (1899), Crane similarly applauds "the spectacle of the common man serenely doing his work, his appointed work."

In his next battle, however, Henry's conviction fails, and he flees to a wooded area where he rationalizes his decision. Tossing a pinecone at a squirrel, he interprets the animal's choice to scurry, rather than "stand stolidly baring his furry belly to the missile," as a sign of nature's law. Yet, the trees and vines and, finally, a dead Union soldier whom he finds propped up in a chapel-like enclosure seem to be casting judgmental eyes on him. Running, he mingles with a procession of wounded soldiers and feels envious, wishing "he, too, had a wound, a red badge of courage." After witnessing the agonizing death of his friend Jim Conklin, he experiences a deepening of his guilt and rage, which become as unbearable as "knife thrusts" when a "tattered soldier," who has been shot twice, asks him about the location of his *own* "hurt." "It might be inside mostly," the man says with unintended irony, "an' them plays thunder." Ashamed, Henry sneaks away.

Henry puzzles over the definition of cowardice. If no one knows he has fled, he considers, he has no need for shame. Further, while, watching more retreating Union soldiers, Henry feels morally vindicated, consoling himself that his army's defeat would render him "a seer" rather than a coward. In reality, though, he is prepared to "throw off himself and become a better." When he asks an infantryman why he fled, the man cracks him over the head with his rifle. Barely conscious, Henry staggers back to his camp. A fellow soldier, believing Henry's lie that he has been shot, looks after him. Henry awakens the next morning certain that he has "opened his eyes upon an unexpected world."

On the battlefield that day, he fights "like a pagan." After Henry wrests his regiment's flag from the hands of the dead color sergeant, the smoke lifts, and he relishes hearing the voices of the retreating enemy, where before "all had been darkness and speculation." Experiencing a sense of "quiet manhood," he suddenly feels more remorse for having deserted the tattered man than for fleeing the earlier battle. He realizes, however, Crane states, that "scars faded as flowers." Crane's final image suggests Henry's rebirth: "Over the river a golden ray of sun came through the hosts of leaden rain clouds."

Discussion Questions

1. Henry Fleming reappears as an old man in Crane's short story "The Veteran" (1896). After reading "The Veteran," discuss how it complements the portrayal of Henry in *The Red Badge of Courage*.

2. The loud young soldier and the cheery man are instrumental in Henry's physical recovery. How might their examples also facilitate his spiritual rejuvenation?

3. In chapter 8, Henry watches his comrades fighting fiercely in what he imagines will be a forgotten battle. Crane's comment on the situation ironically echoes the words used in the Book of Genesis to describe God's reaction toward his creation: "But he saw that it was good." Considering that Henry later reflects on his own fighting with the same biblical reference, why might Crane have chosen this allusion?

4. Other religious references pervade *The Red Badge of Courage*. Analyze Crane's description of Jim Conklin's death in chapter 9, particularly the final simile comparing the sun to a "wafer" pasted in the sky. What role does this scene play in Henry's development?

5. In both "The Open Boat" and *The Red Badge of Courage*, Crane relies heavily on figurative language—particularly personification—to depict the disconcerting circumstances in which both the correspondent and Henry Fleming find themselves. Find examples of such language and explain how each helps to convey the state of mind of the protagonist.

—*John Cusatis*

REFERENCES

Christopher Benfrey, *The Double Life of Stephen Crane* (New York: Knopf, 1992);

Edwin H. Cady, *Stephen Crane*, revised edition (Boston: Twayne, 1980);

James B. Colvert, Introduction, *Great Short Works of Stephen Crane* (New York: Perennial Classics, 2004);

Stephen Crane, *The Red Badge of Courage: A Facsimile Edition of the Manuscript*, edited by Fredson Bowers (Washington, D.C.: NCR/Microcard Editions, 1973);

David S. Gross, "The Western Stories of Stephen Crane," *Journal of American Culture*, 11, no. 4 (1988): 15–21;

Michael W. Schaefer, *A Reader's Guide to the Short Stories of Stephen Crane* (New York: G. K. Hall, 1996);

R. W. Stallman, *Stephen Crane: A Biography* (New York: Braziller, 1992);

Bonnie Szumski, ed., *Readings on Stephen Crane* (San Diego: Greenhaven, 1998);

Stanley Wertheim, *A Stephen Crane Encyclopedia* (Westport, Conn.: Greenwood Press, 1997).

Sharon Creech
(July 29, 1945 –)

WALK TWO MOONS
(New York: HarperCollins, 1994)

SALAMANCA TREE HIDDLE

Salamanca Tree Hiddle is the main character in Sharon Creech's young adult novel *Walk Two Moons*. Thirteen-year-old Salamanca, known as Sal, is trying to deal with many changes in her life, including her mother's desertion and subsequent death and her father's decision to move to Euclid, Ohio, where the one major feature Sal notices is the lack of trees. In Euclid, Sal meets such colorful characters as Mrs. Partridge, who is surprisingly perceptive despite being unable to see; Margaret Cadaver, whose name evokes rumors of husbands and neighbors murdered; and Phoebe Winterbottom, who suspects her mother has been kidnapped.

In an effort to help Sal cope with the loss of her mother, her grandparents encourage her to accompany them on a drive from Ohio to Lewiston, Idaho, where Sal's mother is buried. They plan to arrive by her mother's birthday. To pass the time along the way, Sal tells her grandparents her friend Phoebe's story. Phoebe's mother has mysteriously disappeared, and the Winterbottoms are troubled by mysterious notes and by a young man lurking about whom Phoebe insists is a lunatic.

As she retells Phoebe's tale, which includes glimpses into Sal's relationship with her own mother, Sal gradually realizes that Phoebe's story is like a wall in her former home in Kentucky, where her father found a brick fireplace hidden behind the plaster. Sal says, "The reason that Phoebe's story reminds me of the plaster wall and the hidden fireplace is that beneath Phoebe's story was another one. Mine." In the process of telling her friend's story, Sal comes to terms with her mother's desertion and her father's grief, and she is finally able to confront and accept her loss.

Sal is at once both quirky and kind. Her narration of the novel is sprinkled with colorful turns of phrase such as "fishing in the air" (the way her father describes her hope that her mother will come home) and "jing bang." She is a loyal friend to Phoebe as she helps her find out what happened to her mother, going so far as to break into Mrs. Cadaver's house and trying to convince the local police to investigate Mrs. Winterbottom's "kidnapping." Throughout the novel Sal discovers that she is braver than she thinks; in fact, she learns that "if people expect you to be brave, sometimes you pretend you are, even when you are frightened to the bone." By pretending to be brave, Sal learns to overcome her fears, particularly when she is able to drive her grandparents' car to the site where her mother was killed despite being afraid of car accidents.

Creech describes Sal as "lyrical, stubborn and outdoor loving." In an interview with Hollis Lowry-Moore, Creech explained that she draws on her family and friends to create her characters: "Sal is what you would get if you took me and my daughter and squished us together." Sal's middle name, Tree, evokes Creech's love of the outdoors. "I think I spent half my childhood up in a tree," she recalled.

"They 'live a thousand lives,' appearing to die each autumn." Sal's trip to Lewiston was also inspired by a similar journey the author made when she was twelve, though Creech is quick to note that "none of the things that happen to Salamanca along the way happened to me!"

Salamanca's first name is a marker of her Native American heritage, since her parents were trying to name her after her tribe (Seneca) but got it wrong. Sal's Indian background is a key part of her identity, for she loves the Native American tales her mother told her, and she joins the Indians at Pipestone in smoking a pipe. About Mount Rushmore, Sal says, "you'd think the Sioux would be mighty sad to have those white faces carved into their sacred hill." Still, Sal's Indianness is not made exotic or strange. "For once in a children's book," Hazel Rochman says, "Indians are people. . . . Sal's Indian heritage is a natural part of her finding herself in America."

The title of the book not only hints at Sal's Indian background but also echoes the fortune-cookie message that inspired Creech: "Don't judge a man until you've walked two moons in his moccasins." By the end of the novel Sal has indeed learned to "walk in another's moccasins," and in fact, she and her grandfather have made a game of imagining what it would be like to be in another person's shoes. Sal's journey, which covered the same route her mother took the year before, helps her walk in her mother's moccasins and realize how her mother must have felt when she made the journey. When Sal moves back to Bybanks, Kentucky, at the end of the novel, she realizes that her mother is still with her, in the trees and the hills and the land around her.

The book is about loss and coping with loss, a theme that Creech can relate to because she has experienced both the death of her father and the loss of her daughter, who moved away to attend college while Creech was writing the novel. Many young-adult novels center around the theme of loss and feature a main character trying to cope with the death of a relative, but Sal is different because she uses the power of storytelling and the journey to Idaho to help her come to terms with her sorrow. In the end, Sal realizes that she cannot fix all of the bad things in the world but that "most people seem a lot like us: sometimes brave and sometimes afraid, sometimes cruel and sometimes kind."

Discussion Questions

1. Journeys can be viewed as quests that a character undertakes to achieve a goal or an end. If we view Sal's journey to Idaho as a quest, what is her goal, and how do the various things that happen to Sal along the way help her to achieve that goal?

2. At the end of the novel, Sal tells her grandfather the Navajo folktale of Estsanatlehi, the woman who lives a thousand lives and never dies, a tale both she and her grandfather enjoy. Discuss how other details in the novel reinforce the message this folktale embodies about life and death.

3. In the novel, Mrs. Partridge says that she's been leaving the mysterious notes on the Winterbottoms' porch because she thought they would be "grandiful surprises" for Phoebe and her family. Examine the text of the messages she left for the Winterbottoms. How does each one echo or reinforce a message contained within the novel? Why does Mrs. Partridge leave the same message twice?

4. In the novel, Phoebe repeatedly tells Sal that she's "ever so brave," despite the fact that Sal privately admits to a long list of things she fears. Agree or disagree with Phoebe's statement and, using details from the novel, support your position.

5. *Bittersweet* by Drew Lamm also features a main character, Taylor, trying to cope with the loss of her grandmother to Alzheimer's disease. Discuss the similarities between Sal's struggle to deal with her mother's disappearance and Taylor's attempts to cope with her loss. What do the two books suggest are successful ways to deal with grief?

—*Patti J. Kurtz*

PHOEBE WINTERBOTTOM

Phoebe Winterbottom is the heroine of an "extensively strange" tale from Creech's 1995 Newbery award–winning novel *Walk Two Moons*. Phoebe is not, however, the main character of the book. The novel is a first-person account of a seven-day cross-country road trip from Euclid, Ohio, to Lewiston, Idaho, told by thirteen-year-old Salamanca Tree Hiddle. In order to entertain her grandparents, who are driving her on this journey, Sal agrees to

tell them about one of her friends, Phoebe Winterbottom, and the odd adventures the two girls have recently experienced. Sal's tale is frequently interrupted by the adventures she and her grandparents seem unable to avoid and by Sal's gradual revelations about the events that led the three of them to set off on their trip in the first place.

Sal has angrily resisted her father's decision to move them from their beloved farm in Kentucky to a featureless suburban development in Ohio. For her the change is just one more obstacle in her quest to regain the stability and happiness she enjoyed during the first twelve years of her life before her mother left to visit a cousin in Lewiston. As she stands for the first time on a street in her new neighborhood, Sal contemptuously dismisses the homes as "little birdhouses in a row." Fittingly, the first face she sees is that of Phoebe, a girl with a bird's name, looking out at her from an upstairs window.

Three days later, Sal meets Phoebe in her class at school. As Sal describes her, "Phoebe was a quiet girl who stayed mostly by herself. She had a pleasant round face and huge, enormous sky-blue eyes. Around this pleasant round face, her hair—as yellow as a crow's foot—curled in short ringlets." When Sal joins the Winterbottoms for dinner she is struck by their almost exaggerated conventionality. Mr. Winterbottom works in an office; he sits at the head of the dinner table with his shirt cuffs rolled back and speaks in short, serious sentences. Mrs. Winterbottom bakes, cleans, and shops and sighs over the fact that no one seems to appreciate her work. Seventeen-year-old Prudence is as polite and restrained as her mother. Watching them all, Sal is amazed; "They acted so thumpingly *tidy* and *respectable*."

Sal soon learns, however, that there is more to the Winterbottom family than meets the eye. Phoebe distinguishes herself through a powerful imagination. She sees the world in stark terms; anything out of the ordinary is surely dangerous. And as Sal's grandmother comments, that sort of imagination lends itself to a wild, "pepped up," and "scads more exciting" existence than ordinary people experience. Phoebe flatters Sal by calling her brave, and the two girls soon find mysteries all around them.

Sal, on the other hand, has great confidence in the wonderful and the improbable, a gift she has inherited at least in part from her mother. Like her mother she listens to trees sing and does not hesitate to kiss one in order to learn that the trunks taste just faintly of blackberries. She is easily able to suspend her own disbelief and adopt the odd theories Phoebe creates. Phoebe suspects her neighbor, Mrs. Cadaver, of murdering her husband and burying him under the rhododendrons. She is also on guard against a strange young man who appears to be watching her house and family; she concludes that he is certainly a lunatic of some type and, no doubt, dangerous. The sudden disappearance of Phoebe's respectable and reliable mother only deepens the mysteries. Nor can either girl fathom why someone has inexplicably begun leaving envelopes filled with mysterious adages on the Winterbottom doorstep. Sal eagerly involves herself in Phoebe's life. Not only is it interesting, but Sal unconsciously hopes if Phoebe's mysteries can be resolved, perhaps, the unsettled questions in Sal's life can be as well.

As Sal's story about Phoebe unwinds, parallels and echoes slowly develop between the two girls, though both seem unaware of them. Like Phoebe, Sal finds herself becoming fearful and anxious. Where she was once courageous, she now fears cars, death, and cancer, among other things; only in her willingness to rescue spiders or touch a bug does she retain her old confidence and bravery. Both girls are struggling with a sibling. The "lunatic" Phoebe has observed watching her house turns out to be an older brother given up for adoption by her mother long ago. As Phoebe begins to comprehend this new addition to her family, Sal begins to understand that she is not responsible for her stillborn sister's death. Phoebe learns that her father is as disturbed by her mother's absence as she is, even if he does not show it. Similarly, Sal begins to recognize that her father's friendship with Mrs. Cadaver is not an attempt to replace her mother. Most importantly, Phoebe learns that her mother has not been kidnapped and is coming home, just as Sal finally admits that her mother's death in a bus crash is permanent. Thus, while Sal grows over the course of the novel and comes to terms with the events of her own life, Phoebe shifts from her initial role as a foil to Sal into a fully realized character and a genuinely interesting friend.

Discussion Questions

1. Phoebe is first drawn to Sal because she believes her to be brave. Is Phoebe a brave or fearful person? Is there more than one kind of courage? Compare and contrast Phoebe's fears and her responses to fear with those of Sal.

2. Mrs. Partridge leaves five different messages on Phoebe's doorstep. Perhaps the most important of these is "Don't judge a man until you've walked two moons in his moccasins," since it serves as inspiration for the title of the novel. Choose another one of the other four messages and explain how it relates to Phoebe's experiences.

3. At first glance Phoebe and Sal seem very different from each other. What do you think makes the girls such close friends? How do their worldviews, family structures, and personalities mesh to form a friendship?

4. The events of the story force Phoebe to reevaluate her vision of her parents and, in part, her relationship with them. How does Phoebe perceive her father early in the novel? Why does she tell Sal the tale about the man who guessed people's ages at the state fair? How does Phoebe's perception of her mother change during the course of the novel?

5. Coming to terms with the loss or disappearance of a beloved parent or grandparent provides the theme in many good books for young readers. Compare Phoebe's experiences with those of Summer in Cynthia Rylant's *Missing May* (1992) or Woodrow Pater in Ruth White's *Belle Prater's Boy* (1996).

—*Megan Lynn Isaac*

REFERENCES
Alice B. McGinty, *Sharon Creech* (New York: Rosen, 2006);

Hollis Lowry-Moore, "Creating People Who Are Quirky and Kind," *Teacher Librarian*, 28 (April 2001): 4;

Mary Ann Tighe, *Sharon Creech: The Words We Choose to Say* (Lanham, Md.: Scarecrow Press, 2006).

Mart Crowley

(August 21, 1935 –   )

THE BOYS IN THE BAND

(New York, Theatre Four, 14 April 1968; New York: Farrar, Straus & Giroux, 1968)

HAROLD

Harold, one of the central characters in Mart Crowley's 1968 play *The Boys in the Band,* is a thirty-two-year-old Jewish gay man. The play takes place in New York City at a time when homosexual behavior was a criminal offense and homosexuality was considered to be a psychiatric disease. The central event in *The Boys in the Band* is a birthday party Michael (none of the characters have surnames) is throwing for Harold. All the action takes place in Michael's apartment, and the play occurs in real time. Five other gay men, friends of Michael and/or Harold, attend the party. Each is clearly differentiated through ethnicity and other attributes: Bernard is a well-groomed African American, for example, and Emory is flamboyantly effeminate. Two other characters also appear: Cowboy, a prostitute whose services Emory purchased as a birthday present for Harold, and Alan, Michael's college roommate and the only character whose sexual preference is ambiguous. Defending himself against charges that his characters are stereotypical, Crowley has stated that they are made up of elements of people he knew, and that Michael was based on himself.

Harold does not appear onstage until the end of the first act and is in some ways more an observer than a participant. Nonetheless, he is a central character in *The Boys in the Band* because he functions as a sort of elder statesman, remaining aloof from much of the conversation until he chooses to step in and punctuate it with a well-chosen remark. Harold is obsessed with his appearance, describing himself as "a thirty-two-year-old, ugly, pockmarked Jew fairy"; considers himself too old to be attractive; and hoards sleeping pills so he can end his life if he wishes.

Tension between Michael and Harold builds for most of the second act of *The Boys in the Band* as they compete to gain control of the party. Michael enjoys provoking the other men, particularly during a game that forces them to recall humiliating past encounters. Harold does not participate in the game and remains an observer until he finally explodes at Michael: "You are a sad and pathetic man. You're a homosexual and you don't want to be. But there is nothing you can do to change it. Not all your prayers to your God, not all the analysis you can buy in all the years you've got left to live. You may very well one day be able to know a heterosexual life if you want it desperately enough—if you pursue it with the fervor with which you annihilate—but you will always be homosexual as well. Always, Michael. Always. Until the day you die." With this pronouncement, the party is over, and the emotionally exhausted men head for home.

Earlier American plays had included gay characters, but none enjoyed the success or had the influence of *The Boys in the Band,* whose original New York production ran for more than a thousand performances. Crowley's breakthrough was in setting his play within a circle of friends who are gay in the way that the characters in Lorraine Hansberry's *A Raisin in the Sun* (1959) are African American: it is an obvious fact that affects their lives, but they are not defined by that characteristic alone. The success of the play may have to do with the timing of its premiere: its original run spanned the years immediately before and after the Stonewall riots in June 1969, which most historians consider the beginning of the modern gay liberation movement. Crowley wrote the screenplay for the successful 1970 movie version of *The Boys in the Band,* which stars the cast of the stage production. He also wrote a sequel, *The Men from the Boys,* which centers around a reunion of six of *The Boys in the Band* characters thirty years later. Harold's character retains his sardonic wit in the later play: after revealing that he is infected with HIV, he tells Michael: "Actually I don't care who knows I have AIDS, I just don't want anyone to know I'm gay."

Crowley has offered two explanations for the title *The Boys in the Band.* One is that the men are outlaws of society, like a band of thieves. The other is that it is an allusion to a phrase used in the big band era to refer to the musicians backing up a singer or other soloist. Crowley has been criticized for the negative tone of *The Boys in the Band,* as summed up by Michael: "You show me a happy homosexual, and I'll show you a gay corpse." This negativity of *The Boys in the Band* may have been partly a device to make the play acceptable to mainstream audiences and the censors, but has also been seen as a realistic portrayal of gay men who internalize the homophobia of their society.

Discussion Questions

1. *The Boys in the Band* is set among a circle of gay friends, yet the sexual preference of Alan is deliberately left ambiguous. Why do you think Mart Crowley gave a major role to a character who may not, in fact, be one of the boys in the band?

2. Crowley has been criticized for making the characters in *The Boys in the Band* negative stereotypes. More-recent plays have included gay characters who are both more positive and more complex, for instance, Larry Kramer's *The Normal Heart* and Paul Rudnick's *Jeffrey.* To what extent do you think Crowley's portrayal of his characters was defined by the social conditions of gay men at the time he wrote it, and how much was artistic choice?

3. Midway through the second act, Harold tells Michael: "Oh, I know this game you're playing. And I play it very well. You play it very well too. But you know what, I'm the only one that's better at it than you are. I can beat you at it. So don't push me." What is Harold referring to?

4. Why do you think Crowley decided not to give any of the characters in *The Boys in the Band* surnames?

—*Sarah Boslaugh*

REFERENCES

John L. DiGaetani, "Mart Crowley," in his *A Search for Postmodern Theater: Interviews with Contemporary Playwrights* (Westport, Conn.: Greenwood Press, 1991), pp. 48–53;

John Loughery, "The Boys in the Band," in his *The Other Side of Silence: Men's Lives and Gay Identities: A Twentieth Century History* (New York: Holt, 1998), pp. 291–302;

John Rickard, "*The Boys in the Band,* 30 Years Later," *Gay and Lesbian Review,* 8 (March–April 2001): 9–11.

D

Frederic Dannay

(October 20, 1905 – September 3, 1982)

and

Manfred B. Lee

(January 11, 1905 – April 3, 1971)

SERIES

(1929–1971)

ELLERY QUEEN

Ellery Queen is an amateur detective in a series of 35 novels, 77 short stories, and approximately 294 original radio plays. He was created by two cousins, Frederic Dannay and Manfred B. Lee. Realizing that readers tended to remember the detective's name and not the author's, the cousins signed their work as by Ellery Queen. In *The Roman Hat Mystery* (1929), Ellery is introduced as the son of a New York police inspector, which allows Ellery a semiofficial entrance to criminal investigations. The younger Queen is a tall, athletic man who wears rimless pince-nez glasses; a graduate of Harvard, he talks in a bookish way and uses Latin quotations. Queen is a model of a rational problem-solver utilizing physical clues and timetables (who was where and when).

Complicating this depiction is a series of forewords to the early novels in which J. J. McC., a family friend, explains that the names of Ellery and Richard Queen are pseudonyms, that the inspector has retired and that both are living in Italy, Ellery having married and now with a baby son. Gradually, some of the details are changed, and by the forewords to such books as *The Spanish Cape Mystery* (1935) and *The Adventures of Ellery Queen* (1934), the claimed pseudonyms of the Queens, the retirement to Italy, and the wife and child have been dropped. In the first foreword and most of the others, Queen is said to have fictionalized his own cases; later, after 1936, while he remains a writer, his mystery fiction is separate from the mysteries he solves.

The Spanish Cape Mystery suggests that Queen might be more than a bloodless ratiocinative detective, as indicated by the contrast between two statements he makes: "My work is done with symbols . . . not with human beings. . . . I choose to close my mind to the human elements and treat it as a problem in mathematics. The fate of the murderer I leave to those who decide such things." Later, however, he admits: "I've often boasted that the human equation means nothing to me. But it does, damn it all, it does!"

Queen slowly develops, although partly in response to changes in the market for mysteries as much as internal character growth. His character becomes more emotional, more complex, less purely rational in various ways. For example, in the second of the Hollywood novels, *The Four of Hearts* (1938), Ellery meets Paula Paris, a gossip columnist; his reaction is immediate—he is overwhelmed by her beauty and suffers from "the grand passion." (He has another love interest in the radio plays and in twelve of the short stories and two novels: his secretary, Nikki Porter.) The novels of this period, 1936–1939, suggest works shaped to appeal to women readers—and six of them were condensed in women's magazines.

Dannay and Lee published no new Ellery Queen novel between 1939 and 1942, when they returned with *Calamity Town*, which features a much more mature-seeming Queen in his first visit to the New England village of Wrightsville. In subsequent novels between 1942 and 1958 Queen's adventures were a mix of traditional puzzles and serious examinations of character. Probably the most interesting depiction of Queen as a person comes in a two-novel sequence: *Ten Days' Wonder* (1948) and *Cat of Many Tails* (1949). In *Ten Days' Wonder*—the third novel set in Wrightsville—Queen is tricked into a false solution that causes an innocent person's death, and as a consequence swears off criminal investigations forever. But in the next novel, *Cat of Many Tails*, a serial strangler is active in New York City, and Inspector Queen puts pressure on his son to involve himself in the investigation of the murders. Again Queen finds a false solution first—in this case one that is close to the truth but not quite true, and again one that costs an innocent life—and again he is immersed in guilt. The novel ends with him in Vienna, talking to Dr. Béla Seligmann, a psychiatrist. In the novels of this middle period Queen's character is realistic enough that he must deal with guilt feelings, with the inevitable failures at times of his own rationality.

The last book of this period is *The Finishing Stroke* (1958), not a psychologically complex case but one that is set mostly in 1929–1930, with Ellery as the young author who had just published his first novel, before jumping forward years later to present the resolution of the mystery. As its title suggests, Dannay and Lee may have intended *The Finishing Stroke* to be the last Queen mystery; Dannay suffered from writer's block and other ailments, and subsequent novels in the series—rather heavily stylized puzzles—were written by ghostwriters from Dannay's outlines. The last Ellery Queen novel, *A Fine and Private Place*, was published in 1971.

Discussion Questions

1. Of the shorter fiction of Queen's first period (1929–1936), highly praised are two short stories and a novelette—"The Bearded Lady" and "The Glass-Domed Clock" (from *The Adventures of Ellery Queen*, 1934) and "The Lamp of God" (from *The New Adventures of Ellery Queen*, 1940). Is Ellery Queen in any of these highly plotted works developed with complexity as a personality?

2. *Calamity Town* (1942) is sometimes considered Queen's best novel. It is easy to discuss the details of the setting, but the effect of the tragedy on the people of the town is also well done and could be analyzed. Or, as with most mystery novels, the villain's character is worth discussion—since the motive has to be hidden in order to keep the villain's identity secret, does his or her personality seem realistic after the truth is revealed?

3. Four short stories dealing with sports appear in *The New Adventures of Ellery Queen*: "Man Bites Dog" (baseball), "Long Shot" (horse racing), "Mind over Matter" (boxing), and "Trojan Horse" (football). How do Queen's attitudes toward the four sports affect the plots?

4. *The Origin of Evil* (1951) has a social theme of the animalistic nature of mankind. How is this theme integrated into the characterizations and the plot?

4. Nikki Porter, secretary, is a lightly treated love interest of Ellery Queen. She appears in *"The Adventure of the Murdered Moths" and Other Radio Mysteries* (2005) and in the twelve short stories of *Calendar of Crime* (1952)—these stories were adapted from radio scripts. Using at least the radio scripts, discuss the relationship between Nikki and Ellery.

—*Joe R. Christopher*

REFERENCES

Francis M. Nevins Jr., *Royal Bloodline: Ellery Queen, Author and Detective* (Bowling Green, Ohio: Bowling Green University Popular Press, 1974);

Nevins and Martin Grams Jr., *The Sound of Detection: Ellery Queen's Adventures in Radio* (Churchville, Md.: OTR, 2002);

Ellery Queen and others, *"The Tragedy of Errors" and Others: With Essays and Tributes to Recognize Ellery Queen's Seventieth Anniversary* (Norfolk, Va.: Crippen & Landru, 1999).

Edwidge Danticat
(January 19, 1969 –   )

ᵂᶜᵉ

BREATH, EYES, MEMORY
(New York: Soho, 1994)

SOPHIE CACO

Sophie Caco is the central character in Danticat's novel *Breath, Eyes, Memory*. Sophie comes of age on the island of Haiti, where she is raised by her Aunt Atie and her grandmother. She has a limited relationship with her mother, Martine, who has moved to New York and sends back money to help the family. Martine is a distant image for Sophie, who has developed a strong bond with her aunt. When Sophie is twelve and her mother sends for her, this transition initiates an exploration of the impact of migration on families as well as the relationships between women of different generations. In New York, Sophie must adjust not only to a new culture and environment but to her mother as well. She becomes an "other" in her Brooklyn community, identifiable as different by her language and, according to the African Americans around her, by her smell. Sophie must adjust to a new world that sees her not only as different but also, by virtue of the fact that she comes from the so-called Third World, as more susceptible to various diseases and particularly HIV. Sophie struggles to know herself in the midst of this new environment, and her developing relationship with her mother complicates her self-understanding.

Martine is struggling with her own personal history. She is haunted by being raped as a young adult, which resulted in Sophie's birth. Martine and Sophie thus are marked by this act of violence that bonds them as women but divides them as mother and daughter. Their relationship is further complicated when Sophie reaches puberty and her mother begins to test her virginity. The testing that Martine forces on Sophie was also done to her and Atie. It is a product of the desire to maintain a valued sense of purity that was handed down from generation to generation. Martine and the generations of women before her fail to see the connection between the rape of black women during slavery and the sexual abuse they initiate on their own daughters. Sophie is forced to respond to this act of violence from her mother by taking her own virginity with a pestle, effectively ending the test but beginning her own problems with sex and sexuality.

In order to escape from her mother, who is losing touch with reality, and to escape from sexual abuse, Sophie marries Joseph, a musician who is older than she is. Joseph opens the door to questions of cross-cultural contact and communication. He sees a tangible connection between his African American culture and Sophie's Haitian heritage, making a link between the African diasporic experiences in different nations.

When Sophie has her own daughter, she is forced to deal with her sexual abuse, her relationship with her mother, and with her migration. As the women in Sophie's life reunite in Haiti, they are able to address their personal and collective history. Sophie must deal with her bulimia, a disease her Caribbean relatives, for whom food is not to be taken for granted, cannot understand. She must also come to terms with her mother's personal history, a story that is tied to the history of Haiti and the post-Duvalier era. It is essential that Sophie return to Haiti in order to locate a sense of self; her identity is tied to the history of the place she originally called home despite her migration from the region. Returning to Haiti helps to ground Sophie in her culture and in her womanhood. She learns about not only her mother's history but also of the sacrifices Atie made in order to raise Sophie.

When Sophie returns to America, she brings with her a desire for community that is exhibited in her attempt to find solace in a form of therapy based on Haitian, African, and Latino traditions. Carole Boyce Davies suggests in *Black Women, Writing and Identity* that migrants always take some of their past with them, and Sophie is an embodiment of this ideology. Her therapy is an attempt to amalgamate all aspects of her personal history in order to be a better person.

Sophie's attempt to heal herself is obscured by Martine's continuous struggle with her own sexual identity. Finding herself pregnant, Martine is unable to deal with her life and commits suicide. Sophie takes her mother home to Haiti to be buried, and after the funeral she runs into the cane fields where her mother was raped. Both her grandmother and her aunt see this act as "freeing"; however, the ending of the novel remains ambiguous, offering no easy solution to the question of whether Sophie will continue the tradition by testing her own daughter.

Discussion Questions

1. All the women in the Caco family have suffered because of the legacy of testing that has been part of each of their lives. Is there any evidence in the novel to suggest that Sophie will not test her own daughter?

2. What connection can be made between Sophie's bulimia and her desire to assimilate to American identity?

3. Sophie is raised in a female-centered world. What impact does this have on her relationship with Joseph and with Marc, following her mother's death?

—*J. A. Brown-Rose*

REFERENCES

Carole Boyce Davies, *Black Women, Writing and Identity: Migrations of the Subject* (New York: Routledge, 1994);

Nick Nisbet, *Voicing Memory: History and Subjectivity in French Caribbean Literature* (Charlottesville: University of Virginia Press, 2003).

Rebecca Harding Davis
(June 24, 1831 – September 29, 1910)

ᛕ

"LIFE IN THE IRON-MILLS"
Atlantic Monthly (April 1861); collected in *Life in the Iron Mills and Other Stories*, edited by Jean Pfaelzer (New York: Feminist Press, 1972).

HUGH WOLFE
Rebecca Harding Davis uses Hugh Wolfe, the Welsh worker at the center of "Life in the Iron-Mills" (1861), to explore the contradictions of labor and life under industrial capitalism. Hugh is too inarticulate to explain his intentions, but he is amazingly expressive with pig-metal, the raw material he uses to sculpt his mysterious artistic masterpiece, the korl woman. Dazed and exploited by endless hours at the mill, Hugh forgets to go home for meals, but he somehow has the creative energy to render artwork that impresses even knowledgeable spectators. Limited by a life of labor that has kept him from studying art formally, he instinctually understands the posture of the body, and he easily sculpts the physical manifestations of emotions like hunger or longing. Though he exists in a setting of thankless labor, he is nonetheless—Davis insists readers realize—a "Hugh" just like "you," a figure familiar, who, like everyone else, desires the means and the freedom to cultivate his natural talents. "Life in the Iron-Mills" follows a character prevented from having a life because of the demands of those mills.

Though Hugh works in a setting that demands stamina and brawn, he is oddly feminine, apparently womanly enough to be nicknamed "Molly Wolfe." He devotes his attention to the korl woman, the feminine figure that seems to come to life in his hands, and he neglects Deborah, the mill-worker who wishes to devote her life to him. He dwells in a setting that encourages concentration on mundane labor, but he seems to escape this setting through his imagination, his dreams, and the creative release of his art. He thinks about artistic creation rather than repetitive labor in the mills, and speaks in gruff monosyllables that recall the Welsh expressions of his earlier life. He listens as Mitchell, May, and Kirby, wealthy businessmen who tour the mill, talk about labor unions, democracy, and free enterprise, but when they ask him to explain his statue, "she be hungry" is all he can say. Mitchell, as the most open-minded of these three visitors, suggests that naturally gifted artists such as Hugh deserve the chance to hone their skills. He seems to say that they should have the money and the leisure to spend their lives practicing art instead of laboring at industry. But when Hugh gains enough money to escape—after Deborah poaches Mitchell's wallet—he does not achieve artistic freedom. Confined to a prison cell, he instead loses what little life he had in the first place.

Hugh in the end is the impoverished, under-privileged American—foreign-born, blue-collar, uncomfortable with the idioms of the English language—whom, Davis demonstrates, others so easily ignore, even as they espouse ideals of equal opportunity. Hugh has much in common with slave characters in abolitionist literature, such as the hero of Harriet Beecher Stowe's *Uncle Tom's Cabin* (1852), who experience exploitation and abuse and yet lack the language and the knowledge to fight it. Hugh also looks forward to the heroes of Upton Sinclair's *The Jungle* (1906), who are similarly trapped in heartless industrial enterprises that sap their energy and steal their liberty. Hugh and these kindred figures excite the readers' pities for people suffering from social injustice. He and his ilk, through their inarticulacy, move their more articulate readers to write and speak on their behalf.

The wording of the story seems to insist that readers enter Hugh's muddy, filthy setting of Wheeling, West Virginia, and see for themselves. "I want you to come down and look at this Wolfe," Davis implores, "standing there among the lowest of his kind, and see him just as he is, that you may judge him justly when you hear the story of this night." Readers, who cannot presume to understand what life is like for Hugh, find the story confronting them directly: "What do you make of a case like that, amateur psychologist?" the author addresses the reader. "Is that all of their lives," she asks of laborers; is that all "of the portion given to them and these their duplicates swarming the streets today? nothing beneath? all?" She invites readers to imagine having to share the "vile, slimy lives" of West Virginia millworkers. Hugh functions as a reason for readers to imagine having to leave customary comfort zones.

To Kirby and Mitchell, Hugh's art is a mere curiosity to be abandoned in the mills. To Davis, it is a work of art to be treasured, a statue that stands in the library of her own home at the end of the story. She tells readers that the statue still seems to echo its creator with its "eager wolfish face watching mine: a wan, woeful face through which the spirit of the dead korl-cutter looks out, with its thwarted life, its mighty hunger, its unfinished work." Its lips still seem to be asking something: "Is this the end?" Hugh's hunger and longing live on in his creation. The memory of Hugh, together with the statue's haunting qualities, in effect asks readers to choose sides in a debate about capitalist exploitation. Readers can either be like Mitchell and Kirby, who view works of art from privileged and prejudiced points of view, or they can be like the narrator, who understands Hugh from inside his own setting, appreciates his unrealized potential as an artist, and treasures his unconventional work of art. Choosing a side in such a debate means asking how fairly America treats its aspiring artists, its unconventional dreamers, its citizens who are too inarticulate to speak for themselves. Asking such difficult questions means beginning to imagine an alternative for Hugh, beyond his limited existence, his so-called life in the iron-mills.

Discussion Questions

1. Why does Rebecca Harding Davis's story stress the need for readers to imagine themselves entering the muddy, filthy world of Wheeling, the setting of the story? If it is a place of "mud and foul effluvia," as the story says, why would a reader want to go there?

2. Why does the narrator end the story with the fact that she now possesses Hugh Wolfe's korl woman statue? What attitude or response could she be modeling for her readers when she describes her final attitude toward Hugh's work?

3. What similarities do you see between the struggles of the laborer Hugh Wolfe and those of other exploited or oppressed characters, such as slaves in Harriet Beecher Stowe's *Uncle Tom's Cabin* or the meat-industry laborers in Upton Sinclair's *The Jungle?*

—*Adam Sonstegard*

REFERENCES

Rebecca Harding Davis, *Life in the Iron-Mills: A Bedford Cultural Edition,* edited by Cecelia Tichi (New York: Bedford Books, 1998);

Sharon M. Harris, *Rebecca Harding Davis and American Social Realism* (Philadelphia: University of Pennsylvania Press, 1991);

Jean Pfaelzer, *Parlor Radical: Rebecca Harding Davis and the Origins of American Social Realism* (Pittsburgh: University of Pittsburgh Press, 1996);

Jane Atteridge Rose, *Rebecca Harding Davis* (New York: Twayne, 1993).

Richard Harding Davis
(April 18, 1864 – April 11, 1916)

❦

GALLEGHER AND OTHER STORIES
(New York: Scribners, 1891)

VAN BIBBER AND OTHERS
(New York: Harper, 1892)

CINDERELLA AND OTHER STORIES
(New York: Scribners, 1896)

CORTLANDT VAN BIBBER

Cortlandt Van Bibber is the sophisticated gentleman protagonist of a series of short stories by Richard Harding Davis. First appearing in newspapers and magazines and later collected in several books, the episodes about Van Bibber's life propelled Davis to national fame in the early 1890s. Arthur Lubow, one of Davis's biographers, notes that by the turn of the twentieth century, Davis was one of the best-known men in America, having earned a worldwide reputation as a fiction writer, playwright, travel writer, and war correspondent. As a model for illustrator Charles Dana Gibson's "Gibson Man," Davis came to epitomize the character that he presented in Van Bibber.

According to Fairfax Downey, another of Davis's biographers, Van Bibber was modeled after a character in a French newspaper. Davis recast him to appeal to an American audience, however, and in doing so defined a new American hero— the upper-class gentleman adventurer. Though Van Bibber's social status makes him something of an original among American heroes, he displays familiar heroic traits. As Scott C. Osborn and Robert L. Phillips Jr. note, "the Davis code rests squarely on the Anglo-Saxon code of chivalry." Accordingly, Van Bibber demonstrates the ideals of adventure, courage, and respect toward women.

For Van Bibber, adventure often involves events outside of his routine activities of eating at Delmonico's—the upscale New York restaurant favored by the well-to-do—or paying a visit to his stock broker. In "Love Me, Love My Dog," Van Bibber finds himself enduring the bitter winter weather in search of a lost dog. On another occasion, in "Van Bibber's Burglar," while returning home from a late night on the town, he encounters and captures a burglar. In "Eleanor Guyler," on one of "his many excursions in search of mild adventure," Van Bibber must come to the rescue of a young lady. Unlike heroes who go great distances in search of excitement, Van Bibber discovers his adventures in and about New York City.

Van Bibber enjoys his adventures all the more for the displays of bravery they require. Whether the moment calls for physical fortitude or moral resolve, he is always equal to the challenge. In "Van Bibber's Burglar," he spies a man acting suspiciously. "Because it was curious, and he liked adventure," Van Bibber investigates the man, who "in one hand . . . held a revolver." Although unarmed, he confronts the burglar, disarming him in the ensuing fight. Physical harm is not the only threat that Van Bibber deals with, however, as is apparent in "Van Bibber and the Swan-Boats." He agrees to ride in one of the swan-boats, "the most idiotic inventions he had ever seen." He must summon his courage because he is "so afraid some one would see him" and would be subject to ridicule. For someone of his high social status, the possibility of such ridicule is as intimidating as a loaded revolver.

Davis extends Van Bibber's sense of chivalry by frequently having him come to the aid of a lady in distress. The potentially embarrassing ride in the swan-boat occurs because he has gallantly come to the aid of three young girls who cannot afford an excursion around the lake. On another occasion, he singlehandedly takes on three ruffians who confront Eleanore Cuyler, a "well-born and well-dressed" lady of his acquaintance. In "Love Me, Love My Dog," his hostess has lost her prized dog. In response, Van Bibber says, "to oblige the despondent mistress of this valuable member of the household, I will risk pneumonia." In true heroic form, he repeatedly puts the needs of a lady before his own safety or reputation.

Keeping with the romantic tradition he favored, Davis rewards his hero for his daring deeds. In typical knightly fashion, Van Bibber often wins the admiration of a beautiful woman for having come to her aid. In the story of the swan-boats, Van Bibber is seen riding about by "A Girl He Knew," as she is referred to in the story, just the person whose notice he has sought to avoid. Rather than ridiculing him, however, she tells him that he should "join her, which was to be his reward for taking care of the young ladies." Similarly, for rescuing the dog, Van Bibber finds "Miss Arnett, looking up at him with gratitude in her eyes." For Davis's gentleman adventurer, a lady's warm appreciation for his services is ample reward for a deed well done.

At a time when industrialization and commercialization were rapidly changing America, people eagerly sought out a hero, and Davis provided one that was widely accepted. As Larzer Ziff notes, "courage and the Sunday-school code, loyalty to chums, resistance to blackguards and their cronies, fair play to all," were the values that Richard Harding Davis instilled in his heroes, the most popular of whom was Cortlandt Van Bibber.

Discussion Questions

1. In stories such as "Andy M'Gee's Chorus Girl" and "A Leander of the East River," Davis presents heroes of a lower social status than Van Bibber. In what way are the heroes alike, despite their social differences?

2. Osborne and Phillips note that "Davis through his gentleman heroes argues for a belief in social conventions." What social conventions does Van Bibber adhere to? What does Van Bibber see as a proper code of behavior?

—*Jim Riser*

REFERENCES

Arthur Lubow, *The Reporter Who Would Be King: A Biography of Richard Harding Davis* (New York: Scribners, 1992);

Scott C. Osborn and Robert L. Phillips Jr., *Richard Harding Davis* (Boston: Twayne, 1978);

Larzer Ziff, *The American 1890s: Life and Times of a Lost Generation* (Lincoln: University of Nebraska Press, 1966).

Don DeLillo
(November 20, 1936 –)

UNDERWORLD
(New York: Scribner, 1997)

SISTER ALMA EDGAR

Sister Alma Edgar, like many characters in DeLillo's *Underworld,* spends her life searching for a higher, purer state of existence while also trying to reconcile her own religious doubt and neurotic behaviors. In her first appearance in the novel she is a nun who has retired years previously from teaching and now runs a New York mission that feeds the homeless. She appears again midway through the novel as an intimidating teacher who grills Matt Shay after catching him during recess with a contraband magazine and again at the end as one of the witnesses to the miraculous appearance of the angel Esmeralda.

Visions of the apocalypse haunt Sister Edgar in the same manner that looming nuclear apocalypse preoccupies J. Edgar Hoover. She makes her students wear dog tags so that the authorities can identify bodies in case of nuclear attack and also organizes nuclear-attack drills and emergency plans. Her visions are partially inspired by Pieter Brueghel the Elder's painting *The Triumph of Death,* which Hoover finds in a copy of *Life* magazine at the Dodgers baseball game, where New York Giants outfielder Bobby Thomson hits the home run that fuels most of the narrative of *Underworld.* When recollecting a trip to the catacombs of Rome, for example, she remembers "thinking vindictively that these are the dead who will" return "to punish the sins of the living—death, yes, triumphant."

Both Sister Edgar and Hoover possess a dark conception of the approaching end of humanity, and they exile themselves from society in an effort to purify themselves. This desire for purity manifests itself in several ways for both characters, who are phobic about germs. "At the sink she scrubbed her hands repeatedly," wondering how "can the hands be clean if the soap is not," and that "if you clean the soap with bleach, what do you clean the bleach bottle with?" Her fear of disease runs so deep that she routinely wears latex gloves in public places.

Sister Edgar's students fear her rage and abusive teaching practices, which involve corporal punishment of disobedient children. When she asks her class who "the original parents of us all" are, for instance, she expects them to chant in unison that Adam and Eve are the first parents, and she bangs Michael Kalenka's head against the blackboard when he jokes that the answer is "Tarzan and Jane." In general, she expects the same asceticism from her students that she imposes on herself. When she catches Matt reading movie magazines, however, she quizzes him on his knowledge. The implications are somewhat ambiguous and paradoxical. Sister Edgar knows as much about movie stars as any teenage girl, and yet she feels compelled to warn others about the perils of materialistic culture and chastises them for falling victim to popular culture.

One of DeLillo's more mysterious and quirky characters, Sister Edgar bears comparison to the German nun whom Jack Gladney meets near the end of DeLillo's novel *White Noise* (1985). When Gladney questions the nun about her faith, she responds by pointing out his naiveté. She, like all clergy in the modern world, maintain their faith only because they are the last barrier against complete nihilism. "We make your nonbelief possible," she says. Additionally, she engages in many practices that contradict her stern moral code, hence further emphasizing the impossibility of a totally pure existence in an imperfect world. Aside from the stories that abound of her as one who "used to twirl the big-beaded rosary and crack students across the mouth with the iron crucifix," Sister Edgar has resorted to a shady business of locating stolen and "cannibalized" cars for a gang of graffiti writers in order to fund the homeless shelter operated by the church.

Because Sister Edgar sees humanity standing on the brink of annihilation, she attempts not only to purify herself but also to save others. She demonstrates particular interest in saving a young girl named Esmeralda, a young girl who has run away from a drug addict mother and now lives in a junkyard. Edgar wants not only to save Esmeralda from the squalor of her life but also desires to "buzz her with Spelling and Grammar," as if her salvation

lies in becoming a member of society who adheres to rules and regulations. Her purity involves a deep belief in rules and self-discipline. DeLillo commented in an interview with Anthony DeCurtis that most of his characters "have a deep need for rules and boundaries" in their lives. This need takes many shapes for his different characters, but they all share a fascination and mystic awe of language, which possesses the most intricate and intimate rules and boundaries. Sister Edgar, who sees Esmeralda's salvation in terms of learning proper grammar, is no exception. She approaches her students the same way, diagramming massively complex sentences on the blackboard.

Sister Edgar undergoes a transformation in the final pages of *Underworld,* when she learns of Esmeralda's rape and murder. She initially loses all religious faith and despairs, thinking that the universe is simply composed of "waste with a random emerald star here or there." But her faithlessness only persists until Esmeralda returns as an angel that appears on a Minute Maid billboard advertisement. While Sister Edgar has obsessed over germs and disease most of her life, upon seeing the miracle for herself she immediately takes off her latex gloves "and shakes hands, pumps hands with the great-bodied women who roll their eyes to heaven." The germ-paranoid, sociopathic nun finally embraces humanity, "breathes the same air" as the rest of the world. Her transformation is almost literal as she becomes "a disembodied fact in liquid form, pouring into the crowd." Yet, Esmeralda's appearance on the billboard should not necessarily evoke an inclination toward organized religion over agnosticism. Though DeLillo himself grew up in a Catholic family and even based Sister Edgar on one of his teachers, he routinely challenges traditional faiths in his other works, in particular *White Noise* and *The Names* (1982). Most of his characters search for the assurance of an afterlife, but DeLillo denies them such easy answers. Likewise, as Sister Edgar dies peacefully in a dream-like state in the final paragraphs of *Underworld* as a result of the Esmeralda miracle, readers are left to wonder if Alma's peaceful passing is because of the resurgence of her faith in God or the recent instance in which she has finally embraced other human beings.

Discussion Questions

1. Does DeLillo intend for readers to interpret the appearance of Esmeralda as a genuine miracle or an ironic (false) one? Consider the passages that describe her appearance on a Minute Maid billboard as well as Sister Edgar's reaction.

2. In the conclusion of the novel, does Sister Edgar seem to have reconciled her religious doubt, her obsession with the apocalypse, and her yearning for "authorship and moral form"? How so?

3. What other parallels can one find between the German nun in *White Noise* and Alma Edgar? Acknowledging the fact that both figures appear in the last few pages of both novels, explain what thematic motivation DeLillo might have for ending *Underworld* with Sister Edgar's ostensibly peaceful death. Is this ending meant to address or revise the decidedly more violent and pessimistic conclusion to *White Noise*?

—Brian Ray

NICK SHAY

Nick Shay provides the majority of first-person narration in Don DeLillo's novel *Underworld* and serves as the best candidate for the protagonist of a novel that traces out the lives of several characters. When Shay is introduced, he is in the Arizona desert on his way to a reunion with his former lover, the famous artist Klara Sax. After the meeting between Shay and Sax, *Underworld* begins its retrograde narrative, moving backward in time from 1997 eventually to 1951 and 1952, the focal point from which all the conflicts of the novel originate. He appears throughout the novel, as the victim of a love affair between his wife, Marian, and his best friend, Brian Glassic; then as the perpetrator of an affair with a woman named Donna, whom he meets at a waste-management convention; and later on as a teenager who is sent to juvenile detention for manslaughter. The years 1951 and 1952 turn out to be crucial for Nick Shay. During this period he drops out of school, begins an affair with Klara Sax, the wife of his former high-school science teacher Albert Bronzini, and becomes a surrogate son for George Manza, an illiterate waiter and pool shooter who makes money on the side by dealing in drugs and small-time prostitution. Manza seems to fill an absence left by Nick Shay's father, encouraging Nick to stay in school and offering to find him a better job than his current one. Yet, Manza also ostensibly ruins Nick's life when he shows the seventeen-year-old dropout a sawed-off shot gun, which he claims is not loaded. Shay's profession, waste management, provides an extended metaphor for nearly every aspect of his life. He spends decades trying to rid himself of his own baggage, as it were—his adulterous relationships and, most importantly, the accidental killing of George Manza. His job so affects his life that he can no longer go shopping in peace because he only sees in the new consumer products sitting on shelves a potential for waste. While he attempts to rid himself of negativity, Shay also finds himself in search of it as well. Failure, like waste, becomes an attraction, which explains his fascination with New York Giants outfielder Bobby Thomson's famous home run, the "Shot Heard 'round the World" that propelled the Giants past the Brooklyn Dodgers to win the National League pennant in 1951. Rather than focus on Thomson's victory, Shay instead meditates on Dodgers pitcher Ralph Branca, who gave up the run; to Shay the game signified only "Bad luck, Branca luck. From him to me. The moment that makes the life." Shay sees his possession of the game-winning ball as a means of owning and mastering the various mistakes he has made in his own life.

Shay's religious faith plays a prominent role in the novel. Like Sister Alma Edgar, who has devoted her life to an omnipotent God who will destroy humanity to save only the purest souls, Shay demonstrates an equal and opposite reaction in his agnosticism. His search for a God culminates in his discovery of the phrase *todo y nada*—"everything and nothing"—that is, pure sex. As Shay puts it, sex "is the one secret we have that approximates an exalted state and that we share" with one another. He arrives at this conclusion through a medieval text, *The Cloud of Unknowing*, and soon thereafter understands God as "a long unlighted tunnel, on and on. . . . And so I learned to respect the power of secrets" and how to "cherish his negation." Thus, Shay worships sex and pure creation as opposed to Sister Edgar's Catholic notion of "authorship and moral form."

This denial of God stems from Shay's search for his father, Jimmy Constanza, a bookmaker famous for his incredible memory. Shay spends as much time meditating on the existence of God as he does on the conspicuous absence of Constanza, whose "life closed down the night he went out for cigarettes." As evidenced by frequent arguments with his brother Matt, Shay has never recovered from his father's disappearance and has come up with conspiracy theories. Everyone else in the family, however, seems to silently agree that he simply decided to abandon his family. Shay, already faced with abandonment by God, cannot face the possibility that, as Matt says, "He didn't want to be a father. . . . He was a loner," and that Constanza skipped town to avoid a large horse-betting debt. If Shay has learned that religion is only a way of cherishing God's negation, then this is how he feels toward his own father.

His search for a creator also leads to his affair with Klara, whom he sleeps with while in high school and then seeks out again more than twenty years later, when she has moved to the desert to organize a massive installation called "Long Tall Sally." No doubt Shay is drawn to his old flame because of his attraction to waste management and recycling. Klara's project, which involves dozens of B-52 bombers, is an act of making "art out of war." She and a group of graduate students have stripped the planes of their weapons and are in the process of coating them with paint. Once used to drop bombs over Vietnam, the bombers will now sit in the desert as part of a massive work of art. In many ways Klara shares Shay's need to make new objects from old. Shay realizes the analogy between them: "We were waste brokers. . . . I almost mentioned my line of work to Klara Sax when we had our talk in the desert. Her own career had been marked at times by her methods of transforming and absorbing junk." But, he says, "Famous people don't want to be told that you have a quality in common with them."

A similar connection exists between Shay and Sabato Rodia, the craftsman who makes the Watts Towers, which Shay studies extensively. His interest lies, in particular, in the method by which Rodia has created his own identity from the various components slapped together into the towers. "The towers and birdbaths and fountains and decorated posts and bright oddments and household colors, the green of 7-Up bottles and blue of Milk of Magnesia, the whole complex of structures and gates and panels that were built . . . by one man" who "left his wife and family," someone "whose narrative is mostly blank spaces" and emptiness.

The towers thus remind Shay of his father, who might have left his family to start over and rebuild his life from disparate parts, then to "give away the land and all the art" and go "away . . . to die." The towers serve as a metaphor for all of the struggles in Shay's life—with his "ghost father," and also with his yearning for and ultimate denial of God. Like Rodia, Shay hopes to either rid himself of his life's baggage or to construct something worthwhile from it, thus overcoming his lack of faith and replacing it with confidence and self-reliance.

Nick Shay's victim, George Manza, serves a pivotal role in Shay's life and the novel alike. Manza embodies the notions of failed father and absconding deity that dominate Shay's philosophical quest for meaning and spirituality. Shay is haunted by the moment in which he kills Manza. In one way Shay's actions are accidental. In another way, Shay seems to be conscious of a deeper motivation. By killing Manza, Shay symbolically kills his father. The manslaughter conviction however, seems to rejuvenate Nick Shay, who sees detention as a time when he reconstructs himself and learns the salubrious effects of books, scholastic rigor, and hard physical work. Perhaps the look on Manza's face as he essentially lies to Shay about the gun being unloaded, a look that is "more bright and alive than George had ever looked," should signal an awareness on Manza's part—a suicidal urge but also knowledge that his self-sacrifice will eventually lead to Shay's salvation.

Discussion Questions

1. Has Nick Shay recovered from his troubled teenage years? Remember that he still feels preoccupied by Branca's baseball as a symbol of failure. Is his ownership of the ball a statement of his possession of his own mistakes or a mark of his inability to forget his past?

2. If Shay were presented with verifiable evidence that Jimmy had indeed abandoned him, and not

been kidnapped or murdered by the Mafia, would he accept the evidence or find yet more fanciful reasons to excuse his father? Keep in mind that his denial of the probable truth possesses deeper, spiritually rooted motivations.

3. Why does Shay cheat on his wife, Marian, and then confess of his own volition? Is he trying to hurt her unconsciously, or might his adulterous behavior have something to do with what he tells Donna about pure sex and knowing God (or his father) through absence? Do his actions serve as a way of reenacting his father's failures?

—*Brian Ray*

REFERENCES

Joseph Dewey, Steven G. Kellman, and Irving Malin, eds., *UnderWords: Perspectives on DeLillo's* Underworld (Newark: University of Delaware Press / London & Cranbury, N.J.: Associated University Presses, 2002);

John Duvall, *Don DeLillo's* Underworld: *A Reader's Guide* (New York: Continuum, 2002);

Thomas DePietro, *Conversations with Don DeLillo* (Jackson: University Press of Mississippi, 2003);

Mark Osteen, *American Magic and Dread: Don DeLillo's Dialogue with Culture* (Philadelphia: University of Pennsylvania Press, 2000).

꧁

WHITE NOISE

(New York: Viking, 1985; London: Picador/Pan, 1986)

JACK GLADNEY

Jack Gladney is the narrator and protagonist of Don DeLillo's novel *White Noise*. Gladney, a professor of Hitler studies at the fictional Blacksmith College-on-the-Hill, lives in suburban America with his fourth wife, Babette, and their four children. When his uneventful life is disrupted by a toxic cloud, Gladney details the effect of this occurrence: his preoccupation with death, his wife's identical fear, and his increasingly pessimistic meditations on the banality of modern America.

If DeLillo's preoccupation is with the way Americans live, then Gladney offers a model of supposed normality and its disturbing undercurrents. He is caught in the minutiae of everyday suburban life; his spiritual experiences of supermarkets and his lyrical descriptions of shopping malls are among the most affecting passages in the novel. When not out shopping, Gladney's family retreat to their separate lives, making shared indulgence in commercialism their closest experience of traditional religious or familial bonds. Beyond these rituals, television predominates: it provides the background "white noise" to Gladney's life.

Locating Gladney in such scenes also places him at the center of DeLillo's representation of the postmodern world. Postmodernism has been a preoccupation throughout the author's fiction—the instability of history in *Libra* (1988) and *Underworld* (1997) and the destabilizing of truth and search for meaning in *Mao II* (1991) and early novels such as *Americana* (1971) and *The Names* (1982). In *White Noise*, Gladney is crippled by living in an age that has lost its certainty, and in his home life he retreats from this fear by the promises of belonging and authenticity offered by consumerism. In his professional life his retreat takes another direction: into an academic world of grand ideas of religion, history, and science that provided certainty in an earlier era. Though Gladney is searching for an elusive and perhaps impossible authenticity, his whole life is an experience of simulacrum—copies of phenomena rather than their originals. Early in the novel, Gladney and his friend and colleague Murray Suskind visit the most photographed barn in America to witness individuals finding comfort in a collective tourism that involves "taking pictures of taking pictures." The toxic event is itself a copy of an earlier "simulated evacuation," and one of its reported side effects is a feeling of déjà vu. In his own life Gladney is a model of the inauthenticity he longs to analyze—a professor of Hitler studies who, no matter hard he tries, cannot learn German, making him "the false character that follows the name around." In Gladney's postmodern world, extremes become everyday occurrences, and so he teaches Hitler studies as just another university subject, part of a modern fascination with celebrity. A key episode in the text comes in chapter 15, where Gladney and Murray hold a classroom debate on the parallels between Adolf Hitler and Elvis Presley. This scene illustrates implicitly how extreme figures come to be the subject of everyday discussion and how celebrity has become a field of intellectual endeavor.

Gladney is one of the recognizable characters in DeLillo's fiction through whom he deals with the effect of catastrophe on the lives of individuals. Gladney's response to the toxic cloud forces him to confront his own mortality. It also dramatically removes him from his middle-class comfort zone. Gladney's class position is clearly defined: he locates himself as "not just a college professor. I'm the head of a department. I don't see myself fleeing an airborne toxic event. That's for people who live in mobile homes out in the scrubby parts of the country, where the fish hatcheries are." But the toxic cloud is no respecter of such distinctions. It forces Gladney into precisely the situations that he says he is in "a small-town setting" to avoid.

Ostensibly, Gladney shoots his wife's lover because being poisoned by the toxic cloud has affected his normal reactions. But on another level, his act is a much larger questioning of his own mortality: a refusal to be subject to the will of death and an attempt to take control of that will himself. Like his wife with her pursuit of Dylar, an experimental drug that supposedly relieves one of the fear of death, the increasingly paranoid Gladney (who admits he does not want to die before Babette) also feels he must take control over biological processes, in an age in which the faith that someone else is in charge of such processes has been eroded. Even the nun who Gladney confronts refuses to allay his fears, confessing that her "pretense is a dedication." The farcical nature of Gladney's attempts to gain control of his life only reinforces the sense of his feelings of inescapable powerlessness.

Gladney reflects DeLillo's meticulous construction of narrative voice, which he often claims is a starting point for his novels. The compact sentences of *Cosmopolis* (2003) reflect not only the enclosed nature of the book but also the internalized personality of the protagonist narrator; the sweeping, shifting syntax of *Underworld* captures the multiplicity of voices, each individualized, that it attempts to encompass. In *White Noise,* the short, directed language reflects the banality of Gladney's everyday life but also offers the reader a sense of ominous hyper-normality, of an individual on edge, from whom emotion is only waiting to explode, akin to the "dull and unlocatable roar . . . just outside the range of human apprehension" of the supermarket or, indeed, white noise itself. The shift in Gladney's narrative in the final chapter to an unbroken two-page paragraph is the submission to this underlying hysteria, to his acknowledgment at the conclusion of the novel that he is afraid.

Gladney marks a trend in contemporary American fiction, which focuses not on the hero but on what is suggested is the typical modern American, caught in a postmodern unreality defined by alienation, anxiety, and skepticism. At the end of the novel, nothing tangible has changed in Gladney's reality; his crime blurs into the banal world it springs from, but his acknowledgment of his own fears and the fears of those around him has altered him undeniably.

Discussion Questions

1. In an introduction to an interview with DeLillo in 1998, Maria Moss has stated that "All of DeLillo's characters . . . can be called voluntary exiles." In what ways is Jack Gladney a voluntary exile? How does he exclude himself from American society?

2. To what extent does Gladney represent the "American Everyman"? Is it possible to see him as the hero of the novel?

3. What part does television play in Gladney's life? What point do you think DeLillo is trying to make by representing its influence in the way that he does?

—*Sara Upstone*

REFERENCES

Harold Bloom, ed., *Don DeLillo* (Philadelphia: Chelsea House, 2003);

Thomas Depietro, ed., *Conversations with Don DeLillo* (Jackson: University Press of Mississippi, 2005);

Joseph Dewey, Steven G. Kellman, and Irving Malin, eds., *UnderWords: Perspectives on DeLillo's Underworld* (Newark: University of Delaware Press / London & Cranbury, N.J.: Associated University Presses, 2002);

John Duvall, *Don DeLillo's* Underworld: *A Reader's Guide* (New York: Continuum, 2002);

Frank Lentricchia, ed., *Introducing Don DeLillo* (Durham, N.C.: Duke University Press, 1991);

Lentricchia, ed., *New Essays on* White Noise (New York: Cambridge University Press, 1991);

Mark Osteen, *American Magic and Dread: Don DeLillo's Dialogue with Culture* (Philadelphia: University of Pennsylvania Press, 2000).

Ella Cara Deloria

(January 31, 1889 – February 12, 1971)

ᒡᓓ

WATERLILY

(Lincoln: University of Nebraska Press, 1988)

WATERLILY

The title character of Ella Cara Deloria's novel *Waterlily* is "a girl who lived a century ago, in a remote camp-circle of the Teton Dakotas," as Deloria wrote in a 1948 letter to anthropologist Margaret Mead. Readers follow Waterlily's life from birth through her early twenties as a young wife and mother within the community of her people. Following traditional Dakota educational practices, she learns proper female behavior, kinship obligations, and the seasonal ceremonial obligations of her *tiyospaye* ("group of tipis," the extended family group) primarily from her female relations, particularly her grandmother Gloku and her mother, Blue Bird. A lively, respectful, and pretty young girl, Waterlily grows up firmly grounded in her people's ways. Impending conflicts caused by the encroachment of European American settlers on Dakota homelands remains on the periphery of her childhood.

After a near-death experience at age seven, Waterlily becomes a *hunka* (a child-beloved) when her father, Rainbow, pledges to honor her through this significant initiation ceremony if she recovers. Waterlily survives, thrives, and is an obedient child on all occasions except one. As an adolescent, she defies custom to secretly deliver water to Lowanla, "the youngest and the handsomest of all the [Dakota] singers," who has impressed her at the arduous and highly sacred annual Sun Dance ceremony. Years later, after her first husband, Sacred Horse, has died, the young man to whom Waterlily had delivered illicit water becomes her second husband.

Waterlily's story demonstrates from a female perspective the intricate functioning of Dakota cultural practices prior to the impact of colonial invaders. In the circumstances of her birth, her childhood within the *tiyospaye*, the manner of negotiating her marriage partners, and all aspects of daily life, Waterlily's experiences reveal a Dakota world during "a time prior to white settlement of the western plains," Deloria explained, "when native custom and thought were all there was." Among the sacred circle of her people, Waterlily and her relatives are content and secure, and contact with whites—as in the smallpox epidemic that invades the camp circle at one point through infected blankets left by the army—causes profound disruption to all aspects of Dakota existence. Waterlily's life story does not focus on colonial destruction, however, and instead creates an intimate portrait of Dakota camp life before the reservation period.

Near the close of the novel, Waterlily proudly reflects that "All my relatives are noble. . . . They make their duties toward others a privilege and a delight." Years after her girlhood breach of etiquette at the Sun Dance, Waterlily feels that "It was no struggle to play one's kinship role with people like them [her relatives]. When everyone was up to par in this kinship of loyalty and mutual dependence, life could be close to perfect." The near perfection of Waterlily's life is achieved within conditions that rely upon separate, complementary spheres of male and female activities. The fabric of community is knitted together through the laws of Dakota kinship requiring that people "treat each other at all times with love, honor, and respect," according to Dakota scholar Joyzelle Godfrey. From the daily tasks of household maintenance to sacred ceremonial practices, Waterlily learns that "everyone must cooperate, for that was where the power finally lay."

A trained linguist and ethnographer who worked closely with the distinguished anthropologist Franz Boas, Deloria strove to bring Waterlily to life in a vivid way that ordinary readers could understand. Through Waterlily, she presents a story that "is purely a woman's point of view, her problems, aspirations, ideals, etc." Because of Deloria's extensive ethnographic fieldwork among her own people, Waterlily participates in Dakota life not as it was imagined but as it was remembered by the elders Deloria interviewed who actually lived it. "Only my characters are imaginary," Deloria explains in a letter to Mead; "the things that happen are what the many old women informants have told me as having been their own or their mothers' or other relatives' experiences."

Deloria completed Waterlily in 1944 but did not see it published in her lifetime. What little Native American literature even being produced up to that time did not receive a warm reception from a mass readership. Because of editorial complications and the paper shortage of World War II, Waterlily was not published until 1988; since then, the novel has been enthusiastically received in both academic and popular circles.

Cut by the wishes of both editor and author from thirty chapters to seventeen, Waterlily holds particular significance in Native American literature because of its detailed presentation of Dakota life from a Dakota female point of view at a time when the majority of information about Indians was collected from native males by white male anthropologists. Waterlily thus reveals a female world that the majority of the reading public in Deloria's day knew little about. Although some critics have charged Deloria with idealizing her representations of nineteenth-century Dakota life, her consistent project was to accurately portray, through the use of original oral materials she collected herself from Dakota people, the diversity of her people's longstanding traditions in a way that subverted stereotypes and highlighted Dakota humanity.

Discussion Questions

1. Deloria writes that in Dakota culture "all the women were equally responsible for all the children, being mothers to them all." What Dakota values regarding education does Deloria reveal through the manner in which Waterlily and her brother, Little Chief, receive instruction from their grandmother, Gloku?

2. Some readers are confused by Waterlily's choice not to reveal her secret to her husband at the end of the novel. Why is her decision the right one in the context of Dakota culture and "the cumulative wisdom of Dakota women, gained from way back"?

3. Dorothy Stein, one editor of the Waterlily manuscript before its publication, wrote to Deloria that the portrait she creates of the Dakota people allows readers unfamiliar with Dakota culture to "realize that Waterlily's people were not the savages traditionally pictured in most of our Indian literature, but a well-organized social group functioning smoothly and intelligently." In your opinion, which specific scenes, characters, or events in Waterlily most strongly support Stein's remarks?

4. In her correspondence with editors and colleagues, Deloria expressed concern over maintaining a balance between representing with dignity the details of Dakota traditional life and respecting her people's privacy by not revealing too much personal and/or sacred information. Do you feel Deloria has succeeded in maintaining this balance in Waterlily? Are there specific episodes in the novel where you feel Deloria may have especially struggled with this issue?

—Jane Haladay

REFERENCES

Susan Gardener, "'Though It Broke My Heart to Cut Some Bits': Ella Deloria's Original Design for Waterlily," American Indian Quarterly, 27 (2003): 667–696;

Julian Rice, Deer Women and Elk Men: The Lakota Narratives of Ella Deloria (Albuquerque: University of New Mexico Press, 1992);

Gary Lee Sligh, A Study of Native American Women Novelists: Sophia Alice Callahan, Mourning Dove, and Ella Cara Deloria (Lewiston, N.Y.: Edwin Mellen Press, 2003).

Sarah Dessen

(June 6, 1970 –   )

☙

DREAMLAND

(New York: Viking, 2000)

CAITLIN O'KOREN

Caitlin O'Koren is the main character of Sarah Dessen's novel *Dreamland.* On the morning of her sixteenth birthday, Caitlin's overachieving older sister, Cass, runs away. As her parents struggle first to locate Cass and then to manage their grief over the fact that she has chosen to work as a crew member on a tawdry talk-show rather than attend Yale as had been planned, Caitlin struggles to define herself outside her sister's shadow.

Caitlin sees herself as a dim reflection of her sister; Cass got all A's, was chosen as homecoming queen, spent two years as student body president, and led the soccer team to victory, while Caitlin is a B student who wins the occasional third-place ribbon. Cass embodies popularity, while Caitlin has one close friend, Rina. Caitlin has a small scar over her eye resulting from Cass's hitting her with a plastic shovel when they were small children. Dessen uses the small scar to demonstrate symbolically how Caitlin has been marked by her sister and to suggest how her whole outlook is colored by their relationship.

The title *Dreamland* evokes a variety of images in Dessen's novel. Caitlin fondly recalls how her mother used to stand in the girls' doorway every evening: "'See you in dreamland,' she'd whisper." But much as she loved the idea of spending the night in a beautiful dreamland with her mother and sister, Caitlin regrets "it was never the way I imagined." After Cass leaves, Caitlin slowly realizes how much of her sister's dreams were really only embodiments of her mother's plans. Caitlin's own attempts to define herself are soon co-opted, too. She becomes a cheerleader simply because it is something Cass would never have chosen, but her mother enjoys it much more than Caitlin does. She finds herself rejecting things simply because they represent the sorts of choices her mother and sister might make.

Even as a child Caitlin had trouble imagining her own future. Playing with Barbie and Ken dolls, she would go through the motions of dressing and undressing them. In answer to a neighbor woman's gentle prodding, Caitlin cannot imagine what kind of work Barbie might do or how her life could be filled with anything other than dates with Ken. Her neighbor encourages her to dream, saying, "I think your Barbie can go shopping, and go out with Ken, and also have a productive and satisfying career of her own. . . . She can be anything. . . . And so can you." But Caitlin no longer remembers how to dream. Instead, she begins first to sleepwalk through her life and eventually plunges into a waking nightmare from which she cannot untangle herself.

Cass falls in love with Rogerson Biscoe in part because his checkered past is filled with "long stories" that intrigue her and in part because spending time with him as he drives from parties to trailer parks dealing drugs gives her the sense that she is finally going places, that she is at last creating stories of her own. Rogerson embodies unexplored and unconsidered possibilities: "I saw myself, then, setting out across uncharted territory, places Cass had never been or seen or even heard of. My world was suddenly wide and limitless, as vast as the sky and stars I'd been dazzled by earlier, and it all started there with the door he was holding open for me." When Rogerson begins to physically abuse Cass, she is initially shocked. His violence and her victimization become another one of the secrets she keeps in her attempt to distinguish herself and create an identity separate from those so vividly constructed by her sister and mother.

As Caitlin's life spirals out of control, she recalls part of a T. S. Eliot poem her class studied about voices that awaken people as they drown. She realizes she has lost her own voice, somehow. Finally, when Rogerson's abuse is discovered, it is voices that she clings to. Caitlin slowly wills herself to listen to all the people in her life—to listen to their grief, their apologies, their anger, and their love. These voices also encourage her to discover her own dreams.

The people who surround Caitlin do mostly mean well, though they are often oblivious to her struggles. Caitlin finds the most comfort in her friends Rina and Corinna. Beautiful and viva-cious, Rina serves as a foil to Caitlin. Both girls know their long friendship is an odd pairing, but they also recognize that each finds strength in the other. Rina enjoys the stability of Caitlin's family, and Caitlin admires Rina's easy ability to navigate the dramas of high school. Corinna, on the other hand, serves as a model for Caitlin, despite that she meets her through Rogerson's drug-dealing. At first, Caitlin idolizes the older girl's life. Corinna's long-standing romance and secure little home with her boyfriend are the stuff of Caitlin's dreams, but as she gets to know Corinna better, she realizes how flawed and imperfect Corinna's life really is. Corinna's ultimate willingness to strike out on her own gives Caitlin courage as she struggles to put herself back together after she is sent to Evergreen Care Center to rehabilitate. When she returns home and is greeted by a surprise party attended even by her long-absent sister, Caitlin can celebrate the reunion in part because she is no longer so desperately seeking it.

Discussion Questions

1. Dessen has said that she found many scenes in *Dreamland* difficult to write because of the painful experiences Caitlin undergoes, and that to leaven the depressing qualities of the novel she added humor-ous touches to Caitlin's world. Where in the book do you find moments of humor?

2. What role does photography play in Caitlin's life? What makes it a particularly good form of self-expression for her?

3. How does Caitlin feel about Rogerson at the end of the book? How does Dessen want her readers to feel about him? What textual details does Dessen include to help shape her readers' final vision of him?

4. In the novel the next-door neighbors Boo and Stewart are so much a part of the O'Koren family that Caitlin almost seems to have four parents. How do each of these characters contribute to Caitlin's development as a young woman? What resources do they give her for succeeding in life? What barriers or limitations do they unwittingly impose upon her?

5. Compare Caitlin with a heroine from another of Dessen's novels such as Colie in *Keeping the Moon* (2000), Remy in *This Lullaby* (2002), or Macy in

The Truth about Forever (2004). Consider not only the romantic concerns of the young women but also their relationships with their families.

—*Megan Lynn Isaac*

REFERENCES
Patty Campbell, Dreamland: *A Reader's Companion* (New York: Viking, 2000);
Wendy J. Glenn, *Sarah Dessen: From Burritos to Box Office* (Lanham, Md.: Scarecrow Press, 2005).

Pete Dexter
(1943 –)

PARIS TROUT
(New York: Random House, 1988)

PARIS TROUT

Paris Trout is a store owner in a small Georgia town in the 1950s who stands trial for the murder of a black teenager in Pete Dexter's *Paris Trout*. Trout is a racist in thought and deed. From the first moment he is introduced as the North Main Street store owner who sells .22-caliber shells to fourteen-year-old Rosie Sayers, his behavior exemplifies his belief in treating individuals differently based on their color. "There was a string on the door that tripped a bell when anyone walked in. Colored people stopped just inside the door and waited for him. White people picked out what they wanted for themselves." But thinking of Trout as merely a representative of the values of the Old South is a limited, and not nec-essarily accurate, view. He is different, apart, overly distrustful: "The store in front was locked in two places. Paris Trout was the only man in Cotton Point who put two locks on his doors." Though, because of his success in business, he is seen as a part of the com-munity establishment, his social connections are lack-ing. When attorney Harry Seagraves is deciding he must take Trout as a client after the killing of Rosie, he considers his relationship to "the families that lived on Draft Street, families like his own. He was part of their safety. Paris Trout was not of that group socially—he had no social affiliations—but he owned property and lumber interests and the store and was known to have money." When he needs a companion to go with him to collect his debt, Trout brings his associate Buster Devonne, a "dog off a leash."

Trout is a mean, even a vicious, person without the capacity for warmth or love in any aspect of his life. His relationship with his wife, Hanna, is one of total control and brutality, even before the pressure of his trial and the ostracism of the community push him toward a spiraling descent into paranoia. "He was hard-boiled and cold-blooded and had not bought her a present since the engagement. He had fornicated with her almost nightly. . . . He had never spent a night in her bed, though, or her room." Later in the story, after he has been accused of the shooting death of Rosie, his violence against Hanna increases. When she bends to wipe spilled mineral water from the floor, "there was a slamming noise in her ear, and she was suddenly out of focus. She fell against the desk, beginning to understand that he had hit her, and then his hand was around her neck, his weight pinning her to the desktop." Trout's rape of Hanna with the empty water bottle is the first use of glass in a recurring image throughout the book, including the broken glass on the kitchen floor that severely cuts Hanna's foot, the glass Trout puts under his bed to track his wife's entry into his bedroom, and the repeated discussion of the bottle rape as a prelude to Segraves's and Hanna's intimacy.

Trout's visits to his mother are cold and distant. As the book nears its violent conclusion, he removes her from the nursing home—"Her breathing was quicker now, he saw that she understood he was taking her"— and brings her upstairs in the courthouse, where he shoots her before proceeding with his plan against his enemies. Since Dexter does not include any details of Trout's earlier life, it is difficult to determine if he kills his mother because of love or hatred. His words, however, indicate a determination to sever himself from any remaining tie or limitation: "He put the muzzle of the forty-five against her head. 'I end my connections with everything that come before,' he said."

There is a complexity to Trout, which at times masks his inherent nature. When Hanna reflects on why she had married him, she recalls: "There was a shape to his life, she was sure of that. He was direct and willful and honest, and there was a sureness

about him that was missing in her own life. He did not lie. And yes, at the bottom of it she sensed a darker side, and it had excited her." Later, when his brutality and craziness are revealed, Trout explains: "Nothing is different," he said. "You just misunderstood the way things was." His understanding of his own behavior is generally simple: "I make my deals and live by them, and Jesus save those that don't do the same." This code leads him to conclude that it was Rosie's fault she was killed because of her association with his debtor. He can never understand why he should be convicted of anything, even the minimal offense for which he is found guilty, "just for trying to collect his lawful debts." He can never understand why he should be convicted for second-degree murder, with a sentence of from one to three years, he becomes enraged. After bribing a local judge, he was let out on his own recognizance during the appeal process. During this period he plotted his revenge against his "enemies" and escape for himself. Leaving a note in his store, "To whom it may concern: I just do not care to continue this the way it is going. . . . I was convicted by the highpocket boys and the courthouse gang. . . ," he kills his mother in a hotel room with a view of the town's sesquicentennial festivities, then the prosecutor, Carl Bonner, who responds to the shots. Finally, Trout injures his own defense attorney, Harry Segraves, before turning the gun on himself. He acts consistently with his own internal logic and conviction, disregarding the law, the need to pay taxes, public opinion, or anything beside his fear when finally faced with having lost control over Hanna. "There was a contract he made with himself a long time ago that overrode the law, and being the only interested party, he lived by it. He was principled in the truest sense of the word. His right and wrong were completely private."

Dexter titled his book *Paris Trout,* and Trout appears throughout the novel. The book is not about Trout himself, however, but rather uses him as a catalyst for actions in which the character of the various principals unfolds, and for stimulating thought regarding truth and justice, marital relations, race and changing mores. The book is divided into nine parts, each titled with the name of one of the principal characters. Only sections six and eight are titled "Trout." Though none are written in the first person, each part focuses on observable actions of the character named.

Discussion Questions

1. Paris Trout is considered a man of integrity. His outward demeanor and actions are consistent with his internal values and feelings. Do you agree? Why or why not?

2. Discuss how Trout's racism set the stage for the killing of Rosie. Do you think there would have been a different outcome if Rosie had been white?

3. Trout's behavior increases in its irrationality over the course of the story. Why do you think that occurs? Give examples.

—*Nancy Fowler*

REFERENCES

Richard Predmore, "Ownership in Dexter's *Paris Trout*," *Southern Quarterly*, 33 (Winter–Spring 1995): 147–150;

Deidre Purdy, "Lawyers and Literature: As My Mother Lay Dying," *Legal Studies Forum*, 22, nos. 1–3 (1998).

Philip K. Dick

(December 16, 1928 – March 2, 1982)

৩৫

DO ANDROIDS DREAM OF ELECTRIC SHEEP?

(Garden City, N.Y.: Doubleday, 1968)

RICK DECKARD

Rick Deckard in Philip K. Dick's *Do Androids Dream of Electric Sheep?* is a bounty hunter who stalks humanoid robots. In the futuristic San Francisco that serves as the setting of the novel, "andies" (as the androids are derisively known) who have fled servitude on off-world colonies try to mix in with the remaining human population. Bounty hunters such as Deckard identify the artificial humans by giving them an "empathy test" and then summarily exterminate them. The bounties Deckard collects on each android bring him closer to his dream of purchasing a live animal, a status symbol in a world in which radioactive fallout has made them nearly extinct. As he hunts the latest, most sophisticated model of android, he finds avoiding empathetic feelings toward them increasingly difficult.

In the future society imagined by Dick, a capacity for empathy is believed to be a characteristic peculiar only to humans. It forms the basis for a religion called "Mercerism," in which individuals, through the use of "empathy boxes," telepathically commune by joining Wilbur Mercer as he climbs a hill, alone but persecuted by invisible enemies. Because androids, despite their superior intelligence, supposedly lack the ability to empathize with living beings or other androids, a system has been developed to detect and measure the capacity for empathy in order to distinguish real humans from their extremely convincing simulacra. Deckard interrogates suspect humans with a kind of polygraph and a battery of questions mostly concerning the killing or abuse of people or animals. At the beginning of the novel he is convinced of the distinction between authentic and artificial humans, who represent in his mind the invisible evil that torments Mercer: "an escaped humanoid robot, which had killed its master, which had been equipped with an intelligence greater than that of many human beings, which had no regard for animals, which possessed no ability to feel empathic joy for another life form's success or grief at its defeat—that, for him, epitomized The Killers."

Over the course of a particularly harrowing assignment, Deckard loses faith in the validity of these categories. The Nexus-6 model of android is practically impossible to recognize as an artificial person; some of these androids, in fact, may not realize that they are not human. Deckard has confrontations that challenge his sense of what is human, both with androids, such as Luba Luft, an opera singer whose amazing vocal ability seems to belie the notion that the manufactured people are incapable of deeper feeling, and with other humans, such as Phil Resch, a rival bounty hunter whom Deckard initially suspects of being an android. Resch is probably a psychopath, and the novel suggests that perhaps bounty hunters must have an alienated personality such as Resch's in order to carry out their duties.

The process of interviewing seemingly ordinary people, assessing their humanness, and, if necessary, terminating them on the spot entails physical, emotional, and moral dangers that become more pronounced as the gap between artificial and real humans becomes smaller with each new model of android. In an interview with James Van Hise published in *Starlog* magazine in February 1982, Dick said that "Deckard, to kill the replicants . . . is brutalized and dehumanized. . . . You have Deckard becoming more and more dehumanized and the replicants becoming more and more human, and at the end they meet and the distinction is gone. But this fusion of Deckard and the replicants is a *tragedy*. This is not a victory where the replicants become humanized and there is some victory by humanity over inhumanity." The androids, represented especially by Rachael Rosen, Roy and Irmgard Baty, and Pris Stratton, seem to be Deckard's moral equals: they are cold and self-motivated, but their loyalty to one another and the fact that Roy and Irmgard are married indicate that they actually are capable of some fellow feeling. Deckard's marriage is held together only by his meager potential as a provider and by the various mood enhancers available to the remnants of humanity left on earth. Deckard is unfaithful to his wife, Iran, with Rachael and considers leaving Iran to be with her, even though he knows Rachael is incapable of telling him the truth. When Deckard finally confronts the Batys and Pris, who is the same model as Rachael and thus identical to her, he dispatches them remorselessly, while they respond only in self-defense. The androids are not sympathetic characters—they flagrantly exploit the simple good nature of J. R. Isidore, an artificial-animal repairman who is the only person willing to show them any generosity—but they may in fact be less dangerous than humans such as Deckard and Resch.

As Dick's assertion that the novel is a tragedy suggests, he viewed humanity as a threshold that artificial creations could never cross. Deckard's increasing inability to recognize that threshold represents something of a moral death for him. When Mercerism is revealed as fraudulent and Mercer's archetypal journey as manufactured on a movie set, Iran asks Deckard if he thinks these revelations could be true. His response—"Everything is true. . . . Everything anybody has ever thought"—indicates the extent to which he has become morally unmoored. The lesson he draws from Mercerism is that "Sometimes it's better to do something wrong than right," by which he justifies killing androids for bounty even though he can profess feelings for them and interact with them intimately. Deckard is thus revealed to be as selfish as the androids are. His dream of being able to afford a live animal by hunting down Roy and his compatriots is ultimately thwarted: Rachael vengefully kills the goat he buys on credit after his first bounties. He ends up with an artificial toad he finds in the desert; he is unable to recognize it as fake until Iran shows him that it is. Despite the disappointment, Iran treats him with renewed affection when he returns home from his long, perilous assignment. The novel closes on her ordering by telephone artificial flies to feed the toad—an apparent resignation to artificial reality that undercuts the domestic tranquillity of the scene.

Discussion Questions

1. Deckard tells Rachael that if she were human, he would divorce his wife and marry her. Why does he fall in love with someone he knows is not human?

2. Why does Deckard buy the android Luba Luft a book before he "retires" her? Why does he destroy the book after he retires her?

3. Why does Deckard want to own a living animal? Does it matter what sort of animal? Why or why not?

4. Is Deckard good at administering the Voigt-Kampff Empathy Test? Do the readings he gets with it seem accurate? Why or why not?

5. Why does Deckard remain on earth as opposed to leaving for an off-world colony, as most healthy humans have?

—*Charles Brower*

UBIK

(Garden City, N.Y.: Doubleday, 1969)

JOE CHIP

Joe Chip, the protagonist in Philip K. Dick's novel *Ubik,* is a field tester of psychics for Runciter Associates, a "prudence organization" that exposes and neutralizes mind-readers who infiltrate organizations and threaten their professional secrets. Like many of Dick's protagonists, Chip is a competent professional who in most other respects is a hapless loser. When he is introduced in the novel, he has a hangover and is unable to persuade his computerized, coin-operated appliances to work for him on credit. He is similarly luckless in his relationships with women: when testing powerful psychic Pat Conley, she immediately sizes him up with devastating accuracy: "You're a little, debt-stricken, ineffective bureaucrat who can't even scrape together enough coins to pay his door to let him out of his apt." By the end of the novel, however, Chip, a typical underdog, comes to understand that he has a role of cosmic significance in the fate of the humanity.

Ubik is set in the year 1992, a future in which the recently dead can be preserved in a sort of half-life, a frozen state that enables their loved ones to maintain contact with them. Glen Runciter, Chip's boss, maintains his long-dead wife, Ella, in such a state so that he can confer with her on business matters. When Runciter apparently is killed in an explosive trap engineered by one of his rivals, Chip attempts to rise to the occasion and take control of Runciter Associates in order to keep the company together. Almost immediately, though, he begins to recognize that things are not as they appear: cigarettes crumble into dust; phone directories are out-of-date; and the few coins in his pocket are obsolete and worthless. Moreover, the Beloved Brethren Moratorium, where Ella is kept, claims to be unable to establish half-life contact with her husband, Chip; in addition, the team of Runciter psychics who survived the explosion along with him experience bizarre "manifestations" of their supposedly deceased boss.

In Dick's novels the characters often discover that they are fundamentally misapprehending the reality of the world around them. Confronted by a series of confusing, even contradictory, messages from Runciter, Chip considers and dismisses possible rational explanations for his situation. Ultimately, though, the truth seems impossible to deny: as the graffiti on the wall of an office bathroom puts it, "Jump in the urinal and stand on your head. / I'm the one that's alive. You're all dead." The real situation is exactly the opposite of what Chip originally thought: Runciter survived the assassination attempt, and subsequent events have been a half-life hallucination that Chip and the other psychics are sharing in their cryogenic state. Their boss's manifestations are his attempts to contact them from the visiting room of the moratorium. No stranger to the disappointments of life, Chip accepts the news with bitter resignation, much as he endures the insults of his colleagues and the lack of cooperation of his appliances.

There are degrees of death in the novel, however, and while Chip may approach his half-life with equanimity, he resists a sinister force that is inexorably reducing the other half-lifers to desiccated husks—the same entropy that seems to cause the regression of all the objects in the world to earlier forms. Spaceships, for example, become jet airplanes, then prop-driven biplanes, and finally threaten to disappear as a mode of transportation. Runciter uses various tactics to provide Chip with "Ubik," a mysterious aerosol spray that seems able to arrest the entropy temporarily. The exact nature of Ubik is never made clear, but it provides necessary protection for Chip when he finally learns the threat he faces in half-life—the spirit of a childishly greedy, sadistic boy, Jory, who consumes the souls of other half-lifers. With the enormous power Jory has amassed, he has created the hallucinatory "reality" of half-life as an impish prank.

Chip finally meets the only entity, other than Jory, who isn't a hallucination—Ella Runciter, the inventor of Ubik. She promises him a lifetime supply, but the gift comes with a great responsibility. Ella is about to be reincarnated, and someone must take her place in the perpetual struggle against Jory: "it's a verity," she tells Chip, "a rule, of our kind of existence. . . . It has to be fought on our side of the glass . . . by those of us in half-life, those that Jory preys on. You'll have to take charge, Mr. Chip, after I'm reborn." Thus, Chip, whose attempts to take charge in the living world were thwarted by his impecuniousness and fecklessness, is promoted to champion of the souls of mankind in the face of an implacable devourer. Humbly, he thinks gratefully of the "watching, wise, physical ghosts from the full-life world," particularly Runciter, "the writer of instructions, labels and notes."

Ubik ends with a cryptic coda that nevertheless seems to intimate Chip's new, elevated status. Earlier in the novel, as one of Runciter's manifestations, all of the money in the possession of Chip and his colleagues had their boss's likeness on it. Now, though apparently in the "full-life world," Runciter pulls a coin from his pocket and finds to his surprise a strange but familiar profile—Chip's. Further, "he had an intuition, chillingly, that if he searched his pockets . . . he would find more." The novel concludes with the line: "This was just the beginning."

Discussion Questions

1. Describe Joe Chip's attitude toward women, particularly Pat Conley. How might it be said that Pat knows Chip better than he knows himself?

2. Chip has a reflexive habit of correcting people's grammatical mistakes in conversation. List some of the particular instances when he does this. What does this personality tic indicate about the kind of person Chip is?

3. Why do you think Runciter values Chip as an employee? What skills does he bring to his job? Does he have any professional liabilities?

—*Charles Brower*

GLEN RUNCITER

Glen Runciter in Philip K. Dick's novel *Ubik* is the wealthy owner of Runciter Associates, a "prudence organization" that exposes and neutralizes psychic spies for clients wanting to protect business or personal secrets. At the beginning of the novel, as he usually does when faced with difficult business challenges, Runciter is seeking the advice of the cofounder of the company, his late wife, Ella. In the future portrayed in *Ubik,* people can be preserved in a limited half-life after the deaths of their bodies. Those who can afford the privilege visit their cryogenically preserved loved ones in moratoriums and speak to their disembodied spirits via microphone and headphones. Runciter feels guilt over not having visited Ella more often; but he rationalizes that with each visit, the process of reviving her leaves her a little weaker and vaguer, as what remains of her life dissolves into ether.

Runciter is described as being of indeterminate but advanced age. The manager at the moratorium where Ella Runciter is kept estimates that her husband is at least ninety years old, with "artificial organs grafted into place in his physiological appa-

ratus as the genuine, original ones failed." Nevertheless, he has an imposing physical presence: "tall, . . . with large hands and a quick, sprightly stride. . . . His head, massive like a tomcat's, thrust forward as he peered through slightly protruding, round and warm and highly alert eyes."

Runciter's apparent death, after his business rival Ray Hollis springs an explosive trap on him and his employees, is the primary motivating incident in *Ubik*. Runciter's assistant, Joe Chip, and the team of psychics Runciter and Chip unwittingly lead into Hollis's trap are surprised that they escape the explosion largely unscathed; Chip attempts to keep the company together in the wake of the attack and plots a retaliatory strike against Hollis. Perhaps not surprisingly, in this future society in which the boundary between life and death has become porous, Runciter continues to have a mysterious influence on events in the novel even after Chip has been told by moratorium technicians that they were unable to establish contact with his ethereal essence. Chip, for example, hears (but is unable to speak to) Runciter on the other end of a hotel phone; the other Runciter employees who survived the explosion find the image of their late boss on their pocket change and cryptic, joking references to him on seemingly random objects such as matchbooks.

Chip and the others come to recognize that these "manifestations of Runciter" are becoming omnipresent, in contrast to an entropic effect that seems to be unmaking the world around them: cigarettes have all gone stale, for example, and all the coffee is cold and scummy. More ominously, the survivors of the explosion begin to turn up as desiccated husks, indicating that humans themselves are not immune to the encroaching dissolution. For Chip and Al Hammond, another of Runciter's psychics who survived the attack, Runciter's impossibly coincidental magical manifestations—he leaves a handwritten note for them in a carton of cigarettes in a store and city they randomly choose; a brand-new but already obsolete tape recorder they purchase is, according to its package, the product of a nonexistent Runciter business concern—suggest that their boss has assumed an immanent, almost godlike quality: "the pair of opposing forces were at work. Decay versus Runciter, Al said to himself.

Throughout the world. Perhaps throughout the universe. Maybe the sun will go out, Al conjectured, and Glen Runciter will place a substitute sun in its place." The mystery of what happened to Runciter assumes cosmic proportions: "How much," the characters ask, "can Runciter do?"

Through a particularly rude manifestation—bathroom graffiti that reads "Jump in the urinal and stand on your head. / I'm the one that's alive. You're all dead"—Runciter reveals to Hammond and Chip the truth: far from surviving the explosion, they are the ones currently in a half-life state, and Runciter's manifestations are his attempts to establish contact with them from the world of the living. In yet another appearance, this time as a television announcer, Runciter reveals to Chip the one thing that seems to arrest the deterioration of the world around him, at least temporarily—the all-purpose aerosol spray Ubik.

Dick's novels are considered metaphysical parables as much as science fiction because of their explicit concerns over the nature of reality and the presence of God in the world. In *Ubik* the world experienced by Chip and his cohorts is revealed to be the hallucination of "half-lifers," with reality piercing the veil in the form of Runciter's periodic manifestations. Yet, even Runciter can only partly apprehend the danger facing his deceased employees, the force that is hastening them through their half-lives and into final oblivion. Thus, the messages he manages to convey to Chip are incomplete, confusing, and even contradictory. Ultimately, though bolstered by Runciter and the invigorating properties of Ubik, Chip must stand alone against his adversary—Jory, another half-lifer, who died as a boy and now rapaciously consumes the essences of others with childish selfishness.

Discussion Questions

1. Why does Runciter allow himself and his employees to be drawn into a trap on Luna? Does it seem believable that he would be tricked in this way?

2. What do you make of the ending of *Ubik?* Why does Runciter find Joe Chip's image on the money in his pocket? When Runciter says to himself "This was just the beginning," what does he mean?

3. What can we discern about Runciter's relationship with his wife, Ella, from their conversations and from what Runciter says about her? Does Runciter seem to be a devoted husband? What do you think devotion means to Runciter in a setting where "'Til death us do part" has lost its meaning?

—*Charles Brower*

REFERENCES

Judith Kernan, ed., *Retrofitting Blade Runner: Issues in Ridley Scott's* Blade Runner *and Philip K. Dick's* Do Androids Dream of Electric Sheep? (Bowling Green, Ohio: Bowling Green State University Popular Press, 1991);

Daniel J. H. Levack, *PKD: A Philip K. Dick Bibliography* (Westport, Conn.: Meckler, 1988);

Lawrence Sutin, *Divine Invasions: A Life of Philip K. Dick* (New York: Harmony, 1989);

Sutin, ed., *The Shifting Realities of Philip K. Dick: Selected Literary and Philosophical Writings* (New York: Pantheon, 1995);

Samuel J. Umland, ed., *Philip K. Dick: Contemporary Critical Interpretations* (Westport, Conn.: Greenwood Press, 1995);

Patricia S. Warrick and Martin Harry Greenberg, *Robots, Androids, and Mechanical Oddities: The Science Fiction of Philip K. Dick* (Carbondale: Southern Illinois University Press, 1984).

James Dickey
(February 2, 1923 – January 19, 1997)

ᘓ

DELIVERANCE
(Boston: Houghton Mifflin, 1970)

DREW BALLINGER

Drew Ballinger is one of the quartet of middle-aged Atlanta suburbanites who take a catastrophic canoe trip down the fictional Cahulawassee River in north Georgia one weekend in September. Drew is, in the words of Ed Gentry, the narrator, "a decent city-man, the minor civic leader and hedge-clipper." "Drew was a straightforward quiet fellow. He was devoted to his family, particularly to his little boy

Pope. . . . he worked as a sales supervisor for a big soft-drink company and he believed in it and the things it said it stood for with his very soul." Only the claim by another company that its product had fewer calories spurs Drew into a rage. Of the four he is the most comfortable in his skin and the least bored with his life. Though Dickey worked in advertising for Coca-Cola in Atlanta and led the kind of comfortable suburban life that Drew does, he based the guitar player in the group on his Atlanta friend "Whitewater Al" Brasleton, one of the dedicatees of the novel and the man who taught Dickey to play the guitar.

Drew is also the most apprehensive of the four about the trip; the only aspect of the country that this complacent suburbanite appreciates is its music. The closest he has to a country experience is playing folk songs on the guitar. For this reason he insists on bringing a high-quality (though "stove-in, reconditioned") Martin guitar along for the ride. Drew plays the "really hard finger-picking stuff" and he does it "mighty well, through sheer devotion." Of the rest of the rural life Drew says, "There's not one of us knows a damned thing about the woods or about a river." When he plays a duet of "Wildwood Flower" with a demented mountain boy named Lonnie in Oree, he becomes exhilarated by the experience and his whereabouts. His apprehension returns when he sees how recklessly Lewis gets lost driving to the river "he don't know nothin' about," and he insists on riding in Ed's canoe on the first day.

Drew is as horrified as the others by the events of the second day. When Lewis kills the mountain man who has raped Bobby, Drew's inherent trust of institutions leads him to argue in favor of taking the body down to their destination in Aintry, turning the matter over to the highway patrol, and making a clean breast of things, trusting that the slaying will be found to be justifiable homicide. Lewis asserts that the four of them constitute the law in this wilderness, and the others vote against Drew, who then reluctantly goes along with the burial.

The mystery of Drew's death is offset by Ed's unambiguous expression of admiration for him. After disposing of the dead mountain man, the four city dwellers are flying down the river at dusk when

"something, a puff of wind, but much more definite and concentrated, snatched at some of the hair on the back of [Drew's] head. For a second I thought he had just shaken his head, or been jarred by the canoe in some way I hadn't felt." Drew's canoe capsizes, and Lewis, his thighbone broken when his canoe tosses him into the river, claims that Drew was shot.

Drew's body is not found until after Ed has killed the second mountain man and buried him in the river. Downstream they find Drew caught in a sitting position in the fork of a tree. Examining the corpse, Ed and Bobby find only "a long raw place under the hair just over his left ear, and the head seemed oddly pushed in, dented." Ed knows that Drew must be buried in the river and that he cannot even take Drew's college ring as a souvenir for his wife for fear of giving away their false story. He weights the body and sends it into the river, saying, "You were the best of us, Drew, the only decent one, the only sane one." Thus, Drew, who alive clung the longest to civilized ideals of respect for law and order, in death becomes part of the men's plan to deceive the police. When Ed gets back to Atlanta, he tells Drew's wife the same false story he told the police to maintain the deception.

Drew had wanted to do what would in civilization be the right and honorable thing with the body of the first mountain man, but that kind of innocent trust in others, a quality often associated with the pastoral life, is out of place in the wilderness, where human institutions have no place. The men know they have made an immoral choice necessary to keep alive in a world where there is no law. Drew's corporate mentality led him to be a model citizen in the city, but such an attitude cannot survive a crisis on the river. He is out of sync with his friends, and instead of adapting to circumstances he yields to the will of the unlawful majority.

Drew's character is not without its contradictions. A corporate man, he enjoys the solitary pleasures of guitar playing; the advocate of law and order, he is killed by the mountain man who takes the law into his own hands; he stands up for decency but then acquiesces to the rest in disposing of the rapist.

Discussion Questions

1. Drew's chief characteristic on the trip is his guitar playing. How does this activity reflect his readiness or unpreparedness to survive in the country? What is the meaning of his bringing a high-quality (though beaten-up) guitar on a canoe trip? Is his playing a useful skill or an example of suburban frivolity and naiveté?

2. Drew observes that guitarists develop a sense of touch "beyond what a man with eyes could do." With Drew dead, how does Ed assume this sense of touch in climbing out of the gorge to his ambush spot?

3. Why does Ed, in consigning Drew to the river, call him "the best of us"? Is Drew's corporate mentality a virtue along the river?

4. Drew's death is deliberately left unsolved, and Dickey is clear about the absence of an obviously fatal wound. Why is this so? What does the vagueness of Drew's death say about the mysterious nature and power of the river?

—*Ward Briggs*

ED GENTRY

Ed Gentry is a small businessman who narrates the events that take place during a catastrophic canoe trip down the fictional Cahulawassee River by four Atlanta friends one September weekend. Ed, who as his name implies, is of the gentry, more at home in the manmade structures of Drew Ballinger's business world (a large soft-drink company) and the country-club world of Bobby Trippe than the wilderness where Lewis Medlock tests his survival skills.

Though his workplace is "harmonious" and his fifteen-year marriage is stable, Ed is beset with the meaninglessness of his existence, which comes upon him as he walks home from his office and notices suddenly that "autumn was close." The river trip is in response to his recognition that "Aging with me was going to come on fast" and that "The feeling of the inconsequence of whatever I would do, of anything I would pick up or think about or turn to see was at that moment set in the very bone marrow." The only act that offers "other things, another life, deliverance" is sex with his wife, Martha, though he cannot help fantasizing about a model with a "gold-glowing

mote" in her eye that he had seen in an ad shoot at the office. For Ed and Lewis, this trip down the river will be a tonic for their malaise: "If going up to the woods with Lewis does something about that feeling, I'm all for it," says Ed.

Ed's initial qualms on the drive to Oree, especially after a daredevil ride to the river with Lewis (who gets ominously lost), are allayed when they get to the river, where "something or other was being made good." At the end of the first day he declares, "I'm glad we came. . . . I wouldn't be anywhere else, the way I feel." Their civilizing presence seems to have made their initial encounter with nature successful: "We had colonized the place," says Ed. The harmony is manifest that night when an owl on its evening hunt settles repeatedly at the peak of Ed's tent. When Ed touches a talon as if shaking hands, he seals this imagined communion with nature, starting the process of bringing him back into contact with his instinctual self.

Perhaps it is the owl's touch at night that arouses the hunter in Ed at daybreak. When for the first time he aims an arrow not at a paper target but at a living thing, he breaks the happy concord, introducing hostility into the harmony, even though his arm shakes so badly with a deer in his sights that he misses it.

Ed and Bobby confront hostility and have their civility put to the test when they leave the river and encounter a pair of repulsive mountain men. Ed, tied to a tree, cannot save Bobby from being raped, and Ed is only saved by Lewis ambushing the other mountain man with an arrow through the chest. Ed, who earlier might well have sided with Drew's desire to turn the affair over to the authorities, now sides with Lewis in taking the law into their hands and disposing of the body.

Curiously, Ed's deliverance begins from the exercise of his naturally passive character, which allows him to control nature by submitting to it. When he is swept away by the white water and his every maneuver to fight the force of the water fails, his only defense is finally to yield to the power of the river, a decision that will lead not only to his survival, but his deliverance from the passive boredom that led him to make the trip in the first place: "I turned over and over. I rolled, I tried to crawl along the flying bottom. . . . I felt myself fading out into the unbelievable violence and brutality of the river, joining it." He becomes "a creature I had always contained but never released."

After Drew pitches out of his canoe and is washed downstream, and Lewis is incapacitated by a severely broken leg, Ed must assume the leadership role. This duty is the turning point for his character. In order to be delivered from all that has come before, he must become the deliverer. With Lewis and Bobby secured in a safe haven on the shore with orders to set out at daybreak for their own safety, Ed attempts to enter the mind of his prey, the escaped mountain man, Stovall. Ed says, "I had never thought with another man's mind on life and death, and would never think that way again."

The sex act that could not bring him deliverance in his wife's arms is imitated in the climactic ambush. Climbing the sheer rock face, Ed is all sensuality, "not thinking of anything, with a deep feeling of nakedness and helplessness and intimacy," moving "with the most intimate motions of my body, motions I had never dared use with Martha, or with any other human woman. Fear and a kind of moon-blazing sexuality lifted me, millimeter by millimeter." With the rapist in his bow sight, Ed's sense of power over the man leads him to sexual thoughts; he considers the situation "a peculiar kind of intimacy . . . for he was shut within a frame within a frame, all of my making."

Ed's second shot at a living thing hits Stovall in the neck, bringing Ed harmony, control, and deliverance from his debilitating passivity. The change in him is reflected in his attitude to Bobby. After weighting the mountain man's body with rocks and throwing him into the river, Ed excoriates as "useless" his complacent friend, who has not followed his orders. After Bobby's rape, Ed says that his friend "felt tainted to me." Later, he says that Bobby "would always look like dead weight and like screaming, and that was no good to me."

When they find Drew downstream, they bury him in the river as well and make it down to Aintry, where Ed leads the other two in concocting a false story for the sheriff that finally allows them to return to their suburban lives. "The main thing was

to get back into my life as quickly and as deeply as I could; as if I had never left it."

Submitting to the river gives Ed the elusive harmony with nature that he had only thought he had at the end of the first day: *Deliverance* is not the story of him bringing civilization to the river; it is of the river bringing forth Ed's natural adaptability and strength. At the end of the adventure, Ed controls the river in his mind, for once the area is flooded by a dam to prepare it for development, "The river and everything I remembered about it became a possession, as nothing else in my life ever had. Now it ran nowhere but in my head, but there it ran as though immortally. . . . It pleases me in some curious way that the river does not exist, and that I have it."

Discussion Questions

1. Joseph Conrad wrote about men forced to kill in the depths of a wilderness and far from civilization. How does Conrad's Marlow in *Heart of Darkness* compare with Ed Gentry?

2. What is the significance of touching the talons of the owl who hunts by night from the top of Ed's tent-pole?

3. Joyce Carol Oates called this novel "a savage fable of decent men fighting for their lives and killing and getting away with it." Is the behavior of Ed and the other characters in killing, covering up the truth, and avoiding the institutions of civilization immoral or is it defensible?

—*Ward Briggs*

LEWIS MEDLOCK

Lewis Medlock is the superb physical specimen who leads Ed Gentry, Drew Ballinger, and Bobby Trippe on the disastrous canoeing trip in *Deliverance*. He arouses sheer admiration in Ed, the narrator: "I had never seen such a male body in my life, even in the pictures and in the weight-lifting magazines." At "thirty-eight or nine, at six feet and about 190 pounds," he was "one of the strongest men I had ever shaken hands with." The embodiment of physical strength and courage, Lewis intimidates his friends by the power of his will. "He was the kind of man who tries by any means—weight lifting, diet, exercise, self-help manuals from taxidermy to modern art—to hold on to his body and mind and improve them, to rise above time." Lewis is obsessed with the decay of the body—which he equates with the decay of civilization—both of which he feels are cured by the purifying qualities of nature. Though he wants to live forever as a strong man mentally and physically, "he was also the first to take a chance, as though the burden of his own laborious immortality were too heavy to bear." He leads a comfortable life in Atlanta with his wife, Caroline, but he also believes that machines and political systems are going to fail "and a few men are going to take to the hills and start over." Lewis believes in radical solutions and is prepared to take radical steps.

The key to Lewis's character is his ability to intimidate either physically or intellectually everyone he encounters. The canoe trip is his idea, and he leads the men to try anything. He fears nothing and no one on the river, not the ignorant Griner brothers nor the mountain men, one of whom he kills. He despises Ed's friend, "the chubby boy" Bobby, who is so inept that he steers Lewis's canoe into the first rapids backward. He prides himself on his survival skills, particularly his expertise at archery, whether in securing fish for dinner or saving Ed from sexual assault. On the intellectual side, he browbeats Drew against turning the entire affair with the mountain men over to the law. Lewis assumes power like a tyrant of Greek tragedy, claiming, "You see any law around here? We're the law." As ruler he calls for a vote and wins the day. After they dispose of the corpse in the woods and make their getaway down the river, Lewis is thrown from his canoe and breaks his femur. He ceases at this point to be the leader, and Ed must find the resources within himself to assume Lewis's role. As Lewis tells him: "now you have to play the game."

Lewis, like Ed, is middle-aged, healthy, prosperous, and happily married but bored. "Lewis had every thing that life could give," Ed says, "and he couldn't make it work." In his energetic pursuit of excitement, he is reckless; he gets lost and has injurious accidents. Indeed, though Lewis is the catalyst of Ed's deliverance, once Lewis has got the men into the wilderness, only the reformed Ed can get them out.

Lewis's character is driven by the survival wish, but he wants not only to survive but to prevail. He wants to live as long and as healthily as he can, even if he must risk death to do so. He somehow survives the journey with his broken leg, just as he had once driven all the way home from a previous trip with a broken ankle. Lewis's survival ideas remind us that this novel was conceived in Positano, Italy, in 1962, the very year of the Cuban missile crisis, when air raid shelters and family fallout shelters were common. But Lewis does not believe in such fortifications. "I decided that survival was not in the rivets and the metal, and not in the double-sealed doors and not in the marbles or the Chinese checkers. It was in me. It came down to the man, and what he could do. The body is one thing you can't fake; it's just got to be there." Nevertheless, however much Lewis obsessed on staving off his own mortality, at the end of the novel, when he has survived an injury that might have killed him, Ed says of him "he can die now; he knows that dying is better than immortality."

Lewis Medlock was based in part on Dickey's Atlanta friend Lewis King, an avid outdoorsman who possessed Medlock's physique and fearlessness without his accompanying recklessness. Dickey said, "what fascinated me about Lewis King is what fascinated Ed Gentry about Lewis Medlock. He's the only man with the private means to do what he wanted with his one human life and also the ambition and willpower to realize it." There are also elements of Dickey in the character: Like Dickey, Lewis is a virile outdoorsman and archer, physically imposing but clumsy.

Discussion Questions

1. "This is the whole secret of Lewis," James Dickey said, "he despises himself. . . . He is the victim of a crushing inferiority complex, so that he spends enormous amounts of time on himself . . . so that he can make other people feel inferior." Do you agree with this statement? Support your answer with details from the novel.

2. How does Lewis meet Joyce Carol Oates's statement that *Deliverance* "is about the need of some men to do violence, to be delivered out of their banal lives by a violence so irreparable that it can

never be confessed." Does Lewis need to commit violent acts to be fulfilled?

3. After the men get to Aintry, Ed has to make up a story to tell law enforcement. Lewis tells Ed, "You've got it figured, Ed. You're doin' it better than I could." How does Lewis change in the course of the novel from the alpha male he is at the beginning?

—*Ward Briggs*

BOBBY TRIPPE

Bobby Trippe is a member of the quartet of middle-aged Atlanta businessmen who take a disastrous canoe trip down the Cahulawassee River on a September weekend in northern Georgia. He is distinct from the other members of the party by being single, not a Georgia native ("from another part of the south, maybe Louisiana"), and the only member of the party who is neither killed nor wounded, though he suffers the trauma of rape. In Atlanta he sells mutual bonds for a broker and is known as a sociable companion, "a good dinner or party guest," which is presumably his chief reason for being invited on the trip: Ed Gentry "liked him a good deal," though he knows him the least well of his three companions. "He had smooth hair and a high pink complexion. . . . He was pleasantly cynical and gave me the impression that he shared some kind of understanding with me that neither of us was to take Lewis too seriously." Perhaps he cannot take Lewis Medlock seriously because he is his polar opposite in terms of physical ability, outdoors experience, and courage. Where Lewis is well-muscled and athletic, Bobby is defined by his excess of body fat; Lewis is a master of the canoe, while Bobby is, in Ed's words, "useless."

The key to Bobby's character is his incompetence. Ill at ease on the trip from the beginning, he contributes nothing but a whining companionship ("These bugs like to eat me alive last night"). The first time he gets in the canoe with Lewis, they wind up going backward down the river. On the second day of the trip, Lewis asks Ed to take "the chubby boy" with him in his canoe. As a result, Ed and Bobby take off, leaving Drew Ballinger and Lewis to strike the camp. Thus, they are by themselves, without the strength of Lewis to support them

when they pull in to land to rest and wait for their comrades. Neither knows how to speak to the two mountain men who confront them, the way Lewis had spoken to the Griner brothers about driving his car to Aintry. Unable to intimidate the men, Ed is tied to a tree and Bobby is raped before the helpless Ed's eyes. Bobby is left a sobbing wreck.

After Lewis kills one of the mountain men before he can sodomize Ed, Bobby's anger spills forth when he kicks the dead man in the face. He is now defined by his violation, and after this first vengeful act he simply wants to get away from the place of his assault. Yet, again he is incompetent to exact either vengeance or justice by killing the other mountain man, who may have killed Drew. When the three survivors settle at the end of the second day in a rock crevice beneath a gorge, Bobby is rendered as useless by his simple inability to follow instructions as Lewis is by the broken leg he suffered when his canoe overturned during the getaway from burying Lewis's victim. Bobby cannot even pull Lewis up onto the rock; Ed must do it alone.

Ed's initial attraction to Bobby stems from the easygoing attitude Ed maintains in his business and private life. Now that the situation requires action and courage, he cannot think positively of Bobby in any way. Even the careful instructions to set out with Lewis in the canoe at dawn, given by Ed before he goes off to ambush the second mountain man, are beyond Bobby's meager abilities. Ed, successful in his ambush, finds that Bobby did not set out with Lewis because, as Bobby claims, their companion was in such pain that he could not be moved. Ed rages at him in reply: "You soft city country-club man." Bobby's reduced position is confirmed when they get to Aintry and Ed comes up with a story for the police, while Bobby takes a woman's job of going into town and getting clothes for them to wear.

Bobby is the least suited of the three characters for the ordeal they face and seemingly the least changed. He remains static throughout: he gains no competence, no confidence, and seemingly no understanding. Though he is not wounded as Lewis and Ed are, he is wounded physically and emotionally by his rape in the woods, after which, Ed says, "he felt tainted to me," and their friendship virtually ends. "He would always look like dead weight and like screaming, and that was no good to me," says Ed. As the nature of Ed's experience on the river changes from a social weekend of the sort Bobby is good at to a fight for survival, Bobby's ineptitude, previously a part of his charm, becomes a dangerous and repugnant liability.

Critics have found aspects of Dickey's persona in all four of the main characters in *Deliverance*. Bobby may be a projection of the author's worst image of himself. Dickey was not athletically accomplished, despite the claims he made to be a star athlete. For a while he enjoyed comfort and security in the corporate structure of a large American advertising firm writing advertising copy. But Dickey left that comfortable world, as Bobby could not.

Discussion Questions

1. Bobby is the embodiment of Drew's words, "There's not one of us knows a damned thing about the woods." What has Bobby learned from his experience in the woods? Has he found any kind of deliverance?

2. How common is the "taint" that attaches to the victim of rape, as Ed attaches it to Bobby? Does Ed see Bobby's rape as a sign of his weakness and femininity? How fair is his view in light of the fact that had Lewis not come along, Ed himself might have suffered the same "taint" or worse.

3. Bobby and Ed start out as comrades who share much of the same social life in Atlanta. In what ways does Bobby become the opposite of his friend Ed as the story progresses?

4. When Lewis learns of Bobby's profession, he says, "I've never been insured in my life. I don't believe in it! If you're insured, Ed, there's no risk." Discuss the ways in which Lewis and Bobby are polar opposites.

5. What other characters are used as opposites to a lead character in short stories you have read?

—*Ward Briggs*

REFERENCES

Ronald Baughman, *Understanding James Dickey* (Columbia: University of South Carolina Press, 1985);

Richard J. Calhoun and Robert W. Hill, *James Dickey* (Boston: Twayne, 1983);

Casey Howard Clabough, *Elements: The Novels of James Dickey* (Macon, Ga.: Mercer University Press, 2002);

Harold Schechter, "A Psychological Reading of James Dickey's *Deliverance*," in *Struggling for Wings: The Art of James Dickey*, edited by Robert Kirschten (Columbia: University of South Carolina Press, 1997).

Joan Didion
(December 5, 1934 –   )

RUN RIVER
(New York: Obolensky, 1963)

EVERETT McCLELLAN

Everett McClellan is the husband of the main character, Lily Knight, in Joan Didion's *Run River*. He confronts and kills Lily's lover, Ryder Channing, setting off a chain of memories through which Lily recollects their failed marriage. She remembers her pregnancy with another man's child and her abortion, as well as the death of Everett's sister Martha, who drowns herself after Channing, her longtime suitor, marries another woman. To end what he has come to see as a cycle of destruction on the McClellan ranch and to escape trial, Everett kills himself.

Didion preferred Everett to the other characters in the novel, as she said in a 1978 interview with Linda Kuehl for the *Paris Review*, perhaps because he most directly embodies the themes that *Run River* addresses. "He's the most distinct person in the book for me. I loved him. I loved Lily and Martha but I loved Everett more." His family, as well as Lily's, were the among the first settlers in California. Everett, however, loses more than the other characters in *Run River*. His descent reflects the broader decline of the old California.

The events leading up to Everett's suicide include the death of his father and his wife's unfaithfulness, as well as his sister Sarah's decision to abandon the ranch for an urban life in Philadelphia. Everett routinely shirks his responsibilities as a father, leaving Lily to raise their children as he attempts to recapture the adventurous lifestyle of his ancestors by joining the military. Martha shows her support for Everett's decision when she gives him *The McClellan Journal, an Account of an Overland Journey to California in the Year 1848*. Everett fails to re-create the pioneer days of his forebears—he never sees combat. He refuses to come home for the two years of his military service, returning only when Martha informs him of his father's death. The disintegration of the McClellan family, which begins with the death of Everett's father, causes Everett and Martha to console one another with memories of their childhood—an era that they see as one of innocence and simplicity.

Martha, who likes playing a role game where she is a member of the Donner party, shares many of Everett's dilemmas. Her role-playing evokes the story of an unsuccessful trek west that ends in suicides and cannibalism. Martha's game, in a sense, reflects the family's disintegration. They, too, unable to move further west because the frontier has ended, begin to feed on one another and are ultimately destroyed. When Ryder Channing marries someone else, Martha immediately goes to Everett for comfort, and together they reminisce about their childhoods. Like Everett, she abandons her responsibilities as an adult and chooses to live in the past while her present-day world comes apart. Martha quits her only job at a local television station because of her obsession with time and clocks. She explains to Everett how she could not "work with it going every second . . . she could not take her eyes off it." She is literally frozen by her obsession with time. Her later suicide symbolizes the broader context of the old guard's upheaval. Channing, who believes that "we need everything out of here . . . tabula rasa" represents the new class of people who have come to displace families such as the Knights and McClellans.

When Everett discovers Lily's infidelity and pregnancy, he immediately resorts to drinking as he studies an old photograph for most of the night. The photograph, of a distant birthday party, makes him want to "walk back into that afternoon, walk back into Lily Knight's house, holding Martha by the hand, and begin again." Everett, as well as Lily, is paralyzed by their failed histories but envisions escape in a new frontier, a hope that is made impossible because of what historian Frederick Jackson Turner argued was the end of the end of western expansion. Unable to start over, Everett finds no salvation except in his nostalgia.

Thereafter, he vows never to leave the ranch or let it fall into disrepair. Everett's preoccupation with his work prevents him from bonding with his son and daughter, both of whom demonstrate little interest in his work or the ranch. Thus begins the final stage in his life, in which he exhausts himself by reviving his father's farm and trying to hold the remnants of the family together. He becomes increasingly introverted, alienating himself from friends and family. As Lily's flashback moves closer to the present time of the novel, Everett himself becomes increasingly obsessed with his farm, the hops, and the past. After the death of his sister, Everett no longer has anyone with whom to reminisce and cannot escape his crumbling reality. Because he is a relic of a bygone era, his suicide signals the end of the old social order.

Discussion Questions

1. A key to the novel's theme lies in the difference between Lily's and Everett's reactions to the realization that the old California is vanishing. Explore how Lily's fears and reactions differ from Everett's, using this entry as a jumping point. Why and how does Lily escape the cycle of destruction, while Everett and Martha both commit suicide?

2. Building on the first question, how do their responses to the extinction of the old order distinguish the Knights from the McClellans? Consider such socio-political differences between the families. Lily's father is a politician, for instance, while Everett's father is a farmer.

3. Discuss Lily and Everett's relationship to their children in terms of their relationship to their parents and grandparents. Julia, Lily's daughter, grows up to look like Lily as well as Everett's sister Martha. What does one know about Julia, and what evidence does Didion give to determine whether or not the children will go on to repeat the mistakes of their parents?

—Brian Ray

LILY KNIGHT MCCLELLAN

Lily Knight McClellan is the protagonist of Joan Didion's first novel, *Run River*. When she hears a gunshot at the beginning of the novel, Lily assumes that her husband, Everett, has killed Ryder Channing, with whom Lily has recently been involved in an extramarital affair. The murder inspires a flashback that comprises most of the novel and chronicles the McClellans' marriage, in which Lily knows they were both unfaithful and cruel. Her flashback ends when she and Everett attempt to hide the body. Later that night Lily hears another gunshot signaling Everett's suicide. She walks to the dock where she holds Everett and watches him die, hoping that people will remember him as a good man.

Didion once said in an interview with Linda Kuehl for the *Paris Review* (1978) that "my early novels were ways of dealing with the revelation that experience is largely meaningless." Didion's remark is relevant to the McClellans, who become blind to the present as they attempt to re-create a past that they see as the key to their salvation. Neither Lily nor Everett seem to learn from previous mistakes but instead seem to repeat them.

Run River connects the McClellans' circular existence with the end of the American frontier. This phenomenon was first dealt with by historian Frederick Jackson Turner, who embodied it in the concept of Manifest Destiny. America, he said, flourished so long as it possessed a frontier where those who felt unsatisfied with urban culture could settle and begin what they saw as a fresh life. The bringing of civilization to California, he argued, foreshadowed an end to westward expansion and, therefore, the newness and freedom that had characterized American culture. The McClellans and the Knights, remnants of frontier lifestyle, find themselves unable to cope with the social transformation taking place during the 1930s, 1940s, and 1950s. Set in 1958, *Run River* depicts these two families at the end of a long heritage of pioneering. The Knights are exemplars of westward expansion, having moved to California from Kentucky during the 1800s. Didion expresses a kinship to the family, seeing herself as member of a dying breed. "The ethic I was raised in was specifically a Western Frontier ethic," she once said in an interview. "That means being left alone and leaving others alone. It is regarded by members of

my family as the highest form of human endeavor." The "impulse" for writing the book, she also says, "was nostalgia."

Lily's internal conflict is clear from the beginning of the novel. She and her family can "never seem to get it through their heads that things were changing in Sacramento, that Aerojet General and Douglas Aircraft and even the State College were bringing in a whole new class of people." She realizes that her family has lost the influence and power it once possessed but cannot find a way to cope with her current status. The California in which Lily has come of age is the old one where her father, politician Walter Knight, guarded an idealized perception of the frontier. Lily has come to see the Sacramento Valley the same way her father saw it, as "God's own orchard." When her father loses a bid for governor and his seat in the state legislature, she develops an indifference to the new political current. She ultimately realizes, in spite of Everett and his family, that she and Everett are part of an outdated social class in decline. Lily also knows that "there was one thing that she and Everett and Ryder all had in common . . . they seemed afflicted with memory."

Lily resigns herself to a position of fatalism, believing she has no choice but to live in the world her father and his forbears created until it has altogether vanished. She does not consider her marriage to Everett, for example, as an act of free will, but rather as a decision that she must make. For her, being his wife is nothing more than a scripted role. "Shortly before noon she told Everett that she would marry him. . . . it seemed as inescapable as the ripening of pears, as fated as the exile from Eden." Lily, who has grown up believing that California is a paradise on earth, has suddenly been faced with a reality that there is no such thing as paradise, that, as the epigraph to Didion's novel states, "El Dorado is still farther on."

Lily's marriage is one of convenience. Living with Everett, she remains somewhat capable of sustaining her imagined California. Her identity itself, she asserts routinely, is tied to the land and her heritage: "If my father is dead, then I don't know who I am." Her character is representative of a broader cultural development in American history: the closing of the frontier and, Didion asserts, the end of the possibility of paradise.

Discussion Questions

1. Does Lily's adultery drive Everett to murder and suicide? Discuss also how much of the family's downfall should reside on Lily's shoulders—what she might have done to rescue her husband and sister-in-law.

2. Consider contradictions in Lily's character. She seems helpless, lackluster, and depressed throughout most of the novel. But on the other hand, she responds to emergencies much better than Everett and saves their child's life. What do these contradictions say about the Knights and McClellans and the old California itself?

3. Why does Lily begin an affair with Ryder Channing, when she is aware of how he treated her sister-in-law Martha? Is it a simple matter of cold desire, or is Didion implying something darker about Lily's internal contradictions and unrealized motivation toward self-destruction? Might her complicity in the marital affair symbolize a great acceptance of the new California (developers, bankers, etc.) and the death of the farmer, the old California?

—*Brian Ray*

REFERENCES

Ellen Friedman, ed., *Joan Didion: Essays and Conversations* (Princeton: Ontario Review Press, 1984);

George Plimpton, ed., *Writers at Work: The Paris Review Interviews*, fifth series (New York: Viking, 1981), pp. 341–357;

Mark Royden Winchell, *Joan Didion*, revised edition (Boston: Hall, 1989).

E. L. Doctorow

(January 6, 1931 –   )

BILLY BATHGATE

(New York: Random House, 1989)

BILLY BATHGATE

Billy Bathgate, the title character and narrator of E. L. Doctorow's 1989 novel, is a young man who becomes involved with the criminal gang of mobster Dutch Schultz. Doctorow created in Billy a mixture of American cultural myths and literary stereotypes. His rags-to-riches progression from innocent poverty to experienced affluence connects him to the young protagonists of the nineteenth-century novels of Horatio Alger and, before that, to the national myth of the "self-made man." At the same time, his role as naive witness to complicated events has generated comparisons to characters such as Herman Melville's Ishmael, Mark Twain's Huckleberry Finn, and F. Scott Fitzgerald's Nick Carraway. Just as important, the events that Billy witnesses—the world that he is seduced and transformed by and eventually overcomes—are drawn from a more recent piece of the American mythological tapestry, the mid-twentieth-century urban gangster and his rarified world of gore, glamour, and glory. In the end, Billy himself embodies a struggle between new and old American cultural and literary traditions—between the rags-to-riches, self-made man and the neo-mythical mobster—with his eventual fate spelling out the ultimate theme of the novel.

Billy can be understood only in terms of his relationship to Schultz, who takes Billy under his wing for the duration of the novel. Schultz, while historically real, is an unglamourous figure in the American pantheon of underworld antiheroes. He was crude, brutal, inarticulate, and badly dressed, a violent overachiever in a superficially sophisticated world. An unlikely patron to Billy, he is the catalyst of a violent journey that brings Billy into contact with the most vivid characters and episodes of Schultz's career: genius bookkeeper Abbadabba Berman and hulking gunman Lulu Rosencrantz, the violent gangland war with the Coll Brothers and the Syndicate, the legal struggles with Thomas Dewey, the pivotal trial held in the bucolic setting of upstate New York, and Schultz's bloody assassination in the Palace Chop House in Newark (with Billy taking cover in the restroom) and subsequent "Last Words" uttered at a nearby hospital during a peritonitis-induced stupor.

Much occurs along the way to bring Billy into contact with elements far beyond the traditional self-made-man narrative. Although Schultz's initial instruction to Billy is merely to "keep your eyes open and watch," Billy is more than a simple metaphor for fiction as a means of "witnessing" history while it unfolds or for innocence transformed by experience. Rather, he represents one American myth being transformed by, and ultimately prevailing over, another. Before he meets the Dutchman, Billy is a natural, Rousseauian being: "I was double-jointed," he says. "I could run like the wind, I had keen vision and could hear silence and could smell the truant officer before he even came around the corner." Schultz first takes note of the lad ("a capable boy," he remarks) as Billy juggles on the street, a specialist at keeping aloft all the loose materials of Depression-era America: "Spaldeens, stones, oranges, empty green Coca-Cola bottles . . . rolls that we stole hot from the bins in the Pechter Bakery wagons." During his early days with the gang, Billy feels an "intimation that I might be empowered. That is the feeling you get, that your life is charmed, which means among other things that it is out of your hands." For a juggler, this form of empowerment is a dubious one, symbolic of Billy's loss of identity as he moves from merely "keeping his eyes open" to making numbers-running transactions, witnessing internal murders such as that of former Schultz henchman Bo Weinberg, spying on political figures such as Dewey, and eventually falling into the bed of Schultz's latest "kept woman," Drew Preston.

At the same time, to Billy, Schultz and his henchmen are "all a kind of advanced race," and to them he pays the "deference one gives to the event perceived as *historical*." Billy's immersion into this "historical" world is gradual. First, he senses that his life has come to exist "in the very pulsebeat of the tabloids, distributed in printer's ink and hidden like the fox in the tree leaves on the puzzle page except that I was right in the middle of the centrally important news of our time." At this point no one, least of all Billy's neighborhood cronies, knows of his inclusion in the world of the tabloids. However, upon his return from Schultz's trial, he "realized that wherever I had been, whatever I had done, the people knew about it not in its detail but in its fulfillment of their myth-knowledge of the rackets." At this point, he has emerged as an historical figure and bona fide gangster. Consequently, when he arrives at home for a brief stay,

his mother's first words are "You've grown *out.*" Billy has grown not *up* but *out* into a mythological world populated by a race of "advanced beings who were there before I was and knew more than I knew. . . . It was all quite dazzling to be inserted by birth into their world, to slide out raw through the birth canal to be christened with a great clop, as if from a champagne bottle upside the head, so that life was forever after dazzling, with nothing quite making sense."

Schultz epitomizes the end result of this process to Billy at the same time that his death brings its halt. It is more than Shultz's sudden death, however, that makes him a useful dramatic tool for Doctorow's exploration of intersecting American mythologies. Rather, it is the manner by which Schultz himself attempted in his final hours to voice that myth. Inarticulate as he was in life, Schultz actually manages to describe it aloud in his delirious last words, the meaning of which Billy alone understands. In the last words Billy begins to use his knowledge of the gangster world that has transformed him to his own advantage, as a shortcut in his own original journey as an archetypal self-made man.

Billy has a hard time at first sorting through the ambiguous text of the last words. Historically, the last words are Schultz's actual, transcribed ramblings as he lay on his deathbed in Newark City Hospital, which Billy, in the novel, infiltrates in order to act as second stenographer to the (historically real) F. J. Long of the Newark Police Department. There, Billy says, "I listened for the wisdom of a lifetime. I thought at the end a man would make the best statement of which he is capable, delirious or not. I figured delirium was only a kind of code." Billy admits that in his version of the last words "there are words misheard, mistakes of my own emotion."

Billy's "mistakes" as stenographer result in a text with obvious inaccuracies, but one that leads him directly to a literal treasure: the location of the Dutchman's hidden cash fortune. At this point he finds himself "living in even greater circles of gangsterdom than I had dreamed, latitudes and longitudes of gangsterdom." This is not a regression; it is a reconciliation of Billy the rags-to-riches figure to the violent means by which Billy the gangster has reached that status, a reconciliation of two central American mythologies. This reconciliation is further reiterated in the last scene of the novel, when Billy discovers a final boon, his own son. With money and offspring in hand, Billy reemerges into his original world, walking "on a sunny day along Bathgate Avenue, with all the peddlers calling out their prices . . . and all the life of the city turning out to greet us just as in the old days of our happiness."

Discussion Questions

1. Since the time of Horatio Alger's novels, the American rags-to-riches story has been characterized as a combination of "luck and pluck," "luck" including positive events that happen *to* the hero, and "pluck" including qualities within the hero that contribute to his or her rise. Which parts of Billy's rise can we consider as "luck," and which can we consider as "pluck"?

2. As Billy becomes more and more familiar with Dutch Schultz's world of organized crime, he repeatedly refers to that world as "historical" and refers to himself as a person who is "entering history." In these moments, how can we consider Billy to be a symbol for E. L. Doctorow himself, a fiction writer about historical events?

3. In his essay "False Documents" in the book *Jack London, Hemingway, and the Constitution,* Doctorow argues that "fiction is a kind of speculative history, perhaps a superhistory, by which the available data for the composition are seen to be greater and more various in their sources than the historian supposes." Do you agree with this statement? After reading *Billy Bathgate,* do you feel that you have read a history of Dutch Schultz's gangster empire? What is the basis for your answer?

4. The character of Drew Preston is not based on a specific historical figure, which might seem odd given the fact that the novel contains so many actual historical figures. Why do you think Doctorow included the Drew Preston character in his novel? What role does she play in the story, and how does she contribute to the themes of the novel?

—*John Keener*

RAGTIME
(New York: Random House, 1975)

Tateh

Tateh (Yiddish for father) is an early-twentieth-century Jewish immigrant who endures years of poverty before becoming a success in the fledgling movie business in E. L. Doctorow's *Ragtime.* The novel begins with a description of America that asserts "There were no Negroes. There were no immigrants." The claim is soon belied by the arrival of a boatload of immigrants heading toward Ellis Island. On the boat is the character known throughout the novel as Tateh, along with his wife, Mameh, and his daughter, the Little Girl.

Tateh is a representative of the immigrant class in the novel, just as the characters Mother and Father represent the white, Anglo-Saxon middle class. He is a member of the Socialist Artists' Alliance of the Lower East Side. Through Tateh's daily struggles on the streets of New York and later as a factory worker in Lawrence, Massachusetts, Doctorow depicts the subhuman working conditions of the immigrants and the poor in America during the time. These conditions are effectively set against the comfortable life of Mother and Father and the outrageously lavish homes being designed by architect Stanford White.

In New York, Tateh is a struggling artist, and his wife is a seamstress. The couple is distraught when the government forces their daughter to attend school because, although only a child, the Little Girl also contributes to the family's income. Suffering from this loss of income, Mameh eventually sells her body to her employer for extra money needed to feed and shelter her family. Consequently, Tateh throws her out of their home, calling her a "whore." As the sole guardian of his daughter, Tateh struggles to make a living selling his silhouettes on the street. He is forced to tie her to him with a string as he goes onto the streets to peddle his art because "young girls in the slums are stolen every day from their parents and sold into slavery." Frustrated with the harsh conditions of New York City, Tateh leaves with his daughter. This journey—from one streetcar to another, beginning in Manhattan, journeying through Westchester county and the Berkshires, and stopping in Lawrence—is one of the most compelling scenes in the novel because of its highly imagistic descriptions. In fact, this scene correlates with Doctorow's comments to Jared Lubarsky (collected in *Conversations with E. L. Doctorow*, 1999) on the influence of motion pictures on his writing: "I admit to learning a lot of things from films: the use of the cut, for instance, the use of entirely visual images to create emotion, the use of repetition." On the other hand, Doctorow has "misgivings" about cinema: "I think it involves regression somehow. After building up language and refining the art of linguistic symbol for thousands of years, our use of film suggests a regression of literalism." Doctorow's conflicting attitude toward movies is relevant for Tateh, who by the end of the novel is a successful motion-picture producer.

Before becoming a success, Tateh participates in a union strike in Lawrence. The strike culminates in a riot, with workers being beaten and their children being torn from them. Tateh and his daughter escape this riot by getting on a train heading for Philadelphia. Significantly, after the union wins the strike, Tateh decides not to return to his job in Lawrence: "The I.W.W. has won, he said. But what has it won? A few more pennies in wages. Will it now own the mills? No." This decision determines Tateh's fate "as separate from the fate of the working class." In Philadelphia, Tateh makes the decision to break free from the working class and join the capitalist system as an entrepreneur, selling picture books. These books lead to his success as a producer. The new technology of motion pictures, along with the American capitalist system, frees Tateh from a life of poverty and oppression.

Although Tateh finally finds success through the moviemaking industry and his marriage to Mother, he must make compromises along the way. He refashions himself as the Baron Ashkenazy, a "new man" with a new title: "he invented a baronry for himself. It got him around in a Christian world. Instead of having to erase his thick Yiddish accent he need only roll it off his tongue with a flourish." In his attempts to assimilate, Tateh denies his Jewish heritage. His success has other negative consequences as well. He is now living comfortably with his daughter, and his objective is to erase his past: "he wanted to drive from her memory every tenement stench and filthy immigrant street. He would buy her light and sun and clean wind of the ocean for the rest of her life." Tateh's success has allowed him to forget his idealistic desires for equality for all. He is now only concerned about his own welfare and status. Nevertheless, when Tateh marries Mother, his family becomes a mixture of races. Tateh's Jewish daughter, Mother's WASP son, and their adopted African American son (orphaned after the deaths of his parents, Sarah and Coalhouse Walker) create an assimilated American family and bring together the three main families in the novel.

Discussion Questions

1. Based on details in the novel argue whether Tateh "sells out" to the capitalist system or if he symbolizes the "American Dream."

2. Chapter 3 of *Ragtime* begins with a description of the immigrants flooding into New York City. The narrative voice explains how New Yorkers perceived them: "They were despised by New Yorkers. They were filthy and illiterate. They stank of fish and garlic. They had running sores. They had no honor and worked for next to nothing. They stole. They drank. They raped their own daughters. They killed each other casually." Explain the ways in which Tateh's character debunks such beliefs and stereotypes. Why does Doctorow include this description of the immigrants?

3. In what ways does Tateh's character contrast with Father's?

—*Elise Martucci*

COALHOUSE WALKER

Coalhouse Walker is a successful ragtime musician in E. L. Doctorow's novel *Ragtime* whose attempts to get justice demonstrate the oppressive and unjust conditions African Americans faced during the Ragtime era. Despite his late entry into the work, his story dominates the second part of *Ragtime*, and his fight for justice brings together many of the themes and characters of the novel.

Walker enters the narrative as a stranger who arrives at the home of Mother and Father—representatives of the Anglo-Saxon, middle-class society of the time—in order to court Sarah, the young black woman who is the mother of his child. Sarah refuses to explain who Walker is. The narrator explains that the family "had no idea where she had met him or how. What becomes evident is that Walker impregnated Sarah and now wants to take responsibility for the child and take care of Sarah. Walker's visits to the house demonstrate his perseverance, determination, and self-respect. At first, Sarah will not receive Walker, yet he arrives every Sunday in his brand-new Ford Model T, knocks at the door, and asks to see her. Walker is polite to the family, but he is not subservient. Father is dismayed by Walker's behavior, thinking, "Walker didn't act or talk like a colored man. He seemed to be able to transform the customary deferences practiced by his race so that they reflected his own dignity rather than the recipient's." This observation reveals not only Walker's dignity and confidence but also Father's bigotry. Part of Walker's function in the novel is as a barometer of the other characters' willingness to accept or reject changes in American culture and politics. Father's conservatism and Mother's progressivism are both demonstrated through their reactions to Walker. Additionally, Mother's younger brother is brought out from a life of despondence and passivity and into the role of a revolutionary through his reaction to the injustices Walker suffers.

Walker's sense of dignity and his perseverance remain intact when he is faced with the injustices the white community enacts upon him. These injustices begin when Walker is stopped by a group of firemen, led by Fire Chief Willie Conklin, who attempt to humiliate and degrade him by refusing to let him drive past their firehouse without paying a nonexistent "toll." Walker's first instinct is to file a complaint with the police, but the police refuse to assist him. Walker returns to his Model T to find that the men have defecated inside it and have vandalized the outside. From this incident forward, much of the novel is dedicated to Walker's story. He is arrested, and Sarah is killed while attempting to defend him. After her death, Walker is still determined to receive justice, but he now realizes that

it can only be obtained through violence. Consequently, he begins a campaign of terrorist attacks on local firehouses, culminating in his barricading himself and his followers inside the library of millionaire J. P. Morgan, a symbol of white power and authority in the novel. Walker threatens to blow up the library if his demands are not met. In an attempt to get Walker to surrender, the authorities ask Booker T. Washington to intervene. The meeting of Walker and Washington is an example of Doctorow's tendency in the novel to combine historical figures with fictional ones in order to reveal opposing perspectives. Throughout the ordeal of being arrested, becoming a fugitive, and retaliating with violence against the white community, Walker remains consistent in his demands: to have his car restored to its original condition and to have Conklin executed for causing Sarah's death. Washington urges Walker to surrender and forget about obtaining justice, telling him: "I have had to persuade the white man that he need not fear us or murder us, because we wanted only to improve ourselves and peaceably join him in enjoyment of the fruits of American democracy." He feels that Walker is undoing all of the good Washington has accomplished. Washington fails to recognize that Walker has been one of the model African American citizens he speaks of, playing by the rules of society and rising up in financial and social status through his own hard work. However, the injustices Walker faces demonstrate that Washington's plan for integration will not work until bigotry and prejudice are eradicated from the legal and social systems in the United States. Nevertheless, Walker compromises his demands, now asking only that Conklin repair his car. Once he sees Conklin repair his car to its original condition, thus accomplishing justice, he surrenders and is shot to death outside of Morgan's library.

Walker's story is an adaptation of a German novella, *Michael Kohlhaas* (1810) by Heinrich von Kleist. When asked about Walker, Doctorow responded, "There are several hundreds of thousands of Coalhouse Walkers in this country" (Gussow 5). There is irony in the Walker plot set against the themes and concepts expressed in the novel. The novel begins with the narrative voice explaining that "the best part of Father's income was derived from the manufacture of flags and buntings and other accoutrements of patriotism, including fireworks. Patriotism was a reliable sentiment in the early 1900's." The narrator also informs the reader that "there were no negroes" in this patriotic vision of America. Walker's story demonstrates that patriotic sentiment encourages an ignorance of the real conditions under which the other segments of society, including blacks and immigrants, are forced to live. Mother's younger brother is enlightened through his interactions with Walker and eventually becomes the only white member of his band of terrorists, using the explosives from Father's fireworks business to rig up Morgan's library. Mother winds up raising Walker's child and, consequently, becomes concerned with issues of segregation. Thus, Walker's history galvanizes many of the characters and themes in the novel and presents an alternative view of the historical ragtime epoch.

Discussion Questions

1. Because of Coalhouse Walker's late entry into the novel and his death well before the end, it is arguable whether he is the hero of the novel. Argue for or against this position using details from the novel and drawing from the definition of a literary hero.

2. Explain the similarities and differences between the personality and struggles of Walker and those of Tateh, another of the main fictitious characters in the novel.

3. Critic Barbara Foley notes that "as a 'typical' historical representative of the Ragtime era Coalhouse Walker is a fraud; but as a means of commenting upon the racism continuing in our own time he projects an alarming degree of truth." Do you agree with Foley that Walker is anachronistic? What type of "truths" does the character reveal?

4. What does Doctorow mean when he says, "there are several hundreds of thousands of Coalhouse Walkers in this country"?

—*Elise Martucci*

REFERENCES

Minako Baba, "The Young Gangster as Mythic American Hero: E. L. Doctorow's *Billy Bathgate,*" *MELUS,* 18 (1992): 33–46;

Harold Bloom, ed., *E. L. Doctorow's* Ragtime (Philadelphia: Chelsea House, 2002);

Douglas Fowler, *Understanding E. L. Doctorow* (Columbia: University of South Carolina Press, 1992);

Carol C. Harter and James R. Thompson, *E. L. Doctorow* (Boston: Twyane, 1990);

Christopher D. Morris, *Models of Misrepresentation: On the Fiction of E. L. Doctorow* (Jackson: University Press of Mississippi, 1991);

Morris, ed., *Conversations with E. L. Doctorow* (Jackson: University of Mississippi Press, 1999);

George Plimpton, "The Art of Fiction: E. L. Doctorow," *Paris Review,* 101 (Winter 1986): 22–47;

John Williams, *Fiction as False Document: The Reception of E. L. Doctorow in the Postmodern Age* (Columbia, S.C.: Camden House, 1996).

Stephen R. Donaldson

(May 13, 1947 –)

✺

THE CHRONICLES OF THOMAS COVENANT: THE UNBELIEVER, 3 VOLUMES

(New York: Holt, 1977)

THOMAS COVENANT

Thomas Covenant is the hero of Stephen R. Donaldson's series of epic fantasy novels—*The Chronicles of Thomas Covenant: The Unbeliever* (1977), *The Second Chronicles of Thomas Covenant: The Unbeliever* (1980–1983), and *The Runes of the Earth* (2004)—although a more accurate description would be "antihero." The novels begin with Covenant as a paradox, embodying many contradictions, which cause him to violate expectations of the typical hero of high fantasy. Unlike such heroes, Covenant is an everyman, lacking in status or wealth. In his "real" world, he is a leper and an outcast, a former best-selling author who has lost nearly everything important in his life to his debilitating disease: his wife, his son, and his career.

Outcast by his hometown, where people shun him and deliver his groceries to keep him from coming to town, Covenant's primary focus is on his daily ritual examination of his hands and feet, made necessary by the numbing effects of leprosy, which could allow injuries to go undetected and thus become infected.

When he is hit by a police car, he is transported to a fantasy world called simply "The Land." Though hailed as its savior, Covenant refuses to accept this world as real, and he denies his own role in its defense against the evil Lord Foul, who threatens to destroy the Land. Covenant labels himself "The Unbeliever," shunning the health and vitality of the Land and especially its power to heal his leprosy. He refuses all calls to act on behalf of the Land, no matter how dire the situation becomes, and he repeatedly denies that he possesses any power, claiming, "I'm a leper. I don't know anything about power." He continually demands to be sent back to his own world, and when his adventures conclude, Covenant is not honored as a hero in his primary world. At the end of the first trilogy of novels, he merely returns from the brink of death, while at the end of the second, he dies, further violating reader expectations for a fantasy hero.

Donaldson has admitted that he was influenced in his writing by J. R. R. Tolkien, especially in his choice of genre. "*Lord of the Rings* convinced me that fantasy was worth writing," Donaldson says in an interview (February 1999) on his official web site. Because he found little appreciation for fantasy among his friends at the time, he was inspired to create a character who disbelieves in fantasy but who ends up needing it, as Covenant does. Donaldson says that fantasy explores the human imagination, adding that "Covenant is the Land," though not in an allegorical sense. Rather, in the Land, Covenant confronts his malaise in the tangible form of Lord Foul, and this confrontation is representative of Covenant's internal struggle against isolation and illness.

In contrast to traditional fantasy heroes, Covenant avoids involvement in the problems of the Land for as long as he can, often standing by and watching others suffer or die. When he is first transported to the Land, he tries to kill himself by jumping off Kevin's Watch, the high plateau where he arrives. Later, he watches evil creatures torture and destroy the people of the Land without trying to help. Covenant even manipulates Elena, daughter of a woman he raped on his first visit to the Land, by encouraging her to challenge Lord Foul, so that she will take responsibility for what happens, not him.

In *The Second Chronicles of Thomas Covenant,* Covenant takes a more active role in his attempts to restore the Land because he has lost his unbelief, and thus the health of the Land has become important to him. The Land is now corrupt, however, its earlier vitality and health destroyed. In the end, Covenant's efforts on behalf of the Land cost him his life in the "real world."

W. A. Senior suggests that Covenant is representative of "anyone who has been cast out and left to fend for himself alone or anyone who does not fit into the preconceived molds and forms that society deems appropriate." Even in the Land, Covenant cannot blend in; his deformed hand and his white gold ring continually set him apart and determine the expectations of others who meet him.

But Covenant retains his freedom of choice; the Creator of the Land tells him, "Choiceless, you were given the power of choice. I elected you for the Land, but did not compel you to serve my purpose in the Land." Thus, like all humans, Covenant retains his freedom to choose how to deal with the forces that surround him.

Another distinguishing characteristic of Covenant is his Americanness, according to Senior. In typical American style, he explains away the mystique of the Land by regarding it as a dream or delusion, denying its reality until he gradually broadens his perspective and sees that such things may be possible. Covenant's distrust of power, especially the wild magic embodied in his own wedding ring, also mirrors American fears of such power, especially in the aftermath of Vietnam, when the First Chronicles were written. The ring itself represents a paradox for Covenant, because while it possesses apocalyptic power, he does not know how to use it, nor can anyone tell him. Bearing a talisman of great power, he is powerless, at least until the end, when he remembers the High Lord's statement, "You are the white gold." Only then is he able to tap into the magic of the ring, because the power lies within himself.

Thomas Covenant in many ways breaks the mold of the traditional fantasy hero as Donaldson presents readers with a protagonist and antihero who is both compelling and repelling at the same time. Covenant is a bitter, isolated, and lonely protagonist who must somehow find his path through both his native world and a secondary one.

Discussion Questions

1. Thomas Covenant can be seen as a typical "American" in his reaction to his adventures in the Land. Using examples from the novels, discuss the various ways in which Covenant's actions reveal his essential Americanness.

2. In *The First Chronicles of Thomas Covenant*, a description of white gold says that "he who wields the white wild magic gold is a paradox." Referring to this chant and using examples from the novels, discuss the ways in which Thomas Covenant is a paradox. How does this seemingly conflicted nature help or hinder him in achieving his goals in the Land and in his own world?

3. Discuss the ways in which the character of Thomas Covenant changes from the first trilogy to the second. What are the reasons for this change? How do the changes in his character affect the outcome of the second chronicles?

4. Thomas Covenant has been called an "antihero," the antithesis of traditional epic fantasy heroes. Another example of such a hero is Frodo Baggins, whose adventures also involve a ring and personal sacrifice. Using details from both of Donaldson's Convenant series and J. R. R. Tolkien's *The Lord of the Rings*, compare and contrast these two heroes.

5. Donaldson has said that "Science fiction and fantasy try to answer the question 'What does it mean to be human?'" by contrasting alien and familiar definitions of humanness. Using examples from the two Covenant series, explore how these novels attempt to answer that question. What various options for being "human" do the novels explore? Which ones are ultimately seen as successful or realistic? In what way does Covenant fit into the definition of "human" put forth in the novels?

—*Patti J. Kurtz*

REFERENCES
Matthew A. Fike, "The Hero's Education in Sacrificial Love: Thomas Covenant, Christ Figure," *Mythlore*, 14, no. 4 (1998): 34–38;

Benjamin Laskar, "Suicide and the Absurd: The Influence of Jean-Paul Sartre and Albert Camus: Existentialism in Stephen R. Donaldson's *The Chronicles of Thomas Covenant the Unbeliever*," *Journal of the Fantastic in the Arts*, 14 (Winter 2004): 409–426;

W. A. Senior, *Variations of the Fantasy Tradition: Stephen R. Donaldson's Chronicles of Thomas Covenant* (Kent, Ohio: Kent State University Press, 1995).

Michael Dorris
(January 30, 1945 – April 11, 1997)

A YELLOW RAFT IN BLUE WATER
(New York: Holt, 1987)

RAYONA

Rayona is one of three female characters in Michael Dorris's *A Yellow Raft in Blue Water*, each of whom narrates one section of the book. She begins the narration in a section that takes up about 40 percent of the book; her mother, Christine, narrates the second section, which is roughly equal in length to the first; the last section is narrated by her grandmother, Aunt Ida. As it turns out, Ida is not Christine's mother but her half sister and cousin, who agreed to raise Christine as her own child. Each section of the novel is narrated from a different point of view and a different generational perspective.

Michael Dorris, born in Louisville, Kentucky, in 1945, was of mixed heritage, German/Irish/African American and perhaps Indigenous, although not an enrolled member of the Modoc Nation. The literary characters that Dorris created often reflect this mixed inheritance. Having adopted three Lakota children with fetal alcohol syndrome, he also wrote about the effects that drinking had on the fetus and subsequently how alcoholism affected the lives of families. Dorris's works reflect the themes of identity crises experienced by people of mixed ancestry and the effects of alcoholism, depression, and sexual abuse. The emphasis on the importance of family histories is also evident in his fiction.

From the start of the novel, the reader is aware that all three protagonists are not involved in a "normal" family. Rayona is introduced while playing cards with her mother, who is in the Indian Health Service hospital in Seattle. Rayona knows that Christine is cheating at the game, because she always wins. Her mother is emotionally absent and not paying attention to Rayona's needs. Christine has been hospitalized as a result of her dependency on alcohol and drugs, and her emotional dependence on Rayona necessitates that the daughter assume the role of mother. She assumes responsibilities and makes decisions that are beyond the understanding of a fifteen-year-old girl.

Rayona narrates her story from the perspective of the present, the 1980s, whereas Christine and Ida relate their stories from the past, the 1960s and the 1940s. By the end of the novel their stories overlap. The story moves geographically from Seattle to a reservation in Montana. This narrative structure helps the reader to understand the different perspectives of the story and how the events and actions of previous generations can have devastating effects. This structure also highlights the theme of negotiating one's own identity in the midst of crises.

The major conflict is the crisis of identity within Rayona, who feels both rejected and betrayed by her Native American mother and her African American father, Elgin. She wants to belong and struggles to understand her family and her identity: "As we've moved around from one apartment to another I've changed schools so often that I never get past being the new girl. Too big, too smart, not Black, not Indian, not friendly. Kids keep their distance, and most teachers are surprised, then annoyed, that I know the answers on their tests. I'm not what they expect. About once a year I get discovered, get called a diamond in the rough. Some eager young counsellor has big plans for me, but before they pan out, we're gone, living in another neighborhood, and the whole shooting match starts all over." Unusually tall and thin, Rayona is self-conscious about her physical appearance. Yet, she is remarkably intelligent and observant, able to survive

in the world despite the hardships she experiences. She loves her parents but feels rejected and unloved by both. Her father has abandoned them to live with another woman, and her mother is physically and emotionally unable to care for her.

Rayona does not understand why her mother is unable to care for her and why she abandons and leaves her on the reservation with Aunt Ida, who is supposed to be her grandmother. It is only through the narratives of Christine and then Ida that the reader becomes aware that Rayona is the product of two generations of struggle and misunderstandings. But Rayona displays courage and perseverance as she proceeds to establish a relationship with her mother. She is a product of the problems that have destroyed her family since Ida first agreed to pose as Christine's mother. But Ida keeps this entire past secret. Since Rayona is not aware of this secrecy, however, she cannot begin to understand why her mother and presumed grandmother are alienated from her and from each other. Her mother's lack of connection to her is illustrated by the story of how she got her name: "My Mom couldn't think of a name when I was born since she had planned on me being a boy. When they brought me to her in the hospital, she looked around for an idea and the first thing she saw was a tag on her nightgown. Rayon. She thought that was pretty, so—Rayona."

While Rayona continually searches for her identity, the meaning of her life, and a place in the world, her deepest desire is to be normal and to live in a loving family. She experiences such normalcy for a while when she works at Bearpaw Lake and is adopted for the summer by Evelyn (the cook) and Sky (owner of the local gas station). While working there as a groundskeeper, Rayona finds a scrap of paper, the remnants of a letter that one mother had lovingly written to her daughter, who, as it later turns out, was a lifeguard at the same camp. For a while Rayona keeps this letter among her possessions and daydreams about her "ideal" family.

Rayona's inner strength and need for survival, despite all the disappointments and frustrations, triumph at the end. When Evelyn and Sky take her back to the reservation, there is an Indian rodeo. Her cousin Foxy, who is drunk, asks her to ride a wild bronco for him. Riding disguised as a man, she falls off and gets on three times, showing a great amount of determination and courage. For her effort she wins an unscheduled citation given only on rare occasions—a silver buckle showing a bronco and rider with coral and jet inlay. This event gives her a renewed determination to locate her mother. In the end Rayona emerges as the future hope of the family. If Ida indeed decides that she may one day tell her story to Rayona, "who might understand," the latter will be given the opportunity to understand her family's past and thus move forward into the future with strength. When Ida begins her story, she explains: "No one but me carries it all and no one will—unless I tell Rayona"; it is up to Rayona to break away from the family's secrets, shame, guilt, and misunderstandings. Ida, Christine, and Rayona finally begin to reconcile at Dayton's house—their first family dinner together in years. Dayton (the owner of the horse Rayona was riding) was the good friend of Christine's brother, Lee. After Lee's death he and Christine continue as friends, and Christine decides to spend her dying days at his house.

Discussion Questions

1. The main characters of *A Yellow Raft in Blue Water* are all returning home—looking for places to belong. How do Rayona's travels affect her and what conclusions does she reach?

2. In the novel, the events of the past affect the lives of characters that are too young to know what events have occurred. In what ways do these family secrets affect the different characters of the novel? What is the impact of the fact that these events are kept secret?

3. Discuss the role of "escapist dreams" in *A Yellow Raft in Blue Water*. What does Rayona dream, and how do her dreams affect her reality, and with what results?

4. In the novel *The Window*, Rayona remarks, "Mom once said, and winked at me, 'You know, Ray, it's like we're the same age but I don't know whether that means I'm eleven or you're thirty-two. Let's split the difference and both be twenty.'" How does this statement still hold true in *A Yellow Raft in Blue Water*?

—*Ute Lischke*

REFERENCES

Allan Chavkin and Nancy Feyl Chavkin, eds., *Conversations with Louise Erdrich and Michael Dorris* (Jackson: University Press of Mississippi, 1994);

Louis Owens, "Erdrich and Dorris' Mixedbloods and Multiple Narratives," in his *Other Destinies: Understanding the American Indian Novel* (Norman: University of Oklahoma Press, 1992), pp. 192–224;

Ruth Rosenberg, *A Teacher's Guide to A Yellow Raft in Blue Water* (Jacksonville, Ill.: PermaBound, 1994).

John Dos Passos
(January 14, 1896 – September 28, 1970)

THE 42ND PARALLEL
(New York & London: Harper, 1930)

AMERICAN SOCIETY

John Dos Passos appended a prefatory note to the one-volume edition of the *USA* trilogy published in 1938 that elucidates his purpose. The note concludes: "But mostly *U.S.A.* is the speech of the people." *USA* is an experimental work in which Dos Passos attempted to present a panoramic kaleidoscopic image of American culture during the first third of the twentieth century. The primary character is American society, and each element of the trilogy contributes to his composite portrait.

The 42nd Parallel is the first volume in *USA*; the second volume is *1919* (1932); and the third is *The Big Money* (1936). Heavily influenced by modernist currents in Europe, Dos Passos adapted a variety of artistic techniques from several disciplines. He adapted the technique of overlaying multiple, sometimes distorted, perspectives from cubist painters; from the impressionists, he adapted a style of consciously subjective perspective; from the expressionists, he adapted methods of caricature and the use of common objects juxtaposed to express opinion. From the Russian moviemaker Sergei Eisenstein, he adapted fragmentary presentation of narrative and compression of time lapses.

To create his ambitious composite, Dos Passos incorporated multiple currents of the radical rethinking of science, philosophy, and art called modernism into the form and technique of his trilogy, and he approached his topic from various perspectives. *The 42nd Parallel* introduces four modes of presentation Dos Passos used in his trilogy. First, there is the Newsreel—nineteen sets of fragments of newspaper headlines and articles, popular song lyrics, and bits of poetry. These fragments convey the barrage of diverse information received from the popular media of the day; they suggest the social context of the novel. Second is The Camera Eye, highly subjective memories of Dos Passos's own life from his earliest years (he was born in 1896) through the period of the trilogy; twenty-seven Camera Eyes are included in *The 42nd Parallel*. Third, there are narratives, named for their primary subject. In *The 42nd Parallel* five characters are the focus of 20 narrative sections strategically placed throughout the novel, and their stories overlap; each character interacts with at least one other of the main characters, and certain minor figures reappear throughout. Finally, there are stylized biographical caricatures of both heroic and villainous real people of the time—nine in this novel. Elements in the four modes are strategically arranged so that they complement and elucidate one another. At the beginning of *The 42nd Parallel,* for example, Newsreel I is followed by The Camera Eye (1), followed by the first Mac narrative, followed by The Camera Eye (2).

Each segment gives meaning to the others. Dos Passos carefully planned the order in which the narrative sections of *USA* appeared, so that his recollections of what he experienced, his stories about what others experienced, the media fragments of the time, and the influence of key figures coalesce to provide the portrait of a people. He devised a distinctive technique for each of his modes. The Newsreels are fragmented montages. The Camera Eyes are told in modified stream of consciousness. The narratives are told in what is called free-indirect discourse—a third-person narration that reflects the subjective point of view of the character being portrayed, using the language he might use and recording his impressions. The biographies are a form of literary expressionism, adapting the art techniques of caricature to prose. In all of the modes, Dos Passos was influenced by cinematic technique—presentation of his material in short, sharply focused scenes and abrupt transitions from one scene to another.

The 42nd Parallel lays the thematic groundwork for Dos Passos's *USA*, which moves from the dawn of a new century in which the people face the challenge of making their way in a world governed by technology and commerce, through the war years portrayed in *1919* in which the economic fortunes of the country are bolstered by capitalists who control what Dos Passos called the war machine, and a global perspective replaces the provincialism of the nineteenth century, and into the illusive prosperity of the 1920s depicted in *The Big Money*, when the fortunes of a few, derived at the expense of the rest of society, are threatened by economic chaos.

The Camera Eye
In an interview published in *The Paris Review* in 1966, Dos Passos said about *USA* "in the biographies, in the newsreels, and even the narrative, I aimed at total objectivity by giving conflicting views—using the Camera Eye as a safety valve for my own objective feelings. It made objectivity in the rest of the book much easier."

The twenty-seven chronologically arranged Camera Eye episodes in *The 42nd Parallel* are accurate autobiographical memories. They are the most demanding of the four modes in the trilogy. The technique, which resembles stream of consciousness, can be compared to that used by James Joyce in *Ulysses* (1922), a work Dos Passos admired. But while Dos Passos adapts the impressionist approach of Joyce, he manages to make his personalized memories more accessible.

Some knowledge of Dos Passos's life is required to appreciate these sections fully, and, like the other modes, they require a careful knowledge of the history of the time. For example, the first Camera Eye begins in Belgium, when Dos Passos recalls walking down a street with his mother. By means of subtle clues, readers can infer that the time is 1900, the last year of Queen Victoria's reign (she died in 1901), and the Boer War, raging in Africa, is generating resentment among the Belgians against the colonialism of Great Britain. (Bloemfontein and Ladysmith are South African Boer-War battle sites.) Dos Passos and his mother are mistaken for British and threatened. When they identify themselves as Americans, they are received warmly. Dos Passos is setting historical context for the novel and sharpening the focus to concentrate on the effect the movement of history has on one little boy and his mother. Belgium, the Boer War, the last flourish of British Colonialism, and respect for American values are all skillfully implied, but what matters here are three points: 1) how these historical settings affect one small person, too young to understand what is happening or why; 2) the high regard among foreigners for American character at the beginning of the century; and 3) the feeling the Western world, at least, is at a turning point in history—the Victorian era is in its last days, and a new social order is emerging

The other Camera Eye sections are structured similarly. In The Camera Eye (27), the last in *The 42nd Parallel*, Dos Passos is on the ocean liner *Espagne*, traveling to Europe. The time is late 1916, months before the United States entered World War I. Dos Passos would have expected his readers to know that the Roosevelt boys to whom he refers are the sons of Teddy Roosevelt. There were four Roosevelt boys, and all fought in the war: one was killed in action in 1918, and two were severely wounded. By this time Dos Passos is twenty years old; he is opinionated and cynical, horrified by the war and appalled by the mentality that supports it. He writes that the Roosevelt boys say "We must come in/as if the war were a swimming pool." He believes the war is fueled by money interests at the expense of soldiers' lives: "up north they were dying in the mud and the trenches but business was good in Bordeaux and the winegrowers and the shipping agents and the munitions makers crowded into the Chapon Fin and ate ortolans and mushrooms and truffles." The Chapon Fin, opened in 1825, is a restaurant long regarded as one of the best in the world located in the city of Bordeaux. Ortolans are small songbirds, forcibly fattened, drowned in Armagnac, and in French tradition served to gormands, who eat them with a napkin draped over their heads to preserve the aromas.

Narratives

The narratives in *USA* are heavily influenced by Marxist theory, which attracted Dos Passos when he was writing the work. On the simplest level, there are the radical sentiments introduced as a counterbalance to mainstream political thought in the Mac, Janey, and Charley Anderson segments. Structurally, the characters also play social roles related to Marxist theory in the social fabric Dos Passos constructs in *USA*. Marxists view society as a hierarchy, ranging from workers, who produce the product from which capital is derived to what Thorstein Veblen called the leisure class, who live off the labor of others. In *The 42nd Parallel*, Dos Passos introduces characters at the beginning of their careers who progress to various levels within that hierarchy. The rallying call of the Marxists was "I want to rise with the ranks, not from them." That is Mac's credo, expressed at the beginning of *The 42nd Parallel*, and it is repeated at the end of the novel by a man in the Charley Anderson section. Only Mac refuses to rise above ranks.

In *USA*, Dos Passos gives a human face to representative figures in society, testing Marx's theory in his own way. The narratives in *The 42nd Parallel* introduce the primary types in the society Dos Passos sees: Mac, the committed revolutionary; Janey, the worker seduced by social mobility; Eleanor Stoddard, the aesthetician; J. Ward Moorehouse, the powerbroker; and Charley Anderson, whose ability as an engineer is not exhibited until he reappears in *The Big Money*. Mac supports social revolution; Eleanor Stoddard supports art; Moorehouse manipulates public opinion. Only Janey and Charley Anderson are workers, whom others depend on for their livelihood; Janey abandons her role as she prospers; Charley Anderson, who is only introduced in *The 42nd Parallel*, becomes a technical innovator, then a capitalist boss, depending on labor for his livelihood.

Mac

Mac's narrative is based on stories told to Dos Passos in Mexico by an itinerant radical named Gladwin Bland. Mac's story gets more coverage than any in the novel; he is the subject of the first seven of the twenty narratives plus one more that comes near the end of the book. Like all of the other characters in *The 42nd Parallel*, Mac, the nickname of Fainy McCreary, is from a modest background, but unlike them he has little interest in achieving social success through hard work and perseverance. Unlike the other characters, who gravitate toward New York City from various origins, Mac is born in New York, moves as an itinerant toward California, and ends up in Mexico, choosing to support the Mexican revolution rather than live in the United States. Unlike the other characters, Mac is a revolutionary, a worker who supports Marxist social upheaval. When his first wife's brother offers him an opportunity to advance his social and economic position by becoming a manager, Mac gives it up to socialize at the union hall. With Mac, Dos Passos sets a revolutionary standard against which the other characters can be measured.

Janey

Janey, the second of the narrative characters to be introduced, is given four narrative sections in the novel. She is from a Victorian household in Washington, D.C., headed by an authoritarian father who works in the patent office, a man with Victorian values who believes in strict discipline and order, and who insists that women have no place in public life. Janey's brother Joe aggressively challenges his father's value system, and Janey feels powerless as her brother Joe struggles against their father's domination. Joe rebels, leaving home at the first opportunity; Janey follows soon afterward. Like Dos Passos's other characters, Janey is representative. Just as she is determining to leave home, her father, called Popper, dies. An era died with Popper and his generation; it was replaced by a generation of newly independent men, and newly empowered women.

Janey is introduced to what is called the New Freedom by a male coworker. The reference, which serves to state a theme of the novel, is to *The New Freedom: A Call for the Emancipation of the Generous Energies of a People* (1914), a collection of the campaign speeches of Woodrow Wilson in which he declared a new organization of society based on economic changes and called on the people to exert the energy and the spirit to take advantage of their opportunities. During the course of her narrative, Janey, who does just what Wilson urged, is transformed from a naive young lady with a strong set of values into a self-assured professional woman who

takes advantage of opportunity. When her beloved brother Joe, now AWOL from the Navy and a rough-acting merchant marine, comes to New York, she is ashamed to have her friends see him. She is drawn toward charismatic public relations manager J. Ward Moorehouse by a belief that his work is important, and she becomes devoted to him, to his work, and to the prosperous lifestyle her employment with him brings.

Eleanor Stoddard

Eleanor Stoddard has four narrative sections in *The 42nd Parallel*. Her father works at an office job in the stockyards in Chicago. She cultivates her friends based on their social standing and their wealth. She pretends to be a socialite until she becomes one. After serving an apprenticeship at a department store, she strikes out on her own and establishes herself as a decorator catering to the upper class. Like Janey, Eleanor Stoddard shields her family from her friends, feeling that her parents will embarrass her. After moving to New York, she becomes acquainted through her business with J. Ward Moorehouse. A contract to decorate his office provides a healthy start to her business, and they begin an affair. When Mrs. Moorehouse becomes suspicious of their relationship and threatens to file for divorce, a move that will deprive Moorehouse of financial support, Eleanor Stoddard chooses to confront Mrs. Moorehouse, claiming none but a professional interest in her husband. Eleanor wins her point by deception and the power of persuasion. When the war is declared, Eleanor Stoddard and J. Ward Moorehouse take advantage of the situation by joining the war effort in jobs that will allow them to continue their affair abroad where they can avoid scrutiny.

J. Ward Moorehouse

J. Ward Moorehouse is based on Ivy Lee, the man who is said to have invented the profession of public relations manager. Like the other characters in *The 42nd Parallel*, Moorehouse is from a family of modest means who must find a way to support himself. His narratives are about his transformation from Johnny Moorehouse, a bright, handsome boy from Wilmington, Delaware, into J. Ward Moorehouse, sophisticated New York businessman. As a young man he sells real estate and has some success. Johnny is naive. He falls under the spell of a wealthy and liberated young woman whose family is in a position to make his career. She grooms him to fit in with her friends, calling him Ward, because it sounds more distinguished than Johnny, polishing his language, and arranging for a long European honeymoon. Just before they are married, he learns she is pregnant and has unexpressed doubts about the father. She aborts the baby, and in Europe abandons him to find her own fun as he applies himself to his work. Rather than indulge his wife, Moorehouse divorces her and determines to work even harder. He sells manipulation. Drawing on his background as a salesman, he starts a new kind of business in which he provides his clients useful information and persuasive ways to communicate it, particularly with reference to labor disputes. More cautious in love now, he courts Gertrude Staple, the daughter of a wealthy client. After her father dies, leaving his fortune to Gertrude in a trust controlled by his wife, Moorehouse and Gertrude consummate their love and determine to marry. Moorehouse takes a year off, and the couple convinces her mother to finance a new advertising agency, which is successful in the field of business relations.

Moorehouse is a major character in the next two volumes of *USA*, but there are no other narrative sections named for him.

Charley Anderson

Charley Anderson is the primary character in *The Big Money*, when he becomes a pioneer in the aviation industry; in *The 42nd Parallel* he is simply introduced, and only one narrative section is devoted to him. He is a poor boy from Fargo, North Dakota. He has no education, and makes his way as best he can on his skill as a mechanic. After a misspent youth, Charley makes his way to New Orleans for Mardi Gras. Down on his luck there, he meets an eccentric communist gambler, who buys him passage to New York City, shares his money and his politics. In New York, Charley crosses paths with Janey's brother Joe, who is ranting angrily to a radical crowd in a bar about his sister's boss, J. Ward Moorehouse, pro-war propagandist for the Morgans and Rockefellers. Though not entirely convinced by the communists,

at the end of his narrative Charley has joined the Red Cross Volunteer Ambulance Corps and is on his way to Europe to fight, which turns out later in the trilogy to be a turning point in his life.

Biographies

There are nine biographies in *The 42nd Parallel*. In order, they are Eugene Debs, militant union leader and socialist politician, the man who said, "I want to rise with the ranks, not from them"; Luther Burbank, a brilliant botanist vilified by church leaders for his belief in natural selection and Darwinism; Big Bill Hayward, founder of the radical Industrial Workers of the World, who at the end of his career was exiled to the Soviet Union, where he died; William Jennings Bryan (not named), the populist Democratic politician, orator, and three-time presidential candidate; Minor C. Keith, founder of the United Fruit Company, which ruthlessly monopolized fruit importation to the United States from Latin America; Andrew Carnegie, monopoly capitalist, founder of Carnegie Steel Company, which merged into U.S. Steel, and philanthropist; Thomas Edison, genius whose inventions transformed society but who never thought about the social implications of his work; Charles Proteus Steinmetz, genius electrical engineer whose inventions were the backbone of General Electric; and Robert La Follette, populist Wisconsin governor, senator, and presidential candidate who opposed big business and the war. The biographies include two radical activist social philosophers; three scientists—technologists, to use Veblen's term—who empower the monopoly capitalists; two politicians, who make the laws that structure society; and two "malefactors of great wealth," as Theodore Roosevelt called them, who prospered by virtue of labor and men like Burbank, Edison, and Steinmetz. These are key figures in the primary elements of American society.

Discussion Questions

1. In "The Camera Eye," Dos Passos sketchily charts his own development from about age five until about age twenty-one. What are the key events that shape his character and how do they relate to the development of the American society during the period?

2. Why do you think the Newsreels are presented in such fragmented form? Why does Dos Passos choose to include popular song lyrics and local-interest news stories in the Newsreels among the fragments of national and international news?

3. Dos Passos said that he "aimed at total objectivity by giving conflicting views" in all the modes except for "The Camera Eye," yet in the biographies the narrative voice is clearly opinionated. How do you explain Dos Passos's claim of objectivity?

4. What is the function of the biographies, and why did Dos Passos choose the figures he did? Why, for example, did he not include anyone from the fields of art or literature?

5. Why do you think Dos Passos spaced the narrative segments as he did? Why does Mac get more attention than any other figure, and why are all of his segments bunched together?

6. If Dos Passos meant to characterize American society, why did he not include any figures in the narratives who were born rich, and why do all of the main characters in the biographies except Mac end up in New York?

7. When Dos Passos revised his trilogy for publication as one volume in 1938, he added a short section called USA that is included in most current texts of *The 42nd Parallel* but was not in the original. In the table of contents, the modes of *USA* are typographically distinguished, and the title of the USA segment is in the same typeface as the narratives. What is the function of this segment? What does Dos Passos mean when he says, "But mostly U.S.A. is the speech of the people"?

—*Richard Layman*

◁◎

MANHATTAN TRANSFER
(New York: Harper, 1925)

JIMMY HERF

Jimmy Herf is a central character in John Dos Passos's *Manhattan Transfer*, a work that stands with Theodore Dreiser's *An American Tragedy* (1925), F. Scott Fitzgerald's *The Great Gatsby* (1925), and Ernest Hemingway's short stories as among the best realized expressions of the modern American spirit before World War II. It is a demanding novel to read. Its structure is complex, and its content reflects the most sophisticated intellectual currents of the time during which it was written. The structure is influenced by the cinematic technique Dos Passos more famously employed in his *USA* trilogy—short scenes, abrupt transitions, and interrelated narratives. Thematically, the novel reflects Dos Passos's concerns about the destructiveness of what he called monopoly capitalism—an economic, political, and social force that causes people to subordinate traditional democratic values to social and economic success.

There are some forty characters in *Manhattan Transfer*, each of them reacting to the cultural environment of the American metropolis. Dos Passos drew on his own life when he created Herf. Like Dos Passos, Herf spends his formative years in Europe with his mother, returns with her to the United States as a boy, sees his frail mother die young, and then refuses the offers of well-placed family members to begin a career in commerce. Again like Dos Passos, Herf chooses to become a writer, motivated, finally, by an idealistic urge to record the history of his time.

Herf dreams of making the world better with his journalism. When his best friend, Stan Emery, a brilliant self-destructive cynic, dies in a fire caused by his own carelessness, Herf professes his love for Ellen Thatcher, the mother of Stan's child, which she aborts so she can pursue her career as an actress. World War I defers her dream; she and Herf join the American Red Cross and travel abroad. In Paris they get married and conceive a child, Martin, apparently named after a radical friend of Herf's. After the war Herf has trouble finding a job, and when he does get employment it brings little money and less satisfaction. Ellen hates living in an inelegant apartment with a baby to care for and longs for the freedom and adulation she enjoyed as an actress. Their relationship cools and then dissolves. At the end of the novel, Herf leaves New York, disillusioned and disappointed, striking out for some place "pretty far" away.

The controlling metaphor for Herf and his role in the novel is the story of Jonah, which is told in the Christian Bible and in the Koran, and which Dos

Passos alludes to throughout the novel, namely in the epigraphs for "Metropolis," First Section, II and "Great Lady on a White Horse," Second Section, I; and in "Rejoicing City That Dwelt Carelessly," (an allusion to Zephaniah 2:15) and "The Burthen of Nineveh (the title of the book of Nahum from the Hebrew Bible prophesying the destruction of Nineveh before Jonah's time), Third Section, I and V." Jonah was a prophet instructed by God to warn the inhabitants of the wicked Assyrian city Nineveh, one of the great cities of the world at that time, that God would punish them if they did not change their ways. Jonah shrank from the task, instead taking a boat in the opposite direction. A great storm arose, which Jonah realized was the result of God's wrath at his disobedience. To save the ship's crew, Jonah threw himself overboard, where he was swallowed by a great fish. He stayed in the belly of the fish for three days; he repented and was regurgitated. He then went to Nineveh and prophesied that the city would be destroyed by God in forty days. But the people changed their ways, and God showed them mercy. Angered that God did not keep his word to destroy the city, Jonah left in despair and set up camp on the outskirts of the city to see what would happen. God grew a gourd tree to provide him shade from the sun, then sent a worm to kill the tree. Jonah, left in the light, once again despaired of life.

Jimmy Herf is the Jonah character in *Manhattan Transfer*. At the beginning of his career as a journalist, he fails to regard his job as a responsibility. When the war breaks out, like Jonah, he goes to sea and finds himself in Europe among foreigners. After the war, he returns home with his new wife, Ellen, and their son, Martin, and resumes his work with serious resolve to be a serious writer and a dedicated social activist. When he despairs, Ellen is his gourd tree, but her love for him withers, and Jimmy is left to his own devices. As the novel closes, he is leaving the city, alone, a failed prophet.

Discussion Questions

1. Jimmy Herf arrives in the United States as a boy on the fourth of July. What is the significance of the date and the show of nationalistic spirit that greets him?

2. Compare Jimmy Herf to his friend Stan Emery. Why is Jimmy attracted to Stan's reckless way of life?

3. After Stan's death, Ellen Thatcher tells Jimmy she is pregnant with Stan's baby. He responds by saying her decision to keep the child is "the bravest thing I ever heard of a woman doing." Why, then, does he agree to marry her after she aborts the child for selfish reasons?

4. What are the comparisons to be made between New York City and the ancient city of Nineveh and between Jimmy Herf and Jonah?

5. Do you agree that Jimmy Herf is a failed prophet at the end of the novel, leaving the city in despair because he sees irresponsible behavior rewarded? Is his sense of hopelessness defensible? Where do you think he is going, and why?

—*Richard Layman*

ELLEN THATCHER

Ellen Thatcher is the Broadway starlet who marries her way to success and despair in John Dos Passos's novel *Manhattan Transfer*. New York City is the true central character of the novel, as Dos Passos weaves depictions of characters from all walks of life who are connected only in that they live in Manhattan. The city is depicted as cruel and indifferent to those who inhabit it, and the only way to survive in such a metropolis, Dos Passos argues, is to become just like the city: cool, detached, and void of emotion. Thus, Ellen, who is able and willing to change her name and identity whenever and however it advances her interests, is as adaptable as the city itself and able to rise within it. This quality comes at a price, however, as her mercurial identity strips Ellen of her individuality and leaves her utterly emotionless, "like a tin mechanical toy" who is "all hollow inside."

The novel opens, after a short imagist poem, with Ellen's birth, in which the newborn baby "squirmed in the cottonwool feebly like a knot of earthworms." Born into the harsh realities of a rigid, materialistic environment, Ellen survives because of her desire to succeed regardless of consequence and her willingness to adapt and conform regardless of emotional cost. From early childhood she proclaims that she "wants to be a little boy," since she associates maleness with power and autonomy, and tells her middle-class, hardworking father that she would love him more "if he were rich." Thus begins her fascination with money, power, and male autonomy—all of which she sees as necessary for surviving in a city as large and destructive as Manhattan.

Ellen's path toward such success is through her ability to perform, both in the theatrical profession and in her personal life. She is almost mechanical as she does whatever it takes to get the job done, regardless of moral or ethical codes and without a thought to how her actions might affect those around her. She, like the rest of the inhabitants of the city, is totally isolated by the weight of society, but unlike the majority of those around her, she manages to rise from one class to the next by becoming more like her environment: amoral, adaptive, and cutthroat. She must cast off traditional moral standards and rely upon appearance and adaptability in order to survive. Over the course of the novel, Ellen's name changes from "Ellie" to "Ellen" to "Elaine" to "Helena" as she shifts identities in order to advance her acting career and her sense of power. She marries three men, two of them simply because they advance her position. Her first husband, John Oglethorpe, is a homosexual; her third husband, George Baldwin, is a philandering and disreputable attorney. Thus, she proves, in the words of her dim-witted roommate Ruth Prynne, that she would "marry a trolleycar if she thought she could get anything by it." Her second husband, Jimmy Herf, is a good man, whom she leaves because he cannot provide for her.

Ellen makes every decision with its financial ramifications in mind, because she associates cash with power and success. Her lust for money is often contrasted with the ambition of Cassie, a less successful actress, who wants solely to "live for my dancing." Ellen's choices and her success come at a price, however, as she must repudiate her individuality and her emotional self. Unable to marry Stan Emory—a bright, cynical, reckless drunk, who is the only man she truly loves—or even to follow her desire to leave show business in order to raise his baby, which she is carrying when he dies, Ellen aborts Stan's child. Immediately following the abortion "all the feeling in her fades," and Dos Passos increasingly describes her in relation to inanimate objects such as a painted

"wooden Indian" and a "porcelain figure" that is "rigid" and "enameled."

Ellen's cunning adaptability finally leads her to success on stage and in her personal life, as the novel ends with her married to George Baldwin, a calculating, self-centered lawyer-turned-politician who is set to become the next governor of New York. While her emotional stagnancy might lead her to feel "always alone amidst a growling ocean," she is at least alive in a steamrolling city that crushes most of the characters of the novel and sends Jimmy Herf fleeing the city. Ellen is much like Carrie Meeber in Theodore Dreiser's *Sister Carrie* (1900) in that she becomes a cosmopolitan success because of her ability to adapt and perform in spite of emotional and moral tolls.

Discussion Questions

1. From childhood Ellen "wants to be a little boy." Does she achieve this goal through her actions in the novel? Does the novel treat this quest as a positive one? What is the basis for your argument?

2. Critics often talk about Ellen as an example of "life as performance." How do the qualities necessary to make her successful on Broadway relate to the qualities she demonstrates in her personal life? Is she a success?

3. What is it about Stan Emery that draws real emotion from Ellen? Why does she feel the need to separate herself from Stan and, after his death, abort his baby?

4. Ellen and Jimmy Herf are central characters in *Manhattan Transfer*, followed from their childhoods. Why do these characters merit so much attention? Why does their marriage fail?

—*Todd Kennedy*

THREE SOLDIERS
(New York: George H. Doran, 1921)

FUSELLI, CHRISFIELD, ANDREWS

Dan Fuselli, Chrisfield (his first name is never given), and John Andrews are the three soldiers of the title of John Dos Passos's second novel. Together they represent the geographical and intellectual range of the American soldier: Fuselli is from San Francisco, Chrisfield from Indiana, and Andrews from the East. The three men are in the same unit before being shipped separately overseas. They complement each other as Dos Passos intertwines their stories.

Fuselli is the least complex of the three. More credulous than the others, he is at home in the army. He accepts its values and goals. As a private, he "thought of the day when he would be a non-com too. . . . Overseas, under fire, he'd have a chance to show what he was worth and he pictured himself heroically carrying a wounded captain back to the dressing tent pursued by fierce whiskered men with spiked helmets." The book makes plain where Fuselli's idea of "fierce whiskered" Germans comes from: propaganda movies the soldiers are shown. He believes what he is told and schemes to advance his military career. Given a chance to distribute rations, he sees the army as a way to advance himself that civilian life would not have afforded him and attempts unsuccessfully to parlay a temporary promotion to corporal into a permanent one.

The shallowest of the three, Fuselli has left in "Frisco" a girlfriend whom he believes is committed to him and whom he believes he loves. In France a girl who works in a restaurant, out of boredom, seduces him. When he asks her to marry him, she explodes into laughter. At the same time, in an effort to ingratiate himself with his sergeant, he pimps her to him and then suffers for it when his sergeant contracts a venereal disease. At the end of the novel Fuselli is performing KP in a "labor camp" for an unexplained infraction; his California girl has married someone else, and Fuselli probably has syphilis.

Chrisfield, twenty years old, is a man in conflict from the time he is introduced in the novel. Half of him yearns sentimentally to return to the Indiana farmland that he finds beautiful: "he could almost smell the heavy sweetness of the locust blooms, as he used to smell them sitting on the steps after supper, tired from a day's heavy plowing." The other half of Chrisfield—the other side of his sentimentality—is resentment and violence. Having before almost killed a man, he chafes against army discipline, which he detests even more than he does the enemy forces he has been sent to fight. The focus of these aggressions is Corporal Anderson, who can order Chrisfield about. Chrisfield's chance comes when in the confusion of battle he picks up two grenades and in a forest happens upon Anderson, now a lieutenant, who has been wounded. Without knowing what he is doing, he throws the grenades and kills Anderson. After this incident Chrisfield is temporarily reconciled to the army because he does "not have to think."

Fuselli's conformity and Chrisfield's self-centered rebellion contrast with the radical views of Eisenstein, the true outsider in the company. Jewish and intellectual, Eisenstein wants to "overthrow the capitalist government.—The social revolution." However, Eisenstein is a minor voice in the novel, although the story finally comes close to affirming his ideas.

After centering the narrative on Fuselli and Chrisfield, Dos Passos, in the middle of the story, switches to the one soldier of intellect and sensibility, John Andrews. Based on Dos Passos, the twenty-two-year-old Andrews, unlike his friends, has been to college. Although he tells Chrisfield that "they've tamed" him, Andrews is untamed. Whereas Fuselli wants to fit in and Chrisfield to strike back, Andrews is focused on something outside the military: music. Wounded by shrapnel as his part of *Three Soldiers* begins, Andrews awakes in a convalescent hospital, where he asks the nurse to find him a book by Gustave Flaubert. His concerns are aesthetic.

Armistice is declared, and Andrews goes to school in France while still in the army. Eventually, he goes AWOL to Paris to continue to write and study music. Throughout the novel he is in search of a meaningful inner self. That self can be expressed only through music; yet, he is unable to find a milieu where he can seriously devote himself to art. He temporarily joins a group of disaffected soldiers, some of whom are AWOL as he is and whose disillusionment parallels his own. Their political views are socialistic; however, the needs of this group do not match his. Andrews is a permanently restless, unfulfilled man. The world of *Three Soldiers* has no environment to accommodate this potentially exceptional person.

A love affair gives Andrews some relief from loneliness but no profound understanding. Geneviève Rod wants to show him off as her prize. But Andrews breaks away. Still AWOL, he rents a room and begins to write a symphony in which the story of John Brown figures, but his French landlady betrays him when he no longer has rent money. Stoically, he goes with the American MPs, leaving behind his unfinished symphony.

When it appeared, *Three Soldiers* was seen as grimly pessimistic and bitterly antimilitary. The motivations of Fuselli, Chrisfield, and Andrews are personal rather than patriotic. The casual connections among them proceed from a series of fragments. Dos Passos develops this theme further in *Manhattan Transfer* (1925) and in his trilogy *USA* (1932–1938).

Discussion Questions

1. Why does Dos Passos present Fuselli, Chrisfield, and Andrews in the order he does? What ideas and themes emerge more clearly as a result of this sequence?

2. In "Echoes of the Jazz Age," F. Scott Fitzgerald writes of the "short outbreak of moral indignation" that was "typified by Dos Passos's *Three Soldiers*." To what extent does each of the main characters in the novel share the moral indignation of the reader?

3. *Three Soliders* includes surreal scenes: a soldier is ordered to get out of bed on pain of court-martial but is dead; a Frenchman cheerily chews a glass bottle to earn one franc. What is the function of these surreal episodes? How do they give resonance to the portraits of Fuselli, Chrisfield, and Andrews?

4. How do the minor characters such as Eisenstein, Henslowe, and Geneviève illuminate the predicaments and characters of the three main figures?

5. The titles of the six parts of *Three Soldiers* suggest a metaphor. Identify that metaphor. How does it describe the development of Fuselli, Chrisfield, and Andrews?

—*Roger Lathbury*

REFERENCES

Allen Belkin, ed., *Dos Passos, the Critics, and the Writer's Intention* (Carbondale: Southern Illinois University Press, 1971);

Virginia Spencer Carr, *Dos Passos: A Life* (Garden City, N.Y.: Doubleday, 1984);

Janet Galligani Casey, *Dos Passos and the Ideology of the Feminine* (Cambridge: Cambridge University Press, 1998);

Michael Clark, *Dos Passos's Early Fiction, 1912–1938* (Selingsgrove, Pa.: Susquehanna University Press, 1987);

Iain Colley, *Dos Passos and the Fiction of Despair* (Totowa, N.J.: Rowman & Littlefield, 1978);

Townsend Ludington, *John Dos Passos: A Twentieth Century Odyssey* (New York: Dutton, 1980);

Ludington, ed., *The Fourteenth Chronicle: Letters and Diaries of John Dos Passos* (Boston: Gambit, 1973);

Donald Pizer, *Dos Passos' U.S.A.: A Critical Study* (Charlottesville: University of Virginia Press, 1988);

Robert C. Rosen, *John Dos Passos: Politics and the Writer* (Lincoln: University of Nebraska Press, 1971).

Theodore Dreiser

(August 27, 1871 – December 28, 1945)

AN AMERICAN TRAGEDY

2 volumes (New York: Boni & Liveright, 1925)

CLYDE GRIFFITHS

Clyde Griffiths, the protagonist of Theodore Dreiser's naturalistic novel *An American Tragedy,* is a character whose fate is determined by a combination of deterministic forces. He yearns for the life of material wealth represented by the beautiful Sondra Finchley but feels trapped by his impoverished background and resorts to desperate means to make his escape. The events of the novel unfold in three phases, each associated with distinct settings: Kansas City, where Clyde is raised in the oppressive religious atmosphere of a mission house and where he works as a bellhop at the Green-Davidson Hotel, gaining his first exposure to the allure of money, sex, and good clothes; Lycurgus, a town in upstate New York, where he goes to work for his wealthy uncle in his factory yet is treated as a poor relation; and the courtroom and prison where he faces trial and then execution for the murder of his pregnant girlfriend, Roberta Alden, an employee at his uncle's factory.

The oppressive conditions of the mission house, operated by Clyde's evangelist parents, inspire within him a desire for wealth and status. He reacts against his parents' constrictive morality with rebellious amorality, resolving to pursue an earthly, not a heavenly, paradise. In contrast to the mission house, the Green-Davidson Hotel is an "aladdinish" realm that gives form to Clyde's materialistic dreams. Book 1 establishes the patterns that will shape his destiny: the tension between desire and duty, deceit and betrayal, conflict and vacillation. For example, his desire for the lower-class but sexy Hortense brings him into conflict with his sense of duty to his mother. Clyde's attempts to realize his desires lead to disaster, and he flees in its wake.

In book 2 Clyde similarly vacillates between unrewarding labor in his uncle's factory and the easeful, luxurious life represented by the mansions of the town's wealthy families. When Sondra, the daughter of one of these families, returns his affections, the life of privilege he seeks actually seems attainable. He feels constrained, though, by his relationship with Roberta, a factory girl, who becomes pregnant before he can work up the nerve to break up with her. Pressured by her to marry, Clyde again attempts to flee from responsibility, again with disastrous results. Though he cannot go through with his plan to murder Roberta and make it look like an accidental drowning, when the boat they are in tips over, Clyde swims away. Dreiser leaves unanswered the question of whether he could have saved Roberta, or if he is guilty of murder.

In book 3 the focus of the novel shifts from the tragedy on the lake to the consequences of it. After a brief flight, Clyde is captured and tried for Roberta's murder. In court, a nexus of socio-political forces prevail to determine his fate. The prosecutor, who is running for office, needs a conviction to enhance his political career. The media coverage of the trial whips up public sentiment against Clyde. His defense is hampered by the poor judgment of his lawyer, who mounts an unconvincing insanity defense and is clearly indifferent to his client's fate. Clyde's subsequent conviction is a foregone conclusion given the combination of social, political, and legal forces arrayed against him.

In prison Clyde is little more than a cog in the vast machinery of the institution. The impersonal nature of life behind bars is counterpointed by Dreiser's effective use of Clyde's more personal, intimate point of view, which dramatizes his fears and hopes for a last-minute acquittal or stay of execution. As his terror grows, he is again torn between the possibility of religious redemption and his desire to be free, between his faith and his doubt. This personal point of view enlists the reader's empathy by humanizing the less-than-sympathetic aspects of Clyde's character. He recalls the early events of his life and the flawed characters of those who influenced his destiny, from the impractical (if not hypocritical) evangelicalism of his parents to the negligence of his defense attorney. Although he embraces the promise of salvation offered by the prison chaplain, he goes to his execution still plagued by doubt.

Discussion Questions

1. Explain the significance of the title of the novel with respect to Clyde. In what ways is his fate tragic? In what ways is his story typically American?

2. How does Clyde's "given nature" exert a deterministic influence on his fate? What external forces exert a similarly deterministic influence?

3. Imagine that you are Clyde's attorney for his murder trial. What defense would you offer on his behalf?

—*Stephen Brown and Charles Brower*

THE FINANCIER
(New York & London: Harper, 1912; revised edition, New York: Boni & Liveright, 1927)

THE TITAN
(New York: John Lane, 1914)

AILEEN BUTLER

Aileen Butler is the second wife of Frank Cowperwood, the hero of Theodore Dreiser's "trilogy of desire," which comprises the novels *The Financier, The Titan,* and *The Stoic.* In the course of the first two books, Cowperwood rises to great wealth, loses his money, is imprisoned, is set free, recovers his fortune, and becomes even wealthier, relocating from Philadelphia to Chicago and then to New York. When he first meets Aileen, he is already married to Lillian Semple. The daughter of Cowperwood's business partner, Edward Butler, Aileen is first seen as an object of pure desire: initially, she is not named; she is a "red cheeked maiden . . . a bright, healthy, bounding girl of fifteen or sixteen." With unconscious lust Cowperwood thinks of her as "all vitality," in tacit comparison to Lillian, who is inert and distinctly aged.

The Financier slowly reveals Aileen's qualities as Cowperwood comes to appreciate them. By the time she is eighteen, she is said to have "intelligence of a raw, crude order," and, more crucially for Cowperwood, "she was chronically interested in men." Her high sexual drive matches Cowperwood's. He visits her at her parents' house, where she plays the piano; her hand touching Cowperwood's when they part gives "an electric shock." Two pages later he kisses her, and she admits that she loves him. She is as subject to "chemic" reactions, Dreiser's pseudoscientific, impersonal understanding of sexual attraction, as is Cowperwood. "She was drawn as planets are drawn to their sun."

Aileen is fiercely protective of her love. She deceives her father, who would disapprove, while falling more deeply in love, as her passionate nature dictates. Aileen at that time has no sense of "that ultimate yielding"—sex itself—but accedes willingly to what Cowperwood wants. They do not consummate their relationship until Cowperwood rents a house on North Tenth Street in Philadelphia for Aileen. They are soon spotted together. When an anonymous letter warns Butler about Aileen's "running around" with Cowperwood, Aileen lies to shield him.

Fidelity is another of Aileen's traits. When Cowperwood's business dealings fail, she remains true. "I do hope you don't fail! But it doesn't make any difference, dear, between you and me, whatever happens, does it?" Without being happy about the existence of Cowperwood's wife, she remains unaffected by moral considerations. The obstacle of Lillian may even intensify her devotion: "Her love was unjust, illegal, outlawed; but it was love just the same and had much of the fiery daring

of the outcast from justice." Like many young lovers, Aileen sees her love as something wholly beyond anyone else's experience. When Butler traces Aileen's activities by using detectives and confronts her, Aileen, in classic fashion, feels "her father just did not understand. He did not know what love was. Unquestionably he had never loved as she had."

Aileen is the romantic heroine of *The Financier*. In a sense already Cowperwood's wife, she (as well as Lillian) sends him gifts in prison. The most striking final view of Aileen in *The Financier* is of her crying and kissing Cowperwood as he is about to go to jail. She is ruled by love with the same amorality that rules Cowperwood in his business dealings: "Law—nonsense! People—they were brutes, devils, enemies, hounds!" Matching Aileen's desperation and intensity is Lillian's refusal to grant Cowperwood a divorce. Where Lillian is fueled by selfish rectitude, however, Aileen is driven by passion.

Her story in *The Titan*, the succeeding novel, traces a declining arc. Browbeaten into granting the divorce she had previously refused, Lillian thinks of Aileen as "wretched, vain, empty-headed, ungodly," but the opening chapters show Aileen, after she and Cowperwood are married, en route to Illinois, enthusiastically and adoringly in love with her husband. She is, however, socially unsure of herself. Additionally, she is not yet aware of the realities she will confront when her past history as Cowperwood's mistress is revealed.

Her inexperience is the first challenge that Aileen faces. It is a central one as Cowperwood attempts to make his way into society in Chicago. Not having been brought up in an upper-class social setting, she lacks assuredness and requires Cowperwood's mastery to succeed: "She never quite so much dominated a situation as she permitted it to dominate her." However, even more consequential than her ineptness is the scandal of their past, which results in the Cowperwoods being forced out of the society to which they aspired. When this past is revealed, they are ostracized.

By a "sentimental" but not romantic attachment to acquaintances of Cowperwood's, Aileen brings on their marital crisis. She unconsciously furthers the first of his affairs that doom the marriage. Equally passionate in revenge, Aileen becomes victim to suspiciousness and rage. Still proud, still in love with her husband, she transforms, under the hurt of betrayal, into a vengeful vixen, physically attacking her husband's first mistress. Although Cowperwood's business affairs prosper, his marriage fails. Aileen changes from a fresh, romantic woman into a "gloomy, remote, weary" one. Wearily, too, she comes to accept Cowperwood's philandering as other affairs follow, but the damage is fatal to her self-esteem. She realizes that "he was too passionate, too radiant, too individual and complex to belong to any one individual alone."

She takes vengeance by finding a lover for herself, Lynde Polk, whose manner is like Cowperwood's. Although Polk has to force his attentions on her, after he does so, she tells Cowperwood that "I'm his mistress." Cowperwood sees through her, recognizing that she is still in love with him and in desperation is trying to hurt him.

As their marriage disintegrates, Aileen shows a previously unrevealed capacity for coarseness. Finding that Cowerwood is again seeking the young women to whom he is naturally drawn, she calls for an actor she had known and indulges in an "orgy, in which wine, bestiality, mutual recrimination and despair were involved." When Cowperwood confronts her, she tries halfheartedly to kill herself. He realizes her "histrionic" nature and knows that if he leaves her bereft and in despair—as he does—she will not commit suicide. Her life, however, is essentially over; she has come full circle from triumphant beloved to scorned reject.

Discussion Questions

1. Explain how Aileen's lack of social ease proceeds from her background. Why are social graces more important to her in Chicago than in Philadelphia?

2. Aileen's story could be the basis of a novel in itself. Why does Dreiser center *The Financier* and *The Titan* on Cowperwood when Aileen is a more dramatically exciting character?

3. Do you dislike Cowperwood for his unfaithfulness? How is his behavior to Aileen of a piece with his business dealings? To what extent do you think Aileen understands this point?

4. Do *The Financier* and *The Titan* present Aileen as a more sympathetic character than Cowperwood's other wives? What qualities does Aileen have in common with Lillian, if any? Does Cowperwood's relationship with Berenice Fleming at the end of *The Titan* reenact his relationship with Aileen in *The Financier*? What differences are there, if any?

—*Roger Lathbury*

FRANK COWPERWOOD

Frank Cowperwood is the protagonist in Theodore Dreiser's novels *The Financier* (1912), *The Titan* (1914), and *The Stoic* (1947). His career in Philadelphia—from clerk to bank broker to stock manipulator, through prison and then back to respectability, to grain and stock speculator and philanthropist, and finally, after business, to philosopher—is based on the life of an historical figure, Charles Tyson Yerkes. Yerkes's career and Cowperwood's are examples of the rags-to-riches story popularized early by Benjamin Franklin and formulaically by Horatio Alger in his extended series of boy's books (beginning with *Ragged Dick,* 1868). Cowperwood's story subverts this myth, however, since rather than by steadfast probity, his success comes from his natural magnetism and ruthlessness combined with intelligence and cold-hearted, illegal manipulation.

Cowperwood's relentless pursuit of power is more than narcissism or trivial selfishness. It emanates from an impersonal philosophy of life. This perspective is introduced in the opening chapter of *The Financier,* when, as an inquisitive boy of ten, Cowperwood watches over the course of several days a battle played out in an aquarium between a lobster and a squid. The former slowly eats the latter. "That's the way it has to be, I guess," Cowperwood thinks to himself. "Things lived on each other. . . . What lived on lobsters? Men, of course!" And men, he concludes, live on other men.

This Darwinesque philosophy of survival of the fittest is the guiding principle of Cowperwood's life. It extends to every facet of his existence—most naturally, to business and commerce. Even early in his quest for "wealth, prestige, [and] dominance," he is willing to leave one job suddenly to take a more remunerative one. More imaginative than his father, as a young man he quickly sees that he can earn more money dealing in contracts rather than in goods, so he abruptly leaves his position as a "grain commission man" and switches to "straight-out brokerage."

Survival of the fittest applies to his personal relations as well. In *The Financier* and, less insistently, in *The Titan,* Dreiser argues that power is also the foundation of interpersonal connections. For the young Cowperwood, power equates to sex. His conquest of women complements his business prowess. *The Financier* lists his affairs in a crescendo of complexity, from his interest at age thirteen in Patience Barlow to his early patronage of "the bagnio." Cowperwood desires only attractive, passionate women, about whom his judgment is "temperamental rather than intellectual." He refuses to believe in self-sacrificing women, and prefers to think of women as "frankly self-interested."

Thus, Cowperwood's understanding of existence is totally amoral. Even after he marries a settled older woman, he asks himself, "Was a man entitled to only one wife?" There is nothing to stop him when he finds the sixteen-year-old daughter of one of his business partners, Edward Butler, "all vitality"; he has the right to her since "whether we will or not, theory or no theory, the basic facts of chemistry and physics remain."

Cowperwood is not uniformly successful in his machinations. He is as subject to the randomness and cruelty of outside forces as others are subject to him; the businessmen in association with whom he controls a construction deal are as ready to use him as he is to use them. And larger forces can use everyone. The 1871 fire in Chicago sets up a chain of events that exposes Cowperwood's dealings, although had he been able to persuade his tool, George Stener, to act as immorally as he has acted, his theft of public funds would not have been manifest. As it turns out, short of money and denied loans for several reasons, including exposure of his flirtation with the daughter of one of his partners, Cowperwood loses everything. He gains in stature in the novel, however, because he does not complain. He understands these events as proceeding from the same amoral laws that have justified his previous success.

As a character Cowperwood does not alter throughout the course of *The Financier.* The conclusion of the novel dramatizes this point. Sent to prison by a jury acting "like those scientifically demonstrated atoms of a crystal," he manages to buy as many favors as he can and sets about explaining to his wife, Lillian, that he wants a divorce. When he tells his new love's father of his intentions to marry his daughter, Butler realizes that "he was whipped, literally beaten at his own game," and that Cowperwood's "incarceration had not put him in the least awe." In a monetary panic shortly after his release, Cowperwood keeps calm—as his philosophy enables him to do—and is able to trade shrewdly and recoup the losses he had suffered before his imprisonment.

Nor does Cowperwood's essential nature change in the sequel to *The Financier, The Titan.* His second marriage goes the way of his first as Cowperwood, even wealthier than in *The Financier,* tries to enter Chicago society with his second wife. In line with this goal of buying his way into social position, he becomes a philanthropist. He gives paintings and an observatory to a university, as did his prototype, Yerkes, to the University of Chicago. However, his efforts prove unsuccessful. Society lives under a hypocritical veil of morality.

As ever, Cowperwood pursues other women. He cannot be manipulated by someone less powerful; his wife, Aileen, can only retaliate in kind by having affairs with other men. At the close of *The Titan,* Cowperwood is still moving up the social ladder. He relocates to New York—a move that seems almost compulsory in Dreiser's fiction—where he falls in love with the daughter of a woman who has managed a brothel. This much younger woman becomes his new inamorata. Although his Chicago cronies oust Cowperwood from business, by that point he is too wealthy for it to matter much, and he travels to Europe with his new love.

In *The Stoic,* the last Cowperwood novel, Dreiser tries to present Cowperwood as drawn to Eastern philosophy as an answer to relentless materialism. However, Cowperwood's vision is so strongly presented in *The Financier* and *The Titan* that even in a 1947 review of *The Stoic,* the novelist Nelson Algren could only harken back to the memorable figure of the first two novels: "Cowperwood's conditions were those of America's economic frontiers at the turn of the century, when the great American dream was to acquire, each man for himself, as much of the world's goods as could possibly be labeled, in one man's lifetime, with one's own name. Cowperwood was peculiarly fitted to realize such a dream: there were almost no restrictions, legal or ethical, to hinder his titanic vitality; and his cunning was matched only by his drive for power."

Discussion Questions

1. How does Frank Cowperwood understand those ideas and emotions usually seen as transcendent—above material explanation: love, hope, justice, freedom, art?

2. Why does Cowperwood marry Lillian Semple when clearly he is attracted to women younger than he is? Is he always honest in his dealing with Lillian? With Aileen? How does Cowperwood understand the concept of "honesty"?

3. The Declaration of Independence asserts that among the "inalienable rights" of man are "life, liberty and the pursuit of happiness." Is Frank Cowperwood in his pursuit of these qualities an ideal American? How does the novel make him prototypical? Is Cowperwood ever happy? When and why (or why not)?

4. How does Berenice Fleming in *The Stoic* complement the idea of Eastern thought? Has Cowperwood finally changed in that novel?

—*Roger Lathbury*

THE "GENIUS"
(New York: John Lane, 1915)

ANGELA BLUE

Angela Blue is an old-fashioned wife who is abandoned by her unconventional husband in Theodore Dreiser's 1915 novel, *The "Genius."* Angela comes from the small Midwestern town of Blackwood. She works as a schoolteacher before meeting the man she marries, Eugene Witla. She lives according to what were already outmoded ideals of wifehood and matrimony, believing she exists only to cook and clean for him. He does not live according to the same conventions, however, but pursues an unconventional aesthetic as he becomes a painter and freely pursues other women who take his fancy before and during his marriage. Theirs is forever an unhappy union, as Dreiser shows what happens when married partners look at one another and imagine godlike ideals of romanticism and artistry, and when they do not pause to consider the practical concerns of living together throughout their everyday lives.

Imagined ideals overshadow such practical considerations during their courtship. To Eugene, Angela is a sort of "pure" pastoral maiden, a lovely girl existing in a kind of fairy-tale rural setting of Blackwood. Her family, including her father, Jotham Blue, embodies a folksy image for Eugene that seems more idealized than realistic. To Angela, in turn, Eugene seems a kind of god, a "genius," gifted to rise above his fellow men. It falls to her younger sister, Marietta, to coach Angela on what to wear and how to attract his interest. Even among her siblings, she seems beautiful and attractive but diffident and self-effacing. She seems attached to an older ethic of meek womanhood instead of a progressive spirit of sexual equality. She does not know Eugene's record of dating other women, matching wits with assertive women sculptors and painters who defy convention, and observing nude female models as he supposedly works to perfect his drawing and painting technique. Indeed, she does not know ahead of time what life will be like as an unconventional artist's wife.

Once she is in her husband's shadow, she works to support Eugene through success and failure, subordinating herself to him and only gradually showing her power to resist him. She cannot match the female artists who make bold statements of their own but cooks for Eugene and cleans for him, even standing and smiling in his studio as important art dealers examine his work. He suffers from a nervous illness that prevents him from painting and defeats him for several consecutive years, so she scrimps and saves. When she finds love letters he had written to others and notes that his past amours had written to him, she reads every word, piecing together torn scraps of letters and jealously imagining Eugene's past love life. When he hides the truth, she lashes out in anger, and he is surprised when this side of her personality emerges. When he pursues an artist's life, holding himself to be a genius above the common run of men, he resents her petty presence. He seems disappointed that she fades as his ideal, cannot share his unconventional views on relationships, nor lead a life of her own.

In the last third of Dreiser's novel, when Suzanne Dale comes into Eugene's life, circumstances become increasingly cruel to Angela. Suzanne, twenty years younger than Eugene, once again recaptures his ideal, and Eugene is ready to forget his marriage with Angela and once again impulsively chase after a fairy-tale romance. Angela falls back upon her anger to fight for Eugene and to pose as the wronged wife who could ruin his financial interests. She also reveals she is pregnant with Eugene's baby and uses her condition to convince Eugene to leave Suzanne. When Eugene claims Angela is lying about her pregnancy, Dreiser makes Eugene's self-absorption apparent. Angela is left suicidal, and Eugene all but abandons his pregnant wife.

The novel assigns some of the blame for Eugene's suffering and defeat to Angela, or more generally to womanhood, in terms of the sexual mores of America in 1915. Although common American attitudes toward family planning and birth control in 1915 severely limit Angela's options, Eugene still sees her pregnancy as an attempted trick to keep him. In Dreiser's imagined world of literary naturalism, in which ill-luck and indifferent fate run counter to man's aspirations to become an individual, men such as Eugene fight for recognition as "geniuses," but women such as Angela seem to conspire with fate and bad luck to defeat them. (Dreiser dramatized this theme to an even greater extent in his 1925 novel *An American Tragedy.*) Women's supposed biological destiny to bear children, Angela's conventional ideals as an old-fashioned wife, and widely held mores that insist that a man remain with his wife rather than chase young feminine "ideals" such as Suzanne all check Eugene's potential to realize his "genius" and to live the unconventional life of a defiant artist. Only at the end of the novel, when it is too late to have a happy union with Angela or to return to his artistic career, does Eugene find consolation in studying Christian Science and in raising a child. Dreiser has the baby share the heroine's name, calling her Angela Jr., but he leaves the impression that the family's next generation will not share Angela's tragic fate.

Discussion Questions

1. In reading this novel, did you find yourself feeling pity for Angela, as Eugene seems to abandon her, or feeling frustrated with her, as she fails to stick up for herself or develop her own personality apart from Eugene's? What particular aspects of Dreiser's storyline or of Angela's character have led you to feel this way about her?

2. What is your view of Angela's pregnancy, and of her way of revealing her condition to her husband, in the last portion of the novel? Are her actions here in keeping with her character, as Dreiser has established it, or do they reveal a new, unanticipated side to Angela's personality?

3. In what ways does Eugene and Angela's marriage resemble other unhappy unions in contemporary American literature, such as Tom and Daisy Buchanan in *The Great Gatsby* or Ethan and Zenobia Frome in *Ethan Frome?*

—*Adam Sonstegard*

EUGENE WITLA

Eugene Witla is a man obsessed with proving his distinction as an artist in Theodore Dreiser's 1915 novel, *The "Genius."* The quotation marks in the title of the novel cast doubt on him. As a supposed or so-called genius, Eugene has to prove whether he has the instinctive talent and natural impulses that separate truly gifted artists from common men and women. He readily excels at visual arts, from an unsparing realism in his oil paintings, to a knack for rendering illustrations for magazines, to a gift for designing eye-catching advertisements. His personality also propels him through various trades, including an apprenticeship in newspaper publishing, engagements in day labor and manual construction, and management of a major publishing house's art department. But "genius" in Eugene's case also implies a haughty bearing and a condescending attitude toward others. He thinks it entitles him to a kind of superiority, a license with which he can flout accepted convention and forge his own set of ethics. *The "Genius"* is Dreiser's lengthy record of Eugene's attempts to live according to the ideals of his art rather than the accepted mores of his fellow men.

Eugene recognizes and pursues artistic ideals that mirror Dreiser's aesthetics. After a youth in rural Alexandria, Illinois, he pursues training in art in Chicago, in New York, and eventually in Paris. Eugene works within the "ashcan" school of realism, which presented ordinary, mundane objects instead of showcasing conventionally beautiful or exalted images. "Eugene's pictures," one passage reads, "stood forth in all their rawness and reality—almost as vigorous as life itself." On his canvases "he seemed to lay on his details with bitter lack of consideration. Like a slavedriver lashing a slave he spared no shade of his cutting brush." His pitiless gaze mimics in painting what Dreiser does in prose: both the author and the character present vibrant pictures of life, which may not always be decent or pleasing but always reflect life itself. Dreiser's work of American literary realism, aiming for poignant, ordinary detail instead of romantic ideals, fictionalizes the life of a similarly minded American artistic realist; Eugene reflects Dreiser's own ideas about art and "real life." Like Eugene, the author of the novel hailed from the American Midwest, pioneered an unflinching realism in his artistic depiction of life, and tried to live outside of the more conventional definitions of marriage of his era. Dreiser pursued a series of affairs while married to Sallie Dreiser and suffered from a kind of neurasthenia that—again, like the hero of *"The Genius"*—sometimes kept him from producing his best work. It is not difficult to interpret Eugene as Dreiser's fictional projection of his own ambitions for achieving realism in art, and his hopes for a kind of personal regeneration from pain and nervousness, that he believed could come from cathartic artistic creation.

Eugene's artistic ideas lead him to make impulsive, unconventional choices for his career, his health, and his love life. His artistic apprenticeship includes painting nude women models, an outrageous activity for the late nineteenth century, when the action of the novel is set (and a reason for censorship of the novel when it was published in 1915). His circle of acquaintances includes outspoken and alluring women artists who share his interests and challenge conventional ideas of marriage. But Eugene marries Angela Blue, a former schoolteacher a few years older than himself. She is not an artist like he is but a "pure" rural maiden, who dwells closer to his supposed ideal of romantic perfection. As his wife she supports his efforts and nurtures him through an extended bout of neurasthenia, a nervous disorder that for many years stymies his creativity and destroys his concentration. But she has no life of her own beyond cooking, cleaning Eugene's studio, tending to his things, and smiling brightly beside his portraits when others view them. Eugene as an unconventional artist marries someone so conventional as to be old-fashioned, who initially reflects an artistic ideal but then cannot match wits with her "genius" husband. He soon tires of her; interprets their marriage as his act of giving in or conceding something to her, rather than equally combining his fortunes with hers; and resents her occasional outbursts of anger. When eighteen-year old Suzanne Dale (twenty years younger than Eugene) appears, he is ready to forsake Angela, abandon a successful business career, and break laws surrounding marriage and divorce, all for the impulsive pursuit of the beautiful, impractical ideal Suzanne represents for him. When it looks as though he will attain Suzanne, Dreiser narrates, "nature has intended this as the crowning event of his life. Life recognized him as a genius—the fates—it was heaping posies in his lap, laying a crown of victory upon his brow." He interprets this brief success in love as proof of his genius, his entitlement to a life of art, lived according to his impulses and applauded by the universe. He pursues an aesthetic of idealized perfection in his art, above and beyond ordinary life, while never adjusting his actual life to complement the lives of anyone around him. Even Christian Science, with which he consoles himself after losing Angela, Suzanne, and his artistic career, seems an impulsive and impractical philosophy.

Eugene's history registers a certain disappointment that artists cannot live according to their ideals and moods and still collaborate successfully with fellow men. It reflects the literary realists' view of men who forge their own lives but find themselves turned into machines by circumstances or battered by ill-luck or indifferent fate. It shows that Dreiser did not design Eugene as hero whom all would find to be likeable, but as a likely portrait of a self-absorbed artist who is only nominally married to his wife and more truly married to his career and his artistic ideals.

Discussion Questions

1. What lessons, if any, can aspiring artists of today learn from Eugene's example, in terms of how to excel at the business of art, the management of a career, or the life and character of a successful artist?

2. If readers initially find themselves supporting Eugene and wishing to see him excel as an artist, at what point in the novel (if at all) do they turn against him, suspecting that he might have gone too far or hurt others too much? What makes this particular moment a turning point?

3. What does Eugene have in common with other Dreiser protagonists—such as Hurstwood in *Sister Carrie,* Frank Cowperwood and Clyde Griffiths in *An American Tragedy*—who often make choices that run against conventional ideas of relationships and marriage?

—*Adam Sonstegard*

ᡣᡩ

JENNIE GERHARDT
(New York & London: Harper, 1911)

JENNIE GERHARDT

Jennie Gerhardt is the title character in Theodore Dreiser's second novel, begun almost immediately after he finished *Sister Carrie* but not published until eleven years later. Her career partly parallels that of his previous heroine, but there are important differences between them. Unlike Carrie Meeber, who drifts with circumstances and who enters into liaisons primarily because she sees that the men will provide a way out of poverty for her, Jennie Gerhardt loves the two men with whom she cohabits. Although not ambitious, as Dreiser's males are, Jennie, of the working class, is a willing worker; and unlike Carrie, she approaches life directly. "What scrubbing, baking, errand-running, and nursing there had to do she did. No one had ever heard her rudely complain, though she often thought of the hardness of her lot. She knew that there were other girls whose lives were infinitely freer and fuller, but, it never occurred to her to be meanly envious."

This "daughter of poverty" and unabashed paragon of sweetness accompanies her mother to Columbus, Ohio, to work in a hotel. There she unwittingly strikes the fancy of Senator George Brander, who ingratiates himself with the Gerhardt family. After Jennie has come to love him and to see him as a combination of protector and father—her father being as rigidly religious as Dreiser's own father—he impregnates her, in their single act of sexual intercourse. Brander's own feelings are a mixture of devotion to her and guilt, whereas throughout the story, Jennie, more innocent than Carrie, has no sense of doing anything wrong. There is gossip, and her father disapproves sternly of her conduct, as do others; Jennie, however, like Carrie, is inner-directed. "She could not be readily corrupted by the world's selfish lessons on how to preserve oneself from the evil to come." Although at first she seems a figure in a stock melodrama—the poor girl seduced by the rich older man—Jennie is actually an independent woman who rejects the false or easy morality of the world around her.

This inherent independence and her ability to develop account for Jennie's increased stature and complexity in the last two-thirds of the novel. Jennie takes on various roles in ever-widening circumstances. The first of these is in Cleveland, in the Bracebridge household; it is a sophisticated milieu in which the mistress can speak in Wildean epigrams ("I despise lack of taste; it is the worst crime"). Dreiser describes Jennie's days there as "of a broadening character." In this more worldly menage she meets Lester Kane, "the son of a wholesale carriage builder of great trade distinction." The last two-thirds of the novel are devoted to her growing character as she continues her relationship with him.

Like Senator Brander, Lester is sexually attracted to Jennie, but when she surrenders to him, she is not naive as she was before. Although for a while she has to conceal the existence of her daughter, Vesta, she never conceals her strong sexual nature. When Lester kisses her, "something tremendously vital and insistent was speaking to her." The two of them are entirely suited to each other. For Jennie, love is a supreme fulfillment; it leads to her emotional growth: "She was his natural affinity, though he did not know it—the one woman who answered somehow the biggest need of his nature."

Her self-assurance soon permits her to reveal to Lester the existence of her daughter and, notwithstanding, to preserve their relationship. She grows mentally as well, becoming consciously independent of the confinements of her father's Lutheranism. "She had no particular objection to the church, but she no longer depended upon its teachings as a guide in the affairs of life. Why should she?" She becomes an original thinker through her irregular union with Lester, arriving at a revolutionary conception of relations that startles her more formally educated consort: "Some women think differently, I know, but a man and a woman ought to want to live together, or they ought not—don't you think? It doesn't make so much difference if a man goes off for a little while—just so long as he doesn't stay—if he wants to come back at all." Finally, she grows culturally, when she travels abroad with Lester to Europe and Egypt.

America at the turn of the century was not ready to accommodate these views. Jennie suffers from the narrowness of her neighbors. When Lester buys them a house in Chicago and she receives social callers, the impropriety of their union comes out; she is painfully ostracized. The Kane family ostracizes her as well. A favored son, Lester is the least traditional Kane and the only one to stand up for Jennie; his father and brother, more conventional, cannot accept her because of her class and because her relationship with Lester is not formally sanctioned. Brief encounters between Jennie and the Kanes distress her and intensify the rift. These events do not change Jennie.

Her stature gains when Archibald Kane writes a will in which Lester's inheritance depends upon his son's giving up his mistress. Jennie decides that she and Lester must separate. She sees that if he keeps on with her, Lester cannot realize the possibilities of his life. This is a selfless, heroic act, for she really wants him to stay: "she was in a quandary, hurt, bleeding, but for once in her life, determined." She even has to act for him, for she perceives that he is indecisive. As a consequence, she lives the rest of her life in the diminished circumstances that she has imposed on herself. Her daughter dies. Lester marries a conventional wealthy woman whom he had known before, yet Jennie does not waver in her feelings.

Dramatically and thematically, Jennie Gerhardt is the center of the novel. While his wife is away, Lester, dying, calls for Jennie. He tells her that he loved her before and "I love you now." She will not accept guilt from him: "It's all right. It doesn't make any difference. You have been good to me." In her understanding of fate and the way life works out, she proves herself grand. Foreseeing the fate that awaits her ("Days and days in endless reiteration, and then—?"), the former working-class girl proves herself superior not just to working-class life but to existence itself, which she apprehends in comprehensive, mature terms.

Discussion Questions

1. Dreiser writes of Sister Carrie that she was "a lone figure in a tossing, thoughtless sea," and in general he views the conditions of life as overmastering the will of human beings. Does *Jennie Gerhardt* support this view? To what extent is Jennie able to work her will on her circumstances? Is she a tragic figure or does she not achieve that stature? Why?

2. What do Jennie's actions toward her siblings reveal about her?

3. Compare the attitudes of Jennie toward women, especially her mother, with whom she interacts and her attitudes toward men. What accounts for the difference between them? Solidarity? Sex? Inherent understanding?

4. Examine the roles of class and money in Jennie's giving of herself to Senator Brander and Lester Kane. How do these two affect Jennie's actions at Lester's funeral? How does the funeral tie together the elemental components of Jennie's life and thus make a satisfactory conclusion to the novel?

5. If you have read Thomas Hardy's *Tess of the d'Urbervilles*, compare Jennie to Tess.

—*Roger Lathbury*

LESTER KANE

Lester Kane is one of the lovers of the title character in Theodore Dreiser's *Jennie Gerhardt* (1911). The "son of a wholesale carriage builder of great trade distinction" from Cincinnati, Kane is not introduced until chapter 16 of the novel. He is a friend of the Bracebridges, wealthy people in whose house Jennie is employed as a lady's maid. Unmarried, as is

Jennie's previous lover, Senator George Brander, Lester is older than she. He is "superior to Jennie in wealth, education, and social position" but senses immediately that "there was that about her which suggested the luxury of love."

He is not inexperienced with women, but he does not see Jennie's situation clearly at first, as she conceals that she has had a child by the senator. He yearns for love. "The innocence and unsophistication of younger ideals had gone. He wanted the comfort of feminine companionship, but he was more and more disinclined to give up his personal liberty in order to obtain it." The two poles, of being drawn toward Jennie and of not being willing to commit himself totally, define Lester's connection to the heroine. The book does not judge this refusal of commitment, whatever limitations it puts upon Lester's life, nor does it criticize Lester. Dreiser is not a romantic; Lester is presented sympathetically.

He is pointedly contrasted to his father and to his brother, Robert. The father is the self-made man, the one who rose, with his wife, from poverty; he is more "generous" and "forceful" than his sons. Four years older than Lester, Robert represents success and hardness, the qualities necessary to dominate in commerce. At the same time, he opposes Lester's more open stance on social behavior: "Never overstepping the strict boundaries of legal righteousness, he was neither warm-hearted nor generous—in fact, he would turn any trick which could be speciously, or at best necessitously, recommended to his conscience. How he reasoned Lester did not know—he could not follow the ramifications of a logic which could combine hard business tactics with moral rigidity, but somehow his brother managed to do it."

Lester, by contrast, is "softer, more human, more good-natured about everything." This fundamental decency is both a redeeming quality and a defect. It makes Lester into a more attractive figure than his brother because he lacks Robert's rigidity of judgment; he is human, understanding, and empathetic whereas the other is convention-bound, judgmental, and cold. He is generous and no longer believes in the superiority of class. His sexual drive is keen. His ability to play with Vesta, Jennie's daughter, once he is aware of her existence, is charming: "He liked to invert the

so-called facts of life, to propound its paradoxes, and watch how the child's budding mind took them."

At the base of Lester's attitudes is a distrust in ultimate value. "Life was not proved to him. Not a single idea of his, unless it were the need of being honest, was finally settled." Therefore, if his softness renders him an admirable and attractive mate for Jennie, it also prevents him from committing to her and marrying her. When Jennie writes him a letter intending to leave him and he refuses her, it is, from a business perspective, a "big mistake." The upshot is that this well-meaning man manages to lose both the woman he should have married and the business as well.

Environment triumphs, as it always does in the work of Dreiser. In his will, old Archibald Kane precludes Lester from sharing in most of the family money unless he gives up Jennie. Having been effectively forced out of his father's carriage business and a failure in his real-estate ventures, he is compelled to choose between Jennie and Letty Green, once a would-be lover and now a rich widow. She is "Lester's natural mate, so far as birth, breeding, and position went." Letty tells Lester that she will always love him and that he "can't just drift." Jenny, for her part, magnanimously insists that he accept her leaving. After agreeing and buying her a modest house, Lester marries Letty, but it is a diminishment of the man. He recoups his social position, and his business affairs improve; the novel lists many companies on which he sits on the board of directors. Although he is never again associated with the United Carriage Company, he effects an uneasy, forced, and partial reconciliation with his brother. The Lester Kanes move permanently to New York—a relocation that symbolizes his commitment to the world of high finance and high society.

Lester pays a personal price for his worldly success, however. He thinks of Jennie from time to time and realizes that he has made "a sacrifice of the virtues . . . to policy." He sublimates his physical drives into rich food. He dies at age sixty, on a visit to Chicago, with Jennie called to his side at the end—a martyr to a life lived with insufficient courage.

Discussion Questions

1. Contrast three fathers, or putative fathers, in *Jennie Gerhardt:* old Mr. Gerhardt, Senator Brander,

and Lester Kane. Which seems to you the best father? What are the strengths and limitations of each in respect to their children? How does Jenny's behavior toward Vesta act as a counterpoint?

2. Examine the philosophy of life of Lester Kane, either implied or stated: what he believes and what he has read (for example, Herbert Spencer). How do the big decisions Kane makes reflect that life? Does it affect his dealings equally in his personal and his business life?

3. Is Robert Kane sympathetically or unsympathetically portrayed? Why—in terms of dramatic strategy and reader sympathy—are so few details mentioned about his family life?

4. Of all the factors that induce Lester Kane to accept Jennie's leaving him, which is the most crucial? Why?

—*Roger Lathbury*

"THE SECOND CHOICE"

Collected in *Free, and Other Stories* (New York: Boni & Liveright, 1918).

SHIRLEY

Shirley is a young woman in Theodore Dreiser's short story "The Second Choice" whose relationship with her suitor, Barton Williams, is interrupted by her infatuation with Arthur Bristow. Though previously content with Barton and with her life generally, Shirley becomes dissatisfied and possessed by a romantic ideal of "true love" after allowing herself to be seduced by Arthur. Under the dual influence of her own unrealistic notions of love and the socially conventional expectations of marriage and children, Shirley comes to see anything less than marriage to Arthur as defeat. In her desire to win Arthur, Shirley increasingly reveals herself to be dishonest, selfish, and manipulative in her treatment of the hardworking, devoted, and patient Barton. Once Arthur loses interest and begins treating her in the same way she has treated Barton, Shirley struggles to reconcile herself to the possibility of a commonplace life with her former suitor. Thus, her self-centered and naive view of romance is strongly challenged by

experience, but the extent of her understanding and personal growth remains uncertain.

Dreiser's frank portrayal of Shirley's character and his refusal to pass moral judgment on her reflect Shirley's double-edged role in the story. Torn between Arthur, whose name means "high" or "noble" and is suggestive of the chivalric King Arthur, and Barton, whose name means "barley farm" and is suggestive of common labor, Shirley simplistically views the two men as polar opposites and fails to appreciate their real natures. Shirley's basic selfishness and lack of emotional maturity, as well as her callous and unethical treatment of Barton, are made to seem less objectionable, however, by the fact that the narrative voice remains close to her own point of view. Hence, Shirley demonstrates the restlessness and yearning of young women whose childishly romantic dreams lead to pain and disappointment when confronted with complex and compromising social realities. Nonetheless, she also exhibits the shallowness and self-absorption that were more common among people than typically had been acknowledged in polite society or romantic fiction of the time.

Realizing that Arthur has left her, Shirley feels "for the first time the shame and pain that comes of deception, the agony of having to relinquish an ideal." Even after experiencing the pain of being left by Arthur, Shirley shows scant concern about her own hurtful and unjust actions toward Barton. Thinking primarily of herself, "the thought of saving her own face by taking up with Barton once more occurred to her, of using him and his affections and faithfulness and dulness [sic] . . . to cover up her own dilemma." Having lured Barton back, Shirley still muses: "To see only Barton, and marry him and live in such a street, have four or five children, forget all her youthful companionships—and all to save her face before her parents, and her future. Why must it be? Should it be, really? She choked and stifled." Thus, "by decision of necessity," Shirley forgoes what might be called choice "A" (ironically also the first letter of "Arthur") for choice "B" (also the first letter of "Barton"). She then rationalizes her choice and wallows in self-pity: "My dreams are too high, that's all. I wanted Arthur, and he wouldn't have me. I don't want Barton, and he crawls at my feet. I'm a failure, that's what's the matter with me." Shirley's final act is to assist her mother by setting the table for dinner, suggesting an acceptance of circumstance and the possible beginnings of maturity.

While Dreiser nowhere comments directly on Shirley, she was a character with personal significance for him insofar as she was based in part on a woman named Lois Zahn, whom he became involved with in Chicago almost twenty years before writing "The Second Choice." Arthur, in turn, is something of an idealized image of Dreiser himself. Like Arthur, Dreiser left Lois after about a year and moved to St. Louis, eventually taking work in Pittsburgh. Like Shirley, Lois wrote Dreiser asking for the return of her letters. That Dreiser was attracted to such a woman only to leave her may help to explain the sympathetic yet not uncritical attitude toward Shirley. This ambiguity helps to reinforce the theme, which she herself has yet to learn, that individuals and relationships are often more complex than they first appear.

In her fixation on a romantic ideal, Shirley is similar to the title character of William Dean Howells's "Editha," published thirteen years prior to "The Second Choice." Whereas Howells was a foremost spokesman for literary realism, which tended to depict the average or commonplace, Dreiser's writings are more representative of the naturalistic movement in literature, which often depicted characters and events considered unpleasant or shocking. Moreover, naturalists tended to emphasize the influence of hereditary and environmental forces on people's thoughts and actions. The closely observed social and psychological details of Shirley's life, as well as the nonjudgmental tone of "The Second Choice," are indicative of the characteristics distinguishing naturalism from Howellsian realism. In her restlessness and existential desperation, Shirley also looks forward to characters created by writers of the Lost Generation.

Discussion Questions

1. How does Shirley compare with Ida Zobel in Dreiser's "Typhoon"?

2. How does Shirley compare with the title character in William Dean Howells's story "Editha"?

3. What seems to be Shirley's attitude toward marriage and why?

4. In what ways do Shirley's acting to help her mother set the dinner table affect your attitude toward her character?

5. What, if anything, has Shirley learned from her experience?

—*Ian F. Roberts*

SISTER CARRIE
(New York: Doubleday, Page, 1900)

CHARLES DROUET

Charles Drouet in Theodore Dreiser's *Sister Carrie* is the good-natured seducer and traveling salesman who becomes Carrie Meeber's first lover in Chicago. In this role he performs a vital service to the plot, liberating Carrie from the bleak world of the Hansons to the "aladdinish" realm of George Hurstwood. By virtue of his reappearance at the end of the novel, Drouet also serves as a yardstick for measuring the changes in Carrie and Hurstwood. As his name suggests, he is a "roué," or seducer. Hurstwood symbolizes the kind of man Drouet wishes to become, though the latter cannot overcome his own limitations in "intellect, taste, and sensitivity to hold a girl like Carrie."

Like Carrie and Hurstwood, Drouet is subjected to a deterministic interplay between internal and external forces. The slums and high society of Chicago and New York City are depicted as equally influential in shaping the desires of Carrie, Drouet, and Hurstwood. Chance similarly intervenes to shape Drouet's career, no less than it does the careers of Carrie and Hurstwood, since it governs his initial meeting with Carrie on the train as well as the critical downtown encounter when he makes her a present of a jacket: a gesture that leads her to become his mistress. Consequently, chance, in tandem with poverty-stricken and glittering urban environments, is one of the external forces that determines the careers of the main characters of the novel.

Though chance and external forces are influential in shaping Drouet's destiny, neither are as critical as his basic nature. Drouet has been likened by critics to a male version of Carrie in that he is driven and his choices determined by an insatiable desire for wealth and beauty; he is drawn like a "merry, unthinking moth to the lamp" of affluent Chicago. As David E. E. Sloane observes, Drouet represents "the superficiality of Carrie's personality," as evidenced by his "bright plaid . . . and glassy patent leather" shoes. He is a monument to "shallowness and a kind of self-serving egoism"—a variation of a stock turn-of-the-century character, "the masher . . . who approaches women boldly," a harmless seducer. Drouet is, as Carrie comes to understand, "a kindly soul, but otherwise defective."

He fulfills a vital function in the plot, serving as an intermediate rung on the "ladder of beauty" that Carrie ascends: one that conveys her from a poverty-stricken rural home and a job in a factory to the world of Hurstwood. For Carrie, Drouet is the "perfect all" she has been dreaming about, a striking contrast with the multiple "lacks" embodied by her poverty-ridden family and the dreary routine of the factory. Drouet's actions are driven by sexual impulses beyond his control, by "chemisms" that course like electromagnetic currents through his blood, and by forces of attraction and repulsion that exert a magnetic influence upon his behavior.

As Sloane observes, Drouet's shallow intellect renders him a "foil for higher natures" such as Hurstwood's and a dupe for opportunists such as Carrie. Dreiser writes that he could be "as deluded by fine clothes as any silly-headed girl." Consequently, Drouet is no less a consumer than Carrie: one who is blinded to reality by the illusory nature of his desires. Drawn to Carrie because of her beauty, his feeble intellect blinds him to her materialistic and opportunistic nature: a nature that will prompt her to drop him for a "bigger fish in the pond when the opportunity presents itself." He is as blind to Hurstwood's nature as he is to Carrie's, and is "no more perceptive in sizing up Hurstwood as a rival than he is in analyzing Carrie as a lover."

Drouet mirrors Carrie in another respect as well. At the end, he is "but slightly changed . . . the old butterfly was as light on the wing as ever." Though

"heavier in girth," as Sloane aptly observes, "he is neither deeper in understanding nor shallower in sympathy . . . his egotism prevents him from insight." Drouet's reappearance at the end of the novel functions like a measuring device to assess the progress (or lack thereof) of Carrie's and Hurstwood's lives, as well as his own.

Discussion Questions

1. What service does Charles Drouet perform for the plot of *Sister Carrie*?

2. What role does chance play in shaping the career of Drouet?

3. What aspects of Drouet's given nature help determine his career?

4. How is Drouet a "mirror" to Carrie Meeber and a "foil" (contrast) to George Hurstwood?

—*Stephen G. Brown*

GEORGE HURSTWOOD

George Hurstwood, the main male character in Theodore Dreiser's *Sister Carrie*, is "the suave and socially prominent saloon manager" at Fitzgerald and Moy's who succeeds Charles Drouet as Carrie Meeber's lover. Hurstwood provides a vital service to the plot, dramatizing the destructive effects of deterministic forces. His fate is the result of the interplay between his own nature and the external forces that frustrate his desires and precipitate a decline in fortunes that ends in catastrophe for him. An analysis of Hurstwood's nature, the forces that impinge upon him, and Dreiser's imagery reveal that his destiny is determined by circumstances beyond his control.

Hurstwood is driven by desires for wealth and beauty, desires that bring him into conflict with his sense of duty in general and with his duties as husband and father in particular. He is helpless to stem the force of these passions and instincts, which Dreiser represents as "katastates" that poison the body and undermine health, which course through the body with the deterministic force of "chemisms" and magnetic currents, as if Hurstwood is no more than an "iron filing" subject to the forces of attraction. Like Carrie and Clyde Griffiths, Hurstwood has a fascination with material wealth and physical beauty that he is powerless to resist. Like Carrie, he is drawn to light, color, and wealth and repulsed by shadow, drabness, and poverty. These sexual and material desires exert an influence on Hurstwood's destiny when they interact with yet another fatal trait: his vacillation at critical moments. This characteristic is most evident in the scene that becomes the turning point of his life: when he is burglarizing his employer's safe.

Hurstwood is incapacitated by a conflict between desire and fear: between desire for a girl and fear of the consequences of that desire. On the brink of committing a crime, he is paralyzed by a fatal vacillation. Chance intervenes to resolve his vacillation, sealing his fate. The locus of force, until now equally divided between external and internal forces, shifts to the universe of external forces, embodied in environments and institutions that are indifferent or hostile to Hurstwood's desires.

From this point on, Hurstwood is "beaten down by chance." The dwindling of his money precipitates the decline in his health. His decline in status leads to a decline in his appearance. Even the morbid depression that ensues is depicted as the effect of deterministic causes: of a chemical reaction in the blood, producing toxins that lead to his physical deterioration. As Dreiser observes, "to these, Hurstwood was subject." This social, moral, and intellectual decline is painstakingly documented by Dreiser.

The final sequence of theft-elopement-suicide evidences the extent to which Hurstwood has suffered as a result of the interplay between his nature, chance, and the environment. "He blows money he cannot spare on dinners, booze, and poker" to hide his shame, Dreiser reports. On his final night, Hurstwood is reduced to huddling in the snow outside a flophouse, as one of the "dumb brutes." Yet, even his suicide is redemptive insofar as it restores to him a measure of agency. In contradistinction to the theft, which was more the result of chance than free will, Hurstwood decides to take his own life, finally (if ironically) freeing himself from the control of deterministic forces. Dreiser does not blame Hurstwood for his infidelities, his crime, or his suicide. These incidents are instead attributed to forces embodied in the city and economy, acting in consort with inward forces associated with sexual drives and desires for beauty and wealth, for which the environment provides the fatal stimulus. The characters are mere animals who dream beyond their limitations—and suffer the consequences of those dreams and limitations.

Discussion Questions

1. Compare and/or contrast Hurstwood's career with that one or more of the following: Carrie, Clyde Griffiths from Dreiser's *An American Tragedy*, or Maggie Johnson from Stephen Crane's *Maggie: A Girl of the Streets*.

2. Assess the deterministic influence of chance upon Hurstwood and Carrie's fates.

3. How might Hurstwood's fate be viewed as a critique of the American Dream?

—*Stephen G. Brown*

CARRIE MEEBER

Carrie Meeber, the title character in Theodore Dreiser's *Sister Carrie*, enters Chicago as a small-town girl attracted by the "alladdinish" allure of the city, which promises escape from the dreary existence she leads working in a shoe factory and living with her sister's family. Suiting her virtue to the circumstances, she ascends the social ladder of lovers, from traveling salesman Charles Drouet to George Hurstwood, the manager of a high-class saloon. Her climb culminates in a Broadway theatre career that brings fame and financial independence but neither fulfillment nor happiness. The deterministic forces operating in *Sister Carrie* place the novel as a key early work of American Literary Naturalism.

The event structure of the novel resembles a "ladder of beauty," each rung of which equals an object of Carrie's dreams and stimulates a desire for something higher and better; each time she rises a rung, a higher one acquires an irresistible luster for her. The movement from country to city, from her family to Drouet, from Drouet to Hurstwood, and from Hurstwood to the theatre features a pattern of stimulus and response that plays on Carrie's tropistic attraction to beauty and luxury. Chance adds a final touch to the determinism that shapes this sequence. Carrie's meetings with Drouet on the train and in Chicago are determined by chance.

Chance also governs the discovery of Hurstwood's infidelity by his wife, as it does his theft from the safe and Carrie's discovery of the crime. At critical moments, chance combines with desire to produce the deterministic event, thereby undercutting the individual's free will.

Carrie's "given nature" is also part of the web of deterministic forces governing her career. Her dominant trait is a desire for material comfort that controls the pattern of her movements, the decisions she makes, and ultimately her fate. Underlying Carrie's materialistic yearning is the fear of poverty that exerts a deterministic influence on her career. As Dreiser states, "fine clothes were for her a vast persuasion," or again, "then a new luster would come upon something, and therewith it would become for her the desire—the all," and yet again, "she longed and longed and longed." Carrie Meeber is victimized by her own "commodity fetishism." It is for her "to be the pursuit of that radiance ... which tints the distant hilltops."

Supplementing the novel's deterministic forces is the influence the environment has upon Carrie's career. Chicago is depicted as a massive entity utterly indifferent to the desiring self: "these vast buildings, what were they?" As Dreiser notes, "[I]t seemed as if it was all closed to her." The city and its harsh economic realities are compacted into a universe of force, embodied in the shoe factory where she briefly works and the faceless canyons of the city, quickening her desire to escape this bleak realm of poverty. The impersonal drabness of the factory prompts Carrie to quit her job and become Drouet's mistress, even as Chicago's mansions exert an attraction upon her, prompting her desire to move to the next rung of the ladder and to abandon Drouet for Hurstwood.

Carrie's essential passivity in the face of deterministic forces is reinforced by images of her as a "wisp on the wind" and a "waif on the tide." Her passivity is underscored by her association with an "Aeolian lute" that fortune pipes upon, while images associated with "chemism," "currents," and "magnetism" reinforce the deterministic power of sexual drives. Finally, the rocking chair at the novel's end resonates with multiple connotations for Carrie's "given nature," suggesting that she has moved without going anywhere. It further symbolizes her outward comfort and her inner spiritual restlessness, insofar as she is surrounded by all she has desired, save that which she desired above all: the perfect all. Her seat in the rocking chair suggests that she is doomed to suffer insatiable longing. Her materialism may have brought comfort, fame, and friends, but not happiness. Carrie is the first "bad girl" in American literature to go unpunished—further evidence that Dreiser did not hold Carrie responsible for her discontent but instead blamed the conditions that created her and the false values those conditions enshrined.

Discussion Questions

1. What is Carrie's "given nature?" To what extent is it responsible for her fate?

2. Cite episodes in which environmental forces determine Carrie's destiny.

3. Explicate the final paragraphs of the novel—especially Dreiser's address to Carrie.

—*Steven G. Brown*

REFERENCES

Leonard Cassuto and Clare Virginia Eby, eds., *The Cambridge Companion to Theodore Dreiser* (Cambridge: Cambridge University Press, 2004);

Robert H. Elias, *Theodore Dreiser: Apostle of Nature* (New York: Knopf, 1948);

Richard Lehan, *Literary Masterpieces: Sister Carrie* (Detroit: Manly/Gale Group, 2001);

Richard Lingeman, *Theodore Dreiser*, 2 volumes (New York: Putnam, 1986, 1990);

Jerome Loving, *The Last Titan: A Life of Theodore Dreiser* (Berkeley: University of California Press, 2005);

Margaret Marquis, "The Female Body, Work, and Reproduction in Deland, Cather, and Dreiser," *Women's Studies: An Interdisciplinary Journal*, 32 (December 2003): 979–1000;

F. O. Matthiessen, *Theodore Dreiser* (New York: Sloane, 1951);

Ellen Moers, *Two Dreisers* (New York: Viking, 1969);

Keith Newlin, *A Theodore Dreiser Encyclopedia* (Westport, Conn.: Greenwood Press, 2003);

Donald Pizer, ed., *Critical Essays on Theodore Dreiser* (Boston: G. K. Hall, 1981);

Pizer, *The Novels of Theodore Dreiser* (Minneapolis: University of Minnesota Press, 1976);

Pizer, ed., *New Essays on Sister Carrie* (Cambridge: Cambridge University Press, 1991);

Keith Newlin, *A Theodore Dreiser Encyclopedia* (Westport, Conn.: Greenwood Press, 2003);

Donald David and E. E. Sloane, *Theodore Dreiser's Sociological Tragedy* (New York: Twayne, 1992);

Robert Penn Warren, *Homage to Theodore Dreiser* (New York: Random House, 1971).

E

Edith Maude Eaton
(Sui Sin Far)
(March 15, 1865 – April 7, 1914)

"MRS. SPRING FRAGRANCE" AND "THE INFERIOR WOMAN"

Collected in *Mrs. Spring Fragrance* (Chicago: McClurg, 1912).

JADE SPRING FRAGRANCE

Jade Spring Fragrance, the partially Americanized wife of a successful Chinese businessman, has a central role in two stories by Edith Maude Eaton (Sui Sin Far), "Mrs. Spring Fragrance" and "The Inferior Woman." Mrs. Spring Fragrance seems to be engagingly naive as she assimilates into the strange new world of American freedom and promise. She is, however, a canny observer and interpreter of manners and values. Through her good-hearted meddlesomeness, she targets meanness, exposes hypocrisy, and flouts unswerving allegiance to conservative old-world customs. As a storyteller and clever, comically manipulative do-gooder, she is a mouthpiece for Eaton's passionate belief in justice and right moral action. Eaton was both English and Chinese. She courageously chose to announce her Chinese identity in an era when the Chinese were violently scorned and legally discriminated against, adopting the pseudonym Sui Sin Far (Cantonese for "Chinese lily," or narcissus). Her work heightened awareness of race hatred and the terrible cost of legally sanctioned white "superiority." She advocated scrupulous self-scrutiny, community activism, and bridging the gap between belief and practice. (See her 1909 autobiographical essay, "Leaves from the Mental Portfolio of an Eurasian" for examples of her own moral courage.) She spent her life fighting in print against bigotry and intolerance, and though she was most directly concerned with the plight of the Chinese underclass, she ultimately absolved no one from the crime of heartlessness. The "Mrs. Spring Fragrance" stories are lighthearted in tone but grave in subtext. They are overtly about the collision of old and new attitudes toward romance and marriage, but they are also about women's subordinate status, class, institutionalized racism, abuses of power, and love.

In both stories the young Mrs. Spring Fragrance assumes the traditional role of matchmaker, yet she serves the nontraditional cause of romantic love. In "Mrs. Spring Fragrance," Laura Chin Yuen's parents have arranged her marriage to the son of a Chinese American teacher. Laura and the "American-born" Kai Tzu are in love, but Laura owes allegiance to her father and cannot openly defy him. Mrs. Spring Fragrance soothes Laura by quoting Tennyson (whom she ironically believes is an American poet): "'Tis better to have loved and lost / Than never to have loved at all." The lines from "In Memoriam" baffle Mr. Spring Fragrance and set the stage for a comically poignant misunderstanding. In the end, the schoolteacher's son and his beloved, Ah Oi, are wed; Laura's father approves her union to Kai Tzu; and Mr. Spring Fragrance's trust in his "clever" wife proves grounded in unerring mutual devotion. In "The Inferior Woman," Mrs. Spring Fragrance's intervention opens Mary Carman's eyes to the real worth of her son's choice of marriage partner.

Each story concludes on notes of gentle triumph, with true love winning the day and marriage in the offing. In "Mrs. Spring Fragrance," the initially unyielding Chin Yuen accepts, with "affable resignation," the disarrangement of his arranged marriage plans for Laura. Mary Carman's swift conversion to the loving future mother-in-law of the no longer unsuitably "inferior" Alice happens easily, without conflict or fanfare. The omniscient narrator in the "Spring Fragrance" stories never makes completely clear whether Mrs. Spring Fragrance is artless or calculating. The lack of narrative directive and the thematic hints of deeper troubles help sharpen the ironies implicit in the texts and compound the too-pat resolutions.

Eaton's social realism can be sentimental as well as biting; her characters serve to underscore her themes and are not always meant to be psychologically dimensional. Yet, Mrs. Spring Fragrance is still a vivid, complexly drawn character who, in her good-hearted, comedic way, illustrates the fundamental seriousness of Eaton's prevailing concerns.

The name "Spring Fragrance" is a romanticized evocation of the flowery sweetness of Chinese womanhood. (Eaton's biographer, Annette White-Parks, notes that the name is a common one for women in rural China.) "Mrs." is the decidedly Western designation of respectable social position. Mrs. Spring Fragrance represents the borderland between worlds, the junctures of female independence and subservience, the mating of intellect and heart. She is at once guileless and wise, modest and proud, old-fashioned and forward-thinking, Chinese and American. Like the season in her name, she represents the potential for a new kind of life, one that marries, with sensitivity and grace, old values with new thinking. Her happy marriage to Sing Yook has been traditionally arranged, but she questions the wisdom of forcing young people to betray the dictates of their own hearts. She is modest and self-effacing when catering to her husband's needs but assured and quietly assertive when undermining oppressive social codes. A fairly recent immigrant

from China (in "Mrs. Spring Fragrance" she has been in Seattle for five years), she is comfortably middle class and has both Chinese and American friends. Unlike Eaton's more tragically conflicted or victimized characters (for instance, Lae Choo in "In the Land of the Free" and Pau Lin in "The Wisdom of the New"), this appealing protagonist is at home in both Chinese and American worlds.

She is, though, a kind of "trickster figure," according to White-Parks, subverting notions of the racial "Other" and upsetting the uneasy presumptions on which power is too often balanced. In "The Inferior Woman," Mrs. Spring Fragrance announces her determination to write a book about the "mysterious, inscrutable, incomprehensible Americans," reversing the charged, divisive, patently racist attitude held by many Americans toward Chinese immigrants. Her book will be titled "The Inferior Woman," an allusion to the hardworking, self-made Alice Winthrop, beloved of the young Will Carman. Mrs. Spring Fragrance comes to the aid of the forlorn Will and opens his mother's eyes to her own disturbing snobbery: "Mrs. Mary Carman, . . . you are so good as to admire my husband because he is what the Americans call 'a man who has made himself.' Why then do you not admire the Inferior Woman who is a woman who has made herself?"

Eaton provides Mrs. Spring Fragrance with a kind, openhearted husband who yields to the permissiveness of American social codes with an intelligent interest. His faith in his independent, spirited wife is rewarded by her sweet-natured regard for him. Their marriage models the successful melding of old and new ways. Like a traditional Chinese woman, Mrs. Spring Fragrance defers to her husband, addressing him in her letter from San Francisco as "Great and Honored Man," flattering him, and declaring herself "obedient." She placates him, but she is not insincere. She does what she wants, but she honors the real ties of their marriage. Sing Yook, in turn, adapts to the perplexing mores of his new country. He does not attempt to command, nor does he demand obsequiousness from his wife. Eaton presents their relationship as one based on generosity, selflessness, and tolerance—the qualities needed to foster the humane growth of the land of the free.

Discussion Questions

1. Sing Yook proudly says of his "Americanized" wife: "There are no more American words for her learning." In what ways does Mrs. Spring Fragrance seem like an "Americanized" woman? In what ways is she traditionally Chinese?

2. The lighthearted tone of the "Spring Fragrance" stories contrasts with the disturbingly serious issues they raise. Sing Yook's elder brother, who is being held in a "Detention Pen" at the Immigration Center on Angel Island in San Francisco, is mentioned twice in "Mrs. Spring Fragrance." How do these references deepen and complicate the realism in the story? What other serious social issues are raised in this story and in "The Inferior Woman"?

3. Though their marriage was traditionally arranged, Sing Yook and Mrs. Spring Fragrance enjoy a relationship based on mutual respect and trust. How is their affection for each other demonstrated? How does Eaton's depiction of Sing Yook challenge the stereotypical image of "superior" male authority? Is his attitude toward his wife surprising or unusual? What does this marriage reveal about the real nature of "true love"?

4. Compare Mrs. Spring Fragrance's easy transition into American life with the difficulties experienced by Pau Tsu, the young immigrant bride in Eaton's "The Americanizing of Pau Tsu." Compare the picture presented of Chinese American life in "Mrs. Spring Fragrance" with that shown in Eaton's "In the Land of the Free."

—*Kate Falvey*

REFERENCES

Maude Eaton, *Mrs. Spring Fragrance,* edited by E. Catherine Falvey (Lanham, Md.: Rowman & Littlefield, 1994);

Eaton, *Mrs. Spring Fragrance and Other Writings,* edited by Amy Ling and Annette White-Parks (Urbana: University of Illinois Press, 1995);

White-Parks, *Sui Sin Far/Edith Maude Eaton: A Literary Biography* (Urbana: University of Illinois Press, 1995).

T. S. Eliot
(September 26, 1888 – January 4, 1965)

"THE LOVE SONG OF J. ALFRED PRUFROCK"

Poetry (June 1915); collected in *Prufrock and Other Observations* (London: Egoist, 1917)

J. ALFRED PRUFROCK

"The Love Song of J. Alfred Prufrock" is structured on a proposed journey that the narrator, Prufrock, has invited a friend to embark upon. T. S. Eliot told critic Kristian Smidt in 1949 that the "you" in the first line of the poem "is merely some friend or companion, presumably of the male sex, whom the speaker is at that moment addressing." Some critics, however, interpret the "you" in the invitation as Prufrock's "other self" or "soul." The poem, though structured on fragments loosely connected by a variety of literary and mythic allusions, is a dramatic monologue. In virtually all instances, Prufrock is used in ironic contrast to the virtues or strengths of the characters in the allusions. The major method Eliot uses to characterize Prufrock is to present him in striking contrast to those figures he unconsciously identifies with. The entire poem is built on irony; it defines Prufrock in terms of what he is not.

The opening voice of Prufrock's monologue compares the evening to "a patient etherized upon a table," an image that life for Prufrock is a condition of paralysis lived in a semi-comatose condition. The landscape to which Prufrock invites his companion resembles a classic *Wasteland* condition: "half deserted streets / The muttering retreats / of restless nights in one-night cheap hotels / And sawdust restaurants with oyster-shells. . . ." Clearly, Prufrock is presented as lonely, fearful, even apprehensive of the meaning of his journey. Eliot mixes ennui with fear as the streets follow "like a tedious argument of insidious intent." Fear and ennui become the dominant moods of the poem.

Part of Prufrock's debilitating boredom is his response to the trivialization of great art and artists as seen in a recurring motif: "In the room the women come and go / Talking of Michelangelo."

Prufrock's apathy resembles that of some of Eliot's French poetic influences, such as Charles Baudelaire, Jules LaForgue, and Arthur Rimbaud: these poets view their ennui as a kind of infection, a form of spiritual malaise. Eliot describes the yellow fog—like a serpentine disease—that "slides along the street," infecting the city and its immobilized inhabitants. Prufrock is incapable of not seeing disease everywhere.

The fourth stanza defines the insidious effects of time as destructive duration and alludes to Andrew Marvell's use of time in "To His Coy Mistress" to seduce his mistress before it is too late. Other key lines from Marvell's poem appear toward the end of Eliot's poem and further reinforce Prufrock's inability to take any kind of significant action when it comes to approaching women. Prufrock's paralysis contrasts dramatically to men of accomplishment such as Dante and Michelangelo. Prufrock further proves himself unable to act because he is defeated by time even before he takes action. Allusions to the biblical injunction that there is "time to murder and create" and to Hesiod's *Works and Days* (a practical handbook for the farmer's life) show him unable to murder or to create on any level; nor can he nourish animal or vegetative life as a farmer because of his imaginative and spiritual inertia. Eliot uses rhyme to show the pathetic dilemmas that stultify Prufrock but also enable him to erect a denial system that feeds his illusions that he is conscious of his true feelings: "And time yet for a hundred indecisions / And for a hundred visions and revisions / Before the taking of a toast and tea."

One of the few instances in which Prufrock takes action occurs when he begins to ask questions of himself with "Do I dare?"—even though it is unclear what it is he dares to do. He is thwarted in asking these ambiguous questions because of his tortured sense of being observed and judged and—most devastating of all—of growing old. Again, time paralyzes him when he views himself: a bald spot, thinning hair, frail arms and legs. His fear of taking action applies to the most profound philosophical matters as well as to the most trivial: "Do I dare / Disturb the universe? . . . Do I dare to eat a peach?" Prufrock's penchant for analyzing his every thought, decisions, action—or even proposed action—has

frozen him into stasis. He suffers from paralysis as a result of too much analysis.

Because of Prufrock's fear of taking action, the poem begins to move in a retrograde pattern, and what causes him to reverse himself is the inevitable victory of time: "For I have known them all already, known them all." Prufrock is so self-conscious and embarrassed by his existence that he reaches a condition of complete emotional and spiritual immobility, like a mounted butterfly: "The eyes that fix you in a formulated phrase / And when I am formulated, sprawling on a pin / When I am pinned and wriggling on the wall / Then how should I begin / To spit out all the butt-ends of my days and ways?" The concluding section of the poem lists the vivid, troubled literary and biblical characters he unconsciously identifies with—Hamlet, Polonius, Geoffrey Chaucer's Clerk of Oxenford, and even a stock figure in Shakespeare and medieval drama: the fool.

Prufrock confesses that he has "heard the mermaids singing each to each. / I do not think that they will sing to me." He also admits that he has "seen them riding seaward"—that is, away from him—leaving him alone on the beach. Prufrock has tentatively entered the realm of the imagination which has given him, for a fleeting moment, visions of the mythic mermaids and their promised rapture. But he recoils from such fantasies and confesses, guiltily, that he and his companion—"we"—"have lingered in the chambers of the seas." They have indulged their erotic fantasies too long—a dangerous game—until reality returned and they drowned. Prufrock cannot succeed on any conceivable level of consciousness because his behavior is determined by the memory of his past, his reading, and his threatening desires. The combination of the three paralyzes him.

Discussion Questions

1. Pick out three recurring motifs that establish the prevailing tone of the poem. How does Eliot accomplish this tone in language?

2. What are the three most debilitating weaknesses that consistently paralyze Prufrock's ability to take action?

3. What is Prufrock unable to find that might release him from his recurring obsession with time?

4. How do the many literary and biblical allusions function to define Prufrock's character?

—*Patrick Meanor*

REFERENCES

Caroline Behr, *T. S. Eliot: A Chronology of His Life and Works* (London: Macmillian, 1983);

Jewel Spears Brooker, *Mastery and Escape: T. S. Eliot and the Dialectic of Modernism* (Amherst: University of Massachusetts Press, 1994);

Brooker, ed., *Approaches to Teaching Eliot's Poetry and Plays* (New York: Modern Language Association, 1988);

Ronald Bush, *T. S. Eliot: A Study in Character and Style* (New York: Oxford University Press, 1984);

Denis Donoghue, *Words Alone: The Poet T. S. Eliot* (New Haven, Conn.: Yale University Press, 2000);

Louis Menand, *Discovering Modernism: T. S. Eliot and His Context* (New York: Oxford University Press, 1987);

A. David Moody, *Cambridge Companion to T. S. Eliot* (Cambridge: Cambridge University Press, 1994).

Harlan Ellison

(May 27, 1934 –   )

"'REPENT, HARLEQUIN!' SAID THE TICKTOCKMAN"

Collected in *Paingod and Other Delusions* (New York: Pyramid, 1965).

EVERETT C. MARM

Disguised as the anarchic prankster the Harlequin, Everett C. Marm is the central figure in Harlan Ellison's comic fable of life in a clock-ruled world, "Repent, Harlequin!' Said the Ticktockman." The rebel who represents change in an unchanging society, or chaos in a regimented world, or freedom in a totalitarian state, is a familiar figure in science fiction, and major antecedents of the Harlequin include the character D-503 in Evgenii Zamiatin's *We* (1924) and Winston Smith in George Orwell's *Nineteen Eighty-Four* (1948). But Ellison also draws on the archetypal trickster figure of Harlequin, one of the stock figures in *commedia dell'arte*, the tradition of traveling theater troupes that emerged in mid-sixteenth-century Italy. Often portrayed as an impetuous clown whose resourcefulness and acrobatics are needed to help him extricate himself from the consequences of his own schemes, Harlequin often provided the satirical voice in these plays, commenting on politics and society and sometimes parodying well-known public figures. Significantly, he was traditionally the only character in the *commedia* who was allowed to directly address the audience, just as the narrator of Ellison's story frequently addresses the reader.

Ellison retains most of these classic characteristics of Harlequin but places him in a dystopian, twenty-fourth-century world that carries overt allusions to the increasingly time-bound world of contemporary society. Harlequin's world is so regimented by clocks and schedules that an individual's lateness—to work, meetings, school—can be cumulatively added up and deducted from his or her total life span. The ruler of this world, and Harlequin's opposite, is the dictatorial Master Timekeeper, or Ticktockman, who is responsible for keeping everything on schedule. But Harlequin—who also shares some characteristics with the masked, mysterious superheroes of comic books—deliberately disrupts the city schedules with such pranks as dumping millions of jelly beans on the moving walkways, distracting the workers and gumming up the mechanism, or appearing at a shopping center with a bullhorn, urging people to resist the government. These antics make him a folk hero to the working classes—"a Bolivar; a Napoleon; a Robin Hood; a Dick Bong (Ace of Aces); a Jesus; a Jomo Kenyatta." But his individualism, apart from his subversive antics, is a threat to the system: "He had become a *personality*, something they had filtered out of the system many decades before." As a result, Ticktockman issues an old-fashioned wanted poster for Harlequin.

Like many comic-book heroes, Harlequin has a secret identity, and the tone of the story shifts from manic satire to domestic comedy when the home life of Marm and his partner or wife, Pretty Alice, are introduced. Apologizing to Alice for speaking with too much inflection and then apologizing again for apologizing, Marm is anything but an heroic figure. Instead, he comes across as an almost petulant nebbish, plagued by guilt and self-doubt but nevertheless driven to "*do* something." Alice is clearly at the limits of her patience with his antics, telling him "You're ridiculous" and asking "Oh for God's *sake,* Everett, can't you stay home just *one* night? Must you always be out in that ghastly clown suit, running around an*noy*ing people?" When he promises to return by 10:30, she responds "Why do you tell me that? Why? You *know* you'll be late! You're *always* late, so why do you tell me these dumb things?" He finds himself agreeing with her: *"Why* do *I tell her these dumb things?"* Marm, it seems, is motivated less by heroic ambition than by his efforts to defend and justify his own chronic lateness. Ellison once said that the story was written as a plea for understanding his similar habit, although he also notes that the story was written in a six-hour period in order to make a deadline for a discussion group at a science-fiction writers' conference in Milford, Pennsylvania.

Eventually, the Harlequin is captured and brought before the Ticktockman in the scene that gives the story its title—but, true to his rebellious nature, Harlequin responds to the Ticktockman's command to repent with "Get stuffed!" But when the Ticktockman informs him that Pretty Alice has turned him in, he invites the Ticktockman to activate his "cardioplate," a medical device that enables the government to remotely stop the heart of any citizen. Instead of being "turned off," though, he is sent to "Coventry," where he is reconditioned into a happily conforming citizen, even though Everett C. Marm himself was "destroyed." Alluding to one of the antecedents of the story, Ellison writes: "It was just like what they did to Winston Smith in *1984.*" The idea of Coventry may be borrowed from Robert A. Heinlein's 1940 story "Coventry," in which misfits in a future society must either undergo psychological "adjustment" or live in exile in a country of that name. After the Harlequin is safely reconditioned, however, the Ticktockman learns that he himself has arrived three minutes late for work one morning, suggesting that the Harlequin's rebellion may not have been entirely in vain.

Discussion Questions

1. Ellison introduces his story with a long quotation from Henry David Thoreau's essay "Civil Disobedience." Explain how the figures of the Harlequin and the Ticktockman illustrate specific points from this Thoreau quotation.

2. Ellison explains that his story will "begin in the middle, and the reader will later learn the beginning; the end will take care of itself." Why does he use this jumbled chronology, and how does it add to the effect of the story?

3. At one point the Harlequin is specifically compared to Winston Smith of George Orwell's novel *Nineteen Eighty-Four.* Compare the Harlequin's attitude after he returns to society from Coventry with Smith's attitude at the end of Orwell's novel.

—*Gary K. Wolfe*

REFERENCES

Stephen Adams, "The Heroic and Mock-Heroic in Harlan Ellison's 'Harlequin,'" *Extrapolation,* 26 (1985): 285–289;

Ellen Weil and Gary K. Wolfe, *Harlan Ellison: The Edge of Forever* (Columbus: Ohio State University Press, 2002);

Michael D. White, "Ellison's Harlequin: Irrational Moral Action in Static Time," *Science-Fiction Studies,* 4 (July 1977): 161–165.

Ralph Ellison
(March 1, 1914 – April 16, 1994)

◄◎

INVISIBLE MAN
(New York: Random House, 1952)

UNNAMED PROTAGONIST
The nameless narrator and protagonist of Ralph Ellison's *Invisible Man* is a young black man who once aspired to be president of the Southern college he attended on an academic scholarship; however, he has since taken up residence in an abandoned coal cellar beneath a New York City street, from which he delivers the account of his journey. Ellison explained in an interview that his protagonist's story

is one of "innocence and human error, a struggle through illusion to reality": "The major flaw in the hero's character is his unquestioning willingness to do what is required of him by others as a way to success, and this was the specific form of his 'innocence.'" The narrator explains that he has come to think of himself as invisible "simply because people refuse to see me." While he realizes that people have failed to look beyond his skin color and the preconceptions it triggers, he also recognizes *his* failure to forge his own identity. Ellison remarked, "he creates his own invisibility to a certain extent by not asserting himself." The narrator's ultimate act of self-assertion, however, is the completion of his memoir, which he claims will mark the end of his self-imposed "hibernation."

Ellison noted that he divided his protagonist's journey into three stages, each of which is initiated by his being handed a document offering him a prescribed identity and a promise of success. Each of these promises, however, ends in disappointment and disillusionment. The first, a college scholarship, leads to his expulsion. The second, letters of recommendation from his college president, which he learns are actually disparaging, sends him to New York City, where he is rejected by a succession of potential employers. The third, handed to him by the president of the Brotherhood, a left-wing political group who hires him to deliver speeches in Harlem—only to later betray him and the people of Harlem—gives him his Brotherhood alias. It is the narrator's memoir, a document of his own creation, that finally signifies the discovery of his authentic identity.

In the prologue of the novel the narrator introduces the essential motifs that pervade his story: light and dark, wakefulness and sleep, and sight and blindness. Each pair of opposites symbolizes knowledge and ignorance respectively. He explains that he has installed 1,369 light bulbs to illuminate the blackness of the coal cellar. "Light confirms my reality," he states, "gives birth to my form." He has become such a strong proponent of enlightenment that he recently beat a man to "within an inch of his life" after the "poor blind fool" bumped into him, called him "an insulting name," and refused to apologize. As he begins the story of his own disil-

lusionment, it is clear that passiveness, not aggression, characterized him at the start. As a boy he heard his dying grandfather, a former slave known for his meekness and compliance, urge his father "to keep up the good fight," for he himself had been "a traitor." His words haunt the narrator each time he concedes to the humiliating demands of the white man's world.

The demeaning nature of these demands is typified by the ritual he must undergo before being given his college scholarship. Invited by the prominent citizens of his town to deliver his valedictory speech, he is taunted with the sight of a voluptuous, nude, white woman, then blindfolded and forced to fight a bloody battle royal with nine other black men, and finally prompted to scramble for money tossed onto an electric rug. He proceeds to deliver his speech, squinting through his symbolically battered eye. Along with his scholarship, he receives a briefcase and an ironic piece of advice: "Keep developing as you are and some day it will be filled with important papers that will help shape the destiny of your people."

The narrator depicts his first impressions of his college campus with Edenic imagery; however, his banishment proves inevitable. When a rich white trustee asks to be shown around the area, the narrator unwittingly exposes him to the reality of the rural South, including a brothel called the Golden Day. In his explanation to the college president, Dr. Bledsoe, he reveals his naiveté and idealism. He had merely done what he was told. After chastising him regarding the importance of hiding the truth from white men, Bledsoe explains that a concern for dignity is an obstacle to success: "I've made my place . . . and I'll have every Negro in the country hanging on tree limbs by morning if it means staying where I am." Despite hearing this declaration, the narrator trusts Bledsoe's promise to help him secure a job in New York.

On the bus ride north the narrator encounters one of the patrons he met in the Golden Day, a shell-shocked veteran who prophesies the awakening he will undergo in the city: "Come out of the fog," he tells him; "learn to look beneath the surface." After learning of the malicious content of Bledsoe's sealed letters, the narrator takes a job in a paint factory, where he is injured in an explosion and made to suffer shock treatments. Lying in a glass, tomb-like bed, he is unable to respond to the doctor's symbolic question, "Who are you?" Yet, upon his release, he shows his first sign of self-assertion by standing up for an elderly couple being evicted from their home. This act leads to his being recruited by the Brotherhood, which he gradually learns is as manipulative and self-serving as Dr. Bledsoe. To disguise himself from the followers of a rival street orator, the Black Nationalist Ras the Exhorter, he buys a pair of sunglasses and a white hat and is repeatedly mistaken for a local con man named Rinehart, whose ability to shift his identity intrigues the narrator and awakens him to the possibility inherent in a life lived autonomously. During a race riot in Harlem, in which he contributes to the rebellious destruction, he falls into the dark coal chute where he begins his Thoreau-like exile in an effort to sort out the meaning of his experiences. He creates a torch out of the documents in his briefcase, simultaneously symbolizing the destruction of his past identities and the arrival of his enlightenment.

The narrator of *Invisible Man* has affinities with characters extending from the Bible through the entire canon of Western literature. Critics have compared his spiritual journey to those undertaken by the biblical Jonah, Homer's Odysseus, Voltaire's Candide, Mark Twain's Huck Finn, and James Joyce's Stephen Dedalus, among others.

Discussion Questions

1. In addition to the coal cellar from which the narrator relates his story, many underground settings appear in the novel, such as the subway and the basement of the paint factory. What is the significance of these settings, and how do they help to define the narrator? In what ways might these scenes recall Dante's *Inferno*?

2. Aside from its underground setting, the paint factory carries other symbolic significance, especially considering it is known for its brand of "optic white" paint. In what ways does the narrator's experience in the paint factory contribute to his growing disillusionment?

3. A vivid, recurring symbol in the novel is the plaster bank that protagonist smashes before leaving Mary Rambo's house. Considering that he is separated from and reunited with this item a few times, what might each signify?

4. Water is another symbol that appears frequently in the novel. Consider the narrator's imagining he is "in the center of a lake of heavy water" after the paint factory explosion and the "spray of water that seemed to descend from above" during the Harlem riot scene. What do these references signify regarding the narrator's spiritual journey?

5. What aspects of the narrator's story resemble the struggles of Jonah, Odysseus, Candide, Huckleberry Finn, or Stephen Dedalus? Further, what traits might the narrator share with other post–World War II American literary characters, such as Philip Roth's Neil Klugman, Joseph Heller's Yossarian, or Sylvia Plath's Esther Greenwood?

—*John Cusatis*

REFERENCES

Mark Busby, *Ralph Ellison* (Boston: Twayne, 1991);

John F. Callahan, *Ralph Ellison's* Invisible Man: *A Casebook* (New York: Oxford University Press, 2004);

Robert G. O'Meally, *The Craft of Ralph Ellison* (Cambridge, Mass.: Harvard University Press, 1980).

Louise Erdrich
(June 7, 1954 –   )

THE BEET QUEEN
(New York: Holt, 1986)

MARY ADARE

Mary Adare is one of the narrators of Louise Erdrich's novel *The Beet Queen*. She is introduced, along with her brother Karl, "on a cold spring morning in 1932," in the early days of the Depression. Karl is fourteen, and "His sister was only eleven years old, but already she was so short and ordinary that it was obvious she would be this way all her life. Her name was as squared and practical as the rest of her." The siblings have traveled by boxcars, looking to find their Aunt

Fritzie, their mother's sister, who lives in and owns a butcher shop in Argus, North Dakota. Their mother, Adelaide, abandoned them and their infant brother when she took off with Omar, an airplane stunt flyer at an "Orphan's Picnic" to benefit a local charity. The baby is then taken from them by a young man, who wants to make a present of it to his wife, who had recently lost her own child.

The Beet Queen is the second of four books written by Erdrich that deal with life in and around the imaginary town of Argus. The first is *Love Medicine* (1984), which won the Book Critics Award for Fiction. The others are *Tracks* (1988) and *The Bingo Palace* (1994). Characters, stories, and themes repeat or are alluded to among the four books, providing a deepening understanding of the broader story. *The Beet Queen,* like *Love Medicine,* is told through the voices of six narrators, with a third-person narrator occasionally filling in some gaps. The multiple perspectives weave the lives of characters related by blood and/or circumstances into a broad, rich tapestry. The community itself, rather than any single individual, becomes the protagonist. One character, however, acts as a focal point, even as a catalyst, around which certain aspects of the others develop and reveal themselves. In *The Beet Queen* this character is Mary's niece, Dot, the product of Karl's liaison with her best friend, Celestine James. One night, while Celestine was breast-feeding Dot, she noticed "in the fine moonlit floss of her baby's hair, a tiny white spider making its nest. . . . A web was forming a complicated house that Celestine could not bring herself to destroy." These webs mirror the web of relationships, being woven among the principal characters and holding the community together.

As Karl and Mary walk into town after jumping from the boxcar, they pass a small tree covered in blossoms. "Mary trudged solidly forward, hardly glancing at it, but Karl stopped. The tree drew him with its delicate perfume." The tree owner's dog bounds at Karl. He runs back to the train, while Mary goes toward town and Aunt Fritzie. The abandonment and loss has an immediate effect. Not until many years have passed are they reconnected, after Karl, by then an itinerant peddler, chances upon the home of Mary's friend Celestine and initiates a sexual relationship with her while attempting to

make a sale. Mary becomes an eager helper at home and in the butcher shop. In her first section she narrates, Mary states: "I planned to be essential to them all, so depended upon that they could never send me off. I did this on purpose, because I soon found I had nothing else to offer." Her steadiness and limited aspirations build on themselves. The room she enters her first night at Aunt Fritzie's is the room she sleeps in for the rest of her life. Later, when her aunt and uncle retire to a warm climate, the shop is placed in Mary's dependable hands instead of their daughter Sita's. The butcher shop is the center of Mary's life and becomes her success for many years, until the business declines when a supermarket comes to town. Time goes by, and Mary "seems to have grown heavier in the past few years, not stouter, just more unshakable in word and deed."

A child-like vein remains in Mary, perhaps because of the hard circumstances of her childhood that prevent her from experiencing many of the activities that were common to children. She is always excited by the few birthday parties to which she gets invited, but her fierce desire to make them perfect ruins the fun of them. "Children were afraid of Mary's yellow glare, her gravel bed voice. She organized games with casual but gruesome threats, and the children complied like hostages with a gun trained on them." Mary's lack of social skills and of understanding of other people is partially remedied by her engagement in mysticism and her acceptance of dreams as messages upon which action should be taken. Her mystical bent allows her to interpret and respond to life as it unfolds around her, while also maintaining a safe emotional distance. Her mysticism also fits in well with the native and Catholic traditions of her community. One of the first instances of positive recognition Mary receives occurs when she hurts herself on ice at the bottom of a schoolyard slide, and the nuns and priest who run the school interpret the pattern her blood makes on the cracked ice as resembling the face of Christ. This incident emphasizes to her the power of the miraculous.

Mary's solidity masks her deep insecurity and feeling of low self-worth. Repeated rejection reinforces these feelings. Her one attempt at romance, with her friend Celestine's brother Russell, is unsuccessful. Years later she purchases a dress for Dot to wear to the sugar-beet festival. Dot finds it hideous and says so. In response, Dot relates, "Aunt Mary sighed with pain, as if a knife had twisted deep inside, then set her mouth firm to endure me." Her vulnerability is further emphasized in an incident in which Celestine fills a salad with nuts and bolts and presents it at a school play potluck with Mary's name attached. When the joke is finally revealed, Celestine narrates, Mary's "shoulders slump down and her back relents. And then, in the odd print of her dress, I finally read that she is hurt." Her departure from the potluck event is movingly portrayed. It is also an excellent example of Erdrich's capacity to present her characters in a compassionate light, even while revealing their flaws and failures.

Discussion Questions

1. Erdrich's use of multiple narrators reflects contemporary literary structure, the Native American storytelling tradition, as well as the small-town gossip network. Do you think this approach was effective in telling this story? Why? If Mary were the only narrator, what might have been lost, or gained?

2. When Adelaide finally contacts her children by means of a postcard from Florida, Mary responds to her that her children are dead. Would you expect her to be more forgiving? Why or why not?

3. Erdrich's Native American and German background is reflected in her exploration of multicultural characters and of issues relating that mixed blood. In contrast to much of her work that centers on reservation life, the focus of *The Beet Queen* is on her German roots. Do you think Mary would have been a different person if her aunt lived on the reservation, rather than in a butcher shop? What might be different, or the same?

—*Nancy Fowler*

LOVE MEDICINE
(New York: Holt, Rinehart & Winston, 1984)

MARIE KASHPAW

Marie Kashpaw is one of the major characters in Louise Erdrich's *Love Medicine*. In the chapter "Saint Marie," fourteen-year-old Marie visits the Sacred Heart Convent, where she is sponsored by the nun Sister Leopolda (Pauline Puyat in Erdrich's *Tracks*). Marie wants to become a nun, a saint whom "they would have to stoop down off their high horse to kiss." Although she has the ego and foolish fantasies of a young person who merely wants to be loved, by the time she leaves the convent she is revered much like a saint.

Marie has a love-hate attitude toward Leopolda: "sometimes I wanted her heart in love and admiration. Sometimes. And sometimes I wanted her heart to roast on a black stick." In *Love Medicine*, Marie does not know that Leopolda is her birth mother, a fact revealed in *Tracks;* yet, she has this knowledge in *The Last Report on the Miracles at Little No Horse*. The visit turns into a disturbing scene of physical abuse intended to purify Marie. Leopolda scalds her with boiling water, and in turn, she tries to kick Leopolda into a hot oven. Recovering her balance, Leopolda stabs Marie in her hand with a fork and knocks her out with a poker, but not before Marie can yell, "Bitch of Jesus Christ! . . . Kneel and beg! Lick the floor!" Erdrich renders the horrible treatment of Marie with dark humor, and when Marie regains consciousness, the nuns are worshiping her because they believe Leopolda's story that Marie has been marked with stigmata.

At first, Marie delights in her elevated status; but as she looks at Leopolda, "kneeling within the shambles of her love," she quickly has a change of heart and pities the woman: "It was a feeling more terrible than any amount of boiling water and worse than being forked." Having been humbled, Marie exhibits the feelings of a loving saint and forgives Leopolda for her lies and demented treatment of her, saying, "Receive the dispensation of my sacred blood."

In the next chapter, "Wild Geese," Marie meets her future husband, Nector Kashpaw. Nector has "already decided that Lulu Nanapush is the one," but his encounter with Marie changes his heart, and he decides that he wants her. During a physical struggle between Marie and Nector, he realizes that he is "lying full length across a woman, not a girl." Despite Marie's wounds, inflicted by Sister Leopolda, she never cries out, and Nector is drawn to her strength, the same quality she displayed in sustaining her injuries. The love triangle between

Lulu, Marie, and Nector continues in the future, and Marie eventually extends the same forgiveness to Lulu that she offers to Leopolda.

Marie's character is one of stability, endurance, and perseverance in her marriage and in the role of the good mother; she not only raises her own children but also takes in other children in the community who need a family. She raises her niece, June Kashpaw, and June's son, Lipsha. Marie demonstrates a communal worldview in which the welfare of the group is most important; hence, she cares about those in the tribe who need her help.

Another example of community is the women—Marie's mother-in-law, Margaret Rushes Bear Kashpaw, and Fleur Pillager—who help Marie deliver her baby when she decides not to go to the hospital: "The only thing that wouldn't cost money, I thought to comfort myself, was this baby, as long as she wasn't registered, as long as I did not go to the hospital, as long as I could have her in the house, she was free." Even when Nector urges her to go to the hospital, she refuses because she "was afraid of that place."

This particular birth brings together three women through traditional Ojibwe language and customs associated with having babies. Despite the delivery being "hard enough for her to die," this birthing scene captures the mother's experience told in her own words. Marie suffers the physical abuse of Leopolda, the rough handling by Nector during their initial encounter, and the physical pain of childbirth without anesthesia. Although Nector at first thinks, "She is just a skinny white girl from a family so low you cannot even think they are in the same class as Kashpaws," she is portrayed as a strong Ojibwe woman.

When Nector, Marie, and Lulu are aged and living at the Senior Citizens, Marie asks Lipsha to heal the senile Nector so he will stop chasing after Lulu. When Lipsha's touch fails to heal him, Lipsha decides to use the hearts of geese, which mate for life, as a love medicine. When he goes hunting and cannot obtain the geese hearts, he takes a shortcut and buys frozen turkey hearts at the store; but the love medicine fails because Nector chokes to death when he tries to eat them. Nector's spirit returns to visit Marie, however, and Lipsha tells her that the love medicine is not what brings Nector back: "He loved you over time and distance. . . . It's true feeling, not no magic." Despite Nector's infidelity, Marie volunteers to take care of Lulu after her eye surgery, explaining her motivation to help her by saying that "There's a pattern of three lines in the wood," that the three of them are connected in a natural way to the land and place. Marie tells Lulu: "Somebody had to put the tears into your eyes." Throughout Marie's life, she is a survivor, a pillar of emotional and physical strength, who continues to offer kindness and help to others. Her love and forgiveness are more important for the survival and continuance of the Ojibwes than any resentment and bitterness that she might have felt toward Leopolda, Lulu, and others who have hurt her in her life.

Discussion Questions

1. Considering the signification losses to Native American cultures and languages wrought by the conversion of the Indian peoples to Christianity, why would Marie want to become a nun?

2. During the 1960s and 1970s Native Americans accused the Indian Health Service of sterilizing at least twenty-five percent of Native American women who were between the ages of fifteen and forty-four. Might this statistic account for Marie's fear of going to the hospital? What other reasons might she have?

3. Why does Marie take in the children of others to raise? How does her own childhood influence her motivation for caring for others? Despite enduring physical abuse as a young person, how is she able to offer nothing but love and nurturing to others? She says to Lipsha, "you was always my favorite." Why is Lipsha her favorite child?

4. Indian identity is a complex issue, defined in various ways: by the U.S. government through degree of blood quantum; by the tribe's patrilineal or matrilineal descent criteria; by the tribal community's social acceptance; and by self-definition. Lipsha notes: "Although she will not admit she has a scrap of Indian blood in her, there's no doubt in my mind she's got some Chippewa." As a person of mixed identity, why is Marie considered part of the Ojibwe community?

—Patrice Hollrah

LULU LAMARTINE

Lulu is one of the major characters in *Love Medicine*, Erdrich's novel of forgiveness and contemporary life on and around an Ojibwe (Chippewa) reservation on the North Dakota Plains. As a strong woman, a model of tradition, and a former boarding-school student, she is one strand in a complex network of characters, stories, and themes. Lulu not only serves as a figure to be forgiven but, in fact, also needs to forgive others in her own life so that she, too, becomes transformed through the power of love.

Lulu is one in a continuing family line of tricksters. Her mother, Fleur Pillager, has trickster characteristics, and so does her son, Gerry Nanapush. Trickster figures in American Indian literatures are often cultural heroes who bring good things to the community but who also have lustful appetites, for example, for food, sex, and gambling, which usually cause them trouble. The community learns lessons of how not to behave from the tricksters' examples of inappropriate behaviors. The Ojibwe story of "Naanabozho and the Gambler" establishes the precedent for tricksters to win in games of chance. Consequently, one trickster characteristic that Lulu displays involves her talents as a card player. Lulu passes on her card tricks to her son, Gerry, and grandson, Lipsha—examples of her knowledge that helps her survive even in recreational gambling.

Lulu has a reputation for having sexual relations frequently and with whomever she chooses, as Beverly Lamartine notes when observing her eight children and wondering why they all look so different. As a sexually active survivor, Lulu carries on the trickster tradition from Old Man Nanapush of *Tracks* (another of Erdrich's novels in the North Dakota cycle), who helped raise her. The women on the Ojibwe reservation would have been happier if Lulu had left their husbands alone. She is scorned by the community because she does not practice any self-control. Despite the negative side of her sexual promiscuity, the resulting contempt and isolation she suffers from the other women in the community, the positive side is that she has many children. She not only has creative power to produce Ojibwe offspring but also has political power over the men, the fathers of her children, who are on the tribal council.

Because trickster characters are also humorous and loveable, Lulu has the final word at the tribal council meeting to discuss the government offer of money for the people to move off their land in order to build a modern tomahawk factory, which is headed by Lulu's son, Lyman Lamartine, but originally proposed by his father, Nector Kashpaw. Not wanting to move off of her land, Lulu threatens to name publicly the fathers of her children, a powerful ploy that results in a motion for a financial settlement for her. Although Lulu's goal is not the settlement, her clever tactic is successful, an indication of her power, autonomy, and intellectual sovereignty. Singlehandedly, she controls the entire meeting room, and this power originates in her sexual relationships and the resulting children from those encounters. She knows how to respond to criticism by the community. Thus, there is a tension between her actions as an individual and the repercussions of those actions in the community, which considers Lulu's behavior reprehensible.

As a tribal elder, Lulu passes knowledge on to a younger person in search of personal identity. Her grandson, Lipsha, learns from Lulu that his real parents are Gerry and June Kashpaw, who is the wife of Gordie Kashpaw. As a result, Lipsha forms a new relationship with Lulu because she helps him to connect with his roots and with his communal ties to the Ojibwe tribe. Once again, Lulu is powerful in her role of providing important information to her grandson.

Possibly more important than any of her other roles is Lulu's role as political activist. In her involvement with the American Indian Movement (AIM), she works to maintain respect for the tribe's traditions. Unlike those members who "grew out their hair in braids or ponytails and dressed in ribbon shirts and calico to make their point," Lulu refuses to give up her present-day style and continues to wear her "black spike heels and tight, low-cut dresses blooming with pink flowers," "her makeup, her lipstick, and . . . her 'Dear Abby' wig, a coal-black contraption of curls." She does not care about appearances of the past and rejects the idea that such affectations will solve the problems facing the community today. She wants to make changes of substance that deal with contemporary issues of poverty and unemployment and still maintain a respect for the tribe's history. She cares as much for the land and for the future of the Ojibwe reservation as she does for days gone by; however, she will not give up her contemporary dress or her love life, autonomous choices that reflect her belief in gender complementarity (men and women's roles complement each other and are equally valued for the contributions they bring to the community, one role not having any more importance than another) and intellectual sovereignty (an individual manifestation of the worldview of tribal sovereignty).

Finally, Lulu needs to forgive her lover, Nector Kashpaw, whom she believes deliberately set fire to her house. When Nector comes to her in his senility to ask for forgiveness, Lulu cannot refuse. After Nector dies, Lulu is ready to express her grief, but she still needs Marie Kashpaw, Nector's wife, to help her mourn with tears and to understand that her actions have affected another member of the community in a painful way. After Lulu's eye surgery, Marie volunteers to take care of her, and despite Lulu's claims that she has "no regrets," Marie responds, "Somebody had to put the tears into your eyes." No longer blind to another's feelings, Lulu finally understands "how another woman felt." As Marie forgives Lulu, Lulu also learns forgiveness and absolves those that she holds responsible for some of the misfortune in her life. As Marie puts the eyedrops in Lulu's eyes, Lulu becomes new again and sees the world as a newborn does.

Lulu's characterization is complex with no simple explanations for everything she says and does. Nevertheless, her story, as are others in Erdrich's storytelling cycle, is a tribute to a woman's power, autonomy, and intellectual sovereignty.

Discussion Questions

1. How does the discovery of the dead body in the forest affect Lulu's childhood? Is there a connection between Lulu's not shedding tears and the sight of the dead man? Lulu lives her life the way she wants with no apologies. What connections does she make between life and death?

2. How has Lulu's experience in boarding school changed the way she sees the world? How has the separation from her mother and her Ojibwe community affected her? Read Erdrich's *The Last Report on the Miracles at Little No Horse* and *Tracks* for more of Lulu's thoughts about her boarding school experience.

3. Why is the land so important to Lulu? Why does she refuse to give up her land? What is the connection between the land and her identity?

4. Do you agree or disagree with Lulu's thoughts on the tribe's plans for economic growth, the project of a souvenir factory? Does Lulu have legitimate criticisms, or is she wrong in thinking that their plans play into the stereotypes that the dominant culture has of Indians? What are the economic realities on the reservation?

5. How do you feel about the fact that Lulu has many husbands and lovers? Do you agree with the community that she is irresponsible in her behavior? Do you think that bringing new life—her children—into the community is more important?

—*Patrice Hollrah*

DOT NANAPUSH

Dot Adare Nanapush is a minor character in Louise Erdrich's novel *Love Medicine* and a major character in Erdrich's *The Beet Queen* and *Tales of Burning Love*. In *The Beet Queen* she is the daughter of Ojibwe Celestine James and gay Karl Adare, who have a seven-month relationship that ends when Celestine becomes pregnant. Dot's life is revealed from her conception to her eighteenth year, when she is crowned queen of the Beet Festival. In *Love Medicine* she is the wife of Gerry Nanapush and six months pregnant with a daughter, Shawn Nanapush, who is introduced in *Tales of Burning Love*. Dot is also the fifth wife of Jack Mauser in *Tales of Burning Love*, although she never divorces Gerry. She is a "demanding child, impossible to satisfy," Erdrich writes in *The Beet Queen*, and then a rebellious teenager; later she is a passionate wife who never stops loving her first husband. She functions as the main connection between many of the other characters, bringing together unlikely couples and relationships, illustrating how people can mediate between mainstream society and marginalized groups, non-Native and Native, heterosexual and homosexual, married and single, guilty and innocent.

Dot is a force that people cannot control. Her aunt Mary Adare describes her arrival in the first grade: "Dot was the hawk keenly circling. For seven years, until high school when everything would change, each of these children would be subject to her whim." She knocks out another student's tooth with a rock so the child can collect a quarter from the tooth fairy. Dot has power not only over the children but adults as well. She successfully deceives her aunt Mary when she lies about the punishment doled out by her schoolteacher Mrs. Shumway, claiming that children are forced inside "the naughty box" when they misbehave. When Dot is ten years old, she runs away to Wallace Pfef, her gay namesake and the man who assisted at her delivery. Wallace describes her bold nature: "She feared nothing. Not darkness, heights, nor any type of reptile. She jumped off high dives, climbed my ladders, walked through night as if she owned it." Dot's proclivity for facing the world as if she is ready for a fight speaks to her cultural inheritance of the will to survive.

In the chapter "Scales" in *Love Medicine,* Dot works as a truck-weight inspector, but "what she really did was sleep, knit, or eat all day," behaviors not uncommon for a woman who is six months pregnant. She has a temper and is ready to pick a fight over three things in particular: "Number one was someone flirting with Gerry. Number two was a cigarette leech, someone who was always quitting but smoking yours. Number three was a piss-ant . . . 'a man with fat buns who tries to sell you things. A Jaycee, an Elk, a Kiwanis.'" Dot's pet peeves reflect her contempt for anyone who does not respect marriage boundaries, who does not pay for his own nicotine addiction and exploits the generosity of others, and who is a member of a typically male organization that tries to sell her something in order to take her money. Once coworker Albertine Johnson knows where she stands with the strong-willed Dot, the two have no problems and become good friends.

Dot is a loyal friend and wife and helps hide Gerry whenever he breaks out of prison. She has taken risks before, and in fact, she loves Gerry so much that she is able to conceive during one of her prison visits: "Dot had straddled Gerry's lap in a corner the closed-circuit TV did not quite scan. Through a hole ripped in her pantyhose and a hole ripped in Gerry's coveralls they somehow managed to join and, miraculously, to conceive." She is not discouraged by Gerry's confinement and is willing to engage in sexual relations with him at the risk of being discovered in a prison visiting room, again another sign of her fearless and passionate nature.

Albertine describes Dot's pregnant body, one that comically complements Gerry's "six-foot plus, two-hundred-and-fifty-pound" figure: "Dot weighed over two hundred pounds. . . . She was a short, broad-beamed woman with long yellow eyes and spaces between each of her strong teeth. When we began working together, her hair was cropped close. By the cold months it had grown out in thick quills—brown at the shank, orange at the tip. The orange dye job had not suited her coloring."

Dot gives birth to a girl and names her Shawn. She takes Shawn to work at the scales with her and nurses the baby for long periods: "Her breasts, like overfilled inner tubes, strained at her nylon blouses. Sometimes when she thought no one was looking, Dot rose and carried them in the crooks of her arms, for her shoulders were growing bowed beneath their weight." Although she is portrayed in a humorous way, she is a strong woman, a good mother, one who prepares for her baby's arrival by knitting baby clothes and who willingly nurses her for "what seemed like hours." Despite her troublesome childhood and teenage years, during which she has a volatile relationship with her mother, Celestine, Dot becomes a devoted mother to her own newborn.

In *Tales of Burning Love* Dot marries Jack Mauser, although she has never divorced Gerry. Gerry has escaped from prison and is on the run when Dot picks him up as a hitchhiker. She and three of Mauser's other wives—Eleanor, Candice, and Marlis—are in his red Explorer, which becomes trapped in a snow blizzard. While the other women are asleep in the car, Dot and Gerry make love, and she thinks, "there would always be these times where nothing else existed—no mistakes, no laws, no possible guilt or innocence." Dot is a character who lives her life according to what feels "right" to her, regardless of whether others approve of her decisions. When she loves, she does so with the same tenacity and fearlessness with which she faces everything else in her life. Again, her commitment to her family and loved ones is part of why she survives. As soon as she awakes in the hospital after being rescued in the snow blizzard, her first thoughts are for her daughter, Shawn, and her husband, Gerry.

Discussion Questions

1. Why is Dot so quick to pick a fight with Albertine when she first meets her in a bar?

2. Why does Dot hide Gerry from the authorities? Does she remain loyal to her husband only because she loves him and is pregnant with his child, or does she also have no faith in the United States judicial system?

3. Read *The Beet Queen* to learn about Dot's childhood and discuss how her family life prepares her for a marriage to Gerry. In *Tales of Burning Love*, she is described as a person who "thrived on emergencies." Would you agree with this characterization? Why or why not?

—Patrice Hollrah

FLEUR PILLAGER

Fleur Pillager is Lulu Lamartine's mother and a minor character in Louise Erdrich's novel *Love Medicine*, although she is a major character in Erdrich's *Tracks* and *Four Souls*. In the chapter "The Island" from *Love Medicine*, Lulu begins by noting, "I never grew from the curve of my mother's arms. I still wanted to anchor myself against her. But she had tore herself away from the run of my life like a riverbank. She had vanished, a great surrounding shore, leaving me to spill out alone." Lulu describes her mother sending her to boarding school in *Tracks*, and Fleur goes to Minneapolis to recover her land from John James Mauser, a lumber baron and social scion of Minneapolis in *Four Souls*, but in *Love Medicine* the reader does not entirely understand why Fleur abandons her child. Nevertheless, her presence is felt by Lulu when she hears her mother's voice: "*N'dawnis, n'dawnis.* My daughter, she consoled me. Her voice came from all directions, mysteriously keeping me from inner harm. Her voice was the struck match. Her voice was the steady flame." Despite Fleur's absence, there continues a strong connection between the mother and child. Fleur is a good mother and treats Lulu well when she is young; Lulu describes her in *The Last Report on the Miracles at Little No Horse*: "My mother had always picked me up, given me what I wanted, rocked me, never let me weep. And why did she teach me all this tenderness, this love, if she then threw me in a pit? For that is what the school would be." Fleur values the importance of regaining her land for the tribe over her daughter's happiness, something that Lulu will not understand completely until she is older.

In the chapter "Love Medicine," Lipsha Morrissey, Fleur's grandson, acknowledges Fleur's mythic status and power, partly through her connection to Missepeshu, the Ojibwe water monster: "It had a weakness for young girls and grabbed one of the Pillagers off her rowboat. She got to shore all right, but only after this monster had its way with her. She's an old lady now. Old Lady Pillager. She still doesn't like to see her family fish that lake." This episode is one of the instances of near drowning that Fleur survives, which only adds to her aura of power and the fear that people have of her. She is a medicine woman who has special knowledge that not everyone understands. When Lipsha wants to create a love medicine for Nector Kashpaw, he briefly considers that he should talk to Fleur: "I knew the best thing was to go ask a specialist like Old Lady Pillager, who lives up in a tangle of bush and never shows herself. But the truth is I was afraid of her, like everyone else. She was known for putting the twisted mouth on people, seizing up their hearts. Old Lady Pillager was serious business, and I have always thought it best to steer clear of that whenever I could." Fleur is a complex character who people fear out of respect for her wisdom, knowledge, and power.

Discussion Questions

1. Do you think that Fleur's decision to send Lulu to boarding school was made lightly? Is any evidence provided in *Love Medicine* to support your answer? Should Fleur have kept Lulu at home and not left her, or was Lulu's going away to boarding school necessary? Why?

2. Read *Four Souls* for more information about Fleur's life while Lulu was away at boarding school.

After learning about Fleur's need to regain her land, do you still think that she should not have left Lulu? Research how land was taken away from the Ojibwes by white investors.

3. Read *Tracks* for more information about Fleur's life before Lulu was born. After learning about how she was raped by whites and nearly drowned, do you see her as a victim or survivor? Why?

—*Patrice Hollrah*

PAULINE PUYAT/SISTER LEOPOLDA

Pauline Puyat, a major character in Erdrich's *Tracks* and *The Last Report on the Miracles at Little No Horse*, is a minor character known as Sister Leopolda in *Love Medicine*. Leopolda is Marie Lazarre Kashpaw's teacher at the Sacred Heart Convent where nuns with problems—"nuns that complain too much or lose their mind"—are sent. Erdrich has commented on the dual nature of Christianity and the relationship between Catholicism and Native Americans, saying that on the one hand there is the beauty of the Trinity—the Father, the Son, and the Holy Spirit—and on the other hand there is the brutality in the history of converting the Indians: "a most ticklish concept and a most loving form of destruction."

Leopolda knows that Marie is her daughter, although Marie does not understand her own strange attraction to the nun. Marie thinks that Leopolda has offered her salvation: "But she had loved me, or offered me love. And she had tried to hunt the Dark One down." Marie succinctly summarizes Leopolda's contradictory character, which leads her seemingly to offer goodness to people but in a dark fashion. She knows that Leopolda "was the definite most-hard trial to anyone's endurance, even when they started out with veils of wretched love upon their eyes." When Marie visits Leopolda the first time at the convent, the nun commits unconscionable acts of physical violence on her, scalding her back, cracking her head, and stabbing her hand, leaving a scar. Rather than focus on the love of Jesus Christ, Leopolda watches for Satan: "Leopolda kept track of him and knew his habits, minds he burrowed in, deep spaces where he hid." Hence, she is always looking for the worst in people. As a teacher, Leopolda is the stereotypical nun who doles out punishment with a "long oak pole for opening high windows. It had a hook made of iron on one end that could jerk a patch of your hair out or throttle you by the collar—all from a distance. She used this deadly hook pole for catching Satan by surprise." Leopolda believes that pain is the way in which she must deal with Satan in order to serve the Lord.

Leopolda is consistent in thinking of redemption for her people through pain and suffering. Years later, when Marie takes her daughter Zelda to visit Leopolda on her deathbed, she says, "I knew you would come back." Marie observes that Leopolda "wasn't right in the head after all" when she begins banging a heavy black spoon on her iron bedstead and tries to hit Marie with it. After Marie struggles with Leopolda, trying to take the spoon away from her, she sits with her in silence and realizes that there is nothing she can do to rescue the dying woman. After Leopolda's death, Father Damien, her priest, explains her misdirected behavior: "She regarded herself as one chosen to sacrifice her health, her happiness, after the example of Christ crucified, for the advantage of the Church and the general good of her people."

Discussion Questions

1. Sister Leopolda says to Marie, "Star of the Sea! You'll shine when we burn off the salt!" How do you explain Leopolda's interpretation of Catholicism, the relationship between pain and atonement for sins? Read Erdrich's *Tracks* for background on Pauline Puyat's life before becoming a nun.

2. Leopolda says to Marie, "You have two choices. One, you can marry a no-good Indian, bear his brats, die like a dog. Or two, you can give yourself up to God." What were the objectives of having a convent near the Ojibwe reservation? What are Leopolda's goals in sponsoring Marie? Why does Leopolda reject her own mixed Ojibwe identity?

3. How do you account for Leopolda's treatment of Marie during her two visits to the convent? Read "History of the Puyats by Father Damien Modeste" in Erdrich's *The Last Report on the Miracles at Little No Horse* and discuss how Leopolda's family history might explain her bizarre behaviors.

—*Patrice Hollrah*

REFERENCES

Allan Chavkin and Nancy Feyl Chavkin, *Conversations with Louise Erdrich and Michael Dorris* (Jackson: University Press of Mississippi, 1994);

Allan Chavkin, ed., *The Chippewa Landscape of Louise Erdrich* (Tuscaloosa: University of Alabama Press, 1999);

P. Jane Hafen, *Reading Louise Erdrich's* Love Medicine. (Boise, Idaho: Boise State University Press, 2003);

Patrice Hollrah, "'Women Are Strong. Strong, Terribly Strong': Female Intellectual Sovereignty in the Words of Louise Erdrich," in her *"The Old Lady Trill, The Victory Yell": The Power of Native Women in Native American Literature* (New York: Routledge, 2004), pp. 89–131;

Mickey Pearlman, "A Bibliography of Writings by Louise Erdrich," in *American Women Writing Fiction*, edited by Pearlman (Lexington: University Press of Kentucky, 1989), pp. 108–112;

Greg Sarris, Connie A. Jacobs, and James R. Giles, eds., *Approaches to Teaching the Works of Louise Erdrich* (New York: MLA, 2004);

Lorena L. Stookey, *Louise Erdrich: A Critical Companion* (Westport, Conn.: Greenwood Press, 1999);

Hertha D. Sweet Wong, *Louise Erdrich's* Love Medicine: A Casebook (New York: Oxford University Press, 2000).

F

James T. Farrell

(February 27, 1904 – August 22, 1979)

YOUNG LONIGAN

(New York: Vanguard, 1932)

STUDS LONIGAN

William "Studs" Lonigan, a young Irish tough growing up in Chicago's South Side during the 1910s and 1920s, is at the center of a series of three early Farrell novels—*Young Lonigan, The Young Manhood of Studs Lonigan* (1934), and *Judgment Day* (1935)—republished as a trilogy under the title *Studs Lonigan: A Trilogy* (1935). The novels are classic examples of literary naturalism, a rendering of life in starkly realistic terms. In naturalistic fiction people are treated as a species of animal that lacks a soul and responds to physical drives based on biology. Farrell's depiction of his characters was regarded in his time as so strong that the publisher of *Young Lonigan* included an introduction by a sociologist as a way of avoiding possible censorship.

The character Studs Lonigan was based on an acquaintance of Farrell's from his youth along Indiana Avenue between Fifty-seventh and Fifty-eighth Streets in Chicago. Most of the other characters in this series (and in other works Farrell wrote) were also inspired by people with whom he grew up, though he generally modified their traits and sometimes turned them into composites. Farrell's realistic methods required that he write from what he knew and with an almost photographic accuracy.

Young Lonigan opens as Studs prepares to attend his elementary-school graduation ceremony at St. Patrick's Church. The fourteen-year-old is mugging in front of a mirror, puffing a cigarette, confirming for himself the image he wants to present to his friends, their families, and the priests and nuns who have been his teachers. Through all three volumes Studs strives to project the right image to those around him: his life is devoted to the cultivation of a facade. Studs's reality, however, never quite matches his mental picture of himself, despite his efforts: "He couldn't let himself get soft about anything, because, well, just because he wasn't the kind of a bird that got soft. He never let anyone know how he felt." As he interacts with others—boys, girls, and adults—Studs critiques himself on his actions, replaying incidents in his mind, sometimes rationalizing events, sometimes improving on them.

The first novel in the trilogy captures the physical and psychological world of a handful of Lonigan family members and friends. With minimal plot, the narrative shows what life is like for these lower-middle-class residents of an ethnic neighborhood in a teeming city. Studs's rivalries with other boys are shown primarily through a fight he has with classmate Weary Reilley; his bumbling attempts to relate to girls are invariably colored by his earlier preadolescent worship of Lucy Scanlan; and his undemonstrative love for his parents and siblings comes across through their bickering rather than through scenes of caring family interaction. All these images convey "the life of a community, the tang and sorrow and joy of a people that lived, worked, suffered, procreated, aspired, filled out their little days, and died." Fundamental to that community environment is the Catholic faith practiced by nearly everybody in the neighborhood. Studs vacillates between guilty sinner and tough guy: he prays for forgiveness or for strength and then fights with his peers, steals from local merchants, and makes sexual advances toward usually unwilling girls.

The later volumes of the trilogy follow Studs's growth into adulthood. In *The Young Manhood of Studs Lonigan,* he continues to play the tough, vigilantly protecting his reputation as a street fighter to ensure his place in the neighborhood hierarchy. Bouts of drunkenness, complicated by the inconsistent quality of the illegal booze available during Prohibition, eventually take their toll on Studs's health, despite his occasional attempts to quit drinking. His relationships with and treatment of women mirror the attitudes formed when he was young; he often pictures women in a virgin/whore dichotomy. Despite occasional feelings of guilt, he typically rationalizes his actions and escapes back into the world of the tough street kid. But at a New Year's Eve party concluding the second volume of the trilogy, Studs gets so drunk he cannot defend himself against Reilley, who this time beats him severely. Studs stumbles into the cold Chicago night, where he contracts the pneumonia that eats away at his health.

Studs never fully recovers from that New Year's Eve in 1929. By the opening of *Judgment Day,* he is working for his father, a painting contractor. He soon wears out what remains of his health; his weakened heart troubles him. By 1931 his girlfriend, Catherine Banahan, is pregnant. Under a doctor's orders to find work that does not require the physical exertions of a housepainter, Studs spends a rainy summer day on a job hunt, then falls victim to a fever that puts him in a coma. Lingering for a few days, he dies without marrying Catherine and without reconciling his family to her or to the baby she carries. Studs has been broken and defeated by life.

In an introduction written a dozen years after the first volume of the Lonigan trilogy was published, Farrell said, "Studs is a normal boy, healthy and more or less typical of boys in his own environment. He does not moon and brood over problems of conscience, morals, conduct, as do highly sensitive and extraordinary boys." But he does "moon and brood" over the image he presents to the world. Studs, though dimly aware of the reality of his life, is largely ruled by his passions rather than his intellect. He is a creature driven to maintain his place in his environ-ment. Despite his attempts to survive by cultivating a threatening persona, others in his neighborhood are, in Darwinian terms, more fit to survive.

Discussion Questions

1.Is Studs an example of the person who is "a legend in his own mind"? How does his tendency to act in accord with his image of himself affect his ability to live in the real world?

2.Residents of Lonigan's neighborhood exhibit a moral code embodying strict religious attitudes combined with extreme ethnic, racial, and gender biases. Children have obviously internalized their parents' code. What does that moral code, handed down from generation to generation, tell readers about tendencies within a society? Is there anything universal about the code itself or about the tendency of such a code to transmit values—good or bad—from one generation to the next? Can an individual escape the limitations of such a society?

3. At several points in his life, Studs has a chance to change, to correct his mistakes, and to become a more acceptable member of the greater society. Why doesn't he succeed? What drives him to put image ahead of reality or comfort or even life itself?

4.An early naturalistic depiction of a youth confronting his world is that of Henry Fleming in Stephen Crane's *The Red Badge of Courage.* Both Henry and Studs are concerned with how others view them; both want to be seen as heroic; and both exist largely behind facades. How does Studs's response to the necessity of adaptation differ from the response of Henry Fleming? In what ways is the promise suggested by the closing paragraphs of *The Red Badge of Courage* never more than a distant possibility for Studs Lonigan?

—*Mark D. Noe*

REFERENCES

Edgar M. Branch, *James T. Farrell* (New York: Twayne, 1971);

Laura Browder, *Rousing the Nation: Radical Culture in Depression America* (Amherst: University of Massachusetts Press, 1998), pp. 68–88;

Robert K. Landers, *An Honest Writer: The Life and Times of James T. Farrell* (San Francisco: Encounter Books, 2004);

Donald Pizer, "James T. Farrell and the 1930s," in *Literature at the Barricades: The American Writer in the 1930s,* edited by Ralph F. Bogardus and Fred Hobson (Tuscaloosa: University of Alabama Press, 1982), pp. 69–81.

William Faulkner

(September 25, 1897 – July 6, 1962)

✍

ABSALOM, ABSALOM!

(New York: Random House, 1936)

THOMAS SUTPEN

The central character in William Faulkner's novel *Absalom, Absalom!* is Thomas Sutpen, whose ruthless pursuit of his "design" causes the doom of his house. This theme had previously been developed in two of Faulkner's short stories, "Wash," which describes Wash Jones's murder of Sutpen, and "Evangeline," which focuses on the Henry-Judith-Bon conflict and its aftermath. At the novel's opening Sutpen has been dead for more than forty years. His character and actions—and their effects and consequences on his family—are revealed entirely in retrospect, gradually and piecemeal, filtered through the consciousness of Miss Rosa Coldfield, Mr. Compson, Quentin Compson, and Quentin's Harvard roommate, Shreve.

Sutpen was the quintessential self-made man. Born into a poor family in the mountains of West Virginia, he had a life-changing experience at age fourteen. At the time his family was living in the Tidewater region of Virginia, where his father worked for a wealthy planter. One day Sutpen went to the planter's house to deliver a message from his father but was told by a black servant to go around to the back door. To a boy who had been bred to the independence and egalitarianism peculiar to poor mountainfolk, the incident was a profound shock. After solitary reflection and deliberation, the boy Sutpen formed a "design": to avenge the wrong by becoming a wealthy planter himself, by acquiring "land and niggers and a fine house," for which, he reasoned, he needed only to be "clever and coura-

geous." His design became the god for which he was willing to use and sacrifice everything, including his own children.

Faulkner was very clear about the novel's central theme. When he began writing it, he wrote to his publisher that it was a story of "a man who outraged the land, and the land then turned and destroyed the man's family." Many years after the novel's publication, he explained that Sutpen had said, "I'm going to establish a dynasty, I don't care how," and in doing so he "violated all the rules of decency and honor and pity and compassion, and the fates took revenge on him." The story of Sutpen is the story of his doomed quest for land and a son. For a man of Sutpen's force and courage, land was relatively easy to get, but getting a son who fulfilled his aspirations was a different matter. On his first effort, he acquired land, wife, and son when he married his Haitian employer's daughter after quelling a slave revolt on his plantation. Learning, however, that his wife carried a trace of black blood, he "provided for her and put her aside" because her mixed blood disqualified her from being "adjunctive or incremental to [his] design." He repudiated his wife and son rather than compromise his ideal, his "design," but he felt that he had justly compensated her by making a generous property settlement. The misfortunes that befell the Sutpen family had their source in Thomas Sutpen's heartless treatment of his first wife and son.

Sutpen's second attempt at dynasty took him to Jefferson, Mississippi, where he acquired one hundred square miles of virgin land from an Indian chief and then hacked out a plantation from it. He chose a wife, Ellen Coldfield, who was the daughter of a puritan storekeeper as rigid and calculating as Sutpen himself. She bore him two children—Henry and Judith. But when Thomas Sutpen seemed at last to have achieved his design, the past intruded upon his life in the form of Charles Bon, his rejected son, who had become Henry's dear friend and who fell in love with Judith. Withholding the truth from Bon and Judith, Sutpen told Henry that Bon was his half brother. Henry subsequently renounced his birthright and left with Bon; the two men served together in the Civil War. Near the end of the war Henry seemed willing to allow Judith and Bon's incestuous marriage, until Sutpen finally informed

Henry of Bon's mixed blood. Presumably Sutpen anticipated Henry's response: that he would "calmly and logically" kill Bon.

After the Civil War, Thomas Sutpen returned to a ruined house and Henry, his heir, as good as dead, and immediately set about rebuilding his fortunes. He became engaged to Miss Rosa, but she broke the engagement when Sutpen proposed that they mate first and marry after, if she produced a son. Finally, desperate for an heir and aware of his advancing years, he seduced Milly, the fifteen-year-old granddaughter of his hanger-on, Wash Jones. But Milly gave birth to a girl on the same morning that Sutpen's mare foaled a colt, and his only words to her were: "Well, Milly; too bad you're not a mare too. Then I could give you a decent stall in the stable." Overhearing that heartless remark, Wash, who had always admired him with hero worship, killed Sutpen with a rusty scythe.

Sutpen has been compared to Greek tragic heroes Oedipus and Orestes. Faulkner himself said that Sutpen was one of his most classically tragic characters. The critic Cleanth Brooks has remarked that Sutpen was destroyed by hubris because he violated all codes of human decency for the sake of his "design," his dream of material grandeur. But there is a crucial difference between Sutpen and the Greek heroes: in their suffering the latter gain self-knowledge, but Sutpen does not. Faulkner held that slavery was the curse of the South. In Sutpen he created a character who combined the individual sin of pride and the regional sin of slavery. Further, it might be said that in his pride Sutpen unwittingly enslaved himself to the abstract idea he called his design.

Discussion Questions

1. Sutpen wanted to build a dynasty, for which land and a son were essential. Do you think that Sutpen's treatment of land and his treatment of his sons are related? How are they alike, and how are they different?

2. Ironically, the only surviving descendant of Sutpen is Jim Bond, Bon's idiot grandson. What virtues, if any, does Jim represent?

3. Cleanth Brooks said: "Sutpen's virtues are those of a typical twentieth-century man. So are his vices—his dismissal of the past, his commitment to the future, and his confidence that, with courage and know-how, he can accomplish anything." It might be said that Sutpen's design was his own version of the American Dream. Does Brooks's argument assume that there are higher values than the American Dream? Do you agree with him? Why or why not?

4. Faulkner said that his characters named themselves. Most of the characters' names in *Absalom, Absalom!* are revealing of their owners, whether by likeness or by contrast. For example, Coldfield is the name of the barren, loveless puritan family, and Clytie (Clytemnestra) is the name of Sutpen's loyal, long-suffering mulatto daughter. Sutpen is a very unusual name. What associations or connotations, if any, does the name suggest to you? Try saying the name slowly, drawing it out—Sut-pen, Ssut-pen, Sssut-pen; does the sibilant quality of its sound suggest any word or movement?

—*Joyce Ahn*

AS I LAY DYING
(New York: Cape & Smith, 1930)

THE BUNDREN FAMILY

In William Faulkner's novel *As I Lay Dying* the Bundrens are a poor white family who face a series of hardships to transport the body of Addie, the matriarch of the family, to her hometown for burial. In addition to Addie's husband, Anse, the family includes their children Cash, Darl, Dewey Dell, and Vardaman, and Jewel, Addie's son by an adulterous affair with a local minister. Asked if the individual members of the family represent different parts of one person, Faulkner told a class conference at the University of Virginia: "No. They were—I was writing about people again. . . . I took this family and subjected them to the two greatest catastrophes which man can suffer—flood and fire, that's all." As the Bundrens go through "flood and fire" to bury Addie, they develop from single-trait, flat characters into multidimensional, complex humans.

The oldest son, Cash, a monomaniac carpenter obsessed with his most recent work, Addie's coffin, acquires perseverance and responsibility after he experiences a disabling foot injury during the family's reckless river crossing. The irascibly violent, unruly Jewel demonstrates his love for Addie by volunteering his horse, his beloved mother surrogate, so the family can replace their drowned mules and continue the funeral journey. A seventeen-year-old concealing her pregnancy by an insincere town fellow, Dewey Dell violently assaults her brother Darl, whose knowing eyes make her feel "naked" with her secret exposed. With little or no guidance from surrounding adults, Vardaman leaves behind his initial confusion—expressed by his statement that "My mother is a fish"—as the boy comes to accept that "she" lies dead, or at least dying, in the coffin. Faulkner also offers a complex characterization of Anse, the irresponsibly self-righteous and do-nothing father, who, to his neighbors' puzzled amazement, obtains necessary help through his extreme laziness and manages to keep his word to Addie. Thus, Anse's introduction of a newly picked wife at the end of the novel, which brings to a grotesquely anticlimactic close the family's odyssey, may nevertheless testify to the impressive resilience of an insignificant hill farmer.

Among his siblings, Darl is contemplative and sharp-eyed, as the highly sophisticated language and keen insight of his narration make apparent. The novel comprises fifty-nine chapters of interior monologue from the point of view of Darl and fifteen other characters, with Darl narrating most of them. His penetrating gaze exposes the family's secrets—Addie's affair with Reverend Whitfield that produced Jewel, Dewey Dell's pregnancy, and each member's selfish purpose in visiting the Jefferson town—that at once motivate and complicate the funeral journey. In his last chapter, institutionalized after a mental breakdown, Darl refers metaphorically to his mind-reading perceptiveness as "a little spy-glass he got in France at the war," thus alluding to literary modernists who, disillusioned by the atrocity of World War I, looked beyond humans' self-proclaimed justice into the actual lack of substantive moral values.

Tellingly, Faulkner hinted at such relativity when, asked if Anse was the novel's "villain," he turned rather to "the convention" underlying a society's value judgment: "if there was a villain it was the convention which gave them no out except to carry her through fire and flood twenty miles in order to follow the dying wish, which by that time to her meant nothing." Indeed, the tension between the Bundrens as "protagonist" and the convention as "villain" suggests itself throughout the work. First of all, the family's enterprise itself originates from Addie's "revenge" on the hypocritically restrictive traditions around motherhood, femininity, and selfhood. Addie's only chapter offers her bitter critique of language—the ultimate cause of hypocrisy—as "words go straight up in a thin line, quick and harmless, and . . . doing goes along the earth, clinging to it, so that after a while the two lines are too far apart for the same person to straddle from one to the other." Also, the family's journey serves to expose the uncertainty of conventional values by being at once the noble fulfillment of a promise between a bereaved couple and, as their female neighbors insist throughout, an "outrage" against the dead mother.

Complicating the relationship between the family and the convention, even as Anse's self-righteous appeal successfully enlists the help of respectable Christians, Darl's attempt to cremate Addie's rotting corpse causes his arrest and resulting removal from the society. Amid the confused and confusing workings of social norms, Cash notices the murky boundary between sanity and insanity: "Sometimes I think it aint none of us pure crazy and aint none of us pure sane until the balance of us talks him that-a-way." Indeed, since the novel questions almost all frames of reference (including identity, time, religion, family, and love), even life and death can coexist. On the trip driven by "a motionless hand" of dead Addie, Vardaman struggles with his Addie-fish identification; Dewey Dell cannot help associating childbearing with bodily decomposition ("the agony and the despair of spreading bones"); and Jewel, Addie's favorite son, retrieves her coffin from the fire "riding upon it, clinging to it."

The Bundrens are similar to the Compson family from Faulkner's previous novel *The Sound and the Fury* (1929) in the intensity and depth of the members' psychological interactions and conflicts. Tellingly, Faulkner's comment on their resemblance, made at the University of Virginia, draws upon the idea of family solidarity against the harsh world: "there are certain similarities in family relationships between a family of planters and a family of tenant farmers. The superficial differences could be vast and varied, but basically the same relationship is there because it's based on the need for solidarity in a country which not too long ago was still frontier." Such solidarity eludes the Compsons, but Faulkner presents the Bundrens' strenuous passage somewhat as a process of family disintegration (caused by the loss of mother as the center) and eventual reconstitution effected by Anse's remarriage and the replacement of "insane" Darl with the illegitimate baby Dewey Dell has failed to abort.

Discussion Questions

1. In some of his chapters Darl describes events that take place in his absence—for example, Addie's deathbed scene and the subsequent coffin making by Cash and Tull. Some commentators regard Darl's ability as supernatural clairvoyance; others attribute it to the other characters' predictable simplicity and Darl's lucidity in drawing correct inferences. What is your position on this issue? How would you support your answer with textual evidence? How would your answer help you understand or question Darl's "insanity"?

2. In her only chapter, Addie narrates how she "had been tricked by words older than Anse or love" and suggests that she has asked Anse to bury her in Jefferson to "tak[e] revenge." What does it mean to be "tricked by words older than Anse or love"? How, in her design, would her request serve as "revenge"?

3. Since its publication, *As I Lay Dying* has been considered a comedy as often as a tragedy. How would you read the Bundrens in these terms? Which family members would you categorize as "comic" or "tragic"? Why?

4. How does Faulkner's modernist technique—multiple interior monologues based on character-narrators' streams of consciousness—work to influence the reader's understanding of the Bundren family? What difference would have been made if Faulkner had described the characters through a traditional third-person narrator?

5. Comparing the Bundren family with the Compson family from *The Sound and the Fury*, Faulkner also told a class conference at the University of Virginia: "If there is any relationship it's probably simply because both of them happened to have a sister in a roaring gang of menfolks." How do the two families overlap and differ as regards the relationship between "a sister" and "a roaring gang of menfolks"? What would your answer to the question tell about Faulkner's observation of the gender relations in the 1920s South?

—*Massami Sugimori*

GO DOWN, MOSES
(New York: Random House, 1942)

LUCAS BEAUCHAMP

Lucas Beauchamp is an important character in *Go Down, Moses* and *Intruder in the Dust* (1948), and he also appears in *The Reivers* (1962). Beauchamp's full name, Lucas Quintus Carothers McCaslin Beauchamp, testifies to a genealogy as complex as any in Faulkner's body of work. The son of Tomey's Turl and Tennie Beauchamp, he is the mulatto grandson of the white McCaslin patriarch Lucius Quintus Carothers McCaslin. Lucas grew up on the McCaslin plantation alongside his white cousin, Zack Edmonds, and he identifies most strongly with the McCaslin branch of his family. When a white man directs a string of epithets at Lucas in *Intruder in the Dust*, he objects only to being linked with the Edmonds branch of his family: "I aint a Edmonds," he replies. "I dont belong to these new folks. I belongs to the old lot. I'm a McCaslin." Indeed, Lucas's identification with his McCaslin lineage lies at base of his considerable sense of self-worth, and even his Edmonds relatives see that, as Roth Edmonds says in "The Fire and the Hearth" section of *Go Down, Moses*, *"He's more like old Carothers than all the rest of us put together, including old Carothers . . . intact and complete, contemptuous, as old Carothers must have been, of all blood black white yellow or red, including his own."* Lucas sees himself, as Thadious M. Davis notes, "both as a worthy descendant of old

Carothers and as protected by that position of male privilege despite his race."

Although he stays locked in the Jefferson jail for most of *Intruder in the Dust*, he is the catalyst for all of the action and the focus of the scenes in which he does appear. At the beginning of the novel, Lucas rescues twelve-year-old Chick Mallison, the nephew of lawyer Gavin Stevens, from the icy creek he had fallen into, engendering a sense of obligation in the white boy. When Chick visits Lucas's cabin, he notices the pride of the black man. Lucas wears a heavy gold watch chain, uses a gold toothpick, and wears a hat of "worn handmade beaver such as his grandfather had paid thirty and forty dollars apiece for." Chick later learns that the entire community thinks Lucas "uppity" and knows that even though he "said 'sir' and 'mister' to you if you were white" you knew that he "was thinking neither."

Four years after rescuing Chick, when he is arrested for allegedly shooting Vinson Gowrie, Lucas convinces the boy to dig up Gowrie's body in order to prove that he was not shot with Lucas's gun, setting into motion the events that eventually prove Lucas's innocence. Even in jail, Lucas maintains a powerful, aristocratic air. When Lucas first asks for his assistance, Chick realizes "Lucas was not even asking him to believe anything; he was not even asking a favor, making no last desperate plea to his humanity and pity but was even going to pay him provided the price was not too high." Lucas also takes care to compensate lawyer Gavin Stevens for his services in the last scene of the novel; even though Stevens only allows Lucas to pay two dollars for his expenses, Lucas insists on a business-like exchange and even asks Stevens for his receipt in the novel's last line, proof that he owes him nothing further.

Lucas's agreement to pay Stevens only expenses and to pay Chick nothing at all are significant actions. The reader remembers how Lucas refused Chick's embarrassing attempt to pay him seventy cents for saving him from drowning in the creek. In doing so, he taught Chick that some actions require something more than mere financial compensation. At the end of *Intruder in the Dust*, Lucas acknowledges that Chick has finally paid his childhood debt not with cash or worldly goods, but with kindness and respect.

Discussion Questions

1. Readers have long recognized *Intruder in the Dust* as Faulkner's most obvious fictional attempt to address the racial problems of his own era. In what ways does Lucas's primary allegiance to the white McCaslin branch of his family complicate Faulkner's exploration of racial issues in this novel? How does Faulkner's contemporary treatment of race in *Intruder in the Dust* differ from his treatment of it in his more historical novel, *Go Down, Moses?*

2. Some readers have criticized Faulkner's aristocratic depiction of Lucas Beauchamp in *Intruder in the Dust*. For example, Erik Dussere writes that Lucas "is not a radical figure; rather, he is a version of the perfect Negro Faulkner invokes in his public writings, the one who is required to be *superior* to white people in order to be deserving of equality." Does Faulkner's characterization of Lucas support such claims? Does his depiction of the novel's other characters support them?

3. M-G-M purchased the motion-picture rights to *Intruder in the Dust*. The movie remains largely true to the book, in part because Faulkner acted as an unofficial consultant as M-G-M filmed it in his hometown of Oxford. One significant alteration, though, occurs in the last scene of the movie; rather than the exchange between Lucas and Stevens about debts owed and paid, the movie ends with Stevens and Chick watching Lucas walk down the street discussing, as Cleanth Brooks notes in *William Faulkner: The Yoknapatawpha Country*, "their admiration for him as a man and their indebtedness to him for having given them a lesson in the need for keeping the moral conscience sensitive and alert." How does the ending of the novel depict these same themes? How does it change them?

4. Carl J. Dimitri describes Lucas as "a mystery, a social anomaly, and as a result, he is feared by some and hated by others." Which characters hate Lucas and which ones fear him? Which characters feel both emotions?

—*Lorie Watkins Fulton*

McCaslin Family

The McCaslin family—or, more accurately, the McCaslin-Edmonds-Beauchamp family, the "Negro and the white phase of the same family"—comprises the main characters of William Faulkner's *Go Down, Moses*. Faulkner told a group of students in 1957 that the family was what "held together" the sprawling experimental book. The family's web-like interracial genealogy both mirrors and drives the literary complexities of the book. Instead of being introduced to members of the family in an orderly, linear fashion, readers are plunged from the start into a disorienting search for understanding of characters' names and identities and of the interrelationships between them. The struggle to understand a text about a complicated and disturbing family history itself emerges as one of the key themes of *Go Down, Moses*, as readers follow young Isaac "Ike" McCaslin's efforts in the fifth section, "The Bear," to make sense of his family's cryptic plantation ledgers. Faulkner also uses Ike, along with his mixed-race relative Lucas Beauchamp, to blur the lines between narratives about race relations in the South and hunting stories. Ultimately, Ike and his relatives—white, black, and in between—stand in for an author, a region, and indeed an entire war-ravaged civilization grappling with a dark past and an uncertain future.

Go Down, Moses begins not in the World War II–era narrative present, in which Ike is a childless old widower, but in pre–Civil War Mississippi, before his birth. The section "Was" details a hunt mounted by three white members of the family: Ike's father, "Uncle Buck" McCaslin; his father's twin brother, "Uncle Buddy" McCaslin; and Ike's older cousin, "Cass" Edmonds. Instead of pursuing a fox or deer, they are hunting an escaped slave with the horse-like name of Tomey's Turl. Turl has run, as he regularly does, to visit his enslaved lover, Tennie, on the plantation of Hubert Beauchamp and his sister, Sophonsiba. Tennie and Turl's plight parallels that of the lovelorn Sophonsiba, who would do almost anything to marry the highly unwilling Buck McCaslin. The section's comic plot culminates in a poker game played for human stakes by Uncle Buddy and Hubert Beauchamp; Buddy wins Tennie while simultaneously freeing Buck from having to marry Sophonsiba. Unraveling these complexities, worthy of one of William Shakespeare's comedies, forces readers to grapple with the disturbing implications of a social system in which white women and African Americans of both sexes were hunted, traded, and sold almost exactly like animals. Passing references to Tomey's Turl as a "white half-McCaslin" also foreshadow Ike's attempts in "The Bear" to cope with the news that the racial and familial boundaries he had been raised in the Jim Crow South to view as impermeable had, in fact, been breached.

In the second section of the book, "The Fire and the Hearth," Faulkner clarifies several aspects of the family's genealogy in the process of dramatizing a series of confrontations between white members of the family and their indomitable mixed-raced relative Lucas Beauchamp. Readers learn that Lucas is the grandson—through Tomey's Turl—of white family patriarch "old Carothers" McCaslin. He has capitalized on his genetic proximity to Carothers and his financial independence (thanks to an inheritance left by Carothers to Tomey's Turl) to assert his full manhood in a region whose laws and traditions try to relegate him to the subhuman status of "nigger." In this section Lucas does the hunting, searching for buried treasure he thinks Buck and Buddy may have left behind. Lucas's efforts to lay claim to every aspect of the McCaslin legacy set him apart from Ike, who at age twenty-one mysteriously relinquished his "birthright," the McCaslin plantation, to the Edmonds side of the family.

Faulkner explores Ike's central act of relinquishment in "The Bear." Readers learn that as a young man Ike had decoded entries in the McCaslin plantation ledgers that, in his mind, irredeemably damned both Carothers and the land of his inheritance. Not only had Carothers fathered the slave Tomey's Turl, but Ike believes that Turl's mother, Tomasina (Tomey), was the patriarch's own daughter. Revolted by his grandfather's sins, Ike hands control of the plantation to Cass Edmonds and embarks on a simple life of carpentry in town and hunting in the Big Woods. He also applies his formidable hunting skills to the task of tracking down his mixed-race relatives—not to establish friendly ties with them, but to give them their portions of Tomey's Turl's inheritance.

Ike acts on what he views as honorable intentions, but Faulkner devotes considerable energy to interrogating the efficacy of Ike's choice. For one thing, Ike's wife reacts to the relinquishment by refusing to bear children. In the narrative present, Ike's doe-hunting younger relatives mock him and flout the environmental ethics he has tried to teach them. Ike's beloved Big Woods are clearly doomed. Just as painfully for Ike, his decision does nothing to stop his family's past from repeating itself. In "Delta Autumn" Ike learns that the blood of Carothers will run on through the illegitimate child of the current plantation owner, "Roth" Edmonds, and his mistress, a long-lost descendant of Tomey's Turl. Unable to accept the idea of interracial love, Ike tries to pay the woman off, advising her to return to the North and marry a black man. Like Carothers in spite of himself, Ike views Roth's lover and the child as "niggers" first and as family members second.

Faulkner's complex handling of the McCaslin-Edmonds-Beauchamp family echoes his character Quentin Compson's anguished words at the end of the 1936 masterpiece *Absalom, Absalom!* ("I dont hate [the South] . . . *I dont hate it!*"). Like that novel, *Go Down, Moses*—packed with what scholar Richard Gray calls "rich confusions of region, family and race"—raises more questions than it answers. More than sixty years after its first publication, critics are still debating exactly what, for instance, Ike learns in the family ledgers. One thing is certain, though: *Go Down, Moses* will continue to challenge and inspire readers who, like Ike McCaslin, are drawn to the hard work of trying to understand the human family's tangled past.

Discussion Questions

1. Five of the seven sections comprising *Go Down, Moses* were based on previously published short stories, and the book was originally published with the subtitle "and Other Stories." Faulkner complained in a 1949 letter to publisher Robert K. Haas that this was a mistake, declaring that "Moses is indeed a novel." And yet in 1947 he told students that the book was "simply a collection of short stories." Which genre do you think the book belongs to: story collection, novel, or something else? How does the role played by the McCaslin-Edmonds-Beauchamp family affect your thoughts on the subject?

2. In the key fourth part of the section "The Bear," Cass Edmonds tries to persuade Ike McCaslin not to relinquish the family plantation. Which character do you think makes the stronger argument? What would you do if you were in Ike's position? Why?

3. *Go Down, Moses* is studied frequently by scholars of environmental literature thanks to its fascinating depictions of hunting, wilderness, and environmental destruction. How do these "green" themes mesh, or clash, with Faulkner's explorations of McCaslin-Edmonds-Beauchamp family history? How "green" is *Go Down, Moses* as a whole?

4. Faulkner began compiling and revising *Go Down, Moses* soon after the death of his beloved African American "mammy," Caroline Barr, and the book is dedicated to her. How effectively do you think the book handles the question of interracial love? Does Faulkner, unlike Ike McCaslin, seem to think that such love is real and viable?

5. Compare and contrast Lucas Beauchamp with Joe Christmas in *Light in August*, Charles Bon in *Absalom, Absalom!*, or another mixed-race (or possibly mixed-race) character created by Faulkner or a contemporary such as Nella Larsen. What strategies do Lucas and the other character employ for dealing with the white supremacist order? In what ways do these characters subvert and/or reinforce that order?

—*Bart H. Welling*

༄

THE HAMLET
(New York: Random House, 1940; revised, 1964)

V. K. RATLIFF

V. K. Ratliff, a major character in *The Hamlet*, is William Faulkner's most reliable authority on the Snopes family, a witness to the career of Flem Snopes and a close observer of the entire clan as they establish themselves in Yoknapatawpha County. He plays an important role in the subsequent novels of the Snopes trilogy, *The Town* (1957) and *The Mansion* (1959), and also appears in stories and other works in which the Snopes appear.

Ratliff is known as "V. K. Suratt," or simply "Suratt," in some of Faulkner's fiction. Faulkner wrote to Malcolm Cowley on August 16, 1945 that he renamed the character because "a man of that name turned up at home, so I changed my man to Ratliff for the reason that my whole town spent much of its time trying to decide just what living man I was writing about, the one literary criticism of the town being 'How in the hell did he remember all that, and when did that happen anyway?'" Ratliff functions as a significant narrative presence in *The Hamlet;* even though Faulkner relies on third-person narrative, he filters significant portions of the novel through Ratliff's perceptions and conversations.

A sewing-machine salesman who also trades in other items, Ratliff works not for money but for "his itinerary, his established and nurtured round of newsmongering, the pleasure of retailing it." He sells "perhaps three machines a year" and spends the rest of his time "trading in land and livestock and second hand farming tools and musical instruments or anything else which the owner did not want badly enough" while "retailing from house to house the news of his four counties with the ubiquity of a newspaper and carrying personal messages from mouth to mouth about weddings and funerals and the preserving of vegetables and fruit with the reliability of a postal service." Faulkner writes that Ratliff "never forgot a name and he knew everyone, man mule and dog, within fifty miles." His keen eye for detail and insatiable curiosity about what was going on in his territory make him one of Faulkner's most trustworthy sources of information.

In *The Hamlet,* Faulkner describes Ratliff as "pleasant, affable, courteous, anecdotal and impenetrable." Readers learn little about Ratliff in this novel save that he lives with his sister in Jefferson and that he grew up near the Snopes family on a farm his father rented from Anse Holland. Ratliff never even reveals the details of the mysterious operation that keeps him away from Frenchman's Bend for a year, joking only that the doctor cut out his "pocket book," wryly adding, "I reckon that's why he put me to sleep first." More intriguing than these scant facts, though, are the contradictions of Ratliff's character. For example, he fancies himself a shrewd salesman and trader, yet he sells few sewing machines, and Flem Snopes snook-

ers him phenomenally in his scheme to sell the Old Frenchman place. Ratliff also idolizes Eula Varner, yet he admits to himself that "he would not have wanted" an actual relationship with her to be," adding, "It would have been like giving me a pipe organ, that never had and never would know any more than how to wind up the second-hand music-box I had just swapped a mail-box for." Readers learn more about Ratliff's history in *The Town* via a conversation between Eula and Gavin Stevens when she inadvertently reveals that Ratliff's initials stand for "Vladimir Kyrilytch." She adds that Ratliff descended from a Russian ancestor who fought for the British Army during the American Revolution.

Ratliff's main purpose in the Snopes trilogy seems the same as the one he serves in the hamlet of Frenchman's Bend: he shares information. He is, as Theresa M. Towner points out, a storyteller who participates in Faulkner's method of third-person narration: "Rather than state directly his opinion of the stories he tells, Ratliff works by indirection." Towner adds that Ratliff also functions as the reader's link to the Snopes narratives; readers of *The Hamlet* "look repeatedly to Ratliff for an explanation of what all of the Snopes stories in the novel mean" and "when Flem eventually 'usurps' Ratliff's imagination" readers "too fall victim to Flem." Readers trust Ratliff, at least in part, because of his displays of innate humanity and compassion for others, such as when he leaves money for the retarded Ike Snopes with Mrs. Littlejohn for safekeeping. In another such instance, he allows Mink Snopes's wife and children to stay with him after the sheriff arrests Mink for murdering Jack Houston.

Faulkner admitted his own admiration for Ratliff and curiously humanized him in a 1955 interview with Cynthia Grenier when he remarked, "Ratliff is wonderful. He's done more things than any man I know. Why, I couldn't tell some of the things that man has done." Later, at the University of Virginia, Faulkner praised Ratliff's ability to accept change: "he had accepted a change in culture, a change in environment, and he has suffered no anguish, no grief from it. In—for that reason, he's in favor of change, because it's motion and it's the world as he knows it, and he's never one to say, I wish I had been born a hundred years ago." As Michael Millgate writes in *The Achievement of William Faulkner*, Ratliff is "clearly a character whom Faulkner regarded as being especially important, both for what he did and for what he represented." Ratliff is far from perfect; readers cannot, for example, forget his exploitation of Mink's wife while arranging the goat trade.

Discussion Questions

1. At the University of Virginia, Faulkner said that he used Ratliff's point of view in *The Town* to balance Chick Mallison's and Gavin Stevens's narration. Ratliff, Faulkner said, "practiced virtue from simple instinct, from—well, more than that, because—for a practical reason, because it was better. There was less confusion if all people didn't tell lies to one another, and didn't pretend." Does the narrative lens that Ratliff provides in *The Hamlet* function in a similar fashion?

2. Characters in *The Hamlet* seem compelled to confide things to Ratliff that they do not reveal to other characters. Will Varner, for instance, tells only Ratliff that he likes to sit in his flour-barrel chair at the Old Frenchman place because "I'm trying to find out what it must have felt like to be the fool that would need all this." What qualities make Ratliff so sympathetic that even Will Varner will confide in him?

3. Ratliff seems very wary of trading with Flem Snopes. Just before the spotted horse auction, Ratliff remarks, "I'd just as soon buy a tiger or a rattlesnake. And if Flem Snopes offered me either one of them, I would be afraid to touch it for fear it would turn out to be a painted dog or a piece of garden hose when I went up to take possession of it." How, then, does Flem manage to convince Ratliff to deal with him concerning the Old Frenchman place when the stakes are far higher?

4. Do you agree with Faulkner's description of Ratliff as "a good deal nearer" to Will Varner "in spirit and intellect and physical appearance too than any of his own get"? In what ways are Ratliff and Varner similar? How are they different?

—*Lorie Watkins Fulton*

THE SNOPES FAMILY

William Faulkner either features or refers to various Snopeses not only in the novels of the Snopes trilogy—*The Hamlet, The Town* (1957), and *The Mansion* (1959), collected in *Snopes: A Trilogy* (1964)—but also in many short stories, including "Barn Burning"; the unfinished manuscript of *Father Abraham*; and other novels, including *As I Lay Dying, Flags in the Dust* (and the heavily cut and revised version, *Sartoris*), *Sanctuary, The Sound and the Fury, The Unvanquished,* and *The Reivers.* Many readers new to Faulkner's fiction bring to the texts a bias against the name "Snopes" and equate it with "poor white trash" at best and pure evil at worst. Even a cursory examination of the Snopes characters, though, reveals that not all Snopeses are poor. Flem Snopes, for instance, becomes quite wealthy by the end of *The Mansion.* Nor are they all white or trash. In *The Town* Faulkner introduces the children of Byron Snopes and "a Jicarilla Apache squaw in Old Mexico"; Wallstreet Panic (Wall) Snopes becomes a respectable businessman who operates ethically and eventually, with his wife's help, builds his grocery business into a successful wholesale chain. Faulkner's Snopes clan includes individuals as varied as those in any nonfictional family unit, but notions about "Snopesism" have made them quite possibly the most maligned fictional family in all of American literature.

Most often equated with Flem Snopes's predations and the supposed injury that the upstart Snopeses inflict upon old Southern values, Snopesism has far more to do with perception than with the facts of the Snopeses' behavior that Faulkner relates. As John E. Bassett notes in "Yoknapatawpha Revised: Demystifying Snopes," "the abstraction 'Snopes' is revealed as a fabrication" of such Faulkner narrators as Gavin Stevens and V. K. Rattliff. In *The Town,* for example, Stevens comments that none of the Snopeses "seemed to bear any specific kinship to one another; they were just Snopeses, like colonies of rats or termites are just rats and termites." Although some accept such judgments, most critics now attempt to take Snopesism with all of its complexities into account.

Flem stands as the most visible member of this clan, but technically he is not its patriarch. Abner (Ab) Snopes, Flem's father and the oldest named Snopes in Faulkner's work, stands at the head of this most confusing genealogy. Ab marries two women, Vynie and Lennie, and fathers Flem and three other children, Colonel Sartoris (Sarty) and the twins, Net and Lizzie. Flem marries Eula Varner when she becomes pregnant with Hoake McCarron's child and gives the daughter, Linda, his name. Faulkner refers to a host of Snopeses as Flem's cousins. The cousin who eventually murders Flem, M. C. (Mink) Snopes, marries Yettie and fathers two unnamed daughters. The proverb-spouting I. O. Snopes, another of Flem's cousins, fathers six children by two unnamed wives: Montgomery Ward, Saint Elmo, Clarence Eggleston, Doris, and the twins Vardaman and Bilbo. Eckrum (Eck) Snopes fathers Wallstreet Panic (Wall) by his first wife and Admiral Dewey and two other unnamed children by his second. Wesley Snopes, another of Flem's cousins, fathers Byron and Virgil with an unnamed wife, and he remains unnamed himself until *The Mansion.* Two other cousins include Isaac (Ike) Snopes, the mentally impaired man in love with Jack Houston's cow in *The Hamlet,* and Launcelot (Lump) Snopes, the character who removes the plank from Mrs. Littlejohn's barn so as to spy easily on Ike having sex with the cow. Finally, Faulkner names a couple of Snopeses with indeterminate genealogies: Orestes (Res), a hog dealer, and Watkins Products (Wat), the carpenter who renovates Flem's house in *The Mansion.*

The Snopes tales supposedly grew out of conversations between Faulkner and his friend and early mentor Phil Stone; Faulkner dedicated all three of the Snopes books to Stone, and the dedication to *The Town* reads, "To PHIL STONE / *He did half the laughing for thirty years.*" Faulkner's relationship to these characters, though, included emotions far more complex than simple amusement; as he said of the Snopeses at the University of Virginia, "They have been in—alive and have been in motion, I have hated them and laughed at them and been afraid of them for thirty years now." Yet, Faulkner seemed to admire some traits of the clan as a whole. In the 1938 letter to Robert K. Haas in which Faulkner outlines the initial plot of the trilogy, he refers to one Snopes who "turns out to have all the vices of all Snopes and none of the virtues," so even in his stage of planning the trilogy, Faulkner did not seem to share Stevens's view of the Snopeses as collective soulless monsters. He also thought that they "responded to"

the changing South "pretty well" and knew that they "are the men that can cope with the new industrial age." At the University of Virginia, he even admitted that he grudgingly admired Flem Snopes "until he was bitten by the bug to be respectable, and then he let me down." But Faulkner also described the family as "a tribe of people which would come into an otherwise peaceful little Southern town like ants or like mold on cheese." Faulkner seemed to hate most Flem Snopes's "ability to use people without realizing they're people" and the subsequent "contempt which the ability to use people develops in anyone." Faulkner also admitted, though, that he exaggerated the family's characteristics for literary effect: "there's probably no tribe of Snopeses in Mississippi or anywhere else outside of my own apocrypha. They were simply an invention of mine to tell a story of man in his struggle." He added, "I was not trying to say, This is the sort of folks we raise in my part of Mississippi"; instead, the characters "were simply over-emphasized, burlesqued if you like."

Faulkner offered such conflicting opinions about the Snopes family, at least in part, because of the inherent danger of grouping together such diverse individuals. Certainly, the use of Snopes as a disparaging epithet is justified by the behavior of Flem and some others, including Montgomery Ward with his pornographic postcards and the "revival song-leader," Wesley, whose career in Yoknapatawpha County ends when he is tarred, feathered, and almost castrated for having sex with a fourteen-year-old girl in an empty cotton house. In *The Mansion* Montgomery Ward recollects: "I was probably pretty young, when I realised that I had come from what you might call a family, a clan, a race, maybe even a species, of pure sons of bitches. So I said, *Okay, okay, if that's the way it is, we'll just show them. They call the best of lawyers, lawyers' lawyers and the best of actors an actor's actor and the best of athletes a ball-player's ball player. All right, that's what we'll do: every Snopes will make it his private and personal aim to have the whole world recognise him as THE son of bitch's son of a bitch.*" But not every Snopes makes that "his private and personal aim." Perfectly respectable Snopeses also exist, like Eck and his sons Wall and Admiral Dewey, all of whom Montgomery Ward "dont count" as Snopeses "because they dont belong to us: they are only our shame." In "The Roster, the Chronicle, and the Critic," Theresa M. Towner points out that *The Hamlet* demonstrates that anyone's unexamined assumptions and beliefs can prove his undoing, as Ratliff discovers when he tries to beat Flem Snopes in a deal." Readers who judge Snopeses by their names rather than content of their individual characters run much the same risk.

Discussion Questions

1. In response to a question about similarities between Thomas Sutpen in *Absalom, Absalom!* and Flem Snopes, Faulkner remarked, "Well, only Sutpen had a grand design. Snopes's design was pretty base—he just wanted to get rich, he didn't care how. Sutpen wanted to get rich only incidentally. He wanted to take revenge for all the redneck people against the aristocrat who told him to go around to the back door." Do you agree? What, if anything, does Flem desire besides money?

2. Raymond J. Wilson III suggests in "Imitative Flem Snopes and Faulkner's Causal Sequence in *The Town*" that Flem's imitation of the townspeople of Jefferson corrupts Flem rather than the more commonly held belief that Flem corrupts Jefferson. In a 1939 interview Faulkner described the trilogy as he planned it as telling the story of "a poor white who comes to a little Southern town and teaches the populace corruption in government." Do you think the trilogy plays out in this respect as Faulkner planned it, or does the town also corrupt Flem as Wilson suggests? If so, how?

3. In "Idealism in *The Mansion*," Noel Polk notes, "there is a wide variety of Snopes characters—silly ones, funny ones, sympathetic ones, honest ones and dishonest. In the strictest sense, if the term 'Snopesism' means anything, it describes one extremely active component of all human nature." While the term "Snopesism," as Polk suggests, eludes any one definite meaning, it does mean different things to different characters. How do characters outside the Snopes family such as Gavin Stevens, V. K. Ratliff, and Will Varner seem to define the term? How might Snopeses like Mink, Wall, Eck, and Sarty (from "Barn Burning") define it?

4. John E. Bassett notes that V. K. Ratliff "depends for his fictional existence on Snopes. He is

only in Snopes stories and novels, and he is one creator of the Snopes myth." Bassett adds that Ratliff "is both foil to Snopes and generator of Snopes lore." Given this relationship, why does Ratliff describe the Snopes family as he does? What does he stand to gain (and/or lose) through such depictions?

—*Lorie Watkins Fulton*

FLEM SNOPES

Flem Snopes figures most prominently in the books of William Faulkner's Snopes trilogy—*The Hamlet*, *The Town* (1957), and *The Mansion* (1959)—in which he quickly garners Will Varner's approval and rises from merely clerking in Varner's store to begin doing "what Varner had never even permitted his son to do," settling the yearly accounts between Varner and his tenants and debtors. Ultimately, Flem marries Eula, Varner's daughter, when she becomes pregnant with Hoake McCarron's child, thus giving the daughter, Linda, his name. By the end of *The Hamlet*, Flem's ambitions have taken him from Frenchman's Bend to the town of Jefferson. He makes this transition primarily by turning a profit on the Old Frenchman place when he fools V. K. Ratliff, Henry Armstid, and Odum Bookwright into purchasing the property at his asking price by deliberately allowing himself to be seen digging for the treasure the original owner supposedly buried in the garden. After Ratliff first becomes convinced, he says, "There's something there. I've always knowed it. Just like Will Varner knows there is something there. If there wasn't, he wouldn't never bought it." Shortly thereafter he adds, "And I knowed it for sho when Flem Snopes took it," and his reaction illustrates the effectiveness of Flem's typical mode of operation: he caters to the dreams of others and simply sells people what they want to buy. Noel Polk describes Flem as "Unillusioned . . . not *dis*illusioned, just *un*—," and notes that this condition gives him "almost unrestricted access to the illusions of others, a most powerful position."

The Town opens as Flem replaces Ratliff as Grover Cleveland Winbush's business partner in operating a café in Jefferson. With his shrewd understanding of human nature and willingness to take advantage of any situation that will help him further his own goals, Flem quickly moves from the café to a position as superintendent of the town's power plant, a job that Chick Mallison, the alleged voice of Jefferson in *The Town*, says Manfred de Spain created to facilitate an affair between himself and Eula Varner Snopes. When Colonel Bayard Sartoris dies, Flem becomes vice president of Colonel Sartoris's bank, and by the end of *The Town* he supersedes de Spain as the bank's president by capitalizing on his knowledge of de Spain's affair with his wife. By the end of the Snopes trilogy, Flem attains the outward symbols of success and respectability that he so craves; however, he realizes this dream at quite a high price: Eula kills herself at the conclusion of *The Hamlet*. Years later, in *The Mansion*, Linda Snopes Kohl, Eula's daughter, effectively murders her "so-called father" by engineering Mink Snopes's early release from Parchman, the state prison where he spent most of his thirty-eight-year term planning his revenge against Flem. And Flem, possibly realizing the utter emptiness of his life just before his death, commits a form of passive suicide as he allows Mink to shoot him.

It seems easy enough to dissect Flem's quest for respectability, chart his ascendancy to the upper echelons of Jefferson's social order, and identify the most maligned victims of his machinations, but assessing the content of his character seems a difficult, perhaps even impossible, task. As Joseph J. Arpad puts it, "no amount of generalization upon the divergent views of Flem's character will produce a reliable portrait of the man." In a reading that draws many convincing parallels between Faulkner and Flem and suggests that, in many ways, Flem functions as Faulkner's "darker twin," Joseph R. Urgo similarly notes, "Flem's true character seems to be as difficult to pin down as is Faulkner's own biographical 'true' self." It does seem clear enough that, as Polk suggests, critics misread the trilogy for years by taking Gavin Stevens's evaluations of Flem at face value and deeming Mink's murder of his cousin a just action. Polk instead presents Flem as "the ultimate denizen of the middle class," a product of the world he has become so fully a part of, and adds that if readers fear Flem, they should do so because "he is the picture of what Faulkner believed we would all become if we subscribed to those same middle-

class virtues of security and conformity, as he saw all the modern world rushing to do."

Flem remains so enigmatic, at least in part, because he, like so many of Faulkner's characters, is denied the opportunity to tell his own story. The trilogy records Flem's rise to power, but Stevens and Ratliff, two characters at odds with Flem until his death, narrate large portions of *The Town*, and Faulkner conveys the rest through Chick, a character who claims to speak for the town but is undeniably influenced by his uncle's and Ratliff's opinions. The third-person narration in the other two novels of the trilogy even seems, in places, filtered through these three characters; however, Faulkner never offers readers even a glimpse from Flem's perspective.

Given that Flem does not speak for himself, Faulkner's comments about him offer useful hints as to how readers might read around the collective interests of the narrators of the trilogy in order to begin to see Flem as a flawed human being, something more (or perhaps less) than some sort of Snopesish monster. While Faulkner seemed to hate most Flem's "ability to use people without realizing they're people" and the subsequent "contempt which the ability to use people develops in anyone," he admitted that he grudgingly admired Flem "until he was bitten by the bug to be respectable, and then he let me down." Nevertheless, as Urgo points out, "Faulkner may have laughed at the Snopes clan and their ridiculous given names, their lack of sophistication, their mulish stubbornness, but he held a great respect for their spirit." Perhaps Faulkner's most telling comment is his response to a student at the University of Virginia who asked, "does Flem Snopes understand the woman he is married to at all?" Faulkner replied, "I think he did. He had to teach himself a certain shrewdness about people in order to make the money which he believed was the end of existence." Faulkner's reply references Flem's intuitive understanding of others: how they see themselves, what they desire, and how he might use that knowledge to his advantage. More importantly, it highlights the limits of that perception and suggests that Flem understands little about himself, that he "believed" money "was the end of existence" and perhaps learned too late that that was not the case, if indeed he learned it at all.

Discussion Questions

1. On August 22, 1956, Faulkner wrote to Jean Stein, "Just finishing the book. It breaks my heart, I wrote one scene [presumably concerning Eula's suicide] and almost cried. I thought it was just a funny book but I was wrong." What role does Flem play in making the final section of *The Town* more serious than the earlier segments?

2. The character most sympathetic to Flem is also the one he injures most, his wife, Eula. Early in *The Town* she says to Gavin Stevens of Flem, "You've got to be careful or you'll have to pity him. You'll have to. He couldn't bear that, and it's no use to hurt people if you don't get anything for it. Because he couldn't bear being pitied." In light of Eula's concern, why might Flem deserve pity? Does he deserve Eula's compassion?

3. In *Faulkner's Apocrypha: "A Fable," "Snopes," and the Spirit of Human Rebellion*, Joseph R. Urgo writes, "In Jefferson, Flem comes into his own. Giving off no image of himself but simply reflecting and enlarging the images and values of the community, Flem is able to manipulate and capitalize his way up the social and economic ladder of the community." Can you identify specific examples of this behavior in the trilogy? Is Flem the only character to operate in such a manner?

4. While discussing the Snopes clan during one of his class lectures at the University of Virginia, Faulkner said of the "cavalier spirit": "By cavalier spirit, I mean people who believe in simple honor for the sake of honor, and honesty for the sake of honesty." Although he did not name Stevens specifically as such a cavalier, he may have had Stevens in mind and hinted at such a configuration by juxtaposing such cavaliers against the Snopeses and their capacity to "cope with the new industrial age." Does Stevens embody the "cavalier spirit" that Faulkner speaks of? Does Flem represent some sort of threat to that spirit? Or do the two men share fundamentally similar tactics and purposes, as they unquestionably do when they collude to put Montgomery Ward's peep show out of business? In other words, might Stevens feel so threatened by Flem because he fears that he and Flem share far more similarities than differences? Can you identify specific similarities between the two characters?

5. Gavin Stevens perpetually underestimates Flem; Theresa M. Towner speculates that Stevens does so because he focuses on "imaginative projections of what Flem might be doing rather than clear descriptions of what he is doing. The truth of what Flem does therefore shocks him every time." What are some instances in which Stevens misinterprets Flem's actions or motivations?

—*Lorie Watkins Fulton*

WILL VARNER

Will Varner is described as the "chief man of the country" in William Faulkner's *The Hamlet*, the first volume of his Snopes trilogy. The base of his influence is the hamlet of Frenchman's Bend, located twenty miles from Jefferson in Beat Two, the southeastern section of Yoknapatawpha County. The area derives its unusual name from "a foreigner, though not necessarily French" who was one of the first men to settle there. As *The Hamlet* begins, though, "all that remained of him was the river bed which his slaves had straightened for almost ten miles to keep his land from flooding, and the skeleton of the tremendous house"; even "his name was forgotten." Faulkner describes the area as "Hill-cradled and remote, definite yet without boundaries, straddling into two counties and owning allegiance to neither." Populated largely by the heirs of poor whites and yeoman farmers who "still planted cotton in the bottom land and corn along the edge of the hills and in the secret coves in the hills made whiskey of the corn and sold what they did not drink," it remains an insular community where "Federal officers went into the country and vanished" and "County officers did not bother them at all save in the heel of election years."

Varner, who owns "a good deal of his [the Frenchman's] original grant, including the site of his ruined mansion," is "the largest landholder and beat supervisor in one county and Justice of the Peace in the next and election commissioner in both"; he also owns the store, the cotton gin, and the "combined grist mill and blacksmith shop." Faulkner describes Varner as "the fountainhead if not of law at least of advice and suggestion to a countryside which would have repudiated the term constituency if they had ever heard it." He maintains power by suggesting the benefits of compliance with *his* rules, and the community responds to those suggestions "not in the attitude of *What must I do* but *What do you think you think you would like for me to do if you was able to make me do it.*"

Faulkner provides a detailed physical description of Varner: "He was thin as a fence rail and almost as long, with reddish-gray hair and moustaches and little hard bright innocently blue eyes; he looked like a Methodist Sunday School superintendent who on week days conducted a railroad passenger train or vice versa and who owned the church or perhaps the railroad or perhaps both." Varner seems a force of undirected energy, "at once active and lazy; he did nothing at all (his son managed all the family business) and spent all his time at it, out of the house and gone before the son had come down to breakfast even." In addition to this son, Jody, Varner's daughter, Eula, still lives at home as the novel begins. The other fourteen children of Varner and his wife, identified only as "Mrs Varner," have "scattered, married and buried, from El Paso to the Alabama line."

Varner does not suffer from delusions of his own grandeur and remains a paragon of practicality throughout the novel. In the opening pages, Faulkner positions him in his chair, a rustic throne of sorts made from an old flour barrel, as he surveys the "background of fallen baronial splendor" of the Old Frenchman's homesite and wonders "what it must have felt like to be the fool that would need all this." Later, after Jody learns of Eula's pregnancy and becomes determined to find out which of her suitors fathered the child, Varner logically asks "What for?" and adds, "Dont you know them damn tomcats are half way to Texas now?" He then sets into motion the arrangements that lead to Flem Snopes's marrying Eula two days later.

Varner's relationship to Flem, perhaps another manifestation of this practicality, is an intriguing aspect of *The Hamlet*. Jody first hires Flem to clerk in the store as a form of "fire insurance" in hopes of keeping Ab Snopes, Flem's father and an alleged barn burner renting and farming Varner's land, from destroying the property. Flem quickly rises from merely clerking and begins doing "what Varner had never even permitted his son to do" when he settles the yearly accounts "between Varner and his tenants and debtors." V. K. Ratliff, a close observer of the Snopes family, seems to think that Flem has coerced Varner somehow, and he even tells Varner, "You must have been desperate," upon learning that he deeded the Old Frenchman place to Flem and Eula as her dowry in order, as Ratliff puts it, "to get that patented necktie [a reference to the bow tie that Flem wears daily] out of his store and out of his house." Faulkner, however, never discloses the terms of Varner's arrangement with Snopes. Varner goes about his day-to-day business of inspecting "fields of cotton and corn or herds of cattle or land boundaries" as "cheerful as a cricket and shrewd and bowel-less as a tax-collector" with Flem, rather than the ineffectual Jody, at his side. Varner, who also appears in *The Town*, is one of Faulkner's most realistic patriarchs, imperfectly ruling the remains of his rustic domain with a wry wit and a keen sense of self-preservation.

Discussion Questions

1. In one of Faulkner's lectures at the University of Virginia, a member of the audience commented on *The Hamlet*, "Everyone seemed to be mad at somebody else for something. Is that typical of those people?" Faulkner thought it "typical of the people in *The Hamlet*." Do you agree with this assessment? Which characters seem the most (and the least) sympathetic? Is Will Varner at all sympathetic?

2. Faulkner described the characters in *The Hamlet* as "a pretty poor set of people." He added, "I don't know that there are many of them that I could trust, but I would still be interested in what they did to wonder why they did it." What desires and events seem to motivate Varner?

3. Faulkner published *The Hamlet* in 1940. The next volume of the trilogy, *The Town*, did not appear until 1957. Although Will Varner does not play a major role in *The Town*, how does he seem to evolve between the two novels? In what respects does he remain unchanged?

4. In the first chapter of *The Hamlet*, Will tells Ratliff that he keeps the Old Frenchman place, or "what there is left of it, just to remind me of my one mistake. This is the only thing I ever bought in my life I couldn't sell to nobody." As the novel

progresses, Varner goes on to make other mistakes. Which ones seem most significant? Which ones do you think Varner considers mistakes?

—*Lorie Watkins Fulton*

꩜

INTRUDER IN THE DUST
(New York: Random House, 1948)

CHARLES MALLISON JR.

Charles Mallison Jr., more commonly known as "Chick," first appears in Faulkner's fiction in the 1930s as Yoknapatawpha lawyer Gavin Stevens's nephew and sidekick in the series of detective stories that Faulkner eventually collected in *Knight's Gambit* (1949). Chick makes his last appearance in the final two volumes of Faulkner's Snopes trilogy and narrates large sections of *The Town* (1957), the middle volume of the trilogy. Nowhere does he play a more pivotal role, though, than in *Intruder in the Dust.*

Faulkner began writing *Intruder in the Dust* in January 1948, but he mentioned the project as a potential short story as early as June 1940 when he described it to Robert K. Haas at Random House as "a mystery story, original in that the solver is a negro, himself in jail for the murder" who "solves the murder in self defense." Though Faulkner expanded his idea into a novel-length manuscript, it basically follows this original plot, but the jailed man, Lucas Beauchamp, does not solve the mystery alone. After Sheriff Hope Hampton arrests Lucas for allegedly shooting Vinson Gowrie, Lucas spies Chick in the crowd as he is led to the jail. Lucas says to Chick, "Tell your uncle I wants to see him," and Chick obliges. However, rightly doubting that a lawyer can provide the help he needs, Lucas turns to Chick. As Miss Eunice Habersham, a spinster distantly connected to Beauchamp through his marriage to her childhood companion, Molly, tells Chick, "Lucas knew it would take a child—or an old woman like me: someone not concerned with probability, with evidence. Men like your uncle and Mr Hampton have had to be men too long, busy too long." Lucas convinces Chick to violate Gowrie's grave and help

him obtain the proof that Gowrie was shot with someone else's gun.

Lucas manages to convince Chick to do his bidding because of an encounter the two shared four years earlier, described in the first scene of the novel: twelve-year-old Chick fell into Lucas's icy creek while hunting with his black companion, Aleck Sander. Lucas rescued Chick and took him to his nearby cabin for dry clothes and a hot meal. This circumstance, as well as Lucas's intimidating presence, made Chick uncomfortable because it inverted the established racial hierarchy of the South in the era before the Civil Rights movement. Forced into the unusual position of being dependent upon a black man, Chick tried to regain the upper hand by paying Lucas, but the proud mulatto, descended from two of Yoknapatawpha's oldest families, refused to accept the payment as a "nigger" should. Chick flung the money to the floor in a mixture of rage and embarrassment.

Chick's debt to Lucas lies at the heart of *Intruder in the Dust,* Faulkner's most obvious fictional attempt to address the racial situation of his own era. When Chick, with the aid of Aleck and the elderly Miss Habersham, uncovers evidence of Lucas's innocence, he learns that all of Jefferson—including his beloved Uncle Gavin—wrongly presumed that Lucas murdered Gowrie. Chick's subsequent questioning of the foundations of Jefferson society leads to knowledge that changes his previously vital relationship with the people of his town: "soon there would not even be any contact since the very mutual words they used would no longer have the same significance and soon after that even this would be gone because they would be too far asunder even to hear one another."

Chick's burgeoning awareness of societal inequities seems even more significant given the political climate that existed as Faulkner composed the novel. In 1948 the Democratic National Convention became divided over the controversial civil rights planks added to its platform. In *Intruder in the Dust,* Faulkner promotes through Chick a moderate (albeit impractical) solution to the racial problems of the day, based on individual action. In contrast to his uncle, who talks about abstract racial issues and the plight of blacks in the post–Civil War South but fails to take any sort of effective action, Chick sees a wrong and risks his life to correct it. And Stevens realizes that he stands to learn much from Chick's example. When Chick returns from his overnight grave-digging adventure, Stevens asks him, "When did you really begin to believe him [Lucas]? When you opened the coffin, wasn't it? I want to know, you see. Maybe I'm not too old to learn either. When was it?"

Chick dramatically saves Lucas from a lynch mob at the last minute, but he gains at least as much from the experience as Lucas does. His encounter with Lucas teaches him a life-altering lesson: that a black man is just that, a man, an individual human being worthy of respect. The final exchange between Lucas and Chick harks back to the opening of the novel; Lucas enters Stevens's office to pay his legal fees and asks Chick if he has fallen into any creeks lately. Chick, for the first time, responds with something more genuine than an attempt at one-upmanship motivated by his own feelings of shame as he jokingly replies, "I'm saving that until you get some more ice on yours." This simple remark contrasts starkly with his initial response to Lucas and shows how drastically he has changed. In a 1955 interview Faulkner said that Chick "may grow up to be a better man than his uncle. I think he may succeed as a human being."

Discussion Questions

1. When speaking about his fiction to the citizens of Nagano, Japan, Faulkner suggested that a newcomer to his work begin with *Intruder in the Dust* because it "deals with the problem which is important not only in my country, but, I think important to all people." Assuming that the problem Faulkner referred to is racial discord, in what ways is this issue important not just to Chick Mallison but to all of Jefferson? How do Chick's actions change Jefferson? In what ways do those actions alter him?

2. *Intruder in the Dust* was the first novel that Faulkner had difficulty titling. He knew that he wanted to use the phrase "in the dust" but he never quite found the right word to combine with it. He said that jugglery came closest to the meaning that he searched for, but rejected it because he thought it a "harsh ugly word." In what ways might Chick

act as the intruder of the title? If he is the intruder, what, exactly, does he intrude upon?

3. Many readers have noticed and commented upon the almost paternal relationship between Stevens and Chick as it evolves throughout Faulkner's fiction, especially in the short stories in *Knight's Gambit* and in *The Town*. How does Faulkner invert that relationship in this novel? In other words, what, if anything, does Chick teach Stevens?

4. Just before Faulkner sent the manuscript of *Intruder in the Dust* to Random House, he wrote Robert K. Haas that what "started out to be a simple quick 150 page whodunit . . . jumped the traces" and turned into "a pretty good study of a 16 year old boy who overnight became a man." How has Chick become a "man" by the end of the novel? In light of Faulkner's statement, what, exactly, defines masculinity in *Intruder in the Dust?*

—*Lorie Watkins Fulton*

LIGHT IN AUGUST
(New York: Smith & Haas, 1932)

BYRON BUNCH

Byron Bunch, one of the principal protagonists in William Faulkner's *Light in August*, is a nondescript, long-suffering mill worker and church-choir director, a "quiet little man" whose uneventful life of "celibacy and hard labor" is thrown into disarray precisely when he thinks that he is safest from the "chance to be hurt." In pointed contrast to his closest friend, the defrocked minister Gail Hightower, Byron does not try to escape his present difficulties by going into exile or dreaming about the past. Rather, he takes charge of his own life and, to a large degree, of the lives of other characters. His interventions in the course of events often backfire, and his motives are never purely altruistic. But in struggling to act decently while his little world collapses around him, he comes unusually close (for a Faulkner character) to something like traditional heroism. As Faulkner said of him in a 1957 class conference, Byron demonstrates a "very fine belief in life, in the basic possibility for happiness and goodness." This belief, Faulkner asserted, sets Byron apart from the violent, race-tormented drifter Joe Christmas, who embraces a "tragic view of life" which leads him to "deliberately repudiate man." In daring to "meddle," Byron also aligns himself with Faulkner's authorial perspective to a greater degree than most of the other characters.

Like all the major characters in *Light in August,* the thirty-five-year-old Byron is considered an outsider in the fictional town of Jefferson, Mississippi. Unlike the others, however, his "countrybred" childhood is a virtual blank. (By comparison, Faulkner devotes more than four chapters to Joe Christmas's pre-Jefferson history.) Byron's present life is almost comically drab, and his physical appearance is equally unremarkable; one character describes him as "the kind of fellow you wouldn't see the first glance if he was alone by himself in the bottom of a empty concrete swimming pool."

As the main plot of the novel begins, Byron has spent the last seven years working at the town planing mill every day but Sunday. He spends his short Sabbath break leading the choir at a country church located thirty miles—a hard mule ride—outside of Jefferson. Byron's existence is a "minor mystery" to the people of Jefferson, but Faulkner makes it clear that he has nothing to hide: Byron himself tells Hightower that he had viewed the mill as a place where the "chance to do harm could not have found him." His fellow workers respect "how he stays out of meanness."

One Saturday evening, though, when the other workers have gone to watch the mysterious Joanna Burden's house burn down, the "chance to do harm"—but also to do good—does find Byron at the mill. It comes in the form of Lena Grove, who has traveled from Alabama looking for Lucas Burch, the ne'er-do-well father of her unborn child. Almost unwittingly, and, Faulkner writes, "contrary to all the tradition of his austere and jealous country raising which demands in the object physical inviolability," Byron falls in love with Lena.

Byron begins serving Lena tirelessly, despite knowing that she is bent on marrying Burch—who, unlike Byron, would do practically anything to avoid getting married. Through Burch (who in Jefferson goes by the name "Joe Brown"), this comic love triangle immediately becomes enmeshed with the dark triangle formed by Burch; Burch's bootlegging partner, Christmas; and Christmas's lover, Joanna. Byron learns that the house fire he had avoided seeing may have been set by Burch to cover the killing of Joanna, who was most likely murdered by Christmas. Burch convinces the town that Christmas is a "nigger" rather than the white man they had assumed him to be and joins the manhunt for him in the hope of earning a large reward.

Byron risks everything to shelter Lena from these sordid realities and help her deliver her baby safely. His sense of honor is so strong that he even arranges a meeting between Burch and Lena so that Burch can see his newborn son and, possibly, set up a wedding with Lena. When Burch runs from Lena again, Byron resolves to stop him in a passage that neatly sums up his hopefulness and growing inner strength: "I took care of his woman for him and I borned his child for him. And now there is one more thing I can do for him. I cant marry them, because I aint a minister. And I may not catch him, because he's got a start on me. And I may not whip him if I do, because he is bigger than me. But I can try it. I can try to do it."

When Byron fails to stop Burch, he turns his newfound confidence (combined, admittedly, with a sense of desperation) to the task of persuading Lena to become Mrs. Bunch instead of Mrs. Burch. Despite many rejections, Byron says, "I done come too far now. . . . I be dog if I'm going to quit now." In response to this, Lena gives him the first strong sign that she is taking his offer seriously: "Aint nobody never said for you to quit." While *Light in August* does not end with a wedding, readers are left considering the possibility that Byron and Lena, as Hightower had predicted, may create a family of their own, "peopling in tranquil obedience to it the good earth."

Byron's ascent from anonymity to three-dimensionality entails a series of noteworthy transformations. He overcomes his fear of "public outrage" by defying Jefferson's puritanical sexual standards as he helps Lena. Unlike Quentin Compson in Faulkner's *The Sound and the Fury* (1929), whose horror over his sister Caddy's lost virginity drives him to commit suicide, Byron is able to reject the hurtful fundamentalist standard of "physical inviolability" in women. Moreover, he challenges (even if he does not fully escape) the omnipresent racism of the Jim Crow era by trying to save Christmas from the process that will end in his death at the hands of the white supremacist Percy Grimm. Imperfect as he is, Byron exemplifies many of the virtues Faulkner would later call the "old verities" and joins Lena in contributing a life-affirming dimension to a novel usually remembered for its powerful explorations of human darkness.

Discussion Questions

1. In one of their many conversations, Reverend Hightower tells Byron (in a sardonic allusion to Byron's namesake, the British Romantic poet George Gordon, Lord Byron) that he would have made a fine "dramatist." In what ways does Byron shape the plot of *Light in August*? How does Byron change and grow as a storyteller in his conversations with Hightower?

2. Using as much evidence from the novel as possible, try to prove or disprove that Byron and Lena will get married. If you believe that they will marry, how successful do you think their marriage will be? Will they be happier than some of the other married couples described in the book, such as the Armstids? If you think that they will part ways, what will the future hold for them?

3. Analyze Byron Bunch's relationship with Gail Hightower. How do these very different men evolve as characters? How do they influence each other's ways of thinking and behaving both positively and negatively? Why does Byron reject his friend's advice to leave Jefferson before getting too deeply involved in the main events of the novel?

4. In his Nobel Prize acceptance speech, Faulkner listed what he considered the "old universal truths" of the human heart as "endurance . . . courage and honor and hope and pride and compassion and pity and sacrifice." Show how Byron Bunch embodies, or fails to embody, three or more of these virtues. If *Light in August* has a hero, is he it?

5. Byron Bunch shares numerous similarities with the unnamed tall convict in the "Old Man" section of Faulkner's novel *If I Forget Thee, Jerusalem* (1939; also published under the title *The Wild Palms*). Each is a country man who does his best to help a pregnant woman deliver her baby under chaotic circumstances. The Tall Convict, however, does everything possible to return to his almost monastic life in prison, which is something like Byron's life of "celibacy and hard labor" at the beginning of *Light in August*. How would you explain the difference between the two men? Why is one horrified of female sexuality and childbirth, while the other learns to overcome his paralyzing fear?

—*Bart H. Welling*

LENA GROVE

Lena Grove, one of the principal female characters in William Faulkner's *Light in August*, is a country woman of about twenty who travels from a tiny sawmill settlement in Alabama to Jefferson, Mississippi, the seat of Faulkner's fictional Yoknapatawpha County, looking for "the father" of her unborn child. Faulkner interweaves Lena's story structurally and thematically with that of one of the novel's other major protagonists, Joe Christmas; both characters are orphans raised in bleak physical and social environments. Lena's path, however, leads not to existential despair and violence, as do Joe Christmas's wanderings, but to the creation of new life. Through her intelligence, resourcefulness, and talent for exploiting Southern social conventions without allowing herself to be overwhelmed by them, she accounts for much of the "light" in a novel whose original title was "Dark House."

Readers first encounter Lena in the opening paragraph of the book, in which she contemplates how far she has traveled since leaving the village of Doane's Mill one month before. There she had spent the eight years since the death of her parents with her older brother, McKinley, whom Faulkner describes as a "hard man." The difficult work of caring for her brother's children and his "child-ridden" wife were compounded by the discovery that she herself had conceived a child with a sawmill Casanova named Lucas Burch. Doane's Mill represents an unlivable place for Lena not just by dint of her brother's anger over the pregnancy, but (as environmental literary scholar Lawrence Buell has noted) because of the destruction the sawmill has brought to the forests upon which it depends for its existence. "It had been there seven years and in seven years more it would destroy all the timber within its reach," Faulkner writes, subtly alluding to biblical stories of drought and famine. When the ne'er-do-well Lucas Burch fails to send for her as promised, Lena—whose last name links her to the sacred groves and fertility rites of animist faith traditions—leaves the "devastated hills" of Alabama behind to search for him.

As an unmarried pregnant woman in the early-twentieth-century South, Lena's options are severely limited. This fact becomes obvious to readers in the responses of the men and women who assist her as she makes her way closer to Jefferson. While their version of Christianity requires them to offer her charity, it also prevents them from seeing her pregnancy as anything other than a grave sin. "You keep off your feet now," a farmer's wife snaps at Lena while "clash[ing] the stove savagely" as she prepares food for the unwanted guest, "and you'll keep off your back a while longer maybe." Even Byron Bunch, the Jefferson planing-mill worker who falls in love with Lena and assumes the role of her protector (which she does not need), feels that she has been "wronged and betrayed." In contrast to this narrative of sin and illegitimacy, Lena embodies a pre-Christian faith in the inherent goodness of sexuality and childbirth. Like another unconventional "earth mother," Ántonia Shimerda Cuzak of Willa Cather's *My Ántonia,* Lena resists her culture's efforts to brand her child as "illegitimate" and transform her into the "whore" her brother thought she had become.

Readers sometimes find Lena unintelligent due to her apparent incomprehension both of the strong reactions her condition provokes and of Lucas Burch's flawed nature. But close attention to Faulkner's treatment of her words, facial expressions, and actions reveals that, below Lena's "serene" surface, deeper forms of strength and intelligence are at work. Lena's power manifests itself most clearly when Burch—who, by the time she arrives in Jefferson, has adopted the pseudonym "Joe Brown" and become involved in bootlegging, arson, and (through indirect means) the killing of the reclusive Joanna Burden by her lover, Joe Christmas—is tricked into entering the cabin where Lena lies holding their newborn son. Burch's reaction to meeting his

would-be family counts as one of the most painfully funny moments in Faulkner's fiction. "She just lay there," Faulkner writes, "watching him with her sober eyes in which there was nothing at all—joy, surprise, reproach, love—while over his face passed shock, astonishment, outrage, and then downright terror . . . while ceaselessly here and there about the empty room went his harried and desperate eyes . . . like two terrified beasts." In the first chapter of the novel Faulkner alludes to John Keats's poem "Ode on a Grecian Urn" (1819), comparing Lena and the wagons in which she rides to the figures on Keats's urn. Unlike the frightened women pursued by male figures on that urn, however, Lena takes on the traditionally masculine role of the pursuer, and in Burch's "struggle to escape" from her once again, he becomes (in Faulkner's words) a "fleeing animal."

Later in the book Byron Bunch comes to believe that Lena has known all along that Burch is a "nogood." If this is true, then why does she bother to chase Burch even after he runs away from her this second time? (At the end of the novel Lena is still pursuing Lucas, and Byron is still trying to persuade her to become Mrs. Bunch instead of Mrs. Burch.) One plausible explanation is voiced by a furniture dealer who gives Lena and Byron a ride in Tennessee. The furniture dealer speculates that Lena has "just made up her mind to travel a little further and see as much as she could, since . . . she knew that when she settled down this time, it would likely be for the rest of her life." Whether she will settle down with Byron or another man, or raise the child alone—the novel leaves Lena's future up to the reader's imagination—she is certainly capable of fulfilling the prophecy of Gail Hightower, the defrocked minister who delivers her child. *"That will be her life, her destiny,"* Hightower imagines: *"The good stock peopling in tranquil obedience to it the good earth."* A "rich mine of life" like Cather's Ántonia, Lena will continue to believe in what Faulkner later called the "basic possibility for happiness and goodness" in spite of every reason she might have to lose hope.

Discussion Questions

1. As with many of his characters, Faulkner offers few detailed descriptions of Lena Grove's physical appearance. Why do you think this is so?

How do Faulkner's descriptions of Lena compare to those of other characters in the book?

2. Who "owns" *Light in August:* Lena Grove, Joe Christmas, or another character? Would you describe the book as tragic, comic, or something else? Why does Lena endure while Christmas kills Joanna Burden and allows himself to be killed? Why do you think Lena and Joe never meet each other despite the many points of intersection between their stories?

3. How do you interpret Lena's statement to Byron (reported by the furniture dealer at the end of the novel) that "Aint nobody never said for you to quit"? Will Lena marry him or keep searching for Lucas Burch? Why does Faulkner avoid "marrying her off" to Byron Bunch or Lucas Burch at the end of the novel?

4. At one point the farmer Armstid thinks that Lena's public display of her pregnancy indicates that she wants to "seced[e] from the woman race" like women's rights activists who "dip snuff and smoke and want to vote." The scholar Christina Jarvis, on the other hand, has argued that Lena is focused primarily on "satisfying her desires to eat, to travel, to move freely in (male) public space." How subversive do you think Lena's desires really are? Why does Faulkner draw so much attention to the gap between what other characters think about Lena and what she herself is thinking?

5. Compare and contrast Lena Grove with Cather's Ántonia or Dewey Dell of Faulkner's *As I Lay Dying* (1930). Will Lena's child-rearing practices be similar to those of Ántonia Shimerda Cuzak? Why doesn't Lena seek an abortion in town, while Dewey Dell—another poor, unmarried young woman from the country—does?

—*Bart H. Welling*

GAIL HIGHTOWER

Gail Hightower, D.D., is a defrocked fifty-year-old Presbyterian minister who is a key character in the main plot of William Faulkner's *Light in August.* When readers first encounter him, he has spent more than two decades living in an "unpainted, small, obscure, poorly lighted, mansmelling, manstale" bungalow in fictional Jefferson, Mississippi. There he spends his days in a kind of internal exile on what was once a "principal street" but has since been largely forgotten. This trait is not the only one he shares with Emily Grierson, the protagonist of Faulkner's short story "A Rose for Emily" (1930). Like Emily (and Quentin Compson and other Faulkner characters), Hightower is virtually possessed by the ghosts of the past. "I am not in life anymore," he thinks, believing not only that he is something of a ghost himself, but also that he has "bought immunity" from the pain of life by submitting to the will of the community when he was removed from the ministry. Through his only friend, Byron Bunch, he receives several chances to become involved again in the life of the town. Ultimately, though, readers are left wondering if the townspeople are right that Hightower's D.D., instead of standing for Doctor of Divinity, really means Done Damned.

Hightower would probably say that if he is damned, the damnation began many years before his birth. As an only child raised by elderly parents and former slaves in a house haunted by stories, if not actual ghosts, of the Civil War, Hightower came to believe that he might be the reincarnation of his grandfather. This first Gail Hightower was a Confederate cavalryman who died in connection with an attack on a Union depot in Jefferson. Oddly, Reverend Hightower is not disillusioned to learn that his grandfather was (apparently) killed while stealing chickens *after* the heroic raid; in fact, he sees this as the finest part of the story, since it proves that his grandfather and the other raiders were not "men after spoils and glory," but rather "boys riding the sheer tremendous tidal wave of desperate living." While studying for his theological degree he convinces himself that God must call him to serve in Jefferson because, he thinks, "my life died there, was shot from the saddle of a galloping horse in a Jefferson street one night twenty years before it was ever born." His salvation lies, he believes, in returning "to the place to die where my life had already ceased before it began."

With his warped understanding of religion and history, Hightower would have been perfectly at home (with a few regional adjustments) among the "grotesques" of *Winesburg, Ohio* (1919), a book by Faulkner's mentor, Sherwood Anderson. In that text Anderson defines a "grotesque" as a character who claims possession of one single truth of human nature and tries to live by it so exclusively that the "truth he embraced became a falsehood." Hightower's truth—his grandfather's heroism—transforms him into a grotesque because, as the townspeople tell Byron many years later, it is the only truth he can preach. Instead of ministering to the day-to-day needs of his church and delivering conventional sermons, he goes "wild . . . in the pulpit . . . with his hands flying around him and the dogma he was supposed to preach all full of galloping cavalry and defeat and glory." Hightower differs from other wild religionists who appear in *Light in August*—most notably Eupheus "Doc" Hines, Joe Christmas's brutal grandfather—in that he does not translate his violent rhetoric into equally violent action. But his inaction is almost as troubling as Hines's open violence.

This is particularly true in the case of Hightower's wife. Troubled to begin with, she sinks into a deep depression caused not only by Hightower's wild dream but by his inability to see her misery—to see her at all, really. She dies, possibly by her own hand, at a Memphis hotel where she and a drunk man have been staying under a pseudonym "as man and wife." Faulkner signals how completely she has been destroyed by noting that the police found a paper with her "rightful name" torn up and thrown in a wastebasket. Instead of telling readers what this name was, Faulkner pointedly refuses to identify her as anyone but the "wife of the Reverend Gail Hightower." This refusal raises the possibility that Hightower himself has forgotten the name of a woman he considered "Passive and Anonymous" from the start.

After his wife's death, Hightower's outraged congregants force him to resign, and he is beaten unconscious by members of the Ku Klux Klan. Feeling that he has thus "paid" his debt to the town, Hightower spends his days in almost complete solitude, reading poetry and waiting for twilight, when he can watch the ghosts of his grandfather and the other cavalrymen thunder down the road.

This ghostly half-life is interrupted by Byron. He manages to persuade Hightower to deliver the baby of Lena Grove, with whom Byron (against Hightower's advice) has fallen in love. Byron also tries to enlist Hightower in an effort to save the possibly mixed-race bootlegger Christmas from being killed in retaliation for murdering his lover, Joanna Burden. While Hightower agrees that a public "crucifixion" of Christmas would be "terrible," Hightower's own punishment by the town has convinced him that such things "cant be helped." When Christmas escapes from the police and runs to Hightower's house, the former minister does try to save him, but the attempt fails: Christmas is shot to death and castrated in Hightower's kitchen.

These events do have one positive outcome for Hightower: they prove to him that he has been fully alive all along. In a flash of anguished self-reflection—described in terms that call to mind both the *anagnorisis* (discovery or recognition) central to Greek tragedy and the Christian account of Jesus Christ's suffering in the garden of Gethsemane—Hightower understands for the first time that he was the "instrument of [his wife's] despair and death." But Faulkner forces readers to ask how long this transformation really lasts. In Hightower's last appearance in the book he is sitting alone at his window as usual, where he has watched the Confederate ghosts ride by and it seems he can still hear the "wild bugles and the clashing sabres and the dying thunder of hooves."

Discussion Questions

1. *Light in August* features several characters whose names (patterned after character names in "the old miracle plays" and the works of Geoffrey Chaucer, according to Faulkner) are emblematic of aspects of the characters' identities. Explore the symbolic dimensions of Gail Hightower's name. How does Hightower differ, if at all, from traditional allegorical characters—Christian and Despair in John Bunyan's *The Pilgrim's Progress* (1678–1684), for instance?

2. Like Hightower, William Faulkner was named after a larger-than-life Confederate soldier. Faulkner incorporated family stories about his great-grandfather, the "Old Colonel," in many of his books, but characters based on the first William Falkner (as his name was spelled) are never presented as straightforward military heroes. Analyze the tone

Faulkner uses in describing Hightower's hard-riding, chicken-stealing grandfather. Does Faulkner seem to be satirizing the relationship of his region to its Confederate past, honoring it, or both? Why?

3. Explore Faulkner's treatment of mainstream Christianity and religious extremism by comparing Hightower with "Doc" Hines, Simon McEachern, Joe Christmas, or another religious "grotesque" in *Light in August*. Is Faulkner merely using these characters to attack Christianity, or does he seem to believe that religion has the potential to foster virtues such as compassion and endurance in its practitioners?

4. Why do you think Faulkner presents Hightower's perspective on his past near the end of *Light in August*, long after the town's version of the story has been offered? Do you think Hightower finds redemption from his past, as such critics as Cleanth Brooks have asserted, or drowns in it? Faulkner asserted in a 1957 class conference that Hightower doesn't die at the end of the novel (as many readers have assumed), but could Faulkner be wrong about his own character?

5. Compare and contrast Gail Hightower with Emily Grierson or a relevant character in Anderson's *Winesburg, Ohio* (for example, Reverend Curtis Hartman in the chapter "The Strength of God"). Pay special attention to the gap between the two characters' inner lives and the ways in which they are viewed by their communities. What roles do the communities play in shaping the characters, and vice versa?

—*Bart H. Welling*

Joe Christmas

Joe Christmas, one of several antiheroic protagonists of William Faulkner's novel *Light in August*, is a drifter and ironic Christ figure tormented by the possibility that he may be part black. His wanderings around North America and between white and black identity come to an abrupt end when he murders his lover, Joanna Burden, and allows himself to be killed in the fictional town of Jefferson, Mississippi. Christmas's racial uncertainties lie at the heart of his life and death. Faulkner told graduate students at the University of Virginia that Christmas "didn't know what he was, and so

he was nothing. . . . That was his tragedy . . . that he didn't know what he was, and there was no way possible in life for him to find out." Through his use of unconventional plot structures and a limited omniscient point of view, Faulkner ensures that readers, too, will never know Christmas's racial identity with certainty. In the end, the book suggests that the real tragedy is that the rage to answer questions of this kind with one word—*black* or *white*—has obsessed Americans for so long.

Many scholars have argued that Faulkner based Christmas on an African American lynching victim named Nelse Patton. In 1908 Patton was killed and mutilated by members of a mob of some two thousand people near Faulkner's home in Oxford, Mississippi. Like Patton, Christmas is a bootlegger who outrages the white community by attacking and slitting the throat of a white woman.

In his fictional account, however, Faulkner engineers so many ironies and ambiguities into the murdered man's story that readers can only view the townspeople's racist hysteria as ridiculous. For three years before his death, Christmas had been accepted by the people of Jefferson as a white man. As various puzzled whites put it, "He dont look any more like a nigger than I do." Far from being the stereotypical "black beast rapist" of Jim Crow–era popular literature and oratory, Christmas is a multifaceted and evolving—if deeply enigmatic—modernist creation who anticipates the existentialist characters of such writers as Albert Camus and Jean-Paul Sartre. Christmas's affair with Joanna Burden does violate several taboos, but Burden is anything but an innocent Southern belle: an androgynous but sexually ardent recluse, she comes from a family of Northern abolitionists. By the same token, Christmas *is* violent, but his violence springs from a more complicated source than what many racists in the South viewed as the black man's innate, uncontrollable lust for white women.

Christmas's adult behavior can be traced directly to a childhood marked by racism, misogyny, emotional and physical abuse, and a type of religious extremism so strong as to cross the line into insanity. Many scholars have observed that his life exemplifies Sigmund Freud's ideas on the structure of the human mind and the crucial role played by childhood experience in the formation of adult identity.

Readers, like the people of Jefferson, first experience Christmas as an inscrutable and unsympathetic adult. In the sixth chapter of the novel, Faulkner starts exploring Christmas's origins, and the character (as Faulkner said of well-crafted characters in general) begins to "stand on" his "hind legs and cast a shadow." Christmas's troubles begin in a Dickensian orphanage in Memphis, Tennessee. There he starts wondering if he has "nigger blood" and begins to associate women with deception, punishment, and illicit sexuality. Much later, Faulkner reveals that Christmas was orphaned by his own grandfather, Eupheus "Doc" Hines, a violent white supremacist, enemy of "womanfilth" (that is, female sexuality), and religious monomaniac who had (apparently) killed the baby's father and allowed his unmarried daughter, Milly, to die while bearing the child. It would be wrong to say that Hines abandons his grandson, however, since he obtains a job in the orphanage to spy on "God's abomination" and plant the idea that the light-skinned boy is a "nigger bastard." Hines later returns to play a role in Christmas's death; with "his mouth slavering," the self-proclaimed instrument of God's will tries to whip his fellow whites into a lynching frenzy.

Christmas leaves the orphanage when he is adopted by a "cold, implacable" Calvinist farmer named Simon McEachern, who shares Hines's warped religiosity and misogyny, if not his fanatical racism, and beats the boy regularly. Predictably, on reaching young adulthood Christmas rebels against McEachern—to the extent of attacking and possibly killing his adoptive father—but he unquestioningly accepts McEachern's pathological mistrust of women. And, in sadomasochistic fashion, he comes to associate violence with a sense of fulfillment. This explosive blend of influences renders Christmas's anxiety over his ethnic origins even more damaging.

After Joanna is killed—her death, like many key events in the book, never being reported directly by Faulkner—Christmas ceases to be a man in the eyes of the people of Jefferson and becomes, instead, a "nigger." More than that, he is "someone to crucify," a human sacrifice needed to restore the precarious racial balance upset by the murder of a white woman. The Christian townspeople do not realize how closely their actions parallel those of the people who kill Christ in the New Testament, but Faulkner forces readers to ponder many similarities between the crucifixion of Jesus Christ and the sacrificial killing of Joe Christmas. Like Langston Hughes's controversial 1931 poem "Christ in Alabama" (which begins with the lines "Christ is a Nigger, / Beaten and black . . ."), *Light in August* uses a Southern, modernist Christ figure to attack a version of Christianity that was complicit in the racist order. Likewise, Christmas's story exposes the nearly religious zeal with which many Southern whites embraced racism. Long after Southern lynching has ceased to grab headlines on a regular basis, the novel continues to challenge readers with its explorations of the tensions between the black-and-white life scripts supplied by racism and the lived mysteries of human identity.

Discussion Questions

1. Historian Joel Williamson has observed that Faulkner, a ten-year-old boy at the time, lived no more than a thousand yards from the site of the 1908 lynching of Nelse Patton. Some of his schoolmates were actually involved in capturing and shooting Patton. And yet, in a 1935 letter to his agent, Faulkner denied ever having seen a lynching; and in a letter published in the *Memphis Commercial-Appeal* a few months before he began work on *Light in August*, he offered what scholars Neil R. McMillen and Noel Polk characterize as a "virtual defense of lynching as an instrument of justice." Analyze Faulkner's description of the killing of Joe Christmas in light of these inconsistencies. Is it fair to call *Light in August* an antilynching text, or is it something more complicated? Is Christmas actually lynched, or (as Cleanth Brooks has argued) is it more accurate to call his death a murder?

2. Trace Joe Christmas's fascination with and fear of female sexuality through three or more episodes in his development. How do Joe's views on women and sex evolve? Does Faulkner seem to share in Joe's sexism, as has been alleged by scholars like Louise H. Westling?

3. Using as much evidence from the text as you can find, try to prove—or disprove—that Joe

Christmas killed Joanna Burden. What might have motivated him to kill her? Can it be argued plausibly that someone else did it? Why doesn't Faulkner "show" readers the killing?

4. *Light in August* begins and ends not with murder and insanity but on a humorous note, with Lena Grove remarking how far she has come from her home in Alabama. How does the tragic plot of the book (centering on Joe Christmas and Joanna Burden) engage with its comic elements? How is Christmas similar to, and different from, characters like Gail Hightower and Byron Bunch?

—*Bart H. Welling*

IKKEMOTUBBE (DOOM)

Ikkemotubbe, or "Doom," is an early-nineteenth-century American Indian character who appears in novels and stories spanning most of William Faulkner's career as a writer of fiction. Although important details of Ikkemotubbe's life (including his name, tribal affiliation, and family tree) change between texts, Faulkner was consistent in his handling of one basic narrative. Ikkemotubbe is a usurper who returns to his tribe in north Mississippi after having fled to New Orleans. Using a combination of shrewdness, intimidation, and poison, he becomes "the Man," the leader of his people. But Ikkemotubbe's carefully chosen adoptive name, Doom (from *l'homme* or *du homme*, French for "the Man"), does not just augur death for his political rivals. He helps usher in his tribe's collective "doom," the expropriation of Indian lands by European Americans and the forced removal of the indigenous peoples of Mississippi to Indian Territory (later Oklahoma). Through Ikkemotubbe, Faulkner explores some of the same problems—dispossession, intercultural and internecine conflict, familial decline, the legacy of slavery—that animate fictions featuring better-known characters such as Thomas Sutpen. Unlike such European American characters, however, Ikkemotubbe gave Faulkner the chance to reimagine Mississippi history from the perspective of a radically different culture—a culture with which he was only marginally familiar. Faulkner's evolving efforts to engage in this work of reimagination are both instructive and problematic for modern readers.

In the 1930 story "Red Leaves," Doom (not "Ikkemotubbe") is remembered as a "squat man with a bold, inscrutable, underbred face." In the prehistory of the story, Doom had returned from his New Orleans sojourn to transform his tribe's "matchless parklike forest" into a full-scale plantation, complete with African slaves and an abandoned steamboat for a plantation house. Readers are told that Doom became chief after the sudden, presumably violent, death of his uncle and cousin. His forcefulness stands in marked contrast to the "complete and unfathomable lethargy" of the current "Man" (in the narrative present of the story), Doom's grandson Moketubbe. But the story suggests that Doom was the one who "doomed" Moketubbe and the rest of his tribe by embracing foreign customs and "breeding" more African slaves than the tribe could provide with work. Doom also initiated a pattern of violence that may have resulted in the murder of Doom's son and successor, Issetibbeha, by Moketubbe, Issetibbeha's own son—a pattern that will unquestionably result in the sacrificial death of the slave whose futile efforts to escape the plantation structure the plot of the story. In typical Faulkner fashion, several mysteries remain unsolved by the end of the story. How, exactly, did Doom's uncle, cousin, and son die? What is Doom's real name? Which tribe did he belong to? And why did he leave his ancestral home for New Orleans in the first place?

Faulkner began trying to answer these questions himself shortly after writing "Red Leaves." In "A Justice" readers learn that the birth name of Doom, a Choctaw, was Ikkemotubbe; that he had decided to go to New Orleans—and rename himself "David Callicoat" in the process—after watching the steamboat, piloted by one David Callicoat, pass by four times a year; and that he had used poison to kill his relatives upon coming back. In his ruthlessness and capacity for self-reinvention, this Ikkemotubbe anticipates Thomas Sutpen of *Absalom, Absalom!* (1936).

The two would-be dynasts are actually mentioned in the same breath in *Go Down, Moses*. In the section "The Bear," Faulkner writes that Sutpen purchased his land from Ikkemotubbe. From young protagonist Isaac "Ike" McCaslin's point of view, the two thereby violated God's original intention of giving humans "suzerainty" rather than absolute dominion over the earth, irredeemably "tainting" the land of Ike's inheritance. In the section "The Old People" Ike discovers that Ikkemotubbe, in a Sutpen-like move, sold his own wife and son as slaves to a white neighbor.

Ikkemotubbe's many acts of betrayal did not necessarily "doom" his people financially; readers learn in a belated appendix to *The Sound and the Fury* (1929), first published in 1946, that his descendants in Oklahoma had, in fact, struck it rich in the oil business. But they have taken the pattern of decline first explored in "Red Leaves" to absurd extremes. Like latter-day Moketubbes, they spend their time riding "supine with drink and splendidly comatose" in "specially built scarletpainted hearses and fire-engines." In "Appendix: Compson, 1699–1945," Faulkner seems to have fallen back not just on the old images of the "drunk Indian" and the "lazy Indian" but also on an early version of the "casino-rich Indian" stereotype.

In the 1940s, however, Faulkner also crafted an Ikkemotubbe who achieves a measure of humanity fully equal to that of some of the author's most admirable white characters. Faulkner did this by tackling the biggest question of all: not how but *why* Ikkemotubbe became Doom. Was he simply born evil, as suggested in "A Justice"? If not, what would it have taken to corrupt him? The answers are worked out in "A Courtship," which took first prize in the 1949 O. Henry short-story awards. In "A Courtship" Faulkner employs an Indian narrator to recount Ikkemotubbe's failed, and nearly fatal, attempts to win Herman Basket's sister's hand in marriage. At the end of the story, a weeping Ikkemotubbe and his white friend and rival, David Hogganbeck (a newly three-dimensional version of David Callicoat), try to console themselves with words of philosophy. Hogganbeck, reinforcing the sense of equality between whites and Native Americans that prevails in the story, notes that their philosophies are almost identical: "Perhaps there is just one wisdom for all men, no matter who speaks it." "Aihee," Ikkemotubbe bitterly concurs. "At least, for all men one same heart-break." This exchange looks forward to Faulkner's famous words in his 1950 Nobel Prize address about the "the old universal truths" of "the human heart in conflict with itself." For a moment, Ikkemotubbe actually becomes Faulkner's artistic spokesman.

In Faulkner's later books, Ikkemotubbe functions primarily as a kind of absent presence; his name haunts the county whose haunted name, Yoknapatawpha, Faulkner took from Chickasaw words that he mistakenly believed meant "water flowing slow through the flatland." In *Requiem for a Nun* (1951) Ikkemotubbe and his people are described as having been "swept, hurled, flung not only out of Yoknapatawpha County and Mississippi but the United States too." In *The Town* (1957) Doom's name appears as one of many "phantoms" in the past of the county. Ikkemotubbe, to paraphrase something Faulkner told students at the University of Virginia in 1957, has become the "ghost of that ravishment" that European Americans have perpetrated against American Indian nations. Faulkner was clearly wrong about the future of the indigenous people of Mississippi, and he misrepresented their cultures in many other ways; but an examination of Ikkemotubbe's complex history reinforces the notion that Faulkner was deeply interested in challenging standard American myths of heroic conquest and divinely sanctioned territorial expansion.

Discussion Questions

1. Faulkner rarely provides physical descriptions of Ikkemotubbe, but his descendants and relatives are described in some detail, as in this passage from "Red Leaves": "Issetibbeha was not tall, but he was taller by six inches than his son [Moketubbe] and almost a hundred pounds lighter. Moketubbe was already [at age twenty-five] diseased with flesh, with a pale, broad, inert face and dropsical hands and feet." Why do you think Faulkner avoids supplying readers with a fuller description of Ikkemotubbe? What do his descriptions—and lack thereof—suggest about his view of American Indian history?

2. Examine Ikkemotubbe in the context of one damaging stereotype of American Indians (for example, the "noble savage," the "bloodthirsty killer," the "lazy Indian"). Does Faulkner use Ikkemotubbe to challenge the stereotype? How might Ikkemotubbe help perpetuate it?

3. Howard C. Horsford has argued that "the blunt truth is that [Faulkner] shows very little familiarity with early Mississippi history or with the Choctaws and Chickasaws who were its victims."

Do you think Faulkner represents history correctly or inaccurately through Ikkemotubbe? How might he have represented the past more justly?

4. Compare and contrast Ikkemotubbe's ambitions in "Red Leaves" and "A Justice" with Thomas Sutpen's rise to, and fall from, power in *Absalom, Absalom!* What drives the two men? What thwarts their grand designs?

5. How does Ikkemotubbe compare to a character in a work by a contemporary Native American author—Tayo in Leslie Marmon Silko's *Ceremony* (1977), for instance?

—*Bart H. Welling*

"A ROSE FOR EMILY"

Collected in *These 13* (New York: Cape & Smith, 1931).

EMILY GRIERSON

Emily Grierson, called "Miss Emily" by the townspeople of Jefferson, is the central character in William Faulkner's "A Rose for Emily." The story is told by a narrator who speaks from the perspective of the community upon which Miss Emily had profound effects. The narrative begins with the death of Miss Emily, "a fallen monument" in the deep-South town, and then traces her past to her father's death, which she refused to acknowledge for three days before breaking down and permitting his burial. The townspeople "did not think she was crazy then," but subsequent events reveal her evolving madness and her alienation from the community.

After the death of Miss Emily's father, who had driven away possible suitors of his daughter, Emily in her early thirties became romantically involved with Homer Barron, a flashy "Yankee" foreman come to town to oversee the paving of the sidewalks. Despite the townspeople's gossip, Miss Emily "carried her head high" and bought a man's silver toilet set engraved with the letters "H.B.," causing the community to assume that the two would marry and that Miss Emily would join Barron, who left town when the sidewalks were completed. Barron returns and is observed being admitted through Miss Emily's kitchen door one evening. He is never seen again.

When Miss Emily, with iron-gray hair, dies in her mid seventies, men force open the door of a sealed room upstairs. The rose-colored room is seemingly "furnished for a bridal" with a man's engraved toilet articles on a dresser and his suit over a chair. On the bed lies the decomposed body of a man, and on a second pillow are the imprint of a head and "a strand of iron-gray hair."

A source for "A Rose for Emily," Faulkner's first story published in a magazine with national circulation, is reported by a Faulkner childhood friend to have been a courtship between Miss Mary Louise Neilson and Captain Jack Barron, a Yankee who had come to Oxford to pave the streets. The couple married despite the Neilson family's objections, but the events Faulkner wrote about never actually happened. Faulkner chose to focus his narrative upon the possible consequences of violating entrenched Southern social conventions, the theme of betrayal and alienation, and evolving madness. Much of the story requires the reader to understand inferences. The narrator, for example, never gives specific reasons for the break between Miss Emily and Homer Barron but provides clues. "Homer liked men . . . and was not a marrying man." The narrator observes more subtly that after a collar and tie had been removed from a nightstand in the room where the body lay, a "pale crescent" remained in the dust, suggesting a "horned moon." Faulkner knew from William Shakespeare and other earlier literature that the horned moon is associated with cuckoldry. Therefore, its presence in the story anticipates the narrator's conclusion that love "cuckolded" Homer as well. Although "A Rose for Emily" has many elements of the Gothic genre—a decaying house with spires and cupolas, the haunting influence of the dead upon the living, references to stained-glass windows, and horror—Faulkner scholar Cleanth Brooks maintains that "A Rose for Emily" rises above "cheap Southern Gothic" to the realm of art.

Discussion Questions

1. What evidence in the story can you find that points to Emily's father's dominance? Does that dominance end with the father's death?

2. According to Joseph L. Blotner, Faulkner originally included in the story a scene in which the dying Miss Emily discussed with her Negro servant details about her victim. Do you agree with Faulkner's decision to delete this scene from the story? Why or why not?

3. The narrator has witnessed most of Emily Grierson's lifetime. One critic has said that he has both a sense of community and a sense of history. Do you agree? Why or why not?

4. How does Faulkner use physical objects throughout the story to illustrate the mental states of Emily Grierson?

—John C. Unrue

✐
SANCTUARY
(New York: Cape & Smith, 1931)

TEMPLE DRAKE

Temple Drake, a seventeen-year-old freshman at the state university in Oxford, Mississippi, is the main character of William Faulkner's novel *Sanctuary*. She is also a character in *Requiem for a Nun* (1951). Freed from her father's watchful presence at college, Temple develops a reputation for sneaking out of her dormitory to meet town boys. The university has put her on probation for slipping out at night with them, and she angers several acquaintances, both male and female, by dating different men. Temple's boyfriend and future husband, Gowan Stevens, even sees her name scrawled on a bathroom wall at the train station. While on her way to a baseball game in Starkville, Temple commits a fateful act of rebellion when she jumps off the train at Taylor to join Gowan, her date from the night before and a recent graduate of the University of Virginia. On the way to the game, Gowan wrecks his car near the Old Frenchman place while attempting to purchase a bottle of bootleg whiskey. Tommy, one of the bootlegger's men, takes Temple and Gowan back to the Old Frenchman place, where they spend the night. The next morning Gowan, ashamed and unable to face Temple because of his drunken behavior the previous night, leaves her there. Temple discovers Gowan's absence and hides in a barn near the house as Popeye, one of Faulkner's most menacing villains, shoots Tommy. Popeye, who is sexually impotent, proceeds to rape Temple with a foreign object, later identified as a corncob when the district attorney introduces it into evidence at Goodwin's trial.

Early commentators blamed Temple for somehow contributing to her abuse. For example, in an early review of the novel appearing in the *Saturday Review of Literature* (20 October 1934), Lawrence S. Kubie surmised "That Temple invited the assault with her provocative, if unconscious, exhibitionism is unquestionable." Later critics, such as Diane Roberts, see Temple as a victim of violence and patriarchal oppression rather than an incipient bad seed who, though her experience with Popeye, discovers her affinity for evil.

Some of Temple's actions, though, such as her failure to attempt to escape from Popeye and her false testimony at Goodwin's trials, nevertheless prove problematic in considering her character. Shock and an impulse for self-preservation likely inspire her initial complicity. Scholars have speculated that Temple stays in Memphis and later perjures herself because she has been brainwashed or at least has become completely submissive to Popeye. Others have proposed that she (or, more likely, her father) has arranged some sort of deal with Popeye's lawyer, or that she has repressed her memories of the traumatic experience. Such a variety of speculation about Temple's intentions points back to the only motive that Faulkner makes clear: Temple, a confused and traumatized seventeen-year-old girl, simply makes imprudent, illogical choices and faces serious consequences as a result. She learns that she cannot always rely on the protection of men like her father when Gowan fails miserably in his attempt to defend her.

Several readers have pointed out that Temple fails to maintain a stable, core identity and instead adapts as best she can to whatever situation she finds herself in. Kevin A. Boon, for example, describes her as a "patriarchal cut-out doll, her mind shaped and governed by the men she encounters." It seems fitting, then, that at novel's end Faulkner gives readers a final glimpse of Temple, "sullen and discontented and sad," sitting with her father in the Luxembourg

Gardens and staring "across the pool and the opposite semicircle of trees where at sombre intervals the dead tranquil queens in stained marble mused, and on into the sky lying prone and vanquished in the embrace of the season of rain and death." Similarly vanquished, Temple muses upon her own situation and the dismal prospects for her future, the "season of rain and death" that Faulkner continues to articulate in *Requiem for a Nun*.

At the University of Virginia, Faulkner claimed that he wrote *Requiem for a Nun* after he "began to think what would be the future of that girl" and decided that that story "seemed to me dramatic and worthwhile." It is also inherently tragic. Greatly changed by her experiences of eight years ago in *Sanctuary* and a marriage based not in love but in Gowan's sense of duty, a very different Temple emerges in the later novel. In that novel, in a quest to save Nancy Mannigoe, the "nigger dope-fiend whore" turned nursemaid who murdered Temple's infant daughter, from execution, Temple is, as Roberts puts it, "duped into turning her soul inside out, for her own good, according to Gavin," Gowan's uncle. Gavin convinces Temple to talk about the events of *Sanctuary*, and, as Roberts points out, in doing so he "co-opts and reconstructs her past to insist that her degradation was her own fault." In response to the variety of critical readings of Temple in *Requiem for a Nun*, Roberts writes, "Whether or not Temple is 'redeemed,' as many critics have insisted, or simply humiliated by Gavin Stevens, as Noel Polk suggests, is not a simple issue." Near the end of the first section of the novel, Temple says of the girl she used to be, "Temple Drake is dead." In response, Gavin Stevens utters one of the most memorable phrases in all of Faulkner's fiction: "The past is never dead. It's not even past." Trapped by a past that she cannot change, one that defines a future over which she has precious little control, Temple becomes one of Faulkner's most poignant figures, a lost soul denied even the illusion of salvation that Nancy Mannigoe held so dear.

Discussion Questions

1. Dianne Luce Cox describes Temple's "embrace of the season of rain and death" in the final scene of *Sanctuary* as "slightly optimistic" in that "One cannot withdraw from life to remain in an artificial garden of innocence forever. It may be that Temple is anxious to get on with life; she is ready for another season." How does Cox's speculation play out in *Requiem for a Nun*? Does Temple move on and reach that next "season," or does her marriage to Gowan Stevens, a union Faulkner described as "founded on the vanity of a weak man," simply extend that artificial environment of innocence?

2. The word *sanctuary* has many meanings; it can refer to a sacred space such as a church (or a temple) as well as to the practice of granting sanctuary, or refuge, to criminals and debtors. In *The Town*, Gavin Stevens also defines sanctuary as "a rationality of perspective, which animals, humans too, not merely reach but earn by passing through unbearable emotional states like furious rage or furious fear." How do these different definitions apply to Temple? What types of sanctuary does she give and/or receive?

3. When Temple tells Horace Benbow about the rape, she says that the night before Popeye attacked her she imagined herself several different ways: first, she prayed "to be changed into a boy," then "thought about fastening myself up some way," after the fashion of a chastity belt that had "long sharp spikes on it." As Popeye's "hand was going inside the top of . . . her [Temple's] knickers," she imagined herself "in the coffin" dressed "all in white" wearing "a veil like a bride." Finally, she pictured herself as a teacher with "iron-gray hair and spectacles" before thinking "That wont do. I ought to be a man. So I was an old man, with a long white beard." What do you make of these transmogrifications? What do they say about Temple's state of mind? How does Popeye factor into the passages that include these fantasies?

—*Lorie Watkins Fulton*

POPEYE (VITELLI)

Faulkner probably based Popeye, a character in *Sanctuary*, on a well-known Memphis gangster, Neal Karens (or Kerens) "Popeye" Pumphrey, who was known as "Popeye" because his eyes bulged when he was excited. In 1947 a student at the University of Mississippi asked William Faulkner if Popeye had a "human prototype," and Faulkner responded, "No. He was merely symbolical of evil. I just gave him two eyes, a nose, a mouth and a black suit. It was all allegory." Pumphrey's list of crimes included gambling, bootlegging, assault, and robbery, and Faulkner most likely based his fictional Popeye on an account of Pumphrey that he heard in a Memphis nightclub in 1926. Faulkner heard the story from "a young woman who talked freely about her life, about moving from her village, called Cobbtown, to Memphis, where she had taken up with a rising young gangster." Joseph Blotner writes that the gangster "was probably . . . Pumphrey, a veteran criminal at twenty-three" who "was said to be impotent" but "still persisted in having relations with women, and he had raped one with a particularly bizarre object and kept her in a brothel."

In "Faulkner Reads the Funny Papers" M. Thomas Inge argues that the comic-strip character Popeye serves as another influence for Faulkner's Popeye. This original comic-strip character was different from the more modern, benign, spinach-gulping sailor. Inge writes, "the Popeye of the funny papers was a complex, multifaceted character with more of the bizarre and antisocial in his nature than most people today are likely to know about." Elzie C. Segar's *Thimble Theatre* comic strip debuted the Popeye character in January of 1929, the same month that Faulkner began writing *Sanctuary;* however, Popeye first appeared earlier in Faulkner's fiction in the short story "The Big Shot," which Blotner speculates Faulkner may have written shortly after his encounter in the Memphis nightclub. Faulkner also likely included material in the conclusion of *Sanctuary* that he wrote as early as 1925, but the comic strip could feasibly have influenced Faulkner's Popeye when he reappeared in *Sanctuary.*

Popeye does function as the symbol of evil that Faulkner described; with his dark suits, rough language, brusque manner, and ever-present pistol, he seems the epitome of a 1920s gangster from the popular literature that Faulkner claimed partly inspired the character. Faulkner links Horace Benbow, who later becomes Lee Goodwin's attorney, and Popeye from the first page of the novel when Horace sees Popeye's "shattered reflection" as he drinks from the spring near the Old Frenchman place. In "The Elliptical Nature of *Sanctuary*," John T. Matthews "proposes a radical intimacy between Horace and Popeye defined by a dynamic of projection and self-evasion." In his Freudian examination of *Sanctuary* in *Children of the Dark House: Text and Context in Faulkner,* Noel Polk extends this connection and points out that "Popeye is Horace's twin and alter-ego, at the same time his id and his superego: he is at once the reductio ad absurdum of Horace's darker sexual impulses and the punishing, vengeful father—whom he must inevitably face." Finally, Faulkner also describes Popeye as using sinister language; for example, on the opening page of the novel Faulkner writes, "His face had a queer, bloodless color, as though seen by electric light; against the sunny silence, in his slanted straw hat and his slightly akimbo arms, he had that vicious depthless quality of stamped tin." The text often refers to him as a "black man"; such descriptions likely stem from his dark suits, but they also suggest an ominous aura of corruption.

Faulkner revised *Sanctuary* heavily before publication, making such extensive changes that, in his editorial afterword to Faulkner's original version of the text, Polk describes the "two versions of *Sanctuary*" as "two different books, each written at fairly distinct points in Faulkner's development as a writer." Faulkner made thousands of alterations, and one of the most substantial ones involved adding a chapter offering a biographical sketch of Popeye that significantly complicates any characterization of him as a force of pure evil. Popeye seems to have been doomed even before birth in that his father likely had syphilis and passed it on to Popeye. Faulkner writes of "the disease, the legacy which her [Popeye's mother's] brief husband had left her"; Popeye's impotence, delayed physical and mental development, and the belief that "they thought he was blind" at birth all indicate symptoms consistent with different stages of syphilis. Popeye's father left his mother before his birth, and his grandmother's second husband ran off with her entire savings shortly thereafter. Popeye's grandmother then began to lose her mind. She started setting fires with her grandson in the house and blamed them on someone else; ultimately, she succeeded in burning down the house, and although Popeye survived unscathed, the narrator observes that he "might well have been dead," given his "extensive physical afflictions."

In addition to generating sympathy, or at least pity, with this glimpse of Popeye's difficult childhood, Faulkner shows a favorable side of the adult Popeye when he is arrested on his way to Pensacola to visit his mother, an invalid, the summer after Lee Goodwin's trial. Faulkner writes, "Each summer he would return home to see her, prosperous, quiet, thin, black, and uncommunicative in his narrow black suits. He told her that his business was being night clerk in hotels; that, following his profession, he would move from town to town, as a doctor or a lawyer might." Despite his despicable actions, Popeye still wants his mother's approval. Faulkner also implies that Popeye does not fight being arrested "for killing a man in one town and at an hour when he was in another town killing somebody else," at least in part, because he realizes that, as the narrator earlier observed, he "might well have been dead." The narrator describes Popeye as a "man who made money and had nothing he could do with it, spend it for, since he knew that alcohol would kill him like poison, who had no friends and had never known a woman and knew he could never." At the University of Virginia, Faulkner said of Popeye, "he was to me another lost human being. He became a symbol of evil in modern society only by coincidence." Perhaps the larger tragedy is that Popeye likely realizes the futility of his own life and chooses death by refusing the last-minute efforts of the Memphis lawyer who even asks him, "Are you trying to commit suicide?" Although Popeye does not answer, the lawyer's "baffled and raging unbelief" at his client's refusal to appeal his conviction suggests that the answer would have been an unqualified "yes."

Discussion Questions

1. Temple often calls Popeye "Daddy." While such references could simply reflect her adoption of the slang common to her new environment, parallels exist between Temple's actual father, Judge Drake, and Popeye. What are some of the similarities that Temple might notice? Why might she think of Popeye as a surrogate father?

2. Given Faulkner's juxtaposition of Horace and Popeye in the opening scene of the novel, in what respects does Popeye seem a "shattered reflection" of Horace's thoughts and attitudes?

3. Some readers have suggested that Temple has genuine feelings for Red, the man that Popeye employs as her surrogate sexual partner, and others believe that she simply uses Red in hopes that he will rescue her from Popeye. What clues does *Sanctuary* offer for both of these readings? Does Temple's plan to run away with Red's younger brother, Pete, in *Requiem for a Nun* offer additional evidence of Temple's feelings for Red?

4. Many readers find it troubling that Temple fails to take advantage of several opportunities to escape from Popeye in *Sanctuary*. What are some of the reasons that the text offers for her staying?

—*Lorie Watkins Fulton*

THE SOUND AND THE FURY
(New York: Cape & Smith, 1929)

THE COMPSON FAMILY

The Compson family holds one of the most prominent positions in William Faulkner's fiction. He features the Compsons in *The Sound and the Fury* and *Absalom, Absalom!* (1936) and includes or mentions them in short stories, the "Appendix Compson: 1699–1945," and novels such as *The Unvanquished, Go Down, Moses, Requiem for a Nun, The Town,* and *The Mansion.* In the "Appendix Compson," which he wrote for *The Portable Faulkner* in 1946 (seventeen years after *The Sound and the Fury*), Faulkner details the family's earliest known history, beginning when Quentin MacLachan Compson, the son of a Glasgow printer, flees Culloden Moor, the site of the 1746 battle in which the British defeated the Highland Jacobites. He arrives in Carolina and later relocates to Kentucky at age eighty to avoid becoming involved in the revolutionary conflict. His son, Charles Stuart Compson, fights for the British and, after being left "for dead in a Georgia swamp by his own retreating army and then by the advancing American one," arrives in Kentucky four years later. Charles Stuart fathers Jason Lycurgus Compson, one of Jefferson's first citizens. As Faulkner writes in *Requiem for a Nun,* Jason Lycurgus "came to the settlement a few years ago with a race-horse, which he swapped to Ikkemotubbe, Issetibbeha's successor in the chiefship, for a square mile of what was to be the most valuable land in the future town of Jefferson." Jason Lycurgus seems to be the Compson that Faulkner referred to at the University of Virginia as the "first" Compson (perhaps he excluded the history detailed in the appendix), "a bold ruthless man who came into Mississippi as a free forester to grasp where and when he could and wanted to, and established what should have been a princely line, and that princely line decayed." Jason Lycurgus fathered the "old governor," Quentin MacLachan Compson II, who in turn fathered General Jason Lycurgus Compson II, the Civil War brigadier general who loans Thomas Sutpen his original seed cotton in *Absalom, Absalom!*

The general's son, Jason Richmond Lycurgus Compson III, becomes the first of Faulkner's more-familiar twentieth-century Compsons. Jason III weds Caroline Bascomb, and they create the family Faulkner said had degenerated "into semi-madness" by the time of *The Sound and the Fury*. As the head of an aristocratic clan forced to adapt to the changed post–Civil War world that he inherits, Jason III seems a thwarted gentleman, cynical and disillusioned. He drinks heavily against his doctor's orders to escape the reality of his family's dissolution and, in doing so, effectively commits a form of passive suicide. His oldest son, Quentin III, actively commits suicide by drowning himself in the Charles River after his first year at Harvard. Faulkner thought Quentin "too sensitive to face" the reality of the South, and the final line of *Absalom, Absalom!* including Quentin's paradoxical protest, *"I dont hate it!"* certainly testifies to such conflict. However, far more serious issues plague Quentin than his ambiguous relationship to his Southern heritage, the most obvious of which stem from the problematic notions of sexuality that he learns from his father and their effect on his relationship with his sister.

Critics often refer to Candace or "Caddy," the second child and only daughter, as the "absent center" of *The Sound and the Fury* because, while much of the novel focuses on her brothers' reactions to her, Faulkner does not let her share in their narrative power. Faulkner often called her his "heart's darling," the daring young girl with the muddy drawers who is doomed to get pregnant by one man, marry another, and leave her daughter, Quentin, in Jefferson after her short-lived marriage fails. Although readers never learn what becomes of Caddy with any degree of certainty, according to the Compson appendix, in 1943 librarian Melissa Meek recognizes her (or at least thinks that she does) in a magazine photo with "a German staffgeneral."

Jason IV, the third Compson child, deals with his problematic family in a different fashion from his siblings; Quentin escapes in suicide, and Caddy simply escapes, but Jason's emotions emerge in bursts of anger and vitriolic sarcasm. In the appendix, Faulkner described Jason as the "first sane Compson since before Culloden." Regardless of his mental status, he is one of Faulkner's most unlikable characters. One of Jason's most reprehensible deeds is his theft of the money that Caddy sends to help ensure her daughter's well-being. Faulkner even named Jason as his least favorite character.

Jason finally commits the youngest Compson child, the mentally impaired Benjamin or "Benjy," to the state asylum, but in *The Mansion*, Jason says that "his mother whined and wept" until Jason "gave up and brought Benjy back home." Faulkner said in his interview with Jean Stein, "The only emotion I can have for Benjy is grief and pity for all mankind. You can't feel anything for Benjy because he doesn't feel anything." However, Faulkner did concede that Benjy "recognized tenderness and love though he could not have named them." In *The Mansion* it is revealed that Benjy "had set himself and the house both on fire and burned up in it" less than two years after returning from the asylum.

Faulkner said that the title *The Sound and the Fury*—taken from William Shakespeare's *Macbeth*, in which life is described as "a tale / Told by an idiot, full of sound and fury, / Signifying nothing"—initially referred exclusively to Benjy's section, but he realized, "the more I had to work on the book, the more elastic the title became, until it covered the whole family." Faulkner felt "sorry for the Compsons" because their "blood which was good and brave once . . . thinned and faded all the way out." Faulkner said that they lived with "the attitudes of 1859 or '60," and he described this attitude as inherited. A student at the University of Virginia spoke of Jason III's apparent "lack of values" and wondered if "Quentin winds up the way he does primarily because of that." Faulkner replied, "The action as portrayed by Quentin was transmitted to him through his father. There was a basic failure before that. The grandfather had been a failed brigadier twice in the Civil War. It was the—the basic failure Quentin inherited through his father, or beyond his father." The Compson family is central to much of Faulkner's most significant work, particularly in the early fiction.

Discussion Questions

1. Upon completing the Compson appendix Faulkner wrote to Malcolm Cowley, "I should have done this when I wrote the book. Then the whole thing would have fallen into pattern like a jigsaw puzzle when the magician's wand touched it." However, inconsistencies between the appendix and *The Sound and the Fury* seem to complicate rather than simplify the novel. What are some of these inconsistencies? In what ways are they significant?

2. When a student at the University of Virginia asked Faulkner about the stability of Quentin's character between *The Sound and the Fury* and *Absalom, Absalom!* Faulkner replied, "To me he's consistent. That he approached the Sutpen family with the same ophthalmia that he approached his own troubles, that he probably never saw anything very clearly, that his was just one of the thirteen ways to look at Sutpen, and his may have been the—one of the most erroneous." Faulkner added that although *Absalom, Absalom!* is "Sutpen's story," whenever a "character gets into a book, no matter how minor, he's actually telling his biography." What does *Absalom, Absalom!* add to Quentin's story in *The Sound and the Fury*? How does reading Quentin's history from *The Sound and the Fury* into *Absalom, Absalom!* potentially alter readers' perceptions of both novels?

3. With regard to Caddy's role in *The Sound and the Fury*, Dawn Trouard in "Faulkner's Text Which Is Not One," in *New Essays on The Sound and the Fury* (1993), suggests, "To view Caddy as a unified, single figure, as the criticism has done, distorts, even erases, in practice and spirit, possibilities for understanding Caddy and the complexities of female

experience." She concludes that paying close attention "to the distinct Caddy in each separate section" reveals that she "does not add up; she can't be reconciled—she is more than one." Who are these multiple Caddys? What does Caddy mean to each of her brothers in their sections of the novel? What does she seem to mean to other women, such as her mother and Dilsey, who do not have a narrative voice? Do Faulkner's other fictional representations of her in the Compson appendix and "That Evening Sun" affirm or contradict her brothers' depictions in *The Sound and the Fury*?

4. Faulkner seems consciously concerned with language in *The Sound and the Fury*. Judith Lockyer in *Ordered by Words* (1991) has suggested that each of the Compson brothers "reveals an aspect of the power in language. That power is born out of the relation of language to consciousness." Building upon that idea, Noel Polk describes how "Faulkner uses the mechanics of the English language—grammar, syntax, punctuation, spelling—as a direct objective correlative to the states of each of the narrators' minds." What hallmarks distinguish each brother's use of language? How does Faulkner characterize each narrator through the mechanics of language that Polk describes? How does language function in the novel's fourth section given its third-person narration?

—*Lorie Watkins Fulton*

DILSEY GIBSON

Dilsey Gibson, an African American domestic servant whom Faulkner considered one of his favorite characters, appears as the Compson family nurse, cook, and maid in *The Sound and the Fury* as well as in his 1931 short story "That Evening Sun." Faulkner described her in a 1955 interview as "brave, courageous, generous, gentle and honest." Faulkner's admiration of Dilsey likely stemmed, at least in part, from his affection for her real-life model, Caroline Barr, more commonly known as "Mammy Callie." Barr cared for Faulkner during his childhood, and later did the same for his daughter, Jill.

Faulkner also admired Dilsey because "she was a good human being" who held the Compson family "together for not the hope of reward but just because it was the decent and proper thing to do." She cares for the frequently ailing Caroline Compson, disciplines and comforts the Compson children in the narrative past, and tries to shield Miss Quentin from Jason's tyranny in the narrative present. Perhaps following Faulkner's lead, conventional critical readings of Dilsey contrast her with the Compsons as the moral center of the novel. Cleanth Brooks wrote in *William Faulkner: The Yoknapatawpha Country* (1963), "The one member of the Compson household who represents a unifying and sustaining force is the Negro servant Dilsey. She tries to take care of Benjy and to give the girl Quentin the mothering she needs. In contrast to Mrs. Compson's vanity and whining self-pity, Dilsey exhibits charity and rugged good sense."

Dilsey's own family consists of her husband, Roskus, and their children, Versh, T.P., and Frony. Faulkner, however, limits Dilsey's interaction with her family and is more interested in her role in the Compson household. Blyden Jackson observed in "Faulkner's Depiction of the Negro" (*Studies in English* [1978]), "She is, it can be argued, a black matriarch more dedicated to a white family than to her own." Diane Roberts notes that Dilsey "is especially harsh to her sons and grandsons over care of Benjy."

Dilsey figures prominently in the fourth section of *The Sound and the Fury,* so much so that readers commonly refer to it as "Dilsey's section" even though Faulkner uses third-person narration to relate the events of Easter Sunday, April 8, 1928. The section opens as Dilsey tries on her Easter attire before changing and crossing the yard to prepare breakfast for the Compsons. After Jason discovers that Miss Quentin has run away, Dilsey takes Benjy with her own family to church. They hear a visiting minister, Reverend Shegog, preach a sermon of salvation and sacrifice that takes his congregation "beyond the need for words." Benjy appears "rapt" in "the midst of the voices and the hands" and Dilsey, moved to tears by the service, declares as she walks home "I've seed de first en de last." When Frony asks "First en last whut?" Dilsey replies, "Never you mind," and adds, "I seed de beginnin, en now I sees de endin." A little later Dilsey uses the same statement when she predicts, "Jason aint comin home. Ise seed de first en de last"—meaning, presumably, that she has seen the rise and fall of the Compson family.

For Dilsey's entry in "Appendix Compson: 1699–1945," the genealogical companion to *The Sound and the Fury* written more than fifteen years after the publication of the novel, Faulkner simply writes, "They endured." Dilsey endures, but she does not triumph, and, as Thadious M. Davis noted in *Games of Property,* this "racial epitaph" erases Dilsey as an individual and subsumes her into "the constructed collectivity of a black race." Regardless, she remains, as John Earl Bassett pointed out, the "best black character" in Faulkner's "early fiction, a significant development from Caspey, Isom, and Simon." Faulkner identified Dilsey as one of his three "most nearly perfectly tragic" characters, and wrote of her in his unpublished introduction to *The Sound and the Fury:* "There was Dilsey to be the future, to stand above the fallen ruins of the family like a ruined chimney, gaunt, patient and indomitable." Although in Faulkner's equation that future certainly remains as bleak as the past, Dilsey nonetheless displays great strength in facing it.

Discussion Questions

1. Some readers have criticized Dilsey as too closely related to the stereotypical figure of the plantation "mammy." In what respects does Dilsey conform to this stereotype? How does she defy it?

2. Cynthia Dobbs noted that Dilsey's "voice is full, like Jason's, of a terrifically funny sarcasm" that "discloses key truths about the Compsons." What are some specific textual examples of such moments?

3. Many critics have commented upon the positive power of Dilsey's Christian faith as the source of her ability to endure, but Cleanth Brooks pointed out, "Faulkner makes no claim for Dilsey's version of Christianity one way or the other. His presentation of it is moving and credible, but moving and credible as an aspect of Dilsey's own mental and emotional life." Does *The Sound and the Fury* offer any evidence that Dilsey's belief frees or sustains her in some fashion unavailable to the Compsons?

4. Cheryl Lester suggested in "Racial Awareness and Arrested Development" in *The Cambridge Companion to William Faulkner* (1995), "the body of the black mammy Dilsey herself serves for Faulkner as a sort of twentieth-century ruin or landmark in a South shifting from an agrarian to an industrial economy and from a rural to an urban society." What passages suggest that Dilsey serves such a function?

—*Lorie Watkins Fulton*

REFERENCES

Edwin T. Arnold and Dawn Trouard, *Reading Faulkner:* Sanctuary (Jackson: University Press of Mississippi, 1996);

Harold Bloom, ed., *William Faulkner's* Sanctuary (New York: Chelsea House, 1988);

Joseph L. Blotner, *Faulkner: A Biography,* 2 volumes (New York: Random House, 1974);

Cleanth Brooks, *William Faulkner: First Encounters* (New Haven: Yale University Press, 1983);

Walter Brylowski, "The Theme of Maturation in *Intruder in the Dust,"* in *Readings on William Faulkner,* edited by Clarice Swisher (San Diego: Greenhaven Press, 1998), pp. 172–176;

J. Douglas Canfield, ed., *Twentieth Century Interpretations of* Sanctuary: *A Collection of Critical Essays* (Englewood Cliffs, N.J.: Prentice-Hall, 1982);

Dianne Luce Cox, ed., *William Faulkner's* As I Lay Dying: *A Critical Casebook* (New York: Garland, 1985);

Lewis M. Dabney, *The Indians of Yoknapatawpha: A Study in Literature and History* (Baton Rouge: Louisiana State University Press, 1974);

Thadious M. Davis, *Games of Property: Law, Race, Gender, and Faulkner's* Go Down, Moses (Durham, N.C.: Duke University Press, 2003);

Carl J. Dimitri, "*Go Down, Moses* and *Intruder in the Dust:* From Negative to Positive Liberty," *Faulkner Journal,* 19, 1 (2003): 11–26;

Cynthia Dobbs, "'Ruin or Landmark'?: Black Bodies as *Lieux de Mémoire* in *The Sound and the Fury,"* *Faulkner Journal,* 20 (2004/2005): 35–51;

Don H. Doyle, *Faulkner's County: The Historical Roots of Yoknapatawpha* (Chapel Hill: University of North Carolina Press, 2000);

Erik Dussere, "The Debts of History: Southern Honor, Affirmative Action, and Faulkner's *Intruder in the Dust,"* *Faulkner Journal,* 17, 1 (2001): 37–57;

A. Nicholas Fargnoli and Michael Golay, *William Faulkner A to Z* (New York: Facts on File, 2002);

Frederick L. Gwynn and Joseph L. Blotner, eds., *Faulkner in the University: Class Conferences at the University of Virginia, 1957–1958* (Charlottesville: University of Virginia Press, 1959);

Frederick J. Hoffman, *William Faulkner* (Boston: Twayne, 1966);

Diane Brown Jones, *A Reader's Guide to the Short Stories of William Faulkner* (New York: G. K. Hall, 1994);

Arthur F. Kinney, ed., *Critical Essays on William Faulkner: The Compson Family* (Boston: G. K. Hall, 1982);

Kinney, ed., *Critical Essays on William Faulkner: The McCaslin Family* (New York: G. K. Hall, 1990);

Michael Millgate, *New Essays on* Light in August (Cambridge: Cambridge University Press, 1987);

Richard C. Moreland, "Faulkner's Continuing Education: From Self-Reflection to Embarrassment," in *Faulkner at 100: Retrospect and Prospect: Faulkner and Yoknapatawpha, 1997,* edited by Donald M. Kartiganer and Ann J. Abadie (Jackson: University Press of Mississippi, 2000): pp. 60–69;

John B. Padgett, "*Absalom, Absalom!:* Resources," *William Faulkner on the Web,* edited by John B. Padgett, University of Mississippi, http://www.mcsr.olemiss.edu/~egjbp/faulkner/r_n_aa.html>;

François Pitavy, ed., *William Faulkner's* Light in August: *A Critical Casebook* (New York: Garland, 1982);

Noel Polk, "Idealism in *The Mansion,"* in *Faulkner & Idealism: Perspectives from Paris,* edited by Michel Gresset and Patrick Samway, S.J. (Jackson: University Press of Mississippi, 1983): pp. 112–126;

Polk, *A Rose for Emily* (Fort Worth, Tex.: Harcourt Brace, 2000);

Polk, ed., *New Essays on "The Sound and the Fury"* (Cambridge: Cambridge University Press, 1993);

Diane Roberts, *Faulkner and Southern Womanhood* (Athens: University of Georgia Press, 1994);

Stephen M. Ross and Polk, *Reading Faulkner: "The Sound and the Fury"* (Jackson: University Press of Mississippi, 1996);

Hugh M. Ruppersburg, James Hinkle, and Robert McCoy, *Reading Faulkner:* Light in August: *Glossary and Commentary* (Jackson: University of Mississippi Press, 1994);

Patrick Samway, S.J., "*Intruder in the Dust:* A Re-evaluation," in *Faulkner: The Unappeased Imagination: A Collection of Critical Essays,* edited by Glenn O. Carey (Troy, N.Y.: Whitston, 1980), pp. 83–113;

Theresa M. Towner, *Faulkner on the Color Line: The Later Novels* (Jackson: University Press of Mississippi, 2000);

Joseph R. Urgo, *Faulkner's Apocrypha: "A Fable," "Snopes," and the Spirit of Human Rebellion* (Jackson: University Press of Mississippi, 1989);

Warwick Wadlington, As I Lay Dying: *Stories out of Stories* (New York: Twayne, 1992);

Linda Wagner-Martin, ed., *New Essays on* Go Down, Moses (Cambridge: Cambridge University Press, 1996).

F. Scott Fitzgerald

(September 24, 1896 – December 21, 1940)

◈

"ABSOLUTION"

Collected in *All the Sad Young Men* (New York: Scribners, 1926).

RUDOLPH MILLER

Rudolph Miller, the protagonist of F. Scott Fitzgerald's short story "Absolution," is an eleven-year-old Roman Catholic boy whose lie in confession and consequent interview with a deranged priest confirm his romantic conception of himself and the world that lies before him. The only child of the railroad freight agent for the prairie town of Ludwig in the Red River Valley of North Dakota, Rudolph is experiencing the first stirrings of sexual longing and of rebellion against his family and church. As he encounters the trials of adolescence, he finds refuge in his invented alter ego, Blatchford Sarnemington: "Blatchford Sarnemington was himself, and these words were in effect a lyric. When he became Blatchford Sarnemington a suave nobility flowed from him. Blatchford Sarnemington lived in great sweeping triumphs. . . . as he went by, there were envious mutters in the air: 'Blatchford Sarnemington! There goes Blatchford Sarnemington.'"

In the story of a young person who remakes himself into a fantastically romantic figure, "Absolution" has clear parallels with *The Great Gatsby.* It is, in fact, one of a handful of *Gatsby* "cluster stories"—including "Winter Dreams" and "The Sensible Thing"—in which Fitzgerald experimented with subjects and themes later developed in his novel. Readers have often assumed that Rudolph is the young James Gatz, a view supported by a 1934 letter in which Fitzgerald declared that "Absolution" "was intended to be a picture of his [Gatsby's] early life, but . . . I cut it because I preferred to preserve the sense of mystery." In a June 1922 letter to his Scribners editor, Maxwell Perkins, Fitzgerald had announced that the novel he was planning would have Midwestern and New York settings and "a catholic element." In April of the following year he reported to Perkins that "Much of what I wrote last summer was good but it was so interrupted that it was ragged + in approaching it from a new angle I've had to discard a lot of it—in one case 18,000 words (part of which will appear in *The Mercury* as a short story)." The short story was "Absolution"; but it is most likely that "Absolution" was not simply lopped off the manuscript for *The Great Gatsby,* which does not have a "catholic element," but instead came from a version of the novel that preceded the draft embodying Fitzgerald's "new angle."

Whatever his connection to James Gatz, Rudolph is defined in "Absolution" primarily through his relationships with his father and with his parish priest. Carl Miller is "suspicious, unrestful, and continually dismayed," a weak man whose "two bonds with the colorful life were his faith in the Roman Catholic Church and his mystical worship of the Empire Builder, James J. Hill." Because Miller is unable to measure up to either of these objects of his faith, he bullies his son and is apparently estranged from his wife, who sleeps in a separate bedroom. The angry man's reiterated threats—"First you begin to neglect your religion, . . . the next thing you'll begin to lie and steal, and the *next* thing is the *reform* school!"—provoke a small act of rebellion from Rudolph that brings about a beating of "savage ferocity, outlet of the ineffectual man." Carl Miller later feels regret for his actions, but his forcing his son to perform a second confession before Father Schwartz and then take communion causes Rudolph, hurt and angry, to embrace "the necessities of his [own] ease and pride" and his "'crazy' ambitions and petty shames and fears": "The pressure of his environment had driven [Rudolph] into the lonely secret road of adolescence."

Father Adolphus Schwartz, like Carl Miller, is an ineffectual man, a captive of dark, confined spaces—his office, the church, the confessional. He is haunted by the vitality of the blonde Swede girls with their lovers in the sun-filled wheat fields; only when Rudolph admits in the confessional to "immodest thoughts and desires" does the priest question him closely. Later the boy sits "in a patch of sunshine" in Schwartz's office, and the man notices his beauty, intensity, and enormous blue eyes, which contrast with the priest's "cold, watery eyes." Rudolph wants to tell the priest that he has committed a terrible sin by lying in confession; he has said, "Oh, no, Father, I never tell lies" (an event, according to Fitzgerald's ledger, drawn from his own childhood). But hearing the words "terrible sin," Father Schwartz immediately assumes that the child has committed a "sin against purity." Quite clearly he attributes to Rudolph the longings that he has himself repressed.

Father Schwartz is at least partly correct in his appraisal of Rudolph, though he does not understand how the child's fantasy world relates to his own. During his meeting with Rudolph, the priest indulges in a deranged rant: "When a lot of people get together in the best places things go glimmering. . . . The thing is to have a lot of people in the center of the world, wherever that happens to be. . . . But my theory is that when a whole lot of people get together, in the best places things go glimmering all the time." This refrain brings to Rudolph's mind Blatchford Sarnemington, his own fantasy. Father Schwartz then describes an amusement park: "It's a thing like a fair, only much more glittering. Go to one at night and stand a little way off from it in a dark place—under dark trees. You'll see a big wheel made of lights turning in the air. . . . A band playing somewhere, and a smell of peanuts—and everything will twinkle." What the priest describes is an exotic but meretricious beauty—glimmering and glittering and twinkling

and unreal: "'But don't get up close,' he warned Rudolph, 'because if you do you'll only feel the heat and the sweat and the life.'"

Father Schwartz describes the fantasy world that both he, a mature man, and Rudolph, a child approaching adolescence, embrace. The spuriousness of the image becomes an emblem for the madness that ultimately destroys the priest, who cannot get too close to life. For Rudolph the image propels him into a vision—however false—that is liberating and affirming. The priest's ramblings are "strange," "awful," and terrifying to the boy. "But underneath his terror he felt that his own inner convictions were confirmed. There was something ineffably gorgeous somewhere that had nothing to do with God. . . . At the moment when he had affirmed immaculate honor a silver pennon had flapped out into the breeze somewhere and there had been the crunch of leather and the shine of silver spurs and a troop of horsemen waiting for dawn on a low green hill. The sun had made stars of light on their breastplates like the picture at home of the German cuirassiers at Sedan." The priest collapses; the boy ascends in his heroic, chivalric fantasy. But Father Adolphus Schwartz's experiences may suggest the ultimate direction of Rudolph Miller's experiences. Dreams, no matter how lofty, cannot easily deflect harsh reality.

Discussion Questions

1. Rudolph Miller envisions himself as Blatchford Sarnemington. What does the name suggest about the nature of Rudolph's dreams? What connotations does Fitzgerald intend the name to convey?

2. "Absolution" develops its themes through contrasted images of youth and age, light and dark, natural environments and enclosed human spaces. Using specific details from the text, show how one or more of these contrasted images operates in the text.

3. Explicate the passage, in the fourth-to-last paragraph of the story, beginning "At the moment when he had affirmed immaculate honor" and ending "German cuirassiers at Sedan." Identify the references, and explain why they are described in the language used in the passage. What effect and what message is Fitzgerald conveying in this passage?

4. "Although 'Absolution' has been called a coming-of-age story, it may be more accurately described as a 'pre-coming-of-age story.'" Defend or refute this statement with reference to a well-known coming-of-age story—perhaps John Updike's "A&P," Joyce Carol Oates's "Where Are You Going, Where Have You Been?," or Philip Roth's "The Conversion of the Jews."

—*Judith S. Baughman*

"BABYLON REVISITED"

Collected in *Taps at Reveille* (New York: Scribners, 1935).

CHARLIE WALES

Charlie Wales, the protagonist of F. Scott Fitzgerald's "Babylon Revisited," had made a fortune as a stock-market speculator during the 1920s, enabling him to leave his job and take his wife, Helen, and their daughter, Honoria, to live in Paris. There Charlie and Helen became part of the alcohol-driven, riotous nightlife embraced by certain wealthy Americans in Europe during the boom years. The dissipation in the Waleses' lives exacerbated difficulties in their marriage, and after one drunken quarrel, Charlie locked Helen out of their apartment in the snow. Her exposure to the wet and cold contributed to her death from heart disease. Charlie consequently signed over custody of Honoria to Helen's sister and brother-in-law, Marion and Lincoln Peters, and entered a sanitarium in Switzerland. "Babylon Revisited" focuses upon Charlie's efforts to reclaim both Honoria and his lost honor during a return to Paris in the early 1930s.

When the story begins, the thirty-five-year-old Charlie has once again become a successful businessman—he is now "Charles J. Wales of Prague"—and he hopes to establish a home for himself and nine-year-old Honoria, complete with housekeeper and governess, in the Czech city. He limits himself to one drink a day—"and I take that drink deliberately, so that the idea of alcohol won't get too big in my imagination," he tells Lincoln and Marion, who lead sober, respectable lives in Paris. His relationship with Honoria is loving, playful, and considerate as he reunites with her at the Peterses' home and then treats her to lunch and a vaudeville performance the following day. Yet, Charlie has a difficult adversary in Marion Peters, who blames him for her sister's death, doubts that his sobriety will last, and resents both his affluence and his apparent luck: "she had lived for a long time with prejudice—a prejudice founded on a curious disbelief in her sister's happiness, and which, in the shock of one terrible night, had turned to hatred for him. It had all happened at a point in her life where the discouragement of ill health and adverse circumstances made it necessary for her to believe in tangible villainy and a tangible villain." The relentless attacks of the neurotic, bitter Marion against the well-intentioned Charlie increase the reader's sympathy for him.

At the heart of the story, however, is a very real ambivalence in Charlie's character. Though he has returned to Paris to reclaim Honoria, he begins and ends his quest at a site of his earlier dissipation, the Ritz Bar. In the first scene at the Ritz, now by and large without customers, Charlie seeks information from barman Alix about Americans who had been his companions in the old days; he also leaves the Peterses' address for Duncan Schaeffer, one of these acquaintances who, Alix reports, is in town. Following dinner with Marion, Lincoln, the two Peters children, and Honoria, Charlie tours Montmartre nightspots—bars, cafés, cabarets—that he had earlier frequented. He observes "all the catering to vice and waste" and realizes "the meaning of the word 'dissipate'—to dissipate into thin air; to make nothing out of something." He understands that wasted money, time, and lives "had been given, even the most wildly squandered sum, as an offering to destiny that he might not remember the things most worth remembering, the things that now he would always remember—his child taken from his control, his wife escaped to a grave in Vermont." Through his return to "Babylon"—an Old Testament symbol of wickedness—Charlie confirms his reformation.

However, the drunken Duncan Schaeffer and Lorraine Quarrles arrive at the Peterses' house just as Marion is preparing to surrender custody of Honoria to Charlie. Assuming that her brother-in-law has rejoined bad company, the dismayed Marion determines that he should not take Honoria to Prague for at least another six months. Charlie returns to the Ritz Bar, where Paul the barman says to him, "I heard that you lost a lot in the crash," and Charlie replies, "I did, . . . but I lost everything I wanted in the boom." "Selling short," says Paul. "Something like that," replies Charlie. He clearly admits his squandering of both financial and emotional capital during the riotous 1920s. But he then suggests that his actions were not entirely blameworthy because the standards of behavior were different during the boom years than they are following the stock-market crash: "—The men who locked their wives out in the snow, because the snow of twenty-nine wasn't real snow. If you didn't want it to be snow, you just paid some money." Charlie understands what he has lost through dissipation and failure of character. But he never fully acknowledges his own responsibility for events—particularly the death of Helen—and indulges in constant self-justification. He believes that he can continue to visit his old haunts with their nostalgic appeal, that he can maintain his one-drink-a-day regimen, even that his dead wife would have forgiven him. The last line of the story reads, "He was absolutely sure Helen wouldn't have wanted him to be so alone."

"Babylon Revisited" has obvious sources in Fitzgerald's life. In a November 18, 1930 letter to his literary agent, Harold Ober, he declared that Charlie's conflict with Marion was founded on his own quarrel with Zelda Fitzgerald's sister Rosalind Smith, who blamed Zelda's insanity on Fitzgerald's drinking and who felt that he was not fit to raise their daughter, Scottie, the clear model for Honoria. Charlie's loss of Helen is paralleled by Fitzgerald's loss of Zelda to schizophrenia. Although Fitzgerald felt guilt about the chaos of their life together and the time and opportunities he had wasted through dissipation, he was also inclined toward self-justification. In a 1930 letter to Zelda, he declared, "We ruined ourselves—I have never honestly thought that we ruined each other." This vision of himself and others informs Fitzgerald's complex portrait of Charlie Wales, giving undeniable power to both the character and the story.

Discussion Questions

1. Fitzgerald often used selective detail to reveal character or setting in his fiction. Show how details of speech, action, or appearance define two characters (other than Charlie Wales) in "Babylon Revisited."

2. Show how financial imagery in "Babylon Revisited" helps describe Charlie Wales's surrender to the affluence and dissipation of the expatriate life that have undermined his commitment to responsible behavior.

3. The first and last scenes of the story begin in the Ritz Bar. Explicate the similarities and differences between Charlie's first and second conversations with the bartenders.

4. Deriving evidence from "Babylon Revisited" and two other Fitzgerald stories, "The Swimmers" (1929) and "One Trip Abroad" (1930), discuss the writer's view of the impact of Europe upon American character.

5. Does Charlie Wales deserve to recover Honoria? Support your opinion with details from the text.

—*Judith S. Baughman*

"BERNICE BOBS HER HAIR"
Collected in *Flappers and Philosophers* (New York: Scribners, 1920).

BERNICE

Bernice is the teenage protagonist of F. Scott Fitzgerald's early "flapper" story "Bernice Bobs Her Hair." Fitzgerald's flappers are willful and witty young women who embody Jazz-Age exuberance and rebellion. Marjorie Harvey, the story's antagonist and consummate flapper, declares her generation's philosophy: "At eighteen our convictions are hills from which we look; at forty-five they are caves in which we hide." Fitzgerald's title refers the then-daring practice of young women's having their hair cut mannishly short. In 1920 the Midwestern teenage characters of Fitzgerald's stories would consider a "bobbed" girl as sexually adventurous. Fitzgerald casts Bernice as a pretty, but socially inept, girl from Eau Claire, Wisconsin, visiting her sophisticated cousin Marjorie in St. Paul, Minnesota.

Fitzgerald describes Bernice as "pretty, with dark hair and high color" but "no fun on a party."

Fitzgerald based Bernice on his younger sister. In a 1915 letter, he provided the fourteen-year-old Annabel Fitzgerald with detailed instructions on how to become popular. He stressed the importance of facial expression, as a girl's face "ought to be almost like a mask so that she'd have perfect control of any expression or impression she might wish to use." In the story Bernice learns to adapt her personality and social persona to the flapper model, just as she might assume a role in a play. Fitzgerald opens the story with an extended metaphor comparing the strata of social classes at a country-club dance to different sections of a theatre. He segregates the older generation to the "balcony," where they cannot truly perceive the onstage "drama of the shifting, semicruel world of adolescence." Fitzgerald (twenty-four years old when the story first appeared) declares himself as the spokesman for this "jazz-nourished" younger generation in describing the younger set as occupying center stage socially and as "the only people capable of getting an un-obstructed view of it."

The story traces the birth and development of Bernice's imagination. The "dopeless" girl first learns of the contempt that Marjorie's friends have for her when she overhears her cousin complaining to her aunt, and "the thread of the conversation going on inside pierced her consciousness sharply as if it had been drawn through with a needle." Bernice reluctantly agrees to let Marjorie "re-make" her as a popular girl, one who is perfectly groomed and always ready with witty conversation. Marjorie's instruction works, and Bernice returns from the next dance in triumph. Her most effective social gambit has been in soliciting young men's opinion on her scandalous—and feigned—intention of bobbing her hair. As she goes to sleep a "rebellious thought was churning drowsily in her brain." Bernice begins to dismiss Marjorie as the author of her success, and Fitzgerald introduces the familiar theme of the apprentice rivaling the master. Although Marjorie has provided her with witty dialogue, Bernice realizes that "her own voice had said the words, her own lips had smiled, her own feet had danced."

Yet, Bernice commits a great social sin in attracting the attentions of Warren McIntyre, one of Marjorie's beaux. In revenge Marjorie calls Bernice's hair-bobbing bluff at an afternoon party. Bernice lacks the social skill to extract herself, and in "the face of this direct attack her imagination was paralyzed." But as she rides in a car down to the barbershop her imagination ignites as she has "all the sensations of Marie Antoinette bound for the guillotine in a tumbrel." Despite her terror Bernice remains externally calm, demanding of the shocked barber, "Bob it!" She goes through with the ordeal because this "was the test supreme of her sportsmanship; her right to walk unchallenged in the starry heaven of popular girls."

Bernice's popularity quickly fades after her haircut. Fitzgerald describes her new look as "ugly as sin." He comments that her "face's chief charm had been a Madonna-like simplicity. Now that was gone and she was—well, frightfully mediocre—not stagy; only ridiculous, like a Greenwich Villager who had left her spectacles at home." Later that evening Marjorie offers an insincere apology to her cousin, and the sight of her conspicuously braiding her long blond hair explodes Bernice's imagination: "Fascinated, Bernice watched the braids grow. Heavy and luxurious they were, moving under the supple fingers like restive snakes." Bernice now sees through Marjorie's glamorous exterior and perceives her as a Gorgon-like monster. Refusing to be humiliated by sitting out an important party because of her bobbed hair, Bernice resolves to leave secretly at night for the train station. But as she packs, "an expression flashed into her eyes that a practiced character reader might have connected vaguely with the set look she had worn in the barber's chair—somehow a development of it. It was quite a new look for Bernice—and it carried consequences." Before leaving the house Bernice "amputates" Marjorie's braids. Crossing the house's threshold and "feeling oddly happy and exuberant," she steps "off the porch into the moonlight." Her celebratory final cry "Scalp the selfish thing!" cleverly points back to comments by Marjorie and her mother early in the story on Bernice's alleged Indian blood.

Fitzgerald collected "Bernice Bobs Her Hair" in *Flappers and Philosophers,* and its dust-jacket illustration features Bernice in a barber's chair. The protagonist's development from naive long-haired young girl into an independent and imaginative bobbed adult marks her as a 1920s "New Woman."

She ends both alone and triumphant, stepping into light. When Bernice protests during her flapper education that she has thought Marjorie "despised little dainty feminine things," her cousin responds that she hates "dainty minds!" For Fitzgerald, a woman's attention to social grace and charm is a worthwhile intellectual pursuit. Flapper Marjorie attacks girls like the preflapper Bernice as being "responsible for all the tiresome colorless marriages; all those ghastly inefficiencies that pass as feminine qualities. What a blow it must be when a man with imagination marries the beautiful bundle of clothes that he's been building ideals round, and finds that she's just a weak, whining, cowardly mass of affectations!" Both Marjorie and Bernice transcend this definition.

Discussion Questions

1. Compare Marjorie's plan for making Bernice charming and popular to Jay Gatz's plan for self-improvement in *The Great Gatsby.*

2. At the story's opening party, Fitzgerald describes a secretly engaged couple, Jim Strain and Ethel Demorest. Jim cannot hold a job, and Ethel wonders "why she had trained the vines of her affection on such a wind-shaken poplar." What does this quotation reveal about the choices available to young women in the 1920s? Do they have similar choices today?

3. Marjorie steals much of her witty conversation from Oscar Wilde. Compare Bernice's "play-acting" to Jack's "bunburying" in Wilde's comedy of manners, *The Importance of Being Earnest.*

4. Compare Bernice to one or more of Fitzgerald's other "flappers" (Sally Carrol Happer in "The Ice Palace," Myra in "Myra Meets His Family," and Ardita in "The Off-Shore Pirate").

—*Park Bucker*

৩

THE GREAT GATSBY
(New York: Scribners, 1925)

DAISY FAY BUCHANAN

Daisy Fay Buchanan, the principal female character in *The Great Gatsby,* betrays Jay Gatsby's love and is responsible for his murder. She is lovely, charming, and lethal.

Daisy's conduct is reported and judged by Nick Carraway, the narrator, who is her distant cousin. When he visits the Buchanans at their Long Island estate in June 1922, he is shocked by her acceptance of her husband's unfaithfulness. After she describes to him her feelings about the birth of her daughter, Nick recognizes her essential dishonesty:

> The instant her voice broke off, ceasing to compel my attention, my belief, I felt the basic insincerity of what she had said. It made me uneasy, as though the whole evening had been a trick of some sort to exact a contributory emotion from me. I waited, and sure enough, in a moment she looked at me with an absolute smirk on her lovely face as if she had asserted her membership in a rather distinguished secret society to which she and Tom belonged.

Daisy Fay was the most popular belle in Louisville in 1917 when she and Lt. Jay Gatsby fell in love. "He took what he could get, ravenously and unscrupulously—eventually he took Daisy one still October night, took her because he had no real right to touch her hand." He is penniless, but he allows her to believe that he shares her social background. Gatsby is sent overseas, and he expects to marry her after the war; but Daisy cannot endure the strain of waiting. Before Gatsby returns, she marries the very rich Tom Buchanan.

Gatsby, who nonetheless feels married to Daisy, believes that he lost her because he was poor; he sets out to recover her. He becomes rich through his "gonnegtion" with racketeer Meyer Wolfshiem and purchases a mansion across the bay from the Buchanan establishment, where he hosts lavish parties in the expectation that Daisy will attend one of them. He has not seen her since he left Louisville. When this plan fails, Gatsby persuades Nick to invite him and Daisy to tea. After this reunion, during which Gatsby shows Daisy his expensive possessions, they renew their romance. It is not clear whether the affair is sexual.

Gatsby expects Daisy to leave her husband and marry him. He wants to repeat the past, and she leads him to believe that she shares his intentions. When Gatsby realizes that Daisy doesn't understand the force of his devotion and intentions, he attempts to compel her to tell Tom that she never loved him and that she is leaving him. Tom Buchanan is too hard for her and breaks her weak resolve during the showdown in New York. Tom's exposure of the sources of Gatsby's wealth frightens Daisy. Relishing his victory, Tom tells Daisy to return to Long Island with Gatsby. Daisy, who is driving Gatsby's gorgeous car, kills Tom's mistress, Myrtle Wilson—whom she does not know—in a hit-and-run accident. Gatsby covers for Daisy and claims that he was at the wheel. Nick describes Tom and Daisy together after the accident: "There was an unmistakable air of natural intimacy in the picture and anyone would have said that they were conspiring together." They were. Myrtle's grief-crazed husband comes seeking the owner of the "death car"; Tom—who may not know the truth about the accident—directs him to Gatsby. Wilson murders Gatsby and kills himself. The Buchanans immediately leave on a trip.

Nick's position on Daisy is determined by his class background and the gentleman's code of conduct toward women in the 1920s. He feels that women aren't really accountable for their behavior. The worst he says about Daisy is that she is insincere and that "They were careless people, Tom and Daisy—they smashed up things and creatures and then retreated back into their money, or their vast carelessness or whatever it was that kept them together, and let other people clean up the mess they had made. . . ." She is much more culpable than that. Since Nick speaks for Fitzgerald, it is likely that the novel's treatment of Daisy was influenced by the author's feelings about his wife's involvement with a French aviator while her husband was writing *The Great Gatsby* in 1924.

Discussion Questions

1. Why does Gatsby commit himself to Daisy? What does she represent?

2. Daisy has been called "the great American bitch." Is this fair or accurate? Can you defend her behavior?

3. Why does Daisy cry when Gatsby shows her his shirts?

4. Does Daisy ever really intend to leave Tom for Gatsby?

—*Matthew J. Bruccoli*

NICK CARRAWAY

Nick Carraway is the partially involved narrator of *The Great Gatsby*. Everything in the novel is told by him, and most of the events are witnessed by him. He reports all the scenes in the present time of the novel, and he provides sources for past events. Jay Gatsby is the romantic hero, and it is Nick's function to render this character convincing. The case has been made that Nick is the principal figure in *The Great Gatsby:* that the novel is really about his responses to the events he narrates. He is the moral center, and he judges all the other characters: "Everyone suspects himself of at least one of the cardinal virtues, and this is mine: I am one of the few honest people I have ever known." He means it. Nick had written editorials for the *Yale Daily News,* and the voice of his prose is literary. He is not just the narrator; he functions as a novelist:

> Reserving judgements is a matter of infinite hope. I am still a little afraid of missing something if I forget that, as my father snobbishly suggested and I snobbishly repeat, a sense of the fundamental decencies is parcelled out unequally at birth.
>
> And, after boasting this way of my tolerance, I come to the admission that it has a limit. Conduct may be founded on the hard rock or the wet marshes but after a certain point I don't care what it's founded on. When I came back from the East last autumn I felt that I wanted the world to be in uniform and at a sort of moral attention forever; I wanted no more riotous excursions with privileged glimpses into the human heart. Only Gatsby, the man who gives his name to this book, was exempt from my reaction—Gatsby who represented everything for which I have an unaffected scorn.

Nick Carraway is a Midwesterner—probably from Fitzgerald's St. Paul, Minnesota—and belongs to a "prominent, well-to-do" family. He was educated at Yale and served in World War I. Nick moved to the East in 1922 to work as a bond salesman, and the events of the novel occupy the three summer months during which he rents a cottage in West Egg, Long Island, next to the mansion where the mysterious Jay Gatsby hosts lavish parties.

Nick's cousin Daisy and her enormously wealthy husband, Tom Buchanan, live in East Egg. Nick and Tom had been in the same Senior Society at Yale. When Nick visits them, he learns that Daisy tolerates Tom's open infidelity. Although Nick and the Buchanans share class allegiances, he is shocked by their marital state: ". . . I was confused and a little disgusted as I drove away. It seemed to me that the thing for Daisy to do was to rush out of the house, child in arms—but apparently there were no such intentions in her head."

At his first visit to the Buchanans, Nick meets Jordan Baker, a champion amateur golfer, with whom he conducts an unpassionate romance during the summer. He learns that she is "incurably dishonest"; but despite his pride in his own honesty he accepts her flaw: "Dishonesty in a woman is a thing you never blame deeply—I was casually sorry, then I forgot." Nick becomes more deeply involved with the Buchanans when Tom takes him to a drunken party at the New York apartment he rents for his mistress, Myrtle Wilson, the wife of the proprietor of a garage near the Long Island ash heaps.

Nick does not meet his neighbor until Gatsby invites him to a party, which Nick describes in rich detail: "the lights grow brighter as the earth lurches away from the sun and now the orchestra is playing yellow cocktail music and the opera of voices pitches a key higher." He has reservations about Gatsby's ostentatious conduct and the sources of his wealth after Gatsby introduces Nick to his partner Meyer Wolfshiem, "the man who fixed the World Series back in 1919"; but Nick accedes to Gatsby's request that he be invited to tea with Daisy at Nick's cottage after Jordan tells him that Gatsby and Daisy had been in love when he was stationed in Louisville during World War I but that she had married Tom Buchanan while Gatsby was overseas. Nick expresses no moral ambiguity about his role in arranging the reunion.

Daisy and Gatsby renew their love, although the nature of their sexual conduct is unclear. He expects her to marry him and forces the issue at a New York meeting that includes Daisy, Tom, Nick, and Jordan.

Tom is too hard for Gatsby and Daisy; she is unable to leave him. Daisy and Gatsby drive back to Long Island with Daisy at the wheel of his gorgeous car. She kills Myrtle—whom she does not know—in a hit-and-run accident. Gatsby takes the blame and covers for Daisy.

Wilson, crazed by grief, murders Gatsby—having been directed to him by Tom. The Buchanans leave on a trip, and Nick makes the funeral arrangements. He breaks with Jordan before returning to the Midwest: "I see now that this has been a story of the West, after all—Tom and Gatsby, Daisy and Jordan and I, were all Westerners, and perhaps we possessed some deficiency in common which made us subtly unadaptable to Eastern life."

Despite boasting of his honesty, Nick's role in the novel is morally ambiguous: he conceals Daisy's crime. It is not clear that Tom knows she was the driver—probably not. Nick, the only one besides Daisy who knows that she killed Myrtle, allows the deceased Gatsby to be blamed for the homicide. His final judgment on the Buchanans is scarcely damning: "They were careless people, Tom and Daisy—they smashed up things and creatures and then retreated back into their money or their vast carelessness or whatever it was that kept them together, and let other people clean up the mess they had made. . . ."

Discussion Questions

1. It has been claimed that Nick Carraway is the real protagonist of *The Great Gatsby*—that the novel is about him more than it is about Gatsby. Respond.

2. Is Nick's behavior in arranging the reunion between Daisy and Gatsby morally questionable?

3. Is Nick's conduct influenced by his class allegiances? Why doesn't he clear Gatsby of the hit-and-run charge?

4. Identify points in the novel when Nick alters his judgments on Gatsby.

5. Explicate Nick's final comment: "So we beat on, boats against the current, borne back ceaselessly into the past." Is it tacked on—or is it a proper summing up?

—Matthew J. Bruccoli

JAY GATSBY

Jay Gatsby, who is the main figure in *The Great Gatsby,* is the mysterious host of lavish Long Island parties. Along with Huck Finn, he is one of the two most widely recognized characters in American fiction. Gatsby's history is provided by the narrator, Nick Carraway, who does not tell the story in chronological order. He documents the events in the life of the figure who is the subject of speculation as he learns them. Carraway acts as the moral gauge of the novel. In the first chapter he observes:

> If personality is an unbroken series of successful gestures, then there was something gorgeous about him, some heightened sensitivity to the promises of life, as if he were related to one of those intricate machines that register earthquakes ten thousand miles away. This responsiveness had nothing to do with that flabby impressionability which is dignified under the name of the "creative temperament"—it was an extraordinary gift for hope, a romantic readiness such as I have never found in any other person and which it is not likely I shall ever find again. No—Gatsby turned out all right at the end; it is what preyed on Gatsby, what foul dust floated in the wake of his dreams that temporarily closed out my interest in the abortive sorrows and short-winded elations of men.

Gatsby is a flamboyant, faintly ridiculous figure. He wears silver and gold shirts and suits; his speech is elaborately formal; his defining phrase is "Old Sport."

James Gatz, the son of a North Dakota railroad freight agent, is ambitious to escape his origins through his adherence to the American Dream of success; but his boyhood endeavors to become a self-made man in the Benjamin Franklin tradition fail. He had been a Lake Superior fisherman when he warned millionaire Dan Cody that his yacht was moored in a dangerous place and was hired as Cody's factotum. This was the point at which Jimmy Gatz became Jay Gatsby.

Gatsby did not receive his expected inheritance from Cody. At the time of World War I he was a lieutenant at Camp Taylor in Louisville, where he fell in love with Daisy Fay, the most popular belle in town:

> His heart beat faster and faster as Daisy's white face came up to his own. He knew that when he kissed this girl, and forever wed his unutterable visions to her perishable breath, his mind would never romp again like the mind of God. So he waited, listening for a moment longer to the tuning fork that had been struck upon a star. Then he kissed her. At his lips' touch she blossomed for him like a flower and the incarnation was complete.

Gatsby went overseas expecting to marry Daisy when he returned. He did extraordinarily well in the war. He was a captain before he went to the front, and following the Argonne battle he received his majority. After the Armistice he tried to get home, but he was sent to study at Oxford instead. Daisy, who had grown tired of waiting for him to return, married Tom Buchanan, a very wealthy former Yale football star.

In 1922 Nick Carraway, Daisy's cousin and Tom's classmate, rents a cottage next to Gatsby's mansion in West Egg; the Buchanans' estate is across the bay at East Egg. Nick visits the Buchanans and learns that Tom is openly unfaithful to Daisy. He attends Gatsby's parties and eventually discovers that Gatsby's money comes from his "gonnegtion" with racketeer Meyer Wolfshiem. When Gatsby asks Nick to invite him to tea with Daisy, Nick realizes that Gatsby's parties had been planned in the expectation that Daisy—whom he has not seen since Louisville—would attend one of them; but that has not happened.

After their reunion at Nick's cottage, Gatsby and Daisy renew their romance; but it is unclear whether they engage in a sexual affair. Gatsby believes that he lost Daisy only because he was poor and that his new wealth will recapture her. He does not understand that Buchanan money is better than Gatsby money. Daisy is motivated by her class allegiances, as well as by financial considerations. Gatsby wants her to leave Tom and marry him. Nick warns him that "You can't repeat the past," but Gatsby replies incredulously: "Can't repeat the past? Why of course you can!"

Gatsby attempts to compel Daisy to tell Tom that she never loved him and that she is leaving him. Tom is too hard for them, and the showdown in New York fails. Driving Gatsby's car back to Long Island, Daisy accidentally kills Tom's mistress, Myrtle Wilson, and fails to stop. Gatsby insists on taking the blame for the homicide and covers for Daisy. Tom tells Myrtle's husband where to find Gatsby. Wilson shoots Gatsby in his pool and then kills himself. Only one of Gatsby's party guests, "Owl-Eyes," comes to his funeral and speaks his eulogy: "The poor son of a bitch." Nick, who initially disapproved of Gatsby but has come to admire his idealism, provides an eloquent evocation of Gatsby's relation to American history:

> . . . I became aware of the old island here that flowered once for Dutch sailors' eyes—a fresh, green breast of the new world. Its vanished trees, the trees that had made way for Gatsby's house, had once pandered in whispers to the last and greatest of all human dreams; for a transitory enchanted moment man must have held his breath in the presence of this continent, compelled into an aesthetic contemplation he neither understood nor desired, face to face for the last time in history with something commensurate to his capacity for wonder.

Discussion Questions

1. Gatsby says little in the novel. Select speeches that characterize him, and discuss what these speeches reveal about him.

2. Is Gatsby a convincing racketeer? Could he really have become a successful and powerful criminal—even with Wolfshiem's backing?

3. Gatsby's ostentation borders on absurdity. How does Fitzgerald prevent the reader from judging the character with contempt rather than with affection or admiration?

4. "Gatsby doesn't understand the difference between money and wealth." Explicate.

5. Discuss how Gatsby resembles two of these Fitzgerald characters: Dick Diver, Rudolph Miller, and Dexter Green.

—*Matthew J. Bruccoli*

THE LAST TYCOON
Edited by Edmund Wilson (New York: Scribners, 1941).

THE LOVE OF THE LAST TYCOON: A WESTERN
Edited by Matthew J. Bruccoli (Cambridge & New York: Cambridge University Press, 1993).

MONROE STAHR

Monroe Stahr, the protagonist of F. Scott Fitzgerald's posthumously published novel-in-progress, is his only heroic character. Since Fitzgerald wrote seventeen of the thirty projected episodes, it is uncertain how he would have ended *The Love of the Last Tycoon;* but Stahr is a genius as well as a great man. He is the head of a major movie studio, but he is not just an executive. He is a moviemaker—a creator with high standards—and he is working himself to death.

Stahr was based on Irving Thalberg, "the boy wonder of Hollywood," who was running Universal Pictures at twenty and became, at twenty-four, production head at M-G-M, where he produced classic movies. Thalberg, who had a cardiac condition, worked to exhaustion and died in 1936 at thirty-six. Fitzgerald met Thalberg in 1927, worked for him in 1931, and wrote the novel in Hollywood after his 1937–1938 M-G-M screenwriting contract was not renewed. Fitzgerald, who admired Thalberg's intelligence and taste, regarded him as the most brilliant figure in the motion-picture industry.

Stahr's story is narrated mainly by Cecelia Brady—a college student who is in love with him and is the daughter of his treacherous partner, Pat Brady. She was intended to function the way that Nick Carraway does in *The Great Gatsby,* but there are important events and episodes at which she is not present and for which she does not provide a source. The novel opens on a plane returning to California from the East. The passengers include Stahr and Cecelia. She provides an eloquent assessment of his abilities—explicating the significance of his name:

. . . this was where Stahr had come to earth after that extraordinary illuminating flight where he saw which way we were going, and how we looked doing it, and how much of it mattered. You could say that this was where an accidental wind blew him but I don't think so. I would rather think that in a 'long shot' he saw a new way of measuring our jerky hopes and graceful rogueries and awkward sorrows, and that he came here from choice to be with us to the end. Like the plane coming down into the Glendale airport, into the warm darkness.

Stahr is shown functioning as studio head during a luncheon meeting with his associates; they want to make more money, whereas he wants to make better movies. He is depicted in action as a moviemaker and studio boss: in a script conference, viewing the rushes, firing a director, teaching an English novelist how to write for the movies, and advising the troubled employees who rely on him and his judgment.

Fitzgerald's working title was *The Love of the Last Tycoon: A Western,* which was changed to *The Last Tycoon* when Edmund Wilson edited it for publication in 1941. The alteration obscures Fitzgerald's intention to write a romantic story. Stahr is a lonely widower; his wife was actress Minna Davis, whom he loved. During a studio flood Stahr sees Kathleen Moore, an English woman who resembles his wife. She is not in the movies. Kathleen, who is based on Fitzgerald's Hollywood companion, Sheilah Graham, had been the mistress of a deposed king. She is in California waiting to be married to the man who rescued her from her difficulties in Britain.

Kathleen does not encourage Stahr's attentions; but he persists, and they have a passionate sexual encounter. He persuades her to go away with him, but while he delays a few hours to deal with work problems, Kathleen's fiancé arrives earlier than expected, and she marries him. The effect of Kathleen's marriage on Stahr is powerful; he is seen getting drunk and trying to beat up a union organizer. The draft ends with Stahr spending time with Cecelia: "That's how the two weeks started that he and I went around together. It only took one of them

for Louella [Parsons, Hollywood gossip columnist] to have us married."

The unwritten episodes of the novel were to cover Stahr's struggles with Pat Brady and the other studio executives who want to remove him from control. Kathleen and Stahr were to resume their affair, and Brady would use his knowledge of it to blackmail Stahr. One of the projected endings involved a double murder plot in which Brady and Stahr hire killers; but Fitzgerald did not develop this idea. Stahr was to die in a plane crash, and Fitzgerald probably intended to write about the Hollywood funeral. It is difficult to evaluate the unwritten segments dealing with Stahr's struggle to maintain control of the studio because Fitzgerald's notes convey the impression that Stahr is corrupted by his enemies and employs their methods. It is preferable to believe that Fitzgerald would have maintained Stahr's integrity.

Discussion Questions

1. Fitzgerald observed in his *Notebooks,* "Show me a hero and I'll write you a tragedy." Is Stahr a heroic figure? If so, define his heroism.

2. Most Hollywood novels are about corrupt characters. Is Stahr unspoiled?

3. Why did Fitzgerald reveal Stahr through Cecelia's narration? Is this technique successful?

4. Analyze the description of the plane arriving in California at the end of the opening chapter. Explain how Fitzgerald uses language to convey an impression of Stahr's achievement and destiny.

—*Matthew J. Bruccoli*

"THE RICH BOY"

Collected in *All the Sad Young Men* (New York: Scribners, 1926).

ANSON HUNTER

Anson Hunter, the title figure of F. Scott Fitzgerald's "The Rich Boy," was based on Fitzgerald's wealthy Princeton classmate and lifelong friend Ludlow Fowler. In March 1925 Fitzgerald reported to Fowler that the story "is frank, unsparing but sympathetic and I think you will like it—it is one of the best things I have ever done." Fitzgerald worked on the seventeen-thousand-word novelette during the spring and summer of 1925; *The Great Gatsby* had been published in April of that year. Anson Hunter and his story focus and enlarge upon a theme central to *The Great Gatsby* and to most of Fitzgerald's major works: the effects of wealth on character.

"The Rich Boy," like *The Great Gatsby*, is told from the point of view of a partially involved narrator, though he is not so fully developed nor so clearly reliable as Nick Carraway. The unnamed middle-class narrator, who defines himself as Anson's friend and confidant, insists that he is analyzing an individual rich boy, not a type. Then he delivers one of the most familiar—and most misunderstood—passages in Fitzgerald's fiction: "Let me tell you about the very rich. They are different from you and me. They possess and enjoy early, and it does something to them, makes them soft where we are hard, and cynical where we are trustful, in a way that, unless you were born rich, it is very difficult to understand. They think, deep in their hearts, that they are better than we are because we had to discover the compensations and refuges of life for ourselves. Even when they enter deep into our world or sink below us, they still think that they are better than we are. They are different."

These lines have been used to support the idea that Fitzgerald idolized the rich—or as Hemingway wrote in his 1936 story "The Snows of Kilimanjaro": "He [Hemingway's protagonist] remembered poor Scott Fitzgerald and his romantic awe of them [the rich] and how he had started a story once that began, 'The very rich are different from you and me.' And how someone had said to Scott, Yes they have more money. But that was not humorous to Scott. He thought they were a special glamorous race and when he found they weren't it wrecked him just as much as any other thing that wrecked him." In fact, Hemingway, not Fitzgerald, had been the butt of the quip "they have more money." But Hemingway's vicious, self-serving denunciation reinforced Fitzgerald's image as a writer blindly devoted to the rich. In a July 16, 1936 letter to Hemingway, Fitzgerald replied: "Riches have *never* facinated [sic] me, unless combined with the greatest charm or distinction."

Anson Hunter, who combines extreme wealth with charm and distinction, is the oldest son of a prominent New York family, a Yale graduate, a World War I veteran, and a successful member of a New York brokerage firm. His money, position, and authority make him a natural leader of family, friends, and business associates: "for he had a way, when he came into a room, of putting himself on a footing with the oldest and most conservative people there. 'You and me,' he seemed to say, 'we're solid. We understand.'" Unlike his wealthy predecessors Tom Buchanan in *The Great Gatsby* and Anthony Patch in *The Beautiful and Damned*, Anson is neither villainous nor weak; although he can be "convivial, bawdy, robustly avid for pleasure," he assumes professional and social responsibilities.

Yet, Anson's self-confidence and sense of superiority prove fatal to his romance with Paula Legendre, a beautiful heiress. Their informal engagement is terminated after he becomes drunk in Paula's presence and refuses to express contrition for his behavior: "his despair was helpless before his pride and his knowledge of himself." Later, when Paula offers to abandon another man for Anson, his sense of power over her prevents him from proposing: "No, let it wait—she is mine. . . ." She then marries the other man, and Anson resolutely continues his work and his social life. "But one thing he could not help—for three days, in any place, in any company, he would suddenly bend his head into his hands and cry like a child."

For a Fitzgerald protagonist, the pursuit of wealth and social position is intimately connected with his aspiring love for a beautiful woman: Gatsby's for Daisy in *The Great Gatsby*, Dexter Green's for Judy Jones in "Winter Dreams," George O'Kelly's for Jonquil Cary in "The Sensible Thing." But Gatsby, Dexter, and George are poor boys who seek riches in order to win the wealthy young women they love. When Fitzgerald presents men with inherited wealth, they tend to be morally and emotionally deficient.

In "The Rich Boy" Anson Hunter's pride , which allows him to fulfill so many of his gifts, also prevents him from surrendering himself to Paula or to any other woman. Approaching thirty, he is increasingly isolated from family and friends. He then learns from Paula that she is pregnant and extremely happy in her second marriage: "You see, I'm in love now—at last." Anson's sense of superiority is battered by Paula's denial that she has loved him and by her perception that he is incapable of real love: "You'll never settle down." Depressed, he books a cruise to Europe but, before departing, learns that Paula has died in childbirth. Anson begins a shipboard flirtation with a pretty young passenger, and the narrator comments: "I don't think he was ever happy unless some one was in love with him, responding to him like filings to a magnet, helping him to explain himself, promising him something. . . . Perhaps they promised that there would always be women in the world who would spend their brightest, freshest, rarest hours to nurse and protect that superiority he cherished in his heart." Anson's response to his loss of Paula is to return to his life of self-involvement and isolation.

Discussion Questions

1. In his letter to Ludlow Fowler, Fitzgerald describes his portrait of Anson Hunter as "sympathetic." Defend or refute Fitzgerald's assessment, using evidence from the novelette.

2. Some commentators have suggested that the portrait of Anson Hunter is motivated by the narrator's envy and resentment. Can this interpretation be supported by evidence in the story?

3. Fitzgerald wrote, "I am . . . a moralist at heart and really want to preach at people in some acceptable form rather than to entertain them." If "The Rich Boy" can be read as an expression of Fitzgerald's moral stance, what details from the novelette help define that stance?

4. Fitzgerald's friend Ring Lardner argued that "The Rich Boy" should have been expanded into a novel. But Fitzgerald insisted that the novelette was complete as written and could not be enlarged. What is your judgment? What material might have been added?

5. "The Rich Boy" was written shortly after *The Great Gatsby*. Did Fitzgerald's ideas about the effects of wealth on character change between the two works? Support your opinion with specific details from each text.

—*Judith S. Baughman*

∝

TENDER IS THE NIGHT
(New York: Scribners, 1934)

NICOLE DIVER

Nicole Warren Diver, the principal female character in F. Scott Fitzgerald's *Tender Is the Night*, was born in 1900. A member of a very wealthy Chicago family, she was the victim of incest when she was a child. The resultant trauma caused her schizophrenia, requiring treatment in a Swiss sanitarium. Nicole is introduced in 1925 when she is twenty-four:

> . . .—her face could have been described in terms of conventional prettiness, but the effect was that it had been made first on the heroic scale with strong structure and marking, as if the features and vividness of brow and coloring, molded with a Rodinesque intention, and then chiseled away in the direction of prettiness to a point where a single slip would have irreparably diminished its force and quality. With the mouth the sculptor had taken desperate chances—it was the cupid's bow of a magazine cover, yet it shared the distinction of the rest.

The opening section is followed by the flashback to 1918 when Nicole meets Dr. Richard Diver, a twenty-eight-year-old American psychiatrist studying in Switzerland. Diver understands the risks of marrying a mental patient, but he is persuaded by Nicole's love and need for him. Nicole is beautiful and selfish; she is both hard and vulnerable. At the time of their marriage he is sure that he will not be corrupted by her wealth, but he is. It is too simple to claim that she destroys Dick: he is ruined by his own weaknesses, including his need to be loved and admired—as documented by his decision to marry Nicole. Fitzgerald examines the effects of wealth—or lack of wealth—on male characters in his major fiction; Nicole and her sister, Baby Warren, provide the opportunity to write about rich women. Nicole's name echoes "nickel" and suggests money as well as metallic hardness. The Warren wealth provides a sense of privilege and superiority; it also renders any kind of work inconsequential. Fitzgerald analyzes Nicole's character during a Paris shopping excursion:

Nicole was the product of much ingenuity and toil. For her sake trains began their run at Chicago and traversed the round belly of the continent to California; chicle factories fumed and link belts grew link by link in factories; men mixed toothpaste in vats and drew mouthwash out of copper hogsheads; girls canned tomatoes quickly in August or worked rudely at the Five-and-Tens on Christmas Eve; half-breed Indians toiled on Brazilian coffee plantations and dreamers were muscled out of patent rights in new tractors—these were some of the people who gave tithe to Nicole, and as the whole system swayed and thundered onward it lent a feverish bloom to such processes of hers as wholesale buying, like the flush of a fireman's face holding his post before a spreading blaze. She illustrated very simple principles, containing in herself her own doom.

There are indications that she uses her money to distract Dick from his work because she needs his full attention, as in her stream-of-consciousness account of the early years of her marriage:

When I get well I want to be a fine person like you, Dick—I would study medicine except it's too late. We must spend my money and have a house—I'm tired of apartments and waiting for you. You're bored with Zürich and you can't find time for writing here and you say that it's a confession of weakness for a scientist not to write. And I'll look over the whole field of knowledge and pick out something and really know about it, so I'll have it to hang on to if I go to pieces again. You'll help me, Dick, so I won't feel so guilty. We'll live near a warm beach where we can be brown and young together.

Nicole's relapses and the Divers' travels interfere with his work. By 1925—when the first chapter of the novel opens—they have two children and are living in a villa on the Riviera. They have an active social life, but he does little work on his medical book. One of their frequent guests, soldier of fortune Tommy Barban, is in love with Nicole. Although she is faithful to Dick, she enjoys Tommy's devotion.

In 1925 Dick meets Rosemary Hoyt, an eighteen-year-old American movie star. Nicole's recogni-tion of Rosemary's threat to the Divers' marriage triggers a breakdown. By 1927 the Divers are in residence at the sanitarium where they had met, which has been purchased for Dick by the Warrens. He drinks too much and neglects his work. He sleeps with Rosemary when they accidentally meet in Rome. When Dick is forced out of the clinic, the Divers return to the Riviera where he stops working and gets involved in alcohol-triggered embarrassments. Nicole sleeps with Tommy who wants to marry her. Dick recognizes the situation and forces a break with her because she no longer needs him:

"You're a coward! You've made a failure of your life, and you want to blame it on me."

While he did not answer she began to feel the old hypnotism of his intelligence, sometimes exercised without power but always with substrata of truth under truth which she could not break or even crack. Again she struggled with it, fighting him with her small, fine eyes, with the plush arrogance of a top dog, with her nascent transference to another man, with the accumulated resentment of years; she fought him with her money and her faith that her sister disliked him and was behind her now; with the thought of the new enemies he was making with his bitterness, with her quick guile against his wine-ing and dine-ing slowness, her health and beauty against his physical deterioration, her unscrupulousness against his moralities—for this inner battle she used even her weaknesses—fighting bravely and courageously with the old cans and crockery and bottles, empty receptacles of her expiated sins, outrages, mistakes. And suddenly, in the space of two minutes she achieved her victory and justified herself to herself without lie or subterfuge, cut the cord forever. Then she walked, weak in the legs, and sobbing coolly, toward the house that was hers at last.

Nicole marries Tommy in 1929, and Dick disappears in America.

Nicole's illness was based on that of Zelda Fitzgerald, who suffered a mental breakdown in 1930 and was treated in Switzerland. But she was not the victim of incest, and she was not wealthy.

The characterization of Nicole is in part the result of Fitzgerald's response to his wife's insanity. Nicole is also partly based on Sara Murphy. Sara and Gerald Murphy were wealthy expatriate Americans—though not as rich as the Warrens—who lived on the Riviera during the 1920s. Their Villa America was a model for the Divers' Villa Diana, and *Tender Is the Night* is dedicated to the Murphys.

Discussion Questions

1. Fitzgerald created a string of destructive women in his novels, notably Daisy in *The Great Gatsby*. Do Daisy and Nicole differ in significant ways?

2. How does Fitzgerald balance Nicole's destructive qualities with her charm? What is the source of her appeal to men? To women?

3. Is Dick's marriage to Nicole entirely to blame for his deterioration?

4. Focusing on Nicole, Rosemary Hoyt, and Mary North Minghetti, provide a misogynistic reading of *Tender Is the Night*.

—*Matthew J. Bruccoli*

RICHARD (DICK) DIVER

Dick Diver, the flawed hero of Fitzgerald's most mature and profound novel, is characterized by his name: he dives from a high position to defeat and failure. There is also an obscene meaning. He is introduced to the reader on the Riviera in 1925. There he lives in an elegant villa and presides over admiring—even worshipful—friends and guests. He is intelligent, charming, and handsome. He and his wife, Nicole, are happily married with two children. Dick is a psychiatrist engaged in writing a textbook. The first crack in his perfection is revealed when he encourages the admiration of Rosemary Hoyt, an eighteen-year-old movie star. Dick inspires "carnivals of affection" because he needs to be loved. During the opening section of *Tender Is the Night* Nicole twice suffers hysterical episodes. By the end of Book I it is clear that there are ominous things behind the facade of the Divers' enviable life.

Book II opens with a flashback to 1917 when brilliant young Dr. Diver—educated at Yale, Oxford, Johns Hopkins, Vienna, and the University of Zurich—is in France during World War I. The consequences of the war is a principal theme of the novel. On a visit to a former colleague at a Swiss mental clinic he encounters Nicole Warren, a seventeen-year-old American heiress who had been raped by her father. She falls in love with Dick, but he recognizes the professional impropriety of such a relationship and breaks it off. But in 1919, after she has been discharged from the clinic, he encounters Nicole—who wants him—and they are married. She is nineteen, and he is thirty. Diver believes that he is immune to corruption by the Warren wealth—that it will not interfere with his research and writing. Nicole—who suffers relapses—becomes his only patient, and he abandons his clinical work and research for life on the Riviera. In 1925 Dr. Franz Gregorovious proposes that they become partners in a Swiss clinic—bankrolled by the Warrens. At the end of Book II Dick goes to America in 1928 for his father's funeral, and on the way back to Switzerland he stops off in Rome, where he meets Rosemary. After seducing her he gets into a drunken brawl with the police. He is rescued from jail by Nicole's sister, who has never trusted him: "whatever Dick's previous record was, they now possessed a moral superiority over him for as long as he proved of any use."

At the start of Book III Gregorovious eases Dick out of their partnership. The Divers return to the Riviera, where he does no work, and his alcohol consumption increases. Among the people there are Tommy Barban, a soldier of fortune who has always been in love with Nicole, and Rosemary. Nicole and Tommy commence an affair, which Dick knows about. He forces her to terminate their marriage:

> . . . fighting him with her small, fine eyes, with the plush arrogance of a top dog, with her nascent transference to another man, with the accumulated resentment of years; she fought him with her money and her faith that her sister disliked him and was behind her now; with the thought of the new enemies he was making with his bitterness, with her quick guile against his wine-ing and dine-ing slowness, her health and beauty against his physical deterioration, her unscrupulousness against his moralities—for this inner battle she

even used her weaknesses—fighting bravely and courageously with the old cans and crockery and bottles, empty receptacles of her expiated sins, outrages, mistakes. And suddenly, in the pace of two minutes she achieved her victory and justified herself to herself without lie or subterfuge, cut the cord forever. Then she walked, weak in the legs, and sobbing coolly, toward the household that was hers at last.

Dick waited until she was out of sight. Then he leaned his head forward on the parapet. The case was finished. Doctor Diver was at liberty.

Dick returns to America, where he unsuccessfully attempts to resume the practice of medicine. The novel closes with a perfectly controlled summation of Dr. Richard Diver's failure and obscurity, expressed by means of what Fitzgerald called "the dying fall": "in any case he is almost certainly in that section of the country, in one town or another."

Tender Is the Night was not warmly received in 1934. Readers were bothered by its flashback structure, and reviewers complained that the causes for Dick Diver's destruction were unclear. Fitzgerald was greatly hurt by the failure of his most ambitious novel and prepared an edition in straight chronological order, starting with Dick's high promise in 1917. The restructured edition was published in 1951 and established that Fitzgerald got it right in the 1934 first edition. The reputation of *Tender Is the Night* has steadily climbed, and it now ranks with *The Great Gatsby* in the Fitzgerald canon.

Discussion Questions

1. Do you agree that the causes of Dick Diver's destruction are unclear or unconvincing?

2. What are the causes for his destruction provided by Fitzgerald?

3. Is Dick Diver convincing as a brilliant psychiatrist?

4. Is it believable that Dick Diver would have married Nicole? Why does he decide to do so?

5. *Tender Is the Night* has many references to World War I. Is it useful to regard Dick Diver as a war casualty?

—*Matthew J. Bruccoli*

THIS SIDE OF PARADISE
(New York: Scribners, 1920)

AMORY BLAINE

Amory Blaine is the autobiographical protagonist of Fitzgerald's first novel, *This Side of Paradise*, a bildungsroman—or novel of self-discovery—set at a prep school, Princeton, and New York before and after World War I. The original title of the novel, "The Romantic Egoist" (possibly "The Romantic Egotist"), refers to Amory's idealism, ambition, and need for love. The literary critic Lionel Trilling observed that "Fitzgerald was perhaps the last notable writer to affirm the Romantic fantasy, descended from the Renaissance, of personal ambition and heroism, of life committed to, or thrown away for, some ideal of self." Amory spends the novel seeking a cause or an ideal to which he can devote his life. The first half of the book traces his quest for personal perfection. The second half details his attempt to secure romantic love.

A child of wealth, Amory has great expectations. He is initially unpopular at prep school because he is unable to conceal his belief that he is better—certainly brighter—than the other boys. His ambitions are shaped at Princeton by his reading of English "quest novels" by Compton Mackenzie and H. G. Wells, in which a sensitive and intelligent young man seeks a code of behavior and system of values that will enable him to fulfill his potential. Fitzgerald described *This Side of Paradise* in his *Notebooks* as "a romance and a reading list." At Princeton, Amory develops from a personality to a personage. The distinction is formulated for him by Monsignor Darcy, who serves as Amory's surrogate father: "Personality is a physical matter almost entirely; it lowers the people it acts on. . . . Now, a personage, on the other hand, gathers. He is never thought of apart from what he's done. He's a bar on which a thousand glittering things have been hung . . . but he uses those things with a cold mentality back of them."

Much of Amory's Princeton life is devoted to conversation. He and his friends conduct long discussions about literature, the meaning of life, their destinies, and their responsibility to their intelligence and other superior qualities. As members of an aristocracy of brains and breeding, they accept the code of noblesse oblige—the duties associated with birth and privilege. Amory believes in his potential greatness. He seeks and expects high position, recognition, personal fulfillment—and love. Even when Amory argues for Socialism at the end of the novel, his thinking is anti-egalitarian. He believes in an aristocracy of ability and privilege. He accepts the class system and expects to occupy a position at the top, as befits his natural superiority.

Unexpectedly in a novel that was regarded as a testament of revolt, Amory has a strong puritanical streak, exemplified by his responses to promiscuity: "The problem of evil had solidified for Amory into the problem of sex. He was beginning to identify evil with the strong phallic worship in [Rupert] Brooke and the early Wells. Inseparably linked with evil was beauty. . . ." On two occasions in the novel Amory experiences ghostly visitations when he is with loose women. His affairs do not go beyond "petting"—that is, "necking."

After the war Amory learns that the family fortune has been dissipated and that he is in fact poor. He comes to New York to work in advertising and falls in love with Rosalind Connage, who reciprocates his love. But she requires a wealthy husband who can provide the expensive life she is accustomed to. When she breaks their engagement, Amory quits his job and goes on a binge. In the closing pages he walks from New York to Princeton, commencing a new quest for self-realization:

> There was no God in his heart, he knew; his ideas were still in riot; there was ever the pain of memory; the regret for his lost youth—yet the waters of disillusion had left a deposit on his soul, responsibility and a love of life, the faint stirring of old ambitions and unrealized dreams. But—oh, Rosalind! Rosalind! . . .

The last sentence of *This Side of Paradise* is "'I know myself,' he cried, 'but that is all.'"

This Side of Paradise was influential beyond its sales of 49,000 copies in 1920–1921, and Amory Blaine served as a model for the young men of the 1920s. The novel was read as a guide to Ivy League conduct. His enjoyable social career at Princeton and his indifference to academic requirements were emulated by the next generation of collegians.

Discussion Questions

1. Do you agree that Amory knows himself at the end of the novel?

2. Amory commences another quest at the end of the novel. Why does he return to Princeton? What is he seeking there?

3. Compare *This Side of Paradise* with other American college novels that you have read: for example, *Look Homeward, Angel* or *Stover at Yale*. Do the heroes of these novels want the same things that Amory does?

4. "Fitzgerald's heroes never judge or blame the women who fail them; it is enough for their women to be beautiful and appealing." Agree or disagree, using Rosalind Connage, Daisy Buchanan, and any other female character created by Fitzgerald.

—*Matthew J. Bruccoli*

◖◗

"WINTER DREAMS"

Collected in *All the Sad Young Men* (New York: Scribners, 1926).

DEXTER GREEN

Dexter Green is the protagonist of F. Scott Fitzgerald's "Winter Dreams," one of his most successful stories. Matthew J. Bruccoli comments in *Some Sort of Epic Grandeur*: "One distinction of 'Winter Dreams' is Fitzgerald's control of the narrative voice. The story is told by the third-person omniscient author, who freely comments on the action but whose sensibility is scarcely distinguishable from the hero's." Of all the stories Fitzgerald wrote while thinking through *The Great Gatsby*, "Winter Dreams" is the one most closely related to the novel. According to Bruccoli, "'Winter Dreams' clearly anticipates the major ideas and emotions in *The Great Gatsby*: the ambitious boy whose dreams of success become blended with the image of a rich girl; her inconstancy; his faithfulness; and the inevitable sense of change and loss." Dexterous in every way but in his pursuit of Judy Jones, Dexter is associated with green through golf courses, the money he earns, youthful naiveté, and hope. He is like Gatsby, who "believed in the green light. . . ."

Dexter is the son of the owner of the second-best grocery store in Black Bear, based on the fashionable town of White Bear Lake near Fitzgerald's birthplace of St. Paul. He is a bright and enterprising boy of fourteen caddying at the Sherry Island Golf Club when he makes one of the most important decisions of his life—he quits his job as caddy out of pride because he will not take orders from Judy Jones, an imperious eleven-year-old.

Dexter is, like Gatsby and Fitzgerald, a romantic. "Fall made him clinch his hands and tremble and repeat idiotic sentences to himself, and make brisk and abrupt gestures of command to imaginary audiences and armies." The ambitious Dexter chooses to go to a prestigious eastern university instead of the state university. That "older and more famous university in the East" teaches him valuable social graces. "When the time had come for him to wear good clothes, he had known who were the best tailors in America. . . . He had acquired that particular reserve peculiar to his university, that set it off from other universities." After college, he returns to Minnesota and opens a string of laundries, becoming financially successful by twenty-three when Judy Jones comes back into his life.

Even though Dexter has recognized Judy's flaws from the first, he falls in love with her immediately upon seeing her again. From then on, she determines the course of his life, for this golden daughter of the richest man in Black Bear becomes a part of Dexter's winter dreams of financial and social success, Fitzgerald's version of the American Dream. Judy is the perfect representation of that dream.

When it turns out that Dexter cannot have Judy, he becomes engaged to Irene Scheerer—"light-haired and sweet and honorable, and a little stout," contrasted to Judy, "a slender enamelled doll in cloth of gold." Judy recaptures him and after a month drops him again. Dexter leaves the Midwest for military service and eventually Wall Street and greater financial success.

At thirty-two, Dexter learns in casual conversation that Judy, married to a man who mistreats her,

has faded. Like Gatsby, he devoted himself to a physically beautiful, unprincipled woman incapable of nourishing him in any way. Gatsby is murdered, and Dexter loses his capacity for dreaming—what Fitzgerald called "splendor in the heart," the essence of every romantic character's ability to face life with imagination, vitality, and hope. Dexter, like Gatsby with Daisy, is doomed because of his inability to see Judy for what she is. Perhaps he is blind to her because, representing the American Dream as she does, she may be more of an abstraction than a real person. Or, Dexter may want her simply because he cannot have her—a romantic notion prevalent in Fitzgerald's world. Bruccoli suggests that Fitzgerald's male characters "seek destruction, or at least welcome its potentiality."

Dexter attains one part of his winter dreams, financial success, and the second, social status. But the third, Judy Jones, the embodiment of eternal youth, eludes him. His capacity for dreaming, the splendor in his heart, leaves him in the end. What he loses is the romantic sensibility Fitzgerald brilliantly describes in the moment before Dexter and Judy come together, as Dexter listens to a faraway tune that had been played at a prom "when he could not afford the luxury of proms": "The sound of the tune precipitated in him a sort of ecstasy and it was with that ecstasy he viewed what happened to him now. It was a mood of intense appreciation, a sense that, for once, he was magnificently attuned to life and that everything about him was radiating a brightness and a glamour he might never know again." When he hears of Judy's lost beauty, Dexter knows he will never have such a feeling again. "Even the grief he could have borne was left behind in the country of illusion, of youth, of the richness of life, where his winter dreams had flourished. 'Long ago,' he said, 'long ago, there was something in me, but now that thing is gone. Now that thing is gone, that thing is gone. I cannot cry. I cannot care. That thing will come back no more.'"

Discussion Questions

1. Dexter Green is one of a population of Fitzgerald's poor-boy characters who achieves success in order to win a rich girl. Is his rise convincing?

2. Define "the American Dream." Are Fitzgerald's responses to it ambivalent? Discuss in terms of Dexter Green.

3. "Winter Dreams," published two years before *The Great Gatsby,* has been described as a miniature of that novel. What are the similarities and differences between these works and their heroes?

—*Marvin LaHood*

JUDY JONES

Judy Jones is the main female character in F. Scott Fitzgerald's short story "Winter Dreams." The story, which centers on the romance between the irresistible Judy and the newly successful Dexter Green, was written while Fitzgerald was thinking through the material for *The Great Gatsby;* Judy Jones is a preliminary sketch of Daisy, as is Dexter of Gatsby. In her wealth, social status, and beauty, she symbolizes the golden-girl embodiment of the American Dream that Fitzgerald's heroes desperately seek to possess.

Judy is the daughter of Mortimer Jones, the richest man in Black Bear, the fictional representation of the fashionable town of White Bear Lake where Fitzgerald and his wife, Zelda, lived for a time. Judy's first encounter with Dexter is at the Sherry Island Golf Club. She is eleven and "beautifully ugly as little girls are apt to be who are destined after a few years to be inexpressibly lovely and bring no end of misery to a great number of men. The spark, however, was perceptible. . . . Vitality is born early in such women." She reveals something of her character and the power she will have over Dexter when she shows her smile, "radiant, blatantly artificial—convincing," and tries to strike her nurse with a golf club. Dexter, who "could not resist the monstrous conviction that the little girl was justified in beating the nurse," quits a job he enjoys rather than caddy for her.

Judy and Dexter meet again at the Sherry Island Golf Club after he has graduated from a prestigious Eastern university and is a successful businessman. As she plays through after having driven her ball into the stomach of one of the men in his foursome, Dexter looks at her closely: "She wore a blue gingham dress, rimmed at throat and

shoulders with a white edging that accentuated her tan. . . . She was arrestingly beautiful. The color in her cheeks was centered like the color in a picture—it was not a 'high' color, but a sort of fluctuating and feverish warmth, so shaded that it seemed at any moment it would recede and disappear. This color and the mobility of her mouth gave a continual impression of flux, of intense life, of passionate vitality—balanced only partially by the sad luxury of her eyes."

That evening on Black Bear Lake, Judy asks Dexter to drive her motorboat so she can ride her surfboard. She explains her presence alone on the lake: "I live in a house over there on the Island, and in that house there is a man waiting for me. When he drove up at the door I drove out of the dock because he says I'm his ideal." Judy does not want to be anyone's ideal because she does not want to live up to such expectations. "She was entertained only by the gratification of her desires and by the direct exercise of her own charm." After Judy communicates "her excitement to him, lavishly, deeply, with kisses that were not a promise but a fulfillment," Dexter realizes "that he had wanted Judy Jones ever since he was a proud, desirous little boy."

The intelligent, well-educated, successful Dexter cannot save himself from falling in love with "the most direct and unprincipled personality with which he had ever come in contact": "she was proof against cleverness, and she was proof against charm; if any of these assailed her too strongly she would immediately resolve the affair to a physical basis, and under the magic of her physical splendor the strong as well as the brilliant played her game and not their own." Dexter is one of a varying dozen of men Judy keeps at her beck and call: "Perhaps from so much youthful love, so many youthful lovers, she had come, in self-defense, to nourish herself entirely from within."

Dexter finally drops out and becomes engaged to another girl, but three months before the marriage is to take place, Judy again takes an interest in him. Under her magic, Dexter's will goes slack, and he follows her. She tells him, "I'd like to marry you if you'll have me, Dexter. I suppose you think I'm not worth having, but I'll be so beautiful for you, Dexter." When they reach her home, "Dexter stopped his coupé in front of the white bulk of the Mortimer Joneses' house, somnolent, gorgeous, drenched with the splendor of the damp moonlight. Its solidity startled him. The strong walls, the steel of the girders, the breadth and beam and pomp of it were there only to bring out the contrast with the young beauty beside him. It was sturdy to accentuate her slightness—as if to show what a breeze could be generated by a butterfly's wing." Judy's renewed interest in Dexter lasts just a month, and Dexter leaves the Midwest to serve in the army and eventually to succeed on Wall Street.

When Dexter learns years later that Judy had married and become the dutiful wife of an indifferent husband, that her beauty had faded at twenty-seven, his romantic world crumbles as its symbol is irrevocably lost: "For the first time in years the tears were streaming down his face. But they were for himself now. He did not care about mouth and eyes and moving hands. He wanted to care, and he could not care. For he had gone away and he could never go back any more. The gates were closed, the sun was gone down, and there was no beauty but the gray beauty of steel that withstands all time."

Discussion Questions

1. Fitzgerald's women are destructive to the men who love them. Does Fitzgerald blame Judy Jones for her flaws? Does Dexter Green blame her?

2. Fitzgerald believed in romantic love, but his male and female characters respond to it differently. How is this true of Dexter Green and Judy Jones?

3. Is Judy Jones pitiable? Does Fitzgerald explain why her great appeal fades at twenty-seven?

—*Marvin LaHood*

REFERENCES

Judith S. Baughman with Matthew J. Bruccoli, *Literary Masters: F. Scott Fitzgerald* (Detroit: Manly/Gale, 2000);

Bruccoli, *Classes on F. Scott Fitzgerald* (Columbia: Thomas Cooper Library, University of South Carolina, 2001);

Bruccoli, *F. Scott Fitzgerald: A Descriptive Bibliography*, revised edition (Pittsburgh: University of Pittsburgh Press, 1987);

Bruccoli, *"The Last of the Novelists": F. Scott Fitzgerald and* The Last Tycoon (Carbondale: Southern Illinois University Press, 1977);

Bruccoli, *Some Sort of Epic Grandeur: The Life of F. Scott Fitzgerald*, second revised edition (Columbia: University of South Carolina Press, 2002);

Bruccoli, with Baughman, *Reader's Companion to F. Scott Fitzgerald's* Tender Is the Night (Columbia: University of South Carolina Press, 1996);

Bruccoli, ed., *F. Scott Fitzgerald Manuscripts*, 3 volumes (New York: Garland, 1998);

Bruccoli, ed., *New Essays on The Great Gatsby* (Cambridge & New York: Cambridge University Press, 1985);

Bruccoli, ed., *The Notebooks of F. Scott Fitzgerald* (New York: Harcourt Brace Jovanovich/Bruccoli Clark, 1978);

Bruccoli and George Parker Anderson, eds., *Dictionary of Literary Biography Documentary Volume 219: F. Scott Fitzgerald's* The Great Gatsby: *A Documentary Volume* (Detroit: Bruccoli Clark Layman/Gale, 2000);

Bruccoli and Anderson, eds., *Dictionary of Literary Biography Volume 273: F. Scott Fitzgerald's* Tender Is the Night (Detroit: Bruccoli Clark Layman/Thomson/Gale, 2003);

Bruccoli, ed., with the assistance of Baughman, *F. Scott Fitzgerald: A Life in Letters* (New York: Scribners, 1994);

F. Scott Fitzgerald, *The Great Gatsby*, Cambridge Edition of the Works of F. Scott Fitzgerald, edited by Bruccoli (Cambridge & New York: Cambridge University Press, 1991);

Fitzgerald, *The Short Stories of F. Scott Fitzgerald*, edited by Bruccoli (New York: Scribners, 1989);

Fitzgerald, *Tender Is the Night*, Everyman Centennial Edition, edited by Bruccoli (London: Dent, 1996);

Roger Lathbury, *Literary Masterpieces: The Great Gatsby* (Farmington Hills, Mich.: Manly/The Gale Group, 2000).

Richard Ford
(February 16, 1944 –   )

‹℃

THE SPORTSWRITER
(New York: Vintage, 1986)

INDEPENDENCE DAY
(New York: Knopf, 1995)

THE LAY OF THE LAND
(New York: Knopf, 2006)

FRANK BASCOMBE

Frank Bascombe is the main character and narrator in Richard Ford's *The Sportswriter* and its sequels, *Independence Day* and *The Lay of the Land*. Bascombe, a former sportswriter, in *Independence Day* is working as a real-estate agent. His life has changed in many ways: his former wife has remarried and is taking their children elsewhere; he has ruined his career as a sportswriter; and he is living in New Jersey, apart from his family (both geographically and sentimentally). He has abandoned his life of traveling as a sportswriter to settle down in the suburbs. Furthermore, Frank has many difficulties in reconciling his past life with what the future might bring: he is not expecting anything, but rather trying to cope with problems as they come, with no plans for the future. On the weekend of the Fourth of July, 1988, Bascombe takes his son Paul, a problematic teenager, with him on a trip to the basketball and baseball halls of fame in Springfield, Massachusetts, and Cooperstown, New York, hoping to achieve some kind of connection with his child. The trip shows the strains between both characters, especially Bascombe's difficulty in acting as a father to the troubled Paul. The outing is mostly uneventful until Paul is hit by a pitching machine at the Baseball Hall of Fame: while at the hospital, struggling with feelings of guilt caused only partly by the accident, Frank happens to meet his half brother, Irv, whom he has not seen for many years. This chance encounter and the "uneventful events" of the weekend begin to make Bascombe change his attitude toward his life and relationships. The Independence Day excursion becomes a trip of self-discovery for Frank, who is forced to be reconciled with his own life and to enter a new phase, leaving behind his previous "Existence Period," one that Ford has described in an interview as "the period after the crises have subsided . . . you've survived, and you're nominally happy." Bascombe's modus operandi seems to be "to ignore much of what I don't like or that seems worrisome and embroiling, and then usually see it go away." The new stage of Bascombe's life is what he calls his "Permanent Period," "that long, stretching-out time when my dreams would have mystery like any ordinary person's," when his apathy will disappear and he will start to have hope for the future. Bascombe enters the novel as a middle-aged male with an uneventful life and with worries that are typical of his age and time: a fragmented family, teenage children, and a "learned" or "adopted" inability to commit. His midlife crisis, characterized by his unwillingness to commit (to his present lover, for example) and to make choices, is resolved through this inner change that is symbolized in the passage from one period to another.

As narrator Frank reveals his thoughts, he confronts other characters, making the reader privy to how these thoughts force him to reconsider his own life. In this stage of his life, things are happening to him, but he is not causing them; he is merely taking on whatever comes instead of being an agent of change. A worried but exceptionally perceptive character, whom Ford calls "a good sort of negotiator . . . of ethical issues," he has to come to terms with the death of one of his sons, although it still haunts him; he is troubled by the unexplained death of a colleague, and he acts as a witness to the decay of his neighborhood as a metaphor of his own life. He is still secretly in love with his former wife and estranged from his own children and relatives, apparently unable to commit or unwilling to do so, and still longing for some kind of personal connection, in what Ford has defined as an attempt to "do whatever you can to narrow that space Emerson calls the infinite remoteness that separates people."

In the trilogy of novels about Bascombe, Ford is creating an American everyman, along the lines of

Willy Loman in Arthur Miller's *Death of a Salesman* or Nick Carraway in F. Scott Fitzgerald's *The Great Gatsby:* ordinary individuals who are faced with unheroic, still important dilemmas and choices throughout their lives. Ford reflects, through Frank Bascombe, on suburban American life at the end of the twentieth century: the common lives of common people, and the possibility of finding meaning in everyday experiences as the only way to individual redemption.

While Ford makes the character of Bascombe memorable, the events described in the book, in their simplicity and commonness, are not: however, Bascombe's narration of the events brim with humor, struggle, and the insights that are often the result of such struggle, the common ingredients of everyday life, a life that Ford has defined as "the blueprint you make after the building is built." Frank is making an effort to come to terms with his new choice of career, to cope with troublesome clients and with tenants who will not pay their rent, and he finds himself most often not facing the problems.

Discussion Questions

1. How would you say Frank Bascombe changes between *The Sportswriter* and *Independence Day?* Is he a wiser or a more disenchanted man? Has he been able to assimilate the new direction of his life?

2. Frank considers himself to be an average man, "more or less normal-under-the microscope." How is this view of himself challenged by those around him (for example, his former wife and his current lover)? Is he successful at the many facets of his personal life (father, former husband, colleague, lover)? What about his professional life?

3. Consider the ideas of hero and antihero in characters such as Willy Loman from Arthur Miller's *Death of a Salesman* or Eddie Carbone from Frank Miller's *View from the Bridge.* Does Frank Bascombe fit into the hero or the antihero category? What would be his heroism, if any?

4. Analyze Bascombe's weekend as a spiritual pilgrimage. What are the stages of his "progress"? In what ways does he grow through this journey?

—*Carmen Méndez García*

REFERENCES

Huey Guagliardo, ed., *Conversations with Richard Ford* (Jackson: University Press of Mississippi, 2001);

Guagliardo, ed., *Perspectives on Richard Ford* (Jackson: University Press of Mississippi, 2000);

Elinor Walker, *Richard Ford* (New York: Twayne, 2000).

Hannah Foster
(September 10, 1758 – April 17, 1840)

ᗰ

THE COQUETTE; OR, THE HISTORY OF ELIZA WHARTON; A NOVEL; FOUNDED ON FACT
(Boston: Printed by Samuel Etheridge for E. Larkin, 1797)

ELIZA WHARTON

Eliza Wharton, the protagonist of Hannah Foster's novel *The Coquette*, is a clever, flirtatious, and attractive lady in her mid thirties. She is also a daring, educated individual whose attempts to redefine the possibilities of a post-Revolutionary woman's life backfire, leaving her seduced, pregnant outside of wedlock, impoverished, and ultimately alone. This epistolary novel, written completely in the form of letters between its characters, describes the results of Eliza's romantic choices.

First published in 1797, *The Coquette* was America's first best-selling novel written by an American author. One reason for its popularity was its basis in the true story of Elizabeth Whitman, who died in 1788 and whose seducer was never known; Foster deliberately created a character with a similar name and life history. Whitman's life and death were discussed in many newspapers of the time, and the lesson people derived from the story was a basic equation: if a woman sins, she dies. But this oversimplification of a human life was corrected by Foster's narrative, in which the woman's premarital sexual activity is only one part of a larger story. The book utilizes the epistolary style to deal with enduring issues, such as marriage choices and the difficulty of living within social restrictions.

As the novel opens, the death of Reverend Haly has ended Eliza's first engagement, and her friends and mother are trying immediately to find her another marriage partner. Eliza is rather inclined to enjoy her interval of freedom, as she visits with friends and goes to parties, for she describes herself as "naturally cheerful, volatile, and unreflecting." Her letters suggest that she is actually a thoughtful, fun-loving person. She has a circle of respectable, educated women friends who try to advise her on how to behave properly according to their society, but this sisterhood is not enough to prevent her downfall. The virtuous Lucy Sumner warns Eliza to "act with modest freedom," yet Eliza gambles with her life. She begins losing contact with her friends and becomes isolated. Eliza writes that "marriage is the tomb of friendship" because married women have to focus on their husbands and children.

Eliza knows she lacks the right temperament to be married to a clergyman, but people keep pushing her to pursue that course. She begins a courtship with the overly serious Reverend Boyer, who writes in letters about how he intends to tame her if they marry but then breaks off the engagement because he finds her character unsuitable. He tells Eliza that her flaws include "a levity" or giddiness in her personality, "an unwarrantable extravagance" and excessive attention devoted to fashionable clothing, and inappropriate friendship with Major Peter Sanford, a man of bad character known for seducing women. Eliza's attempt to balance relationships with Boyer and the entertaining Sanford fails, and she loses both suitors. As Lucy states, women must not associate with men of bad character, or they will "be betrayed."

The novel includes both a standard message about the dangers of flirtation and a more subversive message criticizing the limitations on women's lives at the end of the eighteenth century. Writers of "seduction novels" hoped to warn women away from sexual temptation and exploitation by emphasizing the tragic consequences that befall a woman victim of male desire. A woman's morality and personal worth were seen as tied inextricably to her chastity. To relinquish virginity to a rake was a grave mistake for an unmarried woman. When Eliza enters into the affair with Sanford, he states that he loves her; but he will not propose marriage because he wants to marry a woman with more money. When he marries someone else, it makes all three people miserable.

Foster's *The Coquette* also exposes the extreme limitations on women's lives and choices at the end of the eighteenth century. Eliza's only choice is who to marry, not whether to marry or to support herself in some other way. In late-eighteenth-century America, women did not have such opportunities for remunerative employment. Furthermore, they were expected to marry for subsistence and learn to love whomever they married. Eliza challenges such rules by not being married by age thirty-seven and having a premarital affair. Her efforts to determine her own fate lead to her self-destruction.

Sanford exults in his triumph over Eliza's resistance, yet he regrets his immorality by the end of the novel. When Eliza is close to giving birth, he promises he will support her and sends her to an inn outside of town, although he does not see her before her death of puerperal fever, an aggressive infection of the female reproductive system that killed up to 20 percent of new mothers in the 1700s. Their baby is stillborn. Like the historical figure Elizabeth Whitman on whom she was based, Eliza dies alone and leaves behind few material possessions, including some money, baby clothes, and her writing materials. In her last letters she expresses regret, admits her mistakes, and seeks forgiveness from her friends and family. They put up a tombstone to honor Eliza's memory, describing her as "endowed with superior acquirements" and "distinguished by humility and benevolence."

Discussion Questions

1. How does the epistolary style affect your understanding of the characters in the novel? Discuss how Major Peter Sanford presents one image of himself and his intentions to Eliza but reveals his true feelings in letters to Deighton.

2. Why is Eliza and Major Sanford's encounter in the garden in letter 41 the turning point of the novel?

3. What could Eliza have done differently in order to have a better outcome in her life? Considering her range of choices, what other paths in life might she have found, and what do you think she wants?

4. How does the novel reveal a "double standard" of behavior for men and women?

5. The heroines of Foster's *The Coquette* and Nathaniel Hawthorne's *The Scarlet Letter* are both sexual outside of marriage bonds, anc both authors criticize social restrictions involving marriage. In what ways does Eliza Wharton remind you of Hester Prynne in Nathaniel Hawthorne's *The Scarlet Letter*? How too are the situations different?

—*Amy Cummins*

REFERENCES

Cathy Davidson, *Revolution and the Word: The Rise of the Novel in America* (New York: Oxford University Press, 1986), pp. 140–150;

Ian Finseth, "'A Melancholy Tale': Rhetoric, Fiction, and Passion in *The Coquette*," *Studies in the Novel*, 33 (2001): 125–159;

Claire Pettengill, "*Legacy* Profile: Hannah Webster Foster (1758–1840)," *Legacy: A Journal of American Women Writers*, 12, no. 2 (1995): 133–141;

Walter P. Wenska Jr. "*The Coquette* and the American Dream of Freedom," *Early American Literature*, 12 (1977–1978): 243–255.

Jonathan Franzen
(August 17, 1959 –   )

‿◎

THE CORRECTIONS
(New York: Farrar, Straus & Giroux, 2001)

THE LAMBERT FAMILY

Jonathan Franzen's *The Corrections* follows the lives of the Lambert family—two elderly parents, Alfred and Enid, and their three adult children, Gary, Chip, and Denise. The action spans only a few months, from September to Christmas, as Enid tries to orchestrate "one last Christmas together" in St. Jude, Franzen's fictionalized St. Louis; but the novel frequently delves into the past to expose the motivations of the characters and to elucidate their relationships with each other. St. Jude, the stereotypical Midwestern city, is regarded as slow and unsophisticated by the Lambert children, who have moved east to seek their fortunes. The characterization of each Lambert unfolds meticulously within the familial framework. Parents embodying old-fashioned values struggle with deteriorating health, obstinate children, and the preservation of their personal fantasies; children wrestle with failed aspirations, unstable romantic relationships, the burden of aging parents, and general disillusionments of middle age. The primary problem of each Lambert arises from the disparity between reality and the self-deceptions that have been nurtured by the family to avoid confrontation.

A once-imposing patriarch, Alfred Lambert no longer inspires fear and respect from his children. Parkinson's disease has left him, at the age of eighty, palsied, depressed, and delusional. In all facets of his life Alfred has acted in accord with the philosophy of Arthur Schopenhauer; he believes, for example, that humans "were born to suffer" and that intelligent beings "were doomed to be tormented by the stupid." His Depression-era values leave him exceedingly careful with money, and puritanical ideals make him awkward in marriage and fatherhood. In his career as a railroad executive Alfred was a workaholic, work being his drug, according to his older son, Gary. Without work, Alfred finds enjoyment only in vexing his wife and sleeping in his big chair in the basement. He had been an amateur metallurgist in middle age, and one of his patents has recently been used to develop an experimental drug called Corecktall—a pill that promises to cure Parkinson's and similar neurological afflictions. Alfred's children, who deceive themselves about the extent of his declining mental health, sign him up for trial testing of the drug.

Enid, who married for security rather than for passion, appears perpetually optimistic, despite the reticence and pessimism of her husband. Alfred has always been cold and uncommunicative, but Enid dedicates her life to him, even as his infirmity controls their lives. Much of her energy goes into avoiding disturbing realities and constructing the semblance of happiness and order. She admires anything that her Midwestern discernment deems "elegant" and reproves anything that is an affront to this sense (T-shirts on cruise ships, for instance, or public intoxication). Enid envies family friends who have done better financially or who have more attentive children; she lives her life acutely aware of how her family is perceived by others and in endless anticipation of the idealized future—of visits, of vacations, of Christmas. Without genuine fulfillment in her own life, she seeks it through her children's lives, but she inflates their successes and criticizes their choices. Of the three, only Gary offers sympathy for her loneliness and her burdens in nursing a sick husband.

Gary prides himself on his unwavering dependability and financial stability; he has followed the "right" path to making his parents proud. He works as an investment manager at CenTrust Bank of Philadelphia and excels in his position. He lives with his wife, Caroline, and their three sons in a fashionable neighborhood outside of the city. He is devoted to his wife, and, like his mother, even more devoted to upholding the image of blissful domestic life, despite his increasing paranoia and alcoholism. His inability to exercise control over his own life compels him to take control of the lives of his parents. As the oldest child Gary is the responsible one, he thinks, and he disdains the "alternative" lifestyles of his two siblings. That they could find success or happiness following less-conventional paths "undercut the pleasure he took in his home and job and family." His existence has been "set up as a correction of his father's life" as he strives to outdo Alfred at everything the old man has fumbled—fatherhood, marriage, and finances. Gary realizes that he has played by the rules his whole life, perhaps to his disadvantage.

Everyone agrees that Chip is the feckless brother—intelligent, but also impulsive, unreliable, and too willing to blame others for his failures. Yet, everyone but Gary continues to have undue faith in him. Academic life suits Chip's anticapitalist ideas, and he earns a tenure-track position in literary theory at a small Connecticut college. Fired for sexual harassment, he moves to New York, where he borrows money from his sister and maxes out credit cards while chasing women. He proofreads documents for a law firm, writes a screenplay about the alleged injustices in his life, and contributes articles to a transgressive arts publication, the *Warren Street Journal,* which he lets his mother mistake for the *Wall Street Journal.* Pursuing his former girlfriend puts him in the path of her husband, Gitanas Misevičius, a former Lithuanian diplomat who hires Chip for a dot-com start-up in Vilnius established to defraud American investors. He starts his holiday trip to St. Jude as Lithuania collapses, and he overcomes a closed airport, a government coup, masked gunmen, and a cold hike across the Polish border to arrive home on Christmas morning.

Denise, the youngest sibling, is an overachiever—the ideal daughter until a rebellious urge overtakes her in high school. Drawn to culinary arts early on, she quit college to work her way through restaurant kitchens. She has married and divorced Emile Berger, a chef twice her age, who taught her everything she needs to know about cooking. Like her father, Denise enjoys immersing herself in work—at the cost of personal relationships. A lucrative offer puts her in charge of the Generator, Philadelphia's hippest new restaurant, and the endeavor boosts her to celebrity. Months later, just as she achieves the twin success of money and fame, Denise is fired for sleeping with the boss's wife. She faces the family reunion with a life in shambles.

What is supposed to be the perfect last family Christmas culminates in role reversals; children become caretakers, and parents prove as stubborn and helpless as children. Gary bullies Alfred and Enid, insisting that they make realistic decisions about their futures; the reliable son becomes the impatient tyrant, incapable of compassion because of his fear of reality. Chip becomes dependable for the first time in his life, helping Enid to settle Alfred in a nursing home, visiting him every day, and fixing up the old house. After Denise witnesses the extent of her father's decline, she acquires an overdue appreciation of her mother and encourages Enid's new hobbies and travels. Having escaped her oppressive husband, Enid lives her own life for the first time at seventy-five. After years of dishonesty and dysfunction, the Lamberts find strength in their weaknesses, exposing vanities and self-delusions to achieve understanding and forgiveness. They find that they make their "corrections" in time to make amends.

Discussion Questions

1. Compare the way Alfred and Enid view marriage and parenthood with the views of Gary and Caroline.

2. Is there any significance to the lion motif in the story? Consider a connection between Aslan or Mexican A and the character of C. S. Lewis's Narnia books, which Jonah is reading.

3. Considering Alfred's resolute work ethic, why is he drawn more to Chip, a perpetual disappointment, than to Gary, the older, more successful son?

4. At the informational luncheon sponsored by the Axon Corporation, how do Gary's and Denise's reactions differ in response to the Corecktall presentation?

5. Consider the novel as social commentary. What kind of critiques of late capitalist society does the author make? Provide examples.

—*Jill Jividen*

REFERENCES

James Annesley, "Market Corrections: Jonathan Franzen and the 'Novel of Globalization,'" *Journal of Modern Literature,* 29 (Winter 2006): 111–128;

Susanne Rohr, "'The Tyranny of the Probable': Crackpot Realism and Jonathan Franzen's *The Corrections,*" *Amerikastudien/American Studies,* 49 (2004): 91–105;

Catherine Toal, "*The Corrections:* Contemporary American Melancholy," *Journal of European Studies,* 33 (December 2003): 305–322.

Charles Frazier

(November 4, 1950 –   )

꧁

COLD MOUNTAIN

(New York: Atlantic Monthly Press, 1997)

INMAN

After suffering a nearly fatal wound during the fighting around Petersburg, Virginia, in 1864, Inman, a Confederate soldier in Charles Frazier's *Cold Mountain,* deserts from a military hospital in Raleigh, North Carolina, and walks hundreds of miles to his home. When Frazier heard family stories about an ancestor who had also deserted and returned to Cold Mountain, he thought of *The Odyssey,* the ninth-century-B.C. epic poem attributed to the blind poet Homer. "So I went back and reread the *Odyssey* and tried not to write parallel scenes or anything like that but just to have a recognition, as I wrote, that it was a literary ancestor of the story." Allusions to *The Odyssey* can be found throughout the novel. Like Odysseus, Inman endures many trials on his return journey, which is also an opportunity for self-discovery.

Inman enlists after becoming caught up in "the war frenzy in the early days" and at first fights only "to drive off invaders." As the war continues, he questions what the fighting is really about. Frazier has written that those who grow up in the South "get this concept of the war as this noble, tragic thing, and when I think about my own family's experience, it doesn't seem so noble in any direction. To go off and fight for a cause they had not much relation to: that's the part I see as tragic." Inman longs to be reunited with his sweetheart, Ada Monroe, in Cold Mountain, wishing only "to live a life where little interest could be found in one gang of despots launching attacks upon another."

Inman's flight is more than just an escape from the war and death. Rather, it is a journey into life, a search for meaning and redemption. As he slips away from the hospital, he knows the journey "will be the axle of my life." Inman is only one of many thousands of deserters attempting to leave the war, and as he struggles westward toward the mountains and home, his understanding of the conflict deepens. The war is hard not only on combatants but also on civilians. The objectives of the conflict are muddled—a rich man's war and a poor man's fight. People he meets along the way have varying opinions of the conflict, but mostly they, like Inman, just try to survive. Inman wonders if their struggle, like his, is part of the natural order of things.

Inman contemplates nature as he reads William Bartram's *Travels,* an account of the naturalist's journey through North Carolina in the late eighteenth century, and reflects on what he knows of Cherokee myths. Although he has lost his Christian belief in a literal heaven, he holds to the probability of an invisible world, an alternative to "a universe composed only of what he could see, especially when it was so frequently foul." Cold Mountain looms "as a place where all his scattered forces might gather." In a passage used as one of the two epigraphs in the novel, Chinese poet Han-shan, whose name literally means "Cold Mountain," warns that there is "no through trail," no easy way to get there in the spiritual sense. As Inman walks toward home, he becomes a pilgrim, "a dark monk out awander for the good of his soul."

By the time Inman reaches Cold Mountain, where he is reunited with Ada, he believes he is "ruined beyond repair," beyond redemption, incapable of being healed. Throughout his journey he has been pursued by Home Guards, local militia units charged with rounding up deserters and escaped prisoners. As renegades avoiding conscription, the Guards prey on the communities they are supposed to protect. In the vicinity of Cold Mountain, a band of Home Guards finds Inman, who is forced to fight. "There was no sense talking with such men. Language would change nothing, no more than gabbling empty sounds into the air," Inman thinks. He kills them all except for a strange boy named Birch. Inman tells Birch he is "looking for a way not to kill you," but this last attempt to leave the war fails, and Inman is shot by Birch.

Frazier describes the final scene of the novel from the perspective of an "observer situated up on the brow of the ridge" who sees in the distance a man reclining, his head in a woman's lap. "A scene of such quiet and peace that the observer on the ridge could avouch to it later in such a way as might lead those of glad temperaments to imagine some conceivable history where long decades of happy union stretched before the two on the ground." The observer, however, would not know what the reader knows, that Inman is dying and that there will be no long decades of happy union. But an epilogue set a decade later reveals that Ada has given birth to Inman's child and that mother and daughter are living peacefully below Cold Mountain. The epilogue suggests that Inman has finally reached Han-shan's "Cold Mountain" as he is redeemed and regenerated by love.

Discussion Questions

1. Crows appear throughout *Cold Mountain*. What is their purpose in the novel? In what ways do the actions of crows correspond to Inman's fate?

2. Before he leaves the hospital in Raleigh, Inman talks to a blind news vendor. How does this conversation give insight into the war and Inman's feelings about returning to it?

3. Long before Inman deserts from the army, he deserts from school. On the second page of the novel he tosses his hat out the window of a mountain schoolroom during a history lesson and walks away, "never to return." Later in the novel, Inman declines to talk about the people and events he has witnessed during the Civil War, the parts now in history books. What does Inman think about history, and why? What kind of knowledge does he find most important?

4. Some readers call *Cold Mountain* an antiwar novel. Frazier does not paint a romantic picture of the Civil War, but is opposition to war in general a major theme of the novel? Is Inman's desertion a moral act as well as a personal one?

5. Inman and Ada Monroe are changed by the war. In what ways are those changes both similar and different?

—*Paul Ashdown*

ADA MONROE

Ada Monroe, the female protagonist of Charles Frazier's *Cold Mountain*, comes to a hamlet in western North Carolina, from Charleston, South Carolina, several years before the Civil War. She falls in love with Inman, who leaves to fight with the Confederate army when the war breaks out. Ada's father, a minister, dies, leaving her to manage their farm without an inheritance. This responsibility proves difficult, because while Ada is well educated and clever, "her father had kept her back from the hardness of work." She, like her father, thinks of nature as something only to be contemplated. Ada "discovered herself to be frighteningly ill-prepared in the craft of subsistence, living alone on a farm that her father had run rather as an idea than a livelihood." She remains apart from Cold Mountain until she can shed her detachment and draw nourishment from the land and its people. Although mountain customs and folklore are alien to her, she does not want to return to Charleston, believing that "what she could see around her was all that she could count on. The mountains and a desire to find if she could make a satisfactory life of common things here." The arrival of Ruby Thewes as a companion enables Ada to manage on her land. Ruby teaches Ada how to work the farm while Ada reads Dickens and Homer to Ruby. But it is Ruby's worldview that gradually prevails and changes Ada.

Frazier has said that he was not interested in writing about Civil War battles but in discovering "the old lost culture of the southern Appalachians." In his background research for *Cold Mountain*, he was interested in finding out "how things looked and how they worked. Subsistence farming, vernacular architecture, herbal medicines, and the mysterious ways of wild turkeys, for example." As a character, Ada acts as a surrogate for most modern readers. She knows nothing about subsistence farming and relatively little about the natural world. Along with the reader, Ada gradually learns the "language" of Cold Mountain, the names of things, and the processes by which the mountain culture is perpetuated. This new knowledge, as for the modern reader, becomes for Ada a form of initiation.

While Ada masters the language of nature and craft, she becomes increasingly skeptical of the rhetorical language that fuels the war. When a wealthy neighbor tells her about a newspaper account of a glorious battle, Ada rebukes the woman for her credulity. Ada says that the version of events in the newspaper is "the most preposterous thing I have ever heard." War, she insists, is not noble and romantic but "brutal and benighted on both sides about equally. Degrading to all." She learns that Inman has been badly wounded in the fighting in Virginia and taken to a Raleigh hospital. When Inman returns to Cold Mountain, he is killed during a fight with the Home Guard; Ada gives birth to their child, and she and Ruby stay on in Cold Mountain.

Tom Wicker has written that *Cold Mountain* has an unhappy, although not a tragic, ending, because "things had turned out as they should have, as in boundless experience things do. *Cold Mountain* reassures us that life goes on despite all sorts of 'unhappy' events and endings, and yields its joys not alone in ephemeral moments of gratification but continually, in natural compensations—sunsets, a child's discoveries, a task completed, crops in season—that have only to be realized." His view is not inconsistent with the view Frazier attributes to the congregation that hears the Reverend Monroe preach a sermon on death early in the novel. Their grumbling "made it clear that death troubled him to a greater degree than it did them. Many thought it not the tragedy Monroe did, but saw it rather as a good thing." Death is simply a part of life, and life continues in some form.

Ada is more than another tragic lover in a sad story ending in untimely death. She is a participant in a much larger story with universal resonance. John C. Inscoe observes that, as the novel progresses, Ada's life expands "with more scope and greater range, so that by the time she and her lover are reunited, she has undergone a transformation fully as profound as that inflicted on Inman by the traumas of war." By opening herself to a fuller life, Ada becomes part of the lost world Frazier attempts to recover.

Discussion Questions

1. Sometime after she meets Ruby, Ada writes a cousin in Charleston that while "working in the fields, there are brief times when I go totally without thought. Not one idea crosses my mind, though my senses are alert to all around me. Should a crow fly over, I mark it in all its details, but I do not seek analogy for its blackness. I know it is a type of nothing, not metaphoric." How does this passage reveal Ada's changing understanding of nature?

2. Ada plays the piano and loves classical music, but it is the folk music of the mountains that helps open her heart to the community. When she hears Stobrod play a fiddle tune she observes his "utter faith . . . in its ability to lead one toward a better life." How does this music differ in essence from the music she knows? How does it reveal the story of the mountain people? How is it a means of healing?

3. When Ada agrees to hold a mirror and look backward into the well on the Swanger farm, is she abandoning reason for superstition? Why does what she sees in the mirror bring to mind the words of a hymn? How does the vision reveal a change in Ada's character?

—*Paul Ashdown*

RUBY THEWES

When Ruby Thewes arrives at Ada Monroe's farm at the behest of a neighbor to offer assistance, she makes clear that she is to be neither a hired hand nor a servant and that "everybody empties their own night jar." As a character in *Cold Mountain*, Ruby often provides comic relief. At their first meeting Ada "found that she was enormously cheered by Ruby." She offers to teach Ada how to run the farm in exchange for shared meals and shelter. The arrangement becomes an unlikely partnership between two young women who look after one another during the Civil War. Ada is the well-educated, Charleston-born daughter of a minister who has recently died and left her to manage Black Cove farm on her own. Before Ruby's arrival Ada can do little more than search for chicken eggs or pick up apples. She awaits the return of Inman, a Confederate soldier she met shortly before the war began. Ruby is the illiterate daughter of Stobrod Thewes, a shiftless mountain fiddler and drunkard who deserted from the Confederate army and lives with other "outliers" in a mountain cave near Cold Mountain. Stobrod, like Ruby, has comic aspects and is redeemed by his wartime discovery that he can improvise soothing fiddle tunes.

Although Ruby has "not spent a day of her life in school," Ada sees in her "a spark as bright and hard as one struck with steel and flint." Ruby is stalwart, determined, and resourceful, valuing practical experience while the bookish Ada understands things in intellectual terms. When Ada asks Ruby to explain how she knows so much about "how the world runs," Ruby credits "grandmother knowledge, got from wandering around the settlement talking to any old woman who would talk back," listening, and asking questions. One woman knew a great many "quiet things such as the names of all plants down to the plainest weed." Ruby puzzles out the logic of the world, a matter mostly of "being attentive." She understands that nature offers signs and parables useful to observers. She watches, for example, the behavior of birds, "finding a thread of narrative or evidence of character in their minutest customs." She points out that many birds will starve before eating food they do not like, while crows "will relish what presents

itself." Ruby advises Ada to take instruction from the crows and adapt. Ada ultimately learns to take instruction from Ruby, who has all manner of useful skills. She can decapitate a rooster, dig a root cellar, rotate crops, cure tobacco, grind corn, weave wool, crop a sow's ear, build a rail fence, press cider, and split logs.

Ruby, Inman, and Ada all try throughout the novel to sort out their religious and spiritual beliefs during the upheaval of the war. Ruby has a much simpler view of life than the others, but she adapts better to her environment. She tells Ada that when she was four years old, she spent a scary night in the woods while caught on a blackthorn briar. She believes she was protected by "some tender force of landscape or sky, an animal sprite, a guardian that took her under its wing and concerned itself with her well-being from that moment on." Ruby sees a nurturing world "properly put together." Albert Way suggests that the "attractive quality of Frazier's portrayal of Ruby is not that her world view protects the environment from harm but that she is a part of nature rather than apart from it."

Ruby stays with Ada even after Inman's return and death. Ruby marries, and as the novel ends, Stobrod is playing the fiddle for his grandsons and Ada's daughter, passing tradition on to another generation. For many readers, Ruby is the most endearing character in *Cold Mountain*.

Discussion Questions

1. Albert Way suggests that Ruby is a "nature fundamentalist. She reads the environment as a religious fundamentalist would a holy text. . . ." As she learns about the natural world, Ada comes to see Ruby herself as "her principal text."

2. *Cold Mountain* is a novel in which there are many competing "texts"—Reverend Mr. Monroe's Bible, William Bartram's *Travels*, Ralph Waldo Emerson, folklore, Homer, Charles Darwin, Chinese poet Han-shan, newspapers. Because Ruby cannot read, does she have a choice of "texts" in order to make sense of the world? Why does Ada gradually come to find other "texts" lacking when she observes Ruby?

3. Ruby has little reason to care for Stobrod, who often abandoned her when she was a child and has

little concern for her. And yet she seems to have room in her heart even for Stobrod. What binds them together at the end of the novel that was missing earlier in their relationship?

4. Although the novel ends with an image of mothers caring for their children, mothers are often absent in *Cold Mountain*. Like Ada, Ruby "was a motherless child from the day she was born," and Inman apparently has been without a mother from an early age. Where do readers find maternal images in the novel? How does the absence of a maternal presence affect the characters?

—*Paul Ashdown*

REFERENCES

Paul Ashdown, *A Cold Mountain Companion* (Gettysburg, Pa.: Thomas Publications, 2004);

Albert Way, "'A World Properly Put Together': Environmental Knowledge in Charles Frazier's *Cold Mountain*," *Southern Cultures*, 10 (Winter 2004): 34–54;

Carl Zebrowski, *Walking to Cold Mountain: A Journey through Civil War America* (New York: Smithmark, 1999).

Harold Frederic
(August 19, 1856 – October 19, 1898)

〰

"MY AUNT SUSAN"

Collected in *Marsena, and Other Stories of the Wartime* (New York: Scribners, 1894).

AUNT SUSAN

Aunt Susan is the energetic, hardworking young woman at the center of Harold Frederic's short story "My Aunt Susan," a brief, painstaking character study of a single woman rearing a child during the Civil War, narrated by her perceptive young nephew, Ira. Written in 1892, the story stands with Frederic's other wartime tales at a crucial point in his artistic development. He had completed three competent novels, and he was already making notes for his 1896 masterpiece, *The Damnation of Theron Ware*. Thus, he had proven himself a journeyman author, and he was about to demonstrate himself an artist of the

first rank. In the interval he wrote seven stories, one of which was "Aunt Susan."

Frederic was well qualified to portray a woman such as Susan from the perspective of an observant boy. Like Ira, Frederic lost his father as an infant; he was reared by his mother, a strong figure, vigorous and provident, but little given to emotional display. Too, he had experienced the Civil War years as a child in New York State, feeling the effects of war in the sorrow of families and communities in mourning. In reflecting upon the stories he wrote in the 1890s, Frederic noted that they were "by far closer to my heart than any other work of mine, partly because they seem to me to contain the best things I have ever done or ever shall do, partly because they are so interwoven with the personal memories and experiences of my own childhood. . . ."

The opening line of the story, "I held the lamp, while Aunt Susan cut up the pig," suggests a woman who is self-reliant but emotionally cold. Indeed, she works "like a strong man in a hurry." Throughout the rising action, she is emotionally distant, and she offers none of the maternal affection that children seek: "It was not our habit to talk much in that house," Ira states. "She was too busy a woman, for one thing, to have much time for conversation. The impression that she preferred not to talk was always present in my boyish mind." Still more telling is his confession: "I had always had at her hands uniformly good treatment, good food, good clothes. . . .Yet it could never be said that I loved her. Indeed, she no more raised the suggestion of tenderness in my mind than did the loom at which she spent her waking hours." Frederic's description of the loom works well to characterize the insular labor of Susan's life: it is a "diligent loom," and it creates a "monotonous, incessant clatter."

When Ira complains to his aunt that neighbor children call him "wise child"—an insult based on the proverb, "It's a wise child that knows its own father"—reasons for her "frosty curtness" begin to come clear. The name-calling implies that Ira was born to Susan out of wedlock, and that she may have assumed the identity of an aunt upon moving to Juno Mills, New York, to avoid the shame her predicament might have caused in 1862. Such suspicions are confirmed when townspeople refer to Susan as an old maid in Ira's hearing, since, as they do so, they are "winking furtively" over the boy's head. This possibility further emphasizes Susan's coldness: her pain has caused her to deny maternal affection toward her own son. Further, it explains why she isolates herself from the town, why she "kept herself to herself with a vengeance." That such insularity was the least painful option attests to the trauma the woman has experienced.

Readers' perceptions change when Susan's history is revealed at the climax of the story. When Major Blodgett appears at their home, it is clear that he is the boy's father—Susan's one-time lover—but the scene that follows delivers an ironic twist: Susan was not his mother. Blodgett had been Susan's lover, but he had left her to marry her sister, with whom he had fathered Ira. The sister and Blodgett did not get along well, and she died while he was prospecting for gold in California, leaving the spurned Aunt Susan to care for the infant. Thus, the reclusive qualities that had been previously attributable to her shame or even, as Ira puts it, to her "unsociable nature," are more accurately caused by her broken heart and wounded pride. For Susan to have divulged her real situation would have meant recounting the story of her desertion and humiliation to the townspeople. In doing so, she might well have found the comfort of the community's acceptance—but at too high a price: pity. Thus, her pain and her pride have kept her from revealing her actual situation to the town; as a result, the town has assumed the worst.

The story concludes with changes of attitudes, both in the community and within Aunt Susan. Once their garrulous physician has passed the word that Ira's father, Susan's brother-in-law, has arrived—and that he has both wealth and military rank—the little family is no longer outcast. The child notes, "I felt at once the altered attitude of the village toward me." Merchants give him sweets, leading citizens inquire about his father's health, and the children who once taunted him with calls of "wise child" ask him to come out and play. The butcher even finishes cutting up the family's pig.

But more importantly, Susan is transformed from bitter to blessed. Reunited with her lover—and having reached an understanding to renew their relationship—her countenance changes. Ira states, "I could have sworn to the beginnings of a smile about her parted lips. It was not like my Aunt Susan at all." Later she speaks to the boy in "a tone mellowed beyond all recognition" and even, much to his surprise, kisses him. The ending is somewhat too neat for contemporary tastes, but from the perspective of nineteenth-century sentimentality, it remains satisfying. And the psychological complexity that became characteristic of Frederic's later work is manifest in his portrayal of Aunt Susan.

Discussion Questions

1. Even though this story takes place in the relative safety of upstate New York, in what obvious and not-so-obvious ways does the Civil War impact the characters' lives?

2. Why do you think Frederic chose to relate Aunt Susan's story through the eyes of her nephew? How would the story have been different had it been told by the local doctor? By an omniscient narrator? By Aunt Susan herself?

3. Aunt Susan intentionally isolates herself from her neighbors in Juno Mills. Considering her situation, was her choice a good one? Why or why not? What does her decision say about small-town life in the 1860s?

4. At the end of the story, the dissonant relationships are quickly and easily harmonized. Had Frederic chosen to expand the story into a novel, what difficulties might he have introduced into the new family's life together?

5. Harold Frederic was a close friend of Stephen Crane, author of *The Red Badge of Courage*. How do the two authors' stories of the Civil War complete and complement each other?

—*William Jolliff*

THE DAMNATION OF THERON WARE

(Chicago: Stone & Kimball, 1896); republished as *Illumination* (London: Heinemann, 1896)

THERON WARE

Theron Ware is a rural Methodist minister who is intellectually and spiritually crushed by the people he tries to emulate in Harold Frederic's *The Damnation of Theron Ware,* one of the best-selling novels of 1896. When the Reverend Ware is assigned to a congregation in the upstate New York hamlet of Octavius, his new friendships with the leading intellectuals of the town quickly lead to his feeling embarrassed by his own modest knowledge. However, what at first appears to be Theron's intellectual "illumination"—a word used in the ironic title of the British publication of the novel—is slowly revealed to be his "damnation," as Theron imitates his friends at the expense of his identity and values and betrays the trust of his wife and congregation.

The Damnation of Theron Ware is a significant example of American literary realism, a genre that attempted to portray realistically America's changing culture in the final decades of the nineteenth century, exemplified by such authors as Henry James, Mark Twain, Edith Wharton, and William Dean Howells. Frederic intends Ware's transformation from sheltered piety to intellectual pretension and corruption to represent the cultural transformations of the United States from the predominantly rural nation of Frederic's antebellum childhood to the more complex, urbane, self-conscious, yet morally suspect America of the turn of the century. Like the biblical story of Adam and Eve in which eating the fruit of the Tree of Knowledge leads to ruination, Ware's story illustrates Frederic's belief that knowledge can sometimes destroy that which was worth preserving.

At the annual Methodist conference that starts the novel, Ware stands out as a "tall slender, young man with the broad white brow, thoughtful eyes, and features molded into that regularity of strength which used to characterize the American Senatorial type in . . . far-away days of clean-shaven faces and moderate incomes before the War." Upon his arrival in Octavius, the innocent Theron is introduced to three characters who represent modern intellectual, religious, and social changes: Father Forbes, a Catholic priest, is a religious skeptic who speaks to his intellectual circle about "this Christ-myth of ours" and views the church as primarily a social "police force"; Dr. Ledsmar, a scientist who does not believe in God or the soul, conducts Darwinian experiments, one involving his own servant; and Celia

Madden, the daughter of the richest resident of the town, is an assertive New Woman who describes her sensual philosophy as "Greek," meaning "Absolute freedom from moral bugbears . . . [and] the courage to kick out of one's life everything that isn't worth while." Rather than be horrified at the trio's decidedly un-Methodist morality and outright atheism, Ware is instead appalled at his own ignorance of their "modern" ideas and attitudes.

Ware believes he can slip on Forbes's, Ledsmar's, and Madden's philosophies as easily as changing out of his priestly garments. He views his own identity and values, which have taken a lifetime to acquire, as immediately dispensable and treats the Octavius trio's learned philosophies as instantly acquirable. After one of his first visits to Forbes's study, Theron remarks to himself, "it was amazing how much wiser he had grown at all once." Rather than gaining actual intellectual sophistication, he becomes an intellectual pretender, repeating his friends' phrases back to them to seek their approval, believing he has reached enlightenment. Theron's loss of his previous genuine innocence and piety foster his increasingly contemptuous attitude toward his hopelessly unenlightened wife and congregation.

To reconcile his position as a Methodist minister with his newfound "modern" ideas, Theron seeks the help of Sister Soulsby, an itinerant religious revivalist, "debt raiser," and charlatan. Representing a crude version of the prevalent turn-of-the-century philosophy of pragmatism, Soulsby teaches Theron to separate his private lack of belief from his public duty as minister, much as Forbes does—an attitude captured best by Theron's determination "to be a good fraud." Just as Theron is mistaken about his intellectual attainments, he is equally mistaken about Celia's romantic feelings for him. In a climactic scene, Celia informs the minister that while Forbes, Ledsmar, and she were originally "impressed" with his "innocent, simple, genuine young character," the change that Theron "took to be improvement was degeneration." Celia casts Theron out of their lives forever, labeling him "a bore."

The novel ends with a recovered Theron leaving Octavius for the new western territory of Washington, where he plans to get into politics, because "I can speak, you know, if I can't do anything else.

Talk is what tells, these days." Thus, as the novel began with Theron symbolizing the genuineness of antebellum America, it ends with him representing America's future, heading west, devoid of belief, but willing to spin his words for personal and political power.

Discussion Questions

1. In a June 1896 letter Frederic indicates that he believed Theron Ware's demise was fated: "our friend Theron was badly treated. I couldn't save him from it, but it was a grief to me none the less." Based on evidence in the novel, how does Theron's destruction seem unavoidable? Is his deterioration the result of his personality, his circumstances, or both?

2. Analyze Theron's changing relationship with his wife, Alice. How does his treatment and estimation of her change during the novel, and how is this change indicative of changes in Theron's personality? Where does this change come from?

3. Is Sister Soulsby a positive or negative influence on Theron? She does teach him "to be a good fraud," but many readers find her a likable, good-natured character, and it is Soulsby who takes Theron in and nurtures him at the end of the novel. Explain the effects of Sister Soulsby on Theron.

4. William Dean Howells, one of the foremost writers of literary realism, published in 1885 *The Rise of Silas Lapham,* a novel about the near moral ruin of a rural businessman as he becomes enmeshed in the greedy and sophisticated social world of Boston. Harold Frederic wrote that Howells's novel captured "the most distinctive phase of American folk-life." How is Theron Ware's character and fate similar to Silas Lapham's? What are the distinctive differences between the two characters and their outcomes?

—Clay Motley

REFERENCES

Bridget Bennet, *The Damnation of Harold Frederic* (Syracuse, N.Y.: Syracuse University Press, 1997);

Austin Briggs Jr., *The Novels of Harold Frederic* (Ithaca, N.Y.: Cornell University Press, 1969);

Harold Frederic, *The Civil War Stories of Harold Frederic,* edited by Thomas F. O'Donnell (Syracuse, N.Y.: Syracuse University Press, 1992);

Robert M. Myers, *Reluctant Expatriate: The Life of Harold Frederic* (Westport, Conn.: Greenwood Press, 1995);

Robin Taylor Rodger, "Harold Frederic's *The Damnation of Theron Ware:* A Study Guide with Annotated Bibliography" <http://helios.acomp.usf.edu/~rrogers/index.html> (accessed 2 August 2006);

Edmund Wilson, "Two Neglected American Novelists: II: Harold Frederic, the Expanding Upstater," *New Yorker* (6 June 1970): 112+.

Mary E. Wilkins Freeman
(October 31, 1852 – March 13, 1930)

〰

"A NEW ENGLAND NUN"
Collected in *A New England Nun and Other Stories* (New York: Harper, 1891).

LOUISA ELLIS
Louisa Ellis, the protagonist of Mary E. Wilkins Freeman's short story "A New England Nun," likes to be alone. Louisa moves gratefully from an obligation to marry a man she does not love to liberation from their fifteen-year engagement. This complex character, gifted in the homemaking arts, is happy without being married, for her life is already "full of a pleasant peace" that she does not want to lose.

A preoccupation with order and neatness characterizes the "methodical" Louisa. She keeps her house immaculate both inside and out, considering chores as pleasant pastimes. Louisa is so tidy and accustomed to staying by herself that when her affianced, Joe Daggett, pays his twice-weekly visit to her house, she is disturbed by a "mild uneasiness" when he disarranges the books on her table. As she sweeps out the dust Joe tracks into the living room, it seems that she wants to erase all traces of him from her life because he is too disruptive of her routine, bringing "dust and disorder" into her home.

Louisa feels no love or desire for Joe. Fifteen years ago, she consented to marry him, but soon after their engagement, he ventured to Australia to make a fortune with which to support a family. During his fourteen years of absence, Joe and Louisa rarely wrote letters; they do not really know each other now. The "wind" of affection in Louisa's heart for Joe "had never more than murmured; now it had gone down, and everything was still." Her life has taken a path "so straight and unswerving that it could only meet a check at her grave, and so narrow that there was no room for any one at her side." Because Joe was gone for fourteen years and Louisa has been residing alone in her family house, she no longer feels any need to marry him or anyone else. Now with only a week before the scheduled wedding, Louisa knows that marrying Joe means leaving her house and greatly changing her "happy, solitary" habits.

While Joe had made "magnificent alterations" to his family home, the salient point for Louisa is that she would have to leave her own beloved house and be subordinate to Joe's mother, a "domineering, shrewd old matron" who will ridicule her. When Louisa thinks about moving into the Daggett home, she realizes that she and "her neat maidenly possessions" would be "robbed of their old environments" and "would almost cease to be themselves." She does not want to lose her identity. A positive view of Louisa focuses on the happiness she finds in her routines, such as serving herself nice meals on real china, distilling aromatic flower essences, and housekeeping. A more negative view of Louisa emphasizes that, only in her thirties, she is already "slow and still in her movements," seeming prematurely aged and rigid.

Two animals in the story, Louisa's canary and her dog, shed light on her character. Whenever Joe enters Louisa's home, her canary flutters "wildly" in his cage, "beating his little yellow wings against the wires." This symbol may suggest Louisa's nervous discomfort at being in the presence of Joe, or it could suggest her suppression of her desire for him. Alternately, the canary could represent the concept that marriage would be a trap in a gilded cage, whether for Louisa, Joe, or both of them.

Not only does Louisa feed Caesar, her large yellow dog, some of the same food she eats herself, but he has "lived at the end of a chain, all alone in a little hut, for fourteen years," just like she has done. If the dog is a "prisoner," Louisa is also captive, yet she seems satisfied. Louisa fears that Joe will let Caesar run free because he has already "attempted to set him loose." She dreads the time when they are married, because she imagines Caesar "on the rampage," leaving "innocent children bleeding in his path." Because of the way Freeman describes Caesar, many readers believe the dog is a symbol of Louisa's repressed sexuality. Another perspective is that Louisa dreads losing control over herself and her possessions.

The characterization of Louisa is one way in which the author criticizes late-nineteenth-century New England society, which offered only limited roles to women. First published in *Harper's Bazar* magazine in 1887, "A New England Nun" exposes the constraints on women's lives at that time, including cultural stereotypes that they must be selfless and entirely devoted to serving others and that they must marry to have meaningful lives.

Susan K. Harris argues that Freeman's story dramatizes "the dilemma of the woman artist" in the nineteenth century and that Louisa's artistry is apparent in her "extraordinary attention to domestic detail." As the narration of the story states, "Louisa had almost the enthusiasm of an artist over the mere order and cleanliness of her solitary home." Louisa has "throbs of genuine triumph" at her clean windows and rejoices about organized drawers and straight seams. According to Harris's interpretation, Louisa's talents in domesticity, or the aptitude for making a home comfortable and safe, can best be shown "only in an exaggerated form of the very domesticity she appears to have rejected" by not marrying. Thus, the story is a parody of "the domestic ideal" of a perfect home and the unrealistic image of a woman who creates it, as women readers of the time would have recognized.

Louisa is logical in her realization that if she entered the Daggett household, she would have much more housework, company to entertain, Joe's mother to obey, and constant demands on her time. She finds a way to break the engagement for mutually acceptable reasons, because Louisa overhears Joe and Lily Dyer discussing the problem of their love for one another. Louisa realizes that Joe and Lily share the love that brings two people together in companionable marriage and that Lily already gets along well with Joe's mother. So Louisa tells Joe that "she has lived so long in one way that she shrank from making a change." Louisa is now free to enjoy her "serenity and placid narrowness." Louisa is compared with a nun and with a queen who has retained her domains after a struggle. Instead of feeling sad, "her heart went up in thankfulness" for escaping marriage and remaining independent.

Discussion Questions

1. Do you think Louisa Ellis is a sad and lonely person or a happy and independent person? Why does she not want to marry Joe Daggett?

2. Critics have suggested many, even contrasting, meanings of the animals in this story. What do you think the canary and the dog, Caesar, symbolize in this story? What evidence in the text contributes to your perspective?

3. Louisa's ability to choose her way of life relates to her economic independence. How might this story be different if Louisa lacked the money to live alone?

4. Poet and critic Aliki Barnstone has compared Louisa Ellis and the poet Emily Dickinson, noting that both found "freedom and protection" through self-isolation at home. Do you agree or disagree that Louisa Ellis's characterization has similarities with Emily Dickinson?

—*Amy Cummins*

∼

"THE REVOLT OF 'MOTHER'"

Collected in *A New England Nun and Other Stories* (New York: Harper, 1891).

SARAH PENN

Sarah Penn is the unlikely rebel of Mary E. Wilkins Freeman's story "The Revolt of 'Mother.'" She is introduced in the opening lines of the story, in a strained exchange between her and "Father"—her husband, Adoniram Penn. The values of the society of which "Mother" and "Father" are a part are immediately revealed. Sarah's demands to "know what them men are diggin' over in the field for" are quickly squelched by her husband's rebuke to "go into the house" and attend to her "own affairs." As the man of the family, Penn conceives of himself as entitled to manage the family farm; in his view, his wife's appropriate sphere is the home.

Father is not alone in his belief in the traditional division—or unequal distribution—of power between men and women. As she returns to the house and children, Sarah imparts her own investment in these values to her daughter, Nanny. Turning their attention to the work of women, washing dishes after the noon meal, Mother tells Nanny, "You ain't found out yet we're women-folks.... we'd ought to reckon men-folks in with Providence, an' not complain of what they do any more than we do of the weather."

Both mother and daughter have legitimate complaints against "Father." The men "diggin' over in the field" that have raised Sarah's curiosity at the beginning of the story are in fact digging the foundation for a new barn to house four cows and a horse that Penn plans to buy. The barn is to be a grand one, and an unnecessary addition to the Penn farm. The family home, the site of Sarah's limited authority and the space in which she and Nanny perform their labor, is by contrast not grand at all; the house is small, shabby, and inferior to the houses of other women in the Penns' community, whose husbands "ain't got half the means" that Penn does. Moreover, the new barn is to be erected on the spot where Father promised his wife that their new home would be built forty years earlier. In the forty years of their marriage, Father has made significant additions to his property, with the exception of the family home, so that "the house, standing at right angles with the great barn and a long reach of sheds and out-buildings, was infinitesimal compared with them." The house is "scarcely as commodious for people as the little boxes under the barn eaves were for doves."

Even in light of her husband's obvious neglect and misuse, Sarah never responds with the anger or vengeance readers might expect and maybe even hope for. Her defining characteristic is meekness.

Even in appearance, with a forehead "mild and benevolent between the smooth curves of gray hair" and a face permanently fixed in a "saintly expression," Sarah mirrors a pious, traditional New England wife. Though willing to reproach her husband for "lodgin' [his] dumb beasts" better than his "own flesh an' blood," she does not duplicate his neglect. Mother "would never fail in sedulous attention" to Penn's wants no matter how "deep a resentment she might be forced to hold" against him. Such as it is, her house is perfectly kept. To the degree that her husband disregards the needs and comforts of his family, Sarah anticipates and provides for them.

Her "revolt," the decision to move from her family home into the new barn while her husband is out of town buying a horse, further reveals Sarah as exemplary of a pious matriarch. Far from representing a break from the traditional values that she has hitherto subscribed to, the revolt is in fact motivated by them. Drawing on her identity as a mother, and the responsibility toward her children's welfare that role obligates her to, Sarah relocates her brood to the barn. Early in the story it is revealed that Nanny is soon to be married, and the old home's small kitchen is the only space the Penns can offer for the ceremony. While Mother defends Father when Nanny initially voices her embarrassment over the kitchen's inadequacy as a site for her upcoming nuptials, she advocates for Nanny in her private confrontation with her husband. More importantly, the confrontation reveals Sarah's real motivation for wanting a new home. More significant than Nanny's embarrassment, Mother laments that Nanny will "have to go live somewhere else to live away from us." Reminding Penn that their daughter has never been physically strong, Mother worries about Nanny's health in a new home without her motherly presence to spare her the brunt of labor. Sarah's revolt is not motivated at all by a sense of entitlement or a desire for parity with her husband. It is merely a meek woman's meek attempt to fulfill the traditional obligations of a mother to her child.

While concern for her progeny motivates Mother to move to the barn, a belief that she has the blessing of providence justifies the untraditional relocation. The day before Penn plans to move his stock into the new barn, he receives a letter from his brother summoning him to Vermont to buy a horse. Pondering her husband's unexpected journey, Mother reasons that "Unsolicited opportunities are the guide-posts of the Lord to the new roads of life." Scrutinizing her part in the turn of events and concluding that the letter from her brother-in-law did not come as a result of anything she did, Sarah concludes that her husband's departure "looks like a providence." When the minister arrives to pay a visit to Mother in her new home, carrying with him the curiosity and judgment of the community, she promptly informs him that she believes she is "doin' what's right" and that her decision was "the subject of prayer."

The denouement of "The Revolt of 'Mother'" reveals that Sarah's unconventional move has not changed her role as woman at all. In the end, as in the beginning, Mother is a model wife and mother who greets her husband's return from Vermont with his favorite dinner cooked in the new kitchen of the barn-turned-home. The person who is changed is Penn. He has not become more "enlightened." He has not rejected the belief in traditional gender roles that he and his wife have ascribed to for the first forty years of their marriage. Father finally acknowledges his role as husband and father and the obligations for care that role implies. When he tearfully concedes to his wife "I'll—put up the partitions, an'—everything you—want, mother," he is showing remorse for his neglect and promising to care for his family as he should have all along. Sarah has not really staged a revolt; she has managed to put an end to her husband's.

Discussion Questions

1. Why does Adoniram Penn neglect to fulfill his promise to build his wife a new house? What values are reflected in his behavior?

2. Why does Freeman term Sarah Penn's relocation to the barn a "revolt?" What does the word *revolt* connote? How do Sarah's actions constitute a revolt?

3. Is it possible to term Sarah Penn a feminist? Why or why not?

—*Angela Ridinger-Dotterman*

REFERENCES

Aliki Barnstone, "Houses within Houses: Emily Dickinson and Mary Wilkins Freeman's "A New England Nun," *Centennial Review* (Fall 1984): 129–145;

Leah Blatt Glasser, *In a Closet Hidden: The Life and Work of Mary E. Wilkins Freeman* (Amherst: University of Massachusetts Press, 1996);

Susan K. Harris, "Mary E. Wilkins Freeman's 'A New England Nun' and the Dilemma of the Woman Artist," *Studies in American Humor*, 3, no. 9 (2002): 27–38;

Joseph R. McElrath Jr., "The Artistry of Mary E. Wilkins Freeman's 'The Revolt,'" *American Literary Realism* (1980): 255–261;

Michael Tritt, "Freeman's 'The Revolt of "Mother,"'" *Explicator*, 62, no. 4 (Summer 2004): 209–212;

Perry Westbrook, *Mary Wilkins Freeman* (New York: Twayne, 1967).